Real World
Adobe Photoshop CS

Real World
Adobe Photoshop CS
Industrial Strength Production Techniques

David Blatner
Bruce Fraser

Peachpit Press

Adobe

David

For Fay, Harry, Ann, Abe, Katie, and Rita,
who laid the foundation in my family.

Bruce

For the photographers, everywhere.
Without them, we would have no images.

Real World Adobe Photoshop CS

David Blatner and Bruce Fraser

Peachpit Press

1249 Eighth Street
Berkeley, CA 94710
510/524-2178
Fax: 510/524-2221

Find us on the World Wide Web at www.peachpit.com.

Peachpit Press is a division of Pearson Education.

Real World Adobe Photoshop CS is published in association with Adobe Press.

Interior design by Stephen F. Roth/Open House
Cover Design: Aren Howell
Cover Illustration: Ben Fishman, Artifish, Inc.
Image credits and permissions, page 859

ISBN 0-321-24578-4

9 8 7 6 5 4 3 2

Printed and bound in the United States of America

Overview

The Big Picture

Contents

What's Inside

Preface

Photoshop in the Real World

If you're reading this book because you want to produce embossed type, fractalized tree branches, or spherized images in Photoshop, you're in the wrong place. If you're after tips and tricks on how to get the coolest special effects in your images, look elsewhere. There are (at least) half a dozen good books on those subjects.

But if you're looking to move images through Photoshop—getting good scans in, working your will on them, and putting out world-class final output—this is the book for you. Its *raison d'être* is to answer the many questions that people in production environments ask every single day (and not without some frustration).

▶ What settings should I use in the Color Settings dialog box?

▶ How do I bring out shadow details in my images without blowing away the highlights?

▶ What methods are available to neutralize color casts?

▶ How do I calibrate my monitor? (And should I?)

▶ How do I put a drop shadow on top of a process-color tint in Quark-XPress or Adobe InDesign?

▶ What's the best way to silhouette an image for catalog work?

These questions, and dozens of others, face Photoshop users all the time. And unfortunately, the books we've seen on Photoshop—much less Photoshop's own manuals—simply don't address these crucial, run-of-the-mill, day-in-and-day-out production issues. This book does.

Ask Your Printer

We wrote this book for a lot of reasons, but the biggest one was probably our frustration with the knee-jerk advice we kept hearing about desktop prepress: "Ask your printer."

Go ahead. Ask your printer what values you should enter in the Color Settings and Proof Setup dialog boxes. In our experience, with nine out of ten printers you'll be lucky if you get more than wild guesses. In this new age of desktop prepress, there's simply no one you can ask (whether you're a designer, a prepress shop… or a printer). *You're* in the pilot's seat, with your hand on the stick (and the trigger). Where do you turn when the bogies are incoming?

We're hoping that you'll turn to this book.

Developing Your "Spidey Sense"

Flipping through nine hundred pages isn't exactly practical, though, when you've got a missile on your tail. So we try to do more with this book than tell you which key to press, or what value to enter where. We're trying to help you develop what our friend and colleague Greg Vander Houwen calls your "spidey sense" (those who didn't grow up on Spiderman comics may not relate completely, but you get the idea).

When you're in the crunch, you've gotta have an intuitive, almost instinctive feel for what's going on in Photoshop, so you can finesse it to your needs. Canned techniques just don't cut it. So you'll find a fair amount of conceptual discussion here, describing how Photoshop "thinks" about images, and suggesting how you might think about them as well.

The Step-by-Step Stuff

Along with those concepts, we've included just about every step-by-step production technique we know of. From scanning to silhouettes and drop shadows, to tonal correction, sharpening, and color separation, we've tried to explain how to get images into Photoshop—and back out again—with the least pain and the best quality. And yes, in the course of explaining those techniques, we *will* tell you which key to press, and what values to enter in what dialog boxes.

History Is Important

We hear some of you mumbling under your breath, "We've been doing prepress for 30 years, and we don't need to learn a new way of doing it." We believe that the key to succeeding in today's prepress market is understanding both the digital *and* the traditional realms. Our goal in this book is to help you with both. If you're new to prepress, we try to give you the background you need. If you're an old pro, we try to provide an entry into the heart of digital imaging—the world of zeros and ones.

Our goal is not to detract from the way you've been doing things. It's to show you how those approaches can be incorporated with the new tools, improved, and pushed to new limits.

Whither Photography?

This book isn't just about prepress. It's also about photography and about images. We believe that photographers understand tone and color as well as any other skilled group of professionals, and one of our aims has been to help photographers translate their own understanding of images into Photoshop's digital world.

Digital imaging has undoubtedly changed the practice of photography, but images still come from an intentional act on the part of the image maker, and that isn't going to change, whether the photons are captured by goo smeared on celluloid or by photoelectric sensors. We believe that digital imaging offers the photographer as many opportunities as it creates pitfalls. To all the photographers out there who are nervous about the digital revolution, we say, "Come on in, the water's fine." And more to the point, we can't *do* this stuff without you.

The Depth of Understanding

We were crazy to take on this book. If we weren't, we wouldn't have tried to unravel such an insanely complex subject. We don't claim to have the ultimate answers, but the answers we do have are tried, tested, and effective. The methods presented in this book may not be the only way to get good results from Photoshop, but they're the product of endless days and nights of research and testing, of badgering anyone we thought might have an answer with endless questions, then trying to present these insights in some coherent form. (Bruce vaguely remembers wondering, while making coffee at 4 AM, why one of his kitchen faucets was labeled "cyan"....)

While our grasp on reality may have occasionally been tenuous during the production of this book, the techniques we present are firmly grounded in the real world—hence the title.

How the Book Is Organized

The biggest problem we face in writing about Photoshop is not just that it's the "deepest" program we've ever used, but that almost every technique and feature relies on every other technique and feature. It's impossible to talk about Photoshop without circular reasoning.

However, we have tried to impose some structure to the book. In the first five chapters, we attempt to lay the groundwork for the rest of the book, covering *Building a Photoshop System*, *Essential Photoshop Tips and Tricks*, *Image Essentials*, *Color Essentials*, and *Color Settings* (all the color management stuff). We put all this information first because it's patently impossible to be effective in Photoshop without it.

Once we've laid the groundwork, we jump into really working with images. In the next five chapters, we explore techniques you'll want to employ with almost every image you work with in Photoshop: *Tonal Correction Fundamentals*, *Color Correction Fundamentals*, *Selections and Channels*, *The Digital Darkroom*, and *Sharpening*.

The origin and type of the images you work with determine what you can or need to do with them, so the next four chapters discuss these issues: *Spot Colors and Duotones*, *Line Art*, *Capturing Images*, and *Building a Digital Workflow*.

In the course of any book project, the authors find that they have a boatload of information that simply doesn't fit any single category. Fortunately, we're lucky enough to have a chapter called *Essential Image Techniques*. The tips in this chapter are like the tools in your toolbox—you never know when you'll need one, so it's good to have the whole box nearby.

Sometimes it's hard to remember that there is life outside of Photoshop. In the last three chapters of the book, we show how to get those images out of Photoshop into the real world: *Storing Images*, *Output Methods*, and *Multimedia and the Web*.

A Word to Windows Users

This book covers tips and techniques for both the Macintosh and Windows versions of Photoshop. However, we have chosen to illustrate dialog boxes, menus, and palettes using screen shots from the Macintosh version. Similarly, when discussing the many keyboard shortcuts in the program, we include the Macintosh versions. In almost every case the Command key translates to the Control key and the Option key translates to the Alt key. In the case of the very few exceptions to this rule, we have included both the Macintosh and the Windows versions. We apologize to all you Windows users, but because the interface between the two programs is so transparent we picked one platform and ran with it.

Thank You!

We'd like to give special thanks to a few of the many people who helped evolve a shadow of an idea into what you hold in your hands. Rebecca Gulick, our editor of this sixth edition, was helpful, patient, and unflappable as usual; production heroine extraordinaire Lisa Brazieal and our other friends at Peachpit took our work and made it fly. And special thanks to Agen Schmitz, Don Sellers, and Tiffany Taylor for catching an embarrassingly large number of typos and inconsistencies at the 11th hour. Those that may remain are entirely our fault.

A huge vote of thanks must go to Thomas Knoll, without whom there would be no Photoshop. For answering all our ridiculous questions while performing extraordinary feats of engineering to deliver a fine product, we thank Chris Cox, Marc Pawliger, Russell Williams, John Nack, Jeff Chien, David Howe, Scott Byer, and the rest of the Photoshop team.

Several vendors were generous in providing equipment, support, and encouragement. Special thanks go to Parker Plaisted and Eddie Murphy at Epson America, Brian Levey at Colorvisions, Nick Milley and Tom Lianza at Sequel Imaging, Thomas Kunz and Liz Quinlisk at GretagMacbeth, Mark Duhaime at Imacon USA, Kaz Kajikawa at EIZO, and Anne Tramer for Nikon. We owe thanks to Karl Lang for developing the Sony Artisan display, and to the late Carla Ow for making it a reality—Carla will be missed by everyone whose life she touched.

Special thanks go to Stephen Johnson and Michael Kieran for their generosity of spirit, their constant encouragement, and the many hours they spent with us in deep discussions that ranged from the technical to the philosophical; and to Greg Gorman for proving, gracefully but indubitably, that it's possible to immerse oneself in digital imaging yet still have a life. If we see further than others, it's because we stand on the shoulders of true Photoshop giants, including Greg Vander Houwen, Katrin Eismann, Jeff Schewe, Martin Evening, Andrew Rodney, and Deke McClelland, pixelmeisters all.

Bruce. "To photographers everywhere; various musicians who helped keep me semisane while I worked on this book, to my friends, colleagues and peers in the Photoshop community, and to my lovely wife Angela, for more than I can say here."

David. "My deepest appreciation to Debbie Carlson, my friend and partner, and to my family and friends—including Don, Snookie, Damian, and Suzanne—who have had to put up with 'the book is almost done' for way too long. My sincere appreciation to my two sons, Gabriel and Daniel, who helped immeasurably by sleeping at all the right times."

1 Building a Photoshop System

Putting It All Together

Photoshop is about as rich a program as you'll ever encounter, and much of this book focuses on ways to make you more efficient in your use of it. But no quantity of tips, tricks, and workarounds can compensate for hardware that's inadequate to the task, or a poorly configured system. So in this chapter we look at building an environment for Photoshop.

We first look at the hardware resources Photoshop needs, and then at some software add-ons that we find really useful.

Hardware

Photoshop takes full advantage of fast Macs and PCs—the faster the better—but the speed of the computer is only one part of the equation. Even the fastest computer available will seem sluggish if you don't have enough RAM, and Photoshop refuses to work at all if you don't have enough hard disk space. How much is enough? It depends entirely on the size of the files you're working with, and the kinds of operations you're carrying out on them.

Choosing a Platform

Discussions of Macs vs. PCs usually tend to degenerate into "my Dad can beat your Dad"—they produce a lot of heat, but little light. We're firmly convinced that price and performance are at parity on the two platforms. The Mac has richer support in terms of plug-ins and color measurement equipment. The PC has a greater range of general business software.

The bottom line: if you're happy with your current hardware platform, there's probably no reason to switch. You may, however, want to think about upgrading machines that are more than three or four years old: if you're still running Mac OS 10.1 or earlier, or Windows 98, you'll need to upgrade your OS to run Photoshop CS, and the new operating systems make their own heavy demands on hardware.

If you're planning to upgrade to the latest-and-greatest Windows 2000, Windows XP, or Mac OS 10.3, do yourself a favor—get a machine that was designed with the new OS in mind. You'll save yourself a ton of time and frustration. It's possible to run Photoshop CS on fairly old machines—the minimum Mac OS requirement is Mac OS 10.2, and the minimum Windows requirement is Windows 2000 with Service Pack 3—but we can tell you from bitter experience that it will be an uphill struggle. If your time is worth anything, trying to run a third-millennium application like Photoshop CS on a second-millennium machine is a false economy.

Macintosh. Many Photoshop operations involve really large quantities of number crunching, so the speed of your Mac's processor makes a big difference. Photoshop CS unequivocally demands at least a G3—it won't run at all on anything less—and in practice it makes little sense to use anything less than a G4, since Photoshop makes very effective use of the G4's AltiVec acceleration. If you plan to make extensive use of the new high-bit capabilities, particularly if you plan to create layered high-bit files, you want a G5!

Photoshop really benefits from dual processors, as do the operating systems under which it runs. If you're planning to upgrade, a dual-processor Mac with a slightly lower clock speed will generally outperform a somewhat faster single-processor model.

Windows. Photoshop CS demands a Pentium III-class machine, but it's distinctly happier on a Pentium 4, as are Windows 2000 and Windows XP, the required operating systems. At the time of writing, anecdotal evidence suggests that Windows 2000 is more stable and slightly better-supported in terms of drivers than Windows XP, but that's subject to change.

RAM

You can never be too thin, too rich, or have too much RAM. Just how much RAM you need depends on your file size—remember that additional layers and channels increase the size of the file—but we don't recommend even trying to run Photoshop on a system with less than 256 MB of RAM. The absolute minimum configuration, according to Adobe, is 192 MB. It may be doable—barely—but you won't enjoy it. If you typically work on Web-resolution images, use layers sparingly, and use few or no History states, you may be able to run Photoshop quite happily in our minimum suggested RAM complement. But if *any* of the above don't apply, you'll want more—much more. Fortunately, RAM is cheap these days.

We used to have various rules about how much RAM is enough, but as Photoshop has added more features that use scratch space, they've largely gone out the window. Photoshop uses RAM as a cache for its scratch file—if what it needs at any given moment is in the cache, it can fetch it quicker. But unless you only work on small flat files, it's a near-certainty that at some point the scratch disk will come into play. Photoshop will use as much RAM as you can throw at it, up to the 2 GB limit it can currently address.

Copying pixels takes RAM; saving a selection takes RAM; taking a snapshot takes RAM; History states take RAM; in fact, doing anything takes RAM because Photoshop always saves a version of your image in a memory buffer so that you can quickly undo. The History feature takes up gobs of RAM—if you want a supercharged History palette, you may want 20–50 times the file size in RAM for optimal performance. (See "Tip: Turning Off History" in Chapter 2, *Essential Photoshop Tips and Tricks*.)

A reliable way to figure if you'd benefit from more RAM is to keep an eye on the Efficiency indicator while you work (click in the lower-left corner of the document window; see Figure 1-1). If the reading drops below 100%,

Figure 1-1
The Efficiency
indicator

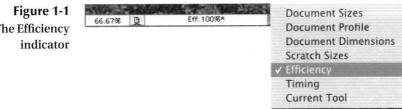

more RAM would help. (If you've already maxed out your machine with as much RAM as Photoshop can address, and your efficiency is still below 100%, see "Scratch disk space," later in this chapter.)

RAM allocation. Under the supported operating systems, memory allocation is dynamic, but you can (and should) still tell Photoshop how much of the available RAM to gobble. A good starting point is to allocate 50% of the available RAM to Photoshop, which you do in the Memory & Image Cache panel of Preferences (see Figure 1-2). If you have a large amount of RAM—a gig or more—you can try increasing that percentage, but if you go too far you'll hear the hard disk start to thrash whenever the OS or another application needs to grab some RAM.

Figure 1-2
Allocating RAM to
Photoshop in Mac OS X
and Windows

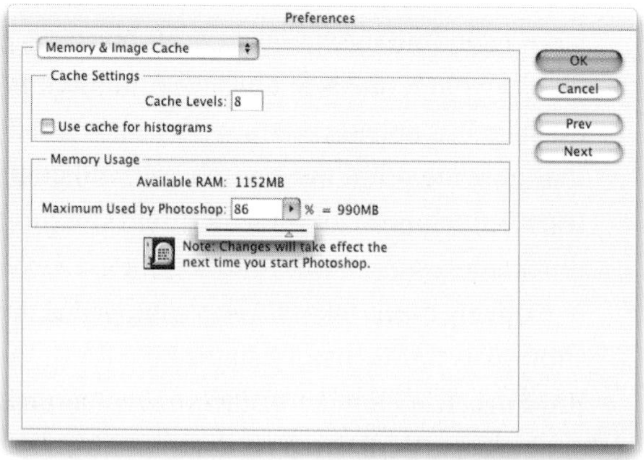

Mac OS X actually gives you an extra clue: when an application is waiting for the computer, you see the all-too-familiar spinning wristwatch cursor, but when the OS is the one causing the delay, you see a spinning multicolored wheel—Bruce calls it "The Spinning Pizza of Death." If you see the SPOD on Mac OS X, or you hear the hard disk thrashing on Windows, when you're working on an image that should fit into RAM, it's a sign that you've set the memory allocation too high and need to back it off a little.

Note that a few Photoshop filters (Lens Flare, for instance) require that you have enough physical RAM to load the entire image into memory. Even though Photoshop has a virtual-memory scheme, if you don't have the RAM, these effects just won't work.

The new Power Mac G5s let you add up to 8 GB of RAM, which may seem like great news for Photoshop power users. However, Photoshop CS is still limited to addressing only 2 GB of RAM, so unless you want to run other RAM-gobbling apps concurrently with Photoshop, there's probably no current reason to configure the box with more than 3 GB or so.

Virtual Memory

Virtual memory is a programming trick that fools the computer into thinking it has more RAM than it really does. It works by reserving a specially marked amount of space on your hard drive that gets treated as RAM. The real, physical RAM is then used as a cache for the "virtual memory" stored on the disk. If the data that the computer is looking for is cached in RAM, you don't see any slowdown, but if the computer has to go searching on the hard disk instead, things can slow down a lot.

Operating systems create a swap file on your hard disk that serves as virtual memory to let multiple applications grab RAM as needed. Photoshop also has its own private virtual memory scheme called Scratch Disk, which it uses to let you do things that wouldn't fit in physical RAM, such as storing 1000 history states on a 300 MB image. To get optimum performance, you need to configure both the OS virtual memory and Photoshop's scratch disk space so that they play nicely together.

Photoshop scratch disk and the OS swap file. Windows and Mac OS X use the startup drive for the swap file unless you have told them otherwise. On Windows systems, you can change the swap file setting by bringing up Properties for My Computer, selecting the Performance tab, clicking the Virtual Memory button, and selecting the "Change" option. This lets you specify maximum and minimum swap file sizes as well as which drive gets used.

On Mac OS X, the procedure for pointing the swap file at a drive other than the startup is much more complex, and not to be contemplated unless you're comfortable logging in as the root user and using the Terminal utility to type UNIX commands. If you're brave enough to try this, go to *http://homepage.mac.com/gdif/virtmem.html* for complete instructions—but make sure that you read the warnings and have a good backup before attempting to do so.

Things go much faster if you put the swap file and Photoshop's scratch file on different physical mechanisms, so a second hard drive is always desirable. If all you have is one single hard disk, you'll have to let Photoshop and the OS fight it out—if you're careful with the percentage of memory you allocate to Photoshop, the conflicts shouldn't be too bad or frequent. Since Photoshop also defaults to using the startup drive for its scratch file, in a dual-drive configuration you'll always want to change the location of either the OS swap file or the Photoshop scratch disk. (See "Scratch disk space," below.) It's easier to move Photoshop's scratch disk than it is to move the swap file—the only reason we can see to do the latter is if your startup drive is also the fastest one, and you want to let Photoshop use it as a scratch disk.

Scratch disk space. Photoshop requires scratch disk space at least equal to the amount of RAM you've allocated to Photoshop—it uses RAM only as a cache for the scratch disk space. That means if you've given Photoshop 120 MB of RAM, you must also have 120 MB of free disk space. If you have less, Photoshop will only use an amount of RAM equivalent to the free space on the scratch disk. In practice, you're likely to need more, and if you work with layered high-bit files or many history states, much more.

Photoshop constantly optimizes the scratch space. Those of you who learned in the stone age to view disk access as a warning that things are about to get very slow should learn to accept it as normal Photoshop behavior. People are often especially concerned when they see disk access immediately after opening a file. This, too, is normal: Photoshop is simply setting itself up to be more efficient down the line. Photoshop has a couple of ways to tell you when you're relying on the scratch disk.

In the lower-left corner of the document window, there's a popup menu that shows, among other things, document size, scratch size, or "efficiency" (see Figure 1-3). If you set this to Scratch Sizes, the first number shows the amount of RAM being used by all open documents, and the second number shows the amount of RAM that's allocated to Photoshop. If the first number is bigger than the second, Photoshop is using your hard drive as virtual memory. When the indicator is set to Efficiency, a reading of less than 100 percent indicates that virtual memory is coming into play.

The ideal configuration is to have Photoshop's scratch space on a separate physical disk from the startup drive, so that the same set of read-write heads don't have to scurry around like gerbils on espresso while trying to serve the dual demands of the operating system swap file and Photoshop's scratch space. It's fine to keep images, applications, or just about anything

Figure 1-3
Scratch size

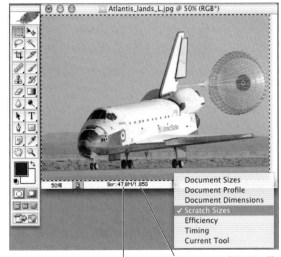

Amount of RAM allocated

Amount of RAM being used

else *except* the OS swap file on the same drive as Photoshop's scratch space, but it's a good idea to dedicate a partition on that drive to Photoshop's scratch space, because otherwise the scratch space may become fragmented and slow Photoshop down. A dedicated partition shouldn't need defragmenting, but you can do so very easily by simply erasing it—you don't need to run a fancy disk optimizer.

RAID arrays. A striped RAID hard disk array can be a very worthwhile investment, particularly if you're dealing with images too large for your available RAM on a regular basis. Photoshop can write to a RAID disk much faster than to a single fixed disk, so your performance will improve. The current speed champ is a dual-channel Ultra320 SCSI array with 1, 2, or 3 15,000-RPM drives on each channel, but fast SCSI drives are small and expensive. A software RAID combining two Serial ATA drives is almost as fast, with a much lower cost per megabyte. FireWire 800 arrays also show great potential, but only if you add multiple FireWire 800 channels by adding extra controllers—a single-channel FireWire 800 array is only about 10–15 percent faster than a single FireWire 800 drive. Three channels will get you almost the same speed as Ultra320 SCSI, and four channels (if you have enough PCI slots to burn) will exceed Ultra320 SCSI on a good many operations. Given the high cost and relatively low capacity of SCSI drives, we recommend exploring the alternatives unless you already have a SCSI array—SATA and FireWire 800 drives in the 250 GB range are relatively inexpensive by comparison.

Opening and saving large files is also faster with a RAID array. But if you have a choice between buying RAM and buying a fast hard drive, max out the RAM first unless opening and saving large files already constitutes a significant bottleneck in your workflow.

Tip: Use the Purge Commands. You know that Photoshop gets sluggish when you run out of RAM. And you know that whenever you take a new snapshot, or copy a large chunk of your document to the clipboard, Photoshop guzzles RAM. When you don't have any more RAM for Photoshop to guzzle, life slows down significantly. You can clear up the amount of RAM that Photoshop is using by "emptying" the Histories, Clipboard, and Undo buffers. We used to need all sorts of clever tricks to do this. Nowadays, we just select Clipboard, Histories, Pattern, Undo, or All from the Purge submenu (at the bottom of the Edit menu). If a Purge command is dimmed, it means the buffer is already empty, so there's nothing there to purge.

Monitors

The CRT versus LCD debate continues to rage. All we can really say is that it's a personal decision. LCDs have improved enormously over the past few years, but the viewing angle is still an issue—the color changes when you move your head from side to side—and it's still difficult to manufacture a large LCD with uniform brightness since all the light is produced by a backlight and a diffuser.

CRT monitors have also improved a lot over the past few years. They're brighter and offer better uniformity than the previous generations. Some CRT monitors, notably the Sony Artisan and LaCie Electron series with BlueEye, feature a USB connection between the monitor and the host CPU that allows the bundled calibration system to automatically adjust the individual R, G, and B gains to achieve the correct white point. Third-party calibrators such as the ones we discuss later in this chapter allow you to do the same thing manually with only slightly more effort, as long as your monitor offers separate R, G, and B gain controls. If you're in the market for a new CRT monitor, look for one that offers this capability—most do nowadays.

Bruce has punted on the question—his main Photoshop system features both a Sony Artisan CRT and an EIZO ColorEdge CG21 LCD. He trusts shadow rendition and overall color a little more on the CRT, but finds the LCD much sharper, and almost as accurate. One thing is clear. CRT technology may still see some improvements, but innovation has pretty much plateaued. That's not true for LCDs. In the long run, the question isn't whether we'll switch to LCDs, it's when.

Video acceleration. There's a widespread but ill-founded belief that accelerated video boards speed up Photoshop screen redraw. The bottleneck in redrawing Photoshop images on the screen is almost never the video system—it's getting the image data out of RAM (or even worse, from disk) to the video system. A super-fast video card may make your system feel faster and more responsive, but if you analyze what's going on, you'll usually find that the difference is a screen redraw of two-tenths of a second rather than five-tenths of a second. (Of course, those tenths of a second can add up—in a month you may even save enough time to grab a cup of coffee.) Most video acceleration these days is aimed at 3D graphics performance—useful if you do a lot of 3D work or play a lot of games—but the 2D performance of just about any current video card is good enough that it won't constitute a significant bottleneck in your Photoshop work.

The only reason we can find to add a third-party video board is to obtain higher resolutions than the built-in video offers. You really need to be able to run at your desired resolution in 24-bit (millions) color—16-bit color is fine for viewing images, but not for editing them.

A fairly widespread misconception is that a video board with a lot of VRAM will be somehow faster than one with less. Not so. More VRAM simply translates into more pixels on the screen—as long as your monitor can display them (see Table 1-1).

	VRAM	Monitor resolution	Bit depth
Table 1-1 **Monitor resolutions** **and VRAM**	2 MB	832-by-624	24-bit
		1280-by-1024	16-bit
	4 MB	1360-by-1024	24-bit
		1600-by-1200	16-bit
	8 MB	1600-by-1200	24-bit

Monitor calibration. If you want to work visually inside Photoshop (which we certainly do), some kind of monitor calibration is essential. The free, eyeball-based, software-only monitor calibrators (such as Adobe Gamma and ColorSync Default Calibrator) are better than nothing, but unless you work in a cave, you'll find it's extremely difficult to get consistent results because your eyes, and hence your monitor calibration, adapt to changing lighting conditions.

We believe that every serious Photoshop user would be better served using a hardware puck to measure the behavior of the monitor, and accompanying software to set it to a known condition and to write a monitor profile. There are several good, relatively inexpensive hardware-based monitor calibration packages available—we like the i1 (or Eye-One) Display from GretagMacbeth, the Optix from Monaco Systems, BasIC-Color Display with the "squid," or OptiCal, and its less-expensive sibling, PhotoCal, from ColorVisions, all of which can calibrate both CRT and LCD monitors.

The Power of Photoshop

Photoshop is not a island, complete unto itself. Rather, it's surrounded by hardware and software that supports or hinders it. If you focus on any piece of the whole and ignore the rest, you'll run into trouble (or at the very least, you'll be less efficient than you might have been).

We're going to focus on Photoshop for the rest of the book, but while you read, keep in mind these other factors: memory considerations, hardware, and third-party software. That way, you'll really be prepared to harness the power of Photoshop.

2 Essential Photoshop Tips and Tricks

Making Photoshop Fly

Photoshop is deep. Really, really deep. It's like those National Geographic movies that talk about the world below the surface of the ocean: on the surface it's smooth and straightforward, but down below you'll find things that'll knock your socks off.

In this chapter, we dive down deep and map out some of the canyons along the sea bed. You can dog-paddle around Photoshop without these tips, but you'll never really swim with the sharks until you've explored these territories.

Don't forget your flippers!

Upgrading to a New Version

There are few things as inevitable as death, taxes, and upgrading your software. Some people upgrade as soon as the box hits the proverbial shelf; others take years, buying a new version only after their service bureau or printer refuses to take their old files anymore. Sooner or later, though, you'll be faced with new features, new challenges, and a new bottle of aspirin.

What's New in Version "CS"

Those of you familiar with Photoshop 6 or 7 will be pleased with most of the interface changes in Photoshop CS, though some might throw you off a little at first. Fortunately, Adobe has left Photoshop's color management features alone this time around. If you really understood Photoshop's Color Settings and Proof Setup dialog boxes in versions 6 or 7, then you're set with Photoshop CS. However, if you still have misgivings about Photoshop's somewhat mysterious color engine, we strongly urge you to take the time to work through Chapter 5, *Color Settings.* Without a thorough understanding of the Color Settings dialog box, you'll be lost before too long (and you may not even know how lost you are).

Here are a few important changes in Photoshop CS (again, we're not listing every new feature here, just the ones you'd better know about before jumping into the rest of the book).

File Browser. The File Browser—which we used to liken to the Open dialog box on steroids—has now become a major force of nature with a host of new features. You can avoid it if you want, but if you have more than a few dozen images on your hard drive you owe it to yourself to use it (unless you work by the hour and you don't want to become more efficient). The File Browser was a palette in the last version, but now it's a hybrid palette/dialog box; you can open and close it with a button in the Options bar. We cover the File Browser in more depth later in this chapter.

16-bit editing. It used to be that very few features in Photoshop worked with 16-bit images (high-bit images). No longer! Now you can do almost everything in 16-bit mode, making color and tonal correction much easier. However, you'd better have a fast machine with a lot of RAM if you're playing with high-bit files.

Layer Comps. So you have 12 layers in your file and you want to view the first, eighth, and ninth but hide the others. Now you want to view the sixth through tenth. At its simplest, this is what Layer Comps is all about: creating sets of layer views that you can turn on and off easily. But Layer Comps goes even farther. We'll get into it later in this chapter.

Metadata. Metadata is one of the most boring-sounding topics on the planet, but it turns out to be one of the coolest features in Photoshop CS. Metadata is text information that is saved along with your image, such as the date and time your photograph was taken and the camera's exposure setting. As we'll see later in this chapter, metadata can also save a record of everything you've done to your files.

Histogram palette. Now you can really see what's going on behind the scenes while you make tonal and color adjustments to your file with the Histogram palette (see Chapter 6, *Tonal Correction Fundamentals*).

Editable keyboard shortcuts. Every power-user's dreams answered: You can now edit the keyboard shortcuts for almost every feature in Photoshop CS, including features that never had keyboard shortcuts before.

Color correction features. Photoshop CS has three new color correction features: Shadow/Highlight Correction, Photo Filter adjustment layers (which mimic traditional camera filters), and Match Color. We cover the first two in Chapter 9, *The Digital Darkroom*. We haven't found any real world use for Match Color yet.

Camera Raw. If your digital camera can save files in the Camera Raw format, you'll be pleased that Adobe has now included a significantly improved version of the brilliant (but formerly sold-separately) Camera Raw plug-in in Photoshop CS, and has vastly improved its integration with the File Browser to let you apply different Camera Raw settings to images for subsequent batch processing. We cover this in much more detail in Chapter 14, *Building a Digital Workflow*.

Text on a path. Is it a photo-editing package or an illustration program? It's getting harder to tell, as you can now place text along a path.

Weird new features. Those wacky software engineers at Adobe have added a number of other features to Photoshop CS that we'll discuss throughout the book. Here's just a few:

▶ You can hold down the Shift key while using the Grabber Hand or Zoom tool to scroll all open windows.

▶ The new Color Replacement tool (which is usually hiding underneath the Healing brush in the Tool palette) lets you paint the foreground color over an image while retaining the image's detail. This is very similar to using the regular Brush tool with the Blend Mode set to Color.

▶ Some sliders (like the Opacity slider in the Layers palette) now have "scrubby" sliders that let you click the label and drag left or right.

▶ The Crop and Straighten feature in the Automate submenu is wonderful when batch scanning a number of photos on a flatbed scanner (see Chapter 15, *Essential Image Techniques*).

▶ A Photomerge feature now lets you stitch together multiple images in a seamless panorama.

▶ You can create preset sizes for documents in the New dialog box.

▶ Photoshop CS lets you automatically upload images to a consumer online service like Shutterfly.com to get prints. It's a small thing, but it's made life so much easier for David (who has a little baby and therefore takes a billion snapshots that need printing).

▶ File sizes can now be so outrageously large that even Bruce hasn't bumped in to the upper limit yet.

Windows

Screen space is at almost as great a premium as memory these days—every little bit helps. We like to work in Full Screen Mode with Photoshop (see Figure 2-1) instead of wasting space on title bars, scroll bars, and the like. You can switch to either of two full-screen modes in the Tool palette or by pressing F. The first time you press F (or when you click on the middle icon on the palette), the image window takes over the screen (up to the menu bar) and the background becomes 50-percent gray. The second time, the menu bar disappears, too, and the background becomes black. (See "Make the Palettes Go Away," later in this chapter, for an important related tip.)

Tip: Full Screen Scroll. Just because your image is in Full Screen mode doesn't mean you can't scroll around using the Grabber Hand tool: Just hold down the space bar and click-and-drag. If the image doesn't take up the whole screen, the Grabber Hand tool moves the whole image around.

Figure 2-1
Full Screen Mode

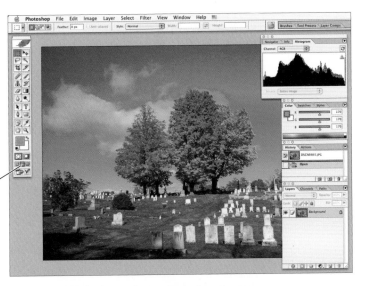

*Click here or press F to
switch to Full Screen Mode.*

*If you have extra
time on your hands,
you can also pick
Full Screen Mode
from the Screen
Mode submenu
(under the View
menu).*

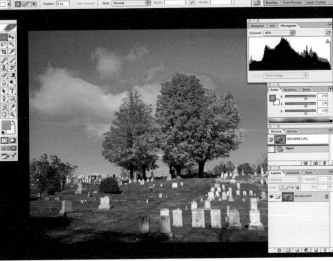

Tip: Showing the Menu Bar. When you're in either of the full-screen modes, you can hide or show the menu bar by pressing Shift-F.

Tip: Changing the Matte Color. You can change the neutral gray background color that surrounds your image when you're in Full Screen mode or when you expand the document window larger than the image itself. Just pick a foreground color and then Shift-click on the background with the Paint Bucket tool (it's in the Gradient tool's popout menu). At first glance, this is nothing more than a good trick to play on your colleagues.

However, it's also a good way to preview how an image will look if you're going to place it on a colored background.

Tip: Spread Out Those Windows. When you have two or more document windows open at the same time, Photoshop will neatly arrange them on your screen if you choose Tile or Cascade from the Arrange submenu (under the Window menu). The difference? Tile resizes and repositions the windows so that you can see all the windows at once. Cascade repositions the windows so that they're stacked on top of each other, with only their title bars showing.

Tip: Rotating Through Your Windows. We often find ourselves in Photoshop with five or more windows open at a time—a frustrating situation when we need to move through them all quickly. You can press Control-Tab to switch from one open document to the next. (In this case, it's the Control key on both Macintosh and Windows.) This way, you can rotate through the windows without taking your hands off the keyboard, even if you're in Full Screen mode with no menus.

Tip: Use New Window. You often want to see your image at Actual Pixels view (where screen pixels equal image pixels) but work at some other magnification. Instead of jumping back and forth between different magnification views, try opening a second window by selecting New Window from the Arrange submenu (under the Window menu). You can leave one window set to Actual Pixels and change the other window to whatever view you want to work at. Whenever you change something in one window, Photoshop updates the other window almost immediately. You can also use this technique to display an image in RGB and CMYK Preview modes simultaneously.

Tip: From Window to Folder. If you want to open an image that you know is in the same folder as one that is currently open in Photoshop, Command-click on the title in the document window's title bar (this is a Macintosh-only feature, as far as we know) and select the folder from the popdown menu that appears. This tells Photoshop to switch to the desktop and open that folder.

Navigation

In this section, we first explore some of the fastest ways to move around your image, including zooming in and out. Then we discuss moving pixels around both within your document, and from one document to another. It's funny, but we find that even expert users forget or never learn this basic stuff, so we urge you to read this section even if you think you already know all there is to know about navigating in Photoshop. Plus, Photoshop CS snuck in a few new zoom and scroll tricks.

Magnification

Images got pixels. Computer screens got pixels. But how does one type of pixel relate to the other type of pixel? When you display an image on your screen, Photoshop has to match image pixels to screen pixels (see Figure 2-2). The percentage in the title bar of the document window tells you how Photoshop is matching up those pixels.

The key to understanding this percentage stuff is to remember two things. First, at 100-percent view (otherwise known as Actual Pixels), each image pixel is represented by a single screen pixel. This view has nothing to do with how big the image will appear in print (or even on the Web, because different monitors have different resolutions). Second, at any percentage other than 100, you're probably not seeing a fully accurate view of your image.

Figure 2-2
Matching pixels

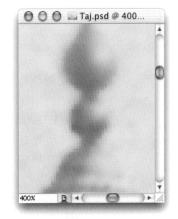

Sixteen image pixels are represented by a single screen pixel.

Sixteen screen pixels represent a single image pixel.

At 400 percent, the image is magnified four times. At 50 percent, it's reduced by half, so you're only seeing half the pixels in the image because you're zoomed farther out and Photoshop has to downsample the image on the fly. When you're viewing at an integral multiple of 100 (meaning 25, 50, 200, 400 percent, and so on), Photoshop displays image pixels evenly. At 200 percent, four screen pixels (two horizontal, two vertical) equal one image pixel; at 50 percent, four image pixels equal one screen pixel, and so on.

However, when you're at any "odd" percentage, the program has to jimmy the display in order to make things work. Photoshop can't cut a screen pixel or an image pixel in half, so instead it fakes the effect using anti-aliasing. The moral of the story is, always return to Actual Size (100 percent) view to peruse your image, particularly if you're trying to evaluate the effects of Unsharp Masking.

By the way, while it's tempting to select Print Size from the View menu (in order to see how large the image will be on paper), this setting is *only* accurate on 72 pixels-per-inch monitors—in other words, on those old 13-inch Apple monitors and hardly anything else. We just ignore it.

Tip: Don't Use Image Cache for Histograms. When the "Use cache for histograms in Levels" option is turned on in the Preferences dialog box (Command-K), the histogram you see is a histogram of what you see on screen, *not* the histogram of your data. The anti-aliasing you get at any view other than 100 percent can produce a very smooth histogram when in fact your data is already severely posterized. We can't really envisage a situation where you need to see a histogram of the screen display instead of a histogram of your data, so leave this option turned off (it is by default).

Tip: Don't Select the Zoom Tool. We never select the Zoom tool from the Tool palette. You can always get the Zoom tool temporarily by holding down Command-spacebar (to zoom in) or Command-Option-spacebar (to zoom out). Each click reduces from actual size to two-thirds (66.7 percent), to one-half (50 percent), to one-third (33.3 percent), and so on when zooming out, and magnifies in 100-percent increments when zooming in. (Actually, it jumps from 800 to 1200 percent, and from 1200 to 1600 percent, which is the maximum magnification available.)

You can also drag around an area with the Zoom tool. The pixels within the marquee are magnified to whatever percentage best fills the screen.

Tip: Zoom with Keystrokes. If you just want to change the overall magnification of an image, press Command-plus (+) or Command-minus (-) to zoom in or out. We find this especially handy because it resizes the window at the same time if necessary. But if any palettes are open, this keystroke won't increase the document window beyond the edges of the palettes unless you click the Ignore Palettes checkbox in the Options bar while the Zoom tool is selected. Note that adding the Option key to this mix tells Photoshop to zoom in or out without changing the size of the window. For some reason, it's just the opposite in Windows: The Ctrl key zooms without resizing, and holding down Ctrl and Alt zooms *and* resizes.

Tip: Get to 100-Percent View Quickly. You can jump to 100-percent view quickly by double-clicking on the Zoom tool in the Tool palette. This is just the same as clicking the Actual Pixels button in the Options bar or choosing Actual Pixels from the View menu. Faster still, press Command-Option-0 (zero).

Tip: Fit Window in Screen. Double-clicking on the Hand tool, on the other hand (no pun left unturned), is the same as pressing Fit on Screen in the Options bar when the Zoom tool or Hand tool is selected, or pressing Command-0 (zero)—it makes the image and the document window as large as it can, without going out of the screen's boundaries.

Tip: Zoom Factor. At the bottom-left corner of the window, Photoshop displays the current magnification percentage. This isn't only a display: You can change it to whatever percentage you'd like (double-click to select the whole field). Type the zoom percentage you want, then press Return or Enter when you're done. If you're not sure exactly what percentage you want, note that you can press Shift-Return instead of Return and the field remains selected after Photoshop zooms in or out, letting you enter a different value (see Figure 2-3).

Figure 2-3
Zoom factor

Type the zoom percentage you want here, then press Return or Enter.

11.65%   rgbMaster

Moving

If you're like most Photoshop users, you find yourself moving around the image a lot. Do a little here . . . do a little there . . . and so on. But when you're doing this kind of navigation, you should rarely use the scroll bars. There are much better ways.

Tip: Use the Grabber Hand. The best way to make a small move around your image is with the Grabber Hand. Don't choose it from the Tool palette. Instead, hold down the spacebar to get the Grabber Hand. Then just click-and-drag to where you want to go.

Grab Every Image. Wouldn't it be cool if you could use the Grabber Hand on more than one open image window at the same time? No problem: Just hold down the Shift key with the Grabber Hand tool (or press Shift-spacebar with any other tool). This works when zooming in and out, too: Just add the Shift key and your magnification change gets applied to all open images.

Tip: End Up Down Home. We like the extended keyboard—the kind with function keys and the built-in keypad. Most people ignore the very helpful Page Up, Page Down, Home, and End keys when working in Photoshop, but we find them invaluable for perusing an image for dust or scratches.

When you press Page Up or Page Down, Photoshop scrolls the image by almost an entire page's worth of pixels up or down. It leaves a small band of overlap, just in case. While there's no Page Left or Page Right button, you can jump a screen to the left or right by pressing Command-Page Up or Command-Page Down. You can scroll in 10-pixel increments by pressing Shift-Page Up or Shift-Page Down (or, again, add the Command key to go left or right).

Also note that pressing the Home button jumps you to the upper-left corner, and the End button jumps you to the lower-right corner of the document. David often uses this technique when using the Cropping tool. He lazily sets the cropping rectangle approximately where he wants it, then zooms in to the upper-left corner to precisely adjust that corner point. Then, with one hit of the End key, he's transported to the lower-right, where he can adjust that corner.

Tip: Match Up Your Images. When you're working on two or more images at the same time, it's often helpful to see the same part of each image at the same magnification. Photoshop CS adds several new features to the Arrange submenu (under the Window menu) that automate this process. The Match Zoom feature sets the magnification percentage for every open image to the zoom level of the current document. Match Location leaves the magnification alone but scrolls each document window to the same part of the image as the current file—for instance, if the current file displays the lower-right corner, then all the images will scroll to the lower-right corner. (Unfortunately, Match Location is only approximate; it won't match to the exact pixel.) The one we use most often is Match Zoom and Location. You can guess what it does.

Tip: Moving Among the Layers. The Grabber Hand and scroll bars only let you move around your image on a two-dimensional plane. What about moving into the third dimension—the layer dimension?

You can move among layers (without ever touching the Layers palette) by using keystrokes: Option-[or Option-] (the square brackets) move to the previous or next visible layer (even if that layer is in a different layer set). If you add the Shift key to that, Photoshop jumps to the bottom or top layer (very helpful if you've got a mess o' layers).

One cool feature here is that if only one layer is visible when you press these keystrokes, Photoshop hides that layer and shows the next layer. This is great for cycling through a number of layers, though it gets confused and doesn't always work when you have layer sets.

By the way, if you want to *move* the layers rather than just select them, you can press Command-Shift-[or Command-Shift-] to move the selected layer to the bottom and top of the layers stack, respectively.

Tip: Faster Layer Selection. Perhaps the fastest way to select a layer is to select the Move tool and then turn on the Auto Select Layer checkbox in the Options bar. Now you can switch to a layer simply by clicking with the Move tool on a pixel on that layer. If you don't have the Move tool selected when you want to switch layers, simply Command-click (which gives you the Move tool temporarily). On the other hand, we personally find Auto Layer Select somewhat infuriating because it's too easy to select the wrong layer. Instead, we like using the Move tool's context-sensitive menu.

Tip: Context-Sensitive Menus. When you Control-click (Macintosh) or click with the right mouse button (Windows), Photoshop displays a context-sensitive menu that changes depending on what tool you have selected in the Tool palette. We find the menu for the various painting tools pretty useless (though if you had to do a lot of painting, it might be helpful). But the menus you get when you Control-click (or right-mouse-button-click) with the Move tool and the selection tools are great.

The context-sensitive menu for the Move tool lets you choose a layer to work on. If you have four layers in an image, and three of them overlap in one particular area, you can Control-click (or right-mouse-button- click) on that area and Photoshop asks you which of the three layers you want to jump to. (Note that you can almost always get the Move tool's context-sensitive menu by Command-Control-clicking or, on Windows, clicking the right mouse button with the Ctrl key held down.)

The context-sensitive menu for the Marquee tool contains a veritable mish-mosh of features, including Delete Layer, Duplicate Layer, Load Selection, Reselect, and Color Range (we have no idea why Adobe picked these and left other features out). Many of these features don't have keyboard shortcuts, so this menu is the fastest way to perform them.

Tip: Click on your Layer. Here's another way to select a different layer without clicking on it in the Layers palette: Command-Option-Control-click (with any tool; in Windows, you Ctrl-Alt-click with the right mouse button). If you click on pixels that "belong" to a different layer than the one you're on, Photoshop jumps to that layer. For instance, if you've got a picture of your mom on Layer 3, and you're currently on the Background layer, you can Command-Option-Control-click (or Ctrl-Alt-right-mouse-button-click) on your mom to jump to Layer 3.

This typically works only when you click on a pixel that has an opacity greater than 50 percent. (We say "typically" because it sometimes *does* work if the total visible opacity is less than 50 percent. See "Info Palette," later in this chapter.) If your mom has a feathered halo around her, you may not be able to get this to work if you click on the feathered part.

Navigator Palette

The Navigator palette acts as command central for all scrolling and zooming (see Figure 2-4). We rarely use this palette because we find that it's usually either too precise or not precise enough, and it takes too much mousing around. Of course, this is largely a personal bias on our part; if you find it useful, more power to you.

Most of the palette is occupied by a thumbnail of the image, with a red frame indicating the contents of the active window. (If your image has a lot of red in it, you might want to change the frame color by choosing Palette Options from the palette's popout menu). Dragging the outline pans the contents of the active window. Command-dragging lets you define a new outline, thereby changing the zoom percentage.

The percentage field at the lower left of the palette works exactly like the one at the lower left of the image window. Clicking the zoom-in and zoom-out buttons has the same effect as pressing Command-plus and Command-minus. David's favorite feature in this palette is the magnification slider, which lets him change the zoom level dynamically. It's not a particularly useful feature, but it's mighty fun.

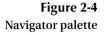
Figure 2-4
Navigator palette

Moving Pixels

If you simply make a selection, then drag it with one of the selection tools, you move the selection boundary but not its contents. If you want the pixels to move as well, you have to use the Move tool. Fortunately, no matter what tool is selected, you can always temporarily get the Move tool by holding down the Command key. Note that you can hold down the Option key while you drag to copy the pixels as you move them (moving a duplicate of the pixels).

When you move or copy selected pixels with the Move tool, you get a floating selection (sort of like a temporary layer that disappears when you deselect). While the selection is still floating, you can use the Fade command (in the Filter menu) to change its opacity or blend mode.

With the Move tool, you can move an entire layer around without selecting anything. When you do have something selected, you don't have to worry about positioning the cursor before you drag. This is a great speedup, especially when you're working with heavily feathered selections.

Tip: Arrow Keys Move, Too. When moving pixels around, don't forget the arrow keys. With the Move tool selected, each press of an arrow key moves the contents of your selection by one pixel. If you add the Shift key, the selection moves 10 pixels. Modifier keys work, too: hold down the Option key when you first press an arrow key, and the selection is duplicated, floated, and moved one pixel (don't keep holding down the Option key after that, unless you want a *lot* of duplicates).

Remember that you can always get the Move tool temporarily by adding the Command key to any of these shortcuts. Pressing the arrow keys with any tool other than the Move tool moves the selection without moving the pixels it contains. This is an essential technique for precision placement of a selection.

If you've got the Move tool selected (press V), and nothing is selected when you press the arrow keys, the entire layer moves by one pixel. Add the Shift key to move 10 pixels instead.

Tip: Moving Multiple Layers. One of the problems with layers is that you often can't do the same thing to more than one layer at the same time. But remember: There are always workarounds!

If you want to move more than one layer at a time with the Move tool, you can link the layers by clicking in the second column of the Layers palette (see Figure 2-5). Whichever layer tile you click on (other than the one that's already active) is linked with the current layer. Now when you use the Move tool (with no selections), both layers move.

Tip: Duplicating Layers. Duplicating a layer is a part of our everyday workflow, so it's a good thing that there are various ways to do it.

▶ You can drag the layer's tile on top of the New Layer button in the Layers palette.

▶ You can press Command-J (if some pixels are selected, then only those pixels will be duplicated).

Figure 2-5
Linking layers for moving

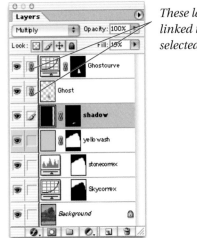

These layers are linked to the selected layer.

▶ You can select Duplicate Layer from the Layer menu.

▶ You can select Duplicate Layer from the context-sensitive menu you get when Control-clicking (Macintosh) or right-mouse-button-clicking (Windows) with the Marquee, Lasso, or Cropping tool.

The method you use at any given time should be determined by where your hands are. (Keyboard? Mouse? Coffee mug?)

Tip: Duplicating and Merging Layers. You can merge a copy of all the currently visible layers in a document into the currently selected layer (without deleting the other layers) by holding down the Option key when selecting Merge Visible from the Layer menu (or, better yet, just press Command-Shift-Option-E). Generally, you'll want to create a new layer just before doing this, so the merged layers end up there.

Tip: Copying Pixels. Layers are a fact of life, and with Photoshop it's not uncommon to find yourself with more layers than you know what to do with. If you make a selection and select Copy, you only get the pixels on the currently active layer (the one selected on the Layers palette). If you want to copy all the visible layers, select Copy Merged instead (or press Command-Shift-C).

However, we find some people using this technique in order to make a merged copy of the entire image (not just a selection). Sure, you can do it, but it's faster and less memory-intensive to use Duplicate (under the

Image menu) and turn on the Duplicate Merged Layers Only checkbox. (This label makes no sense to us; it really should be called "Merge Visible Layers in Duplicate.")

Tip: Pasting Pixels. Pasting pixels into a document automatically creates a new layer (unless your image is in Indexed Color mode). So what about the Paste Into (Command-Shift-V) and Paste Behind (Command-Shift-Option-V) features (which are available when you've made a selection)? When invoked, each of these adds a new layer, but it also adds a layer mask to that layer in the form of the selection. This is one of the fastest ways to build a layer and a layer mask in one step: Draw a selection the shape of the layer mask you want, then perform a Paste Into or a Paste Behind (depending on the effect you're trying to achieve).

Tip: Drag-and-Drop Selections and Layers. Most Photoshop users can't envision a world without Cut and Paste. However, there are times to use the clipboard and times not to. In Photoshop, you often want to avoid the clipboard because you're dealing with large amounts of data. Every time you move something to or from the clipboard, you eat up more RAM or hard drive space, which can slow you down.

If you want to move a selection of pixels (or a layer) from one document to another, you can do so by dragging it from one window into the other (if you've got a selection, remember to use the Move tool, or else you'll just move the selection boundary itself). Photoshop moves the pixels "behind the scenes," so as to avoid unneeded memory requirements. If you're trying to copy an entire layer, you can also just click on its tile in the Layers palette and drag it to the other document's window.

Tip: Placing your Drag-and-Drop Selection. In the last tips we talked about how you can drag and drop a selection or layer from one image into another. When you let go of the mouse button, the selection is placed into the image right where you dropped it. However, if you hold down the Shift key, Photoshop centers the layer or selection in the new image. If the two images have the same pixel dimensions, the Shift key "pin-registers" it—the layer or selection falls in exactly the same place it was in the original document.

Guides, Grids, and Alignment

Moving pixels is all very well and good, but where are you going to move them to? If you need to place pixels with precision, you should use the ruler, guides, grids, and alignment features. The ruler is the simplest: you can hide or show it by pressing Command-R. Wherever you move your cursor, faint tick marks appear in the rulers, showing you exactly where you are (you can also follow the coordinates on the Info palette).

Guides. You can add a guide to a page by dragging it out from either the horizontal or vertical ruler. Or, if you care about specific placement, you can either carefully watch the measurements on the Info palette as you drag, or select New Guide from the View menu. (If you don't think in inches, you can change the default measurement system; see "Tip: Switch Units," later in this chapter.)

You can always move a guide with the Move tool (don't forget you can always get the Move tool temporarily by holding down the Command key). Table 2-1 lists a number of grids and guides keystrokes that can help you use these features effortlessly.

Tip: Snap to Ruler Marks. We almost always hold down the Shift key when dragging a guide out from a ruler; that way, the guide automatically snaps to the ruler tick marks. If you find that your guides are slightly sticky as you drag them out without the Shift key held down, check to see what layer you're on. When Snap To Guides is turned on, objects snap to the guides *and* guides snap to the edges and centers of objects on layers.

Tip: Switching Guide Direction. Dragged out a horizontal guide when you meant to get a vertical one? No problem: just Option-click on the guide to switch its orientation (or hold down the Option key while dragging out the guide).

Table 2-1 Grids and guides keystrokes	To do this...	Press this...
	Hide/Show All Extras (grids, guides, etc.)	Command-H
	Hide/Show Guides	Command-' (quote)
	Hide/Show Grid	Command-Option-'
	Snap To Guides	Command-; (semicolon)
	Lock/Unlock Guides	Command-Option-;

Tip: Mirroring Guides. If you rotate your image by 90 degrees, or flip it horizontally or vertically, your guides will rotate or flip with it. You can stop this errant behavior by locking down the guides first (press Command-Option-semicolon).

Tip: Guides on the Pasteboard. Just because your pixels stop at the edge of the image doesn't mean your guides have to. You can place guides out on the gray area outside the image canvas and they're still functional. This is just the ticket if you've got a photo that you need to place so that it bleeds off the edge of your image by .25 inch.

Tip: Changing Guides and Grids. Guides are, by default, blue. Grid lines are, by default, set one inch apart. If you don't like these settings, change them in the Guides, Grid & Slices pane of the Preferences dialog box (you can select this from the Preferences submenu), or just double-click on any guide with the Move tool (or Command-double-click with any other tool).

Alignment and distribution. People often use the alignment features in page-layout applications, but Photoshop has alignment and distribution features, too, and they're a godsend for anyone who really cares about precision in their images (we find them particularly useful when building images for the Web). Here's how you can align objects on two layers.

1. Choose which layer you want "locked"—that is, which one stays put while the other layer moves—by selecting it in the Layers palette.

2. Click in the second column of the Layers palette next to the layer you want to move (a link icon should appear next to it). If you want to align more than two layers, link all of them.

3. Make sure you have no selections by pressing Command-D (or choosing Deselect from the Select menu), and then choose among the options on the Align Linked submenu (under the Layer menu; see Figure 2-6). Or, even faster, click on one of the Align buttons in the Options bar. If you don't deselect first, Photoshop aligns to the selection instead of to the layers.

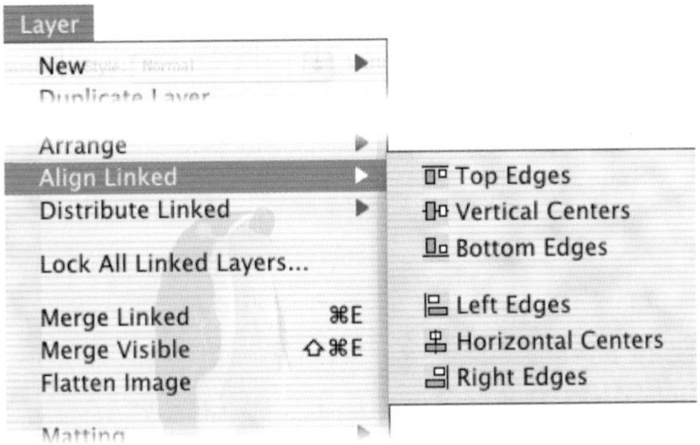

Figure 2-6
Aligning layers

Layer	
New	▶
Duplicate Layer	
Arrange	▶
Align Linked	▶
Distribute Linked	▶
Lock All Linked Layers...	
Merge Linked	⌘E
Merge Visible	⇧⌘E
Flatten Image	
Matting	▶

Align Linked submenu:
- ▯ᵈ Top Edges
- ▯◦ Vertical Centers
- ▯◦ Bottom Edges
- ▯ Left Edges
- ▯ Horizontal Centers
- ▯ Right Edges

4. When you're done aligning objects, don't forget to turn off the link icon in the Layers palette (unless you want these layers to be linked so that they move in tandem from now on).

If you select three or more layers (or, to be more precise, select one layer in the Layers palette, and then link two or more other layers to it), you can also distribute the layers instead of aligning them. For example, if you have four small pictures that you want evenly spread across your Photoshop image, you can put each one on a separate layer, link them all together, and choose Horizontal Centers from the Distribute Linked submenu (under the Layer menu; see Figure 2-7).

Note that Distribute Linked doesn't care which layers are selected and which are linked. When distributing layers vertically, Photoshop "locks" the layers that are closest to the top and the bottom of the image canvas; when distributing horizontally, it locks the left-most and right-most layers. All the layers in between get moved. For example, if you choose Vertical Centers from the Distribute Linked submenu, Photoshop moves the layers so that there is an equal amount of space from the vertical center point of one layer to the next.

We think this interface is pretty clunky (after all, when you link layers together, they aren't supposed to move independently of each other), but after you align or distribute layers once or twice, you'll find that it's not that bad.

Tip: Aligning to the Canvas. Aligning two layers together is all well and good, but we often find we want to align something to the image canvas itself. For instance, you might want to center some text horizontally in the picture. Here's how you can do it.

Figure 2-7
Distributing layers

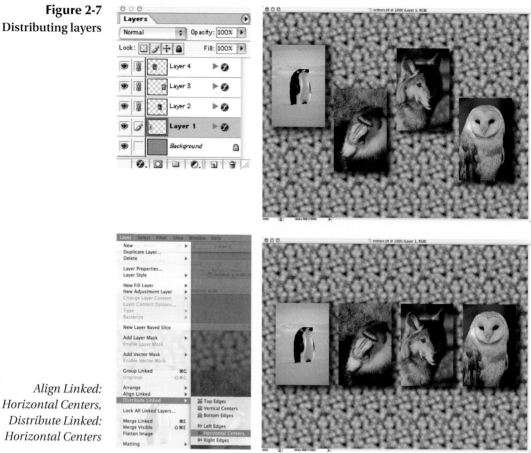

Align Linked:
Horizontal Centers,
Distribute Linked:
Horizontal Centers

1. Press Command-A to select the whole image.

2. Select the layer you want to move.

3. If you want to align more than one layer, link those layers to the selected layer.

4. Choose from among the Align buttons in the Options bar or the Align to Selection submenu (under the Layer menu). If you choose the Horizontal Centers button, then Photoshop centers your layer to the selection (which, in this case, is the size of the canvas).

   Note that when you have a selection, the Align Linked submenu changes to the Align to Selection submenu (which is why you have to deselect your selections before aligning two or more layers).

Dialog Boxes

Dialog boxes seem like simple things, but since you probably spend a good chunk of your time in Photoshop looking at them, wouldn't it be great to be more efficient while you're there? Here are a bunch of tips that will let you fly through those pesky beasts.

Tip: Scroll 'n' Zoom. The most important lesson to learn about dialog boxes in Photoshop is that just because one is open doesn't mean you can't do anything else. For instance, in many dialog boxes—such as the Levels and Curves dialog boxes—you can still scroll around any open documents (not just the active one) by holding down the spacebar and dragging. You can even zoom in and out of the active window using the Command-spacebar and Command-Option-spacebar techniques. Note that some dialog boxes, most notoriously the Distort filters, don't let you scroll or zoom at all. Pity.

Tip: Save your Settings. Many dialog boxes in Photoshop have Save and Load buttons that let you save to disk all the settings that you've made in a dialog box. They're particularly useful when you're going through the iterative process of editing an image.

For instance, let's say you're adjusting the tone of an image with Curves. You increase this and decrease that, and add some points here and there.... Finally, when you're finished, you press OK and find—much to your dismay—that you need to make one more change. If you jump right back into Curves, you degrade your image a second time—not good (see Chapter 6, *Tonal Correction Fundamentals*). If you undo, you lose the changes you made the first time. But if you've saved the curve to disk before leaving the dialog box, you can undo, go back to the dialog box, and load in the settings you had saved. Then you can add that one last move to the curve, without introducing a second round of image-degrading corrections.

Tip: Instant Replay. There's one other way to undo and still save any tonal-adjustment settings you've made. If you hold down the Option key while selecting *any* feature from the Adjust submenu (under the Image menu), Photoshop opens the dialog box with the last-used settings. Similarly, you can add the Option key to the adjustment's keyboard shortcut.

For instance, Command-Option-L opens the Levels dialog box with the same settings you last used. This is a great way to specify the same Levels or Curves (or Hue/Saturation, or any other adjustment) for several different images. But as soon as you quit Photoshop, it loses its memory.

Tip: Opening Palettes from Dialog Boxes. We almost always work with the Info palette open. However, every now and again it gets closed or covered up with some other palette. Unfortunately, while you're in a dialog box (like the Curves or Levels dialog box), you cannot click on any palette without leaving the dialog box by pressing OK or Cancel. Fortunately for efficiency, you *can* select a palette from the Window menu. To display the Info palette, select Show Info from this menu. (Unfortunately, this doesn't work for palettes that are docked in the palette well.)

Keystrokes in Dialog Boxes

We love keystrokes. They make everything go much faster, or at least they make it *feel* like we're working faster. Here are a few keystrokes that we use all the time while in dialog boxes.

Option. Holding down the Option (or Alt) key while in a dialog box almost always changes the Cancel button into a Reset button, letting you reset the dialog box to its original state (the way it was when you first opened it). If you want to go keystrokes the whole way, press Command-Option-period to do the same thing (this doesn't work on Windows).

Command-Z. You already know Command-Z because it's gotten you out of more jams than you care to think about. Well, Command-Z performs an undo within dialog boxes, too. It undoes the last change you made. We use this all the time when we mistype.

Arrow keys. Many dialog boxes in Photoshop have text fields where you enter or change numbers (see Figure 2-8). You can change those numbers by pressing the Up or Down arrow key. Press once, and the number increases or decreases by one. If you hold down the Shift key while pressing the arrow key, the number changes by 10. (Note that some dialog box values change by a tenth or even a hundredth; when you hold down Shift, they change by 10 times as much.)

Figure 2-8
Numerical fields
in dialog boxes

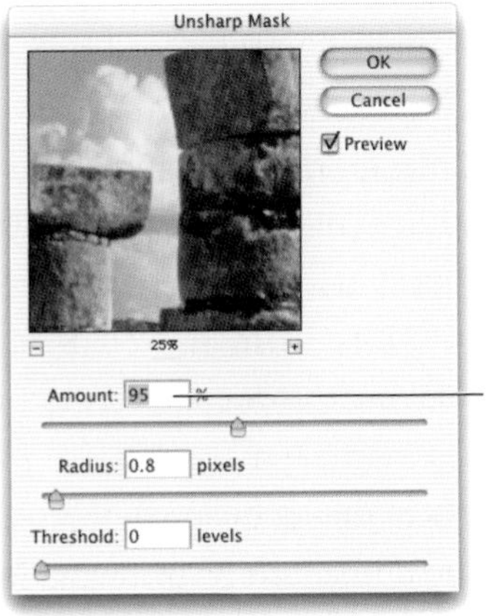

Pressing the Up or Down arrow key changes this number.

Add Shift to change in increments of 10.

A few dialog boxes use the arrow keys in a different way, or don't use them at all. In the Lens Flare filter, for instance, the arrow keys move the position of the effect, and arrow keys just don't do anything in most of the Distort filters.

Tab key. As in most Macintosh and Windows applications, the Tab key selects the next text field in dialog boxes with multiple text fields. You can use this in conjunction with the previous tip in dialog boxes such as the Unsharp Mask filter, or you can simply tab to the next field and type in a number if you already know the value you want.

Previewing

Most of Photoshop's tonal- and color-correction features and many of its filters offer a Preview checkbox in their dialog boxes. Plus, all the filters that have a dialog box have a proxy window that shows the effect applied to a small section of the image (some dialog boxes have both). If you're working on a very large file on a relatively slow machine, and the filter you're using has a proxy window, you might want to turn off the Preview checkbox so that Photoshop doesn't slow down redrawing the screen. However, most of the time we just leave the Preview feature on.

Before version 6 of Photoshop, the Preview checkbox in all the Image Adjust dialog boxes (Levels, Curves, Hue/Saturation, and so on) acted as a switch to turn on and off the Video LUT Animation feature. When the Preview option was off, the video LUT ("look up table") kicked in, altering the entire screen instead of just the image or portion of an image. This was much faster on slow machines, but it wasn't always accurate (and didn't work in Windows anyway). In Photoshop 6, Adobe removed Video LUT Animation entirely. Fortunately, they left in our favorite video LUT trick: finding white and black clipping points in the Levels dialog box (see "Levels Command Goodies" in Chapter 6, *Tonal Correction Fundamentals*).

Today, we primarily use the Preview checkbox to view "before" and "after" versions of our images, toggling it on and off to see the effect of the changes without leaving the dialog box.

Proxies. The proxy in dialog boxes shows only a small part of the image, but it updates almost instantly. Previewing time-consuming filters such as Unsharp Mask or Motion Blur on a large file can take a long time, and some very time-consuming filters such as the Distort filters don't offer a preview at all, so we rely on the proxy a lot.

Tip: Before and After in Proxies. You can always see a before-and-after comparison by clicking in the proxy. Hold down the mouse button to see the image before the filter is applied, and release it to see the image after the filter is applied.

Tip: Changing the Proxy View. To see a different part of the image, click-and-drag in the proxy (no modifier keys are necessary). Alternatively, you can click in the document itself. The cursor changes to a small rectangle—wherever you click shows up in the Preview window.

Similarly, you can zoom the proxy in and out. The *slow* way is to click on the little (+) and (-) buttons. Much faster is to click the proxy with either the Command or Option key held down—the former zooms in, the latter zooms out. However, we rarely zoom in and out because you can't see the true effect of a filter unless you're at 100-percent view.

Note that proxies only show the layer you're working on at any one time. This makes sense, really; only that layer is going to be affected.

New Dialog Box

Before we move on to essential tips about tools, we need to take a quick look at the New dialog box, which has a few very helpful (and in some cases hidden) features. For instance, note that the New dialog box now has an Advanced button; when you press this, you're offered two additional settings: Color Profile and Pixel Aspect Ratio. Color Profile lets you specify a working space for your image (we cover working spaces in Chapter 5, *Color Settings*). Pixel Aspect Ratio lets you choose a non-square pixel, in case your image is destined for video. If video isn't in your game plan, then avoid this popup menu entirely. (Neither of us are video experts, so we're pretty darn happy with plain ol' square pixels.)

Tip: Preset Document Sizes. The Preset popup menu in the New dialog box lets you pick from among 24 common document sizes, such as A4, 640 × 480, and 4 × 6 inches. In Photoshop 7, if you didn't like these default presets, you could use a text editor (like Windows Notepad or BBedit) to edit a special text file on disk. In Photoshop CS, editing what appears in the Preset popup menu is both more limited and easier. It's more limited because you can no longer delete built-in presets, even if you don't need them. It's easier because all you have to do is set up the New dialog box the way you want it and then click the Save Preset button (see Figure 2-9).

When you save a document preset, Photoshop gives you the choice of which settings to remember: Resolution, Mode, Bit Depth, Content, Profile, and Pixel Aspect Ratio. For example, let's say you turn off the Profile checkbox; when you later choose your preset from the Preset popup menu, Photoshop leaves the image's profile set to the default (whatever you last used, typically) instead of overriding it.

If you tire of your preset, you can always select it from the Preset popup menu and then press the Delete Preset button to erase it. Note that some built-in presets (those having to do with video), can also automatically

Figure 2-9
The New
dialog box

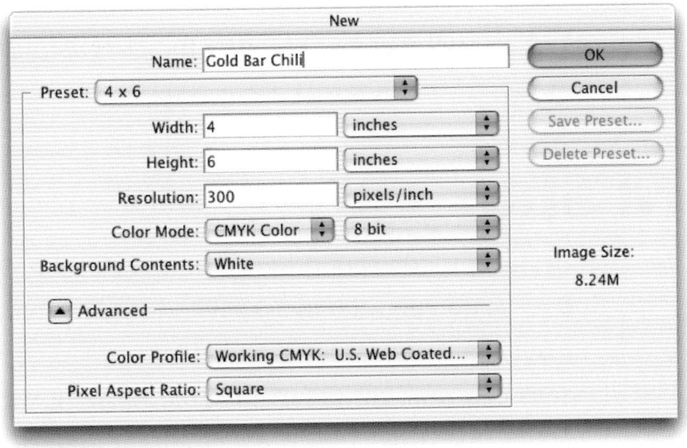

add guides to the document. Unfortunately, there's currently no way to save presets with guides yourself.

Tip: Clairvoyant Image Size. The New dialog box tries to read your mind. If you have something copied to the Clipboard when you create a new document, Photoshop automatically selects Clipboard from the Preset popup menu and plugs the pixel dimensions, resolution, and color model of that copied piece into the proper places of the dialog box for you. If you'd rather use the values from the last new image you created, hold down the Option key while selecting New from the File menu (or press Command-Option-N).

Tip: Breaking Up Measurements. Photoshop is just trying to help make your life easier: When you select a measurement system (inches, picas, pixels, or whatever) in the New dialog box—or the Image Size or the Canvas Size dialog box—Photoshop changes both the horizontal and vertical settings. If you want vertical to be set to picas and horizontal to be millimeters, then hold down the Shift key while selecting a measurement system. That tells the program not to change the other setting, too.

Tip: Copying Sizes from Other Documents. Russell Brown, that king of Photoshop tips and tricks, reminded us to keep our eyes open. Why, for instance, is the Window menu not grayed out when you have the New dialog box open? Because you can select items from it!

If you want your new document to have the same pixel dimensions, resolution, and color mode as a document you already have open, you can select that document from the bottom of the Window menu or the bottom of the Preset popup menu. Voilà! The statistics are copied.

This trick also works in the Image Size and Canvas Size dialog boxes.

Keyboard Shortcuts

In the early days of desktop publishing software, programmers figured it was good enough to assign various keyboard shortcuts to menu items. Even if the keyboard shortcut (which engineers abbreviate KBSC) made no sense, we users were forced to memorize it if we were to become efficient. Today, the times they are a changin', at least for some programs. While

QuarkXPress is still living in the dark ages, Photoshop CS now lets you edit every keyboard shortcut to your own liking, and even add shortcuts where there weren't any before. (Actually, you can't edit *every* shortcut; while the documentation says you can edit the shortcuts in the File Browser, the currently-shipping version doesn't yet let you do this.)

Of course, the ability to change keyboard shortcuts is great for users, but wreaks havoc for those of us who write books about the software! Throughout this book we describe the keyboard shortcuts in the Photoshop Defaults set. (Someday you'll know you're really living in the future when you change your shortcuts and our book—printed on "digital paper"—automatically updates.)

Tip: Use Your Own Set. To change or add a keyboard shortcut, select Keyboard Shortcuts from the bottom of the Edit menu. Now stop! Before you do anything else, create a new shortcut set. (Or, if you have already made one, ensure that it's selected in the Set popup menu of the Keyboard Shortcuts dialog box.) To make a new set, press the New Set button (see Figure 2-10); by default, Photoshop saves the set in the proper location on your hard drive (inside your Photoshop application folder, in Presets>Keyboard Shortcuts). Actually, even if you edit the default set, you can still get the original default back (just choose Photoshop Defaults from the Set menu). But it's still better etiquette to make your own set first.

After selecting the shortcut set you want to use, follow these steps.

Figure 2-10
Edit Keyboard
Shortcuts

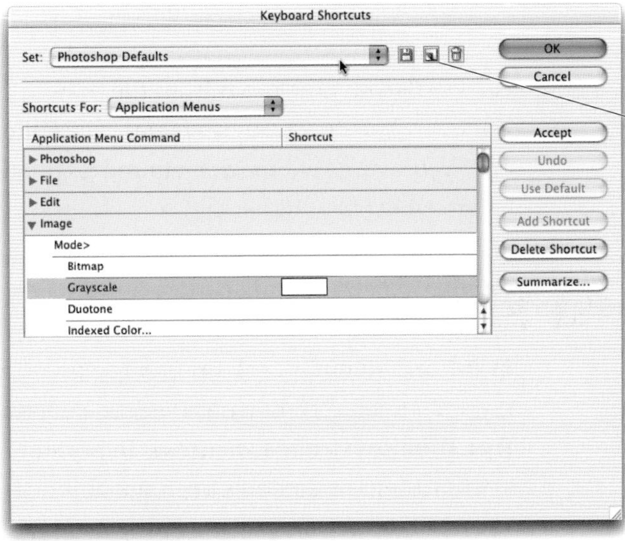

Click here to create a new set based on the current set.

1. Pick Application Menus, Palette Menus, or Tools from the Shortcuts For popup menu. All of Photoshop's shortcuts fall into one of these three areas.

2. Choose from the feature list (you have to click on the little "expand" icon to the left of a menu or palette name to see its features).

3. Note that the field in the Shortcut column is highlighted; now you can type the keyboard shortcut you want to apply to this feature. If the shortcut is already in use, Photoshop alerts you—if you proceed, the shortcut is removed from the other feature and applied here.

4. If you want to create another shortcut for the same feature (there's no reason you can't have more than one shortcut that does the same thing), press the Add Shortcut button. If you're done with this feature and want to change another, press the Accept button. When you're done applying shortcuts, press OK.

Tip: What Was That Shortcut Again? With the advent of editable keyboard shortcuts, there are now hundreds of different shortcuts you can keep track of. It's too much for any mortal brain. Fortunately, you can press the Summarize button in the Keyboard Shortcuts dialog box to export a list of every feature and its shortcuts. Photoshop saves this file in HTML format, so you can open it in any Web browser and print it out for future reference.

Tools

After you're finished moving around in your image, zooming in and out, and moving pixels hither and yon, it's time to get down to work with Photoshop's tools. Photoshop's tools have all sorts of hidden properties that can make life easier and—more important—more efficient. Let's look at a number of tips and techniques for getting the most out of these instruments of creation.

Tip: Tool Keystrokes. The most important productivity tip we've found in Photoshop to date has been the ability to select each and every tool with a keystroke. Unlike most programs, the keystrokes for Photoshop's tools do not use any modifier keys. You press the key without Command, Control, or Option. Figure 2-11 shows the keystroke for each tool.

Some tools in the Tool palette have multiple modes. For instance, the Dodge tool also "contains" the Burn and the Sponge tools. The slow way to access the different modes is to press the tool icon to bring up the popout palette containing the different modes. A faster method is to press the tool's keystroke once to select it, and then hold down the Shift key while pressing it again to toggle among the choices. Press M once, and you jump to the Marquee tool; then press Shift-M, and it switches to the elliptical Marquee tool; press Shift-M once more, and it switches back to the rectangular Marquee tool. Note that this keystroke doesn't cycle through the single-row marquee or the single-column marquee.

(Photoshop lets you change this behavior: If you turn off the "Use Shift Key for Tool Switch" checkbox in the General panel of the Preferences dialog box—see "Preferences," later in this chapter—then you don't have to hold down the Shift key to rotate through the tools; each time you press M, you'll get a different tool.)

Tip: Changing Blend Modes. You can also change blend modes (Normal, Screen, Multiply, and so on) by pressing Shift-minus and Shift-plus, or by holding down Shift and Option and pressing the first letter of the mode (such as Shift-Option-S for Screen). If you have a painting tool selected (like the Brush tool), this changes the mode of the selected tool; otherwise, it changes the mode of the layer itself.

Tip: Swap Tool Effect. While we rarely use the Blur, Sharpen, Dodge, or Burn tools (the first two are kind of clunky and we prefer to use adjustment layers rather than the last two), it is kind of fun to know that if you hold down the Option key, the Blur tool switches to the Sharpen tool (and vice versa), and the Dodge tool switches to the Burn tool (and vice versa).

Tip: Options Bar Keystrokes. The tools on the Tool palette only go so far. You often need to modify the tool's default settings on the Options bar. Try this: select a tool, then press Return. The Options bar, even if hidden, appears at this command. Plus, if there is a number-input field on the Options bar, Photoshop selects it for you. When you press Return with the Lasso or Marquee tools selected, for example, the Feather field becomes highlighted on the Options bar.

Figure 2-11
Keystrokes for tools

*Of course, these are
just the defaults;
you can edit the
shortcuts by
selecting Keyboard
Shortcuts in the
Edit menu*

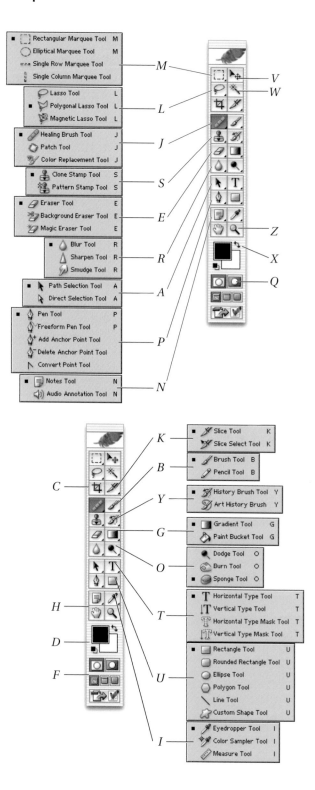

If there is more than one number-input field on the Options bar, you can press Tab to jump from one to the next. Finally, when you're finished with your changes, press Return again to exit from the bar and resume work.

Tool Presets

Each tool in the Tool palette offers one or more options, such as how large a brush diameter, or whether a selection is feathered, or what mode a tool will paint in (Multiply, Screen, and so on). It's a hassle to remember to set all the tool options, but fortunately Photoshop can remember them for you if you use the Tool Presets feature.

The Tool Presets feature lives in two places: at the far left side of the Options bar, and in the Tool Presets palette (which you can select from the Window menu). We find that the palette is most useful for fine artists who need to switch among various tool presets often within the same image (see Figure 2-12). Production folks like us tend to keep the palette closed and select tools from the Tool Presets popup menu in the Options bar (see Figure 2-13).

Figure 2-12
Tool Presets palette

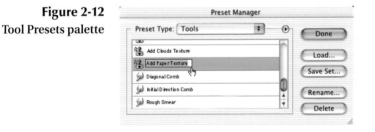

To create a new tool preset, select any tool in the Tool palette, change the Options bar to the way you want it, click on the Tool Presets popup menu in the Options bar, then click the New Tool Preset button (it looks like a little page with a dog-eared corner). Or, faster, after setting up the tool, you can Option-click on the Tool Presets icon in the Options bar. When Photoshop asks you for a name, we suggest giving the tool preset a descriptive name, like "ShapeTool Circle 50c20m."

Photoshop also comes with several pre-made collections of tool presets, such as Art History and Brushes. The trick to finding these (and doing all sorts of other things with tool presets, like saving your own sets), is to click once on the Tool Presets popup menu in the Options bar, and then click once on the popout menu icon (the little triangle on the side of the menu). Or, if the Tool Presets palette is open, you can find all these same options in the palette's popout menu.

Unfortunately, there's no way to edit a tool preset once you make it—you can only create a new one and delete the old one by choosing Delete Tool Preset from the Tool Preset popout menu.

Figure 2-13
Tool Preset
popup menu

Tip: Renaming Tool Presets. You can't edit a tool preset name in the Options bar's Tool Preset popup menu, but you can in the Tool Presets palette. Just double-click on the preset name. Similarly, you can edit preset names by double-clicking on them in the Preset Manager dialog box (select Preset Manager from the Edit menu).

Tip: Resetting the Tools. Photoshop power users are forever changing the settings for the tools on the Options bar. But every now and again, it's nice to level the playing field. You can reset the tool options for either a single tool or for all the tools by Control-clicking on the Tool Presets popup menu on the far left edge of the Options bar (or right-mouse-button in Windows).

Eyedropper

Matching colors by eye can be difficult. Instead, use the tool designed for the job: the Eyedropper.

Tip: Eyedropper Keystroke. You can always grab the Eyedropper from the Tool palette (or press I), but if you already have a painting tool selected, it's faster just to use the Option key to toggle between the Eyedropper tool and the painting tool.

Tip: How Many Pixels Are You Looking At? Almost every image has noise in it—pixels that are just plain wrong. If you're clicking around with the Eyedropper tool, there's a reasonable chance that you'll click right on one of those noise pixels, resulting in a color you don't expect (or want). The key is to change what the Eyedropper is looking at.

David usually changes the Sample Size popup menu in the Options bar to 3 by 3 Average. This way, the Eyedropper looks at nine pixels (the pixel you click on, plus the eight surrounding it) and averages them. If he's working on a very high-resolution image, however, he switches to 5 by 5 Average. Bruce, on the other hand, lives on the edge: he always leaves the Eyedropper set to Point Sample. If he thinks there's a danger of picking up a noise pixel, he just zooms in far enough to see exactly which pixel he's sampling.

Tip: Don't Limit your Eyedropping. Don't forget that when you're working with the Eyedropper tool, you can click on *any* open Photoshop document, or even the Picker, Swatches, or Scratch palettes. This usually even works when a dialog box is open. If you want to select a color from someplace else on screen (outside of Photoshop), first click down inside a Photoshop document, and then drag the mouse (with the button held down) over the color you want. Note that this only captures the RGB color values of whatever is visible on screen (there's no way for Photoshop to find out what the underlying color value is if you sample, say, a CMYK color from a QuarkXPress document).

Tip: Lock your Sample Points. The Color Sampler (which is hidden as an alternate to the Eyedropper tool) lets you place a sample point at any location in your image and expands the Info palette to show the readings at this coordinate (see Figure 2-14). This is most helpful when performing

Figure 2-14
Locking sample points

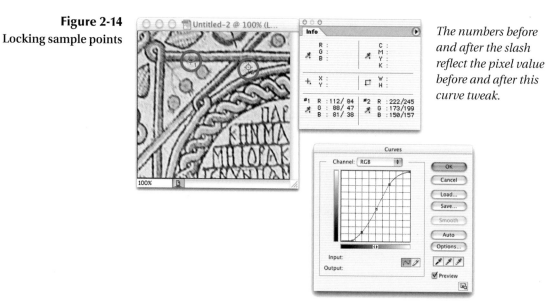

The numbers before and after the slash reflect the pixel value before and after this curve tweak.

color or tonal adjustments, because you can quickly see how your tweaks are affecting various areas of your image while you're making changes. (See Chapter 6, *Tonal Correction Fundamentals,* for more on this technique.)

We almost never choose the actual Color Sampler tool from the toolbox. Instead, we just Shift-click with the normal Eyedropper tool (or Option-Shift-click with any of the painting tools), which does the same thing. If you want to move a sample point someplace else, you can just click-and-drag it with the Color Sampler tool (or Shift-drag with the Eyedropper tool). To delete a sample point, just Option-click with the Color Sampler tool (or Option-Shift-click on it with either the Eyedropper tool or any painting tool).

Gradient Tool

One of the complaints Adobe heard most in times gone by was that blends in Photoshop resulted in banding. The answer they always gave was to "add noise" to the blend. It's true; adding noise reduces banding significantly. Fortunately, Photoshop adds noise for us. Of course, you can stop it by turning off the Dither checkbox in the Options bar, but there's almost no reason to do so. You *may* want to turn dithering off if you're doing scientific imaging or printing to a continuous-tone device that can actually reproduce the gradient without banding.

Tip: Adding More Noise. If you're still getting banding even with Dither turned on, you may want to add even more noise to a blend. However, note that you don't always need to apply the Add Noise filter to the entire gradient; use the filter selectively.

Instead, you might find it better to add noise to only one or two channels. View each channel separately (see Chapter 8, *Selections and Channels*) to see where the banding is more prevalent. Then add some noise just to the blend area in that channel.

Tip: Blends in CMYK. Eric Reinfeld pounded it into our heads one day: if you're going to make blends in Photoshop images that will end up in CMYK mode, create them in CMYK mode. Sometimes changing modes from RGB to CMYK can give you significant color shifts in blends.

Tip: Gradients on Layers. Some people make hard work of creating a blend that fades away into transparency. They go through endless convolutions of Layer Masks and Channel Options, or they spend hours building custom gradients, and so on. They're making it difficult for themselves by not opening their eyes. When you have the Gradient tool selected, the Options bar offers a popup menu with various gradients in it, and one of the defaults blends from Foreground to Transparent, or from Transparent to Foreground. If that option isn't available, someone may have edited your gradient presets. You can create or edit a gradient by clicking once on the gradient swatch in the Options bar. You can also select a different set of gradient presets from the popout menu to the right of the swatch (see Figure 2-15).

Paint Brushes

We can't tell you how to make great art using Photoshop's painting tools, but we can give you some hints about how to use them more efficiently.

Photoshop 7 dramatically increased the ability to customize your brushes (see Figure 2-16). It's important to remember that these brush styles aren't only for painting with the Brush tool—they also work with the Eraser tool, the Clone Stamp tool, the History Brush tool, and so on. While most of the new brush features are designed for fine art work (simulating charcoal, water colors, and so on), every now and again you may find them helpful in a production environment, too—especially for detailed

Figure 2-15
Gradient options

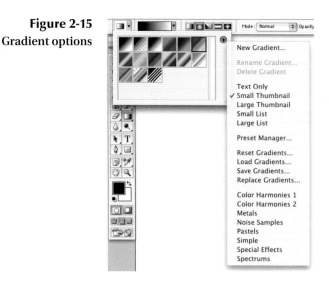

Figure 2-16
The Brushes palette

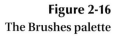

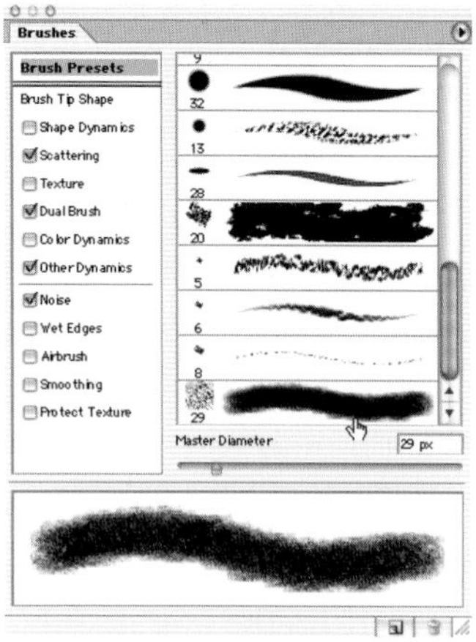

retouching. Note that beginning in Photoshop CS you can use the Brush tool in 16-bit images, too.

Tip: Brush Keystrokes. Did you know that the [and] keys (the square brackets) increase and decrease the diameter of a brush? Plus, Shift-[and Shift-] change the brush's hardness. We now keep one hand on the keyboard and one on our mouse (or tablet pen); when we want to change tools, we press the key for that tool. When we want to change brush size, we cycle through the brushes with the [and] keys until we find the size we like. Here's one more shortcut, too: the Command and period keys move up and down through the brush presets.

Tip: Fastest Brush Selection. Actually, one of the best ways to select a brush is probably via the context-sensitive menu. On the Macintosh, hold down the Control key when you click with any of the painting tools and Photoshop displays the Brushes menu wherever you click. In Windows, right-mouse-button-click to see the menu. After selecting a brush size, press Enter or Esc to make the palette disappear.

Tip: Hovering Pseudo-Selections. Instead of selecting a brush from the Brushes palette, then painting with it to see how it will really look, hover the cursor over the preset for a moment and Photoshop will display a sample of that brush at the bottom of the palette. If you don't like it, hover over another brush. When you find one you like, click on it to select it.

Tip: Opacity by the Numbers. In between changing brush sizes, we're forever changing brush opacity while painting or retouching. If you're still moving the sliders around on the Options bar, stop it. Instead, just type a number from 0 to 9. Zero gives you 100-percent opacity, 1 gives you 10 percent, 2 gives you 20 percent, and so on. For finer control, press two number keys in quick succession—for example, pressing 45 gets you 45-percent opacity. If you have a non-painting tool selected in the Tool palette, then typing a number changes the opacity of the layer you're working on (unless it's the Background layer, of course). Note that if the Airbrush feature in the Options bar is turned on, then typing numbers affects the Flow percentage rather than the Opacity setting.

Tip: Touching Up Line Art. We talk about scanning and converting to line art in Chapter 12, *Line Art*, but since we're on the topic of painting tools, we should discuss the Pencil tool for just a moment. One of the best techniques for retouching line-art (black-and-white) images is the Auto Erase feature on the Options bar. When Auto Erase is turned on, the Pencil tool works like this: if you click on any color other than the foreground color, that pixel—along with all others you touch before lifting the mouse button—is changed to the foreground color (this is the way it works, even with Auto Erase turned off). If you click on the foreground color, however, that pixel—along with all others you encounter—is changed to the background color. This effectively means you don't have to keep switching the foreground and background colors while you work.

Tip: Use All Layers. If you're working on a multilayer image, you may find yourself frustrated with tools like the Smudge, Blur, Magic Wand, or the Clone Stamp tools. That's because sometimes you want these tools to "see" the layers below the one you're working on, and sometimes you do not. Fortunately, Photoshop gives you a choice for each of these tools with the Use All Layers checkbox on the Options bar. (Note that in older versions, this was called Sample Merged.)

When Use All Layers is turned off, each tool acts as though the other layers weren't even there. But if you turn it on, look out! Photoshop sees the other visible layers (both above and below it) and acts as though they were merged together (see Figure 2-17).

The benefit of this is great, but people often don't see the downfall. Let's say your background contains a blue box, and Layer 1 has an overlapping yellow box. When you paint or smudge or blur or whatever with Use All Layers turned on, Photoshop "sucks up" the blue and paints it into Layer 1. If you think about it, that's what it should and has to do. But it can really throw you for a loop if you're not prepared.

Cropping Tool

We almost always scan a little bigger than we need, just in case. So we end up using the Cropping tool a lot. The nice thing about the Cropping tool (as opposed to the Crop feature on the Image menu) is that you can make fine adjustments before agreeing to go through with the paring. Just drag one of the corner or side handles. Here are a couple more ways you can fine-tune the crop.

Tip: See What Gets Cropped. By default, Photoshop darkens the area outside the cropping rectangle so that you can see what's going to get cropped out before you press Enter. However, David likes to change this behavior so that it ghosts the cropped out pixels instead (turns them near white). You can do this by clicking on the Color swatch in the Options bar (when the Cropping tool is selected) and picking white from the Color Picker instead of black. You may want to increase the opacity of the color in the Options bar, too (David usually uses 80 percent).

Tip: Rotating and Moving While Cropping. If cropping an image down is the most common postscan step, what is the second most common? Rotating, of course. You can crop and rotate at the same time with

Figure 2-17
Use All Layers

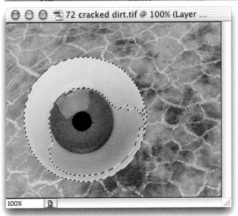

When Use All Layers is turned off and we click on the eyeball,
Photoshop only selects portions of the eye.

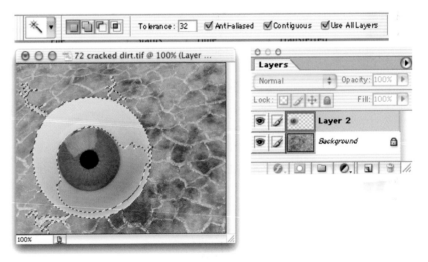

When Use All Layers is turned on, the selection extends past the eye
because there is some white in the background.

the Cropping tool: after dragging out the cropping rectangle with the Cropping tool, just place the cursor outside the cropping rectangle and drag. The rectangle rotates. When you press Return or Enter, Photoshop crops and rotates the image to straighten the rectangle. It can be tricky to get exactly the right angle by eye—keep an eye on the Info palette. Also, if the cropping rectangle isn't in the right place, you can always move it—just place the cursor inside the cropping rectangle and drag.

Tip: Adjusting for Keystone. What do you do about lines in your image that are supposed to be vertical or horizontal but aren't? For example, if you take a picture of a tall building from the sidewalk, the vertical lines of the building appear skewed (they look like they get closer together near the top). Fortunately, our faithful Cropping tool offers a cool option: adjusting for perspective. The key is to turn on the Perspective checkbox in the Options bar after drawing the cropping rectangle; this lets you grab the corner points and move them willy-nilly where you will.

However, positioning the corner points of the cropping "rectangle" can be tricky. You must first find something in the image that is supposed to be a rectangle, and set the corner points on the corners of that shape. In the example of a building, you might choose the corners of a window. Then, hold down the Option and Shift keys while dragging one of the corner handles; this expands the crop but retains its shape. When you have the cropping shape the size you want it, drag the center point icon to where the camera was pointing (or where you imagine the center of the focus should be). Then press Enter or Return.

Our favorite use for this technique is photographing framed paintings (or anything hanging on the wall). If you shoot the painting straight-on (especially with a flash), you get a nasty reflection. Instead, try photographing it slightly from one side. The image becomes distorted by this perspective, but this Perspective feature can quickly straighten it out (see Figure 2-18).

By the way, we find that when using this tool Photoshop often alerts us that either the center point or the corner points are in the wrong position. This usually happens when you haven't selected the corner points of something that *should* be rectangular. In other words, Photoshop acts as a safety net, stopping you when you choose a distortion that isn't likely to happen in a real photograph. Sometimes simply moving the center point to a different location (by trial and error) does the trick.

Tip: Save that Layer Data. In early versions of Photoshop, the cropping tool would throw away pixels outside the cropping rectangle. If you changed your mind and wanted to crop the image differently, you would have to select Undo and then try again. But Photoshop now gives you the option (by selecting the Hide button in the Options bar after dragging the cropping rectangle) of saving the cropped-out pixels as *big data*—material that hangs outside the actual visible image rectangle. Then, if you didn't get

Figure 2-18
Adjusting perspective
with the Cropping tool

*The cropping
corners set to
a rectangle in
the image*

*It was impossible
to photograph this
floor mosaic without
keystone distortion.*

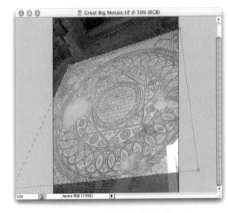

*The crop is extended by holding down
Option and Shift while dragging
the corner points.*

*Press Enter or Return to crop
and adjust for perspective.*

the crop just right, you can either move the image around with the Move tool or re-crop using a different rectangle (see "Tip: Expand the Canvas by Cropping," later in this chapter). Note that this only works on layers other than the Background layer.

Tip: Resampling While Cropping. Warning: the Cropping tool may be changing your resolution or even resampling your image data without you knowing it! The Height, Width, and Resolution fields in the Options bar (when you have the Cropping tool selected) let you choose a size and resolution for your cropped picture. Basically, these fields let you save the step of visiting the Image Size dialog box after cropping. But remember that when you use them, they always change your image resolution or resample the image (see Chapter 3, *Image Essentials*, for more on the pros and cons of resampling).

In ancient versions of Photoshop, if you left the Resolution field blank and you specified a Height and Width without specifying any units (like pixels, inches, and so on), the program would constrain the cropping size to a particular aspect ratio (like four-by-six) but it wouldn't mess with your resolution. Alas, now the Height and Width fields always have units attached to them. If you leave the Resolution field blank, Photoshop adjusts the image resolution to accommodate the change in size. That means your image resolution can drop or increase without you realizing it. (In this case, Photoshop is *not* resampling the data—just adjusting the size of the pixels.) Instead, see the next tip for how to crop to an aspect ratio.

If you type a value into the Resolution field, Photoshop resamples the image to that value. This resampling behavior is handy when you want to resample down, but be careful that you don't ask for more resolution than you really have; resampling up is usually best avoided. (Note that you can only set the Height, Width, and Resolution values *before* you start cropping; once you draw a cropping rectangle, the Options bar changes.)

Tip: Cropping to an Aspect Ratio. Let's say you want to crop your image to a four-by-six aspect ratio (height-to-width, or vice versa), but you don't want to resample the image (which adds or removes pixels, causing blurring) or change the image resolution. The Cropping tool can't perform this task anymore, so you need a different technique. First, select the Marquee (rectangular selection) tool and choose Fixed Aspect Ratio from the Style popup menu in the Options bar. The Options bar then lets you type values in the Height and Width fields (here you'd type *4* and *6*). Next, marquee the area you want cropped, and then select Crop from the Image menu. See Chapter 8, *Selections and Channels,* for tips and tricks for the Marquee tool.

Tip: Expand the Canvas by Cropping. Once you've created a cropping rectangle with the Cropping tool, you can actually expand the crop past the boundaries of the image (assuming you zoom back until you see the gray area around the image in the document window). Then, after you press Enter, the canvas size actually expands to the edge of the cropping rectangle. This is David's favorite way to enlarge the canvas.

Tip: Cropping Near the Border. If you're trying to shave just a sliver of pixels off one side of an image, you'll find it incredibly annoying that Photoshop snaps the cropping rectangle to the edge of the image whenever you drag close to it. Fortunately, you can turn this behavior off by selecting Snap in the View menu (or pressing Command-Shift-;). Or, you can hold down the Control key to temporarily disable the snapping behavior.

Eraser Tool

The Eraser tool has gotten a bad rap because people assume you have to use a big, blocky eraser. No, you can erase using any brush—soft or hard, like an airbrush or even with the textured brushes in the Brushes palette. And what's more, you can control the opacity of the Eraser (don't forget you can just type a number on the keyboard to change the tool's opacity). This makes the eraser fully useable, in our opinion. However, just because a tool is useable doesn't mean you have to use it. Whenever possible, we much prefer masking to erasing. The difference? Masks (which we cover in Chapter 8, *Selections and Channels*) can "erase" pixels without actually deleting them. Masks just hide the data, and you can always recover it later. Nevertheless, the Eraser tool can on occasion get you out of a jam. Here are a few tips.

Tip: Erase to History. The Erase to History feature (it's a checkbox on the Options bar when you have the Eraser tool selected) lets you use the Eraser tool to replace pixels from an earlier state of the image (see "When Things Go Worng," later in this chapter, for more on the History feature). Erase to History more or less turns the Eraser into the History Brush tool. For instance, you can open a file, mess with it until it's a mess, then revert *parts of it* to the original using the Eraser tool with Erase to History turned on.

The important thing to remember is that you can temporarily turn on the Erase to History feature by holding down the Option key while using the Eraser tool.

Tip: Watch Preserve Transparency When Erasing. Note that the Eraser tool (or any other tool, for that matter) won't change a layer's transparency when you have the Preserve Transparency checkbox turned on in the Layers palette. That means it won't erase pixels away to transparency; rather it just paints in the background color. Don't forget you can turn Preserve Transparency on and off by pressing / (slash).

Tip: Erasing to Transparency. When you use a soft-edged brush to erase pixels from a layer (rather than the Background layer), the pixels that are partially erased—that is, they're still somewhat visible, but they have some transparency in them—cannot be brought back to full opacity. For example, if you set the Eraser to 50-percent opacity and erase a bunch of pixels from a layer, there's no way to get them back to 100-percent again. The reason: You're not changing the pixel's color, you're only changing the layer's transparency mask. This isn't really a tip: it's just a warning. What you erase sometimes doesn't really go away.

Measurement Tool

We still sometimes hear people complain that Photoshop doesn't have a Measurement tool. Actually Photoshop does have one, but for some reason people don't notice it. That's too bad, because the Measurement tool is extremely useful for measuring distances and angles. The keyboard shortcut for this tool is "I" (or Shift-I if it's hiding under the Eyedropper tool). Here's a rundown of how this tool works.

▶ To measure between two pixels, click-and-drag from one point to the other with the Measurement tool.

▶ Once you have a measuring line, you can hide it by selecting any other tool from the Tool palette. To show it again, select the Measurement tool.

▶ You can move the measuring line by dragging the line (not the endpoints). If you drag an endpoint, you just move that one end of the line.

▶ You can't really delete a measuring line, but you can move it outside the boundaries of the image window, which is pretty much the same thing.

▶ You can turn the measuring line into a V-shaped compass in order to measure an angle by Option-clicking on one end of the measuring line and dragging (see Figure 2-19).

Where do you find the measurement? On the Info palette or the Options bar, of course. The palette displays the angle and the horizontal and ver-

Figure 2-19
Measuring up

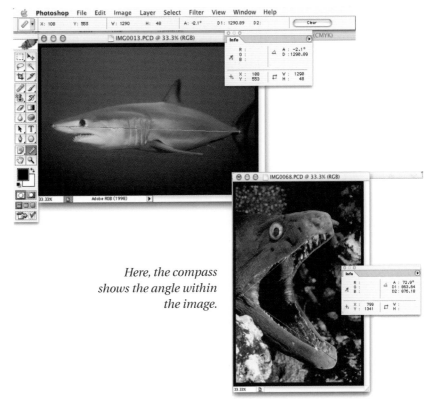

*Here, the compass
shows the angle within
the image.*

tical distances, along with the total distance in whatever measurement system you've set up in Units Preferences.

Tip: Measuring Before Rotating. We know you always make sure your images are placed squarely on the scanner before you scan them, but you may occasionally have to level someone else's crooked scan. Again, the Measurement tool can help immensely. If you select Arbitrary from the Rotate Canvas submenu (under the Image menu) immediately after using the Measurement tool, Photoshop automatically grabs the angle and places it in the dialog box for you.

There are two things to note here. First, the angle in the Rotate Canvas dialog box is usually slightly more accurate, so the number you see there may be slightly different from the one on the Info palette (usually within half a degree). Second, if the angle is above 45 degrees, Photoshop automatically subtracts it from 90 degrees, assuming that you want to rotate it counterclockwise to align with the vertical axis instead of the horizontal axis.

Notes Tools

While the majority of images touched by Photoshop are edited by a single person, people are increasingly working on pictures in teams. Perhaps the team is a retoucher and a client, or perhaps it's four Photoshop users, each with specific skills—whatever the case, it's important for these folks to communicate with each other. Enter Photoshop's Notes tools (press N). Photoshop has two Notes tools: one for text annotations and one for audio annotations. We suggest using audio annotations to your images only if you've never learned to type or if you're tired of having so much extra space on your hard drive—audio notes can make your files balloon in size (each 10 seconds of audio you add is about 140 K compared to about 1 K for 100 words of text notes).

To add a text annotation, click once on the image with the Notes tool and type what you will. If you type more than can fit in the little box, Photoshop automatically adds a scroll bar on the side. In addition, you can change the note's color, author, font and size in the Options bar at any time.

Double-clicking on a note opens it (so you can read or listen to it) or closes it (minimizes it to just the Notes icon). Single-clicking on the Notes icon lets you move it or delete it (just press the Delete key). Or, if you want to delete all the notes in an image, press the Clear All button in the Options bar.

Tip: Move the Notes Away. By default, Photoshop places your notes windows at the same place in your image as the Notes icon. However, that means the little notes window usually covers up the image so you can't see what the note refers to. We usually drag the Notes icon off to the side slightly (just click-and-drag the note's title bar to move it), or—if there aren't many notes in a file—most of the way off the image, onto the gray area that surrounds the picture.

Tip: Show the Notes. If you can't see notes in your Photoshop file but you suspect they're there, make sure the Annotations item is turned on in the Show submenu (under the View menu). When this is off, no Notes icons appear.

Palettes

Bruce has a second monitor set up on his computer just so he can open all of Photoshop's palettes on it and free up his primary monitor's precious space. There's little doubt that palettes are both incredibly useful and incredibly annoying at times. Fortunately, Photoshop has some built-in but hidden features that make working with palettes a much happier experience. For instance, palettes are "sticky"—if you move them near the side of the monitor or near another palette, they'll "snap-to" align to that side or palette. (Even better, hold down the Shift key while you drag a palette to force it to the side of the screen.) This (if nothing else) helps you keep a neat and tidy screen on which to work.

Tip: Make the Palettes Go Away. If you only have one monitor on which to store both your image and Photoshop's plethora of palettes, you should remember two keyboard shortcuts. First, pressing Tab makes the palettes disappear (or reappear, if they're already hidden). We find this absolutely invaluable, and use it daily.

Second, pressing Shift-Tab makes all palettes except the Tool palette disappear (or reappear). We find this only slightly better than completely useless; we would prefer that the keystroke hid all the palettes except the Info palette.

Tip: Making Palettes Smaller. Another way to maximize your screen real estate is by collapsing one or more of your open palettes. If you double-click on the palette's name tab, the palette collapses to just the title bar and name (see Figure 2-20). Or if you click in the zoom box of a palette (the checkbox in the upper-right corner of the palette), the palette reduces in size to only a few key elements. For instance, if you click in the zoom box of the Layers palette, you can still use the Opacity sliders and Mode popup menu (but the Layer tiles and icons get hidden).

Tip: Mix and Match Palettes. There's one more way to save space on your computer screen: mix and match your palettes. Palettes in Photoshop have a curious attribute—you can drag one on top of another and they become one (see Figure 2-21). Then if you want, you can drag them apart

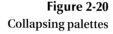

Figure 2-20
Collapsing palettes

Full palette

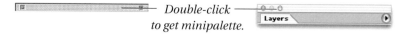

Click in the zoom box
to get partial palette.
(Unavailable on Mac OS X.)

Double-click
to get minipalette.

again by clicking and dragging the palette's tab heading. (In fact, these kinds of palettes are called "tabbed palettes.")

For instance, David always keeps his Layers, Channels, and Paths palettes together on one palette. When he wants to work with one of these, he can click on that palette's tab heading. Or better yet, he uses a keystroke to make it active (see "Actions" in Chapter 15, *Essential Image Techniques*, for more on how to define your own keyboard shortcuts).

Bruce, on the other hand, always keeps his Layers and Channels palettes separate, even when he's working on a single-monitor system. Neither of us ever mixes the Info palette with another palette, because we want it open all the time.

Photoshop offers one more way to combine palettes: by docking them. Docking a palette means that one palette is attached to the bottom of another one. Docked palettes always move together, and when you hide one they both disappear. To dock one palette to another, drag it over the other palette's bottom edge; don't let go of the mouse button until you see the bottom edge of the palette become highlighted.

Tip: In-and-Out Palettes. You can store palettes in the Options bar as well: when your screen resolution is above 800 pixels wide, the Options bar contains a "palette well," onto which you can drag palettes. Then, to use one of these palettes, just click on its tab. When you press Enter or

Figure 2-21
Mixing and matching
palettes

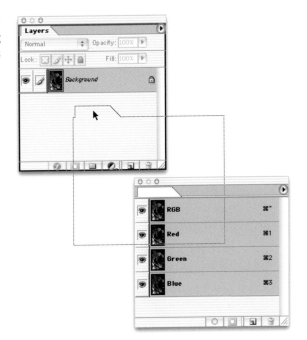

Return, or as soon as you start doing anything else (like use a tool or a menu), the palette minimizes into the well again. This behavior is perfect for the Swatches and Colors palettes, but is inappropriate for palettes you need open a lot, like the Info or Layers palettes.

Tip: Scrubby Sliders. Some palettes—notably Layers, Character, and Paragraph—sport a hidden new feature called "scrubby sliders," which lets you change values by clicking and dragging to the left or the right. For example, you can change the Opacity field in the Layers palette by clicking *on the title* "Opacity" and dragging to the left (to reduce opacity) or the right (to increase it). Not all fields in all palettes have this feature yet, but you can always tell a scrubby slider by hovering the cursor over the title of a field—scrubby sliders change the cursor icon to a pointed finger with left and right arrows. For faster scrubbing, hold down the Shift key, which multiplies the normal adjustment by ten.

Tip: Reset Palette Positions. Every now and again, your palettes might get really messed up—placed partly or entirely off your screen, and so on. Don't panic; that's what Reset Palette Locations (in the Workspace submenu, in the Window menu) is for.

Saving Workspaces

If you have a favorite way you like your palettes to be arranged on your screen, and your co-worker is forever moving them, don't go berserk and throw your carrot sticks at him. Instead, use the Workspace feature to save your palette setup and then recall it whenever necessary. It's easy to save a workspace: just arrange the palettes exactly the way you want them, and then choose Save Workspace from the Workspace submenu (under the Window menu; see Figure 2-22).

Later, when you want to recall your carefully customized creation, you can select it from the Workspace submenu. Workspaces are useful even if only one person is using the computer, too. For instance, David has one workspace for when he works on Web graphics (which has the Swatches palette and the Styles palette open) and another for print images (which has those palettes closed). In Photoshop CS, workspaces now apply to File Browser configurations, too, so Bruce has various workspaces which change the layout of the File Browser (one for big thumbnails, one for editing metadata, and so on).

Tip: Save Info Palette Configurations. If you're like us, you probably use different info palette setups for different kinds of work. For example, when Bruce works on RGB files destined for CMYK output, he sets one

Figure 2-22
Workspaces

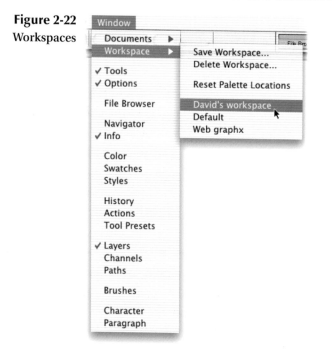

readout to RGB and the other to CMYK. But if he's working on RGB files for RGB output on an inkjet or film recorder, he sets the Info palette to read RGB and Lab. When you save a workspace, it records not only palette locations, but also the Info palette configuration, so you can use workspaces to switch easily between different Info palette setups.

Layers Palette

In every version since 3.0 (the first time that the layers feature was introduced), the Layers palette has become increasingly important to how people use Photoshop. With such a crucial palette, there have to be at least a few good tips around here. No?

Tip: Displaying and Hiding Layers. Every click takes another moment or two, and many people click in the display column of the Layers palette (the one with the little eyeballs in it) once for each layer they want to show or hide. Cut out the clicker-chatter, and just click-and-drag through the column for all the layers you want to make visible. Or, Option-click in the display column of the Layers palette. When you Option-click on an eyeball, Photoshop hides all the layers except the one you clicked on. Then, if you Option-click again, it redisplays them all again. Even though this trick doesn't save you a lot of time, it sure feels like it does (which is often just as cool).

Tip: Creating a New Layer. Layers are the best thing since sliced bread, and we're creating new ones all the time. But if you're still making a new layer by clicking on the New Layer button in the Layers palette, you've got some learning to do: Just click Command-Shift-N (or Command-Option-Shift-N, if you don't want to see the New Layer dialog box). If you're trying to duplicate the current layer, just press Command-J (if you have pixels selected when you press this, only those pixels will copy to a new layer).

Tip: Rename your Layers. It's a very good idea to rename your layers from Layer 1 or Layer 2 to something a bit more descriptive. However, don't waste time looking for a "rename layer" feature. Instead, just double-click on the layer tile to rename it. Note that this works in the Channels, Paths, and File Browser palettes, too.

Tip: Creating Layer Sets. The more layers you have in your document, the more difficult it is to manage them. Fortunately, Photoshop now offers layer "sets" in which you can group contiguous layers (layers that are next to each other). Layer sets are so easy to use that they really don't require a great deal of explanation. Here are the basics, though.

▶ To create a layer set, click on the New Layer Set button in the Layers palette (see Figure 2-23).

Figure 2-23
Layer sets

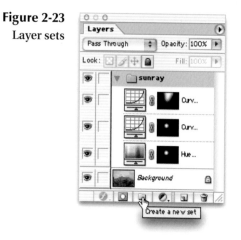

▶ To add a layer to a set, just drag it on top of the set. Or, to create a new layer inside the set automatically, select the set or any layer within the set (in the Layers palette) and press the New Layer button. You can remove a layer from a set simply by dragging it out.

▶ You can move layer sets in the same way you move layers: just drag them around in the palette. You can also copy a whole set of layers to a different document by dragging the layer set over.

▶ If you have more than one layer set, it's helpful to color code them: just double-click on the layer set's name and pick a color in the Layer Set Properties dialog box. You should probably name the set, too, while you're there (the default "Set 1" doesn't help identify what's in it). Watch out, though: if you drag a color-coded layer out of the set, it still retains its color-coding!

▶ If you want to move all the layers within a layer set at the same time, select the layer set in the Layers palette. This is easier and faster than linking the layers together.

▶ You can add a layer mask to the layer set (see Chapter 8, *Selections and Channels,* for more on masks) and it'll apply to every layer in the set. Similarly, locking a set locks every layer within the set.

▶ Photoshop CS lets you nest one layer set inside another; just drag a set on top of another set, as though you were dragging a folder inside another folder. Or, if you select a layer inside a set first, when you create a new set, it will also be nested. You can nest your layer sets up to five deep.

▶ Layer sets act almost like a single layer, so when you show or hide the set, all the layers in that set appear or disappear.

▶ When you delete a layer set, Photoshop lets you choose to delete the set *and* the layers and sets inside it or just the set itself (leaving the layers and nested sets intact).

Unfortunately, you can't apply a layer effect (see Chapter 15, *Essential Image Techniques*) to a set or use a set as a clipping group (see Chapter 8, *Selections and Channels*).

Tip: Layer Sets and Blending Modes. If you had your coffee this morning, you'll notice that you can change the blending mode of a layer set. Normally, the blending mode is set to Pass Through, which means, "let each layer's blending mode speak for itself." In this mode, layers inside the set look the same as they do if they were outside the set. However, if you change the set's blending mode, a curious thing happens: Photoshop first composites the layers in the set together as though they were a single layer (following the blending modes you've specified for each layer), and then it composites that "single layer" together with the rest of your image using the layer set's blending mode. In this case, layers may appear very different whether they're inside or outside that set.

Similarly, when you change the opacity of the set, Photoshop first composites the layers in the set together (using their individual Opacity settings) and then applies this global Opacity setting to the result.

Layer Comps Palette

We arrive, at last, at David's favorite new feature in Photoshop CS: the Layer Comps palette. David loves keeping his options open, and is forever trying to decide among various permutations of reality. For instance, he'll picture in his mind's eye five different ways to drive to the grocery store before committing to one. Photoshop's Layer Comps palette won't help him with his driving choices, but it's an awesome help when making decisions about how to edit an image in Photoshop.

The Layer Comps palette is like a clever combination of the Layers palette and the History palette: It lets you save the state of your document's layers so you can return to it later. It seems like the Layer Comps feature should be part of the Layers palette, but perhaps Adobe figured the Layers palette was already complex enough. (Besides, you know those engineers at Adobe—they're always game for adding a new palette!) While the snapshots feature of the History palette can perform most of the same tasks as the Layer Comps palette, the History palette is significantly more memory-intensive and—this is important—layer comps can be saved with the document while snapshots disappear when you close the file. Saving a layer comp makes almost no difference to your file size (each comp is only a few K on disk).

Tip: Layer Comps Don't Only Record Visibility. A "comp" details how each layer in the layer palette is composed. At first glance, it appears that each layer comp just records which layers are visible and which are hidden, but they can actually remember the position of items on each layer, layer effects, and the layer's blending mode, too. To create a layer comp, press the New Layer Comp button in the Layer Comps palette. Now Photoshop displays the New Layer Comp dialog box, which lets you name the layer comp, specify which settings Photoshop should remember, and insert a comment about the comp (see Figure 2-24).

It's a good idea to get into the habit of naming your layer comps and even writing a quick one-line comment about the comp. After you create three or four comps, you'll start to get confused as to what is what; and then if you save the file and come back to it later, you'll be totally lost if these aren't named or commented.

Photoshop can remember three kinds of information about your layer comps: Visibility, Position, and Appearance.

▶ By default, layer comps just remember the *visibility* of each layer—that is, which layers and layer sets are are visible and which are hidden in the Layers palette.

▶ When you turn on the Position checkbox, the layer comp remembers the geometry of all your layers—where on the layer the pixel data is sitting. For example, let's say you save a layer comp with Position turned on, and then use the Move tool to reposition the image or text on that layer. When you return to the saved layer comp, the image or text reverts back to where it was when you saved the comp.

▶ The Appearance option tells the program to remember any layer effects and blending modes that you've applied to your layers. For example, let's say you save a layer comp with Appearance turn *off*, then you change the blending modes of one or more layers in the Layers palette. When you return to the saved layer comp, the blending mode changes remain because you hadn't told the layer comp to retain the appearance of the layers.

For a quick and dirty layer comp with the default name, no comment, and the same attributes as the last comp you made (by default, just the Visibility option), hold down the Option (Alt) key while clicking the New Layer Comp button. Remember that, like layers and channels, you can always rename a layer comp by double-clicking on its name in the palette. If you double-click on the tile (anywhere other than its name), you open the Layer Comp Options dialog box.

Tip: Quick Display of Comps. Once you have saved one or more layer comps in the Layer Comps palette, you can return to a comp state by clicking the small square to the left of the comp name. You can also press the left and right arrow icons at the bottom of the Layer Comps palette. Better yet, if you have ten comps, but only want to cycle through three of them, select those three (Command- or Ctrl-click on the comps to select more than one) and then use the arrow buttons in the palette. If you use layer comps much, we strongly suggest that you use the Keyboard Shortcuts feature (in the Edit menu) to apply keyboard shortcuts to the Next Layer Comp and Previous Layer Comp features so you don't have to click those silly arrow buttons all the time.

Figure 2-24
Layer Comps
palette

Here, we're telling Photoshop to remember everything about the Layer palette and the position of the data (here, the text) on the layers.

Click here to create a new layer comp.

Layer comp comments appear here when you click on the triangle.

Clicking here applies this layer comp to the file.

Cycles through selected layer comps

You'll notice a layer comp called Last Document State in the Layer Comp palette. This is just the state of your document before you chose a layer comp. For example, let's say you display a layer comp, then hide some layers and move some text around. Now if you select any layer comp, your changes disappear—but if you click on the Last Document State comp, the changes return.

Tip: Updating Comps. Need to change the layer comp? You don't have to delete it and start over. Just set up the Photoshop document to reflect what you want the comp to look like, then select the comp in the palette, and press the Update Layer Comp button (that's the one that looks like two rotating arrows).

Tip: Sending Comps to Clients. The fact that Photoshop saves layer comps—comments and all—with your files is pretty cool. That means you can save a file as a PSD, TIFF, or PDF file and have someone else open the file in Photoshop and browse through the Layer Comp palette. Even cooler, however, are the three Export Layer Comp scripts in the Scripts submenu (under the File menu): Export Layer Comps to Files, Export Layer Comps to PDF, and Export Layer Comps to WPG. Each of these lets you save all (or the currently-selected) layer comps to one or more flattened files on disk. The PDF can even be a slide-show presentation which progresses automatically every few seconds if you want. It took us some time before we figured out what WPG is: It's a Web Photo Gallery of your comps, ready to post on a Web site.

Note that when you run the last two of these scripts (each written in Javascript, by the way), you'll see each of your comps appear twice. The first time, Photoshop is flattening and saving to disk; the second time, it's opening that flattened version and adding it to the presentation.

Tip: Clear Comp Warnings. If, after making one or more layer comps, you delete or merge a layer, you'll notice that small warning icons appear in the Layer Comps palette. These tell you that Photoshop can no longer return to the layer comp as saved (because the layer no longer exists like it did when you made the comp). You can still choose a layer comp that has a warning icon—it'll still apply to all the layers that still do exist. If you delete a layer and you don't want to see the warning icons anymore, Control-click (or right-click on Windows) on one of the icons and choose Clear All Layer Comp Warnings from the context menu.

Info Palette

In a battle of the palettes, we don't know which Photoshop palette would win the "most important" prize, but we do know which would win in the "most telling" category: the Info palette. We almost never close this palette. It just provides us with too much critical information.

At its most basic task, as a densitometer, it tells us the gray values and RGB or CMYK values in our image. But there's much more. When you're working in RGB, the Info palette shows you how pixels will translate into CMYK or Grayscale. When working in Levels or Curves, it displays before-and-after values (see Chapter 6, *Tonal Correction Fundamentals*). Especially note the Proof Color option, which shows the numbers that would result from the conversion you've specified in Proof Setup, which may be different from the one you've specified in Color Settings (see Chapter 5, *Color Settings*). The Proof Color numbers appear in italics—a clue that you're looking at a different set of numbers than the ones you'd get from a mode change.

But wait, there's more! When you rotate a selection, the Info palette displays what angle you're at. And when you scale, it shows percentages. If you've selected a color that is out of the CMYK gamut (depending on your setup; see Chapter 5, *Color Settings*), a gamut alarm appears on the Info palette.

Tip: Finding Opacity. When you have transparency showing (*e.g.*, on layers that have transparency when no background is showing), the Info palette can give you an opacity ("Op") reading. However, while Photoshop would display this automatically in earlier versions, now you have to do a little extra work: you must click on one of the little black eyedroppers in the Info palette and select Opacity (see Figure 2-25).

Tip: Switch Units. While we typically work in pixel measurements, we do on occasion need to see "real world" physical measurements such as inches or centimeters. Instead of traversing the menus to open the Units dialog box (on the Preferences submenu under the File menu), we find it's usually faster to select from the Info palette's popout menu. Just click on the XY cursor icon (see Figure 2-26). Another option: double-clicking in one of the rulers opens the Units Preferences dialog box. You can also do this by Control-clicking (Mac) or Right-button-clicking (Windows) on one of the rulers. (Press Command-R if the rulers aren't visible.)

Figure 2-25
The Info palette

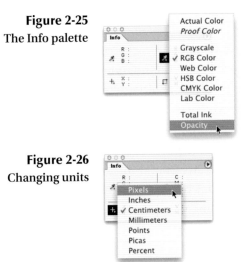

Figure 2-26
Changing units

Color Palettes

The Color Picker and the Color palette both fit into one category, so we almost always group them together into one palette on our screen and switch between them as necessary. Or better yet, we just put them in the Options bar's palette well.

Most novice Photoshop users select a foreground or background color by clicking once on the icons in the Tool palette and choosing from the Color dialog box. Many pros, however, have abandoned this technique, and focus instead on these color palettes. Here are a few tips to make this technique more... ah... palettable.

Tip: Switching Color Bars. Instead of clicking on the foreground color swatch in the Tool palette, you might consider typing values into the Color palette. Are the fields labeled "RGB" when you want to type in "CMYK" or something else? Just choose a different mode from the popout menu on the palette. If you like choosing colors visually rather than numerically, you can use the color bar at the bottom of the palette (no, the Color Bar is not just another place to meet people). While the spectrum of colors that appear here usually covers the RGB gamut, you can switch to a different spectrum by Shift-clicking on the area. Click once, and you switch to CMYK; again, and you get a gradient in grayscale; a third time, and you see a gradient from your foreground color to your background color. Shift-clicking again takes you back to RGB. You can also use the context menu to choose a color space.

Tip: Editing the Color Swatches. You've probably ignored all those swatches on the Swatches palette because they never seem to include colors that have anything to do with your images. Don't ignore... explore! You can add, delete, and edit those little color swatches on the Swatches palette. Table 2-2 shows you how. If you're looking for Web-safe colors, or other useful colors, check out the popout menu at the top of the palette.

You can't actually edit a color that's already there. Instead, you can click on the swatch (to make it the current foreground color), edit the foreground color, then Shift-click back on the swatch (which replaces it with the current foreground color).

	To do this...	Do this...
Table 2-2 **Editing the** **Swatches palette**	Add foreground color	Click any empty area
	Delete a color	Command/Alt-click
	Replace a color with foreground color	Shift-click (Mac only)

The File Browser

If you're like us, you've got way too many images floating around on various disks, and finding the right image at the right time can be a hassle. Fortunately, Photoshop has made this process a giant step easier with the File Browser window, which acts like an Open dialog box on steroids (see Figure 2-27). You can browse through the images on your disk, create folders, move images in and out of folders, rename files, or even delete images from disk.

In Photoshop 7, the File Browser was a palette; however, now it's a strange hybrid—it looks like a dialog box, but it has some palette-like attributes. For instance, the File Browser stays visible even after you open an image. That means that if you have two monitors, you can display the File Browser on one and work on your images in the other. To open the File Browser, select Browse from the File menu, or press Command-Shift-O, or click the File Browser button on the right side of the Options bar.

The File Browser can only display one folder of images at a time. You can choose which folder in the navigation portion in the Folders palette. (Yes, the File Browser now has palettes of its own!) There's also a popup menu at the top of the File Browser which contains recently-viewed folders and a list of "Favorites." To add a folder to the favorites list, navigate to it and then choose Add Folder to Favorites from the File menu inside the File Browser (which is different than the normal File menu).

Once you're looking at a folder-full of images, you can double-click on one to open it, or select more than one image at a time by Shift-clicking (for contiguous selections) or Command-clicking (for selections that aren't next to each other).

Tip: Turn Each Way. The File Browser lets you rotate images. In this case, the image on disk isn't actually changed. Instead, the File Browser itself remembers to rotate the image as soon as you open it inside Photoshop. To set one or more selected images to rotate, click on one of the two Rotate buttons at the top of the File Browser window. Each click rotates the image 90 degrees clockwise or counter-clockwise. You can also rotate an image by Control-clicking (Mac) or right-button-clicking (Windows) on it and selecting Rotate from the context-sensitive menu. Or, if you're trying to impress your supervisor, press Command-] (to turn selected images counter-clockwise) or Command-[(clockwise).

Figure 2-27
The File Browser

Rotate file.

Drag to change size.

You can edit some of this metadata.

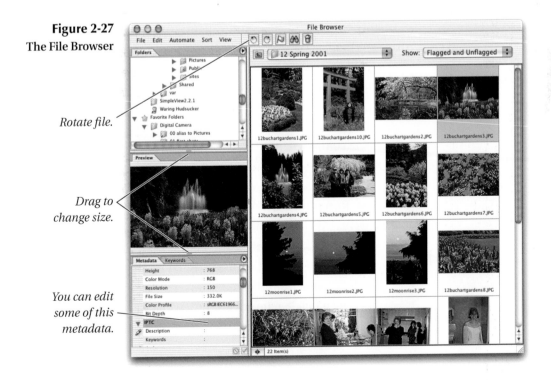

Tip: Flag On, Flag Off. Usually, the first thing we do when looking at a folder full of images is to separate out the duds. It's a "yes or no" first pass, so the File Browser's Flag feature is perfect: We just select one or more files and click the Flag button at the top of the File Browser. A little flag icon appears next to the thumbnails; the flag doesn't affect the image at all, it's just for sorting purposes. After you flag images, you can select Flagged Files or Unflagged Files from the Show popup menu to see one group or the other.

Tip: Drag Those Files. Got an urge to drag images around the File Browser window as though they were slides on a big lightbox? Go for it! Photoshop CS now lets you drag and drop images. Note that the File Browser's Sort menu is automatically set to Custom when you do this; if you choose any other Sort (like sort by filename), your drag-order is lost.

Tip: Rank and File. You can change a file's name by clicking on it in the File Browser (or select the image and press Enter). This actually changes the file name on disk. You can also change a file's Rank by clicking in the Rank area (which is only visible when you have turned on "Show Rank" in the File Browser's View menu). Rank is simply an additional way of ordering images. For instance, if you take five snapshots of a model, you can rank them in the order of preference for easy reference later. Then, to view all the "A" ranked images, you could select Rank from the File Browser's Sort menu (see Figure 2-28).

Note that you can jump from one file name field to the next by typing Tab (or back to the previous file name field with Shift-Tab). Similarly, if you're editing a Rank field, you can jump the next or previous image's Rank field with Tab or Shift-Tab.

Tip: Renaming a Folder. Most digital cameras assign names like P0001924.JPG to each image. Is that useful to anyone? If you have a folder full of these kinds of files, the File Browser can rename them all. First, make sure no thumbnails are selected in the File Browser. Then, choose Batch Rename from the File Browser's Automate menu. Photoshop displays the Batch Rename dialog box, which gives you a number of options for naming files (see Figure 2-29). Careful with this one; you can't undo it after pressing OK.

Figure 2-28
View By Rank

Figure 2-29
Batch Rename

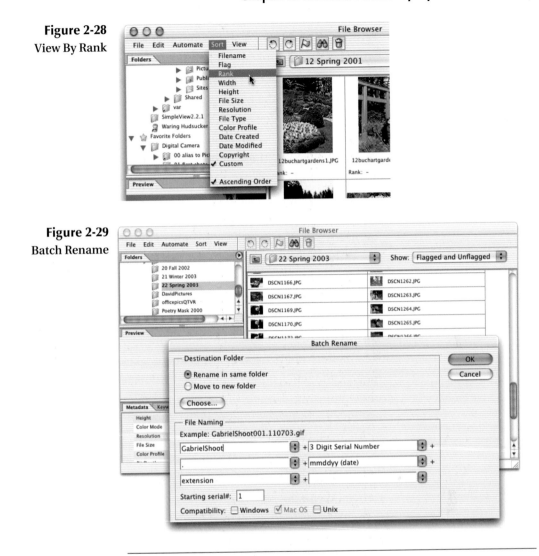

Tip: Jump to File by Name. If your folder has dozens of images in it, it's a hassle to use the scroll bars in the File Browser. Instead, just click on any image in the File Browser window and then type the first few letters of the name of the image you're looking for. (Don't click on the image name, or else you'll rename it!) You can also use the arrow keys to move around this window.

Tip: Copying Images. You can move files from one folder into another by dragging the file's thumbnail into any other folder in the navigation area of the File Browser. Add the Option key and the file is copied instead of moved.

Extended File Info. Perhaps our favorite File Browser feature is the extended file information (also called *metadata*) in the lower-left corner of the window. Here, the File Browser displays whatever information it can cull from the file. At a minimum, it shows you the file's creation date, file format, and size. However, if the capture device or software application that created the image saved more information in the EXIF (exchangeable image file) format, then Photoshop can display it here, too. This is particularly useful for people who use digital cameras, which typically save a plethora of data, including the date and time the picture was snapped, the exposure setting, and focal length.

Photoshop also lets you edit some of the metadata, such as keywords, description, and copyright information. You can later search for this information, or view it in the File Info window, or even view it from within InDesign CS's Links palette.

Tip: Exporting the Cache. The first time you use the File Browser to view a folder of files, you'll notice that it takes some time to gather information and build a thumbnail for each image. It's usually worth waiting until Photoshop is done, as it's difficult to do anything in the File Browser while it's busy making thumbnails. However, the next time you browse that folder, the images show up almost instantaneously. The trick? Photoshop saves the thumbnails in a cache—along with file information, ranking, and rotation setting. The cache is saved in a compressed and proprietary format on your local hard drive.

We thought this was all just fine and dandy until our colleague Deke McClelland pointed out two problems. First, if your images are on a network server, having rank and rotation information saved on your local hard drive doesn't help anyone else who needs to see those images. Second, the cache references a specific folder name, so if you change the name of the folder, all the thumbnails, ranking, and so on, are lost.

Fortunately, Photoshop lets you save a folder's cache file within the folder itself. To do this, select Export Cache from the File Browser's File menu. When the exported cache files (which are called AdobeP8P.tb0, Adobe P8T.tbo, and AdobeP8M.md0) are present in a folder, Photoshop uses them instead of creating new cache files.

If you later write the folder full of images to a CD, Photoshop can even read the cache off the CD. However, any subsequent changes you make to the rankings or image rotation are only stored in your local cache (not on the CD, as it is read-only).

Tip: Purge the Cache. Photoshop builds a cache for every folder you open in the File Browser. If you're looking at images all day, the cache will grow to take up an enormous amount of hard drive space. That's why it's a good idea to empty the cache folder every month or so by selecting Purge Cache from the File Browser's popout menu. Of course, this will delete *all* the ranking and rotation settings, too, which could be disastrous, depending on your workflow.

Tip: Opening the Composite. Do you have a large .TIF or .PSD file with a lot of layers, but you only want to open a flattened version? No problem: hold down Option and Shift while double-clicking on the image in the File Browser or in the Open dialog box. Note that for .PSD files, this only works when the file was saved with a composite image. If you turn off the Always Maximize Compatibility for Photoshop (PSD) Files option in the Preferences dialog box, you won't be able to open the composite because there will be no composite to open (see "Preferences," later in this chapter).

Tip: Change the File Browser Boundaries. To maximize the views of the thumbnails (on the right side of the File Browser) and hide the navigation view (on the left), click on the Expanded View button at the bottom of the File Browser window—that's the little button with the double-headed arrow. Or, note that you can also just expand the File Browser window to any size you want and then move the borders between each section of the window by dragging them. For example, if you want more space to display the additional file information, you can just click-and-drag the border area between it and the thumbnail preview. To collapse one of the File Browser palettes, double-click on the palette's name tab—this leaves more room for the other File Browser palettes.

Of course, you can also save various configurations of the File Browser using the Workspace feature (see "Saving Workspaces," earlier in this chapter). One workspace might have a really large preview image and no metadata; another might have tiny thumbnails; and so on.

Tip: Close the Browser. You can leave the File Browser open all the time as a free-floating window, but we don't recommend it. When open, the File Browser is constantly working in the background and it will slow you down.

Preferences

There's a scene in Monty Python's *Life of Brian* where Brian is trying to persuade his followers to think for themselves. He shouts, "Every one of you is different! You're all individuals!" One person raises his hand and replies, "I'm not."

This is the situation we often find with Photoshop users. Even though each person uses the program differently, they think they need to use it just like everyone else. Not true. You can customize Photoshop in a number of ways through its Preferences submenu (in the Edit menu on Windows, and in the Photoshop menu in Mac OS X).

We're not going to discuss every preference here—we're just going to take a look at some of the key items. First we'll cover the General Preferences dialog box (press Command-K); then we'll look at some other preferences. (We also discuss preferences where relevant elsewhere in the book; for example, we explore Photoshop's color preferences more in Chapter 5, *Color Settings*.)

Tip: Return of Preferences. If you make a change in one of the many Preferences dialog boxes and then—after pressing OK—you decide to change to some other preference, you can return to the same dialog box by pressing Command-Option-K.

Tip: Navigating Through Preferences. The Preferences dialog box contains eight different "screens" (also called "panels" or "tabs"), each of which offers a different set of options (see Figure 2-30). Sure, you can select each screen from the popup menu at the top of the dialog box, or by clicking the Next and Prev buttons. But the fastest way to jump to a particular screen is by pressing Command-1 (for the first screen), Command-2 (for the second screen), and so on up to Command-9.

Tip: Propagating your Preferences. Any time you make a change to one of the Preferences dialog boxes, Photoshop remembers your alteration, and when you quit, saves it in the "Adobe Photoshop CS Prefs" file.

Figure 2-30
General panel of the
Preferences dialog box

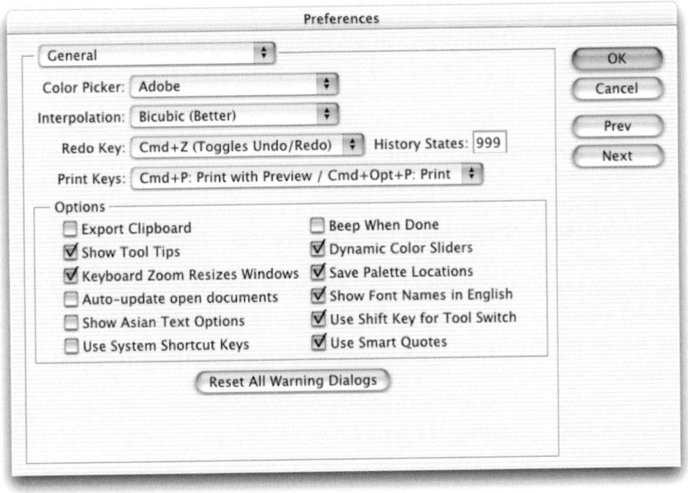

(In Mac OS X, it's in User>YourName>Library>Preferences>Adobe Photoshop CS Settings. On Windows systems, it's hidden.) If anything happens to that file, all your changes are gone. Because of this, on the Macintosh, we recommend keeping a backup of that file, or even the whole settings directory (people often back up their images without realizing they should back up this sort of data file, too).

Certain kinds of crashes can corrupt Photoshop's Preferences file. If Photoshop starts acting strange on us, our first step is always to replace the Preferences file with a clean copy (if no copy of the Preferences file is available, then Photoshop will build a new one for you). To reset the preference files, hold down the Command, Option, and Shift keys (Ctrl, Alt, and Shift keys on Windows) immediately after launching the program—Photoshop will ask if you really want to reset all the preferences.

Note that if you administer a number of different computers that are running Photoshop, you may want to standardize the preferences on all machines. The answer: copy the Photoshop Prefs file to each computer. Finally, note that Photoshop doesn't save changes to the preferences until you Quit. If Photoshop crashes, the changes don't get saved.

Export Clipboard. When the Export Clipboard checkbox is on, Photoshop converts whatever is on the clipboard into a PICT or WMF format when you leave Photoshop. This is helpful—indeed, necessary—if you want to paste a selection into some other program. But if you've got a megabyte or two or 10 megabytes on the clipboard, that conversion is going to take some time. In situations when you're running low on RAM, it may even crash your machine, though this is now rare. We recommend leaving Export Clipboard off until you really need it.

Save Palette Locations. This does what it says—it remembers which palettes were open, which were closed, and where they were located on the screen the last time you quit. But if you change your monitor resolution, the palettes return to their default locations. We leave this turned on, but we tend to rely on the Save Workspace feature to manage our palettes instead.

Tip: Use System Shortcut Keys. In Mac OS X, Apple appropriated two keyboard shortcuts that were crucial for Photoshop users: Command-H and Command-M. Photoshop users know these as "Hide Selection" and "Curves dialog box." The Mac OS X folks use these shortcuts for "Hide Application" and "Minimize Application." In Photoshop, the Photoshop keyboard shortcuts always win. However, you can hold down the Control key, too, to get the system shortcuts (press Command-Control-H to get Hide Application, and so on).

Image Previews. When you save a document in Photoshop, the program can save little thumbnails of your image as file icons. These thumbnails can be helpful, or they can simply be a drag to your productivity. We always set Image Previews to Ask When Saving, so we get a choice for each file (see "Preview Options" in Chapter 16, *Storing Images*).

Ask Before Saving Layered TIFF Files. Most people don't realize that TIFF files can include Photoshop layers. We discuss this in detail in Chapter 16, *Storing Images*, but we should point out one thing here: When the Ask Before Saving Layered TIFF Files option is turned on in Preferences (it is by default), Photoshop will always alert you when you try to save a file that was a flat (non-layered) TIFF but now has layers. For example, if you open a TIFF image and add some type, the text shows up on a type layer. Now if you press Command-S to save the file, Photoshop displays the TIFF Options dialog box, in which you can either flatten the layers or keep them.

If you find yourself staring at this dialog box too much, and you keep thinking to yourself, "If I wanted to flatten the image, I would have done it myself," then go ahead and turn this option off in the Preferences dialog box. Then Photoshop won't bother you anymore. David likes this option and leaves it turned on, Bruce finds it annoying and keeps it turned off.

Maximize PSD File Compatibility. We used to think that the Maximize PSD File Compatibility feature (previously known as "Maximize Backwards Compatibility in Photoshop Format," "Include Composited Image with Layered Files," or "2.5 Format Compatibility") was completely brain-dead. Now we think it's only "mostly useless." Basically, when you set the popup menu to Always, Photoshop saves a flattened version of your layered image along with the layered version. The main problem is that this feature makes your image sizes larger on disk (sometimes several times larger) than they would otherwise be.

We've always said: turn this off (by setting the popup menu to Never) and leave it off. However, there are now several very good exceptions which have tempered our opinion so that we now set this to Ask. (This tells Photoshop to add a checkbox in the Save As dialog box so you can choose whether or not you want it on a per-image basis.)

First, turn it on if you're using some other program that claims to open native Photoshop files, like Macromedia FreeHand, but which requires this flattened version to work. InDesign CS can import layered Photoshop files without this composite as long as they only have 8 bits per channel—16-bit per channel images require the composite. Another reason to leave it on is that future versions of Photoshop may interpret blending modes slightly differently than they do today. Adobe won't say what might change (or even if there will be changes), but if they do change something, and that change affects the look of your file, then you would at least be able to recover the flattened version if there is one. We discuss this in more detail in Chapter 16, *Storing Images*.

Brush Size. By default, the Painting Cursors preference (in the Display & Cursors panel of the Preferences dialog box) is set to Brush Size (see Figure 2-31). However, if you'd prefer to see a little brush cursor icon instead of setting the cursor to the shape of the brush, you can change the preference to Standard. We can't figure out why anyone would want to do this, but ain't it great that Photoshop lets you?

Figure 2-31
Brush Size

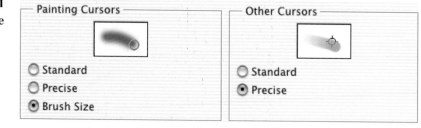

Tip: What Pixel? Because it's often difficult to tell which pixel a small painting tool will affect, Photoshop implemented the handy crosshairs feature: when Caps Lock is down, the cursor switches to a crosshair icon displaying precisely which pixel Photoshop is "looking at."

Gamut Warning. Bruce thinks the Gamut Warning is basically useless—he'd rather just see what's happening to the out-of-gamut colors when they're converted—but for the record, when you turn on Gamut Warning from the View menu (or press Command-Shift-Y), Photoshop displays all the out-of-gamut pixels in the color you choose here. (For more on the out-of-gamut display features, see "Gamut Alarm" in Chapter 7, *Color Correction Fundamentals*.)

If you do want to use this feature (David likes it), we recommend you choose a really ugly color (in the Transparency & Gamut Preferences dialog box) that doesn't appear anywhere in your image, such as a bright lime green. This way, when you switch on Gamut Warning, the out-of-gamut areas are quite obvious.

Transparency. Transparency is not a color, it's a state of mind. Therefore, when you see it on a layer, what should it look like? Typically, Photoshop displays transparency as a grid of white and gray boxes in a checkerboard pattern. The Preferences dialog box lets you change the colors of the checkerboard and set the size of the squares, though we've never found a reason to do so (see Figure 2-32).

Legacy Photoshop Serial Number. Photoshop CS has an all-new serial number scheme—old serial numbers won't work. This could create problems if you want to use third-party plug-ins whose copy-protection serializes them to your old Photoshop serial number, so Photoshop lets you

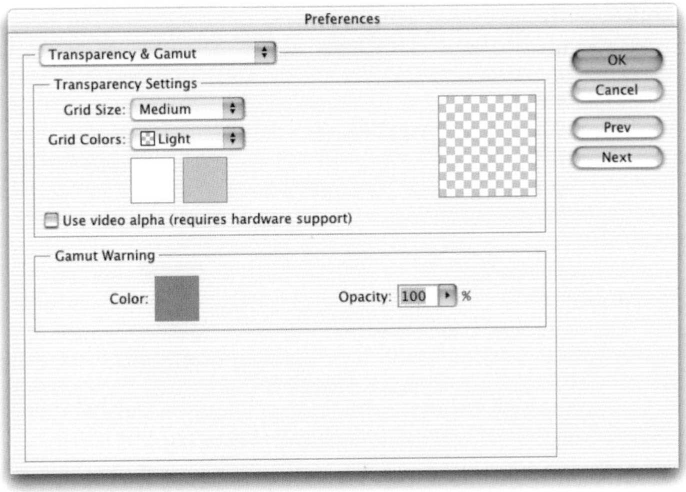

Figure 2-32
Transparency
Preferences

enter your old serial number in the Plug-Ins & Scratch Disks panel of the Preferences dialog box. Your old plug-ins can then find the serial number they're expecting, and run happily in the new version.

Image Cache. Adobe has been getting yelled at for years about Photoshop's handling of large images. Way back in version 4, Photoshop introduced a nominal concession towards large-image handling with the Image Cache feature. It wasn't a great step forward, but it was a step nonetheless. Unfortunately, Photoshop hasn't progressed any farther down the road since then. Here's the one concession: When Image Cache is on (as it is by default), Photoshop saves several downsampled, low-resolution versions of your image. That way, if you work on your image in a zoomed-out view, Photoshop can update your screen preview more quickly by displaying the cached image instead of downsampling the full-resolution one.

If you're low on RAM, you should probably turn off image caching (set the number of caches to 1 in the Image Cache Preferences dialog box; see Figure 2-33), because these downsampled versions of your image take up extra RAM (or space on your scratch disk, if you don't have enough RAM available). If you've got plenty of RAM and you spend a lot of time working at zoom percentages less than 100 percent, an Image Cache setting of 4 or higher could help speed you up. Each cache level caches one increment of zoom, so a setting of 4 caches the 66.7-, 50-, 33.3- and 25-percent views, while a setting of 6 adds the 16.7-percent and 12.5-percent views. The highest setting, 8 levels, caches all views down to 6.25 percent. This is

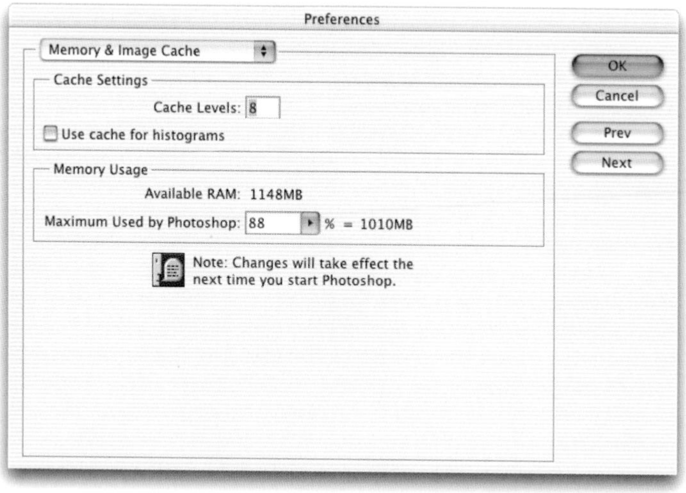

Figure 2-33
Image Cache
Preferences

really only useful on very large images, but the incremental difference in RAM footprint between 6 levels and 8 levels is so small that even if you'd benefit from a setting of 8 only occasionally, you'd probably be best off just setting the Image Cache to 8 and leaving it there.

Note that we *strongly* urge you to keep the "Use cache for histograms in Levels" checkbox in this Preferences dialog box turned off. While turning it on will speed up your histograms at views other than 100 percent, it renders these histograms useless (see "Tip: Turn Off Use Image Cache For Histograms" in Chapter 6, *Tonal Correction Fundamentals*).

When Things Go Worng

It's 11 PM on the night before your big presentation. You've been working on this image for thirteen hours, and you're beginning to experience a bad case of "pixel vision." After making a selection, you run a filter, look carefully, and decide that you don't like the effect. But before you can reach Undo, you accidentally click on the document window, deselecting the area.

That's not so bad, is it? Not until you realize that undoing will only undo the deselection, not the filter... and that you haven't saved for half an hour. The mistake remains, and there's no way to get rid of it without losing the last 30 minutes of brain-draining work. Or is there? In this section of the chapter, we take a look at the various ways you can save yourself when something goes terribly wrong.

Undo. The first defense against any offensive mistake is, of course, Undo. You can find this on the Edit menu, but we suggest keeping one hand conveniently on the Command and Z keys, ready and waiting for the blunder that is sure to come sooner or later. Note that Photoshop is smart enough not to consider some things "undoable." Taking a snapshot, for instance, doesn't count; so you can take a snapshot and then undo whatever you did just before the snapshot. Similarly, you can open the Histogram, hide edges, change foreground or background colors, zoom, scroll, or even duplicate the file, and Photoshop still lets you go back and undo the previous action.

Revert to Saved. You'd think this command is pretty easy to interpret. If you've really messed up something in your image, the best option is often simply to revert the entire file to the last saved version by selecting Revert from the File menu. In most applications, it's the same as closing the file without saving changes, then reopening it, but in Photoshop, Revert doesn't go back to the file that's saved on disk unless you actually selected Save from within Photoshop after opening the file. If you open an image in Photoshop, do a bunch of stuff, then choose Revert, what you get is the file as it first appeared in Photoshop. What's the difference?

The big difference is that anything you do using the Missing Profile or Profile Mismatch warnings doesn't get undone when you revert. For example, when you open an Untagged image, and use the Missing Profile warning to assign the Adobe RGB profile, if later you choose Revert you'll get an Adobe RGB image, not an Untagged one. What's worse is that when you make a conversion using the Profile Mismatch warning—actually changing the numbers in the file—choosing Revert will give you the image *after* the conversion, not the image that was saved on disk.

Worse still, when *all* you've done to the image is to change its profile or make a color conversion using the Profile Mismatch warning, the Revert command is dimmed and unavailable. We think this is a bug, and we hope it gets squashed, but keep an eye out for it—it's quite obscure. If you run into this situation, the only way to get back to the original image is to close it without saving, then re-open it (which is what we think Revert should do under all circumstances). If you do choose Revert, any changes you've made since the file was opened are lost, however, so proceed with caution. Note that the Revert feature *is* undoable.

The History Palette

There is a school of thought that dictates, "Don't give people what they want, give them what they need." The Photoshop engineering team appears to advocate this—they spend hours listening to and thinking about what people ask for, then they come back with a feature that goes far beyond what anyone had even thought to request. For example, people long asked Adobe for multiple Undos (the ability to sequentially undo steps that you've taken while editing a Photoshop image). The result is the History palette, which goes far beyond a simple Undo mechanism into a whole new paradigm of working in Photoshop.

The History palette, at its most basic, remembers what you've done to your file and lets you either retrace your steps or revert back to any earlier version of the image. Every time you do something to your image—paint a brush stroke, run a filter, make a selection, and so on—Photoshop saves this change as a *state* in the History palette (see Figure 2-34). At any time, you can revert the entire image to any previous state, or—using the History Brush tool or the Fill command, which we'll discuss in a moment—selectively paint back in time.

There is, however, an itty-bitty problem with the History palette: it can take up a lot of RAM. Sorry, did we say "a lot"? We meant "vast, awe-inspiring, mind-boggling quantities" of memory, particularly since Photoshop's old 100-state limit was increased to 1000 in Photoshop 7. As we pointed out in Chapter 1, *Building a Photoshop System*, Photoshop can require as much as 10 to 20 times your file size in RAM—or more—to perform efficiently when it is saving history states (that's 200 to 400 MB of RAM for a 20 MB image). Performing simple tasks such as opening, rotating,

Figure 2-34
The History palette

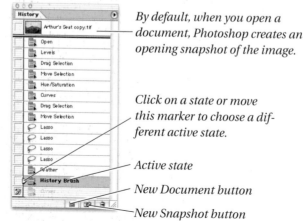

By default, when you open a document, Photoshop creates an opening snapshot of the image.

Click on a state or move this marker to choose a different active state.

Active state

New Document button

New Snapshot button

sharpening, and saving may take significantly longer when the History feature is turned on.

Tip: Turning Off History. If you're doing straight-laced production work all day (the kind of work for which a single Undo is perfectly adequate), you may want to avoid the History feature's heavy RAM overhead by changing the History States value to 1 in the Preferences dialog box (press Command-K). Similarly, you can turn off "Automatically Create First Snapshot" in the History Options dialog box (which you can find on the History palette's popout menu). You might also want to turn off these functions if you're going to batch-process a number of images using actions or the Automate "wizards" (because in these cases, History isn't necessary).

The History palette has two sections: snapshots and states. Let's take a look at each of these and how you can use them.

Snapshots. The History palette lets you save any number of snapshots—representing a moment in time for your image—so that at any time you can go back to a specific state. There are two main differences between snapshots and states.

▶ Photoshop records almost everything you do to an image as a state. By default, snapshots are only recorded when you first open an image and when you click the New Snapshot button in the History palette.

▶ When the number of states recorded on the History palette exceeds the Maximum Remembered States value (set in the History Options dialog box), the oldest states start dropping off the list. Snapshots don't disappear until you close the document.

Tip: What's in the Snapshot. When you click the New Snapshot button on the History palette (or select New Snapshot from the palette's popout menu), Photoshop saves the whole document (individual layers and all). Depending on how many layers you have and how large your document is, this might require a lot of RAM. If you Option-click the button, Photoshop offers two other less-memory-intensive snapshot choices: a version of the image with merged layers, or just of the currently selected layer. (If you find yourself Option-clicking the button a lot in order to get these options, then turn on the Show New Snapshot Dialog By Default checkbox in History Options. That way, you don't have to press the Option key anymore.)

Stepping through states. As we mentioned above, Photoshop saves every brush stroke, every selection, every anything you do to your image as a state on the History palette (though the state only remains on the palette until you reach the maximum number of states or you close the document). There are three ways to move among states of your image.

▶ To revert your image back to a state, you can click on any state's tile in the History palette.

▶ You can move the active state marker to a state on the History palette.

▶ You can press Command-Z to step back to the last state (just as you've always been able to do). But you can also press Command-Option-Z to move backward one state at a time, and Command-Shift-Z to move forward one state at a time.

In general, when you move to an earlier state, Photoshop grays out every subsequent state on the History palette, indicating that if you do anything now these grayed-out states will be erased. This is like going back to a fork in the road and choosing the opposite path from what you took before. Photoshop offers another option: if you turn on the Allow Non-Linear History checkbox in the History Options dialog box, Photoshop doesn't gray out or remove subsequent states when you move back in time (though it still deletes old states when you hit the maximum number of states limit).

Non-Linear History is like returning to the fork in the road, taking the opposite path, but then having the option to return to any state from the first path. For example, you could run a Gaussian Blur on your image using three different amounts—returning the image to the pre-blurred state in the History palette each time—and then switch among these three states to decide which one you wanted to use.

The primary problem with Non-Linear History is that it may confuse you more than help you, especially when you're dealing with a number of different "forks in the road."

The History Brush. Returning to a previous state returns the entire image to that state. But Photoshop's History feature lets you selectively return portions of your image to a previous state, too, with the History Brush and the Fill command. Before painting with the History Brush, first select the source state in the History palette (click in the column to the left of the state from which you want to paint). For instance, let's say you sharpen a picture of a face with Unsharp Masking (see Chapter 10, *Sharpening*) and find that the lips have become oversharp. You can select the History Brush, set the source state to the presharpened state, and brush around the lips (though you'd probably want to reduce the opacity of the History Brush to 20 or 30 percent by pressing 2 or 3 first).

The History Brush tool (press Y) is very similar to the Eraser tool when the Erase to History checkbox is turned on in the Options bar, but the History Brush lets you paint with modes, such as Multiply and Screen. Additionally, unlike Erase to History or Fill from History, the History Brush works on high-bit files.

Tip: Snap Before Action. If you run an action in the Actions palette that has more steps than your History States preference, you won't be able to "undo" the action. That's why before running the action you should either save a snapshot of your full document or set the source state for the History Brush to the current state. The latter works because Photoshop never "rolls off" the source state in the History palette, so you don't have to worry about its getting deleted after reaching the maximum number of states.

Fill with History. One last nifty technique that can rescue you from a catastrophic "oops" is the Fill command on the Edit menu (press Shift-F5). This lets you fill any selection (or the entire image, if nothing is selected) with the pixels from the current source state on the History palette. We usually use this in preference to the History Brush or Eraser tools when the area to be reverted is easily selectable. Sometimes when we paint with those tools, we overlook some pixels (it's hard to use a brush to paint every pixel in an area at 100 percent). This is never a problem when you use the Fill command.

You've always been able to press Option-Delete to fill a selection or layer with the foreground color. In version 4, Photoshop added the ability to automatically preserve transparency on the layer when you add the

Shift key (slightly faster than having to turn on the Preserve Transparency checkbox in the Layers palette). Similarly, you can fill with the background color by pressing Command-Delete (add the Shift key to preserve transparency). To fill the layer or selection with the current history source state, press Command-Option-Delete. And, of course, you can add the Shift key to this to fill with Preserve Transparency turned on.

Tip: Persistent States. Remember that both snapshots and states are cleared out when you close a document. If you want to save a particular state or snapshot, drag its tile over the Create New Document button on the History palette. Now that state is its own document that you can save to disk. If you want to copy pixels from that document into another image, simply use the Clone Stamp tool (you can set the source point to one document and then paint with it in the other file).

Tip: Revert When Revert Doesn't Work. Deke McClelland taught us a trick at a recent Photoshop conference that has already saved David's buttocks several times. Because David has a tendency to type fast and loose, he'll often press Command-S (Save) when he really meant to press Command-A (Select All) or Command-D (Deselect). Of course, this saves over his file on disk, often ruining his original scan. The History palette to the rescue! Remember that the default preference for the History palette is to create a snapshot of the image when you first open it. If you save over your original image, you can drag the snapshot's tile over the Create New Document button in the History palette to recreate the original data in its own file.

Tip: Copying States. Although Photoshop lets you copy states from one document to another simply by dragging them from the History palette onto the other document's window, we can't think of many good reasons to do this. The copied state completely replaces the image that you've dragged it over.

Tip: When History Stops Working. Note that you cannot use the History Brush or the Fill from History feature when your image's pixel dimensions or color mode has changed. Pixel dimensions usually change when you rotate the whole image, use the Cropping tool, or use the Image Size or Canvas Size dialog boxes.

Tip: Purging States. As we said earlier, the History palette takes up a lot of memory. If you find yourself needing more RAM, you might try clearing out the History states by either selecting Clear History from the popout menu on the History palette or choosing Histories from the Purge submenu (under the Edit menu). The former can be undone in a pinch; the latter cannot. Curiously, neither of these removes your snapshots, so you have to delete those manually if you want to save even more RAM. Remember that closing your document and reopening it will also remove all snapshots and history states.

Easter Eggs

It's a tradition in Macintosh software to include Easter Eggs—those wacky little undocumented, nonutilitarian features that serve only to amuse the programmer and (they hope) the user. Note that if your friends think you have no sense of humor, you might want to skip this section; it might just annoy you.

There are (at least) three Easter Eggs in Photoshop—two hidden screens and one quote list.

Dark Matter. A tradition even more venerable than Easter Eggs is code names. Almost all software has a code name that the developers use before the product is christened with a real shipping name. Photoshop 4 was code-named Big Electric Cat (it's an Adrian Belew reference, if you care). Photoshop 5 was code-named Strange Cargo. Photoshop 6 was called Venus in Furs. Photoshop 7 was called Liquid Sky. Photoshop CS was called Dark Matter. To see the original Dark Matter splash screen, hold down the Command key while selecting About Photoshop from the Photoshop menu. In Photoshop for Windows, press Control-Alt and select About Photoshop from the Help menu.

Quotes. If you watch either the standard About Photoshop screen or the Dark Matter splash screen, you'll notice that the credits at the bottom of the screen start to scroll by, thanking everyone and their dog for participating in the development process. Don't get impatient—the last person on the list is someone special. (Actually, if you are the impatient type, try holding down the Option or Alt key once the credits start rolling; that speeds them up.)

Here's even more fun: In the Dark Matter splash screen (see the previous tip), try clicking once just above the first line of text (where it says "Protected by U.S. Patents..."). If the screen disappears, you've clicked in the wrong place. If nothing happens, you've done it right. Now just wait until the scrolling credits are finished, and you'll be treated to some very funny quotations.

Merlin lives! Finally (at least, this is the last one we know about), there's a little hidden dialog box nestled away. When you hold down the Option key while selecting Palette Options from the popout menus in either the Paths, Layers, or Channels palettes, Merlin happily jumps out. If you're on a Mac, don't forget to try clicking on Merlin for that extra kick.

The World of Photoshop

If our publisher weren't screaming bloody murder to get this book to the printer, we'd still be writing tips. But instead of waiting until the next edition of the book, try finding them for yourself. The more you *play* with Photoshop, the more you'll be rewarded with treasures from the deep.

3 Image Essentials

It's All Zeros and Ones

Let's get one thing perfectly clear: this book is not about pictures or work flow or even computers. This book is about zeros and ones. As Laurie Anderson so plainly pointed out, no one wants to be a zero, and everyone (at least in America) wants to be "number one." The digital age is built entirely on the interplay between the two.

To be sure, the digital world (in which zeros and ones, offs and ons, and whites and blacks frolic together in cooperation, not competition) is not as confusing as some people make it out to be. And, as it turns out, you can't really be efficient with digital imaging without knowing a little bit about that dark underworld. In this chapter we're going to break it all down for you. To some of you, most of this chapter is going to sound pretty basic, but we urge you to peruse it anyhow. You might be surprised at how many power users find themselves stumped by something as small as a misunderstanding of how—and why—bitmapped images work.

Bitmapped vs. Vector Graphics

In all the grand canon of computer imaging, there are really only two kinds of graphics: bitmapped and vector.

Bitmapped images. Bitmapped images are simply collections of dots (we call them *pixels* or *sample points*) laid out in a big grid. The pixels can be different colors, and the number of dots can vary. No matter what the picture is—whether it's a modernist painting of a giraffe or a photograph of your mother—it's always described using lots of dots. This is the only way to represent the fine detail and subtle gradations of photorealistic images.

Just about every bitmapped image comes from one of three sources: capture devices (such as scanners, video cameras, or digital cameras), painting and image-editing programs (such as Photoshop), and screen-capture programs (like Snapz Pro, the System, and a host of others). If you create a graphic with any of these tools, it's a bitmapped image.

Vector graphics. Vector graphics, often called object-oriented graphics, are both more complex and simpler than bitmapped images. On the one hand, instead of describing a rectangle with thousands (or millions) of dots, vector graphics just say, "Draw a rectangle this big and put it here." Clearly, this is a much more efficient and space-saving method for describing some images. However, vector graphics can include many different types of objects—lines, boxes, circles, curves, polygons, and text blocks. And all those items can have a variety of attributes—line weight, type formatting, fill color, graduated fills, and so on.

To use an analogy, vector graphics are like directions saying, "Go three blocks down the street, turn left at the 7-11, and go another five blocks," while bitmapped images are more like saying, "Take a step. Now take another step. And another …." Photoshop has traditionally worked with bitmapped images, but in Photoshop CS you can create a variety of vector graphics that retain their object-oriented characteristics, or use them as selections and masks on bitmapped images.

Outside Photoshop, vector graphics come from two primary sources: drawing programs such as FreeHand, Canvas, Illustrator, and so on, and computer-aided design (CAD) programs. You might also get vector graphics from other programs, such as a program that makes graphs.

Bitmaps as objects. The distinction between bitmapped and vector graphics is slightly fuzzy, because vector graphics can include bitmaps as objects in their own right. For instance, you can put a scanned image into an Adobe Illustrator illustration. The scan actually acts like an object on the page, much like a rectangle or oval. If you include a bitmap as an

Words, Words, Words

While terminology might not keep you up at night, we in the writin' business have to worry about such things. In fact, one of our first controversies in writing this book concerned the term *bitmap*.

Bruce maintains that, strictly speaking, bitmaps are only black-and-white images. This is how Photoshop uses the term. He prefers to describe images made up of colored dots as *raster* images (the word "raster" refers to a group of lines—in this case, lines of pixels—that collectively make up an image). David thinks that only people who wear pocket protectors (some of his best friends do) would use the word "raster." With this controversy comes our first compromise: we'll call these creatures *bitmapped images*—whether they're black and white, grayscale, or color.

Another problem we've encountered is what to call all those little dots in a bitmapped image. As we mentioned earlier, when we talk about points in a bitmapped image, we like to call them *pixels, samples,* or *sample points.*

The phrase "sample points" comes from what a scanner does: it samples an image—checking what color or gray value it finds—every 300th of an inch, every 100th of an inch, or whatever. But nowadays, many bitmapped images are captured with a digital camera rather than being scanned, which makes the concept of sample points more questionable. Pixel is a more generic term because it specifies the smallest "picture element" in an image. Some people still call pixels *pels.* They may not wear pocket protectors, but they've almost certainly had an unnatu-

rally close relationship with an IBM mainframe somewhere in their past.

When we talk about scanning an image in, or printing an image out, we talk about samples or pixels per inch (while samples is closer to reality, everyone we know uses the latter, or *ppi*); and when we talk about the resolution of a bitmapped image saved on disk, we just talk about the total number of pixels. Note that many people use "dots per inch" (*dpi*) for any and all kinds of resolution. We reserve the term "dots per inch" for use when speaking of printers and imagesetters, which actually create dots on paper or film.

We use the term "pixels" for one other thing: screen resolution. But to be clear, we always try to specify "screen pixels" or "image pixels."

object in an illustration, you can rotate it and scale it, but you can't go into the image and change the pixels.

Note that a vector graphic file might include a bitmap as its *only* object. In this situation, the file is a bitmapped image that you can open for editing in a painting or image-processing application. Photoshop's EPS (Encapsulated PostScript) files are good examples of this. While EPS is typically a vector file format, you can create a bitmap-only EPS in Photoshop.

Vectors in bitmapped graphics. Just to round out the confusion, Photoshop lets you include vector graphics in bitmapped images, either as stand-alone objects (like text) or as clipping paths. A clipping path in an image is invisible; it simply acts as a cookie cutter, allowing you to produce irregularly shaped images such as the silhouetted product shots you often see in ads (see "Clipping Paths" in Chapter 16, *Storing Images*).

Bitmapped Images

Photoshop lets you open, create, edit, and save bitmapped images. Bitmapped images are its *sine qua non*, its *raison d'être*, its "precious bodily fluid." So to get the most out of Photoshop, you've got to understand bitmapped images inside and out.

Every bitmapped graphic has three basic characteristics: dimension, bit depth, and color model (which Photoshop refers to as *image mode*).

Dimension

Bitmapped images are always big rectangular grids. Like checkerboards or chessboards or parquet floors in your kitchen, these big grids are made of little squares (see Figure 3-1). The *dimensions* of the bitmap grid refer to the number of pixels wide and tall it is. A chessboard is always eight squares by eight squares. The grid of pixels that makes up your computer screen might be 1200 by 1600.

A bitmapped image can be any dimension you like, limited only by the capabilities of your capture device, the amount of storage space you have available, and your patience—the more pixels in the image, the more space it takes up, and the longer it takes to do anything with it.

Figure 3-1
Bitmaps as
grids of squares

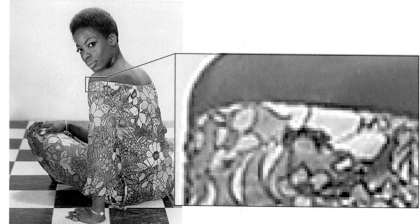

Note that *dimension has nothing to do with physical size* in inches or picas. Bitmapped images in their pure digital state have no physical size; they're just data. They exist as Platonic ideals, waiting to be realized by reproduction in some physical form. No matter how you stretch or shrink a bitmapped image, it still contains the same number of pixels.

When you print a bitmapped image, you print it at a specific size, and the relationship between that size and the number of pixels the image contains is called the *resolution* of the image. But it's very important to understand that resolution isn't innate to the digital image; it's a flexible measurement that changes depending on the physical size at which you reproduce the image. We'll discuss resolution and why it's important in more detail later in this chapter.

Bit Depth

Each pixel in a bitmapped image is represented by a particular number of zeros and ones, otherwise known as *bit depth* (one bit can be either a zero or a one). That number dictates the range of possible values for each pixel, and hence the total number of colors (or shades of gray) that the image can contain. The number of possible values is 2 to the power of the number of bits.

A 1-bit image (one in which each pixel is represented by one bit) can only contain black and white. If you have two bits of information describing a pixel, there are four possible combinations (00, 01, 10, and 11), hence four possible values (2^2), and four possible colors or gray levels (see Figure 3-2). Eight bits of information give you 256 possible values (2^8); 24 bits of information result in over 16 million possible colors. (With 24-bit RGB images, each sample actually has three 8-bit values—one each for red, green, and blue; see Figure 3-3.)

Figure 3-2
Bit depth

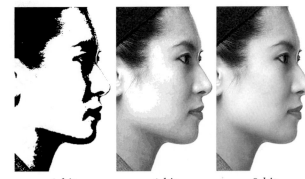

1-bit   4-bit   8-bit

Figure 3-3 When RGB and CMYK combine

Color images (like the one in the upper-left corner) can be described with RGB data (on the left) or CMYK data (on the right). This figure is somewhat complicated by the need to print the red, green, and blue versions using cyan, magenta, and yellow inks.

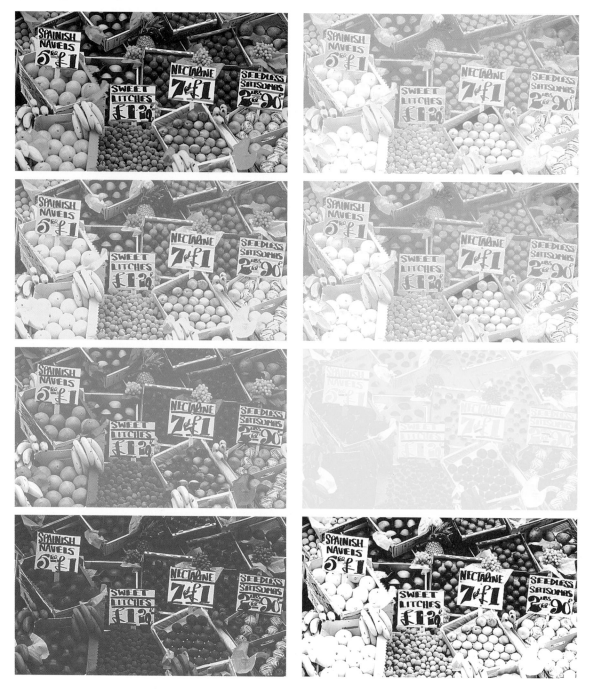

Figure 3-4
A "deep" bitmap

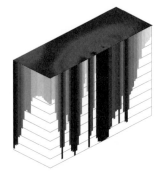

We call 1-bit images *flat* or *bilevel* bitmaps. A *deep* bitmap is any image that has more than one bit describing each pixel (see Figure 3-4).

Photoshop also allows you to use 16-bit-per-channel images. Sixteen bits of information (2^{16}) can in theory describe 65,536 possible values, but Photoshop's implementation is a little different. Photoshop's 16-bit values range from 0 to 32,768, which to some people may seem more like 15-bit color. Rather than take sides, we simply note the following: the range 0–32,768 has a midpoint, which is very useful in blending operations; it takes 16 bits to represent ($2^{15}+1$); and it represents many more discrete values than our capture devices can capture.

Nowadays, even entry-level flatbed scanners capture at least 10 bits per channel (1,024 levels), "prosumer"-level digital cameras capture 12 bits per channel (4,096 levels), and high-end scanners and cameras capture 14 bits per channel (16,384 levels). But that's still less than half the number of levels Photoshop can represent, so we don't feel that Photoshop's 16-bit implementation presents any undue limitations.

In fact, when we consider that, though we can display a maximum of 16.7 million possible colors on our monitors, we can see perhaps seven or eight million discrete colors at best, and we can print at most a few tens of thousands of colors on the best printing processes available, the question becomes, what do 16-bit channels offer except massive overkill?

Why capture many more colors than we print, or even see? The simple answer is that the larger number of bits gives us much more editing flexibility. When you start out with only 256 shades per channel, each edit you make has the inevitable result of reducing that number. As you'll see in "Stretching and Squeezing the Bits" in Chapter 6, *Tonal Correction Fundamentals*, every edit opens up gaps between some adjacent pixel values and smooshes others together, reducing the total number of shades.

This discarding of data is a normal and inevitable part of image editing, but we've always advocated holding on to as much data as possible for as long as possible. If you start out with a 16-bit-per-channel image, you'll be able to edit your image with much less risk of losing detail or introducing posterization or banding than you would with an 8-bit-per-channel image. In some cases, you can squeeze a little extra editing headroom from an 8-bit image by converting it to 16 bits—doing so doesn't increase the amount of information in the image, but it gives the data points more places to land.

Bit depth has an important relationship to the quality of an image, which we'll cover more fully later in this chapter.

Image Mode

The problem with bit depth is that it doesn't really tell you (or Photoshop) what each color (numerical value) means. A 1-bit image is easy: Each pixel can only be on or off. It doesn't have to be black or white, though; if you were twisted enough, you could make this orange or blue.

But as we've seen, each pixel in an 8-bit image can be described using one of 256 values. Are those 256 levels of gray? Or 256 colors? Or something else? We'll let you in on a sad, sordid little secret here. Everyone who works with color on computers discovers it eventually, anyway: Computers don't understand color at all. They just understand numbers: zeros and ones.

The color model—otherwise known as *image mode*—is the missing piece of the puzzle, the magic decoder ring that tells how to translate each pixel's numerical value into a color or a shade of gray. Actually, image mode and color model aren't exactly the same thing, but they're so closely related that it makes sense to discuss them as aspects of the same thing.

If the image mode is set to Grayscale under the Mode menu, the value of each pixel is a grayscale value: 0 is black, 255 is white. If the image mode is Indexed Color, then each value is tagged to a specific, arbitrarily chosen color. (An indexed color image can have only 256 different colors in it; see "Indexed Color," later in this chapter.)

However, if the image mode is set to RGB, Lab, or CMYK, then the color of the pixel is actually made up of multiple 8-bit or 16-bit values. For instance, in a 24-bit RGB image, each pixel is described using three 8-bit values, each of which specifies a level of brightness for the red, green, and blue channels (see Figure 3-3, earlier). In a CMYK image, Photoshop looks at and composites four 8-bit images.

You can look at the individual channels and view each one as a gray-scale image. The color image is made by colorizing each channel with the appropriate color and stacking them one atop the other.

Note that unless you're working with esoteric scientific or medical imaging equipment, you won't have to tell Photoshop which image mode to use: Virtually every file format that Photoshop recognizes has the secret decoder ring built in. But you need to understand image modes and their related color models if you want to do much useful work with Photoshop. (For a fuller discussion of color models, see Chapter 4, *Color Essentials.*)

We look at each mode that Photoshop uses, and why you'd want to use one or another, later in this chapter.

Resolution

Resolution is one of the most overused and under-understood words in desktop publishing. People use it when they talk about scanners and printers, images and screens, halftones, and just about anything else they can get their hands on. Then they wonder why they're confused. Don't worry; resolution is easy.

As we noted earlier, a bitmapped image in its pure digital state has no physical size—it's just a bunch of pixels. But you can't see a pure digital image unless you can decipher zeros and ones in your head. So whenever you give an image tangible expression, whether it's as an ephemeral representation on the screen or as a permanent printed form, you confer upon it the property of physical size. And with size comes resolution.

The resolution of a bitmapped image is the number of pixels in each unit of measurement. If we're talking in inches, then we talk about the number of pixels per inch (ppi), which is what most people mean when they say "dots per inch" (dpi).

If your bitmapped image has 72 pixels per inch, and it's 72 pixels long on each side, then it's an inch long on each side. If you print it at half the size, you'll still have the same number of pixels, but they'll be crammed into half the space, so each inch will contain 144 of them. If you take the same bitmapped image and change it to 36 pixels per inch (changing its resolution), suddenly the image is two inches on each side (same number of pixels, but each one is twice as big as the original; see Figure 3-5).

Figure 3-5
Scaling and
resolution

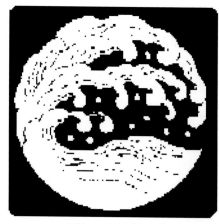

25 percent
(288 ppi)

50 percent
(144 ppi)

100 percent (72 ppi)

50 percent
(144 ppi)

100 percent (72 ppi)

300 percent (24 ppi)

You can also look at bitmap resolution in another way: If you know the size of an image and its resolution, you can figure out its dimensions. When you scan a picture that is three inches on each side at 100 pixels per inch, you know that the bitmapped image has 300 pixels on each side (100 per inch). If you scan it at 300 pixels per inch, the dimensions shoot up to 900 pixels on each side.

The key to making resolution work for you (rather than against you) is knowing how many pixels you need for the intended purpose to which you'll put the image. We discuss how much data you need for different purposes in the next section.

How Much Is Enough?

If bigger were better, we'd be out of business (you'd be hard pressed to call us statuesque). And when it comes to resolution of bitmapped images, bigger isn't necessarily better. The higher the resolution of an image, the longer it takes to open, edit, save, or print. Back in Neolithic times, we used to point out the money you could save by working with smaller images. With storage costs hovering around $1 per gigabyte, that's a less compelling argument, but large images still take longer to transmit over a network, and even 250 gigabyte hard drives fill up eventually.

Of course, smaller isn't necessarily better, either. If your image resolution is too low, your image will look pixelated (see Figure 3-6); you'll start seeing the pixels themselves, or adverse effects from excessively large pixels. Loss of detail and mottling are the two worst offenders in this category.

Maybe you thought you could save time by reducing your images to 150 ppi. However, when the client rejects the job because the image is too pixelated, any savings will be more than wiped out when you have to redo the job. So if bigger isn't better, and too small is even worse, then how much

Figure 3-6
Pixelation in images
when the resolution
is too low

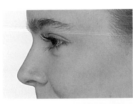

100 percent
200 ppi

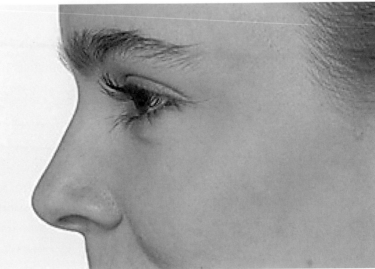

300 percent
66 ppi

Terms of Resolution

Not everyone talks about resolution in terms of ppi. Depending on the circumstance, your personality, and the time of day, you might discuss a file's resolution in a number of ways, but they're all different ways of talking about the same essential concept: *how much information* the file contains. Here's a quick rundown of your options.

Image size. The first way to discuss resolution is the way we've done it up until now (and the way we do it in most places in this book): spec both the physical size and number of pixels per inch. For example, you might say a file is 4 by 5 inches at 225 ppi. This makes the most sense to someone doing page layout, because they're typically concerned with how the image is going to look on the printed page. Note, however, that you have to specify both the

size and the resolution; otherwise you're telling only half the story.

Dimensions. You can sidestep the question of resolution by simply specifying the dimensions of the bitmapped image; that is, the number of pixels on each side of the bitmap grid. This doesn't tell you what physical size it is, but if you understand how much resolution you need for different output methods, it's useful shorthand for expressing how big the image *could be*, depending on what you wanted to do with it. It tells you how much information is in the file. Hard-core Photoshop users like to talk in dimensions because they don't necessarily know (or care) how large the final output will be.

For instance, you could say a scan from a 35 mm original is a 2,048-by-3,076 image. What does that tell you? With experience,

you'd know that your file size is 18 MB, and at 225 ppi you could print a full-bleed letter-size page. Later in this chapter, we discuss ways how you can figure all this out for yourself.

File size. The third way to discuss resolution is by the file's size on disk. You can quickly get a sense of the difference in information content of two files when we tell you that the first is 900 K and the second is 12 MB. In fact, a lot of digital imaging gurus *only* think in file size. If you ask them, "What's the resolution of that file?" they look at you like you're an idiot.

Once you become accustomed to working with a number of different sizes, you'll recognize that the 900 K RGB file is about the size of a 640-by-480 RGB image. At 72 ppi (screen resolution) that's pretty big, but at 300 ppi (typical resolution for a high-quality print

is enough? How much image data do you need? The first consideration is image mode: The requirements are very different for line art than they are for grayscale and color.

Line Art

For bilevel (black-and-white, 1-bit) images, the resolution never needs to be higher than that of the printer you're using. If you're printing to a 600-dpi desktop laser printer, there's no reason to have more than 600 pixels per inch in your image (the printer can only image 600 dots per inch, so any extras just get thrown away). However, when you print to a 2,400-dpi imagesetter, that 600-ppi image appears jaggy.

job), the image is only about two inches wide.

The resolution of Photo CD images is often specced by file size. The highest-resolution Photo CD image is 18 MB; the highest resolution of Pro Photo CD is 64 MB.

Single-side dimension. People who work with continuous-tone film recorders, such as the Solitaire or the Kodak LVT, frequently talk about a file's resolution in terms of the dimension of one side— typically the width—of the image. For instance, they might ask for "a 4 K file." That means the image should be exactly 4,096 pixels across.

K usually means file size (kilobytes). However, in this case it's 1,024 pixels (see Table 3-1).

The height of the image is relatively unimportant in this case, though if you're imaging to film, it's usually assumed that you know the other dimension of the image because it's dictated by the aspect ratio of the film you're using. High-quality film recorders usually

Table 3-1 Resolution in K

K	Number of Pixels Across
1	1,024
2	2,048
3	3,072*
4	4,096
5	5,120*
6	6,144*
7	7,168*
8	8,192

* rarely used

write out to 4-by-5-inch chromes (positive transparencies), so if you want to fill the image area, it's usually assumed that the short side of your 8 K image will contain somewhere around 6,550 pixels.

Res. One other method of discussing resolution uses the term *res*. Res is simply the number of pixels per millimeter, and if we had anything to say about the matter, it'd be stricken from common usage. People usually talk about res when they're discussing

Table 3-2 Resolution in res

Res	Pixels per Inch
1	25.4
2	50.8
3	76.2
4	101.6
5	127
6	152.4
7	177.8
8	203.2
9	228.6
10	254
11	279.4
12	304.8
20	508
40	1,016
60	1,524
80	2,032

scanning resolution. For example, a file scanned at res 12 is scanned at 12 sample points (pixels) per millimeter—which is 120 sample points per centimeter, or—in common usage—304.8 sample points per inch (see Table 3-2).

If you're printing to an imagesetter, you should plan on using an image resolution of *at least* 800 ppi—preferably 1,000 ppi or more (see Figure 3-7). Line art with an image resolution of less than 800 shows jaggies and broken lines. Of course, if you're then going to print that artwork onto newsprint or porous paper, you can often get away with a lower resolution such as 400 or 600 ppi, because the jaggies will disappear with the spreading ink.

See Chapter 12, *Line Art*, for techniques to increase the resolution and improve the appearance of line art images at lower resolutions.

Figure 3-7
Resolution of
line art

144 ppi *300 ppi*

800 ppi *1,200 ppi*

Grayscale and Color Halftones

There's a relatively simple formula for figuring out the proper resolution for printing grayscale and color ("deep") bitmapped images to halftoning devices like laser printers and imagesetters or platesetters: Image resolution should be twice the screen frequency *at most*. For instance, if you're printing a halftone image at 133 lines per inch (*lpi*), the image resolution should be no larger than 266 ppi (see Figures 3-8 and 3-9). Any higher resolution is almost certainly wasted information.

We've heard from people who claim to see a difference between 2 times the screen frequency and 2.5 times the screen frequency, but no one has ever shown us a print sample that supported this contention. It's an absolute certainty that anything higher than 2.5 times the screen frequency is wasted if you're printing to a PostScript output device.

If you go to print an image whose resolution exceeds that multiplier, Photoshop warns you, and PostScript just discards the extra information

Figure 3-8 Resolution and image reproduction

How much resolution do you need? All of these images are printed using the same 133-lpi halftone screen, but they contain different numbers of pixels. Look for details, such as readability of type.

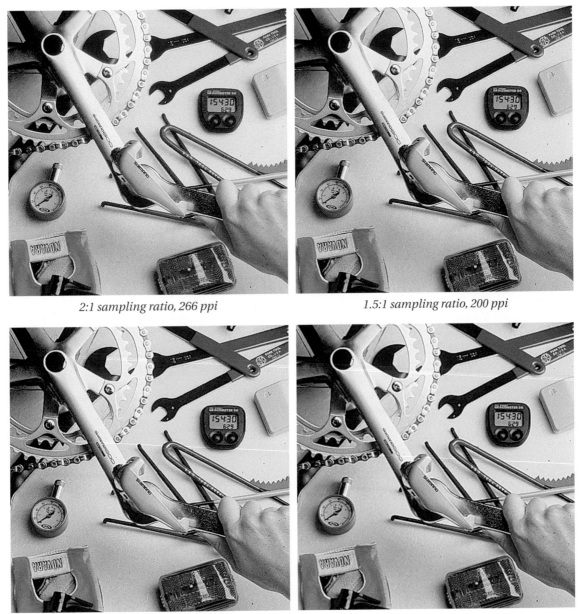

2:1 sampling ratio, 266 ppi

1.5:1 sampling ratio, 200 ppi

1.2:1 sampling ratio, 160 ppi

1:1 sampling ratio, 133 ppi

when it gets to the printer. You can print the image, but it takes longer to print, and you don't get any better results than you would with a lower-resolution version.

Figure 3-9 Resolution of grayscale images

2:1 (266 ppi)

1.5:1 (200 ppi)

1.25:1 (166 ppi)

1:1 (133 ppi)

In fact, we rarely use even twice the line screen. With a good 80 percent of images, you can use 1.5 times the screen frequency, and you can often get away with less, sometimes even as low as 1.2 times the screen frequency. That means the resolution of the image you're printing at 133 lpi *could* be as low as 160 ppi (but if you want to play it safe, you might use 200 ppi).

So which multiplier should you use? It depends on your quality requirements, the quality of your reproduction method, the kind of images you're reproducing, and your system. If you're working with a slower computer, less RAM, or a smaller hard drive, think lower resolution.

Quality requirements. The only reliable way we've found to answer the question of what's "good enough" is whether the person paying for the job smiles when they sign the check. There's no absolute index of quality, and clients have widely differing expectations. The best course of action is to prepare Matchprints, Kodak Approvals, or other high-quality dot-based proofs of a few different images, using different multipliers to see where the trade-off works for you.

Reproduction method. Images destined for uncoated stock and newsprint can generally withstand a lower multiplier than those printed on coated stock at a high screen frequency, because the more porous stock causes greater dot gain: The halftone dots grow larger because the ink bleeds into the paper. If you're producing a rag or a newspaper and you're still using the two-times-frequency rule, you're wasting someone's time and money—we hope it's not yours.

Image detail. The need for higher resolution also depends on the content of the image itself. Reducing the multiplier reduces the clarity of small details, so higher resolution is most important with images that have small (and important) details.

Most pictures of people work fine at 1.25 times the screen frequency, but trees with fine branches and leaves might do best with 1.5 times screen frequency. And if the image has a lot of fine diagonal or curved lines (such as rigging on a sailboat, or small text), you may want to use a resolution of 2 times the frequency, particularly if you're paying through the teeth for a 200-lpi print job on high-quality coated stock. Of course, in those cases it's probably worth spending a little extra on high-quality proofs to test some of the more difficult images at different resolutions.

Many Photoshop neophytes assume that if they have a 300-ppi scanner, they should scan at 300 ppi even if the image is going to be reproduced at actual size with a 133-lpi screen. If you use a 2× multiplier or 266 ppi instead, that's a savings of 1 MB for a little 4-by-5-inch image. A 1.5× multiplier saves you almost 3 MB, and 1.25× brings your original 5 MB image down to only 1.58 MB. That could mean quite a large difference in printing time or costs. (See Chapter 17, *Output Methods,* for more on halftone output issues.)

If a lot of this halftone talk is going over your head, we recommend a book that David coauthored with Steve Roth, Conrad Chavez, and Glenn Fleishman called *Real World Scanning and Halftones, 3rd Edition.*

Grayscale and Color Inkjet Output

The vast majority of photo-inkjets don't use halftoning. Instead, they use a quite different technique of laying down dots, called *error diffusion*. (See Chapter 17, *Output Methods,* for more on the differences between halftone and diffusion dithers.) A common mistake is to look at the resolution of the printer in dots per inch, and then send the printer a file with that same resolution in pixels per inch. You do *not* want to send an inkjet printer with a resolution of 1440 × 2880 dpi a 2880 ppi file, or a 1440 ppi file, or even a 720 ppi file! If you do, you'll create an uneccessarily huge file, and you'll drown the printer with data, actually obscuring detail rather than revealing it.

There are all sorts of theories as to the "best" resolution for inkjet printing, some more grounded in reality than others. We'll spare you the more esoteric details and simply tell you that we've obtained good results using resolutions between 180 ppi for very large prints and 480 ppi for small prints. Most of the time we print at somewhere between 240 and 360 ppi, depending on the print size and the available resolution in the image. We've yet to find a reason to send more than 480 ppi to any inkjet printer.

Grayscale and Color Continuous-Tone Output

If you're printing to a continuous-tone output device such as a dye- sublimation printer or a film recorder, you can forget all that fancy math. In an ideal world, you simply want the resolution of your file to match the resolution of the output device. If you're printing to a 300-dpi dye-sub printer, you want 300-ppi resolution—about 18 MB for a letter-size page. If you're printing to an 8 K film recorder, you really do want 8,096 pixels on the short side of the image, or an approximately 240 MB scan.

Sometimes, your scan or digital capture may have fewer pixels than you ideally need. Some film recorders and digital printers have excellent built-in upsampling capabilities that rival even the new resampling options in Photoshop CS, in which case you can save a good deal of time, effort, and disk space by letting the output device do the upsampling. But if you're a driven control freak, you'll probably want to control the upsampling process yourself. (See "Resampling," later in this chapter.)

On-Screen Output (Multimedia and the Web)

Multimedia is another form of continuous-tone output, but where you often need very high resolution for film recorders, on-screen multi- media projects require very little. It's generally misleading to think in terms of resolution when you prepare images for use on screen. All that really matters is the pixel dimensions.

When people talk about monitor resolution, they almost invariably specify the number of pixels on the screen—640 by 480, 800 by 600, 1,024 by 768, and so on. The polite fiction that screen resolution is 72 ppi is no more than that. You can run a 21-inch monitor at 640 by 480 (great for games) or a 17-inch monitor at 1,600 by 1,200 (great for images, bad for reading small type). These extreme cases produce actual resolutions much lower and higher than 72 ppi. You can't control the actual size at which your images will appear on other people's monitors. All you can do is suggest the ideal number of pixels on the screen for viewing your project.

We almost never scan an image at screen resolution, however. We like to scan at a higher resolution so that we can crop and resize the image to get it just right; then we downsample it (see the next section).

Resampling

One of the most important issues in working with bitmapped images—and, unfortunately, one which few people seem to understand—is how the resolution can change relative to (or independently of) the size of your image.

There are two ways that you can change resolution: scaling and re-sampling. You can scale or resample an image or part of an image in several ways, but you get the most control through the Image Size dialog box (see "Tip: Faster File Figuring," later in this chapter).

In Photoshop, you can scale an image without altering its resolution. Or you can change the resolution of an image without changing its size. These processes are called *resampling*, because you're changing the number of pixels in the image. You're adding or removing pixels.

If you take a 2-by-2-inch, 100-ppi image and change the size to 1 inch square without changing the resolution, Photoshop has to throw away a bunch of pixels; that's called *downsampling*. If you double the size by *upsampling*, the program has to add more pixels by *interpolating* between the other pixels in the image.

Upsampling vs. Downsampling

We used to have a very simple rule regarding upsampling: "Just don't do it if you can avoid it; and if you *can't* avoid it, use bicubic interpolation." Our thinking was that, while adding pixels to a file can reduce aliasing (a.k.a. the jaggies) and mottling in some situations (and exaggerate them in others), it can't add details that weren't there in the first place.

When your images are scanned from film, that simple rule may still apply, but the lack of film grain in digital captures makes them much more tolerant of upsampling than film scans ever were. We often upsample digital captures by 200 percent, sometimes even more. Upsampling still doesn't add details that weren't there in the capture, but sometimes it does an uncannily good impersonation!

Downsampling is much less problematic, because it's just throwing away data in a more or less intelligent manner. In fact, it's a common and necessary practice: We often scan at a higher resolution than is strictly necessary, to allow for cropping and for unanticipated changes in output size or method. We downsample to the required resolution before printing to save time and storage space.

Resampling methods. Photoshop can downsample and interpolate using five methods: Nearest Neighbor, Bilinear, Bicubic, Bicubic Smoother, and Bicubic Sharper, the last two of which are new in Photoshop CS. You choose which you want in the General Preferences dialog box or in the Image Size dialog box (see Figure 3-10).

▶ **Nearest Neighbor** is the most basic, and it's very fast: To create a new pixel, Photoshop simply looks at the pixel next to it and copies its value. Unfortunately, the results are usually lousy unless the image is made of colored lines or shapes (like an image from Illustrator or FreeHand).

▶ **Bilinear** is slightly more complex and produces somewhat better quality: the program sets the color or gray value of each pixel according to the pixels surrounding it. The effect is similar to averaging the neigh-

Figure 3-10

Photoshop's resampling
(interpolation) methods

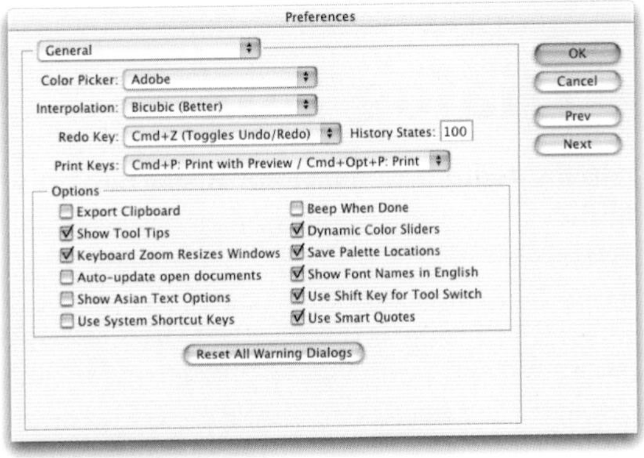

General Preferences

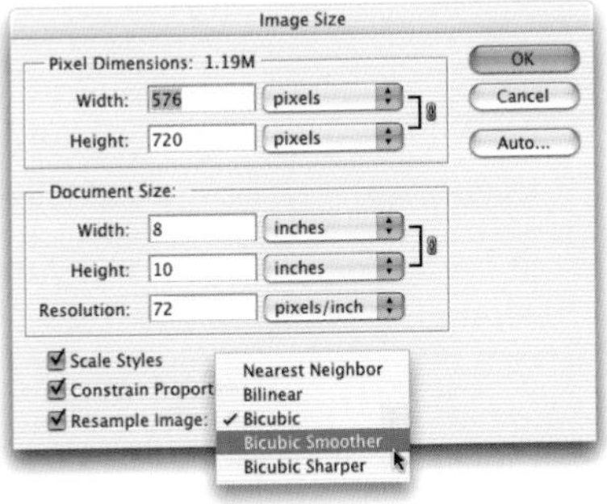

Image Size

boring pixels, but Photoshop uses a more sophisticated algorithm. The result is that some pictures can be upsampled pretty well with bilinear interpolation. However, we really have never found a good reason to use it; instead, we use one of the bicubic options.

▶ **Bicubic** interpolation creates better effects than Nearest Neighbor or Bilinear, but takes longer. Like Bilinear, it looks at surrounding pixels, but the equation it uses is much more complex and calculation intensive, producing smoother tonal gradations.

▶ **Bicubic Smoother** is a new interpolation method specifically designed for upsampling. As its name suggests, it provides a smoother result that responds better to subsequent sharpening than does the old Bicubic sampling.

▶ **Bicubic Sharper** is another new interpolation method, only this time designed for downsampling. It does a better job of preserving detail than does Bicubic.

The differences are quite subtle (see Figure 3-12). The new simple rule: Use Bicubic Smoother for upsampling (but don't expect miracles, particularly with film scans) and Bicubic Sharper for downsampling.

Image Size Dialog Box

For those of us who have to teach Photoshop as well as use it, the Image Size dialog box is always one of the biggest sources of confusion, because the results you get depend not only on which buttons you click and which fields you type numbers into, but also on the order in which you do so.

The Image Size dialog box is split into the two most important ways of describing an image's resolution: its pixel dimensions and its print size.

Figure 3-11 Image Size dialog box

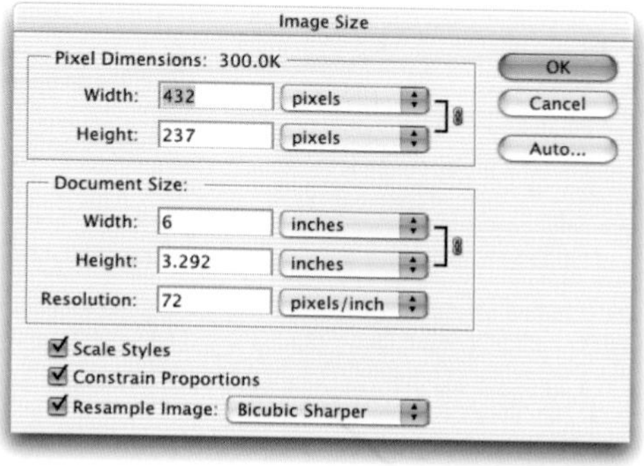

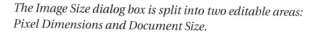

The Image Size dialog box is split into two editable areas: Pixel Dimensions and Document Size.

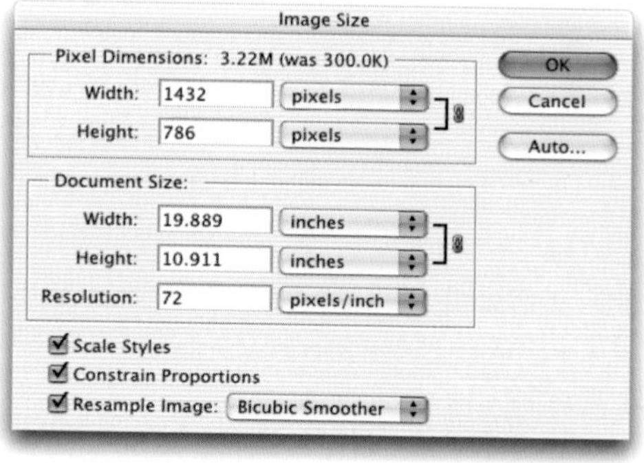

▶ **Pixel Dimensions.** The best way to specify an image's size is by its pixel dimensions—these tell you exactly how much data you have to work with. The Pixel Dimensions section shows you both the dimensions and the file's size, in megabytes (or K, if it's under 1 MB).

▶ **Document Size.** A bitmapped image has no inherent size—it's just pixels on a grid. The Document Size section lets you tag the image with a size and resolution, so that when you import the file into some other program, it knows the image size.

Resample Image. The most important feature in the Image Size dialog box is the Resample Image checkbox. When this is turned on, Photoshop lets you change the image's pixel dimensions; when it's off, the dimensions

With Resample Image turned on, when you change the Pixel Dimensions, the Document Size changes, but the Resolution doesn't.

are locked. In other words, unless you turn on this checkbox, you cannot add pixels to or remove pixels from the image (upsample or downsample).

Although the dialog box is split into two areas, you really have three interdependent values you can adjust. With Resample Image turned on, you can change the pixel dimensions, the document size, or the resolution. You also

have the ability to choose which resampling method Photoshop should use (see "Upsampling vs. Downsampling," earlier in this chapter).

Note that when the pixel dimensions change, so does the size of the file. Photoshop displays both the old and new size in the Pixel Dimensions section of the dialog box.

Figure 3-11 Image Size dialog box, continued

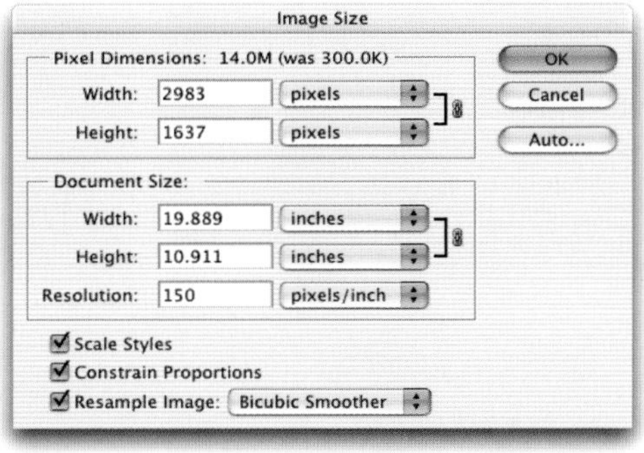

With Resample Image turned on, when you change the Resolution, the Pixel Dimensions change, but the Document Size doesn't.

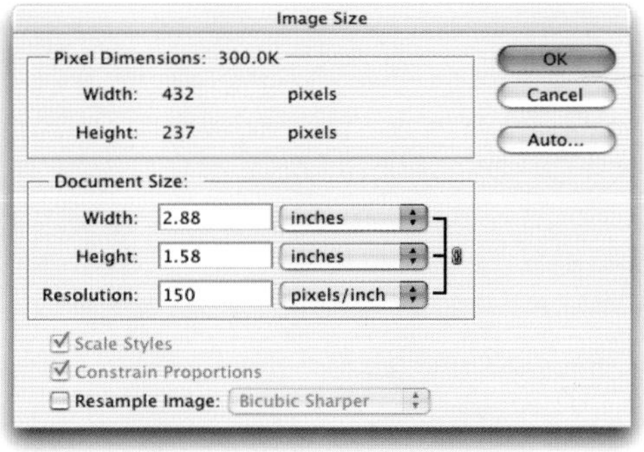

With Resample Image turned off, the Pixel Dimensions never change. Changing Document Size affects Resolution and vice versa.

The key is that Document Size and Resolution are independent of one another when Resample Image is turned on. Just change one, then the other.

When Resample Image is turned off, the Pixel Dimensions never change, and changing either Document Size or Resolution always affects the other one (see Figure 3-11).

If the previous two paragraphs didn't make any sense, don't bother trying to memorize them; just go and play with the Image Size dialog box until you see what's going on.

Tip: Adjusting by Percent. The word "percent" appears in both the Pixel Dimensions and the Document Size popup menus. Percent isn't a size; it's based on the current size of the image you're working on. For example, if you have a 2-by-2-inch image and you type in 200 percent for Document Size Width and Height, the result will be a 4-by-4-inch image. The number of pixels in the image will depend on whether you have Resample Image turned on or off.

We find this especially helpful when we have to recreate an image that was scaled "for position only" in a layout program. First we write down the scaling values on a piece of paper, and then we open the image in Photoshop and type the percentages into the Image Size dialog box.

Changing sizes. Like we said, the Image Size dialog box takes some getting used to. One confusing element is that whenever you make a change to one field, some other fields change and others don't. Here's a quick summary of what to watch for.

When Resample Image is turned on and you change the Pixel Dimensions, the Document Size changes, but the Resolution does not. If you change the Document Size, the Pixel Dimensions change, too, and the Resolution remains unchanged. If you change the Resolution, the Pixel Dimensions change, and the Document Size stays the same. An often overlooked subtlety is that Image Size allows you to change the Document Size and the Resolution in a single operation (which then changes the pixel dimensions).

Figure 3-12 Results of different interpolation methods when upsampling

Original (82 dpi)

Nearest Neighbor (165 dpi)

Bilinear (165 dpi)

Bicubic (165 dpi)

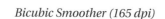

Bicubic Smoother (165 dpi)

Bicubic Sharper (165 dpi)

Image Mode

As we said earlier, pixel depth can tell you that pixel number 45 has a value of 165, but that doesn't mean anything until you know what image mode the bitmapped image is saved in. That 165 could represent a level of gray, or a particular color, or that might be only one value in a set of three or four other 8-bit values. Fortunately, Photoshop makes it easy to see what image mode a bitmapped image is in, as well as to convert it to a different mode, if you want.

Ultimately, an image mode is simply a method of organizing the bits to describe a color. In a perfect world, you could say to a printer, "I'd like this box to be navy blue," and they'd know exactly what you were talking about. However, even Bruce and David can't agree on what navy blue looks like, much less you and your printer. So color scientists created a whole mess of ways for us to describe colors with some precision—to each other and to a computer.

Photoshop reads and writes only a handful of the many different color modes they came up with. Fortunately, they're the most important of the bunch, at least for those in the world of graphic arts. Each of the following image modes appears on Photoshop's Mode menu. Note that the mode your image is in determines the file formats you can save in. For instance, you cannot save as PICT if the file is in CMYK mode. We'll talk more about this in Chapter 16, *Storing Images*.

Bitmap

David really wishes that Adobe had picked a different word for this image mode. All images in Photoshop are *bitmapped*, but only "flat" black-and-white images, in which each pixel is defined using one bit of data (a zero or a one), are *bitmaps*. Perhaps "B&W" would have been more user-friendly to those of us who think that "rasters" have something to do with reggae.

One-bit pictures have a particular difference from other images when it comes to PostScript printing: the white areas throughout the image can appear transparent, showing through to whatever the image is printing over. Ordinarily, images are opaque, except for the occasional white silhouetted background made with clipping paths (see "Silhouettes" in Chapter 15, *Essential Image Techniques*).

There's another major difference between the other image modes and Bitmap mode: You're much more limited in the sorts of image editing you can do. For instance, you can't use any filters, and because there's no such thing as anti-aliasing in 1-bit images, you just cannot use tools that require this, such as the Smudge tool, the Blur tool, or the Dodge/Burn tool.

Bilevel bitmaps are the most generic of images, so you can save them in almost any file format (though there are some quirks that can cause transparency weirdnesses; see "Drop Shadows" in Chapter 15, *Essential Image Techniques*).

Grayscale

Although you can spec grayscale images with various numbers of bits per pixel in other programs, grayscale files in Photoshop are always either 8- or 16-bit images: Anything less than 8-bit gets converted to 8-bit; anything more than 8-bit gets converted to 16-bit. Eight-bit is still more common, although most scanners now allow you to bring more than 8 bits into Photoshop.

With 8-bit grayscale, each pixel has a value from 0 (black) to 255 (white), so there are a maximum of 256 levels of gray possible. With 16-bit grayscale, each pixel has a value from 0 (black) to 32,768 (white), for a theoretical maximum of 32,769 possible gray shades.

However, in practice, few scanners can actually deliver all those gray shades, so 16-bit files usually have rather a lot of redundancy. In Photoshop CS, 16-bit files are much better supported than in any previous version, so with scanners that capture 12 or more bits per pixel, it's well worthwhile bringing the high-bit data into Photoshop.

Eight-bit grayscale images are also pretty generic, so you can save them in almost any format this side of MacPaint. You can save 16-bit grayscale images in a number of formats, but if you add layers, your choices are limited to Photoshop, Large Document Format, PDF, and TIFF.

Duotone

When you print a grayscale image on a printing press, those 256 levels of gray often get reduced to 100 or so because of the limitations of the press. You can counter this flattening effect considerably—increasing the tonal range of the printed image—by printing the image with more than one color of ink. This is called printing a *duotone* (for two inks), a *tritone* (for three inks), or a *quadtone* (for four).

The key is that the extra colors aren't typically used to simulate colors in the image; rather, they're used to enhance the underlying grayscale image. Those expensive Ansel Adams books on your coffee table were very likely printed using three or four (or even five or six) *different* black and gray inks.

Duotones also allow you to exploit the presence of a spot color in a two-color job. However, you have to take some care in matching the spot color to the subject in a duotone: Duotones of people generally look ghastly if the second color is a green shade.

Photoshop has a special image mode for duotones, tritones, and quadtones, and even though the file may appear to be in color, each pixel is still saved using only eight bits of information. The trick is that Photoshop saves the 8-bit grayscale image along with a set of contrast curves for each ink.

Creating a good duotone is an art as much as a science. We'll discuss it in detail in Chapter 11, *Spot Colors and Duotones*. Note that if you want to place duotone images in a page-layout application for spot-color separation, the safest choice is to save in EPS format, though InDesign supports Photoshop and, in theory, PDF formats for duotone-mode images.

Indexed Color

As we said, each pixel in a grayscale image is defined with eight bits of information, so the file can contain up to 256 different pixel values. But each of those values, from 1 to 256, doesn't have to be a level of gray. The Indexed Color image mode is a method for producing 8-bit, 256-color files. Indexed-color bitmaps use a table of 256 colors, chosen from the full 24-bit palette. A given pixel's color is defined by reference to the table: "This pixel is color number 123, this pixel is color number 81," and so on.

While indexed color can save disk space (it requires only 8 bits per sample point, rather than the full 24 in RGB mode—see below), it gives you only 256 different colors. That's not a lot of colors, when you compare it to the 16.7 million different colors you can get in RGB. But the relatively tiny files make indexed-color images useful for Web graphics.

There are a few (severe) limitations with Indexed Color mode. First, you can't use any filters or tools that require anti-aliasing (such as the Smudge tool or the Dodge/Burn tool) because Photoshop can't anti-alias in this mode. Therefore, you should always do your image editing in RGB mode and then convert to Indexed Color mode as a last step.

Another issue with indexed color stems from a problem with the color lookup tables. If the table changes when you move the picture from one program to another, so do all the colors in the image. Pixel number 123 might still have a value of 81, but "color number 81" may have changed from red to blue in the process.

Last, note that you can't separate indexed-color images into CMYK values using a program such as QuarkXPress or Adobe InDesign. If you're printing these images to paper, you might consider converting them to RGB or CMYK while still in Photoshop. However, you won't improve the image any in the process—you're still getting only 256 colors.

You can save indexed-color images in Photoshop, GIF, PNG, PICT, Amiga IFF, or BMP format (see "Reasonable Niche File Formats" in Chapter 16, *Storing Images*).

RGB

Every color computer monitor and television in the world displays color using the RGB image mode, in which every color is produced with varying amounts of red, green, and blue light. (These colors are called *additive primaries* because the more red, green, or blue light you add, the closer to white you get.) In Photoshop, files saved in the RGB mode typically use a set of three 8-bit grayscale files, so we say that RGB files are *24-bit* files.

These files can include up to approximately 16 million colors—more than enough to qualify as photographic quality. This is the mode in which we prefer to work when editing color images. Also, most scanners save images in RGB format. High-end drum scanners include "color computers" that automatically convert files to CMYK mode (see below), but RGB scanning is becoming more common even in shops with these scanners.

If you're producing images for multimedia, or you're outputting files to a film recorder—to 35 mm or 4-by-5 film, for instance—you should always save your files in RGB mode (see Chapter 17, *Output Methods*).

Tip: To RGB or to CMYK. A great philosophical debate rages on whether it's better to work in RGB or in CMYK for prepress work. As with most burning philosophical questions, there's no easy answer to this one, but that doesn't deter us from supplying one anyway. If you get CMYK scans from a drum scanner, work in CMYK. In all other cases, we recommend staying in RGB for as long as possible. We discuss this question in much more detail in Chapter 7, *Color Correction Fundamentals*.

You can save 24-bit RGB files in Photoshop, EPS, TIFF, PICT, Amiga IFF, BMP, JPEG, PCX, PDF, Pixar, Raw, Scitex CT, or Targa format, but unless you have compelling reasons to do otherwise, we suggest you stick with Photoshop, TIFF, PDF, or EPS.

Photoshop also lets you work with 48-bit RGB files, which contain three 16-bit channels instead of three 8-bit ones. Now that Photoshop supports layered 48-bit images, we're bringing more and more 48-bit files into Photoshop for the great editing flexibility they offer (see "Working with High-Bit Images," also in Chapter 7, *Color Correction Fundamentals*).

Of course, if you're building images for multimedia or the Web, you want to stick with RGB and avoid ever switching to CMYK.

CMYK

Traditional full-color printing presses can print only four colors in a run: cyan, magenta, yellow, and black. Every other color in the spectrum is simulated using various combinations of those colors. When you open a file saved in CMYK mode, Photoshop has to convert the CMYK values to RGB values on the fly, in order to display the image on your computer screen. It's important to remember that when you look at the screen, you're looking at an RGB version of the data.

If you buy high-end drum scans, they'll probably be CMYK files. Otherwise, to print your images on press or on some desktop color printers, you'll have to convert your RGB images to CMYK. We discuss Photoshop's tools for doing so in Chapter 5, *Color Settings*.

You can save CMYK files in Photoshop, TIFF, DCS, EPS, JPEG, PDF, Scitex CT, and Raw formats, but the first five are by far the most common.

Lab

The problem with RGB and CMYK modes is that a given RGB or CMYK specification doesn't really describe a *color*. Rather, it's a set of instructions that a specific output device uses to produce a color. The problem is that different devices produce different colors from the same RGB or CMYK specifications. If you've ever seen a wall full of television screens at a department store, you've seen what we're talking about: The same image—with the same RGB values—looks different on each screen.

And if you've ever sat through a printing press run, you know that the 50th impression probably isn't exactly the same color as the 5,000th or the 50,000th. So, while a pixel in a scanned image may have a particular RGB or CMYK value, you can't tell what that color really *looks like*. RGB and CMYK are both *device-specific* color modes.

However, a class of *device-independent* or *perceptually-based* modes has been developed over the years. All of them are based, more or less, on a color space defined by the Commission Internationale de l'Éclairage (CIE) in 1931. The Lab mode in Photoshop is one such derivative.

Lab doesn't describe a color by the components that make it up (RGB or CMYK, for instance). Instead, it describes *what a color looks like*. Device-independent color spaces are at the heart of the various color management systems now available that improve color correspondence between your screen, color printouts, and final printed output.

A file saved in Lab mode describes what a color looks like under rigidly specified conditions; it's up to you (or Photoshop, or your color management software) to decide what RGB or CMYK values are needed to create that color on your chosen output device.

Photoshop uses Lab mode as a reference when switching between CMYK and RGB modes, taking the values in your RGB Setup and CMYK Setup dialog boxes into account (see Chapter 5, *Color Settings*, for more information on this conversion). You can save 24-bit Lab images in Photoshop, DCS, EPS, PDF, TIFF, or Raw format. (You can only save 48-bit Lab images as Photoshop, Large Document Format, PDF, TIFF, or RAW.)

It's a good thing that there's seldom a reason to work in Lab mode, because it's almost impossible to wrap your head around this model. While RGB or CMYK can actually make some sense, Lab is much stranger. The Lightness channel is reasonably intuitive, but the "a" and "b" channels represent how red or green, and how blue or yellow a color is, respectively. Worry for your sanity if this mode starts to makes sense to you. Nonetheless, Lab mode is handy for some techniques (like cleaning up images from digital cameras or doing subtle brightness tweaks).

Tip: L is for Luminosity. One useful property of Lab mode is that it stores the luminance information (the "L" channel) separately from the color information (the "a" and "b" channels). This can be handy if you want to adjust the tonal values in the image without affecting the hues. It's also useful for some sharpening tricks.

Multichannel

The last image mode that Photoshop offers is Multichannel mode. This mode is the generic mode: like RGB or CMYK, Multichannel mode has more than one 8-bit channel; however, you can set the color and name of each channel to anything you like.

This flexibility can be a blessing or a curse. Back in the days when color scanners cost a fortune, we used to scan in color on grayscale scanners by scanning the image three times through red, green, and blue acetate, combining the three images into a single multichannel document that we then turned into RGB. Fortunately we don't have to do that anymore.

These days, many scientific and astronomical images are made in "false color"—the channels may be a combination of radar, infrared, and ultraviolet, in addition to various colors of visible light. Some of our gonzo digital photographer friends are using Multichannel mode to combine infrared and visible-spectrum photographs into composite images of surreal beauty.

We mostly use Multichannel mode as an intermediary step. For instance, you can use it to store extra channels for transparency masks or selections in other images. Your only options for saving multichannel images are the Photoshop, Raw, Large Document Format, and DCS formats.

Bitmaps and File Size

As we said at the beginning of this chapter, bitmapped images are rectangles with hundreds, or thousands, or hundreds of thousands of pixels. Each of those pixels has to be saved on disk. If each pixel is defined using 8 bits of color information, then the file is eight times bigger than a flat bitmap. Similarly, a 24-bit file is a full three times bigger than that, and a 48-bit file is twice the size of a 24-bit one.

Big files take a long time to open, edit, print, or save. Many people who complain about how slow editing is in Photoshop are simply working with files much bigger than they need. Instead, you can save yourself the complaining and reduce your file size when you can. Here's a quick rundown of how each attribute of a bitmapped image affects file size.

Dimensions and resolution. When you increase the number of pixels in a bitmap, you increase the file's size by the square of the value. That means if you double the resolution, you quadruple the file size (2×2); triple the resolution, and your file is nine times as large (3×3). There can easily be a multimegabyte difference between a 300-ppi and a 225-ppi image.

Bit depth. Increasing bit depth increases file size by a simple multiplier. Therefore, a 24-bit image is three times as large as an 8-bit image, and 24 times as large as a 1-bit image.

Image mode. Image mode doesn't necessarily increase file size, but going from RGB (24-bit) to CMYK (32-bit) mode does. It adds an extra 8-bit channel, thereby increasing bit depth (because each pixel is 32 bits deep).

Figuring File Size

Now that you know the factors that affect the size of bitmaps, it's a simple matter to calculate file size using the following formula.

$$\text{File size} = \text{Resolution}^2 \times \text{Width} \times \text{Height} \times \text{Bits per sample} \div 8{,}192$$

For example, if you have a 4-by-5-inch, 1-bit image at 300 ppi, you know that the file size is 220 K ($300^2 \times 4 \times 5 \times 1 \div 8192$). A 24-bit image of the same size would be 5,273 K (just about 5 MB). In case you were wondering, this formula works because 8,192 is the number of bits in a kilobyte.

Tip: Faster File Figuring. There's an even easier way to calculate file sizes than doing the math yourself—let the computer do it for you. Photoshop's New Document and Image Size dialog boxes are very handy calculators for figuring dimensions, resolution, and file size. Simply type in the values you want, and Photoshop shows you how big the file would be (see Figure 3-13).

Figure 3-13
The Image Size
dialog box

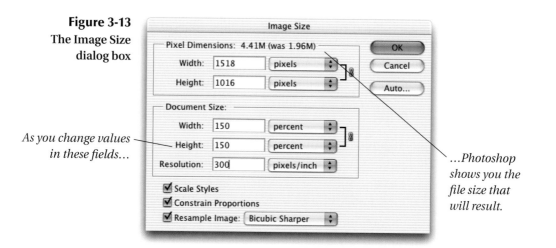

As you change values in these fields…

…Photoshop shows you the file size that will result.

Of course, all these calculations apply only to flat files. When you start adding layers, layer masks, and alpha channels, it becomes quite difficult to figure file size with any degree of reliability. Each channel or mask adds another 8 or 16 bits to the bit depth (depending on whether the document was in 8-bit/channel or 16-bit/channel mode), but layers are much harder to figure because Photoshop divides each layer into tiles. Empty tiles take up almost no space, but if a tile contains just one pixel, it takes up the same amount of space as a tile that's full of pixels. It's possible, and sometimes useful, to place layered TIFF or Photoshop files in a page-layout application, but we recommend flattening all files before final handoff to keep final files to a managable size.

Some file formats also offer compression options. It's important to bear in mind that the file size that Photoshop reports is always the amount of RAM that the uncompressed, flattened image will occupy. We'll discuss compression options and file formats in much greater detail in Chapter 16, *Storing Images*.

Billions and Billions of Bits

Would you hire a carpenter who didn't know anything about wood? Bit-mapped graphics are the wood of Photoshop; they're the material you use to construct your images. Without a firm understanding of the strengths as well as the weaknesses of your material, you won't get very far with this power tool of a program.

In the next chapter, we move away from the wood and start looking at the hammer-and-nails aspects of Photoshop: the essential tools you need to get your work done efficiently.

4 Color Essentials

What Makes a Color

You may have been taught back in kindergarten that the primary colors are red, yellow, and blue, and that all other colors can be made from them. Bruce still vividly recalls the day when his first-grade teacher, Mrs. Anderson, told him that he could make gray by using equal amounts of red, yellow, and blue. After looking at the lurid, weird, multicolored mess that was supposed to be a gray cat, he quite sensibly started over using a 2B pencil, and concluded that Mrs. Anderson was either color-blind or clueless. He traces his sometimes-inconvenient tendency to question authority to that day.

The details of Mrs. Anderson's lesson were certainly fallacious, but they contained an important kernel of truth—the notion that we can create all colors by combining three primary constituents. People have many different ways of thinking about, talking about, and working with color, but the notion of three ingredients that make up a color occurs again and again. Art directors may feel comfortable specifying color changes with the terms *hue*, *lightness*, and *saturation*. Those who came to color through the computer may be more at home with levels of RGB. Scientists think about color in all sorts of strange ways, including CIE Lab, HSB, and LCH. And dyed-in-the-wool prepress folks think in CMYK dot percentages.

Although Photoshop tries to accommodate all these ways of thinking about color—and it does a pretty good job—many Photoshop users find themselves locked into seeing color in only one way. This is natural and understandable—we all have one way of thinking about color that seems more sensible than the others—but it can make life with Photoshop more difficult than it needs to be. If you understand that all the different ways of looking at color are based on the same notion—combining three ingredients—you can learn to translate among the ways Photoshop lets you work with them, and choose the right one for the task at hand.

"Wait a minute," you say. "CMYK has four constituents, not three!" You question authority too, when that authority doesn't make sense. Well, in our role as temporary authority figures, we'll do what authority figures often do when asked hard questions: We ask you to trust us. Set this issue aside for the moment. We promise we'll deal with it later.

In this chapter, we take a hard look at some fundamental color relationships and how Photoshop presents them. This stuff might seem a little theoretical at times, but we urge you to slog through it; it's essential for our later discussions about tonal and color correction.

Primary Colors

The concept of *primary* colors is at the heart of much of the color work we do on computers. When we work with primary colors, we're talking about three colors that we can combine to make all the other colors. We can define colors by specifying varying proportions of primary colors, and we can color-correct images by adjusting the relationship of the primary colors. Ignoring for the moment which specific colors constitute the primaries, there are two fundamental principles of primary colors.

- ▶ They are the irreducible components of color.

- ▶ The primary colors, combined in varying proportions, can produce an entire spectrum of color.

The *secondary* colors, by the way, are made by combining two primary colors and excluding the third. But we don't much care about that.

Additive and Subtractive Color

Before becoming preoccupied with the behavior of spherical objects like apples, billiard balls, and planets, Sir Isaac Newton performed some experiments with light and prisms. He found that he could break white light down into red, green, and blue components, a fairly trivial phenomenon that had been known for centuries. His breakthrough was the discovery that he could *reconstitute* white light by recombining those red, green, and blue components. Red, green, and blue—the primary colors of light—are known as the *additive primary* colors because as you add color, the result becomes more white (the absence of colored light is black; see Figure 4-1). This is how computer monitors and televisions produce color.

Figure 4-1
Additive and subtractive primaries

But color on the printed page works differently. Unlike a television, the page doesn't emit light; it just reflects whatever light hits it. To produce color images in print, you don't work with the light directly. Instead, you use pigments (like ink, dye, toner, or wax) that *absorb* some colors of light and reflect others.

The primary colors of pigments are cyan, yellow, and magenta. We call these the *subtractive primary* colors because as you add pigments to a white page, they subtract (absorb) more light, and the reflected color becomes darker. (We sometimes find it easier to remember: You *add* additive colors to get white, and you *subtract* subtractive colors to get white.) Cyan absorbs all the red light, magenta absorbs all the green light, and yellow absorbs all the blue light. If you add the maximum intensities of cyan, magenta, and yellow, you get black—in theory (see Figure 4-1).

Mrs. Anderson had the right idea about primary colors; she just picked the wrong ones. No matter how hard you try, you'll never be able to make cyan using red, yellow, and blue crayons.

An Imperfect World

A little while ago, we asked you to trust us on the subject of CMYK. Well, we just told you that combining cyan, magenta, and yellow would, *in theory,* produce black. In practice, however, it produces a muddy brown mess. Why? In the words of our friend and colleague Bob Schaffel, "God made RGB . . . man made CMYK." To that we add: "Who do you trust more?"

Imperfect pigments. If we had perfect CMY pigments, we wouldn't have to add black (K) as a fourth color. But despite our best efforts, our cyan pigments always contain a little red, our magentas always contain a little green, and our yellows always contain a trace of blue. So when we print in color, we add black to help with the reproduction of dark colors. Plus, by adding black, we can reduce the total amount of ink needed to create dark areas, which not only saves money but solves some . . . uh . . . *sticky* printing problems. See Chapter 5, *Color Settings,* for more on this.

Imperfect conversions. If we only had to deal with CMY, life would be a lot simpler. However, a large part of the problem of reproducing color images in print is that scanners—since they deal with light—see color in RGB, and we have to translate those values into CMYK to print them. Unfortunately, this conversion is a thorny one (see Chapter 5, *Color Settings,* for more on this subject).

The Color Wheel

Before moving on to weightier matters such as gravity, calculus, and his impending thirtieth birthday, Sir Isaac Newton provided the world of color with one more key concept: if you take the colors of the spectrum and arrange them around the circumference of a wheel, the relationships among primaries become much clearer (see Figure 4-2).

The important thing to notice about this color wheel is that the additive and subtractive primary colors are opposite each other, equidistant around the wheel. These relationships are key to understanding how color works. For instance, cyan sits opposite red on the color wheel because it is, in fact, the opposite of red: Cyan pigments appear cyan because they absorb red light and reflect blue and green. Cyan is, in short, the absence of red.

Figure 4-2
The color wheel

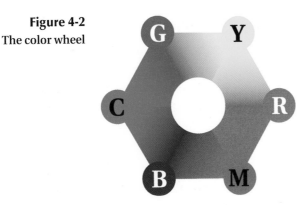

Emitted and reflected (additive and subtractive) colors are complementary to one another. Red is complementary to cyan, green to magenta, and blue to yellow.

Colors that lie directly opposite each other on the wheel are known as *complementary* colors.

Figuring Saturation and Brightness

So far, we've talked about color in terms of three primary colors. But there are other ways of specifying color in terms of three ingredients. The most familiar one describes color in terms of *hue* (the property we refer to when we talk about "red" or "orange"), *saturation* (the "purity" of the color), and *brightness*.

Newton's basic two-dimensional color wheel lets us see the relationships between different hues, but to describe colors more fully, we need a more complex, three-dimensional model. We can find one of these in the HSB (Hue, Saturation, Brightness) color cylinder (see Figure 4-3).

In the HSB cylinder, you can see the hues are arranged around the edge of the wheel, and colors become progressively more pastel as we move into the center—the farther in you go, the less saturated or pure the color is. The Apple Color Picker (which many programs use to specify color, but not Photoshop) is a graphical representation of the HSB color model—it displays a color wheel to pick hue and saturation, with a slider to control brightness.

Tristimulus Models and Color Spaces

Ignoring the inconvenience of CMYK, all the ways we've discussed of specifying and thinking about color involve three primary ingredients. Color scientists call these *tristimulus* models. (A *color* model is simply a way of thinking about color and representing it numerically: A tristimulus model represents colors by using three numbers.) If you go deep into the physiology of color, you'll find that our perceptual systems are

Figure 4-3
The HSB color cylinder

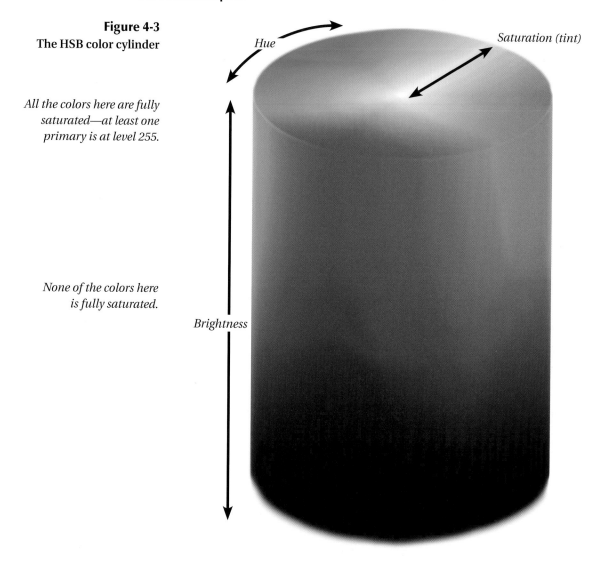

Hue

Saturation (tint)

All the colors here are fully saturated—at least one primary is at level 255.

None of the colors here is fully saturated.

Brightness

actually wired in terms of three different responses to light that combine to produce the sensation of color. So the tristimulus approach is more than just a mathematical convenience—it's dictated by the way our perceptual systems work.

But tristimulus models have another useful property. Because they specify everything in terms of three ingredients, you can (with very little effort) view them as three-dimensional objects with *x*, *y*, and *z* axes. Each color has a location in this three-dimensional object, specified by the three values. These three-dimensional models are called *color spaces*, a term that gets thrown around a great deal in the world of color.

We like to think of the HSB color space as a giant cylinder; the brightness slider in the Apple Color Picker determines which slice of the cylinder we're looking at. But, like any metaphor, there's a good side and a bad side to looking at color this way.

▶ **The good side.** The Apple Color Picker is a great way to start learning about color and how changing a single primary changes your colors.

▶ **The bad side.** The simple HSB model can't really describe how you *see* colors. For instance, you know that cyan appears much lighter than blue; but in the HSB cylinder, they both have the same brightness and saturation values.

Therefore, while the color picker is a step in the right direction, we have to go further to understand how to work with color.

How Colors Affect Each Other

There are a lot of times in Photoshop when we find ourselves working with one color space, but thinking about the changes in terms of another. As you'll see in Chapter 7, *Color Correction Fundamentals*, for instance, we often recommend that you use curves to adjust RGB values, but base your changes on the resulting CMYK percentages as displayed in the Info palette. So, it will speed up your work if you take some time to figure out how color spaces interact—what happens in one space when you work in another.

Here are some ways to think about RGB, CMY, and HSB colors, and how they relate to each other.

Tone. One of the least understood—yet most important—effects of adding colors together is that adding or removing primaries not only affects hue and saturation; it also affects tone. When you increase any RGB component to change the hue—adding light—the color gets lighter. The reverse is true with CMY because you're adding ink, making the color darker.

Hue. Every color, except the primaries, contains opposing primary colors. In RGB mode, red is "pure," but orange contains red alongside a good dose of green (and possibly some blue, too). In CMYK, magenta is pure, and red is not—it contains some amount of yellow in addition to magenta. So to change a color's hue, you add or subtract primary colors.

In the process, you will probably affect the color's tone—adding or removing light (or ink) so the color gets lighter or darker.

Saturation. A saturated RGB color is made up of only one or two primaries; the third primary is always zero. When you add a trace of the third color—in order to change the hue slightly, for instance—you desaturate the color.

Likewise, if you increase the saturation of a color using the Hue/Saturation dialog box (or any other), you're removing one of the primaries. If you get out to the edge, where one of the primaries is maxed out and the other two are still changing, you'll change the hue and the tone.

There's another important consideration pertaining to saturated colors. When you saturate a color in an RGB image, you wind up with detail in only one of the three channels. One of the others is always solid white, and the other is always solid black. It's this—not just the difficulty of reproducing them—that makes saturated colors in images difficult to handle, because all the detail is being carried by only one channel.

Neutrals. A color made up of equal values of red, green, and blue is always a neutral gray (though you may have to do quite a bit of work to make it come out that way on screen or—once you've converted it to CMYK—on press). The "darkness" of the gray depends on how much red, green, and blue there is—more light makes for a lighter gray. This is useful in a number of situations, including making monitor adjustments and correcting color casts.

For a quick summary of relationships among the color spaces, see the sidebar "Color Relationships at a Glance," later in this chapter.

Device-Independent Color

Basically, the problem with HSB, RGB, and CMY (and even CMYK) is that they don't describe how a color looks; they only describe the color's ingredients. You've probably walked into a television store and seen about a hundred televisions on the wall, each of them receiving the same color information. But *none* of them displays the colors in the same way.

Color Relationships at a Glance

It's worth spending however long it takes to understand the color relationships we're discussing in this chapter. We all have a favorite color space, but if you can learn to view color in more than one way—understanding how to achieve the same results by manipulating CMY, RGB, and HSB—you'll find the world of color correction much less alien, and you'll be much more able to select the right tool for the job.

We suggest memorizing these fundamentals.

▶ 100% cyan = 0 red

▶ 100% magenta = 0 green

▶ 100% yellow = 0 blue

▶ Increasing RGB values corresponds exactly to reducing CMY values, and vice versa.

▶ Reducing saturation (making something more gray) means introducing the complementary color; to desaturate red, for example, you add cyan.

▶ The complement of a primary color is produced by combining equal amounts of the other two primary colors.

▶ Lightening or darkening a saturated color desaturates that color.

▶ Changing the hue of a color often changes lightness as well.

▶ Saturation changes can cause hue changes.

Saturated Primaries—CMY versus RGB

100C	255G 255B
100C 50Y	255G 128B
100C 100Y	255G
50C 100Y	128R 255G
100Y	255R 255G
50M 100Y	255R 128G
100M 100Y	255R
100M 50Y	255R 128B
100M	255R 255B
50C 100M	128R 255B
100C 100M	255B
100C 50M	128G 255B

The colors at left are fully saturated—each contains 100 percent of one or two primaries. The additive and subtractive primaries have an inverse relationship.

Desaturating Saturated Colors

	255R 255G
	64R 128G 192B
	128R 128G 128B
	64R 192G 128B
	255R 255B

Desaturating the reds removes red and adds other primaries to the red areas. Adding a third primary "pollutes" the saturated color, causing it to go gray. It may or may not affect lightness.

Lightness and Saturation

Lightening or darkening a saturated color (here, +50 and -50) desaturates it; either it pulls the primaries back from 100 percent, or it pollutes them with a third primary, or both. Also note the hue shift in the darkened version.

50C	100C 50M 50Y
50C 50Y	100C 50M 100Y
50Y	50C 50M 100Y
50M 50Y	75C 100M 100Y
50M	50C 100M 50Y
50C 50M	100C 100M 50Y

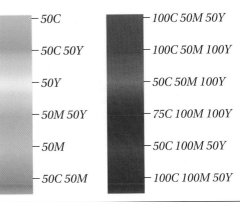

In fact, if you send the same RGB values to ten different monitors, or the same CMYK values to ten different presses, you'll end up with ten different colors (see Figure 4-4). We call RGB and CMYK *device dependent,* because the color you get varies from device to device.

So, Photoshop has a problem in trying to display colors properly on your monitor: It doesn't know what the colors should *look like* to you. It doesn't know what those RGB or CMYK values really mean.

Plus, the program has to take all the little quirks of human vision into account. For instance, our eyes are more sensitive to some colors and brightness levels than to others, and we're more sensitive to small changes in bright colors than we are to small changes in dark ones (if you've had trouble teasing all the subtle shadow details out of your scanned images, this is one reason why). RGB and CMYK don't give Photoshop the information it needs to know what color is actually being described.

Figure 4-4 **Device-dependent color and color gamuts**
Since this figure is printed with process inks on paper, it can only simulate the results of sending the same RGB or CMYK values to various devices. It depicts relative appearances, not actual results. Likewise, the color chart just represents the gamuts of different devices, rather than actually showing those gamuts.

Screen display

Dye-sublimation printer

Process inks, coated stock

Process inks, newsprint

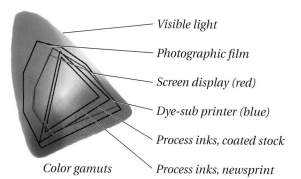
Color gamuts

— Visible light
— Photographic film
— Screen display (red)
— Dye-sub printer (blue)
— Process inks, coated stock
— Process inks, newsprint

Lab Color

Fortunately, there's CIE Lab, which appears on the Mode menu simply as Lab. Lab is designed to describe what colors *look like*, regardless of the device they're displayed on, so we call it *device independent*.

Whereas in HSB the hues are represented as lying around a wheel, Lab color uses a more accurate but significantly less intuitive arrangement. In Lab, the third axis (which lies perpendicular to the page and is roughly equivalent to brightness in HSB) is the luminance axis—it represents how bright the color appears to the human eye. But unlike brightness in HSB, it takes into account the fact that we see green as brighter than blue.

Whole books have been written on Lab color (we've even read some of them), and while they may be of great interest to color scientists, they're unlikely to help you get great-looking images on a deadline. For now, there are really only three things you need to know about Lab color.

▶ While HSB, HSL, and LCH are based on the way we think about color, and RGB and CMYK are based on the ways devices such as monitors and printers produce color, Lab is based on the way humans actually *see* color. A Lab specification describes the color that most people will see when they look at an object under specified lighting conditions.

▶ Photoshop thinks in Lab when it does mode changes. For instance, when you switch from RGB mode to CMYK mode, Photoshop uses Lab to decide what *color* is being specified by each device-dependent RGB value, and then comes up with the right device-dependent CMYK equivalent. You'll see why this is so important in the next chapter, *Color Settings*.

▶ Finally, you shouldn't feel dumb if you find it hard to get your head around Lab color. It *is* difficult to visualize, because it's an abstract mathematical construct—it isn't based on amounts of things we can understand readily, like RGB or HSB. It uses differing amounts of three primaries to specify colors, but those primaries don't really correspond to anything we can actually experience.

Working with Colors

When you work with Photoshop, it lets you view and adjust your colors in all sorts of different ways. It's difficult to adjust saturation in an image, for example, by manipulating RGB or CMYK values directly, so Photoshop provides tools that let you apply changes in hue, saturation, and brightness to the underlying RGB or CMYK data. Likewise, if you have an RGB image but you plan to print it in CMYK, you can use Photoshop's Info palette to keep track of what's happening to the CMYK values you'll eventually get when you do the mode change from RGB to CMYK.

You face two fairly large problems, however. The first is that every time you do a mode change, you lose some image information; your images only have 256 shades of each color, and as you convert from one color space to another, some of these get lost due to rounding errors. Photoshop lets you work around this by providing information about what you'll get after you've done the color-space conversion, without your actually having to do so until we've perfected your images. We discuss this in much more detail in Chapter 7, *Color Correction Fundamentals*.

The second problem is that the color spaces in which most of your images are stored, RGB and CMYK, are device dependent—the color you'll get varies depending on the device you send it to. Worse, each device has a range of colors it can reproduce—called the *color gamut*—and some devices have a much wider gamut than others (see Figure 4-4, earlier in this chapter). For example, color film can record a wider range of colors than a color monitor can display, and the monitor displays a wider range of colors than you can reproduce with ink on paper; so no matter what you do, some of the colors captured on film simply can't be reproduced in print.

Fortunately, Photoshop has tools that let us remove some (if not all) of the variability from your RGB and CMYK color definitions, and it lets you specify the gamut of your monitor and your CMYK output devices. The next chapter, *Color Settings*, is devoted to explaining what those tools are, how they work, and how to use them.

5 Color Settings
Configuring Photoshop's Color Settings

Welcome to the heart of *Real World Photoshop CS*. We consider every topic in this book to be important, but when push comes to shove, Photoshop's deepest, darkest secrets lie right here in the Color Settings chapter. Without understanding how Photoshop handles color behind the scenes, there's no way to get great color (or black-and-white) images out of Photoshop. It's dense stuff, but it's worth slogging through. (For maximum benefit, we recommend reading the whole chapter once, and then reading it again.)

Back when Photoshop 5 arrived, we knew its new way of handling color would cause headaches. And it did, so the folks at Adobe made sweeping changes to the way Photoshop 6 handled color. If you're coming from an earlier version than Photoshop 6, be prepared to re-learn a lot. If you're familiar with the way Photoshop 6 or 7 handled color, you'll be glad to know that this time, there are no wrenching paradigm changes. But whether you're a Photoshop newbie or an old pro, be prepared to spend some time in this chapter, 'cause we're going spelunking deep into Photoshop's dark color caverns; without this information, you'll be one lost puppy.

In the last chapter, we broke the sad news that RGB and CMYK are very ambiguous ways of specifying color, since the actual color you get will vary from device to device. In this chapter, we'll look at the settings Photoshop gives you to keep your color consistent and to make what you see on the screen at least resemble, if not actually match, what you get in your printed output.

Controlling Color

It may seem strange to devote a whole chapter to a handful of commands, but the settings that deal with defining, converting, and displaying color are so important that you really need to understand what they do, and when and how they do it. Use these features correctly, and you'll produce predictable, repeatable color more easily than ever; use them incorrectly, or ignore them, and you'll be doomed to "chase color" through cycle after cycle of corrections and proofs.

In this chapter, we'll focus on five features:

▶ Color Settings

▶ Assign Profile

▶ Convert to Profile

▶ Proof Setup

▶ Print with Preview

We'll explain what each does, how they interact, and how you can use each one, both to communicate color clearly and to see what your output will look like ahead of time, whether it's print CMYK, print RGB, or the Internet.

If you're new to the concepts behind color management, you'll likely find that just diving into Photoshop's dialog boxes is more than a tad overwhelming. Even experienced Photoshop users may find a 30,000-foot overview helpful. So before we look in detail at the color management features in Photoshop CS, let's step back a little and look at just what color management is and how it's supposed to work.

Color Management Systems Explained

A color management system (CMS) is a set of software tools that attempts to maintain the appearance of colors as they're reproduced by different devices. We stress the word "appearance" because it's simply impossible to reproduce many of the colors found in the world in print, or even on a color monitor.

Color management often gets dressed up in much fancier clothing, but it really does only two things.

▶ It lets you assign a specific color appearance to RGB or CMYK numbers that would otherwise be ambiguous.

▶ Within the physical limitations of the devices involved, it allows you to preserve that specific color appearance on different displays and output devices.

The options may sometimes appear more complex, but if you keep the two concepts listed above firmly in your mind, you'll find that color management really is relatively simple.

CMS Components

All CMSes employ three basic components:

▶ The *reference color space* (also known as the *profile connection space*, or PCS) is a device-independent, perceptually based color space. Most current CMSes use a CIE-defined color space, such as CIE Lab or CIE XYZ. You never have to worry about the reference color space; it's the theory behind how the software works.

▶ The *color-matching engine* (sometimes known as the *color matching method*, or CMM) is the software that does the conversion between different device-specific color spaces. Photoshop CS supports other color matching engines besides the Adobe-branded one (ACE) that it shares with the other Adobe Creative Suite applications, but the only reason we can see for using a different engine is if you absolutely must obtain exactly the same conversions from non-Adobe products. In general, the differences between the various CMMs are slight.

▶ *Profiles* usually describe the behavior of a device like a scanner, monitor, or printer. For instance, a profile can tell the CMS "This is the reddest red that this device can output." A profile can also define a "virtual color space" that's unrelated to any particular device (the Adobe RGB space is an example of this; we'll see how it's useful later on). Profiles are the key to color management. Without a profile, 100-percent Red has no specific meaning; with a profile, the color management system can say "Oh, *that* color red!" Thanks to the ICC (International Color

Consortium), device profiles conform to a standard format that lets them work with all CMSes on all platforms. ColorSync profiles on the Mac and .icm or .icc profiles on Windows both follow the ICC spec and are interchangeable between platforms.

The arrangement is similar to the way ancient versions of Photoshop (prior to version 5) used Lab color as a reference when they converted color between device-specific color spaces using the information in Monitor, Printing Inks, and Separation Setups. The major differences are that the device profiles provide a much more detailed description of the device's color space than Photoshop's old Color Settings did, there's more flexibility in translating between them, and they're understandable by lots of other applications rather than being Photoshop-specific settings files.

Conveying Color Meaning

The key concept in using a CMS is conveying color meaning—making those ambiguous RGB and CMYK values unambiguous. As we said earlier, if the system is going to keep the color consistent among different devices, it needs to know how each device in the process sees, displays, or prints colors. If a CMS knows enough about a scanner, it can interpret the incoming color information to find out what the colors in the original really look like. Then, if it knows how colors appear on your screen, it can adjust the image's colors to make the image on your screen match the original. Finally, if it knows about a printer, the CMS can adjust the colors to make them look right on that printer.

Profile embedding. When you embed a profile in an image, you aren't changing the image. You're simply providing a definition of what the numbers in the file mean in terms of actual colors you can see—you're assigning a specific color appearance to the RGB or CMYK numbers. If you don't embed profiles in your images, the numbers in the file are ambiguous and open to many different interpretations. Embedding a profile simply tells color-management-savvy applications which interpretation you want to place on the numbers. Profile embedding is the easiest way to convey the color meaning—the intended color appearance—of the numbers in the digital image.

Source and target profiles. When you ask the color management system to make a conversion—to change the numbers in the file—the CMS needs to know where the device-specific color values came from and where you want to send them. Whenever you open or create an image, you have to give the CMS this information by specifying a source profile and a target profile.

The source profile (which is sometimes already embedded in the file) says, "This RGB data is from such-and-such a scanner," or "This RGB data is from such-and-such a monitor." This tells the CMS what the colors really look like. The target profile tells the CMS where the image is going, so that it can maintain the color in the image.

For example, imagine that color management systems work with words rather than colors. The purpose of the word-CMS is to translate words from one language to another. If you just feed it a bunch of words, it can't do anything. But if you give it the words and tell it that they were written by a French person (the source), it all of a sudden can understand what the words are saying. If you then tell it that you speak German (the target), it can translate the meaning faithfully for you.

The process. Back to pictures: When you scan some artwork, you end up with a lot of RGB data. But for Photoshop to know what specific colors those RGB values are meant to represent, you have to tell it that the RGB data came from this particular scanner. When you choose your scanner's device profile as the source profile, you're telling Photoshop that this isn't just any old RGB data; it's the RGB data carefully defined by the scanner's device profile.

To make the image on your printer match the original, you choose your printer profile as the target profile. The CMS takes the RGB values in the image and uses the scanner profile as the secret decoder ring that tells it what colors (in the reference color space) the RGB values represent. Then it calculates new RGB or CMYK values based on the printer profile, to produce the same colors when they're printed on your printer.

This is really the only thing CMSes do. They convert color data from one device's color space (one "language") to another. Pretty much everything you do with a CMS involves asking it to make the colors match between a source and a target profile, and this same two-step is integral to the way Photoshop CS handles color.

Rendering intents. There's one more wrinkle. Each device has a fixed range of color that it can reproduce, dictated by the laws of physics. Your monitor can't reproduce a more saturated red than the red produced by the monitor's red phosphor. Your printer can't reproduce a cyan more saturated than the printer's cyan ink. The range of color a device can reproduce is called the *color gamut*. Colors present in the source space that aren't reproducible in the destination space are called *out-of-gamut* colors. Since you can't reproduce those colors in the destination space, you have to replace them with some other colors.

The ICC profile specification includes four different methods of handling out-of-gamut colors, called *rendering intents*. (In Photoshop CS, they're simply called intents.) The four rendering intents act as follows:

▶ **Perceptual.** The Perceptual intent attempts to fit the gamut of the source space into the gamut of the target space in such a way that the overall color relationships, and hence the overall image appearance, is preserved, even though all the colors in the image may change some-what in lightness and saturation. It's a good choice for images that contain significant out-of-gamut colors.

▶ **Saturation.** The Saturation intent maps fully-saturated colors in the source to fully-saturated colors in the target without concerning itself with hue or lightness. It's good for pie charts and such, where you just want vivid colors, but not much else.

▶ **Relative Colorimetric.** The Relative Colorimetric intent maps white in the source to white in the target, so that white on your output is the white of the paper rather than the white of the source space, which may be different. It then reproduces all the in-gamut colors exactly, clipping out-of-gamut colors to the closest reproducible hue. For images that don't contain significant out-of-gamut colors, it's often a better choice than Perceptual because it preserves more of the original colors.

▶ **Absolute Colorimetric.** The Absolute Colorimetric intent is the same as Relative Colorimetric, except that it doesn't scale source white to target white. If your source space has a bluish white, and your output is on a yellowish-white paper, Absolute Colorimetric rendering makes the printer lay down some cyan ink in the white areas to simulate the white of the original. It's generally only used for proofing (see "Soft-Proofing Controls" later in this chapter).

When you use a CMS to convert data from one color space to another, you need to tell it three pieces of information: the source profile, the target profile, and the rendering intent. You can think of these three elements as where the color comes from, where the color is going, and how you want the color to get there. But before you go hog-wild, converting images willy-nilly from one space to another, a cautionary note is needed.

Space conversions and data loss. Bear in mind that even the best CMS degrades your image when you convert it from one color space to another. Even though the conversions may be very accurate, you still want to limit their number (any color space conversion involves some loss, due to rounding and quantization errors). That's why Photoshop has taken a somewhat different approach to color management than most other applications. Rather than make you transform images continually from one device's color space to another's, thus degrading the image, Photoshop offers a reasonable place for images to live: a device-independent RGB working space.

Color Management in Photoshop

A little history: In versions of Photoshop prior to 5, the program acted like almost all other applications at the time and simply sent RGB values straight to the screen. A little-understood feature called Monitor Setup let you tell Photoshop how your monitor behaved—what its white point, primaries, and tone reproduction characteristics were, in effect providing Photoshop with a monitor profile. If the information was correct, Photoshop knew what color you would see when a set of RGB numbers was displayed on the monitor, and it would attempt to preserve that color during color space conversions. You can think of this approach as a crude color management system, albeit a limited, closed, proprietary one.

But it had a fundamental flaw. Even when used correctly, this approach had no mechanism for telling other users how your monitor behaved and hence no mechanism for conveying what colors the RGB numbers represented; so the image would appear different on each system, and would convert to other color spaces differently on each system. Most users just left Monitor Setup alone, so images converted the same but appeared different on different systems, giving rise to the myth that it's impossible to trust the monitor.

With Photoshop 5, Photoshop started using industry-standard ICC profiles to define the various color spaces, a practice continued in all subsequent versions. In Photoshop 5, your image's RGB space (called the *working space*) became uncoupled from the monitor's RGB space, or for that matter from any other physical device. Instead of keeping hundreds of images in different device-specific color spaces (each tied to whatever monitor last worked on it), Photoshop more or less forced you to convert all your images into a single RGB working space. Photoshop displayed images by performing an on-the-fly transform from this one RGB space to your monitor's RGB space—but only to the data that it sent to the monitor; the actual image data wasn't changed. The huge advantage was that images displayed correctly on different systems, as long as they had accurate monitor profiles. But this also had some disadvantages.

One disadvantage of this approach was that it forced a one-time conversion of the image from whatever RGB space it was captured in to the RGB working space, which many users found scary. But the bigger problem was that nobody could agree on *which* working space to use (though there was general agreement that the default, sRGB, was a Really Bad Idea). As a result, lots of people were confronted with strange dialog boxes warning them about profile mismatches and scary-looking progress bars that announced that Photoshop was "Converting colors"—which created confusion and discomfort, even when Photoshop was doing the right thing.

So Photoshop 6 replaced the strict (or, as some of the Photoshop team labelled it, "fascist") approach to working spaces with a more flexible approach (which we labelled "anarchist"), introducing the notion of *per-document* color. Documents could exist in any profiled space—a working space, a capture space, an output space. There are good reasons why you may still want to convert most of your images into a working space—we'll look at these in detail a little later—but the huge difference (and benefit) with per-document color is that you aren't forced to do so.

The consensus is that Photoshop 6 finally got color management right, and its approach has been carried over largely unchanged through Photoshop 7 to today's Creative Suite applications, including Photoshop CS.

But if you just jump into the Color Settings dialog box (press Command-Shift-K, select Color Settings from the Edit menu, or, on Mac OS X, the Photoshop menu), and start clicking buttons, you may wind up sinking in a morass o' confusion (see Figure 5-1). Color Settings is very deep indeed, and the interactions between the controls are often quite subtle. So rather than just waltzing through the various options in order, we need to step back a little and look at some of the concepts the controls embody. If you're used to Photoshop 5, we recommend that you read the next section carefully. Even if you're comfortable in Photoshop 6 or 7, you may benefit from reviewing the fundamentals one more time. If you just want the CliffsNotes version, see the sidebar "Photoshop Color Management at a Glance."

Figure 5-1
The Color Settings
dialog box

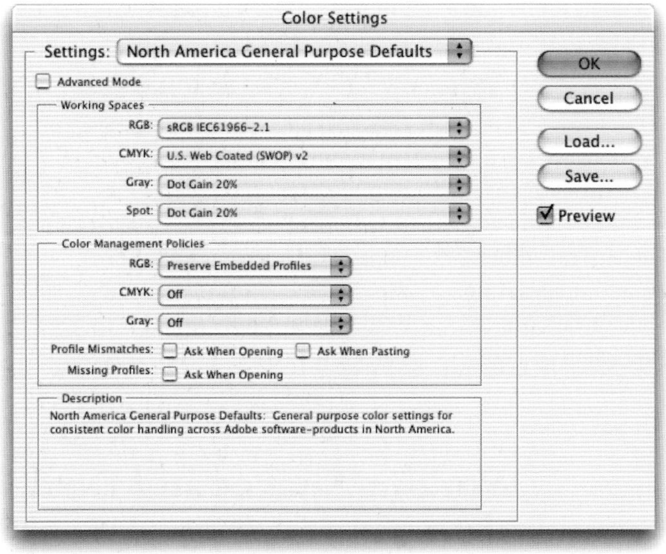

The Conceptual Framework

Photoshop 6 introduced several new concepts and made some old ones more important than they used to be. Getting a handle on these will give you a much clearer understanding of how the various settings work and why you'd want to choose one option over another. So before we dive into the depths of the Color Settings dialog box, let's look at an overview of the controls and the kinds of things they do.

Photoshop Color Management at a Glance

The color architecture in Photoshop CS is deep but straightforward. Here, in a nutshell, are the controls you need to know about to make Photoshop CS produce the results you want.

▶ The Color Settings dialog box lets you set default working spaces for RGB, CMYK, and Grayscale, and set Color Management Policies, which dictate how Photoshop uses (or ignores) embedded profiles in images. It also lets you set warnings for missing or mismatched profiles.

▶ The default working spaces are the ones Photoshop always uses when it encounters untagged images (those with no embedded profiles), and are also the ones Photoshop always uses as the destination when you convert between color modes by choosing RGB, CMYK, or Grayscale from the Mode submenu on the Image menu.

▶ Untagged images use whatever working space is currently set for that color mode. If you change the working space, Photoshop reinterprets the image as being in the new working space. Tagged images stay in the space represented by the embedded profile unless you explicitly ask for a conversion to another space.

▶ Color Management Policies let you control Photoshop's color management behavior. Preserve Embedded Profiles makes Photoshop open each image in the space represented by its embedded profile. Convert to Working RGB/CMYK/Grayscale forces a conversion from the embedded profile space to the working space. Off ignores embedded profiles and treats all images as being in the working space. Untagged images—those that don't contain an embedded profile—are always treated as being in the current working space.

▶ Photoshop *always* displays images through your monitor profile, which it picks up from the operating system. It performs an on-the-fly conversion on the data sent to the video card from the document's space (either the document's own embedded profile or the current working space) to your monitor space. This conversion is only for display—it doesn't affect the contents of the file.

Working Spaces and Device Spaces

In the Bad Old Days, you could use only one RGB space and only one CMYK space at a time. That rule no longer applies, because "per-document color" means you can now have multiple RGB and CMYK documents open at the same time, each one using a different color space. This is a giant leap forward for service bureaus and others who work with images from many different sources, but it also opens several cans o' worms. We now have to draw a distinction between the working space and the document space(s), and between working spaces and device spaces.

Most of us have become used to switching CMYK spaces as our output needs dictate (each output device or method requires a different CMYK space), but we've generally followed the practice of sticking with a single RGB space, mainly because Photoshop forced us to do so. Now that we're

▶ The Assign Profile command lets you assign a profile to any image. Assigning a profile doesn't change the numbers in the image, it just attaches a new meaning to those numbers, and hence it changes the appearance, sometimes dramatically.

▶ The Convert to Profile command lets you convert images to any profiled space, with a choice of rendering intents. Unlike Assign Profile, Convert to Profile changes the numbers in the image but preserves the appearance. Convert to Profile offers more control over color space conversions than changing modes from the Mode submenu, because it lets you preview different rendering intents, and it allows you to perform RGB-to-RGB or CMYK- to-CMYK conversions, which are impossible using the Mode commands.

▶ The Proof Colors command offers a live preview of conversions to any RGB, CMYK, or Grayscale output space. You can work in a working space while previewing the output space. Proof Colors offers separate control over the rendering from source space to proof space, and proof space to the monitor, providing very accurate previews.

▶ The Color Management Options panel of the Print with Preview dialog box lets you perform a conversion on the data that's sent to the printer. The conversion can be a simple one from document space to the output space, or a more complex one from the document space to the Proof Colors space to the output space. The former is handy for printing final art on a composite printer directly from Photoshop. The latter is useful for proofing final press output on a composite printer.

If you learn how to use all these controls effectively, you'll have achieved mastery of Photoshop's color management in its entirety. Maybe you should write a book!

On your way to mastering Photoshop's color management, just remember the basic principle that color management only does two things: assign a color appearance to the numbers, and change the numbers to preserve that appearance in a different scenario. Learn to figure out whether you're assigning an appearance or making a conversion.

freed from the tyranny of the RGB working space, it's important to look at the pros and cons of leaving RGB images in the space in which they were opened or converting them to an RGB working space.

With per-document color, your chosen working space is just a fall-back position for untagged images (images that don't have embedded profiles). Photoshop offers several different RGB working spaces, and enterprising third parties have created still more. It may seem sensible to edit in the space in which the image was captured—a scanner or digital camera space—or in the final output space, such as an RGB inkjet. But working spaces have important properties that make them more suited to image editing than the vast majority of device spaces.

▶ Most device color spaces are not *perceptually uniform*. That means that when you edit your file, the same editing increment in Levels, Curves, Hue/Saturation, or whatever, may have a much larger effect on some parts of the tonal range and color gamut than on others.

▶ Most device color spaces aren't gray-balanced. One of the key features of the abstract RGB working spaces built into Photoshop (as well as most third-party working spaces) is that when R=G=B, you know you have a neutral gray. This isn't true for most scanner RGB spaces, many digital camera RGB spaces, and pretty much all printer RGB spaces.

▶ Output device spaces typically clip some colors in the image because their gamut is almost always smaller than the original capture. For instance, if you simply apply a monitor or inkjet printer profile to an image you just scanned, you may not get all the colors you deserve. (Note that we don't say "never" edit files in final RGB output space—you may want to do some final tweaking there, just as you would in CMYK, but you wouldn't want to start out making big edits there.)

Working spaces, in contrast, tend to be uniform, and are invariably gray-balanced. They do, however, differ widely in their gamuts, so gamut size is one of the key considerations when choosing an RGB working space for a particular job (see "Choosing an RGB Working Space," later in this chapter).

So while you're no longer forced to use abstract RGB working spaces, you probably should for any serious image editing. Of course, there are always exceptions. If you're shooting on a high-end digital camera with a good profile, and you'll be making only minor tweaky adjustments to your images in Photoshop, you might consider just leaving the file in the camera's source space. But if you need to make significant changes to tone and color, you'll be better off converting your images into one of the working spaces.

Tagged and Untagged Images

Whenever you open or create an image, Photoshop treats it as a Tagged or an Untagged image from the moment of opening or creation, depending on how you set the Color Management Policies in Color Settings. Tagged and Untagged images behave differently as follows:

Tagged images. Tagged images have an embedded profile, which may be different from the current working space profile. A Tagged image keeps its original profile and stays in the "document space" rather than the working space, unless you explicitly assign a new profile, convert to a new profile, or untag the image, discarding the profile. The Color Management Policies let you automatically keep documents in their own space, convert them to the working space, or discard the profile.

Untagged images. Untagged images have no embedded profile. They exist as a bunch of numbers whose actual color meaning is open to interpretation. If you change the working space while an Untagged image is open, the image gets reinterpreted to be in the new working space. If you move pixels (by either copy and paste or drag-and-drop) to another image in the same color mode, the numerical values are moved to the new document. For operations where Photoshop needs to make an assumption about the actual colors the numbers represent, such as mode changes or displaying on the monitor, Photoshop treats Untagged images as being in the current working space for that mode. It also does so when you move pixels to a document in a different color mode, such as pasting from an RGB document to a CMYK one.

Almost every image should be tagged with an embedded profile. The only instance we can think of when you'd want to specifically *not* tag an image is when the numbers in the file are more important than the colors those numbers represent. This includes calibration targets and Web interface elements that must remain in Web-safe color. For everything else, you'll want to keep them as tagged images.

You can always convert a tagged image to an untagged one, or vice versa, by using the Assign Profile command (on the Mode submenu, under the Image menu), or the Embed Profile checkbox in the Save As dialog box, to embed a profile.

Tip: Document Profiles at a Glance. You can tell at a glance whether a document is tagged or untagged by choosing Document Profile from the popup menu at the lower left of the document window (see Figure 5-2). For tagged images, it shows the profile name. For untagged images, it displays "Untagged RGB" (or CMYK, or Grayscale, depending on the document's mode).

Figure 5-2
Watching the
document profile

Proofing Simulations

One of the hardest—and most important—tasks in Photoshop has long been proofing what your final output will look like on your screen or on a color printer. Photoshop gives you very fine control over both, which we'll talk about in great depth later in this chapter and in Chapter 17, *Output Methods*. Here's the quick version, though:

▶ The Proof Setup command (in the View menu) gives you full control over on-screen proofing simulations. Proof Setup's simulations are window-specific, so you can simultaneously view the same file in different simulations.

▶ You can view how different rendering intents will convert an image to a destination space before actually making the conversion.

▶ You can see how an image prepared for one output process will behave when sent to another without adjustment: This is particularly useful when you're faced with the prospect of repurposing CMYK files made for one printing condition to work with another.

▶ You can work inside an accurate output simulation to optimize your image for a particular output process.

Finally, you can see what will happen to your images on any kind of output device, before you output them. But if you want to work visually, relying on what you see on screen, then before you start configuring Color Settings, you need to calibrate and profile your monitor, and you need to take steps to control your viewing environment (see the sidebar "Creating a Consistent Environment").

Photoshop and the Monitor

To display color accurately, Photoshop needs to know how your monitor behaves—what color white it produces, what sort of tonal response it has, and what actual colors it produces when it's fed pure R, G, or B. Photoshop gets all its information about the monitor from an ICC profile. If you want the color on your monitor to be accurate, that means you *must* have a customized ICC profile that accurately describes the behavior of your monitor. (Making a profile for your monitor is called *characterizing* it.) And since monitors drift over time, you also have to calibrate them to make sure that the profile still describes them accurately. In theory, calibration and characterization are two distinct processes—calibration actually changes a device's behavior, while characterization simply measures and describes—but in practice, monitor calibration and profiling packages combine the two processes.

In ancient versions of Photoshop, you always had the option to make Photoshop send the values in RGB files directly to the monitor. The actual color that came out depended on the quirks of your particular monitor, which was almost certainly a bit different from anyone else's. You still have the option of doing this (though we wouldn't recommend it) by loading your monitor profile as your RGB working space, but even to do that, you need a monitor profile; and if you want the color to display correctly, it needs to be an accurate one.

When you work in any space except monitor RGB, Photoshop uses the monitor's profile to transform the data on the fly as it gets sent to the video card so that the monitor displays the color correctly. The great benefit of this approach is that it makes it possible for people using very different monitors on different platforms to view the same image virtually identically.

Tip: If You Just Want to Go by the Numbers... It's possible to do good work with Photoshop using an uncalibrated, uncharacterized monitor—you just can't trust what you see on the screen. If you want to simply go by the numbers—reading the RGB levels and the CMYK dot percentages—you can use the Info palette to check your color and simply ignore what you see on the monitor. Even with a calibrated monitor, it's usually a good idea to check those numbers anyway.

If you aren't concerned with the monitor appearance, open Color Settings, pull down the RGB menu in the Working Spaces section, and choose Monitor RGB. We don't advocate this—we much prefer being able to work visually—but it is possible, particularly if you're working in a closed-loop environment where you always go to the same output conditions. Of course, if you do this, you may as well ignore the rest of this chapter....

Bruce has several very different monitors, some CRTs calibrated to varying white points and gammas, and other LCDs that aren't calibrated at all, but were simply measured in their native state. Within the limits of their varying color gamuts and dynamic ranges, all the monitors display the same image identically in Photoshop, because Photoshop corrects the data that gets sent to the display on each machine. If you've ever tried to make two monitors from different vendors show the same result, you'll realize right away that this is a Big Deal!

To make this magic happen for you, you need an accurate profile for each monitor, and you need to let Photoshop know which profile it should use for the monitor. Some folks think they can get away with using a preset "canned" profile supplied by their manufacturer. Not so! Just as two televisions from the same manufacturer at a television store display a slightly different image, two monitors show different color, too (especially after someone has gotten their paws on the Brightness and Contrast knobs). You may be able to get away with using vendor-supplied profiles for all your other devices, but you *must* make a custom display profile in order for Photoshop's color management (or any other color management, for that matter) to work. It's as simple as that.

Creating a profile is basically the same for Macintosh and Windows, (though there are minor differences, which we'll explain). There are three basic scenarios: using a measuring instrument with a smart monitor, using a measuring instrument with a dumb monitor, and measuring by eyeball using Adobe Gamma (Windows) or the OS X Calibrate feature (Mac). Note that both Adobe Gamma and the OS X Calibrate feature were designed with CRT monitors in mind. You can use them on LCD displays, but the results are pretty variable. If you're at all serious about working visually in Photoshop, trusting what you see on the screen, we strongly recommend using a display calibration package with a measuring instrument.

Creating a Consistent Environment

Three factors combine to produce the sensation we describe as color: the object, the light source that illuminates that object, and the observer. You are the observer, and your color vision is subject to subtle changes brought on by things as disparate as age, diet, mood, and how much sleep you've had. There isn't a lot you can do about those, and their effects are relatively minor, but it's good to bear them in mind because they make the phenomenon of color very subjective. The other factors that affect your color vision are, fortunately, easier to control.

Lighting. Consistent lighting is vital if you want to create a calibrated system. In the United States, color transparencies and print proofs are almost always evaluated using light with a controlled color temperature of 5000 Kelvins (K). In Europe and Asia, 6500 K is the standard—it's a little more blue. (Strictly speaking, the relevant standards—D50 and D65—are daylight curves that aren't absolutely identical to the black-body radiation described by the Kelvin scale, but for all practical purposes they're interchangeable.)

You need to provide a consistent lighting environment for viewing your printed output; otherwise the thing you're trying to match—the original image or the final output—will be constantly changing. You can go whole hog and install D50 lighting everywhere, bricking up any offending windows in the process, but for most of us that's impractical. But you can situate your monitor so that it's shielded from direct window light, turn off room lights for color-critical evaluations, and use a relatively inexpensive 4700 K Solux desk lamp for evaluating photographs and printed material. Be careful, though—many D50 lamps require a special fixture to avoid overheating, because the unwanted wavelengths are reflected through the back of the lamp into the fixture.

Theoretically, the ideal working situation is a low ambient light (almost dark) environment. This maximizes the apparent dynamic range of the monitor and ensures that no stray light is distorting your color perception. However, some shops that have tried this have noted a significant drop in the productivity of the employees forced to work in dark windowless rooms, so go as far toward approaching that ideal as you feel is reasonable.

Consistency is much more important than the absolute color temperature of the light source— the variations we've measured in the color temperature of viewing booths at various commercial printers are strong evidence of that. If you work in a studio with a skylight and floor-to-ceiling windows, the color of the light will change over the course of the day, and hence so will your perception of color. In a situation like that, you really need to create an area where you can view prints and transparencies under a light source that's shielded from the ambient light.

A hood to shield the monitor from stray reflections is also very worthwhile—a cardboard box spray-painted matte black may not be elegant, but it's every bit as effective as more expensive solutions, and doesn't distort the color the way most antiglare shields do.

Context. Your color perception is dramatically affected by surrounding colors. Again, you can go to extremes and paint all your walls neutral gray. (Bruce wound up doing this because his office was painted pale pink when he first moved in, and he found that it was introducing a color cast into almost everything— including his dreams.)

It's easier and more important, however, to make your desktop pattern a neutral, 50-percent gray. Pink-marble, green-plaid, or family-snapshot desktop patterns may seem fun and harmless, but they'll seriously interfere with your color judgment. We also recommend not wearing Hawaiian shirts when you're making critical color judgments. Designer black, you'll be happy to know, is just great.

Using a Smart Monitor

A smart monitor is one that has a USB connection to the host computer, allowing the calibrator to set the white and black points by adjusting the gain and bias on the voltage amplifiers that drive the electron guns. Examples include the Sony Artisan and the LaCie Electron Blue series purchased with the BlueEye calibrator. While advances in third-party calibration packages have reduced the advantages of a smart monitor primarily to convenience, they also offer superior accuracy because the software can make finer adjustments to gain and bias than can be achieved using the controls offered by the monitor's on-screen display.

Smart monitors make it easy to calibrate to a known standard and then generate a profile that describes this standard. The question then becomes, to what standard should you calibrate?

We used to advocate calibrating CRT monitors to D50 white, with a gamma of 1.8. Several factors have brought us to change that recommendation. If you've been using a D50/gamma 1.8 monitor calibration and you're happy with the brightness of the monitor at D50 (that is, it looks white, not dingy yellow), then by all means continue to do so. Otherwise, we offer the following suggestions:

How White Are Your Whites?

For several years, we advocated calibrating monitors to a white point of D50 and a gamma of 1.8 to match the proofing illuminant and dot gain of the commercial printing industry. Hard lessons taught by bitter experience made us back away from that recommendation.

It's very difficult for a monitor to achieve satisfactory brightness when calibrated to a D50 white point, because the blue phosphors are the most efficient of the three, and calibrating to D50 invariably involves turning down the blue channel. Often, the result is a monitor that looks dingy and yellow. Our eyes respond to brightness in a quite non-linear way, and when the brightness of the monitor is too low (below about 70 candelas/m^2) we see yellow instead of white.

A second problem seems to arise when you attempt to compare an image on the monitor side-by-side with hard copy in a D50 light box. We've been able to achieve close matches, but we've also noted that the highlights on the monitor tend to appear redder than those of the hard copy, even when both monitor and light box are calibrated to D50 and balanced to the same level of illumination.

We haven't yet heard a technical explanation of this phenomenon that completely satisfies us (and we're not sure we'd understand one anyway), but we've experienced it ourselves, and we've heard enough reports from others that we believe it's a real issue. Part of the explanation may be that, while a theoretically ideal D50 illuminant produces a

- ▶ Calibrate to a white point of D65 (6500 Kelvins) rather than D50. Monitors find it much easier to achieve satisfactory brightness levels at D65 than at D50. Yes, we know that most of the graphic arts industry worldwide uses D50 as the proofing illuminant, but when it comes to monitors, D65 makes more sense (see the sidebar "How White Are Your Whites?").

- ▶ If you're using an LCD display, simply leave the white point at its native setting. The color termperature is determined by the backlight, and while some LCDs let you adjust the white point, they do so by filtering the backlight, so you lose some luminance and possibly some levels.

- ▶ If you're running Windows, shoot for a target gamma of 2.2 rather than 1.8. PC-based systems generally aim for a gamma of 2.2, and you'll lose fewer levels in the video card's lookup table the closer to the native monitor gamma you aim. In theory, Mac displays' native gamma is 1.8, but in practice, gamma 2.2 works just fine. Under Mac OS X, the entire user interface is color-managed, so it doesn't matter which gamma you use as long as the profile is accurate.

continuous spectrum, both the lamps in light boxes and the phosphors in monitors produce spiky, discontinuous output that's concentrated in fairly narrow bands. There are many different combinations of wavelengths that add up to a D50 white point.

Bruce believes that there's also a perceptual effect in play. One of the well-documented tricks our eyes play on us is something called "discounting the illuminant"—if we look at a red apple under red light, we still see it as red rather than white, because

we know it's red, and we discount the red light. But when we look at a monitor, we can't discount the illuminant because the image *is* the illuminant!

One solution is to separate the monitor and the light box—Bruce has taken to working with the monitor in front of him and the light box behind him, switching from one to the other—which seems to resolve the problem in large part. Interestingly enough, though, others have reported that calibrating the monitor to D65 rather than D50

creates a much better match with a D50 light box.

Obviously this subject needs a great deal more research, but we've come to the conclusion that it makes more sense to calibrate the monitor to D65 than to D50. If you're happy with a D50 monitor white, don't fix what isn't broken; but if you're running into any of the aforementioned issues, if your monitor highlights look red, or if your monitor seems overly dim, we strongly recommend that you try D65 instead.

Using a Dumb Monitor

We don't mean anything pejorative by the term "dumb monitor"—just that it doesn't talk back to the host computer through a special cable. Most monitors are dumb devices. In this scenario, most or all of the calibration is done by changing the lookup table in the video card. This almost invariably means that the monitor ends up displaying fewer than 256 levels per color channel. How many fewer levels depends on how far you're trying to take the monitor from its native state—the further you go, the more levels you lose.

Some third-party calibration packages, such as ColorVision's OptiCal and GretagMacbeth's EyeOne (both of which we like a lot), allow you to set the white point by manually adjusting the RGB guns on monitors that offer individual gun control. If your monitor and calibration package offer this feature, use it—you'll lose fewer levels than you would if the calibrator had to tweak the lookup tables in the video card to achieve the requested white point.

If your calibrator and monitor lack these features, there's a trade-off. You can simply measure the monitor's native behavior and create a profile from the measurements. That way, you'll get your monitor to perform optimally, delivering the full range of brightness and color of which it's capable. The downside to this approach is that monitors drift—some drift a lot more than others—so you need to check the measurements and update the profile on a regular basis (every few weeks, probably). If you do this, note that you can simply overwrite your old monitor profile each time you update it—there's basically no reason to save old monitor profiles.

If your monitor allows calibration, we suggest setting it to something close to its native white point and gamma to minimize losses in the video lookup table. A good place to start would be D65 gamma 2.2.

Visual Calibration

We strongly recommend hardware-based monitor calibration and characterization: Our eyes are good at comparing small differences between two color samples viewed simultaneously, but lousy at determining absolute color values. That said, if you don't have a measuring instrument (one of those suction-cup devices) for the monitor, you can still perform a reasonably good characterization on CRT monitors using Adobe Gamma on Windows or the Display Calibrator on the Mac. (Adobe Gamma has been discontinued for the Mac because it's pretty much the same as the

LCD Monitors

LCD (Liquid Crystal Display) monitors are in many ways more appealing than traditional CRTs. They produce a very sharp, flicker-free image, they consume a fraction of the power of CRT (cathode-ray tube) monitors, they're much brighter than CRTs, and you can lift a 22-inch LCD with one hand, which we don't recommend trying with an equivalent-size CRT! In fact, Apple Computer has stopped selling CRT monitors entirely.

But LCDs aren't without their downsides. Viewing angle can be a major issue: The color shifts noticably as you move your head from side to side. Expensive LCDs such as the Apple Cinema Display suffer less from viewing angle problems than do less-expensive LCDs, but for some people at least, it's still an issue, particularly for grayscale work.

Lack of uniformity in the brightness across the face of the monitor is a bigger problem. In an LCD monitor, all the light comes from the backlight—typically a fluorescent tube with a diffuser. It's difficult to make this light even, more so with larger LCDs than with smaller ones, so you'll often find significant differences in brightness at different spots on the display.

LCDs are also a lot more expensive to buy than CRTs—for the price of an Apple Cinema Display, you can buy five 19-inch CRTs. The upfront expense is offset by the lower power consumption of LCDs, making them less expensive to own.

Calibrating and profiling an LCD is less straightforward than calibrating a CRT, simply because many more tools are available for the latter than for the former. Solutions based on eyeballs like Adobe Gamma and the Display Calibrator don't work well with LCDs—they're really designed for CRT controls and CRT behavior. LCDs don't have brightness and contrast controls, for example—just a brightness control that adjusts the intensity of the backlight. If you use an LCD monitor for Photoshop work, you really have only two choices.

▶ Use the factory-supplied ICC profile. LCDs don't vary nearly as much in manufacturing as CRTs, and they don't have the brightness and contrast controls that constitute such a huge variable in CRTs, so the factory profiles are generally more accurate for LCDs than they are for CRT monitors.

▶ Use a hardware-based profiling tool designed for LCDs. GretagMacbeth's EyeOne and Spectrolino instruments measure LCDs and are supported by both third-party software and GretagMacbeth's own. Colorvisions' Monitor Spyder colorimeter and OptiCal software, and Monaco Systems' Optix package likewise do an excellent job of profiling LCDs.

If you've paid a premium for a high-end LCD, don't be pennywise and pound-foolish. Spring for a hardware profiling solution. But *don't* use a colorimeter with a sucker cup for attaching to a CRT—it will rip the coating right off the front of your LCD!

If we seem ambivalent about LCD monitors, we are. But while Bruce talks about some of his peers as having "drunk the LCD Kool-Aid," he's quick to acknowledge that people whose judgment he respects are using them happily to produce great work. LCDs are the wave of the future—they're improving at a much faster rate than CRTs—and the question isn't whether to buy into LCDs, but when.

For critical work, we still prefer CRTs, but that's just our opinion. Like any proofing system, you have to learn to interpret an LCD display. Before buying an LCD monitor, look at a variety of grayscale and color images, and see if the quirks are something you can live with. If they are, more power to you. If not, buy a CRT that displays the same number of pixels for much less money. By the time it wears out, our current quibbles about LCDs will have long been put to rest.

ColorSync Display Calibrator, and having both just confused people.) If you're using an LCD monitor, the factory profile is likely to be more reliable than anything you can create by eyeball.

We do have some observations that supplement the on-screen instructions. Eyeball-based calibration and characterization are *extremely* dependent on the ambient viewing conditions. A stable viewing environment is absolutely vital for the process to work. (See the sidebar "Creating a Consistent Environment," earlier in this chapter.)

Launching the calibrator. Adobe Gamma and Display Calibrator are extremely similar, so we'll treat them as being the same and point out the few differences as we run into them. You launch the Display Calibrator by choosing the Displays System Preference (Mac OS X), clicking the Color tab, and then clicking Calibrate. But before you click Calibrate, check which profile is currently assigned to your monitor in the Color list.

The results of the calibration will vary depending on how far away this profile is from your monitor's real behavior. If you don't have a profile that's even close to your monitor, you'll have opportunities to address this later in the process, but if you do have a profile that describes at least your model of monitor, choose it now. Adobe Gamma is a standalone control panel. Unlike the Display Calibrator, it offers the opportunity to load a different profile as your starting point—again, try to use one that bears some resemblance to your monitor (see Figure 5-3).

Figure 5-3
Adobe Gamma and
ColorSync Display
Calibrator

Before launching the Display Calibrator, check the current monitor profile. Adobe Gamma lets you do this later...

Both calibrators have similar introductory screens. With Adobe Gamma, we recommend using the Step By Step version rather than the all-in-one control panel, at least when you're starting out. With the Display Calibrator, make sure you check the Expert Mode checkbox (see Figure 5-4).

Figure 5-4
Introductory screens

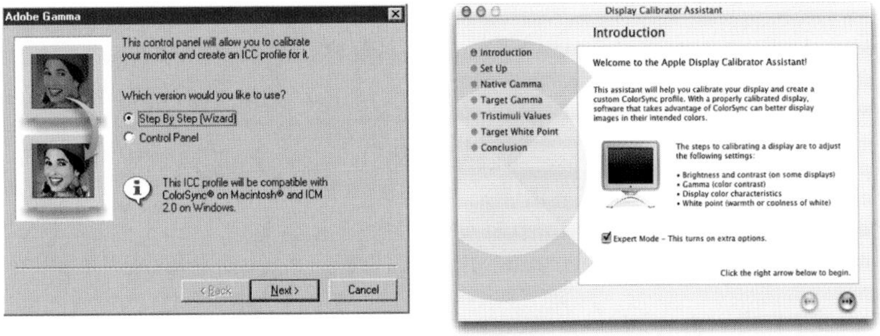

Choose Step By Step.　　　　　　　*Check Expert Mode.*

In Adobe Gamma, make sure you enter a description into the Description field (we usually insert the date, too, so we know when we created the profile) before you move to the next window. The description you enter here is the profile's menu name, which is not necessarily the same as the filename—it's the name under which the profile will appear in menus (see Figure 5-5).

Figure 5-5
Entering a menu name

The description you enter in this field is the name by which the profile will appear in menus. It can be different from the filename.

Setting brightness and contrast. The next screen deals with setting the brightness and contrast. Note that this is really designed for use in a low ambient light setting: If you're working in bright surroundings, some of the recommendations given by the assistant may be problematic.

Both calibrators suggest starting out by setting your monitor's contrast control to its maximum setting. For most users this will work well, particularly if the monitor is more than a year or two old.

Next, you're instructed to set the brightness control (which is actually the "black level") so that the center target is as dark as possible while still being distinguishable from the black background. Note that in Adobe Gamma there are three concentric boxes. The center box should wind up being a dark gray, the outer box should be white, and the one in between should be a true black (or as close to a true black as your monitor can display; see Figure 5-6).

Figure 5-6
Setting brightness and contrast

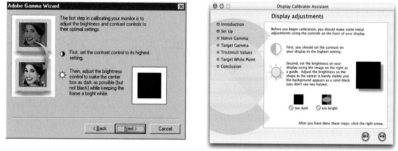

Adjust the brightness and contrast until the center target is very slightly lighter then the black surround.

Choosing phosphors (Adobe Gamma only). The next screen gives you the opportunity to choose a phosphor set to override those indicated by the starting profile (see Figure 5-7). If you know that your starting profile was incorrect, this is your chance to fix it. While it's fun to bandy about terms like "phosphor sets," the concept is very simple: the profile needs to know what are the reddest red, the greenest green, and the bluest blue your monitor can produce. That is, what the little phosphors in the monitor look like when you hit 'em with an electron beam—like measuring the color of an ink.

If you know that your monitor uses one of the phosphor sets listed in the menu, you can choose it there. Or you can obtain the phosphor chromaticities from your monitor's documentation or, failing that, from the vendor. If the monitor is more than a few months old, the phosphors will have changed some from the factory spec, but the right phosphor set is still a better starting point than the wrong one.

Figure 5-7
Choosing phosphors

If you know your starting profile has the wrong primary values, you can choose the right ones from the popup menu, or choose Custom to enter custom values.

Setting the gamma. The next screen (two screens in the Display Calibrator) lets you set the monitor gamma (see Figure 5-8). Without getting into a long discussion about what gamma is, here's our advice: Unless you have compelling reasons to do otherwise, we suggest using a gamma of 2.2 on both platforms. We've found that the notion that Mac displays have a gamma of 1.8 is something of a myth—Bruce has measured the native gammas of many Mac monitors as something very close to 2.2. If you use an LCD display, you may find that you get smoother gradients checking the Uncorrected Gamma (native) checkbox instead.

We strongly recommend turning off the View Single Gamma Only checkbox, which lets you adjust the red, green, and blue gamma values independently. When you're adjusting these, it helps to move as far back from the monitor as you can while still being able to adjust the sliders,

Figure 5-8
Setting the gamma

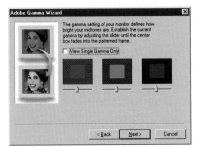
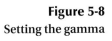

Follow the onscreen instructions to select and adjust the gamma.

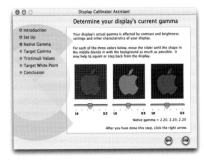

and defocus your eyes so that the red, green, and blue squares become slightly blurry. This makes it much easier to find the sweet spot where the solid center boxes merge with the striped backgrounds.

If you're like us, you'll probably find that it's much harder to make the blue square merge into the background than it is the red and green. Try this: Use a neutral gray desktop pattern, first adjust the red and green sliders, and then watch the color balance change as you manipulate the blue slider. When the desktop looks neutral gray, you've probably come as close as you can to making the central blue square match its background.

Setting the white point. If your monitor has hardware white-point settings (usually chosen from an onscreen menu called up by a button on the front panel), we suggest you choose D65—the D50 setting will probably look dim and yellow, while settings higher than D65 will likely be very blue. Adobe Gamma offers a Measure button that lets you estimate the white point visually. Once you've gone through the Measure routine, you can proceed to the next screen (see Figure 5-9).

Here, you're offered the option of allowing Adobe Gamma to adjust your monitor's white point. If you need to work with a specific white point to deal with non-color-managed applications, you may wish to choose it from the popup menu. Otherwise, we suggest choosing Same as Hardware, which again minimizes any losses in the video lookup table. Display Calibrator lets you correct the white point or use the native one.

Saving the profile. In the next screen, you can compare the before-and-after results of the calibration. If you've picked the correct phosphors, and you use the Same as Hardware setting for the white point, probably the only difference you'll see is a slight midtone shift from the gamma correction. (If you see a big shift, you're probably changing the monitor's behavior more than necessary—you can try living with the resulting calibration for a while, or you can start over, double-checking each step.) If at this stage you find that the "after" setting makes the monitor too dim, your best bet is to turn up your monitor's contrast setting and start at the beginning again. If the contrast was already set at its maximum, it may be time to replace the monitor (see the sidebar "Evaluating Your Monitor").

On the Macintosh, the final screen contains a text field that allows you to type in an appropriate file name (we usually include the date in the file name so we know when we made it), and click Create. With Adobe Gamma,

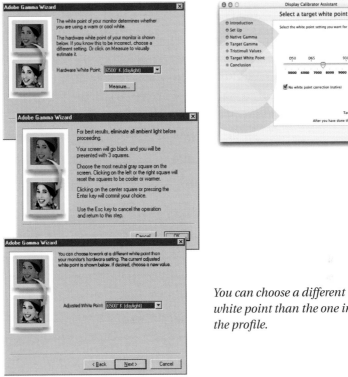

Figure 5-9
Setting the white point

You can choose a different white point than the one in the profile.

you'll be prompted to save the profile. On Windows 2000 and Windows XP, save the profile in the WinNT/System/Spool/Drivers/Color directory. On Mac OS X, see the sidebar "Mac OS X and Profiles."

Evaluating Your Monitor

Monitors lose brightness over time, and eventually they simply wear out. Long before the menu bar is burned into the screen, the monitor has lost so much of its brightness range that it probably can't be accurately calibrated to ideal settings.

Calibration utilities work by selectively *reducing* the brightness of the red, green, and blue channels (making them dimmer). So when you calibrate your monitor, the first thing you'll notice is that it's not as bright as it was in its original uncalibrated state. If it wasn't very bright to begin with, it's a problem.

Here's our simple rule of thumb: turn the contrast control all the way up. If the monitor is brighter at that setting than you like, it's a worthwhile candidate for hardware calibration. If it isn't as bright as you'd like, it's a candidate for replacement—it's only going to get dimmer over time, and you'll find it very difficult to bring it to a specific white point. You can still get some life out of the monitor by running it in its raw state and simply profiling that state, but it won't last forever.

Bad Monitor Profiles

There's one further gotcha. A fairly large number of users wind up creating profiles with Adobe Gamma or Display Calibrator that turn all colors in Photoshop into a psychedelic mess. If accepting the situation and calling it art works for you, fine. Otherwise, start over. The problem is almost invariably caused by starting out with a bad profile. Pick a known good profile like sRGB or Apple RGB as the starting point, and repeat the whole exercise. This time it should work.

Color Settings

Once you've created a custom monitor profile, it's time to get to the meat of Photoshop's built-in color controls. The Color Settings dialog box (from the Edit menu, or press Command-Shift-K) is color central, letting you set up working spaces and color management policies for RGB, CMYK, and grayscale images. It also lets you tell Photoshop what you want to do about missing or mismatched profiles. You can choose each of these settings individually or just use one of the presets, which then makes all the

Mac OS X and Profiles

Mac OS X offers a bewildering variety of places to store profiles. You'll find them in the System/Library/ColorSync/Profiles folder, in the Library/ColorSync/Profiles folder, in the Library/ColorSync/Profiles/Displays folder, in the Library/Application Support/Adobe/Color/Profiles folder, in the Library/Application Support/Adobe/Color/Profiles/Recommended folder, in the Users/UserName/Library/ColorSync/Profiles folder, and in some cases, buried several levels deep in subfolders in the Library/Printers folder.

As David would say with characteristic understatement, "Oy!"

Here's the deal. There are really only three places where users may want to store profiles.

If you want to make a profile available to everyone who uses the Mac, save it in the Library/ColorSync/Profiles folder. Don't try to put it in the System/Library/ColorSync/Profiles folder—a good rule of thumb is that the only thing that should mess with the OS X System folder is the OS X installer, or a hard-core UNIX geek who is comfortable driving the Mac from the Terminal window.

If you want to make a profile available only to you (or to someone else logged in as you), save it in the Users/YourUser Name/Library/ColorSync/Profiles folder. (If you're the only user, you may as well save all your profiles there.)

If you want to make a profile available from Photoshop's Color Settings dialog box when the "Advanced" checkbox is unchecked, save it in the Library/Application Support/Adobe/Color/Profiles folder.

choices for you (customizing the settings is more powerful, of course). If you turn on the Advanced Mode checkbox, Photoshop also lets you change the color engine (CMM) and the default rendering intent for conversions, as well as a few more esoteric controls we'll discuss later in this section.

Color Settings Presets

The Settings menu at the top of the Color Settings dialog box lets you load presets to configure Color Settings with a single menu command that sets working spaces, policies, and warnings for you (see Figure 5-11). Presets are a reasonable place to start, but if you've gotten this far into this chapter, you're obviously the kind of person who believes presets are made to be overwritten.

The real power of the Settings popup menu isn't what ships with Photoshop, but rather the fact that you can save your own settings to disk and then recall them quickly later. Even better, while you can always load a Color Settings preset from anywhere on your hard drive (using the Load button), if you save your settings in the right place, they become available from the Presets popup menu. (On Mac OS X, the "right place" is inside the Library/Application Support/Adobe/Color/Settings folder; on Windows,

Figure 5-11
Color Settings presets

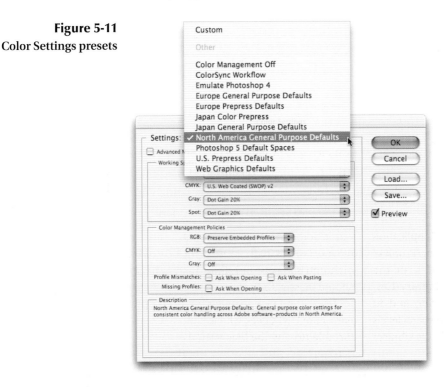

it's inside Program Files/Common Files/Adobe/Color/Settings.) Saving presets that appear on the Settings menu offers an easy way to configure Photoshop for an entire workgroup.

The presets that Adobe offers fall into two broad categories: those that ignore color management, and those that use it. As you can probably guess, we fall squarely into the "use it" camp.

General Purpose Defaults. New to Photoshop CS, the three General Purpose Defaults (North American, Europe, and Japan) are Adobe's latest sop to those users who just want color management to go away. They set the RGB working space to sRGB and the RGB policy to Preserve Embedded Profiles; they set the CMYK working space to U.S. Web Coated (SWOP) v.2 (North American), Euroscale Coated v2 (Europe), or Japan Color 2001 Coated (Japan) respectively; and they set the CMYK policy to Off. They disable missing profile and profile mismatch warnings, and just to confuse matters, they set the default rendering intent to Perceptual. These presets provide relatively safe settings for an all-RGB color-managed workflow or an all-CMYK by-the-numbers workflow, but their basic goal seems to be to prevent users from understanding color management.

Color Management Off. As its name suggests, Color Management Off tells Photoshop not to use color management, setting all the policies to Off (again, we discuss the individual policies later in this chapter). It treats all your documents as though they are in the working space for that color mode, ignoring any embedded profiles.

Web Graphics Defaults. The only difference between Web Graphics Defaults and Color Management Off is that the latter sets your monitor profile as the RGB working space, while Web Graphics Default sets the working space to sRGB. It still doesn't really manage color.

Emulate Photoshop 4. Choosing Emulate Photoshop 4 is like reminiscing about the good old days, back when life was simpler. Somehow we always forget all the terrible aspects of the "good old days." This option ignores color management for the most part, setting different working spaces for RGB, CMYK, and grayscale (it uses Apple RGB as the working space on the Mac, and sRGB as the RGB working space on Windows). If you're in a strictly-by-the-numbers all-CMYK print, or an all-RGB Web workflow, and you're firmly convinced that color management has nothing to offer you, one of these non-CMS choices may make sense. Otherwise we suggest you avoid them.

Prepress settings. The three prepress settings—Europe, Japan, and U.S. Prepress Default—tell Photoshop to use color management wherever possible, and to give you as much feedback as possible about missing and mismatched profiles. They differ only in their choice of CMYK profiles and the assumed dot gain for grayscale and spot colors (20 percent in the U.S., and 15 percent in Europe and Japan). If your work is destined for a printing press and you don't have a custom profile for your printing or proofing conditions, one of these choices may be a good starting point.

Photoshop 5 Default Spaces. Photoshop 5 Default Spaces is a setting you should consider only in the unlikely event that you've been working with Photoshop 5 or 5.5, you've never changed the default color settings, and you're happy with the results you've been getting. It sets the policies and warnings to the same settings as the prepress defaults, but uses sRGB (unfortunately) as the RGB working space and Photoshop 5's default CMYK as the CMYK working space. We're not sure why someone would pick this, but we guess it's nice that Adobe gave us the option.

ColorSync Workflow. Macintosh users have one more option: ColorSync Workflow. This sets the ColorSync Default Profiles as the RGB, CMYK, and Gray working spaces. Photoshop dynamically updates the settings—when you change the profiles in ColorSync System Preferences, Photoshop picks up those changes and resets the working spaces accordingly. (If the Color Settings dialog box is open when you change the ColorSync System Preferences settings, close and reopen Color Settings to see them take effect.)

Unfortunately, choosing the ColorSync Workflow option also makes Photoshop use the CMM specified in the ColorSync System Preferences. We're less happy about this because we've found that the Adobe (ACE) engine has fewer bugs than any of the other CMMs out there. Its only disadvantage is that you can use it only inside Adobe products—you can't load it under ColorSync. ColorSync Workflow was a nice idea, offering a single place to configure the profiles for all color-managed applications. But since OS X 10.3 will reportedly remove the default ColorSync profiles feature, it's also doomed.

Why Use RGB Working Spaces?

So what are these strange things, the RGB working spaces, that you choose from the Color Settings RGB menu? They're arbitrary, device-independent RGB spaces. Some real techno-geeks will quibble with applying the term "device-independent" to an RGB space, preferring to reserve the term for purely synthetic perceptually-based color spaces like CIE Lab. To those folks, we suggest that while a useful distinction can be made between perceptually-based spaces and RGB spaces, that distinction does not revolve around device-independence. Photoshop's RGB working spaces don't depend on the vagaries of any given piece of hardware, so we feel it's truthful to call them "device-independent RGB."

Why is device-independent RGB better than monitor RGB? In non-color-managed applications, the RGB working space is always monitor RGB, because those applications just send the numbers in the RGB file to your monitor. The *only* situation where it makes sense to use your monitor profile as the RGB working space is when you're doing Web design or multimedia, and you need to make Photoshop's display match the RGB that non-color-managed Web applications use. For any other purpose, it's a bad idea, for several reasons.

▶ Your monitor is unique, a little or a lot different from everyone else's, so unless you use a device-independent RGB working space your images will look different on everyone else's machine.

▶ Monitor gamuts, while considerably larger than those of most CMYK print processes, are much smaller than those of film or high-end digital cameras. Limiting RGB to the gamut of the monitor means that you compress the gamut of the original file, which is undesirable if you plan to output your image later on an RGB film recorders, or another such device with a wider gamut than the monitor.

▶ A common misconception is that monitors can display all printable CMYK colors. Monitor gamuts actually clip a considerable part of the CMYK gamut, particularly in the pure cyans (and those greens and blues adjacent to them), and in the pure oranges and yellows. Limiting RGB to the monitor's gamut prevents you from producing all the colors the CMYK output process can reproduce.

▶ Monitor color spaces aren't perceptually uniform. When you edit in a monitor space, the same editing increment in Levels, Curves, and Hue/Saturation may have a much larger effect on some parts of the tonal range and color gamut than on others.

Abstract RGB working spaces can address all of these problems. You can choose an RGB working space that has a large enough gamut to encompass all your output devices and that is perceptually uniform for maximum editing flexibility.

Why is device-independent RGB better than scanner or camera RGB? While we generally advocate putting images through as few color space conversions as possible, most capture (scanner or digital camera) spaces just don't make good editing spaces. A very few capture spaces, such as those from a gray-balanced scanning-back digital camera, may work as editing spaces, but the vast majority of capture spaces are neither gray-balanced nor perceptually uniform, which makes them hard to edit. So if your images need any significant amount of editing, you'll almost certainly want to convert them to a perceptually uniform, gray-balanced RGB working space.

Why not just use Lab? After all, Lab is by design a device-independent, perceptually uniform color space. But Lab has at least two properties that make it less than ideal as a standard editing space.

First, Lab is pretty non-intuitive when it comes to making color corrections—small adjustments to a* and b* values often produce large changes in unexpected directions. A bigger problem, however, is that Lab, by definition, contains all the colors you can see. (It actually also contains many "colors" you can't see.) When we use eight bits per channel to represent this whole range of color, the distance from one value to the next becomes large—uncomfortably large, in fact. And since any real image from a scanner or digital camera contains a much smaller range of color than Lab represents, you wind up wasting bits on colors you can't capture, display, print, or even see. If you work with 16-bit-per-channel images, the gamut problem is much less of an issue, but editing in Lab is still not particularly friendly.

Working Spaces

The working spaces for RGB, CMYK, Gray, and Spot Color define the default assumptions Photoshop makes about images in those color modes. Photoshop needs to know what colors the numbers in your files represent, both to display them correctly on your monitor, and to convert them to other color modes.

Depending on how you set your policies (see "Color Management Policies," later in this chapter), the working space may apply to all documents, to only some documents, or, conceivably, to no documents—in which case you might as well choose a more relevant working space!

Unless you're lucky enough to always print to the same CMYK output process, you'll probably need to change your CMYK working space to suit the output requirements of the job at hand. Ditto for Gray if you produce grayscale images for printed output. (In other words, because printing on a web offset press in America is drastically different than printing to a sheetfed press in Japan, you'll need to change the settings.) But the RGB working space is a rather different animal. CMYK spaces are based on the behavior of real physical devices, but the RGB working spaces typically are not.

Old versions of Photoshop more or less forced you to choose a single RGB working space and stick to it. In Photoshop CS, you have the freedom to use a different space for every image, but that doesn't mean you should exercise that freedom willy-nilly. If an image has an embedded profile, we recommend that you open the image in that profile's space, at least for an initial evaluation. But in many, perhaps even most cases, you'll want to convert the image to an RGB working space for editing (see "Why Use RGB Working Spaces?" earlier in this chapter).

Choosing an RGB Working Space

In choosing between the various RGB working spaces that Photoshop CS offers, the most important consideration is almost certainly the color gamut. All the spaces offered are gray-balanced (that is, when R=G=B, you've got a neutral gray), but they differ dramatically in the size of the gamut they offer. You may think you should just choose the largest gamut available so that you'll be sure of encompassing the gamuts of all your output processes, but you'd be wrong. There's a trade-off involved—at least if you're using 8-bit-per-channel images.

As we explained in Chapter 3, *Image Essentials*, RGB images are made up of three grayscale channels, in which each pixel has a value from 0 to 255. This holds true for every 24-bit RGB image, irrespective of the working space it lives in. If you choose a very large-gamut space, the 256 possible data values in each channel are stretched to cover the entire gamut—the larger the gamut, the further apart each value is from its neighbors.

The practical implication is that you have less editing headroom in a large-gamut space than you do in a small one: When you edit images, you invariably open up gaps in the tonal range as levels that were formerly adjacent get stretched apart. In a small-gamut space, the jump from level 126 to level 129 may be visually insignificant, whereas in a larger space, you'll get obvious banding rather than a smooth transition.

So, when you work in 24-bit RGB, you have to balance gamut size and editing headroom. If you work with images that typically need major corrections, you probably want to choose a working space that's just big enough to encompass your output requirements. If your images come out more or less perfect from your capture device and need only light editing, you can afford to use a larger-gamut RGB working space. And if you work with 16-bit channels (high-bit images), the issue goes away.

The simplest option may be to settle on a single RGB editing space for all your work, but you may wish to use a larger space for 48-bit images than you do for 24-bit ones. In a service bureau environment, you'll have to support all sorts of RGB spaces, which is easy in Photoshop CS. But no working space is ideal for all purposes, so the default working space should simply be the one you use most.

In the Color Settings dialog box (without the Advanced Mode turned on), you can choose one of the four recommended RGB working spaces, plus Monitor RGB. (Mac users get a sixth option, ColorSync RGB, which simply grabs the profile you've set as the RGB Default profile in the Default Profiles panel of the ColorSync System Preferences.)

Adobe RGB (1998). This is the largest of the built-in RGB spaces, with a gamut that comes very close to encompassing all likely CMYK gamuts. It also encompasses the gamut of most RGB output devices—it may clip some very saturated orange-yellows, but to avoid that you'd need to use a very large RGB space indeed. The gamma 2.2 is perceptually uniform, and Adobe RGB (1998) is also inherently gray-balanced, so equal values of R, G, and B always produce a neutral.

The only downside of Adobe RGB (1998) is that it has a huge excursion into the greens, and hence wastes some bits on colors that you're unlikely to be able to capture, let alone display or reproduce. But as long as you're working with reasonably high-quality capture devices (which means pretty much any scanner made after the year 1999, and any digital camera that costs more than $300), the gamut size is unlikely to be a problem.

If your work is aimed at hard-copy output, Adobe RGB (1998) is the best of the built-in RGB working spaces. (And David uses this even for preparing Web graphics.)

AppleRGB. This is a legacy—it's basically the Photoshop 2.0 default space. It's based on an Apple 13-inch RGB monitor (how many of those are in use for Photoshop work?), and while it has a slightly wider gamut than sRGB, its lower 1.8 gamma tends to posterize shadows more quickly than sRGB. The only reason to use this space would be to get Photoshop CS to emulate Photoshop 4 or earlier on default Mac settings. We strongly recommend against doing so.

ColorMatch RGB. Based on the long-dead Radius Pressview monitor space, ColorMatch RGB is the other reasonable choice—besides Adobe RGB (1998)—for print work. But it's basically a legacy space, and the only reason we can see for choosing it rather than Adobe RGB (1998) is if you have large numbers of images already in a D50 gamma 1.8 space. Color-Match RGB has a reasonably large gamut but is significantly smaller than Adobe RGB (1998), so it clips more of the cyans and oranges. It also has a gamma of 1.8, which is less perceptually uniform than the gamma 2.2 of Adobe RGB (1998).

It's certainly possible to produce exquisite work using ColorMatch RGB, but unless legacy files offer a compelling reason to choose it, we recommend Adobe RGB (1998) instead.

sRGB. The default RGB space in Photoshop 5 was sRGB, a color space developed by Hewlett-Packard and Microsoft that purports to represent the "average" monitor. However, we believe that most Photoshop users have monitors much better than the sRGB spec, which we think represents a really bad 15-inch VGA monitor (the kind you might pick up at a garage sale).

sRGB has a serious mismatch with the gamut of offset printing. It clips the cyans—and those blues and greens adjacent to cyan—quite drastically. With a typical sheetfed printing setup, you'll never get more than 75-percent cyan ink when you convert an RGB image in sRGB to CMYK.

sRGB is useful as an output RGB space for images destined for the Web (since Hewlett-Packard and Microsoft have used their considerable clout to push sRGB as the standard RGB space for the Web). But even if all your work is destined for the Web, we still recommend doing the majority of your edits in a larger space than sRGB, and converting to sRGB only when the image is complete. If your work is destined for print, then sRGB is a very poor choice indeed.

Note that the Web Graphics Default preset uses the sRGB working space. However, if you use this space and later import the images in a non-color-managed application such as Macromedia Dreamweaver, they'll look different from how Photoshop displays them (since the non-color-managed apps simply send the values in the file to your monitor). See "Monitor RGB," below, for our suggestions for this kind of work.

Monitor RGB. When you choose Monitor RGB, Photoshop uses your monitor profile as the RGB working space: It's listed in the RGB Working Space menu as "Monitor RGB–YourMonitorProfileName."

Tip: Check Your Monitor Profile. Photoshop CS always displays images through your monitor profile. The only way to find out *which* monitor profile it's using is to look at the Monitor RGB listing in the RGB menu in the Color Settings dialog box; the name of the profile is listed there.

If you choose Monitor RGB, Photoshop displays RGB images by sending the numerical values in the RGB file directly to the video card. It uses the definition of those RGB values supplied by the monitor profile to convert RGB to other color spaces. Older (pre-7) versions of Photoshop would "simplify" monitor profiles that used lookup tables, approximating them with a gamma value, but Photoshop CS uses whatever's in the monitor profile directly.

The only reason we can think of to choose Monitor RGB as your working space is if you're working exclusively on Web graphics, and you need the RGB color in Photoshop to match the RGB color in non-color-managed applications like Dreamweaver. Using your monitor profile as the working space will ensure that RGB in Photoshop looks exactly the same as RGB in all your non-color-managed applications—unfortunately, it will also ensure that RGB looks different on your machine than it does on everyone else's. (That's why Photoshop introduced the idea of an RGB working space in the first place.)

If you're a Windows user, you'll likely find that the differences between Monitor RGB and sRGB are quite small. Mac users, though, will typically see a bigger difference. Web designers who work on the Mac may want to do most of their work using Monitor RGB, and then convert the final result to sRGB. That way, Windows users will see something close to what was intended, while Mac users who use Safari, or Internet Explorer with ColorSync turned on, will also see something close to the intended color. Mac users who use Netscape will see dark images, but they should be used to that....

On the other hand, many images destined for the Web also end up in print as repurposing becomes increasingly important. So even when he's creating Web graphics, David uses the Adobe RGB (1998) working space and then uses Photoshop's soft-proofing controls to see what the image will look like on the Web (see "Soft-Proofing Controls," later in this chapter).

Other. Those of you with sharp eyes will notice a grayed-out menu item labelled Other. It's just a placeholder for custom settings, which you can create only when the Advanced Mode checkbox is turned on. Other is always either grayed out, or replaced with the name of the Advanced profile or setting (see "Color Settings Advanced Mode," later in this chapter). Aren't you glad you know that?

Other RGB Working Spaces

If you turn on the Advanced Mode checkbox in Color Settings, the RGB menu expands to include every RGB profile installed on your machine. In Advanced Mode, Photoshop allows you to use any RGB profile as an RGB working space, or even to create your own. Don't go hog-wild with this! Editing in your SuperHamsterScan 9000 Turbo Z profile's space is possible, but it probably won't be perceptually uniform, and, worse, it probably won't be gray-balanced. It's extremely hard to edit images well in a space that isn't gray-balanced, and almost impossible to do so in one that has color crossovers, which many capture profiles do.

However, you may want to consider some working spaces that aren't installed in Photoshop's Recommended folder. If you're really courageous, you may even want to define your own RGB working space, in which case you've definitely earned the title of Advanced User.

In addition to Adobe RGB, Bruce uses several different RGB working spaces for different purposes. It isn't absolutely necessary to load these as working spaces in Color Settings—you can always use the Assign Profile command (see "Assign Profile" later in this chapter) to assign a profile other than the working space to an image—but if you're going to be working with a bunch of images in the same space, it makes life slightly easier to load that space as the working space. The following is by no means an exhaustive list, but we've found each of these spaces useful.

ProPhoto RGB. Formerly known as rgbMaster, and before that as ROMM (Reference Output Metric Method) RGB, Kodak's ProPhoto RGB is an extremely wide-gamut RGB space, so wide that its primaries are imaginary—there is no light source that could produce these colors, and we couldn't see them if there was. It needs these extreme primaries to be able to accommodate the very saturated yellows attainable on E6 transparency film. It's also wide enough that we recommend doing major edits only on high-bit files—small tweaks to 8-bit-per-channel files, however, are safe.

ProPhoto RGB has a wide enough gamut to absolutely, definitely cover the entire gamut of transparency film. Bruce uses it for most of his work, particularly as a rendering space for color neg scans (see "Interpreting Color Negatives" in Chapter 7, *Color Correction Fundamentals*). To set it as the RGB working space, turn on the Advanced checkbox in Color Settings and choose it from the RGB working space menu.

EktaSpace. Developed by photographer Joseph Holmes, EktaSpace is a large-gamut space that's a little more conservative, and hence a little more manageable, than ProPhoto RGB. There's been some debate over whether EktaSpace really covers the entire E6 gamut. Our experiments suggest that, while it may be possible to capture colors in-camera (without resorting to games like exposing the film with a monochromatic laser) that will be clipped by EktaSpace, it's not likely. EktaSpace will hold any colors you're likely to encounter on E6 film that's shot and processed under normal conditions. It's possible to use 8-bit-per-channel images in EktaSpace, but you'll get much more editing headroom with 16-bit files.

Bruce uses EktaSpace for transparency scans when it's important to preserve the characteristics of the individual film stock. He finds it's easier to do this in EktaSpace than in any other space he's tried. You can download it from www.josephholmes.com.

BruceRGB. Unlike both ProPhoto RGB and EktaSpace, BruceRGB is a small-gamut space. Bruce designed it to offer the maximum editing headroom on 8-bit-per-channel images destined for CMYK printing. It's basically a compromise between Adobe RGB (1998), which is a little too big, and ColorMatch RGB, which is too small. It covers most of the gamut of CMYK offset printing and is also a good fit for most RGB inkjet printers. It does clip some cyans and oranges, but a *much* larger RGB space would be required to encompass these.

Nowadays, Bruce uses it as an "emergency" space on difficult images that require massive editing, either because they were scanned badly or because they were captured under far-from-ideal lighting conditions with point-and-shoot or low-end digital cameras. He notes that today's scanners and cameras are so much better than those from 1998, when he developed the space, that he has much less need for BruceRGB. But it still comes in handy for images that simply fall apart in larger spaces. You can define it yourself using the Custom RGB setting (see the next section).

Custom RGB Spaces

If you're a hard-core imaging geek who likes to live dangerously, you can define your own RGB working space. It's not that difficult, because an RGB working space is defined by just three primary xy values for red, green, and blue; a white point; and a gamma value. For example, if you use a high-quality scanning-back digital camera that lets you set the gray balance for each image, you may want to define a working space whose primaries are the same as the camera's, thereby (in theory) ensuring that your working space matches your input device.

To define a custom RGB working space, you first need to check the Advanced checkbox in Color Settings. This lets you choose Custom RGB from the RGB menu, which in turn opens the Custom RGB dialog box (see Figure 5-12). Custom RGB allows you to choose a name for your custom space, as well as specify the gamma, the white point, and the primaries. If you're not already intimate with these terms, then you should probably just skip down to "Choosing a CMYK Working Space."

Gamma. The Gamma field lets you enter a value for the gamma of your working space. This is completely independent of your monitor gamma—there's no reason to match your working space gamma to your monitor gamma, and there may be plenty of good reasons not to do so. To oversimplify (the long explanation would be very long), the gamma of the editing space controls the distribution of the bits over the tone curve. Our eyes don't respond in a linear fashion to changes in brightness: A gamma of 2.2 is generally reckoned to be more or less perceptually uniform, so we recommend using that value for your working space gamma. It has the added benefit of devoting more bits to the shadows, which is where we find we usually need them during editing.

White Point. This setting defines the white point of the RGB working space. You can choose one of the ten built-in white points, or choose Custom to define a custom white point by entering xy chromaticities (the xy components of a color defined in CIE xyY). As with the gamma setting, the white point of the working space is quite independent of the monitor white point. It's also independent of the output white point. For a variety of reasons, we suggest using D65 as the white point for most RGB spaces. (For a more detailed discussion of white points, see the sidebar "How White Are Your Whites?" earlier in this chapter.) If you use one of the built-in spaces, this setting will be made for you automatically.

Figure 5-12
Custom RGB

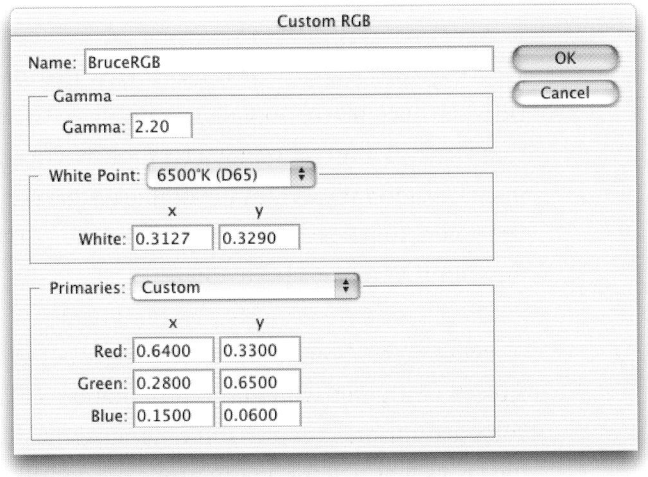

The Custom RGB dialog box lets you define custom RGB working spaces by defining the gamma, white point, and primaries.

Primaries. The Primaries setting lets you choose from the Primaries menu, which contains six sets of phosphor-based primaries for common monitors and three sets of abstract primaries. Or you can enter custom xy values for R, G, and B to set the boundaries of the color gamut.

Tip: Finding the xy Values for Primaries. To find the xy chromaticities of the primaries for a chosen built-in space, first load that space from the RGB menu, and then choose Custom from the Primaries menu. The Primaries dialog box appears, showing the xy chromaticities for the red, green, and blue primaries. If you wish, you can even plot them on a chromaticity chart like the one in Figure 5-13.

For example, here are the settings for BruceRGB:

▶ White point = 6500K

▶ Gamma = 2.2

▶ Red xy = 0.6400 0.3300

▶ Green xy = 0.2800 0.6500

▶ Blue xy = 0.1500 0.0600

Defining custom RGB spaces isn't for the faint of heart, and there are now so many RGB spaces available that relatively few people should need to build their own. But it's always nice to know that you can.

Tip: Custom RGB Settings and ICC Profiles. When you save custom RGB settings, you're actually creating an ICC profile. On Mac OS X, save them in the Library/ColorSync/Profiles folder. On Windows 2000/XP, save profiles in the WinNT/System/Spool/Drivers/Color directory. That way, the profile that describes your RGB working space will be readily available to other ICC-aware applications.

Figure 5-13 shows a chromaticity plot of some of Photoshop's built-in spaces, compared with the chromaticities of SWOP inks. A word of caution: color gamuts are complex three-dimensional objects, and a chromaticity plot is very much an abstraction. We include this figure primarily as a visualization tool to help you get your head around the implications of different RGB primaries, not as an exact comparison of their color gamuts.

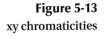

Figure 5-13
xy chromaticities

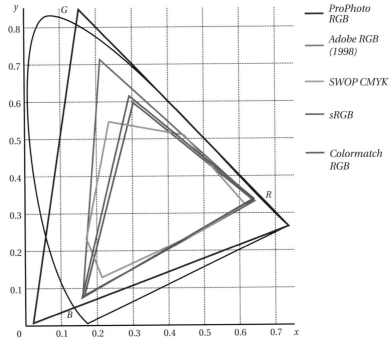

This figure shows the gamuts of several of Photoshop's working RGB working spaces and the gamut of SWOP CMYK, plotted in CIE xyY space. It illustrates the trade-off inherent in choosing an RGB space between clipping the gamut of CMYK and wasting bits on unprintable colors.

RGB Output

It's possible to load an RGB output profile as your working space. This may even seem like a good idea if you're one of the many Photoshop users whose final output is a desktop inkjet printer. But even if you only ever print to an RGB printer, using your RGB output profile as your RGB working space is a bad idea. RGB output spaces almost always have two properties that make them very difficult to use as working spaces: They're almost never gray-balanced, and they're usually far from perceptually uniform.

You may find that you want to make small adjustments to your image after converting it to your RGB printer space, but with a good output profile you can obtain the same results more easily by keeping your image in the working space and using Photoshop's soft-proofing controls to provide an accurate simulation of your output on screen (see "Soft Proofing Controls," later in this chapter).

To make the actual conversion from the working space to your printer's RGB output space, you have several choices as to where to apply your RGB output profile. (See "Print with Preview" and "Print," later in this chapter.) The one place you *don't* want to use your RGB output profile is as an RGB working space!

Choosing a CMYK Working Space

Unlike RGB working spaces, which may be entirely abstract and not based on any real device, CMYK working spaces always reflect some real combination of ink (or toner, or dye) and paper. The ideal situation is to have a custom ICC profile for the specific CMYK process to which you're printing, but in the real world that's still the exception rather than the rule. However, if you do have a custom ICC profile for your CMYK print process, or for an industry-standard proofing system such as Kodak Polychrome Matchprint or Fuji ColorArt, turn on the Advanced Mode option and load that profile into the CMYK menu in the Color Settings dialog box.

With Advanced Mode unchecked, your choices of CMYK working space are limited to the seven new press profiles installed by Photoshop, plus Custom CMYK, which users of older versions of Photoshop may recognize as the old "Built-in" panel of Photoshop 5's CMYK Setup (what we tend to call "Photoshop Classic").

In the absence of a custom profile, Adobe's new press profiles are much, much better than the old Photoshop Classic mechanism. They typically produce smoother gradations and better saturation than the old CMYK Setups, and the ink colors are more accurate.

However, they do differ substantially from the old defaults, so exercise caution. Table 5-1 shows the rough equivalents of each of the preset CMYK settings.

We should emphasize "rough equivalents"—the black generation and dot gain compensation differ substantially from the old setups; the real dot gains are different for each ink, and as full-blown ICC profiles; the new profiles support perceptual rendering as well as the colorimetric renderings to which the old setups were limited. Unfortunately, though, there is no documentation for these profiles—the settings we've provided in Table 5-1 represent our best educated guesses.

Table 5-1
Inside the CMYK presets

Setting	TIL	K	GCR	Dot gain
U.S. Web Coated (SWOP)	300	90	Light	21%
U.S. Web Uncoated	260	95	Medium	18%
U.S. Sheetfed Coated (175 lpi)	350	85	Light	26%
U.S. Sheetfed Uncoated	260	95	Medium	18%
Euroscale Coated	350	90	Light	19%
Euroscale Uncoated	260	95	Medium	25%
Japan Standard	300	90	Light	13%

However, if you're more comfortable with the old-style Photoshop CMYK setups, they're still available. Choosing Custom CMYK from the CMYK popup menu opens the Custom CMYK dialog box, as shown in Figure 5-14.

Figure 5-14
Custom CMYK

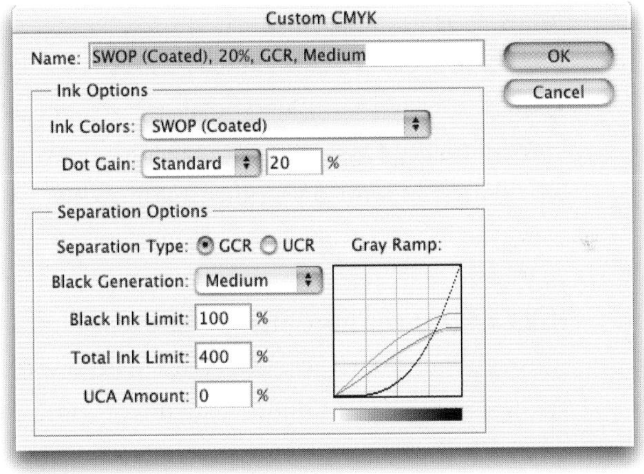

Should You Use Custom CMYK?

Before we get into the details of the Custom CMYK dialog box, a disclaimer is in order. The Custom CMYK feature in Photoshop CS was born at the introduction of CMYK capabilities in Photoshop 2.0 (which shipped in June of 1991, long before "color" and "management" were combined into a scary phrase, and before ColorSync was a twinkle in Apple's eye). The fact that it has persisted in one form or another through all subsequent revisions of Photoshop shows that it's perfectly possible to make great color separations using this mechanism.

If you're a relatively experienced Photoshop user and you're comfortable with defining CMYK settings this way, we have a few tricks that you may find useful. But if you're relatively new to the world of color and Photoshop, you'd be *much* better off spending your time and ingenuity investigating some of the many packages available for creating and editing ICC profiles (like GretagMacbeth ProfileMaker Pro or Monaco Profiler). Or, if you're outputting film and making traditional proofs (like Matchprint), you might consider just buying a profile for the proofing system instead and using that.

Ultimately, Adobe left Custom CMYK in Photoshop mostly for backward compatibility. ICC profiles are the wave of the future, and if you're at the beginning of your learning curve, you're better off concentrating on those instead.

That said, there's still some life in the old dog, and we've even been able to teach it a couple of new tricks!

Editing Custom CMYK

The Custom CMYK dialog box has two sections: Ink Options, which lets you define the colors of your inks and the way they behave on your paper stock; and Separation Options, which lets you tell Photoshop how you want the inks to build color when converting to CMYK.

Ink Colors. The Ink Colors setting tells Photoshop about the color of the inks you'll be using. You can create your own custom ink set or use one of Photoshop's built-in ink sets such as SWOP, Eurostandard, or Toyo, each of which has ink definitions for coated, uncoated, and newsprint stock (see Figure 5-15). The SWOP ink sets differ substantially from the current SWOP spec; but a great many Photoshop users have been using them for years, so you should talk to your commercial printer about which ink definitions to use.

Bear in mind that the built-in ink sets are paper-specific (that is, if you print cyan on a slightly pink paper, it'll look different than if you print it on a slightly blue paper). Unfortunately, no one seems to remember which paper stocks the built-in sets specify. Plus, even though there are rough standards for inks used on web presses, they actually vary widely, and a magenta on the west coast might be different than one on the east coast.

You can generally produce good results using one of the built-in ink sets, but if you're printing direct-to-plate, if you're using waterless inks, if

Printing to Desktop Printers

If you're one of the growing number of Photoshop users who print exclusively, or mainly, to desktop printers, rest assured that the vast bulk of the material contained in this chapter applies as much to you as it does to those whose printing is done on a commercial press. If you're printing to an inkjet printer, you'll have less variation to worry about on output since inkjet printers are stable, and inkjet inks are generally consistent from batch to batch. True photographic printers such as the Fuji Pictrography and the Durst Lambda also offer much better consistency than any printing press. So in some ways, your task is easier than printing on a press. But in other ways it's more complicated.

The main question you have to answer is whether you drive the printer as an RGB or a CMYK device. Photographic printers are true RGB devices—they expose photosensitive paper using red, green, and blue lasers or LEDs— so the CMYK color mode simply doesn't apply. Inkjet printers use cyan, magenta, yellow, and black inks (plus, sometimes, light cyan, light magenta, and even light black, which we used to know as gray), which in theory at least makes them CMYK devices. But in practice, unless you're printing through a PostScript RIP, desktop inkjet printers function as RGB devices because traditionally, the Macintosh Quickdraw and Windows GDI graphics languages lack

any facility for passing CMYK to printers. Quartz, the graphics engine in Mac OS X, has the theoretical capability to hand off CMYK, but we've yet to see a printer driver that exploits it. Photoshop will let you send CMYK to these printers, but the printer driver will immediately convert it to RGB before doing anything else with it.

A PostScript RIP may seem to allow more control over the printing process by letting you control the individual inks, but that usually isn't the case. PostScript RIPs that use the printer's native screening algorithms usually send RGB to that part of the print process: Those that truly provide ink-level control use their own screening, which usually looks much worse than the printer's native screening. A PostScript RIP makes sense from a workflow standpoint if you're using a desktop printer as a proofer, but if your desktop print is your final output, we recommend using the RGB driver, or a specialized RIP designed for photo output, such as Colorbyte's ImagePrint.

RGB output. If you're printing RGB, you can skip the entire CMYK section in this chapter since it doesn't apply to you. You should, however, read the sections "Choosing an RGB Working Space," "Soft Proofing Controls," and "Print with Preview" carefully. We recommend using ICC profiles for your printer. If you print us-

ing the printer vendor's inks and papers, the canned profiles that come with the printer work fairly well. If you're using third-party inks and papers, though, a custom profile will improve your output immensely. Inexpensive scanner-based profiling packages such as Monaco EZColor work very well with inkjet printers, and will likely pay for themselves quickly in savings on ink and paper. Don't use your RGB printer profile as an RGB working space, though, because RGB printer spaces aren't gray-balanced or perceptually uniform, making editing difficult. Instead, use a working space such as Adobe RGB (1998), and fine-tune your image for output using Proof Setup to create a simulation of the printed output.

CMYK output. If you're printing CMYK through a PostScript RIP, almost everything we say in this chapter about press CMYK applies equally to desktop printers. Ideally, you should use a custom ICC profile for your inks and papers. If you always print using the same inks and paper, consider building a custom profile or commissioning one from one of the many companies and individuals offering such services. Or use some of the techniques we discuss in Custom CMYK to make a custom CMYK space for your printer in Photoshop, especially if you experiment with different inks and paper stocks.

Figure 5-15
Preset ink sets

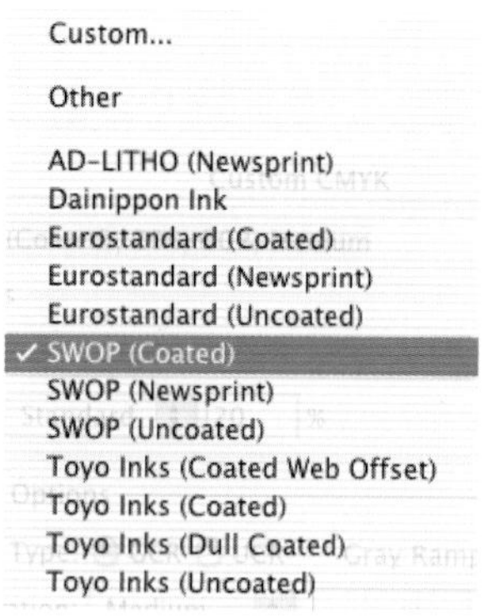

Custom...

Other

AD–LITHO (Newsprint)
Dainippon Ink
Eurostandard (Coated)
Eurostandard (Newsprint)
Eurostandard (Uncoated)
✓ SWOP (Coated)
SWOP (Newsprint)
SWOP (Uncoated)
Toyo Inks (Coated Web Offset)
Toyo Inks (Coated)
Toyo Inks (Dull Coated)
Toyo Inks (Uncoated)

The Ink Colors menu lets you choose one of Photoshop's built-in definitions for ink sets, or choose Custom to define your own.

you're using a very yellow or very blue-white paper stock (or any colored stock at all, for that matter), or if you're printing with non-standard inks, you can almost certainly improve your results by creating a custom ink set. You're unlikely to get as good a result as you would using a package that's designed to build ICC profiles, but the Custom CMYK dialog box lets you do it with no additional software, it's relatively easy, and it produces decent, if not spectacular, results.

The Custom setting at the top of the Ink Colors popup menu allows you to define your own colorants (see Figure 5-16); when you open the Ink Colors dialog box, it's loaded with the values from the previously selected Ink Colors option. There are two ways of using this feature, one much more exact (and more exacting) than the other.

Colorimetric measurement. The Ink Colors dialog box lets you set the CIE xyY or CIE Lab values for the eight progressive colors (cyan, magenta, yellow, black, cyan+magenta, cyan+yellow, magenta+yellow,

Figure 5-16
Ink Colors dialog box

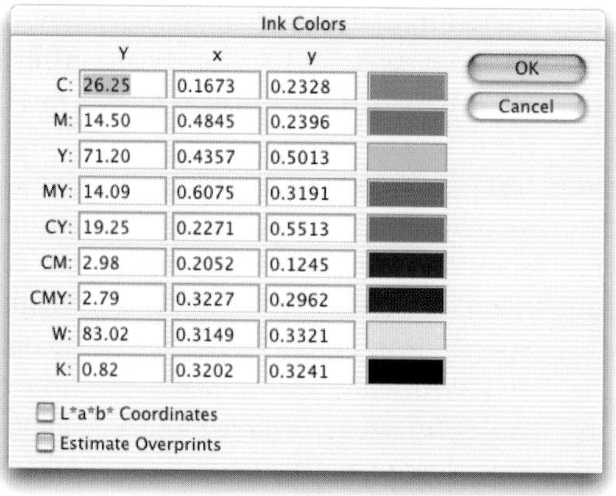

	Y	x	y
C:	26.25	0.1673	0.2328
M:	14.50	0.4845	0.2396
Y:	71.20	0.4357	0.5013
MY:	14.09	0.6075	0.3191
CY:	19.25	0.2271	0.5513
CM:	2.98	0.2052	0.1245
CMY:	2.79	0.3227	0.2962
W:	83.02	0.3149	0.3321
K:	0.82	0.3202	0.3241

☐ L*a*b* Coordinates
☐ Estimate Overprints

The Ink Colors dialog box lets you enter custom xyY or Lab values for your inks, or click the color swatches to open the Color Picker and choose an ink color by eyeball.

cyan+magenta+yellow), and the white of the paper stock. The only way to determine these accurately is to measure them from press output with a colorimeter or spectrophotometer (you can do this by eye, too, as we'll discuss in a moment).

We've encountered several situations where measuring these values is well worth the trouble. A newspaper that uses a bright red as a spot color prints process color, using red in place of magenta to save money. A fine-art printer needs to use permanent lightfast inks for archival-quality prints, and the closest thing available to magenta in a nonfugitive ink is a vermilion. A photographer wants to use a quadtone black inkset (black plus three shades of gray) to print black-and-white images on an inkjet printer through a CMYK RIP. A previous edition of *Real World Photoshop* was printed direct-to-plate using a yellow ink that was considerably more orange than the SWOP standard. All these situations have exactly the same problem and are able to use the same solution.

First, you need to print a set of color bars using the nonstandard inks. The color bars must be specified as CMYK colors in Photoshop. At this stage, it doesn't matter whether or not you're using a reasonable CMYK setting because you're simply sending ink values to the output. Then you measure each color swatch with a colorimeter or spectrophotometer and enter the CIE xyY or CIE Lab values into the Ink Colors dialog box. (On the

Canned vs. Custom Profiles

Canned profiles—profiles supplied by a third party that are based on something other than measurements of your specific device—have earned a bad reputation, often deservedly so. But under the right circumstances, generic ICC profiles can be very useful. It's true that each combination of printing press, ink, and paper is unique. However, virtually all press operators pride themselves on their ability to match a contract proof such as an Imation Matchprint or Fuji ColorArt—if

they couldn't, color printing would be almost impossible.

Proofer profiles. Proofing systems are generally very consistent from shop to shop. This makes them good candidates for canned profiles—stable, repeatable, consistent output processes like contract proofers simply don't need custom profiles. You need to make sure that the profile you choose has the correct ink limits, black generation, and substrate for your job, but as long as you pay attention to these

variables, you can produce excellent results using generic proofer profiles.

Sheetfed press. While sheetfed presses vary a little more than do proofing systems, we've seen excellent results from generic sheetfed press profiles too, providing the paper stock isn't too weird. Bear in mind that the press operator has a great deal of control over the final result—a profile only has to be a reasonable match to the press.

same target, we also suggest you print a "gray" ramp for each ink, with swatches for 2, 4, 6, 8, 10, 20, 30, 40, 50, 60, 70, 80, and 90 percent ink, which you can then use to measure the dot gain—see "Dot Gain," later in this chapter.) If you ask nicely, your printer can often print these swatches outside the trim area of some other job that is being printed on the same paper stock and with the same inks.

Photoshop can accept CIE xyY or CIE Lab values. In either case, you should measure these values with your instrument set to D50, 2-degree observer (even if you don't know what that is, your device's software will).

Eyeball. The second technique is a lot less accurate—in fact, it's a kludge— and we only recommend using it as a way to improve the color from desktop four-color inkjet and thermal-wax color printers driven by a CMYK RIP (though in a pinch we might use it for a digital press or direct-to-plate scenario too). It doesn't work with three-color CMY printers, or with inkjets that take RGB data and print through a Quickdraw or GDI driver, or on dye-subs—we've tried. But it doesn't require measuring equipment other than your eyeballs.

Again, you need to print a set of color bars, which you must specify as CMYK colors (don't make them in RGB and then convert). Then, choose Custom from the Ink Colors popup menu to open the Ink Colors dialog box. Clicking on each color swatch opens the Color Picker dialog box (see Figure 5-17). You can then edit each progressive color to match your printed output. Generally, desktop printers use colorants that are purer and more saturated than press inks, so head in that general direction.

Don't expect miracles from this technique—the results you get depend on your monitor calibration, your lighting, and your skill in matching colors by eye. It should get you into the ballpark, but given the amount of work involved and the uncertain quality of the results you get, we recommend that you investigate obtaining, building, or commissioning an ICC profile instead.

Tuning CMYK Previews. If you find that CMYK images don't look right on your screen (that is, they don't match what you're printing), there's a good chance your monitor profile isn't correct. However, if the problem doesn't lie with the monitor profile, you can try to create a custom CMYK ink set just for viewing your images. You can sometimes improve the accu-

Figure 5-17
Ink Colors dialog
box with Color Picker

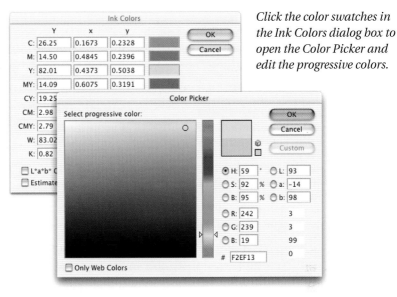

Click the color swatches in the Ink Colors dialog box to open the Color Picker and edit the progressive colors.

racy of the CMYK Preview by fine-tuning the ink colors, then saving the result with a name that clearly indicates it's only to be used for viewing CMYK, not for creating it. The easiest way to do this is to open the CMYK image or images you're trying to match, make a Duplicate, and use Assign Profile to make it an Untagged CMYK image (see "Assign Profile," later in this chapter). Then go to Color Settings, turn on the Preview checkbox, choose Custom CMYK, choose Custom from the Ink Colors menu, and adjust the Ink Colors until you see the match you want. You may have to wait a second or two for the changes to show up in your image.

To save this setting, select Save CMYK from the Color Settings CMYK menu. This saves the settings as an ICC profile. Remember to name it something that tells you that it's for viewing only; using this to convert RGB to CMYK could be disastrous. To use this profile for viewing, you'll load it into Proof Setup (see "Proof Setup," later in this chapter). When you're done making it, hit Cancel so you leave the dialog boxes without actually using this new setup.

Using Estimate Overprints for spot inks. The Estimate Overprints checkbox in Custom Ink Colors is primarily useful if you substitute Pantone spot inks (or other inks for which you have known CIE values) for CMYK—you can use Estimate Overprints to see how they'll interact with one another. Be aware that this is a highly experimental procedure, and the strongest possible, closed-track, professional-driver, don't-try-this-at-home caveats apply. But if you're in a situation where you're forced to do a job using spot inks instead of process, loading the spot inks into Custom Ink Colors and using Estimate Overprint will give you at least some idea of what'll happen when you overprint them (see Chapter 11, *Spot Colors and Duotones*). Using Estimate Overprints to save taking four measurements for the various CMY combinations is a very silly idea—the minimal savings of time simply aren't worth it.

Dot gain. When ink hits paper, it smooshes some, bleeds some, and generally "heavies up on press" (even if your "press" is a little desktop printer). That means that your 50-percent cyan halftone spot won't look like 50 percent when it comes off a printing press. It's your responsibility to take this dot gain into account when building your images, and if you don't, your pictures will always appear too dark and muddy. Custom CMYK gives you two methods to compensate for dot gain (see Figure 5-18). The simpler method, entering a single percentage value, is also the less accurate. Using individual dot gain curves for each ink will generally yield better results, but it takes a little more time and effort.

Tip: Where to Adjust Dot Gain. Photoshop automatically compensates for dot gain when it converts images to CMYK for printing. It's much less work to build the dot-gain compensation into the separation process than to try to compensate for it manually on an image-by-image basis. In a pinch, you can make slight compensations for dot gain in an already-separated CMYK file using Curves, but you'll generally get better results going back to the original RGB image, adjusting the dot-gain value in Custom CMYK, and generating a new CMYK file using the new settings. In fact, one of the few advantages Custom CMYK has over ICC profiles is the ease with which you can adjust for minor variations in dot gain between different papers.

You'll hear all sorts of numbers bandied about with reference to dot gain, so it's important to be clear about what Photoshop means, and what your service providers mean, by a given dot gain percentage—they're often different (see the sidebar "Dot Gain: Coping with Midtone Spread"). All the built-in ink sets contain default dot gain values, but these shouldn't be considered as much more than a starting point. As we said earlier, the ink sets are paper-specific—the ink colors typically don't vary much from

Figure 5-18
Custom CMYK/Dot Gain
field highlighted

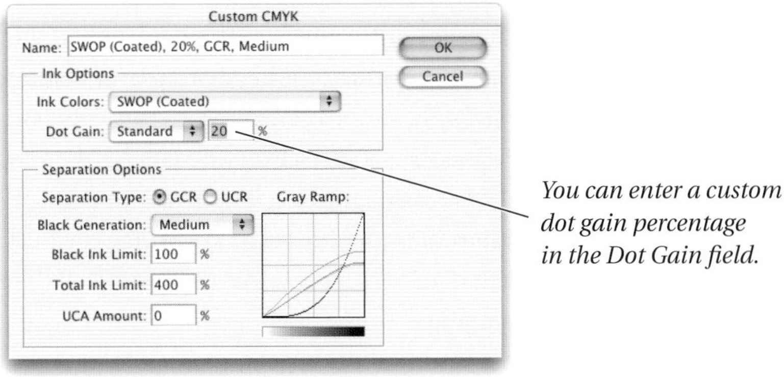

*You can enter a custom
dot gain percentage
in the Dot Gain field.*

paper stock to paper stock (unless you're printing on puce, lime green, or goldenrod paper), but the dot gain can vary tremendously from one paper to another.

Table 5-2 shows some rough-and-ready numbers for typical dot gain, but they're guidelines, not rules. If you come up with values vastly different from these, double-check your calculations or measurements, reread the sidebar "Dot Gain: Coping with Midtone Spread," and talk to your service providers to make sure that there isn't some misunderstanding. Bear in mind that higher halftone screen frequencies have more dot gain than low ones. The values in the table are based on 133- to 150-line screens with the exception of newsprint, which is based on an 85-line screen.

Table 5-2
Dot gain
settings

Press and stock	Typical dot gain
Web press, coated stock	17–22%
Sheetfed press, coated stock	12–15%
Sheetfed press, uncoated stock	18–22%
Newsprint	30–40%
Positive plates	10–12%

Dot Gain Curves. Single-value dot gains work reasonably well if you're using one of the built-in ink sets—the differential gain for each ink has already been factored in—but Photoshop CS offers an easy, unambiguous way to define the anticipated dot gain in the form of the Dot Gain Curves feature.

The only disadvantage to using Dot Gain Curves is that you need to use a densitometer (or a colorimeter or spectrophotometer that can read dot area) to read printed swatches. (You can almost always piggyback the swatches onto another job by printing them in the trim area, and if you don't have one of these devices, your printer or service bureau probably does.)

Choosing Curves from the Dot Gain popup menu opens the Dot Gain Curves dialog box (see Figure 5-19). It allows you to enter the actual dot values measured from 2, 4, 6, 8, 10, 20, 30, 40, 50, 60, 70, 80, and 90 percent patches for each ink. Measuring all the patches is probably overkill. At a pinch, you can simply measure the 50 percent dot and type in the measured value, but we recommend taking measurements of at least the 4, 6, 8, 10, 40, 50, and 80 percent swatches for each ink. Don't be tempted by the All Same checkbox—it's very unusual to find exactly the same dot gains on all four inks.

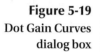

Figure 5-19
Dot Gain Curves
dialog box

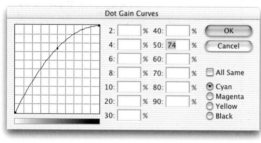

Enter the measured dot area for a swatch to build a custom dot gain curve. You can enter a single value for the 50-percent dot, or take more measurements to increase accuracy.

It's worth noting that the combination of Custom Ink Colors and Dot Gain Curves provides a somewhat effective means of profiling a press or other halftone output device with a relatively small number of measurements—most profiling tools require hundreds or even thousands of measurements. You can even create an ICC profile from this setup—see "Tip: Creating ICC Profiles from Custom CMYK Settings," later in this chapter.

Separation Options. The Separation Options section is where you tell Photoshop how you want to use the inks you've defined in the Ink Options section (see Figure 5-20). It lets you control the total amount of ink you'll put on the paper, as well as the black generation—the relationship between black and the other colors. Note that unlike the Ink Options settings, the Separation Options have no effect on the display of CMYK images—these only control how colors will convert to CMYK.

The decisions you make in Separation Options can make or break a print job, and there's no single correct answer, no hard-and-fast rules—

every combination of press, ink, and paper has its own optimum settings. When it comes to determining what these are, there's no substitute for experience. But understanding the way the Separation Options work is key to making sense of your own experience, and even if there are no rules, there are at least some valuable guidelines.

Figure 5-20
Separation
Options

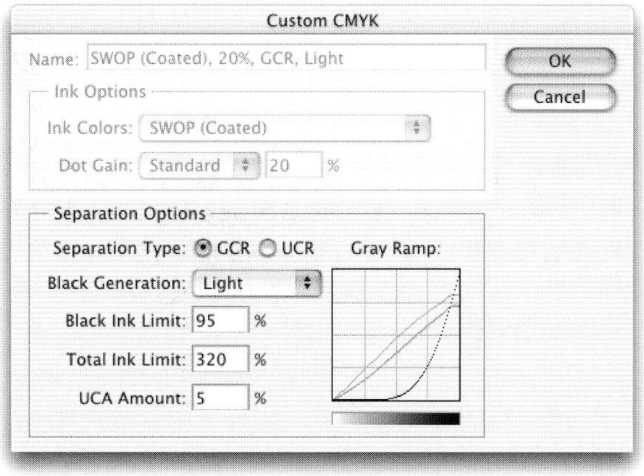

Separation Options lets you specify a total ink limit, a black ink limit, and a black generation method.

Rules, guidelines, and caveats. It's important to remember that these guidelines are useful starting points, nothing more. You'll hear all sorts of recommendations from experts; most are valid, but it's unlikely that any of them will apply perfectly to your particular situation. Just how far it's worth going to optimize your color seps for a specific press depends in part on the economics of the situation, and in part on the degree of process control used by the commercial printer. It's the exception rather than the rule for every impression in a print run to be identical, but the amount of variation within a press run varies widely from shop to shop—typically, the less variation, the higher the prices.

Creating ideal separations for a given press is often an iterative process—you run press proofs and measure them, then go back to original RGB files, reseparate them, and repeat the whole process until you arrive at the optimum conditions. This is both time-consuming and expensive, and for most jobs the economics simply don't justify it. If you're willing to dedicate a print run to testing, you're better off ignoring the whole Custom CMYK mechanism and building (or commissioning) a good ICC profile instead.

Dot Gain: Coping with Midtone Spread

Dot gain is the name given to the tendency for halftone dots to increase in size from film to press. The biggest cause is the ink spreading as it hits the paper—the more absorbent the paper, the greater the dot gain—but some dot gain occurs when the ink is transferred from the ink roller to the blanket roller on press, and some may even creep in when the film is made into plates. Because dot gain makes your images print darker than anticipated, compensating for it is essential.

Photoshop's dot gain is always measured at the 50-percent value, because that's where its effect is greatest. The larger the circumference of the halftone dot, the more it's subject to dot gain; but above 50 percent the dots start to run together, so they don't gain as much. For the same reason, high screen frequencies are more prone to dot gain than low screen frequencies, because there's more circumference to the dots.

The subject of dot gain attracts more than its share of confusion because people measure different things under the name "dot gain." Then, to make matters worse, they have different ways of expressing that measurement.

Photoshop's dot gain. The Photoshop documentation states that Photoshop's dot gain value is the dot gain from film to press. However, since Photoshop also assumes that it's printing to a linearized imagesetter—one that will produce a 50-percent dot when asked for one—we think it's less confusing to say that Photoshop's dot gain is really talking about the difference between the digital data and the final printed piece.

Photoshop's reckoning of dot gain is the absolute additive amount by which a 50-percent dot increases. So if a 50-percent dot appears on the print as 72 percent, Photoshop would call this a 22-percent dot gain.

When you ask your printer about the dot gain anticipated for your job, he may give you the gain from color proof to final print. There's a simple way to remove this ambiguity. Ask your printer, "What will happen to the 50-percent dot in my file when it hits the press?" If the response is that it will print as a 78-percent dot, that's 28-percent dot gain as far as Photoshop is concerned, and that's the number you should use for your Dot Gain setting in Custom CMYK.

But Photoshop CS offers an even simpler way to remove the ambiguity: just measure the dot area of the 50-percent dot, then simply plug that value into the 50-percent field in Dot Gain Curves—that way, no guesswork or arithmetic is involved.

Who makes the proof? Many service bureaus will make a laminated proof such as a Matchprint when they run your film, but it's unlikely that their proofing system is set up to match the press and paper stock on which your job will run. If you give this proof to your printer, he may tell you he can match it, but he's guessing. If the printer makes the proof, there's no guesswork involved, and responsibility is clear.

Tip: Testing on a Budget. Remember that a printer can sometimes piggyback a test onto someone else's print job, particularly if you show that you can offer them a significant amount of business. Preparing several different versions of an image (and a few color bars, too) and ganging them on a page can tell you a lot when they're printed.

UCR vs. GCR. The Photoshop Classic separation engine offers two different methods of black generation: UCR (Undercolor Removal) and GCR (Gray Component Replacement). Both reduce the total amount of ink used to compensate for ink-trapping problems that appear when too much ink is applied to the page. (In this context, *trapping* is the propensity for one ink to adhere to others—it has nothing to do with building chokes and spreads to compensate for misregistration on press.)

► UCR separations replace cyan, magenta, and yellow ink with black only in the neutral areas. This uses much less ink in the shadows.

► GCR extends into color areas of the image as well—it replaces the proportions of cyan, magenta, and yellow that produce neutral gray with a corresponding percentage of black ink.

GCR separations are generally considered easier to control on press than are UCR separations, at least by the theoreticians. The downside of GCR is that it can make the shadow areas look flat and unsaturated since they're being printed only with black ink, so many commercial printers distrust GCR separations. UCA (Undercolor Addition) allows you to compensate for flat shadows by adding some CMY back into the neutral shadow areas (see "Undercolor Addition (UCA)," later in this chapter).

Even though some experts contend that UCR separations are better for sheetfed presses and that GCR is better for web presses, we just don't buy it. We almost always use GCR separations with some UCA. On the other hand, we've found that UCR sometimes works better than GCR when printing to newsprint with a low total ink limit—say, 220 to 240 percent—but your mileage may vary. Ask your printer, but test whenever possible. We suspect that many printers who profess to hate GCR seps often run them unknowingly, usually with good results, as long as the black generation amount isn't too extreme.

There are also image-specific issues with black generation: If we take the extreme examples represented by two images—one, a pile of silver coins, the other, a city skyline at night—the first is an ideal candidate for a fairly heavy black plate using Medium or Heavy GCR, since there's little color, and carrying most of the image on the black plate improves detail and makes it easier to maintain neutral grays on press. The second image, though, will have significant color and detail in the deep shadows, and too heavy a black will make it flat and lifeless.

Black Generation. The Black Generation popup menu is available only when Separation Type is set to GCR. This feature lets you control the areas of the tonal range that Photoshop replaces with black (see Figure 5-21). For the vast majority of situations we prefer a Light black setting, in which Photoshop begins to add black only after the 40-percent mark. Often, however, a Medium black (where black begins to replace colors after only 20 percent) may work better for newsprint. We almost never use the Heavy or Maximum black settings, with one exception: A Maximum black setting can do wonders when printing images that were captured from your screen (like the screen shots in this book).

Custom black generation. The Custom option allows you to create your own black generation curve. This isn't something you should undertake lightly—the black plate has an enormous influence on the tonal reproduction of the image. However, if you want to make slight modifications to one of the built-in black generation curves, you can—choose the curve you want to view, then choose Custom. The Black Generation dialog box appears with the last selected curve loaded (see Figure 5-22).

If your printer asks for a "skeleton black," you can use the Custom option to create a skeleton black curve—a very light black setting that still extends high up into the tonal range, typically to 25 or 30 percent. You should attempt to do this only if the printer demands it, and even then only if you have considerable experience in evaluating images by looking at the individual color plates—the values on the black plate are critical, and you'll almost certainly need to run press proofs to get it right.

Black Ink Limit. Black Ink Limit does just what it says—it limits the amount of black ink used in the deepest shadows. In general, we recommend leaving this set at 100 percent, because it seems to produce the best overall balance between the black and the CMY inks. This is a recommendation that has often been misunderstood. It doesn't mean that you'll actually wind up laying down 100-percent black ink. You can (and in most cases should) reduce the black shadow dot for individual images by changing the target black color of the black eyedropper in Levels or Curves (see "Reducing the Black with the Eyedropper" in Chapter 7, *Color Correction Fundamentals*). On the other hand, if you're working with newsprint or another process that requires low total ink densities—280 percent or less—you may want to try setting the Black Ink Limit between 70 and 85

Figure 5-21
Black generation

A UCR separation uses black ink only in the neutral areas. It produces rich shadows but can be difficult to control on press because it uses a lot of ink compared to GCR separations.

A Light GCR setting replaces slightly more CMY with K than does a UCR separation. In this image, Light GCR puts slightly more black into the sky and the water than does the UCR separation.

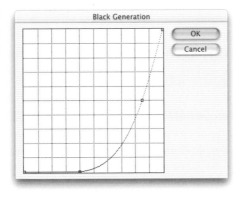

Maximum GCR replaces all neutral components of the CMY inks with black. It's easy to control on press because the black plate carries most of the image, but it can make shadow areas look flat.

Figure 5-22
Custom Black
Generation dialog box

Choose Custom to create a custom black generation curve.

percent, particularly if you're using UCR rather than GCR. Your printer is the best source of advice on the maximum black the press can handle.

Total Ink Limit. Total Ink Limit also does what it says—it limits the total amount of ink used in the deepest shadows. The ideal value depends on the combination of press, ink, and paper, but bear in mind that it isn't necessarily desirable to use the maximum amount of ink that the printing process can handle. It's generally true that more ink will yield a better image (within the limits of the press), but it also creates more problems with ink trapping and drying, show-through, and offsetting, and (for printers) it costs more because you're using more ink. Your printer will know, better than anyone else, the trade-offs involved.

For high-quality sheetfed presses with coated stock, a total ink limit of 300 to 340 percent is a good starting point—you may be able to go even higher with some paper stocks. For newsprint, values can range from 220 to 280 percent (see "Typical Custom CMYK Setups," facing).

Undercolor Addition (UCA). UCA is used with GCR to compensate for loss of ink density in the neutral shadow areas. Using UCA lets you bring back richness to the shadows, yet still retain the benefits of easier color-ink balancing on the press that GCR offers.

The need for UCA is image-dependent. If your shadows look flat, the image can probably benefit from modest amounts of UCA. We rarely use more than 10 percent, and typically use less. (Because David doesn't like to think a whole lot, he usually sets this to 5 percent and forgets about it.)

	Press and paper	Inks	Dot gain
Table 5-3 Suggested separation settings	Sheetfed Coated	SWOP (Coated)	12–15%
	Sheetfed Uncoated	SWOP (Uncoated)	17–22%
	Web Coated	SWOP (Coated)	17–22%
	Web Uncoated	SWOP (Uncoated)	22–30%
	Newsprint 1	SWOP (Newsprint)	30–40%
	Newsprint 2	SWOP (Newsprint)	30–40%

Typical Custom CMYK Setups

Table 5-3 gives some general guidelines for different types of print jobs. The dot-gain values are based on 133- to 150-line screens, except for newsprint, which assumes an 85-line screen. If you use these values, you should get acceptable separations; but every combination of press, ink, and paper has its own quirks, and your printer should know them better than anyone else. View these values as useful starting points, and get as much advice from your printer as you can.

Tip: Creating ICC Profiles from Custom CMYK Settings. Once you've made a Custom CMYK setting, you can save it as an ICC profile by choosing Save CMYK from the Color Settings CMYK menu. Photoshop saves the settings as an ICC profile that you can use in any ICC-aware application. Profiles made this way support only relative and absolute colorimetric renderings, not perceptual or saturation, so they're more limited than profiles produced by full-blown profiling packages.

Advanced CMYK settings. When you turn on the Advanced Mode checkbox in Color Settings, you can choose any CMYK profile installed on your system as the CMYK working space. Bear in mind that the Convert to Profile command lets you convert images to any CMYK profile, so it isn't necessary to load a particular CMYK profile as the CMYK working space. It's simply more convenient to load the CMYK profile you're going to use most as the CMYK working space.

Black generation	Black limit	Total ink	UCA
GCR, Light	100%	320–340%	0–10%
GCR, Light	100%	270–300%	0–10%
GCR, Light	100%	300–320%	0–10%
GCR, Light	100%	280–300%	0–10%
GCR, Medium	95–100%	260–280%	0–10%
UCR	70–80%	220–240%	

Tip: Adding Profiles to the Recommended List. You can easily add profiles to the Recommended list (the list that appears in the CMYK menu when the Advanced Mode checkbox is turned off) by storing the profile, or an alias to the profile, in the right place. In Mac OS X, the right place is inside the Library/Application Support/Adobe/Color/Profiles/Recommended folder. In Windows, it's inside the Program Files/Common Files/Adobe/Color/Profiles/Recommended folder. This lets you access your favorite profiles without having to keep Advanced Mode turned on, so you don't have to wade through the entire list of profiles installed on your system, or deal with all the Advanced Mode controls.

Choosing a Gray Working Space

Grayscale is a first-class citizen in Photoshop CS, with its own profiles independent of RGB or CMYK. However, note that grayscale profiles only contain tone reproduction information; they have no information about the color of the black ink or of the paper.

When Advanced Mode is turned off, you can choose among grayscale dot gains of 10, 15, 20, 25, or 30 percent, depending on your printing conditions. You can also choose either gamma 1.8 or 2.2, which are good choices for grayscale images destined for the screen. Of course, there's nothing to prevent you from using these gamma values for print images, or the dot gain curves for onscreen use, but generally speaking, gammas are designed for onscreen and dot gain curves are designed for print. Note that on the Macintosh platform, you can also choose the black channel of the ColorSync Default Profile for CMYK Documents, which is particularly useful if you print grayscale and color images in the same job.

Custom Gray

When you check Advanced Mode, you gain access to all the grayscale profiles installed on your system, as well as the ability to define custom grayscale working spaces (which you can then save as Grayscale ICC profiles, if you want).

Custom Dot Gain. If you print a lot of grayscale work on the same sort of paper stock, it may well be worth it to build your own custom dot gain (remember, the more you customize, the better results you'll get). You can define a custom dot gain by choosing Custom Dot Gain from the Gray menu in the Color Settings dialog box. The Custom Dot Gain dialog box (see Figure 5-23) lets you plug in values for the 2, 4, 6, 8, 10, 20, 30, 40, 50, 60, 70, 80, and 90 percent dots. You can enter a single value for the 50-percent field (for example, to define 18-percent dot gain, you'd enter 68 in the 50-percent field), but you'll get much better results if you first print a ramp with patches for all the values in the dialog box, then measure the actual dot area for each one, and enter them all in the dialog box. This gives you a very accurate grayscale profile.

Of course, it's not absolutely necessary to measure every single patch, but we strongly recommend that you at least measure the highlight (2, 4, 6, 8, and 10 percent) patches plus the 40- and 80-percent patches. Obtaining accurate measurements for the highlights lets you set your all-important highlight detail quickly and easily.

Figure 5-23
Custom Dot Gain for grayscale

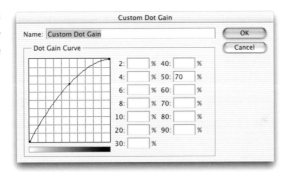

The Custom Dot Gain dialog box lets you specify a precise dot gain compensation for grayscale images.

Custom Gamma. Grayscale gamma settings are designed primarily for on-screen images. We can't envisage too many situations where you'd need to define a gamma other than the gamma 1.8 and gamma 2.2 built into Photoshop, but if for some reason you need to do so, choose Custom Gamma from the Color Settings Gray menu. Permissible values range from 0.75 to 3.0 (see Figure 5-24).

Figure 5-24
Custom Gamma for grayscale

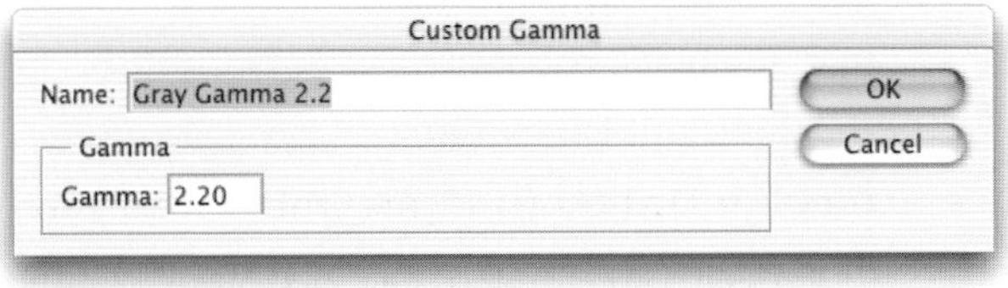

The Custom Gamma dialog box lets you create a custom gamma setting for grayscale images.

CMYK black channel. If you need to mix grayscale and color images in the same job, you might find it useful to simply load the black channel of your CMYK profile as your Gray working space. To do so, choose Load Gray from the Gray menu, then select the CMYK profile you wish to load from the dialog box and click Load. The profile appears in the Gray menu as Black Ink—ProfileName.

Note that the Black Ink Limit in a CMYK profile has no effect on grayscale images (because Black Ink Limit is used only when you convert to CMYK). The grayscale setting only uses the tonal response of the black ink, and lets you use the entire dynamic range of the black channel.

Save Gray. To use a custom grayscale setting elsewhere in Photoshop (for instance, in the Proof Setup, Assign Profile, or Convert to Profile dialog boxes) and in other ICC-savvy applications, you need to save your grayscale setting as an ICC profile. To do so, choose Save Gray from the Color Settings Gray menu, browse to the appropriate folder or directory for your platform, and click Save. Your grayscale profile will now be available for use in any application that understands grayscale ICC profiles. (The only ICC-aware applications we know that don't support grayscale profiles are PageMaker, which crashes on encountering them, and InDesign, which just ignores them.)

Spot Spaces

The Spot feature in the Color Settings dialog box allows you to specify a dot gain for spot colors. Like grayscale settings, spot color settings know nothing about the actual color of the ink and paper, and they contain no information about the way the spot ink interacts with other inks. Spot settings essentially behave identically to grayscale ones.

The Spot popup menu in the Color Settings dialog box contains dot gain settings for 10, 15, 20, 25, and 30 percent dot gain. In Advanced Mode, you can also define a Custom Dot Gain, choose a custom grayscale profile, or load the black channel of a CMYK profile. The procedure for doing any of these is identical to that for Grayscale mode. But spot inks differ widely in how they behave on paper, and the only way to know what will happen is to print a tint build. If you've got money to burn, go for it.

Loading the black channel of a CMYK profile for Spot is primarily useful if you need to use black as a spot color in a CMYK image: making type, callouts, or drop shadows print with only black ink are good examples. But using tints of spot colors, which spot dot gains seem to invite, is a very uncertain process. The dot gain curve will ensure that the tint you request is the one you'll get, but the only way to find out how the spot color interacts with the process inks is, unfortunately, to print it.

Color Management Policies

If you ever got stuck trying to figure out what those dang "Profile Mismatch" or "Missing Profile" alerts were saying in Photoshop 5, you might appreciate the relative simplicity of the Photoshop CS Color Management Policies feature. While the working space definitions allow you to tell Photoshop what colors the various numbers in your images represent, the Policies and Warnings sections of the Color Settings dialog box (see Figure 5-25) do something quite different: They let you tell Photoshop how to use the interpretations of the numbers.

Figure 5-25
Color Management
Policies

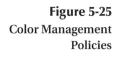

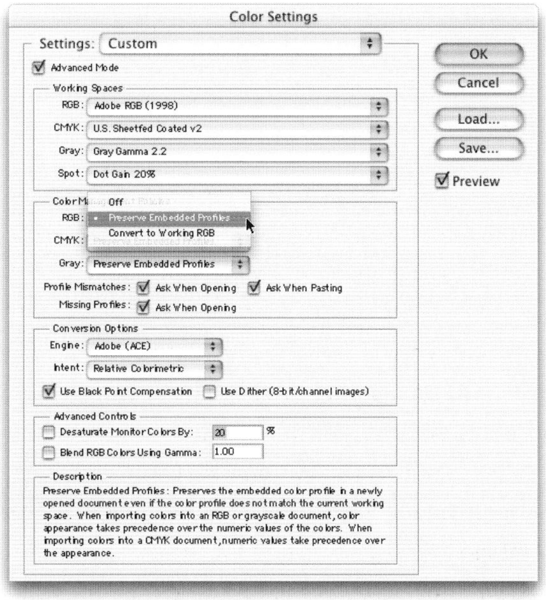

Color Management Policies let you tell Photoshop how to manage your color.

The policies control how Photoshop handles several aspects of color management. When you open a document with an embedded profile, the policies tell Photoshop to:

▶ use the embedded profile instead of the working space, opening the document as a Tagged document in its own "document space" (which may or may not be the same as the current working space), or

▶ convert the image from the document space represented by the embedded profile to the current working space, or

▶ ignore the profile and treat the document as Untagged (in which case the numbers in the file are interpreted according to the current working space), or

▶ ignore the profile and treat the document as a Tagged document in the working space.

When you create a new document, the policies tell Photoshop to treat it as an Untagged document, or as a Tagged document in the working space.

When you move pixels between documents (by copying and pasting or by dragging), the policies tell Photoshop to move either the numerical values of the pixels or the colors those numerical values represent.

When you save a document, the policies tell Photoshop whether or not to embed the profile currently associated with the document. You can override the policy's setting for profile embedding in the Save As dialog box, but the policy dictates whether the Embed Color Profile checkbox is turned on or off when the dialog box appears.

You can set individual policies for RGB, CMYK, and grayscale images, but the policies themselves behave almost identically in each color mode. The thumbnail characterizations of the three policies are:

▶ Off means "behave like Photoshop 4."

▶ Convert to Working Space means "behave like Photoshop 5."

▶ Preserve Embedded Profiles means "behave sensibly."

If this characterization displays some bias on our part, we admit to it cheerfully. Nevertheless, there are some situations where one of the less-sophisticated policies make sense, as you'll soon see.

Off. The Off choice is somewhat misleadingly named, as there's really no way to turn color management entirely off in Photoshop CS. It is, however, pretty close to the way Photoshop behaved prior to version 5. When you set the policy for a color mode to Off, Photoshop behaves as follows:

▶ When you open a file that contains an embedded profile, Photoshop discards the embedded profile and treats the image as Untagged, *unless* the embedded profile happens to match the current working space. In that case, the image is treated as a Tagged document in its own document space, which in this case happens to be the same as the working space. If you change the working space in the Color Settings dialog box, all your Untagged images will change, taking on the new working space definition, but the Tagged images keep the old working space definition, now acting as a document space. (If you find this confusing and counterintuitive, you're not alone. We think it would be a whole lot simpler if Off simply treated all your documents as Untagged.)

▶ When you save the document, no profile is embedded (unless you turn on Embed Profile in the Save As dialog box, in which case the current working space profile is embedded), *unless* Photoshop is handling the document as a Tagged document because its embedded profile matched the working space that was in effect when it was opened. In that case, the profile that was embedded in the file when it was opened is re-embedded when you save, unless you turn off the Embed Color Profile checkbox in the Save As dialog box (see figure 5-26).

▶ When you open a file that has no embedded profile, Photoshop treats it as Untagged. When you save the document, no profile is embedded (unless you turn on Embed Color Profile in the Save As dialog box, in which case the current working space profile is embedded).

▶ When you create a new document, Photoshop treats it as Untagged. When you save the document, no profile is embedded (unless you turn on Embed Color Profile in the Save As dialog box, in which case the current working space profile is embedded).

▶ When you transfer pixels between images in the same color mode by copy and paste or by drag-and-drop, the numerical values get transferred. That means if the two documents are in different color spaces,

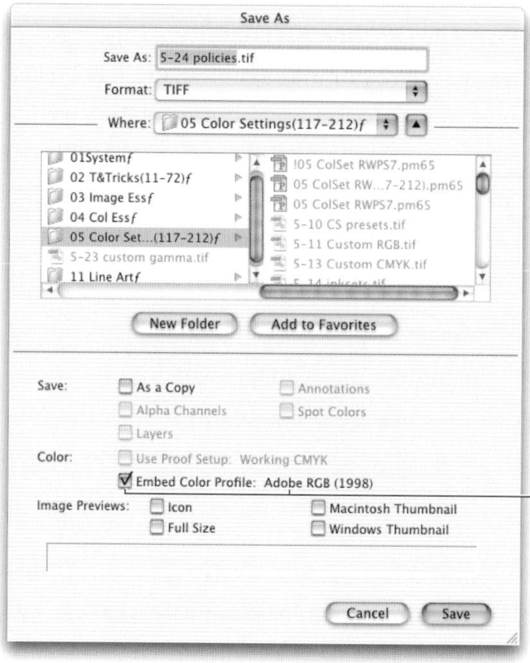

Figure 5-26
The Embed Color
Profile checkbox

You can control whether or not Photoshop embeds a profile by checking or unchecking the Embed Color Profile checkbox in the Save As dialog box. Photoshop always tells you which profile will be embedded (if you choose to embed a profile).

the colors change even though the numbers are preserved. (If the two images are in different color modes—CMYK and RGB, for instance—the color appearance is always preserved.)

Off is the policy you want if you're a dyed-in-the-wool, by-the-numbers type who has been cursing at Adobe for years for stuffing color management down your throat. Of course, you don't have to set all the policies to Off. If you're in an all-CMYK, by-the-numbers workflow, you can set the policy to Off just for CMYK, and still get the benefits of color management in the other spaces. Similarly, if your work is mostly for the Web, and you need Photoshop's RGB to behave the same as RGB in the vast majority of Web browsers, you can set the policy to Off for RGB. (Well, actually, as we noted earlier in the chapter, on the Mac you may also want to set your RGB working space to Monitor RGB to ensure that RGB in Photoshop matches RGB in your other, non-color-managed applications.)

However, if you want to use color management in Photoshop, you'll want to choose one of the other policies and simply untag documents that need to be untagged on a case-by-case basis (see "Assign Profile," later in this chapter).

Preserve Embedded Profiles. This is the third-millennium, industrial-strength color management approach. Preserve Embedded Profiles is the "safe" policy, in that it makes sure Photoshop doesn't do color conversions when you don't want it to. With this policy, the working spaces in Color Settings are there only as a convenience because each image can live in its own document space. On the other hand, it can also be the "dangerous" policy because if you're not at least a little careful, you can wind up editing images in color spaces that are wildly inappropriate for editing. For instance, if your scanner software embeds its own profile in an image, this policy might mean you're editing the image in the scanner's space, which is significantly less than optimal.

Overall, though, it's a welcome addition to Photoshop's color management, and it's the one that we typically use.

▶ When you open an image that contains an embedded profile, Photoshop preserves the profile and treats the image as Tagged, using the embedded profile as the document space (which may or may not be the current working space). When you save the document, the document space profile (the profile the image had when you opened it) is once again embedded in the saved file.

 If the embedded profile is different from the current working space, Photoshop throws up a dismissable alert telling you that the document you just opened has a different profile than your current working space (see Figure 5-27). You can just press Enter whenever you see this, but we suggest that you simply turn on the "Don't show again" checkbox the first time you see this annoying and useless dialog box. If you need a warning, you can use the Profile Mismatch warning instead (see "Profile Warnings," later in this section).

Figure 5-27
The dumb Embedded
Profile Mismatch alert

The Embedded Profile Mismatch alert isn't terribly useful. If you want to be warned about mismatched profiles, turn on the Profile Mismatch warning instead.

▶ When you open an image with no embedded profile, Photoshop treats the image as an Untagged image (it preserves the lack of an embedded profile, if you will). When you save the document, no profile is embedded (unless you turn on Embed Color Profile in the Save As dialog box, in which case the current working space profile is embedded).

▶ When you create a new document, Photoshop treats it as a Tagged document and assigns the current working space profile as the document space. When you save the document, Photoshop embeds the document space profile (even if you change the working space in the Color Settings dialog box, it has no effect on the image, which stays in the document space).

▶ When you transfer pixels between two RGB or two grayscale images (by copy and paste or drag-and-drop), the actual color gets transferred. If the two images are in different color spaces, the numbers change even though the color appearance is preserved.

▶ When you transfer pixels between two CMYK images, the numerical values get transferred. If the two CMYK documents were in different CMYK spaces, the color appearance changes even though the numbers are preserved. While this routine is the reverse of what happens with RGB and grayscale files, it is actually more logical and useful.

We believe quite strongly that Preserve Embedded Profiles is the best policy for the vast majority of Photoshop users. It keeps track of color for you and rarely performs any conversions that aren't explicitly requested (and *never* does so if you keep the Profile Mismatch warnings turned on). If you have to deal with files from many different sources, this is almost certainly the policy you want to use. It does a good job of keeping color management out of your face, but it also offers tremendous power and flexibility for hard-core color geeks.

Convert to Working Space. Convert to Working Space tells Photoshop CS to behave very much like Photoshop 5, where you're strongly encouraged, if not actually forced, to convert everything into your working RGB, CMYK, or Gray space. It tells Photoshop to convert images from their own space into the current default working space automatically. We find this method a bit too authoritarian, though if your workflow relies on picking a single RGB, CMYK, or grayscale color space and sticking to it, you'll almost certainly want to use this policy.

▶ When you open a file that already has the current working space profile embedded, Photoshop preserves the profile and treats the image as a Tagged image, using the embedded profile as the document space. When you save the document, the document space profile (the profile the image had when you opened it) is once again embedded in the saved file, even if you change the working space in the Color Settings dialog box when the image is open.

▶ When you open a file that has an embedded profile different than the current working space, Photoshop converts the image from the embedded profile's space to the current working space. From then on, it treats the image as a Tagged image, with the working space profile that was in effect when it was opened as the document space.

 Note that Photoshop alerts you with a dialog box telling you that the document you just opened isn't in the current working space, and that the current policy is to convert to the working space. You can just hit Enter, but we suggest that you turn on the "Don't show again" checkbox the first time you see this alert. If you need a warning, use the Profile Mismatch warning instead (see "Profile Warnings," later in this section). This new profile is preserved even if you change the working space while the image is open. Later, when you save the document, that profile is embedded by default.

▶ When you open an image with no embedded profile, Photoshop treats the image as Untagged. If you change the working space, Photoshop keeps the numbers in the file unchanged and reinterprets them as belonging to the new working space (so the appearance changes). When you save the document, profile embedding is turned off by default (though you can turn it on in the Save As dialog box).

▶ When you create a new document, Photoshop treats it as a Tagged document in the current working space. If you later change the working space, Photoshop preserves the working space profile that was in effect when the document was created. When you save the document, that same profile is also embedded.

▶ When you transfer pixels between two images (whether it's RGB-to-RGB, RGB-to-CMYK, or whatever), the color appearance gets transferred, even if that means Photoshop changes the numbers (which it'll have to do if the files are in different color spaces).

Convert to Working Space is a useful policy when you need to have all your images in the same space, such as when you're compositing RGB images or repurposing CMYK images from several different sources for a single output. You can think of it as an automation feature, whenever you need to convert a bunch of pictures quickly. However, unless you're very sure about what you're doing, we still think it's safer to use Preserve Embedded Profiles instead, and perform the conversions manually whenever you need to change an image's working space (see "Applying Profiles Outside Color Settings," later in this chapter).

Profile Warnings

Although they appear in the Color Management Policies section of the Color Settings dialog box, the Missing Profile and Profile Mismatch warnings operate independently from the policies. (You can think of it this way: The policy determines the initial default setting of some of the warnings.) Unless you're adamantly opposed to the use of color management, we suggest you turn all the warning checkboxes on and keep them on. They're much more useful than the dismissable, information-only alerts you get when they're turned off, because they actually allow you some choices, letting you override the default behavior of the policy you've chosen for a specific color mode.

Profile Mismatch: Ask When Opening. When Profile Mismatch: Ask When Opening is turned on, Photoshop alerts you when you open a document with an embedded profile that's different from the current working space (see Figure 5-28). Even better, this Embedded Profile Mismatch dialog box offers you three choices for handling the profile mismatch.

▶ **Use the embedded profile (instead of the working space)** tells Photoshop to keep the embedded profile, treating the document as a Tagged image in the embedded profile's space. The embedded profile is then used to display the image, and is also used as the source profile for any subsequent color conversion. This is typically what you'd want to do.

Figure 5-28
Embedded Profile
Mismatch dialog box

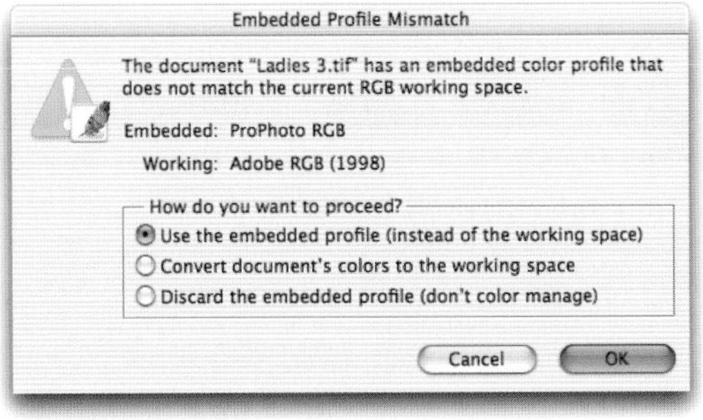

*The Embedded Profile
Mismatch warning offers
three choices for handling
images whose embedded
profile differs from the
working space.*

▶ **Convert document's colors to the working space** does what it says:
It performs a conversion from the embedded profile's space to the
current default working space. This makes sense if you need several
images in the same working space (for example, to composite them).

▶ **Discard the embedded profile (don't color manage)** strips off the
embedded profile and opens the document as an Untagged image.
The numbers in the document are left unchanged and are interpreted
according to the current working space definition. You might use this
if you know you're going to significantly edit the color and tone of the
image and you don't care about any color interpretations that were
already assigned. Similarly, this might be appropriate for an image
destined for the Web, especially if you'll be saving it in the sRGB space.
It's pretty rare that we use it, though.

The Embedded Profile Mismatch dialog box chooses one of these three
as the default (the one that you'll get if you just hit the Enter key). The
default it picks depends on the policy you've chosen for that color mode.
Of course, the dialog box always allows you to override the default behavior
for the policy on an image-by-image basis.

Profile Mismatch: Ask When Pasting. The second checkbox, Ask When
Pasting, comes into play when you move pixels between two images that
are in the same color mode, but in different color spaces (like sRGB to
AdobeRGB, or from one CMYK setup to another). When this is on, Photoshop asks you whether you want to paste the numerical values or the
color appearance (see Figure 5-29). Note that when you copy and paste
or drag-and-drop between images that are in different color modes (like
RGB to CMYK), this alert doesn't do anything because Photoshop only lets
you paste the color appearance.

Figure 5-29
Paste Profile Mismatch
dialog box

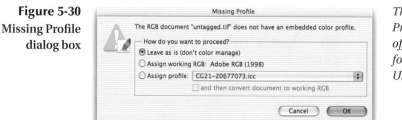

The Paste Profile Mismatch warning lets you choose whether to paste the numerical values or the perceived color those values represent.

Just to be clear: In this dialog box, "Convert (preserve color appearance)" tells Photoshop to change the numbers in the image so that you get roughly the same color. It's like doing a profile-to-profile conversion. We add the caveat "roughly" just in case a color in one profile simply cannot be represented in the gamut of the target profile. The "Don't convert (preserve color numbers)" option simply copies the numbers from the source file into the target file, without worrying about color changes. As with Profile Mismatch: Ask When Opening, the default option (the one you get if you just press Enter) is set to match the current policy for the color mode.

Missing Profile: Ask When Opening. The third warning, Missing Profile: Ask When Opening, comes into play when you open a document with no embedded profile. When this is turned on, Photoshop lets you choose how you want it to interpret the numbers in documents with no embedded profiles (see Figure 5-30).

▶ **Leave as is (don't color manage)** tells Photoshop to treat the file as an Untagged document. The numbers in the file are preserved and interpreted according to the current working space (which means that the appearance may change radically).

Figure 5-30
Missing Profile
dialog box

The Missing Profile warning offers four choices for handling Untagged images.

▶ **Assign working space** tags the document with the current working space profile. As with the previous option, the numbers in the file are preserved, and interpreted according to the current working space. The difference is that the document is treated as Tagged, so it keeps that profile if you subsequently change the working space.

▶ **Assign profile** lets you tag the document with a profile other than the working space profile. Again, the numbers in the file are preserved, but in this case they're interpreted according to the profile you choose.

▶ **Assign profile and then convert document to working space** lets you assign a source profile to the document, and then convert it to the working space. Let's say you've taken a picture with a digital camera that doesn't embed a profile. If you have a profile for the camera, you can use this option to force Photoshop to interpret the data using that profile (just choose it from the popup menu), and then automatically convert it to the current working space (because you almost certainly don't want to edit the image in the digital camera's space). This is the only option of the four that actually changes the numbers in the file.

If you're in a workflow in which you know where images are coming from and you know where they're going, you can probably turn off the warning dialogs off. When you don't need them, they do get kind of annoying after a while.

Color Settings Advanced Mode

When you turn on the Advanced Mode checkbox in the Color Settings dialog box, you gain access to further controls as well as to a wider range of profiles (we've discussed that earlier in the chapter). A few of the Advanced Mode controls can be useful in typical workflows. However, ultimately, the Advanced Mode section is a grab-bag that offers a couple of options that may be useful to a very small number of serious players, and are "hurt-me" buttons for almost everyone else.

The Conversion Options section of the dialog box lets you control useful things like Photoshop's default rendering intent and color management

Figure 5-31
Advanced Conversion
Options

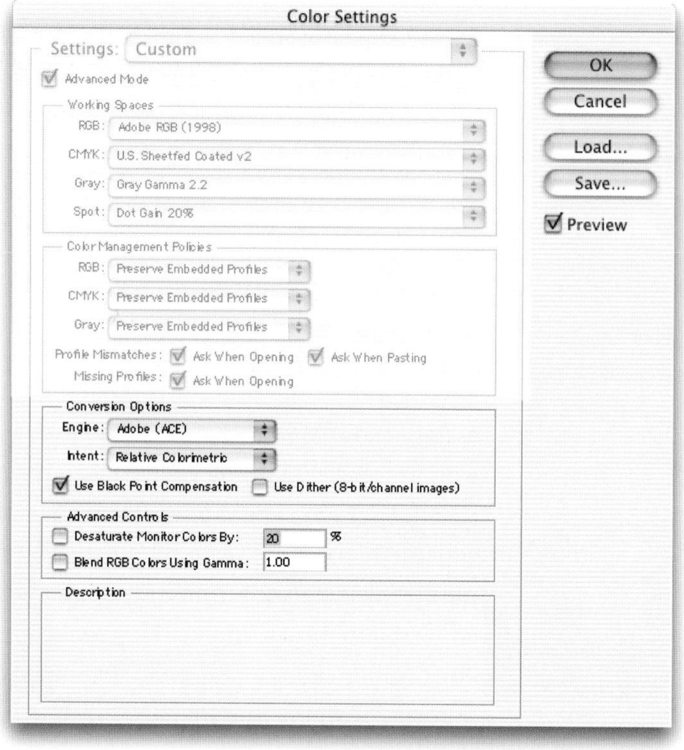

engine (CMM)—things you probably won't need to change very often, but might want to occasionally (see Figure 5-31).

Engine. The Engine popup menu lets you select the CMM that Photoshop uses for all its color space calculations. The options that appear on the menu depend on which CMMs are installed on your system. Unless you have really pressing reasons to use a different CMM, we recommend just sticking with the Adobe (ACE) engine. Bruce has found bugs in all the other CMMs he's tried (though they're pretty dang obscure), and has yet to find any in ACE. Of course, no complicated software is entirely without bugs…. The thing is, when the engines work correctly, there is only a tiny (less then 2 percent) change in pixel values with the different engines; except for the bugs, we've never noticed a visual difference.

Mac users will notice separate entries for the Apple CMM and Apple ColorSync. Apple CMM means that the Apple CMM will always be used. Apple ColorSync uses whatever CMM is set in the ColorSync System Preferences.

Intent. The Intent popup menu is significantly more useful for the average user. Intent lets you choose the default rendering intent that Photoshop uses in any of the following color space conversions:

▶ Converting documents on opening

▶ Converting documents by choosing a different mode from the Mode menu (like separating RGB to CMYK)

▶ Calculating the numbers that appear on the Info palette for color modes other than the one the document is in

Every other feature in Photoshop that lets you convert colors from one profile's space to another has its own rendering intent controls. Photoshop's default rendering intent is relative colorimetric with the sole exception of the new General Purpose Defaults, where it's perceptual. These defaults are always the subject of some pretty heated debate. We offer three observations:

▶ While some users may prefer perceptual rendering as the default choice (conventional wisdom says this is best for scanned images), relative colorimetric renderings may actually do a better job than perceptual rendering when your images don't have a lot of significant out-of-gamut colors.

▶ Photoshop's color conversions have always been relative colorimetric in the past.

▶ It's just a default. Don't get your knickers in a twist; you can always override it to suit the needs of the image at hand.

Since Photoshop CS makes it very easy to both preview and apply different rendering intents for each image, the rendering intent setting here is more a matter of convenience than of necessity.

Use Black Point Compensation. Use Black Point Compensation, when turned on, maps the black of the source profile to the black of the target profile, ensuring that the entire dynamic range of the output device is used. In many cases you'll find little if any perceptible difference whether it's turned on or off, because it depends on the contents of the particular profiles involved. See the sidebar "Black Is Black (or Is It?)" for a detailed look at the Black Point Compensation feature.

Black Is Black (or Is It?)

We usually think of black as being "just black," but of course black on different devices appears differently (solid black on newsprint is much grayer than solid black on glossy sheetfed stock, for instance). Photoshop's Black Point Compensation forces us to think about this fact. The information here is fairly complex, but the basic principle is simple. When you transform from one color space to another, there are two ways of transforming the black point: absolute and relative.

Transformations involve first mapping the source gamut to the reference color space (also known as the Profile Connection Space, or PCS), which in most cases is Lab, and then mapping the Lab values to the destination space. In a relative black-point transformation, the source black is mapped to a L* value of 0 in the PCS, but in an absolute black-point transformation, it's mapped to the actual L* value that the source device can produce, which is usually substantially higher than zero. (A zero L* value represents the total absence of any reflected light, which is blacker than anything other than a black hole can reproduce.) The ICC profiles themselves specify whether the transform should be absolute or relative.

This can lead to undesirable results. For example, Radius Color-Match RGB profiles map RGB 0,0,0 to L*a*b* 3,0,0 in the PCS. A CMYK profile that uses absolute black transformation may map to a black value in the PCS of L*a*b* 7,0,0. If you convert an RGB image to CMYK using this pair of profiles, your shadow detail will get clobbered because the first few levels in the RGB document will convert to L* values in the PCS between 3 and 7. Since these are all darker than the output device can produce, they'll be clipped to black, and your shadow detail goes bye-bye.

If the same RGB profile is used with a CMYK profile that maps device black to L*a*b* 2,0,0, you'll get very different, equally undesirable results. The RGB black will convert to L*a*b* 3,0,0, which is lighter than the black the output device can produce. The resulting image will appear slightly washed out because it contains no true blacks.

If you want a transform that uses the entire dynamic range of the output device, you need a relative black transform both from source to PCS and from PCS to output. Photoshop's Black Point Compensation forces this to happen, no matter what the profiles say. It works by estimating the black point for the source and the target.

If they're the same, as they would be if both profiles use relative black encoding, the feature does nothing. But if the black levels are different, it adds an extra processing step: After the source color is converted into the PCS, Black Point Compensation adjusts the PCS to map the source profile's black to the destination profile's black via a straightforward linear transformation of the L* values in the PCS. This ensures that the entire dynamic range of the source is mapped into the entire dynamic range of the target, without shadow clipping or washed-out blacks. Again, we now turn this on and leave it on.

While in earlier versions of Photoshop we offered a complex set of rules about when to turn this on and off, we now recommend that you just leave Use Black Point Compensation turned on at all times.

Use Dither (8-bit/channel images). The Use Dither feature is somewhat esoteric. All color space conversions in Photoshop are performed in a high-bit (16 bits per channel) space. When Use Dither is turned on, Photoshop adds a small amount of noise when the 8-bit channels are converted into the high-bit space. This makes banding or posterization much less likely to occur (that's a Good Thing). However, there are some situations where you may want to turn this feature off. If your final output is JPEG, this tiny dithering is likely to produce a larger file size (because it introduces more discrete colors into the image). Also, if you're using Photoshop for scientific work, where you need to perform quantitative analysis on colors, you should turn this off, as it will introduce noise in your data.

Desaturate Monitor Colors By. The Desaturate Monitor Colors feature attempts to solve a problem with large-gamut working spaces: Rendering to the monitor is always relative colorimetric, so colors in the working space that lie outside the monitor gamut get clipped to the nearest equivalent the monitor can display. You can think of desaturating the monitor as the poor man's perceptual rendering. (We would tell you how this works, but Earth-based humans cannot pronounce the words.) Unless you're working with a very large space like Kodak's ProPhoto RGB, don't even think about messing with this.

For those brave (or foolhardy) souls who want to experiment with it, a setting in the 12 to 15 percent range seems somewhat useful for Kodak ProPhoto RGB, and 7 to 10 percent seems good for EktaSpace. If you're working with one of these spaces, try turning the feature on and off to see if it's doing anything useful for you. Whatever you do, don't forget to turn it back off before you try to do any normal work; otherwise you'll find yourself producing excessively colorful imagery!

Blend RGB Colors Using Gamma. The Blend RGB Colors Using Gamma feature controls how RGB colors blend together. To see its effect, try painting a bright green stroke on a red background with the checkbox turned off, and then again with the checkbox turned on and the value set to a gamma of 1.0. With the checkbox turned off, the edges of the stroke have a brownish hue, as they would if you were painting with paint. With it turned on, the edges are yellowish, as they would be if you were painting with light. You can think of the behavior with the checkbox off as artistically correct, and with it turned on as colorimetrically correct. Permissible values are from 1 to 2.2.

Applying Profiles Outside Color Settings

The settings in the Color Settings dialog box represent the "fallback" position for performing color conversions. But two commands on the Mode submenu (under the Image menu) offer much more flexibility for applying profiles and performing conversions on an image-by-image basis. In fact, Bruce hardly ever converts colors (like from RGB to CMYK) using plain ol' Mode changes, because he likes to be able to preview and select the rendering intent that does the best job on the image at hand.

Assign Profile

Assign Profile lets you tag an image with a specified profile, or untag an image by removing its profile. It doesn't do any conversions; it simply attaches a description (an interpretation, as it were) to the numbers in the image, or removes one (see Figure 5-32).

Figure 5-32
Assign Profile
dialog box

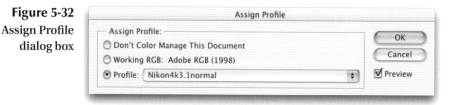

We find Assign Profile particularly useful when we're trying to decide what profile should be attached to an Untagged document. Unlike the profile assignment in the Missing Profile dialog box, Assign Profile lets you preview the results of applying various profiles. This gives you the opportunity to make an educated guess rather than a blind one.

The Assign Profile dialog box offers three options, which are identical to the first three options in the Missing Profile warning (see "Color Management Policies," earlier in this chapter).

Don't Color Manage This Document. Don't Color Manage This Document tells Photoshop to treat it as an Untagged document. The numbers in the file are preserved and are interpreted according to the current working space, and the embedded profile is stripped out. If you're delivering final CMYK to shops that are scared or confused by color management, if you're delivering images in sRGB for the Web, or if you've inadvertently embedded a profile in a calibration target, you can use this option to strip out the profile.

Assign Working Space. Assign Working Space tags the document with the current default working space profile (whatever is set in the Color Settings dialog box). As with the previous option, the numbers in the file are preserved, but reinterpreted according to the current working space. The difference is that the document is treated as Tagged, so it keeps that profile if you later change the working space. If you've opened an Untagged document and decided that it really does belong in the working space, use this option to make sure that it stays in the working space.

Assign Profile. Assign Profile lets you tag the document with a profile other than the default working space profile. Again, the numbers in the image are preserved, but in this case they're interpreted according to the profile you assigned. If you have a profile for your scanner, but the scanner uses an Acquire plug-in (so the image just shows up right in Photoshop), then you can use Assign Profile to assign color meaning to the image you've just scanned. You'll then probably want to use Convert to Profile (below) to move the image into a more reasonable editing space, like AdobeRGB.

The Preview checkbox lets you preview the results of applying or removing a profile (it's rare that we turn this off—the preview is pretty fast, even on a 2.5 GB file). That's all there is to Assign Profile—it's a handy tool that's simple to use and doesn't involve much in the way of mysteries.

Convert to Profile

Convert to Profile, as its name suggests, lets you convert a document from its profile space (or, in the case of an Untagged document, the current working space) to any other profiled space, with full control over how the conversion is done (see Figure 5-33).

The Convert to Profile dialog box displays the source profile and allows you to choose a destination profile, engine, and rendering intent. It also allows you to turn black point compensation on and off, decide whether or not to use dithering for 8-bit-per-channel images, and specify whether to flatten the image. Best of all, it lets you preview the results of the conversion correctly while the dialog box is still open.

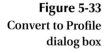

The Convert to Profile dialog box gives you full control over conversions, allowing you to choose the destination space, engine, and rendering intent.

The engine, rendering intent, black point compensation, and dithering options all work identically to those in the Advanced Mode Color Settings dialog box (see "Color Settings Advanced Mode," earlier in this chapter). A quick recap: Generally we leave the Engine set to Adobe (ACE) and turn on both Black Point Compensation and Use Dither. The Intent is image-specific; however, unless there are significant areas of the image that are out of gamut, we leave this set to Relative Colorimetric. (If there is important detail that is out of gamut, we'd probably use Perceptual.)

The Flatten Image option is there as a convenience, when you want to produce a final flat file for output. When we use Convert to Profile, we usually make a duplicate of the layered file first (choose Duplicate from the Image menu), and then run Convert to Profile on the duplicate, with Flatten Image turned on—that way we can keep our layered master files intact.

Bruce tends to use Convert to Profile instead of Mode change for most of his conversions (whether it's RGB-to-CMYK, cross-rendering CMYK-to-CMYK, or whatever), because it offers more control, and especially because it allows him to preview different rendering intents. Rendering intents only know about the color gamut of the source color space—they don't know anything about how much of that gamut is actually used by the source image—so applying perceptual rendering to an image that contains no significant out-of-gamut colors compresses the gamut unnecessarily. With Convert to Profile, you can see how the different rendering intents will affect a particular image, and choose accordingly.

Soft-Proofing Controls

If you're sane, you probably want to get some sense of what your images are going to look like before you commit to the $50,000 print run. There are three ways to proof your pictures: traditionally (print film negatives and create a laminated proof like a Matchprint), on a color printer (like one of the new breed of inkjet printers), or on screen. On screen? If you've been paying attention during this chapter, you know that you can set up your system well enough to start really trusting what you see on screen. Proofing images on screen is called *soft-proofing*, and Photoshop CS offers soft-proofing capabilities whose accuracy is limited only by the accuracy of the profiles involved.

In Photoshop CS, soft-proofing has its own set of controls, separate from the Color Settings dialog box. These allow you to preview your output accurately, whether it's RGB or CMYK. This is a huge advantage for those of us who print to RGB devices like film recorders or to those photorealistic inkjet printers that pretend so assiduously to be RGB devices that we're forced to treat them as such. But soft-proofing is a big improvement for those of us who print CMYK too, because we can soft-proof different conversions to CMYK while we're still working in RGB, and have them accurately depicted on screen. (For example, you can quickly see how the same image would look on newsprint and in your glossy brochure.)

The Proof Colors command on the View menu lets you turn soft-proofing on and off. It even has the same keyboard shortcut, Command-Y, as the old CMYK Preview it replaces. But the real magic is in the Proof Setup submenu, which governs exactly what Proof Colors shows you (see Figure 5-34). The settings you make in Proof Setup are specific to the image window that's in the foreground when you make the settings, not to the image itself. This means that you can create several views of the same image (by choosing New View from the View menu), and apply different soft-proofing settings to each view, letting you see how the image will work in different output scenarios.

The default setting for Proof Colors (what you get if you don't change anything in the Proof Setup dialog box) works as follows:

▶ It first simulates the conversion from the document's space to working CMYK, using the rendering Intent and Black Point Compensation settings specified in Color Settings.

Figure 5-34
Soft-proofing controls

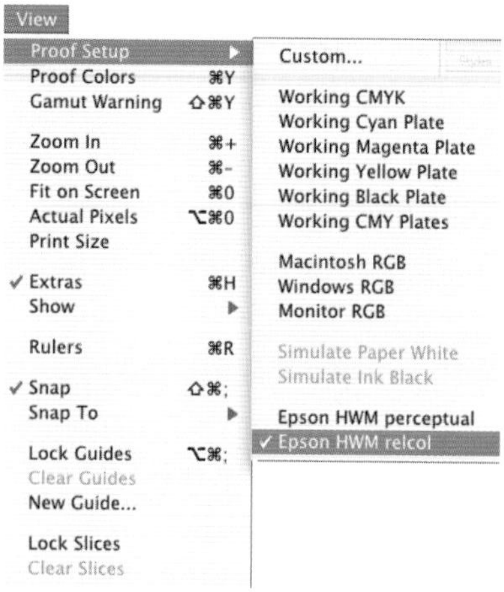

View
Proof Setup ▶
Proof Colors ⌘Y
Gamut Warning ⇧⌘Y
Zoom In ⌘+
Zoom Out ⌘–
Fit on Screen ⌘0
Actual Pixels ⌥⌘0
Print Size
✓ Extras ⌘H
Show ▶
Rulers ⌘R
✓ Snap ⇧⌘;
Snap To ▶
Lock Guides ⌥⌘;
Clear Guides
New Guide...
Lock Slices
Clear Slices

Custom...
Working CMYK
Working Cyan Plate
Working Magenta Plate
Working Yellow Plate
Working Black Plate
Working CMY Plates
Macintosh RGB
Windows RGB
Monitor RGB
Simulate Paper White
Simulate Ink Black
Epson HWM perceptual
✓ Epson HWM relcol

The Proof Setup menu lets you choose a wide variety of soft-proofing options, including your own custom settings.

▶ It then renders that simulation to the monitor using relative colorimetric rendering. If Black Point Compensation is turned on in Color Settings, it's also applied to the rendering from the proof space to the monitor.

This essentially duplicates the behavior of the old CMYK Preview, except that it's a bit more accurate (because it doesn't use an intermediate transformation from CMYK to working RGB; instead, it goes straight from working CMYK to the monitor).

However, to really unleash the power of the new soft-proofing features, you need to visit the Proof Setup dialog box, which gives you an unprecedented degree of control over your soft proofs.

Proof Setup Dialog Box

Proof Setup lets you independently control the rendering from the document's space to the proof space, and from the proof space to the screen. Ultimately, it allows you to preview accurately just about any conceivable kind of output for which you have a profile. You can open the Proof Setup dialog box by choosing Custom from the Proof Setup submenu (under the View menu; see Figure 5-35).

Setup. The Setup menu lets you recall proof setups that you've saved in the special Proofing folder. (On Mac OS X, this is the Library/Applications Support/Adobe/Color/Proofing folder. In Windows, it's in the Program Files/Common Files/Adobe/Color/Proofing folder.) You can save proof setups anywhere on your hard disk by clicking Save, and load them by

Figure 5-35
Proof Setup dialog box

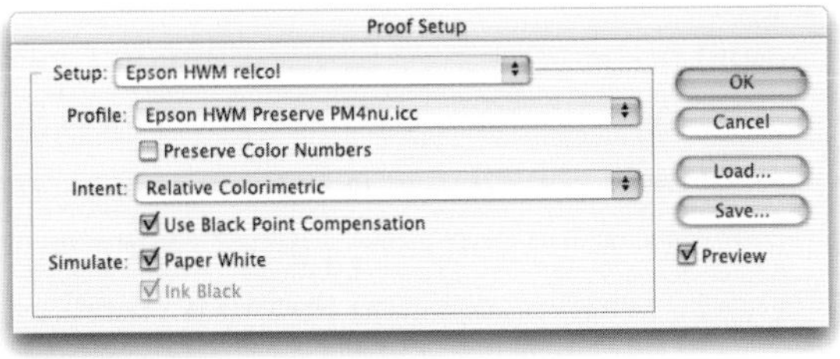

The Proof Setup dialog box lets you control conversions from document space to proofing space, and from proofing space to the monitor.

clicking the Load button, but the setups you save in the Proofing folder appear on the list automatically. (Even better, they also appear at the bottom of the Proof Setup submenu, where you can choose them directly.)

Profile. The Profile menu lets you specify the proofing space you want to simulate. You can choose any profile, but if you choose an input profile (for a scanner or digital camera), the Preserve Color Numbers checkbox becomes checked and dimmed, and all the other controls become unavailable. (We're not sure why you would choose an input profile, but we suppose it's nice to have the option.) Generally, you'll want to choose an RGB, CMYK, or grayscale output profile.

Preserve Color Numbers. The Preserve Color Numbers checkbox, when on, tells Photoshop to show you what your file would look like if you sent it to the output device without performing a color space conversion. It's available only when the image is in the same color mode as the selected profile (as when both are in RGB); when you turn it on, the Intent menu becomes unavailable, since no conversion is requested.

We've found that this feature is particularly useful when you have a CMYK file that was prepared for some other printing process. It shows you how the CMYK data will work on your output, which can help you decide whether you need to edit the image, convert it to a different CMYK space, or just send it as is. It's also useful for seeing just how crummy your image will look if you send it to your desktop inkjet printer without converting it to the proper profile (see "Converting at Print Time," later in this chapter).

Intent. The Intent popup menu lets you specify the rendering intent you want to use in the conversion from the document's space to the proof space. This is particularly useful for helping you decide whether a given image would be better served by perceptual or relative colorimetric rendering to the output space. It defaults to the Color Settings default rendering intent until you change it, whereupon it remembers what you last used. However, when you save a proof setup, your selected rendering intent is saved with it; so, if you find that you're continually being tripped up by the wrong intent, you can just save a proof setup with your preferred rendering intent.

Simulate. The checkboxes in the Simulate section—Paper White and Ink Black—control the rendering of the image from the proofing space to the monitor. When both Paper White and Ink Black are turned off, Photoshop does a relative colorimetric rendering (with black point compensation if that option is turned on in Color Settings). This rendering maps paper white to monitor white and ink black to monitor black, using the entire dynamic range of the monitor. If you're using a generic monitor profile, this is probably as good as you'll get (of course, with a canned monitor profile, you can't trust anything you see on screen anyway). With a good monitor profile, though, you should check out the alternatives.

▶ When you turn on Ink Black, it turns off black point compensation in the rendering from proof space to the monitor. As a result, the black you see on the monitor is the actual black you'll get on output. (Within limits—most monitor profiles have a "black hole" black point. The black ink simulation will be off by the amount that real monitor black differs from the monitor profile's black point. On a well-calibrated monitor, the inaccuracy is very slight.) If you're printing to a low-dynamic-range process like newsprint, or inkjet on uncoated paper, turning on Ink Black will give you a much better idea of the actual blacks you'll get in print.

▶ Turning on the Paper White checkbox makes Photoshop do an absolute colorimetric rendering from the proof space to the monitor. When you turn on Paper White, Black Ink becomes checked and dimmed, since black point compensation is always disabled in absolute colorimetric conversions. In theory at least, turning on Paper White should give you the most accurate soft-proof possible.

In practice, the most obvious effect of turning on Paper White isn't that it simulates the color of the paper, but rather that you see the compressed dynamic range of print. If you look at the image while turning on Paper White, the effect is dramatic—so much so that Bruce looks away from the monitor when he turns on Paper White, and waits a few seconds before looking at the image to allow his eyes to adapt to the new white point. He also makes sure that he hides any white user interface elements, so that his eyes *can* adapt.

Obviously the quality of the soft-proofing simulation depends on the accuracy of your monitor calibration and on the quality of your profiles. But we believe that the relationship between the image on screen and the final printed output is, like all proofing relationships, one that you must learn. We've never seen a proofing system short of an actual press proof that really matches the final printed piece—laminated film proofs, for example, often show greater contrast than the press sheet, and may have a slight color cast too, but most people in the print industry have learned to discount the slight differences between proof and finished piece.

It's also worth bearing in mind the limitations of the color science on which the whole ICC color management effort is based. We still have a great deal to learn about color perception, and while the science we have works surprisingly well in many situations, it's only a model (see the sidebar "CIE Limitations and Soft Proofing"). The bottom line is that each of the different soft-proofing renderings to the monitor can tell you something about your printed images. We recommend that you experiment with the settings and learn what works for you and what doesn't.

Proof Setup Submenu

The Proof Setup submenu (under the View menu) contains several other useful commands that we should discuss. For instance, when you're viewing an RGB or grayscale image, you can view the individual CMYK plates (or the CMY progressive) you'd get if you converted to CMYK via the Mode submenu (in the Image menu). You can also use these commands to view the individual plates in CMYK files, but it's much faster and easier to use the keyboard shortcuts to display individual channels, or click on the eyeballs in the Channels palette.

The next set of commands—Macintosh RGB, Windows RGB, and Monitor RGB—is available only for RGB, grayscale, and indexed color images, not for CMYK or Lab. They show you how your image would appear on a "typical" Macintosh monitor (as defined by the Apple RGB profile), a "typical" Windows monitor (as defined by the sRGB profile), and on your

CIE Limitations and Soft Proofing

All ICC color management is based on the system of mathematical models developed by the Commission Internationale de L'Éclairage (CIE), starting with CIE XYZ (1931), and including later variants such as CIE Lab and CIE xyY. These models were all developed with a very specific purpose in mind, which was to predict the degree to which two solid swatches of reflective material of a specific size on a specific background at a specific distance under a known illuminant would appear to match.

By design, the CIE models ignore many of the contextual effects that modulate our color perception, such as surround color, simultaneous contrast, and the dozens of effects named after the color scientists (Abney, Hunt, Stevens, Bezold-Brücke, and Bartleson-Breneman, to name but a few) who documented them. For solid colors viewed under tightly controlled conditions, these effects don't matter much, but for pixels in images, they almost certainly come into play. Moreover, the CIE models were never designed for cross-media comparisons like that between a monitor and hard copy.

We know quite a lot about white point adaptation—the tendency of our perceptual system to see the brightest thing in the scene as white—but science knows relatively little about black point adaptation, which is very likely equally important in soft-proofing. It's not that CIE color-imetry is wrong, just that we've taken to applying the CIE models to situations for which they weren't designed. With our current understanding of color perception, it's probably unrealistic to expect an exact match between an image on a monitor and a hard copy of that same image, because we experience them differently. But Photoshop's soft proofs are better than any other we've seen, and with a little experience, we believe you'll be able to make important judgements about your printed images based on what you see on your monitor with Proof Colors turned on.

---

personal monitor (as defined by your monitor profile) if you displayed it on these monitors with no color management. These might be useful when producing Web graphics, for instance.

The Simulate Paper White and Simulate Ink Black commands are available for documents that are in profile spaces that actually contain paper white and ink black information (most, but not all output profiles for RGB, CMYK, or grayscale). If these commands are dimmed, either the document isn't in an output space or the output profile doesn't contain the necessary information.

The Simulate Paper White and Simulate Ink Black commands do the same things as the Paper White and Ink Black checkboxes in the Proof Setup dialog box; they change the default rendering from an output space to your monitor from relative colorimetric with black point compensation to relative colorimetric without black point compensation (Simulate Ink

Black), or to absolute colorimetric (Simulate Paper White). The rest of the menu lists custom proof setups saved in the Proofing folder.

Photoshop's soft-proofing features let you see how your image will really appear on output, so you can optimize the image to give the best possible rendition in the selected output space. They also help you to be lazy by letting you see if the same master file can produce acceptable results on all the output conditions to which you plan on sending it, relying on color management to handle the various conversions. So whether you're a driven artist seeking perfection, or a lowly production grunt doing the impossible on a daily basis, Photoshop's soft-proofing tools will become an invaluable addition to your toolbox.

Converting at Print Time

Photoshop lets you perform color conversions as it sends the data to a printer—converting from the working space to a selected printer profile using a selected rendering intent, or from the document space to your Proof Setup space using the rendering intent in Proof Setup, and then to the printer profile using the intent you specify while printing.

The latter lets you print an RGB file to a composite printer and make it simulate the CMYK output you've been soft-proofing—that is, it gives you a hard copy of your soft-proofed image without your having to first convert the image to final output CMYK. The Print with Preview command lets you exercise either of these options.

Print with Preview

We cover most of the cool new features in Print with Preview (choose Print with Preview from the File menu, or press Command-Option-P) in Chapter 17, *Output Methods;* however, we'll cover the color management aspects of the dialog box here. These features let you use color management to control the color that gets sent to the printer.

To use the color management features in the Print with Preview dialog box, turn on the Show More Options checkbox and choose Color Management from the unnamed menu that appears immediately below the checkbox (see Figure 5-36).

The color management options let you set source and target spaces and a rendering intent to convert the data that's sent to the printer.

Figure 5-36
Print with Preview Color
Management controls

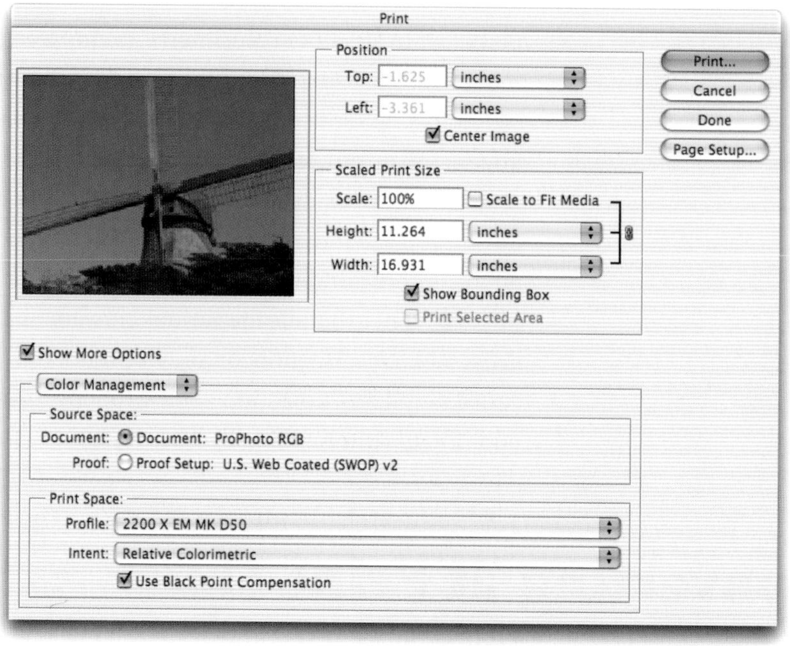

The dialog box is titled Print, but it's really Photoshop's Print with Preview...

Source Space. The Source Space radio buttons let you choose the Document space (to reproduce the image as well as your printer allows) or the Proof space (to produce a hard copy of your soft-proof simulation). If the image window from which you're printing has a custom proof setup, it will appear as the Proof option; otherwise you get Working CMYK.

Print Space. The Print Space popup menus let you choose a print profile and a rendering intent for the conversion. In addition to all your installed profiles, the Profile menu offers two additional options:

▶ **Same As Source** sends the source data unconverted. Use this option if you've already converted the image to the output space.

▶ **PostScript Color Management** (or Printer Color Management in the case of non-PostScript printers) sends the source data along with the profile that describes it. Use this option if you want the printer, rather than Photoshop, to manage the color. Color-managing CMYK images on PostScript printers requires PostScript 3—on a PostScript Level 2 printer, choose Lab Color instead—and PostScript color management varies enormously. Use it at your own risk.

Intent. The Intent popup menu lets you specify the rendering intent from the Source Space to the Print Space. If you use Proof as your Source Space, the rendering intent you chose in Proof Setup is used to convert from the Document space to the Proof space, and the rendering intent you choose in Print with Preview controls the conversion from the Proof space to the Print space.

Print

All the color management options you set up in Print with Preview are applied by Photoshop to the data that gets sent to the printer driver. You won't see any trace of them in the Print dialog box. If you use Print with Preview to convert the image for output, make sure that you don't have another conversion specified in the Print dialog box—otherwise you'll get a double correction and a nasty print.

The print color management features allow you to control your printing precisely—whether you're trying to reproduce an original image as exactly as possible, or to make your printer simulate all sorts of other output conditions—from a single master RGB source file. This helps you by saving time and by cutting down on the number of different versions you need to prepare for a given image.

Isolating Variables

The information in this chapter may seem insanely complex, and to some extent it is. The important thing to keep in mind is that you're dealing with several independent variables. Before you change one of them, make sure you know what you're changing and why you're changing it. As you gain experience working with a particular press or output device, examine the results closely and see where you can improve things. Your first print job may prove disappointing, but your second one should be better, and the third one should be better still. If we could afford to print everything twice, life would be easy!

6 Tonal Correction Fundamentals

Stretching and Squeezing the Bits

Tonal manipulation—adjusting the lightness or darkness of your images—is one of Photoshop's most powerful and far-reaching capabilities, and sometimes it can seem like magic. But really, there's nothing magical about it. Once you understand how tonal manipulation is done—it all comes back to those ubiquitous zeros and ones—it starts to look downright pedestrian. But your increased understanding of how Photoshop works (and more important, your ability to spend more time playing around) should more than make up for any loss of the sense of wonder.

Tonal manipulation is the key to setting the right contrast for images. It makes the difference between a flat image that lies lifeless on the page and one that pops, drawing you into it. And tonal correction is the central method for avoiding those dark, muddy images that you're forever seeing produced using Photoshop.

But the role of tonal correction goes far beyond that. When you correct the color balance in an image, you're really doing tonal manipulation on the color channels. And when you work with masks and alpha channels, you'll find that much of their power stems from the ability to use Photoshop's tonal controls to isolate objects from their background, emphasize edges, or control the intensity of filters and other effects.

In fact, just about every edit you make in Photoshop involves tonal manipulation. In Chapter 9, *The Digital Darkroom*, we'll show you some

229

more esoteric techniques for doing so, but in this chapter we'll concentrate on the fundamentals—the basic tonal manipulation tools and their effects on pixels. In this chapter we'll talk exclusively about grayscale images, but you'll use the same tools to perform both tonal and color correction on color images, so it's important that you get acquainted with them on an intimate basis.

Stretching and Squeezing the Bits

If you're working with images in Photoshop, they're probably made up of one or more 8-bit channels, in which each pixel is represented by a value from 0 (black) to 255 (white). Grayscale images have one such channel, while color images have three (RGB or Lab) or four (CMYK). If you're more adventurous, you may work with *high-bit* images, where each channel uses 16 bits per pixel to represent a value from 0 (black) to 32,768 (white).

The key thing to bear in mind is that when you use Photoshop's tonal controls, you're stretching and squeezing various parts of the tonal range, and in doing so, you inevitably lose some information. A key point to understand is that you lose a great deal more information in 8-bit-per-channel files than you do in high-bit ones. To demonstrate this, try the following simple experiment.

1. Create a new grayscale file in Photoshop, 7 inches wide by 5 inches tall, at 72 dpi, in 8-bit mode.

2. Use the Gradient tool to create a horizontal gradient from black to white across the entire width of the image (it's the third gradient in the default Gradients palette in the Options bar).

3. Choose Levels (from the Adjust submenu under the Image menu), change the gamma (the middle Input setting) to 2.2, and click OK (see Figure 6-1). You'll notice that the midtones are much lighter, but you may already be able to see some banding in the shadows.

4. Choose Levels again, and change the gamma to 0.5. The midtones are back almost to where you started, but you should be able to see that, instead of a smooth gradation, you have some distinct bands in the image (see Figure 6-2).

Figure 6-1
Adjusting
the gamma

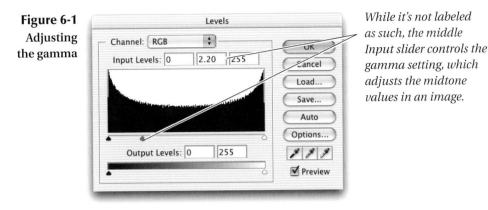

While it's not labeled
as such, the middle
Input slider controls the
gamma setting, which
adjusts the midtone
values in an image.

What happened here? With the first gamma adjustment, you lightened the midtones—stretching the shadows and compressing the highlights. With the second gamma adjustment, you darkened the midtones—stretching the highlights and compressing the shadows.

Figure 6-2
Data loss due to
tonal correction

While the effect of
successive tonal-
correction moves on
images may be subtle, the
effect on the data within
the image—as expressed
in the histogram—
is profound.

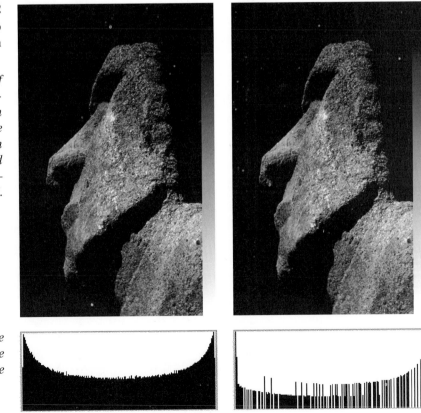

Histogram for the
gray wedge at the
right side of the image

Before tonal correction   *After two gamma moves*

But with all that stretching and squeezing, you lost some of the levels. Instead of a smooth blend, with pixels occupying every value from 0 to 255, some of those levels became unpopulated—in fact, if we're counting right, some 76 levels are no longer being used.

If you repeat the pair of gamma adjustments, you'll see that each time you make an adjustment, the banding becomes more obvious as you lose more and more tonal information. Repeating the gamma adjustments half a dozen times will give you a file that contains only 55 gray levels instead of 256. And once you've lost that information, there's no way to bring it back.

Now repeat the experiment, but create a 16-bit-per-channel file instead of an 8-bit one (in the New dialog box, choose 16-bit from the menu to the right of the Color Mode popup menu). The difference in the result is dramatic, as shown in Figure 6-3.

Figure 6-3
Data loss due to
tonal correction

With a high-bit file, you still lose some data, but the effect is much less drastic, as shown by the histogram of the edited image. The lesson is that high-bit files give you much more editing headroom than do 8-bit-per-channel ones.

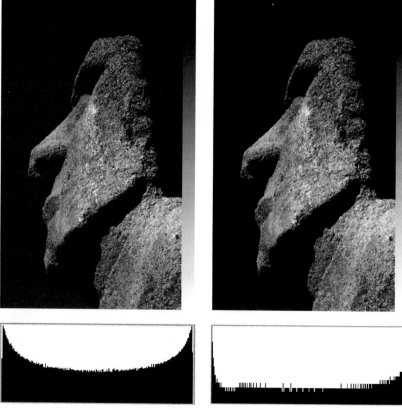

Histogram for the gray wedge at the right side of the image

Before tonal correction   *After two gamma moves*

Data Loss in Perspective

This loss of image information may seem scarier than it really is. Most corrections you make to images are less drastic than in the previous example. Nonetheless, this simple demonstration should serve to hammer home the following lessons and the ensuing pieces of advice.

▶ All tonal manipulations incur some data loss.

▶ Once the data is gone, you can't bring it back.

▶ You lose much less data making corrections in high-bit mode.

▶ Successive tonal manipulations lose data at an increasing rate.

Get good data to begin with. If you've got a high-bit capture device, (which you almost certainly do), it's better to get the image as close to "right" as you possibly can while the image is in high-bit form. The whole point of high-bit capture is to let you manipulate the high-bit data, so that you get the *right* 8-bit data when you downsample to 8 bits per channel.

Use adjustment layers. You can avoid the penalties incurred by successive corrections and cover yourself by using an adjustment layer instead of applying the changes directly to the image. Adjustment layers use more RAM and create bigger files, but the increased flexibility makes the trade-off worthwhile. But since the various tools offered in adjustment layers operate identically to the way they work on flat files, we're going to discuss how the features (Curves, Levels, Hue/Saturation, and so on) work on flat files first. For a detailed discussion of adjustment layers, see Chapter 9, *The Digital Darkroom*.

Use high-bit data. If your scanner or camera allows it, you can bring the 10-, 12-, 14-, or 16-bit-per-channel data directly into Photoshop—you are, in effect, telling your capture device "just give me all the data you can capture"—and then edit it in Photoshop. In the 16-bit-per-channel space, you have much more editing headroom before you run into posterization. Photoshop CS lets you do just about anything to a high-bit file that you can do to an 8-bit one, so the main reason for downsampling is to keep file sizes managable. If you bring digital captures into Photoshop using Camera Raw, note that Camera Raw always operates on the high-bit data.

Difference Is Detail: Tonal-Correction Issues

What do we mean when we talk about image information? Very simply, adjacent pixels with different values constitute image detail. If the difference is very slight, you won't be able to see it (especially in shadows); but it's there, waiting to be exploited. You can accentuate those differences—making those adjacent pixels *more* different—to bring out the detail.

The color of noise. Difference isn't always detail, though. Low-cost scanners, and digital cameras shot at high speeds, introduce spurious differences between pixels (see Figure 6-4). Those differences aren't detail, they're just noise (like static on the radio that drowns out the weather report), and they're one of our least favorite things. Photoshop can't tell the difference between genuine image information and device-induced noise. You need to decide what is desirable detail and what's noise, accentuating the detail while minimizing the noise.

Posterization. Noise isn't the only problem to deal with when you're doing tonal correction, though. There's also *posterization*—the stair-stepping of gray levels in distinct, visible jumps rather than smooth gradations (see Figure 6-5).

Unless you're working with a high-bit image, Photoshop gives you only 256 possible values for a gray pixel. When you start making dark pixels more different, you eventually make them *so* different that the image looks splotchy—covered with

Figure 6-4 What noise looks like

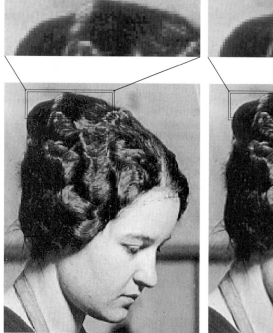

A dirty scan. This type of noise poses problems during tonal correction.

A cleaner scan makes it much easier to adjust tone.

Minimize tonal correction. Small tonal moves are much less destructive than big ones. The more you want to change an image, the more compromises you'll have to make to avoid obvious posterization, artifacts due to noise, and loss of highlight and shadow detail.

Figure 6-5 The effects of posterization

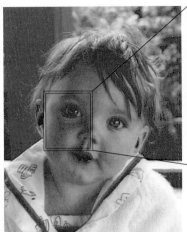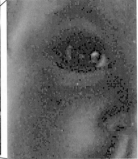

patches of distinctly different pixels rather than smooth transitions. This is a problem especially with noisy images, because those distinct patches may be noise, not detail. And the posterization is accentuated by sharpening.

Lost highlight detail. When you accentuate detail in one part of the tonal range, making slightly different pixels more different (*expanding* the range), you lose detail in other areas, making slightly different pixels more similar (*compressing* the range).

For instance, when you stretch the shadow values apart to bring out shadow detail, you inevita-

bly squeeze the highlight values together (see Figure 6-6). If you make two different pixels the same, that detail is gone forever. That's what we mean in real-world terms when we say that information is "lost."

Photoshop's tonal controls allow you to improve your images immeasurably, but they'll also let you wreck an image irreparably. Various clichés come to mind— you can't make a silk purse out of a sow's ear, there's no such thing as a free lunch, and so on—but however you slice it, *any* tonal manipulation you do in Photoshop throws away some image information. The trick is to make the image look better than it did before, even though it contains less information (which is what this book is about).

Figure 6-6 Loss of highlight detail

Bringing out shadow detail with tonal correction inevitably loses some highlight detail.

Before tonal correction   *After tonal correction*

Be decisive, or use adjustment layers. If you push an edit too far, don't try to correct it with a second edit—go back and fix the problem. On a flat file, you can use History to step back and fix the problem. With adjustment layers, you have the freedom to keep changing your mind right up to the point where you flatten the image.

Cover yourself. Since the data you lose is irretrievable, you should try to leave yourself a way out by working on a copy of the file, by saving your tonal adjustments in progress separately (without applying them to the image) by applying your edits using adjustment layers, or by using any combination of the above. Or you can use the History feature to leave yourself an escape route—just remember that History only remembers the number of states you specify in general preferences, and it can consume mind-boggling amounts of RAM, particularly if you autocreate snapshots in high-bit files.

Data loss can be good. Sometimes you want to throw away information. For example, none of these restrictions applies when you're working on masks or alpha channels—in fact, you usually *want* to throw away data on those, since you're often trying to exaggerate a feature or isolate it from its background. (See "Step-by-Step Silhouettes" in Chapter 8, *Selections and Channels.*)

With these caveats in mind, let's look at Photoshop's tonal-manipulation tools.

Tonal-Correction Tools

Almost everything you need to do to tone your images can be accomplished using only four of Photoshop's tools.

▶ Histogram palette

▶ Info palette

▶ Levels dialog box

▶ Curves dialog box

The Histogram and Info palettes let you analyze the image and the effect of your tonal manipulations. Levels and Curves are the tools you use to actually make the adjustments (if you're still using Brightness/Contrast, check out the sidebar "The Nonlinear Advantage," later in this chapter). These four tools simply offer different ways of viewing and changing the same data.

The Histogram Palette

A *histogram* is a simple bar chart that plots the levels from 0 to 255 along the horizontal axis, and the number of pixels at each level along the vertical axis (see Figure 6-7). If there are lots of pixels in shadow areas, the bars are concentrated on the left; the reverse is true with "high-key" images, where most of the information is in the highlights.

Some of the information offered by the Histogram palette may not seem particularly useful—for most image reproduction tasks you really don't need to know the median pixel value, or how many pixels in the image are at level 33. But histograms show some very useful information at a glance.

Figure 6-7
Histogram
palette

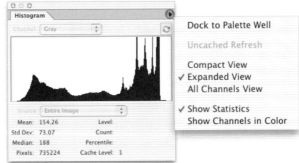

Highlight and Shadow Clipping

With a quick look at the histogram, you can immediately see whether or not your scanner has clipped the highlights or shadows (see Figure 6-8). If there's a spike at either end of the histogram, the highlight or shadow values are almost certainly clipped—we say "almost" because there are some images that really do have a very large number of pure white or solid black areas. But they're pretty rare.

Figure 6-8
Highlight and
shadow clipping

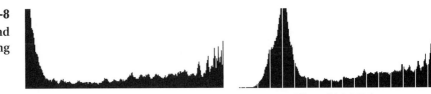

Clipped shadows   *Clipped highlights*

How Much Information is Present?

The overall appearance of the histogram also gives you a quick, rough-and-ready picture of the integrity of your image data (see Figure 6-9). A good scan uses the entire tonal range, and has a histogram with smooth contours. The actual location of the peaks and valleys depends entirely on the image content, but if the histogram shows obvious spikes, you're probably dealing with a noisy scanner. If it shows a comb-like appearance, it's likely that the image has already been manipulated—perhaps by your scanning software.

Figure 6-9
Comb-like histogram suggesting a noisy (or previously manipulated) image

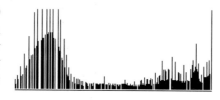

The histogram also shows you where to examine the image for signs that you've gone too far in your tonal manipulations. If you look at the histograms produced by the earlier experiment in applying gamma adjustments to a gradient, you can see at a glance exactly what each successive adjustment did to the image—spikes and gaps start to appear throughout the histogram.

Note that a gap of only one level is almost certainly unnoticeable in the image—especially if it's in the shadows or midtones—but once you start to see gaps of three or more levels, you may begin to notice visible posterization in the image. The location of the gap gives you a good idea of where in the tonal range the posterization is happening.

Histograms Are Generalizations

Once you've edited an image, the histogram may look pretty ugly. This is normal; in fact, it's almost inevitable. The histogram is only a guide, not a rule. Histograms are most useful for evaluating raw captures. A histogram will show clipped endpoints and missing levels, but a good-looking histogram isn't necessarily the sign of a good raw image. And an image with a bad histogram can still look good.

Fixing the histogram doesn't mean you've fixed the image. We have plenty of tricks that will make the histogram look better: smoothing out the peaks and filling in the gaps (resampling the image), or rotating the image clockwise, then counterclockwise by the same amount will do it, for example (as will a Gaussian Blur). But none of those tricks brings back image detail that was lost through overly aggressive tone manipulation. They just interpolate pixels in the missing levels, based on the data that's left. You can use tricks to salvage a posterized image when there's really no other alternative, but it's better to avoid the posterization in the first place. Extract what useful information you can from the histogram, but don't let yourself be ruled by it.

Our next tool, however, is very specific. It tells you exactly what's happening to a specific pixel or group of pixels in the image.

Tip: Don't Forget to Refresh the Histogram. For performance reasons, while you work on an image, the Histogram palette shows you values based on the antialiased screen display of your image. This view can hide posterization, giving you an unrealistically rosy picture of your data. Photoshop warns you of this by displaying a warning icon when the histogram is showing you an approximation of your data. To see what's really going on, click the Refresh button in the Histogram palette. (See Figure 6-10.)

Figure 6-10
Histogram
warning

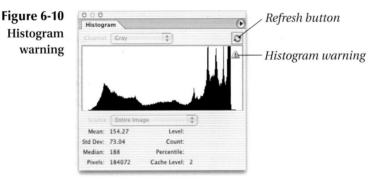

Refresh button

Histogram warning

The Info Palette

Like the Histogram palette, the Info palette is purely an informational display. It doesn't let you do anything to the image besides analyze its contents. But whereas the Histogram palette shows a general picture of the entire file, the Info palette lets you analyze *specific* points in the image.

When you move the cursor across the image, the Info palette displays the pixel value under the cursor and its location in the image. More important, when you have one of the tonal- or color-correction dialog boxes (such as Levels or Curves) open, the Info palette displays the values for the pixel before and after the transformation (see Figure 6-11).

Figure 6-11
Info palette

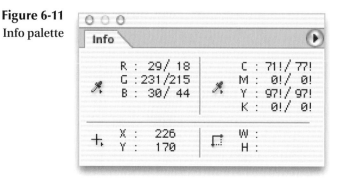

When you're working in one of the Adjust dialog boxes, such as Levels or Curves, the Info palette shows the pixel value before and after the correction.

Tip: Look for Differences. The Info palette lets you sample the actual values of different pixels, but it also lets you hunt down hidden detail, particularly in deep shadows and bright highlights where it can be hard to see on the monitor. Move the cursor over a deep shadow, and watch the Info palette. If the numbers *change* as you move the cursor, there's difference lurking in there—it may be detail waiting to be exploited or it may be noise that you'll need to suppress, but *something is* hiding in there.

Palette Options

You can control what sorts of information the Info palette displays in one of two ways. First, you can select Palette Options from the Info palette's popout menu (see Figure 6-12). The second method is to use the Info palette's hidden popup menus (see Figure 6-13). We have several different palette setups that we use for different kinds of work, and we use the Workspace feature, which captures the Info palette settings in addition to all the other palette locations, to load them as needed (see "Workspaces" in Chapter 2, *Essential Photoshop Tips and Tricks*).

For grayscale, duotone, or multichannel images, we generally set the First Color Readout to RGB, and the Second Color Readout to Actual Color. (Actual Color causes the readout method to change, depending on what type of image you're viewing.) We just about always display the mouse coordinates as pixels, because it makes it easier for us to return consistently to the same spot in the image.

Figure 6-12
The Info palette's Info
Options dialog box

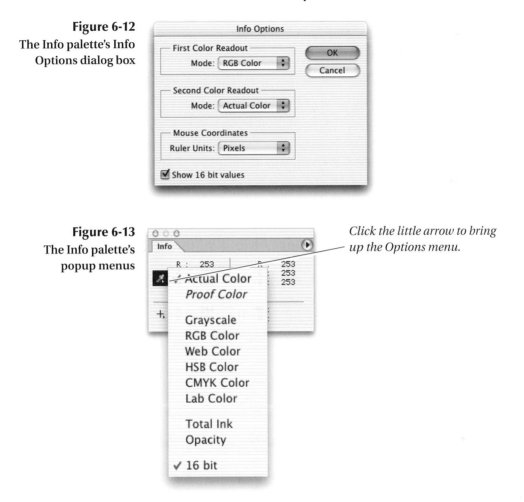

Figure 6-13
The Info palette's
popup menus

*Click the little arrow to bring
up the Options menu.*

Why display RGB values for a grayscale image? Simply for the precision. Grayscale and Total Ink show percentages instead, on a scale of 100 instead of 255. For outrageous precision, Photoshop CS even displays the 16-bit values—ranging from 0 to 32,768—when you work on high-bit files. (If these numbers make your head explode, you're not alone! We'd really like to be able to see the 8-bit and 16-bit values side by side, at least until we get used to thinking of midtone gray as 16,384.) The numbers for R, G, and B are always the same in a grayscale image, so the level just displays three times. Setting the second readout to Actual Color lets you read the dot percentage, so you can display levels and percentages at the same time. We use different setups for color, which we cover in Chapter 7, *Color Correction Fundamentals.*

Now let's look at the tools you can use to actually change the image.

Levels and Curves

Levels and Curves are the two fundamental Photoshop tools for global tonal and color correction. Levels is the easier of the two for beginning Photoshop users, and (in some situations) for experienced ones, too. Curves is a little more difficult to master, but a lot more powerful. We liken Levels to an automatic transmission and Curves to a stick shift. Levels is quick and easy. Curves lets you do all the same things (and more), but it demands a bit more skill, coordination, and experience.

Levels and Curves let you change existing (input) pixel values to new (output) pixel values—but they offer different ways of controlling the relationship between input and output. They share an important property that differentiates them from the Brightness and Contrast controls: They let you apply nonlinear transformations, instead of the linear transformations applied by the Brightness and Contrast controls (see the sidebar "The Nonlinear Advantage," later in this chapter).

Levels

Photoshop's Levels command opens a tonal-manipulation powerhouse (see Figure 6-14). For grayscale images, it's often the only tonal manipulation feature we use. This deceptively simple little dialog box lets you identify the shadow and highlight points in the image, limit the highlight and shadow dot percentages, and make dramatic changes to the midtones,

Figure 6-14
How Levels works

This tonal range is being expanded…

This tonal range is being compressed…

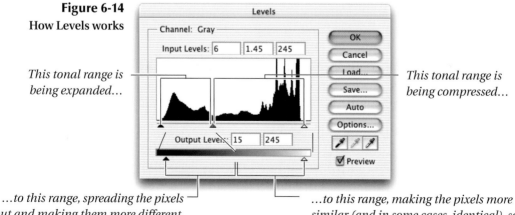

…to this range, spreading the pixels out and making them more different, so detail is more apparent.

…to this range, making the pixels more similar (and in some cases, identical), so detail is less visible or completely lost.

The Nonlinear Advantage

Linear transformations (such as those applied by Brightness/Contrast) discard your image's information, and they do so in a pretty dumb way. They're called linear transformations because they do exactly the same thing to each pixel in the image. If you're trying to modify the brightness or contrast of an image, using Brightness/Contrast is a bad idea, because you lose detail at one or both ends of the tonal range and probably do severe violence to the image in the process.

For example, the Brightness control simply shifts all the pixel values up or down the tonal range. Let's say you increase Brightness by 10. Photoshop adds 10 to every pixel's value, so value 0 becomes 10, 190 becomes 200, and every pixel with a value of 245 or above becomes 255 (you can't go above 255). This is called "clipping the highlights" (they're all the same value, so there's no highlight detail). Plus, your shadows go flat because you lose all your true blacks.

The Contrast control stretches the tonal range as you increase the contrast, throwing away information in both the highlights and the shadows (and potentially posterizing the tones in between); and it compresses the tonal range when you reduce the contrast, so either way, you lose gray levels.

Don't use the Brightness and Contrast controls on images! You can use them to good effect with channels and masks, but that's another story.

The nonlinear transformations applied by Levels and Curves throw away some image information too (losing some highlight detail, in most cases), but they don't discard nearly as much, and they do it in a more intelligent way (see Figure 6-15). They let you adjust the values in the middle of the tonal range without losing the information at the ends, so you can improve your images dramatically while still preserving vital highlight and shadow detail.

Figure 6-15 Linear versus nonlinear correction

| Uncorrected | Brightened | Increased contrast | Corrected with Levels |

while providing real-time feedback via the on-screen image and the Info palette. For more detailed tonal corrections, we use the Curves command instead; but there are a couple of things that we can only do in Levels, and for a considerable amount of grayscale work, it's all we need.

The Levels dialog box not only displays a histogram of the image, it lets you work with the histogram in very useful ways. If you understand what the histogram shows, the workings of the Levels controls suddenly become a lot less mysterious.

Input Levels

The three Input Levels sliders let you change the black point, the white point, and the gamma in the image. As you move the sliders, the numbers in the corresponding Input Levels fields change, so if you know what you're doing, you can type in the numbers directly. But we still use the sliders most of the time, because they provide real-time feedback—by changing the image on screen—as we drag them. Here's what they actually do.

Black- and white-point sliders. Moving these sliders in toward the center has the effect of increasing the overall contrast of the image. When you move the black-point slider away from its default position at 0 (zero) to a higher level, you're telling Photoshop to turn all the pixels at that level and lower (those to the left) to level 0 (black), and stretch all the levels to the right of the slider to fill the entire tonal range from 0 to 255.

A look at the histogram in Figure 6-16 shows that the tweak clips some extreme shadow details, but increases contrast and detail in the remaining shadows (as a result, a few gaps appear in the histogram).

Moving the white-point slider does the same thing to the other end of the tonal range. As you move it from its default position at level 255 (white) to a lower level, you're telling Photoshop to turn all the pixels at that level and higher (those to the right of the slider) to level 255 (white), and stretch all the levels to the left of the slider to fill the tonal range from 0 to 255.

Gamma slider. The gamma slider lets you alter the midtones without changing the highlight and shadow points. When you move the gamma slider, you're telling Photoshop where you want the midtone gray value (50-percent gray, or level 128) to be. If you move it to the left, the image gets lighter, because you're choosing a value that's darker than 128 and making it 128. As you do so, the shadows get stretched to fill up that part of the tonal range, and the highlights get squeezed together (see Figure 6-17).

Conversely, if you move the slider to the right, the image gets darker because you're choosing a lighter value and telling Photoshop to change it to level 128. The highlights get stretched, and the shadow values get

Figure 6-16 Black- and white-point tweaks

*These pixels
go black...*   *...and these
                              go white.*

*Postcorrection histogram,
displaying some black- and
white-point clipping*

squeezed together. (David likes to think of this as grabbing a rubber band on both ends and in the middle, and pulling the middle part to the left or right; one side gets stretched out, and the other side gets bunched up.)

If you make too large a gamma correction, you end up with obvious posterization where levels get stretched too far apart; but smaller moves (less than 1.4) are very effective. You may be forced to make larger corrections with images from low-cost capture devices, but that's just one of the trade-offs inherent in digital imaging.

Figure 6-17
Gamma tweak

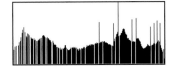

*Adding a gamma adjustment of
1.2 to the image in the previous
figure brings out some shadow
detail, though highlight detail is
lost, and the histogram displays
some additional combing.*

Output Levels

The Output Levels controls let you compress the tonal range of the image into fewer than the entire 256 possible gray levels. Mostly, they're useful for final optimization—setting the maximum shadow and minimum highlight dot on grayscale images without *specular highlights* (the small, very bright reflections you get from glass or highly polished metal)—and for editing masks. If you know that the press for which the image is destined can't hold a dot smaller than 5 percent, for example, you can compress the tonal range so that the brightest pixels have a value of level 242, corresponding to a 5-percent dot on the press.

When we have a grayscale image where we want small specular highlights to blow out to white paper, we use the black and white eyedroppers instead, and we use them later in the image-editing process (after sharpening). But even then, if we're dealing with a low-quality reproduction medium like newsprint—where the minimum highlight dot is more like 8 percent—we use the Output Levels sliders to do some preliminary tonal compression, then use the eyedroppers for fine tuning. (In color work, we don't use the Output sliders because good ICC profiles do much of the work for us—though we may still fine-tune with the eyedroppers.)

Black Output Levels. When this slider is at its default setting of 0, pixels in the image at level 0 will remain at level 0. As you increase the value of the slider, it limits the darkest pixels in the image to the level at which it's set.

This is different from the behavior of the black *Input* Levels control, which actually clips the data: If you set the black Input Levels slider to 5, then all pixels at levels 0 through 5 turn to level 0. If you set the black *Output* Levels slider to 5, on the other hand, the loss is from compression rather than clipping; the pixels that were at level 0 go to level 5, those at level 1 go to level 6 (or thereabouts), and so on. You lose contrast and some image detail as the tonal range gets compressed, but this is quite different from clipping the black input levels.

White Output Levels. This behaves the same way as the black Output Levels slider, except that it limits the lightest pixels in the image rather than the darkest ones. Setting the slider to level 240, for instance, will turn all the pixels at level 255 to 240, and so on (see Figure 6-18).

You might think that compressing the tonal range would fill in those gaps in the histogram caused by gamma and endpoint tweaks, and to a

Figure 6-18
Output levels

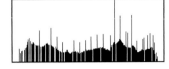

Compressing the tonal range with the Output sliders to the limits of the printing process (we used 12 and 243—about 5 and 95 percent) makes the darkest shadow detail more visible while reducing contrast overall.

It also points out the limitations of this targeting approach with images that include specular highlights (or headlights). They go gray.

limited extent it will; but all that number crunching introduces rounding errors, so you'll still see some levels going unused.

Tip: Leave Some Room When Setting Limits. Always leave yourself some room to move when you set input and output limits, particularly in the highlights. If you move the white input slider so that your highlight detail starts at level 254, with your specular highlights at level 255, you run into two problems.

▶ When you compress the tonal range for final optimization, your specular highlights go gray.

▶ When you sharpen, some of the highlight detail blows out to white.

To avoid these problems, try to keep your significant highlight detail below level 250. Shadow clipping is less critical, but keeping the unoptimized shadow detail in the 5 to 10 range is a safe way to go.

Likewise, unless your image has no true whites or blacks, leave some headroom when you set the output limits. For example, if your press can't hold a dot smaller than 10 percent, don't set the output limit to level 230. If you're optimizing with the output sliders in Levels, set it to 232 or 233 so you get true whites in the printed piece. If you'll be optimizing later with the eyedroppers or Curves, set it somewhere around 237 or 240. This lets you fine-tune specular highlights using the eyedroppers or Curves, but brings the image's tonal range into the range that the press can handle.

Levels Command Goodies

There are a few very useful features in the Levels dialog box that aren't immediately obvious. But they can be huge time-savers.

Preview. When you turn on the Preview checkbox in the Levels dialog box, Photoshop redraws the image—or the part of the image that is selected—to reflect any Levels tweaks you've made, so you can see the effect before you click OK.

Instant before-and-after. In any mode, you can see instant before-and-afters by turning the Preview checkbox on and off. (This is true in any Photoshop dialog box that has a Preview checkbox.)

Black-point/white-point clipping display. Black-point and white-point clipping is the one feature that keeps us coming back to Levels instead of relying entirely on Curves to make tonal adjustments. Long ago, this was pretty much a Mac-only feature since it relied on video LUT animation, but it's now built right into Photoshop on all platforms. Even better, it works with Levels adjustment layers, too. It doesn't work in Lab, CMYK, Indexed Color, or Bitmap modes—just Grayscale, RGB, Duotone, and Multichannel—but it's immensely useful.

When you set the black and white points, you typically want to set the white point to the lightest area that contains detail, and the shadow to the darkest point that contains detail. These aren't always easy to see. Hold down the Option key while moving the black or white Input Levels sliders to see exactly which pixels are being clipped (see Figure 6-19).

Tip: Look for the Jumps When Clipping. When you're Option/Alt-dragging the input sliders to view the clipping display, watch out for big clumps of pixels turning on or off. You generally want to stay outside of these clumps of image pixels, because moving past them removes a lot of detail.

These types of jumps are also what we look for when we're evaluating scans and scanners. A good scan gives you a smooth growth of pixels as you Option-move the sliders. Lesser-quality scanners tend to provide scans with distinct jumps between gray levels.

Figure 6-19
The clipping
display in Levels

*Holding down Option
as you move the left and
right input sliders shows
which pixels are being
clipped to white or (in
this illustration) black.
The display is really
handy for setting white
and black points, but it's
useful in many other sit-
uations as well.*

Input Levels: 24 | 1.00 | 255

Input Levels: 48 | 1.00 | 255

Input Levels: 72 | 1.00 | 255

Auto. Auto Levels and Auto Contrast work identically on grayscale images, though they differ in their handling of color ones. For grayscale, we advise avoiding both unless you want to auto-wreck your images. They automatically move the black and white input sliders to clip a pre-determined amount of data separately on each channel. If you have a large number of images that you know will benefit from a preliminary round of black and white clipping, you *may* want to consider running Auto Levels, but you'll probably want to reduce the default clipping percentages from 0.50 percent to something lower (the minimum is 0.01 percent). To change the clipping percentage, click the Options button, and enter your desired percentages in the dialog box that appears.

Auto-reset. If you hold down the Option key, the Cancel button changes to Reset (if you click this, all the settings return to their default states).

   We'll take you through the process of using Levels to correct an image a little later in this chapter, but first we'll look at the other major tonal-manipulation tool: Curves.

Curves

As we said earlier, if Levels is an automatic transmission, Curves is a stick shift. It's indispensable when you're stuck in the snow or mud, but it takes a bit more effort to master. The Curves command offers a different way of stretching and squeezing the bits, one that's more powerful than Levels. But it also uses a different way of looking at the data.

When you use Levels, the histogram shows you the shape of the data you're working with. Curves doesn't do that (except through the Histogram palette). Instead, it displays a graph that plots the relationship between input level and output level (unaltered and altered). Input levels run along the bottom, and output values run along the side. When you first choose the Curves command, the graph displays a straight 45-degree line—for each input level, the output level is identical (see Figure 6-20).

Curves versus Levels. Anything you can do in the Levels dialog box, you can also do with Curves (see Figure 6-21). When you move the middle input slider in Levels to adjust the gamma, for instance, it's almost the same as moving the midpoint of the curve right or left. Setting the other four sliders is equivalent to setting the endpoints of the curve.

Tone curves are probably the most useful global image-manipulation tool ever invented—they're indispensable for color correction, but they're also very useful for fine control over grayscale work. Gamma corrections

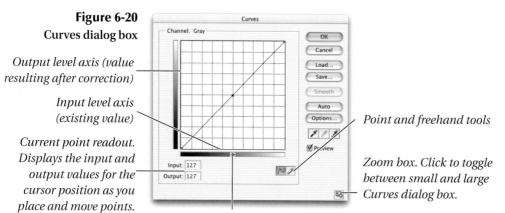

Figure 6-20
Curves dialog box

Output level axis (value resulting after correction)

Input level axis (existing value)

Current point readout. Displays the input and output values for the cursor position as you place and move points.

Point and freehand tools

Zoom box. Click to toggle between small and large Curves dialog box.

Percentage/levels selector. Click to toggle between black on the left, with level readouts (0–256), and black on the right, with percent readouts (0–100).

Figure 6-21
Levels and Curves

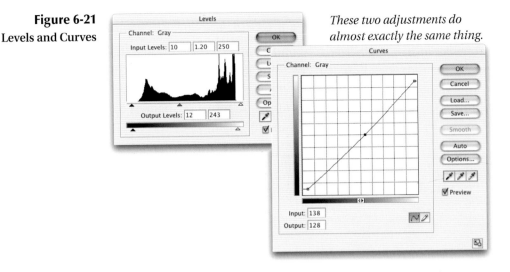

These two adjustments do almost exactly the same thing.

like the one in Levels let you change the broad distribution of midtones, but they only let you create very basic curves ("move the 50-percent point to here") with two endpoints and a single midpoint. Curves lets you make very precise adjustments to specific parts of the tonal range.

You change the relationship between input level and output level by changing the shape of the curve, either by placing points or by drawing a curve freehand (with the pencil tool). We vastly prefer placing points on the curve to drawing freehand, because it's much easier to be precise that way. All the settings you can make with Levels—white point, black point, midtones, maximum shadow, and minimum highlight—you can make with Curves too, but the way you go about it is slightly different.

Before we get into adjusting curves, though, there are a couple of ways to customize the Curves dialog box to your preferred way of working.

Tip: Customizing the Curves Dialog Box. Some people are happy thinking of tone in terms of levels from 0 to 255. Others want to work with dot percentages. The Curves dialog allows you to switch from one to the other by clicking the arrowheads in the middle of the gray ramp.

When you display levels, the 0,0 shadow point is at the lower left and the 255,255 highlight point is at the upper right. When you display using percentages, the 0,0 highlight point is at the lower left and the 100,100 shadow point is at the upper right. You can switch freely between the two modes at any time.

Tip: Change the Grid. You can also change the gridlines of the Curves dialog box. The default displays gridlines in 25-percent increments, but if you Option-click anywhere in the graph area, the gridlines display in 10-percent increments instead (see Figure 6-22). The 25-percent grid lets prepress folks think in terms of shadow, three-quarter-tone, midtone, quarter-tone, and highlight, while the 10-percent grid provides photographers with a reasonable simulation of the Zone System.

Figure 6-22
Changing the grid
in Curves

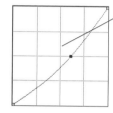

Option-click anywhere in the grid area to toggle between 25-percent and 10-percent gridlines.

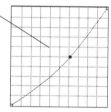

The curve. The great power of the Curves command comes from the fact that you aren't limited to placing just one point on the curve. You can actually place up to 16 curve points, though we rarely need that many. This lets you change the shape of the curve as well as its steepness (remember, steepness is contrast; the steeper an area of the curve, the more definition you're pulling out between pixel values).

For example, an S-shaped curve increases contrast in the midtones, without blowing out the highlights or plugging up the shadows (see Figure 6-23). On the other hand, it sacrifices highlight and shadow detail by compressing those regions. We often use a small bump on the highlight end of the curve to stretch the highlights, or on the shadow end of the curve to open up the extreme shadows.

The info readout. Whenever you move the cursor into the graph area, the Input and Output levels display (at the bottom of the dialog box) changes

Figure 6-23
S-curves

More contrast

Less contrast

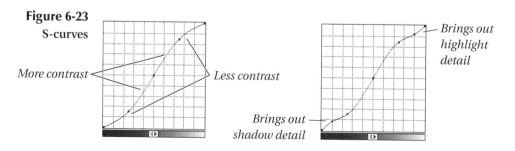

Brings out highlight detail

Brings out shadow detail

to reflect the cursor's x,y coordinates on the graph. For example, if you place the cursor at Input 128, Output 102 and click, the curve changes its shape to pass through that point, and the readouts become editable fields. All the pixels that were at level 128 change to level 102, and the rest of the midtones are darkened correspondingly (see Figure 6-24).

Figure 6-24
The numeric entry fields

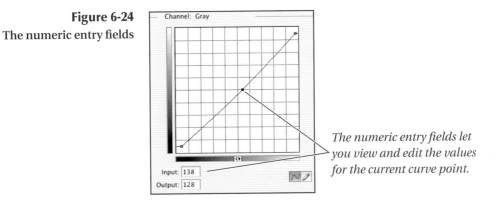

The numeric entry fields let you view and edit the values for the current curve point.

Taking the midpoint of the curve and moving it left or right is analogous to moving the gamma slider in Levels. You can follow the shape of the curve with the cursor, and watch the info readout to determine exactly what's happening to each level.

Handling black and white points. You can clip the black or white points by moving the endpoints of the curve horizontally toward the center of the graph (just like moving the input sliders in Levels; see Figure 6-25). For instance, if you move the black end of the curve directly to the right so that the info readout reads Input 12, Output 0, you've clipped all the pixels at level 12 or below and made them all level 0. This is exactly the same as moving the black input slider in Levels from 0 to 12.

Figure 6-25
Clipping and compressing in Curves

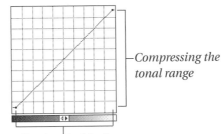

Compressing the tonal range

Clipping the black and white pixels

You can also limit the highlight and shadow dots by moving the endpoints of the curve vertically toward the center of the graph (like moving the output sliders in the Levels dialog box). For example, to limit the highlight dot to 5 percent, move the highlight end of the curve until the Output level displays as 243—or (if you're displaying percentages) 5 percent.

The eyedropper. While the Curves dialog box lacks the black and white clipping displays of Levels, it has an extra cool feature that shows you at a glance where any point in the image lies on the tonal curve. When the Curves dialog box is open, the cursor automatically switches to the eyedropper when you move it over the image. If you hold down the mouse button, the info display in the Curves dialog shows the input and output levels of the pixel(s) under the eyedropper, and a hollow white circle shows the location of that point on the curve (see Figure 6-26). This makes it very easy to identify the levels in the regions you want to change, and to see just how much you're changing them.

For some reason the eyedropper feature doesn't work when you're adjusting the composite (CMYK) channel in a CMYK image, though it does when you're adjusting individual channels.

Automatic curve point placement. A nifty feature in Curves is automatic curve point placement. When you Command-click in the image, Photoshop automatically places a point on the curve for the input value of the pixel on which you clicked. Once the point is placed, you can adjust it by dragging, by pressing the arrow keys, or by using the following tip.

Tip: Numeric Curve Entry. An equally nifty feature in Curves is that you can specify curve points numerically. We use this in two ways:

▶ When we know the input and output values we want, we place a curve point by clicking anywhere on the curve, type in the input value, press Tab to move to the Output field, and type in the output value.

▶ When we want to set a specific point in the image to a specific output value, we Command-click on the image to place the curve point, and then we press Tab and type in the output value.

Figure 6-26
Curves dialog
with eyedropper

The circular marker shows
the position on the curve of
the current pixel value.

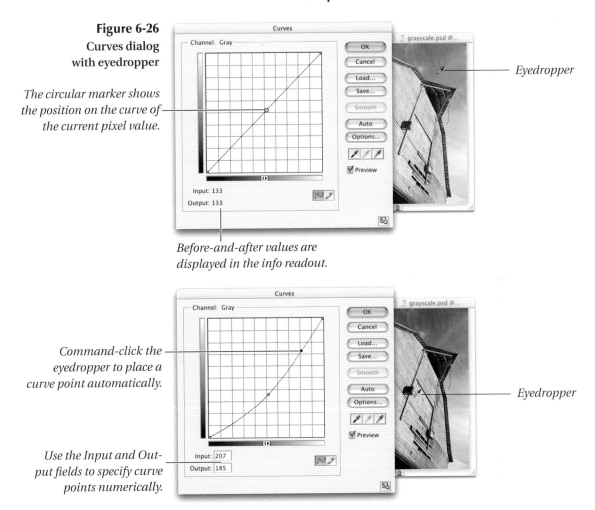

Eyedropper

Before-and-after values are
displayed in the info readout.

Command-click the
eyedropper to place a
curve point automatically.

Eyedropper

Use the Input and Out-
put fields to specify curve
points numerically.

Other Curves command goodies. Like Levels, Curves has some hidden goodies. The Preview feature and the instant before-and-after work exactly the same as in Levels, as do the Auto and Options buttons, and the Option/Alt key provides the same auto-reset feature—Option-click Cancel to reset the curve. Mac users can press Control-Tab to cycle through the points on the curve, selecting the next one with each press—there doesn't seem to be an equivalent Windows shortcut, alas. We'll take you through the process of using Curves to correct an image a little later in this chapter, but first let's look at those oft-misunderstood yet extremely useful little critters, the black and white eyedropper tools.

White Points and Black Points and Grays, Oh My!

Correcting grayscale images is only half the battle. You also have to optimize them—you have to compensate for the shortcomings of the output process the images are aimed at. If you're going to an output process other than halftone printing, optimizing grayscale images is simply a matter of matching the contrast of your image to the contrast behavior of the output device. But when the image is destined for print, you have to do two things.

▶ Set the endpoints of the tonal range so that your highlights don't blow out and your shadows don't plug up.

▶ Adjust your midtones to compensate for dot gain on press.

You can build in these adjustments while you correct flaws in the image, or you can perform them as a separate step after you've fixed all the other problems in the image. With color work, ICC profiles do a lot of the work for you, but reliable grayscale profiles are still somewhat rarer than hens' teeth.

Endpoints and limits. Some people use the terms *white point* and *minimum highlight*, or the terms *black point* and *maximum shadow* interchangeably. But an important distinction can be drawn between the two.

▶ The white point and black point are defined by the image itself. They're simply the lightest and darkest pixels in the image, often but not always levels 255 and 0, respectively.

▶ The minimum highlight and maximum shadow values, on the other hand, are dictated by the limitations of your output process. Each combination of printing press, ink, and paper has limits for both the smallest and largest dots it can print. Dots that are too small don't print (you get white paper instead), because the ink doesn't adhere to the plate. Dots that are too large simply plug up and print as solid ink coverage. In either case, the detail in those areas is lost, because the differences between adjacent pixels are gone—they're all black or white.

Setting Endpoints with Levels

In some cases, you can simply set your white point to the value that you know will produce the minimum highlight dot, and your black point to the maximum shadow dot. With many images, however, the white and black points need to lie inside or outside of the printable range.

True blacks and whites. If the image has detail all the way up to the level-255 highlight and all the way down to the level-0 shadow, you can simply set these values to your minimum highlight and maximum shadow dots. To do so, use the Output Levels sliders in Levels (see Figure 6-27).

For example, if you know that a particular press can handle a minimum highlight dot of 5 percent and a maximum shadow dot of 95 percent, you can set the white Output slider to 243 and the black Output slider to 13. This ensures that all your gray values fall into the range the press can reproduce.

This approach works fine for many images, but it can cause difficulties with images that have important detail in the highlights or shadows.

Highlight problems. One source of trouble in setting the highlight is the *transition zone*—the point at which the press can no longer handle a dot and simply drops out to white paper. It's especially problematic with newsprint (or desktop laser printers), where the minimum dot is often quite large—in the region of 10 percent or so.

We see a lot of newspaper images where highlights on faces appear as large, leprous white patches, or where skies have huge white holes in them.

Figure 6-27
Setting endpoints
with Levels

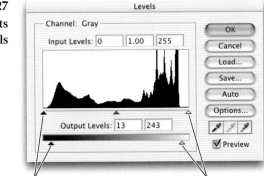

Pixels at level 0
change to level 13
(a 95-percent dot).

Pixels at level 255
change to level 243
(a 5-percent dot).

The jump from white paper to a 10-percent dot is sudden and obvious, so when you're dealing with output that has a large minimum dot size, you often want to be a little more conservative and set the minimum dot even larger. The trade-off is that you lose contrast, because the brightest areas in the image are still being reproduced as a 10-percent gray (see Figure 6-28).

Shadow problems. If you set the black point in your image to the maximum shadow dot, and the image has significant detail in the shadows stretching up through level 20 or so, the image will appear flat when it prints, because there will be very little true, solid black in the shadows.

You can deal with this using Levels by setting the black Output slider to a lower value than the maximum dot that the press can produce. For example, if the press plugs up at anything over 85 percent, instead of setting the black Output slider to 38, you may want to set it to 35 instead. You'll sacrifice some shadow detail, but the overall contrast will be much improved.

Specular highlights. The compress-the-output-levels approach outlined here works well in many images, but it doesn't work well at all when the image contains small specular highlights—the very bright highlights that appear on shiny surfaces such as glass, metal, or a well-polished apple. If you compress this type of image with the normal output controls, you'll

Figure 6-28
Trouble in the
transition zone

Because of the sudden jump from no dot to a 10-percent dot, images printed to newsprint can display a severe case of "highlight psoriasis."

To emphasize the newsprint effect, we've printed this image with an 85-lpi screen.

get a flat, low-contrast look. Your images will have much more snap on the page if you let those highlights blow out to white paper, rather than print with the minimum dot. You want to reserve the minimum dot for those parts of the image that are very bright but still contain some detail.

You can do this with the Output sliders in Levels, but not with any great degree of precision. If you set the white Output slider to a value a little higher than the minimum highlight dot, the very brightest pixels in the image will blow out to white paper. But you won't really know just how much highlight detail is going to blow out, or which parts of the image will actually print with the minimum highlight dot.

You can also run into problems with the transition zone in newsprint. The specular highlights *may* drop out to white. It's equally likely, though, that some will and some won't. Fortunately, Photoshop offers some more precise ways of setting endpoints; we'll look at those next.

Setting Endpoints with the Eyedropper Tools

When you're dealing with specular highlights, you want to set the minimum highlight dot to a level a little darker than the absolute whites in your image. You want the minimum highlight dot to reproduce the lightest parts of the image that still hold detail, and let the small specular highlights blow out to white paper.

The same holds true for deep shadows, though to a much lesser extent. In theory, the maximum shadow dot is the point at which the press plugs up the dots and prints solid ink. In practice, this isn't a hard-and-fast rule. If the press can only print a 95-percent dot and you have a few theoretically unprintable 97-percent dots sprinkled in your shadows, they'll probably provide a little more texture than if you simply set a 95-percent limit.

Photoshop's black and white eyedropper tools (in both the Levels and Curves dialog boxes) let you set your minimum highlight and maximum shadow dots very accurately. These tools are shrouded in mystery and provoke more than their fair share of confusion, in part because they can do so many things. For a detailed description of what the eyedroppers do, see the sidebar "The Math Behind the Eyedroppers," later in this chapter.

Eyedropper confusion. Many people find the eyedropper tools in the Levels and Curves dialog boxes so confusing that they give up on them after trying them once or twice. Others believe that they're as useless as Brightness and Contrast. There are four sources for the confusion.

▶ The tools give misleading feedback. When you use them, they move the Levels sliders or change the endpoints of the curve in Curves. But those changes *don't reflect what the eyedroppers are really doing!* If you try to duplicate their effect by moving the sliders or changing the curve, you get a different result. This is incredibly frustrating, because you have to ignore the signals the dialog box is giving you.

▶ Using either eyedropper sets the tonal curve to a straight line, so if you make a Levels or Curves tweak and then use the eyedroppers, your tweak is immediately undone. If you use the eyedroppers first, and then do a Levels or Curves tweak, you're likely to change what you did with the eyedroppers!

▶ People keep trying to use these tools for tonal correction rather than optimization. Since they're designed to make small tonal moves, the larger moves involved in tonal correction tend to push their limits.

▶ While they live in the Levels and Curves dialog boxes, which apply non-linear transformations, these tools apply a linear transformation. Nonetheless, this linear transformation is not necessarily bad.

Nevertheless, once you understand how and when to use them, the eyedroppers let you set your minimum and maximum dots very precisely.

What the eyedroppers do. The black, white, and gray eyedroppers do similar things, but each is specialized to operate on a different part of the tonal range. For now, we'll discuss the black and white eyedroppers. The gray eyedropper is a color-correction tool—it isn't available for grayscale images—so we'll deal with it in the next chapter, *Color Correction Fundamentals*.

Each eyedropper lets you choose a target color and a source color. All pixels in the image with the value of the source color are turned to the value of the target color, and all the other pixels in the image are changed proportionally. The black eyedropper operates on the shadows without affecting the highlights, while the white eyedropper operates on the highlights without affecting the shadows.

The Math Behind the Eyedroppers

For the terminally curious, or for those who want to know exactly what will happen to each value in the image, this is what the two eyedroppers do.

White eyedropper. The white eyedropper simply multiplies all the pixels in the image by *target value ÷ source value*. For example, if we choose a target value of 243 (a 5-percent dot) and click the tool on a pixel with a value of 248, all pixels at level 248 are turned to level 243. All the other values in the image are multiplied by 243 ÷ 248, or approximately 0.98.

So pixels with an input value of 255 produce an output value of 250, because 255 × 0.98 = 249.85. Pixels with an input value of 128 produce an output value of 125, and so on down the tonal range until you get to level 25, which remains unchanged (because 25 × 0.98 = 24.5, which gets rounded back up to 25).

If you make a much smaller move by choosing a source value of 246 and a target of 243, the multiplier is 0.99, so an input value of 255 produces an output value of 253, 128 produces an output value of 127, and values below 50 remain unchanged.

Note that you can use the white eyedropper to stretch the highlights (rather than compress them) by choosing a source color that's darker than the target color. This produces a multiplier with a value greater than 1, so the pixel values are increased rather than decreased.

Black eyedropper. The black eyedropper essentially does the reverse of the white eyedropper, but the arithmetic is a little more complicated. To limit the effect to the shadows, the algorithm uses the inverse brightnesses of the input value and of the difference between source and target color—the inverse brightness of any value x is 255-x.

If we call the difference between source and target values y, then for each pixel value x, the output value equals (($(255-x)$ ÷ (255-y) 2 y) + x.

If this makes your head hurt, don't worry—the net result is very similar to that produced by the white eyedropper, only in reverse. The source value is changed to the target value, and all other values in the image change proportionally, with the change becoming progressively smaller as you go toward the highlights.

The advantage they offer over the other methods of tonal compression is that they let you set a specific pixel value *other than black or white* to the minimum and maximum dot values the press can hold. Thus you can hold detail in highlight areas while still letting your specular highlights blow out, and maintain texture in deep shadows without making them go flat.

Using the eyedroppers. You can use the eyedroppers from either the Levels or the Curves dialog box, but we prefer using Levels, because of the cool black-point/white-point clipping display in the Levels dialog box. This tool makes it much easier to identify good candidate values for black and white source colors, and to find pixels in the image that have those values. Follow these steps:

1. Set the target value by double-clicking the black or white eyedropper and entering the value in the color picker that appears. You can specify the color in any color space, but for grayscale images, just enter identical values for red, green, and blue, or use the Brightness field.

   Set the target black and white colors to the maximum shadow and minimum highlight values that the output process can handle. For example, a target black value of 13 and a target white value of 243 correspond to a 95-percent maximum shadow dot and a minimum 5-percent highlight dot (as Brightness values, they would be 5 and 95, respectively).

2. Option-drag the black or white Input Levels slider, and note the value at which detail starts to appear. Make sure you return the Input Levels sliders to their original places (at 0 and 255).

3. Now comes the tricky part: Find a pixel in the image with that exact value, and click it with the eyedropper. Photoshop changes that pixel to the output value and compresses or expands the tonal range to compensate for that change.

   This takes a little practice. Use the clipping display in Levels to get a general idea of where to look, check values in the Info palette as you go, and if necessary zoom in and out using Command-spacebar and Command-Option-spacebar, or Command-plus and Command-minus.

Tip: Use a Gray Wedge to Select Your Source Color. It's easy to identify the value where your highlight detail really lies using the clipping display in Levels. It's much harder to find a pixel with that value to set as the source, using the eyedropper tool. Fortunately, you can pick up the source color for the eyedropper from any open image—it doesn't have to be in the active image.

To make it easy to find source values, keep a file containing a gray wedge open while you're targeting images.

1. Create a 300-pixel-wide, 72-ppi image, and use the Gradient tool to fill it with a ramp from black to white; turn off dithering first in the Options bar.

2. Use the clipping display to identify the value you want to select for the source pixel. For this example, let's assume your highlight detail goes up to level 252.

3. Select an eyedropper and, while holding down the mouse button, drag the white eyedropper through the gray wedge until the Info palette reads 252. Release the mouse button, and you've picked up your source value. Just make sure you don't make the gray wedge the active image, or you'll change it instead of the image you were working on.

Tip: Keep the Mouse Button Down. If you're picking up the source value from the active image, it's still handy to hold down the mouse button while searching for the perfect pixel. When you find the one you want, you can just release the mouse button to select it. When the cursor hits the edge of the window, the image autoscrolls, which is sometimes useful.

Depending on where you click the eyedropper, the Input or Output sliders may move (or if you're in Curves, the endpoints of the curve may change). *Ignore this feedback*—it doesn't provide an accurate picture of what's going on. Trust the values in the Info palette instead.

If you don't like the result, or if you click on the wrong pixel by accident, you can click on another pixel to undo the bad tweak and apply another one. To undo both a black and a white eyedropper tweak, hold down the Option key to change the Cancel button in the dialog box to Reset. The changes aren't made permanent until you click OK to close the Levels (or Curves) dialog box.

Setting Endpoints with Curves

The beauty of using the white eyedropper tool to set the minimum highlight dot is that it lets values brighter than the one you select as the source color fade out softly to white paper. But in some situations, that can also be its biggest liability. If you're dealing with newsprint or low-quality web printing, the transition zone—that ambiguous area between white paper and the minimum reliable dot—can make your specular highlights messy and inconsistent. Some may drop out, while others may print with a fairly large dot.

This calls for a more desperate remedy: using the pencil tool in the Curves dialog box. (It's actually just about the only time we use the pencil tool in Curves.) You need to make a curve that sets your brightest highlight detail to the minimum highlight dot value, and then blows everything brighter than that directly out to white. This is a two-step process.

1. Select the highlight point by clicking it, then use the numeric fields to set your input point to a value corresponding to your brightest real detail, and an output value corresponding to your minimum printable dot. Figure 6-29 shows a point that sets the input value at 253 and the output value at 231, corresponding to a 10-percent dot. (This is an extreme case.)

   This sets all the pixels with a value of 253 to 231. Unfortunately, it also sets pixels with values of 253 through 255 to 231, which isn't what you want. You want them to be white.

2. Select the pencil tool, and *very carefully* position it at the top edge of the curve graph, until the input value reads 253 and the output value reads 255, then click the mouse button. (See Figure 6-29.)

   This keeps pixels with an input value of 252 set to an output value of 231, but blows out pixels with a value of 253 through 255 to white paper. Your highlight detail will print with a reliable dot, and your specular highlights will definitely blow out.

Click the Save button to save the curve. Don't click the Smooth button, because it will smooth the curve—which in this case is not what you want.

When to Set the Endpoints

Conventional wisdom usually dictates that sharpening your image is either the very last thing you do, or (with RGB color images) the second-to-last step before converting it to CMYK. But conventional wisdom predates Photoshop. We think it's crazy to set your endpoints before sharpening the image, because sharpening with Unsharp Mask always increases contrast at the ends of the tonal range, forcing some pixels to black or white. In short, it undoes your work in setting the endpoints.

No matter which method you use to set your endpoints, we strongly recommend that you do so after you've applied Unsharp Mask. For a deeper discussion on sharpening your images, see Chapter 10, *Sharpening*.

Figure 6-29
Blowing out
the speculars

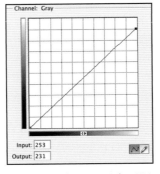

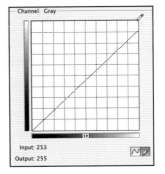

*A curve point at 253 in, 231
out compresses the image to
the printable range.*

*A little touchup with the
pencil tool makes all the
white pixels white.*

Compensating for Dot Gain

The second part of targeting your images is compensating for dot gain. In older versions of Photoshop, the mechanism for modelling dot gain on grayscale images was complicated and drove us to all sorts of esoteric tricks. In Photoshop CS, grayscale is a first-class citizen with its own gamma or dot gain setting. In the Color Settings dialog box, you can create and load custom dot gains and dot gain curves for Gray (see "Dot Gain: Coping with Midtone Spread," "Custom Dot Gain," and "Custom Gray" in Chapter 5, *Color Settings*). If you've actually measured a dot gain curve for the black ink, and your monitor gamma is correctly reflected by your monitor profile, your display of grayscale images should be a very close match to the printed result.

If you've simply measured the dot gain and entered a single value, you may still need to tune the highlights and possibly the three-quarter-tones. The best cure for this is to measure the dot area for the black ink and create a dot gain curve. Failing that, you have two choices.

▶ Change the image data itself.

▶ Use a transfer function and Save as EPS.

The latter approach has the advantage of not changing the original image data, and it allows you to compensate for dot gain very precisely (though no more so than building a dot gain curve for the black ink); but it limits you to using the EPS format. We recommend this approach only when you have to repurpose a large number of grayscale images.

Tip: Figuring Dot Gain. When your printer tells you to expect 12-percent dot gain, that means (or should mean) that a 50-percent dot on film will result in a 62-percent dot on press. (See "Dot Gain: Coping with Midtone Spread" in Chapter 5, *Color Settings*.)

Changing the image to compensate for dot gain. The easiest way to compensate for dot gain is to change the image itself. The disadvantage is that you end up with an inflexible image optimized for a specific set of output conditions. You can usually repurpose an already optimized image for *more* dot gain, but if you try to repurpose it to print with less dot gain, you may encounter posterization when you darken the midtones again.

If you have a black dot gain curve, you can load it as your Gray working space in Color Settings to make the monitor simulate the effects of dot gain, and change the image by working visually.

Failing that, if you have a printed sample to go by, you can display the image, then simply mess with the dot gain curve in Custom Dot Gain until your display matches the print—make sure you have Preview turned on in the Color Settings dialog box. If you don't have a printed image, you can probably get your printer to supply a set of control bars. If possible, talk your printer into measuring the dot areas for the patches in the control bars—they should have the equipment to do so—but if that's not possible, you can eyeball the patches to make a reasonable dot gain curve.

First, create a grayscale image that contains swatches of the same value as the control bars (they're often 40, 60, 80, and 100 percent). Then, with the grayscale file open, choose Color Settings, then choose Custom Dot Gain from the Gray popup menu. Adjust the dot gain curve until the printed control swatches match the ones in the grayscale image on screen. This works as long as your monitor profile is accurate (see Figure 6-30).

When you're done, you can save the Custom Dot Gain curve as a grayscale ICC profile. You'll still have to do more fine-tuning of the highlights than you would with a curve based on measurements that included the 2, 4, 6, and 8 percent dots, but the results will be more accurate than ones based on single dot gain values.

Use a transfer function to compensate for dot gain. If you're faced with the prospect of repurposing a large number of grayscale images, one very efficient way to do so is to use a transfer function. The downsides

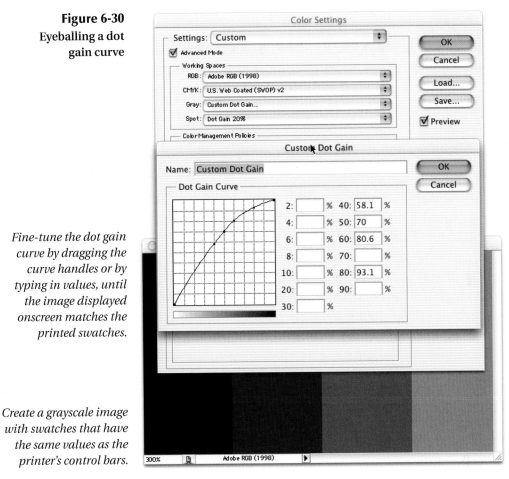

Figure 6-30
Eyeballing a dot
gain curve

*Fine-tune the dot gain
curve by dragging the
curve handles or by
typing in values, until
the image displayed
onscreen matches the
printed swatches.*

*Create a grayscale image
with swatches that have
the same values as the
printer's control bars.*

to this approach are that you're limited to EPS format, and your file has
something hiding in it (the transfer function) that changes the way the
image prints. When the image is rasterized by a PostScript RIP, it alters the
gray values according to the curve.

To create a transfer function, do the following.

1. Choose Print with Preview from the File menu.

2. Click the Transfer button to open the Transfer Functions dialog box.

3. Enter the desired value for the 50-percent dot (and, ideally, the 80-
   percent dot) in the appropriate field(s).

4. Optionally, save the transfer function, then click Done.

5. Save the image as EPS and turn on Include Transfer Function.

Tonal Correction in Practice

Theory is all very well and good, but there's no substitute for practice, practice, practice. Every image is different, presenting its own challenges and opportunities; here are a couple of examples of how we use these tools together to enhance images quickly and efficiently.

Using Levels to Correct a Good Scan

Figure 6-31 shows an image scanned from color negative using a Leafscan 35. Since the Leafscan is a high-bit scanner, we tapped its capabilities, setting reasonable black and white points to avoid tonal clipping, and applying a gamma move of 2.2 (to match our working space gamma). This yielded a scan that was very usable but needed some fine-tuning to increase contrast, bring out detail, and get it ready for print.

Option-dragging the white input slider shows us that we don't want to clip any of the highlight detail—it's all good, useful stuff. Option-dragging the black input slider shows us that there's very little important detail in the extreme blacks—we can definitely afford to clip some of it. In so doing, we'll intensify the blacks, increase the overall image contrast, and bring out detail throughout by expanding the tonal range.

The amount of clipping is largely dictated by our output process. If we were going to a film recorder that could record all that subtle detail, or preparing a premium print job, we'd be very conservative and clip only two or three levels; but for a midrange job like this book, we can easily clip to level 14 or so. There's some detail below that, but it isn't important detail; we know we won't be able to reproduce it under these printing conditions, and if we clip it we can use the available levels to show more important detail in the midtones and highlights.

This intensifies the blacks nicely. There's relatively little detail in the highlights, so we pull them back to 245 to brighten the whites overall, but not so much that they'll blow out (see Figure 6-32).

In this case we target the image with the fast-and-dirty approach: set the output sliders to compress the tonal range, and make a quick curve move to compensate for projected dot gain. But by being conservative in our compression, we can avoid graying out our whites and blacks and flattening the image excessively (see Figure 6-33).

Figure 6-31 The raw lighthouse image

The histogram shows that the scan has succeeded in capturing the entire tonal range of the image, without clipping the highlights or the shadows. The problem is that it looks flat, with no really dense blacks.

Shadow clipping at level 16

Highlight clipping at level 240

Figure 6-32 The lighthouse after correction with Levels

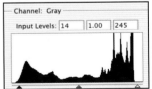

Channel: Gray

Input Levels: 14   1.00   245

This Levels adjustment results in the image at left and the histogram below.

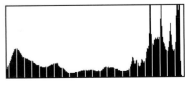

Figure 6-33 The lighthouse after targeting

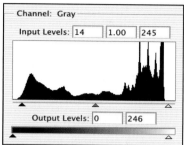

Our measured dot gain curve maps the highlights and shadows accurately to the dot limits, so we need to do relatively little in the way of targeting. We'll combine the targeting move with the tonal-correction move to minimize data loss.

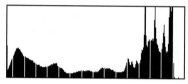

The final histogram after correction and targeting

Using the Info palette as our guide, we pull the white output slider back to make sure that we hold a dot in the highlights. Setting the white output slider to 246 gives us a 4% dot.

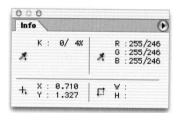

Correcting an Old Image with Levels

The old photograph in Figure 6-34 presents more of a challenge. The picture of Bruce's grandmother was scanned using an Agfa Arcus Plus from a very old print (c. 1928) that had been stored for years under less-than-ideal conditions. The ink in the inscription is much darker than anything in the photograph itself, and insects have eaten through the emulsion to produce tiny white spots that are brighter than any real image detail. Together, they fooled the scanner's autoexposure algorithm into using a much wider tonal range than the image really contains, so the scan appears washed out even though the histogram shows some data at almost every level. As with the lighthouse image, we applied a 2.2 gamma adjustment to the high-bit data at scan time.

Figure 6-34 The uncorrected Ella scan

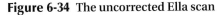

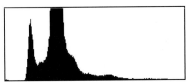

The black and white points for this scan were wide of the mark, resulting in an excessively flat image.

Shadow clipping at level 28   *Highlight clipping at level 225*

The clipping display for this image tells a very different story. Setting the white input slider to 240 creates small specular highlights on the bracelet, without clipping anything else in the image. At the shadow end, approximately the first 25 levels are taken up by the ink on the inscription. The darkest pixels in the image itself are in the shadows on the dress, but they also display the noise that's characteristic of flatbed scanners, so we set the black Input slider to level 27. A gamma tweak of 1.14 retrieves a little shadow detail (see Figure 6-35).

If we were in a hurry, this is pretty much all we'd do to the images before sharpening and using the eyedroppers to fine-tune the endpoints. Given more time, we'd cancel out of the Levels dialog box and use Curves instead, remembering what we'd learned about the shadow and highlight values from the clipping display.

Figure 6-35 Ella corrected and optimized

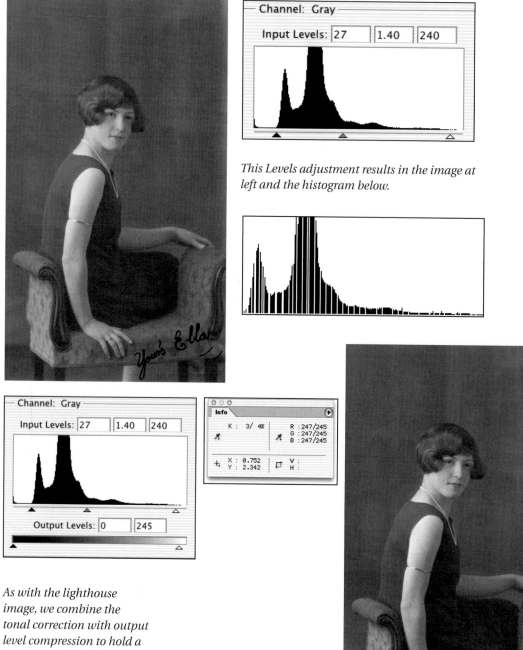

This Levels adjustment results in the image at left and the histogram below.

As with the lighthouse image, we combine the tonal correction with output level compression to hold a highlight dot, checking our highlight values with the Info palette. You can see the result in the image and histogram at right.

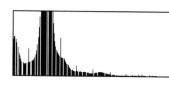

Deep Fixes with Curves

Levels lets you produce decent-quality images, but with Curves you can do much more. Curves lets you isolate specific parts of the tonal range for adjustment. Usually there's a trade-off involved—you emphasize some parts of the image at the expense of others. Learning how to manipulate images is easy; learning what needs to be done for each image is hard and takes practice. The examples we give here are based on our subjective opinions; you may have different ideas on what we should have done.

In practice, it's rare nowadays for us to build curves as detailed as the ones in these examples. Everyone knows that Photoshop offers a gazillion ways to accomplish any given task, and we created these examples back in the days when Photoshop only offered a few million ways to accomplish a given task.

But Curves is such a powerful and fundamental tool that it's well worth spending the time needed to master it. Mastery constitutes not only understanding the effect a curve has on the image, but also becoming efficient in working with Curves as a process, using all the feedback it provides, auto-placing points, learning when to use numeric entry, when to drag points with the mouse, and when to nudge them with the arrow keys. Everyone has their own working style and rhythm, and Curves can seem deceptively simple, but it's really a very deep feature.

Long after you've graduated to using nested layer sets with masks and esoteric blending modes to edit tone and color, you'll find that in a significant number of cases, Curves still offers the quickest fix, so take the time to learn all its features.

Tip: Nudge Curve Points with the Arrow Keys. You can move curve points up, down, left, or right using the up, down, left, and right arrow keys on the keyboard—it's often the easiest way to make precise adjustments. (Bruce never drags curve points with the mouse.) The increment by which the points move depends on whether you use the small or large Curves dialog (click the Zoom box to toggle between the two). In the large dialog, each press of the arrow key moves the point by one level. Adding Shift moves ten levels. In the small dialog, each press of the arrow key moves the point by two levels, adding the Shift key moves the point by 15 levels. So the difference between the two sizes of Curve dialog isn't just cosmetic.

Lighthouse. Our first three curve points establish the overall contrast. Remembering what we've learned from the clipping display in Levels, we clip the extreme shadows to add density to the blacks. The midtones are still too bright, so we darken them with a second point. This makes the whole image too dark, so a third point brings the midtones and highlights back to a reasonable range (see Figure 6-36).

Our remaining points bring out specific features in the image. We Command-click on the whitecaps to place point 4, and on the water to place point 5, then move them apart to increase the contrast between the whitecaps and the water. This drastically blows out the highlights, so we add point 6 by Command-clicking the bright area on the lighthouse. We nudge it back to 240 to bring some detail back into the highlights.

We're left with a tight kink in the curve, so we add point 7 by Command-clicking the shadow on the lighthouse, and pull it back to level 210 to add some solidity to the shadow, and to darken the sky.

Turning Preview off and on in the Curves dialog to get a quick before-and-after, we can see that we've improved the contrast in almost all areas. The rocks have solidity, and the whitecaps on the waves snap. The image is now ready for sharpening and targeting with the eyedroppers.

Your's Ella. Remembering what we saw in the Levels clipping display, we set the endpoints of the curve first. In this case, we clip both the shadows and the highlights considerably because they contain no real image information (dealing, we hope, with any scanner-induced noise that may have been lurking in the shadows). We make sure that our highlight detail is still well below level 250, so we can target it later. A third curve point deepens the shadows, improving the overall contrast.

Three further moves go after specific areas in the image. The first increases contrast in the face but makes the highlights on the shoulder a little hot. If this were a modern image, we might let it go, but part of the charm of this photograph is its obvious age. We don't want to make the contrast too harsh, so our fifth curve point pulls back the highlights on the shoulder. A quick before-and-after obtained by turning Preview off and on shows us that we've lost some contrast around the left eye, so our final move lightens that side of the face slightly, and improves its contrast with the background (see Figure 6-37).

Figure 6-36 Correcting the lighthouse with Curves

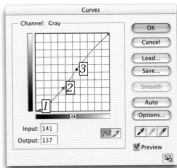

Point 1. 11 in, 0 out. Gives us solid black in the shadows.

Point 2. 94 in, 74 out. Brightens the midtones on the rocks.

Point 3. 141 in, 137 out. Brings the highlights back under control.

Our first three curve points establish the overall contrast. We clip the shadows slightly (1) to get solid blacks and disguise noisy pixels, then darken the midtones (2), concentrating on the rocks. This makes the sky too dark, so we use point (3) to bring the highlights back into a reasonable range. Curve points 4 and 5 increase the separation between the whitecaps and the water.

Brightening the whitecaps blows out all our highlights, so we add point 6 to bring the highlights on the lighthouse down to a manageable level. Point 7 darkens the sky a little further and adds some solidity to the shadow on the lighthouse.

Point 4. 161 in, 192 out. Brightens the whitecaps.

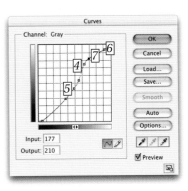

Point 7. 177 in, 210 out. Darkens the sky and strengthens the shadow on the lighthouse.

Point 6. 233 in, 240 out. Corrects for point 4, bringing the highlights back under control.

Point 5. 124 in, 110 out. Darkens the water.

Figure 6-37 Ella corrected with Curves

Point 3. 52 in, 23 out.
Darkens the background.

We clip the highlights (1) to 250 (the lightest point on the shoulder, reserving the higher levels for the small specular highlights on the bracelet) and the shadows (2), spreading the real image information across the tonal range, and increasing contrast. Point 3 deepens the shadows so that the darkest areas are almost the same shade as the ink of the inscription.

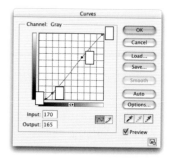

Point 4 lightens the face and also increases its contrast—too much, in fact. It also makes the highlights on the shoulder uncomfortably hot. Point 5 pulls back the highlights on the shoulder and softens the contrast on the face, producing a result we feel is more in keeping with the photograph's obvious age. Point 6 produces just a hair more contrast on the shadowed side of the face, bringing out the sparkle in the eyes.

Point 6. 73 in, 51 out. Emphasizes the catchlight in the right eye.

Point 1. 250 in, 255 out. Clips and brightens the highlights.

Point 2. 28 in, 0 out. Clips unwanted noise and creates true blacks.

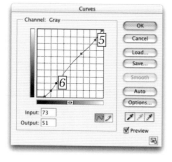

Point 4. 170 in, 165 out. Brightens the lighter tones of the face and increases its contrast.

Point 5. 225 in, 219 out. Pulls back the highlights on the shoulder.

Save the Curves

We're done with the curves for now—this is as close as we can get without pulling a proof. But before we click OK to apply them to the image, we save the final curve by clicking the Save button. Because we're working on a copy of the image, if something goes wrong or we decide that some of the changes aren't quite to our liking, we can go back to the original file and load this curve as a new starting point.

After we see proofs, we may want to make some changes, and these are better made by going back to the original data and modifying the curve. A look at the histograms reveals why. We already have some gaps of more than one level; so if we want to do more manipulation, we're better off going back to the original 8 bits, rather than stretching and squeezing the remaining ones even further (see Figure 6-38).

Figure 6-38
Histograms of
corrected lighthouse
and Ella images

Sharpen Before Final Tonal Compression

Every scanned image needs some unsharp masking, and it's a rich and complex enough subject that we've devoted an entire chapter to it later in the book. For now, trust us on the sharpening we apply to the two images before we do final tonal compression (see Figure 6-39).

Figure 6-39
Sharpening settings
for lighthouse and
Ella images

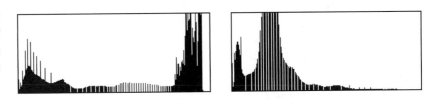

The lighthouse image needs considerably more sharpening than the studio portrait, which we deliberately leave soft since it preserves more of the feel of the original. Note that we use a much smaller sharpening radius for the lighthouse image, because it contains more small details than the portrait.

Final Compression with the Eyedroppers

You can use the eyedroppers from either the Levels or the Curves dialog box, but we always use Levels because we find the clipping displays indispensable. We use them to check where our highlight and shadow details really are after sharpening.

We set the highlight target for a 4-percent dot (our printer told us that their press could probably hold a 3-percent dot, but we decided to err on the side of caution), and set the shadow target for a 96-percent dot (see Figure 6-40).

The moves we make with the eyedroppers are small and have a barely perceptible effect on the images overall, but they let us nail the extremes of the tonal range precisely (see Figures 6-41 and 6-42).

Figure 6-40
Setting
eyedropper
targets

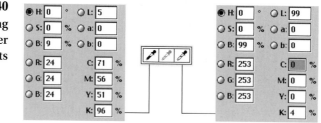

If you like to think in dot percentages, the fast, easy way to set the eyedropper targets for grayscale print work is to use the K field in the CMYK color picker.

Figure 6-41 Lighthouse, sharpened and targeted

We set 4 percent as the source value for the white eyedropper, because that's what our press can hold. The edge of the middle attic window has several pixels in the 0-3 percent range, so we zoom into that area, find a 3-percent pixel along the edge of the window, and click on it. We may end up with a very few pure white highlights, but we've ensured that anything that contains detail will print with a dot. Repeating the process for the black eyedropper, we click on a 98-percent pixel in the extreme shadow at the left of the image.

Figure 6-40
Ella, sharpened
and targeted

We want to make sure that we hold a dot in the skin tones, but we also want the specular highlight on the bracelet to blow out to white paper, so we choose a 3-percent pixel in the necklace as the source color, forcing it to 4 percent. This ensures that the only area in the image that won't hold a dot on press is the small specular highlight on the bracelet.

Tonal Magic

Levels and Curves are real powerhouses, and becoming fluent with them is key to mastering Photoshop's production capabilities. We've introduced these tools by looking at grayscale manipulation, but they play an even more important role in color correction.

When you correct color, you're still stretching and squeezing the bits; but you're working with three or four channels simultaneously, so it's a lot more complex. If you master the operation of the tools thoroughly in grayscale, the color-correction techniques we present in the next chapter will come much more easily.

7 Color Correction Fundamentals

The Basic Tools and Concepts

If you opened this book and went straight to this page looking for easy answers, stop. Go directly to jail. Do not pass Go. Do not collect $200. While you're in jail, you should take some time and read through a few other chapters.

First off, take a look at Chapter 4, *Color Essentials*. Then, if you're looking to convert your image from RGB to CMYK, or if you're trying to make decisions based on what you see on the monitor, or if you're confused about the brave new world of color management systems and device profiles, you're going to need to know about RGB, CMYK, and Gray working spaces, and color management policies (so go read Chapter 5, *Color Settings*). And when you make color corrections in Photoshop, you're really manipulating the tone of the individual color channels, so you need to understand how to tweak grayscale images before you touch color ones—they're at least nine times more complicated! (So you'd better read the last chapter, *Tonal Correction Fundamentals*, too.)

That said, if you want to plunge in, go ahead. Just bear in mind that when things get sticky, you may want to refer back to those chapters to get a better handle on what you've actually been doing.

Changing Modes and Losing Information

We've stressed throughout this book that almost everything you do to an image in Photoshop throws away some information. But too many people, including some so-called experts, don't realize that changing to a different color mode throws away information faster than almost anything else. With 16-bit-per-channel files, you have so much data that the losses are entirely affordable, but with 8-bit-per-channel files, every bit counts.

The subject of mode conversion is surrounded by confusion and by more than its share of mythology. We'll discuss the arguments in detail throughout this chapter, but let us say up front that mode changes lose considerable amounts of information, no matter which color space you're going to or from (with one exception—the conversion from grayscale to RGB). Mode changes between RGB and Lab, Lab and CMYK, and RGB and CMYK all discard image information to a greater extent than most people realize. (Conversions between different color spaces in the *same* mode—RGB-to-RGB or CMYK-to-CMYK—also throw away information, particularly when they have different gammas or dot gains.) The color conversion algorithms in Photoshop CS are as good as they come, but they still entail some data loss.

Dithering and Data Loss

Photoshop 6 introduced the option of dithering 8-bit conversions (see "Use Dither (8-bit/channel images)" in Chapter 5, *Color Settings*). Dithering will help you avoid posterization, but it's important to realize that it doesn't eliminate data loss; it only masks it by adding back some noise after the data has already gone into the bitbucket. Dithering may help you avoid obvious posterization, but it doesn't preserve detail—remember, difference is detail—because the noise is random.

If you want to replicate our experiments here, you need to turn off "Use Black Point Compensation" and "Use Dither (8-bit/channel images)" in the Color Settings dialog box. The results also depend on the specific color spaces—we used Adobe RGB (1998) and US Web Coated (SWOP) v2—the length of the gradient (these are 2048 pixels long), and the rendering intent, which in these examples is Relative Colorimetric.

RGB to Lab

There's a lingering impression in the Photoshop community that you can switch between RGB and Lab color without losing significant amounts of image information. In fact, the conversion between 24-bit RGB and 24-bit Lab is far from lossless. You lose differences between levels, and hence you lose possibly-significant detail.

For instance, try converting an RGB step wedge to Lab and back to RGB, and then examine the results: Depending on your working space gamma, *between 20 and 35 of the possible 256 levels simply disappear* (see Figure 7-1). This loss may not be visually significant—you probably can't see it on the screen, and you're unlikely to see it in print—but if you try to stretch the now-degraded tonal range after the conversion, it will start to show up as posterization.

Figure 7-1
RGB-to-Lab-to-RGB
data loss

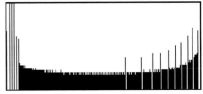

Histogram of a gray wedge in Adobe RGB (not terribly interesting)

Histogram of the gray wedge after RGB-to-Lab-to-RGB conversion

The gaps in the histogram show unused levels after RGB-to-Lab mode conversion, but they don't tell the whole story about the loss of image information. The spikes in the histogram indicate where values have been rounded (made the same). These also represent loss of image detail. It may not have been visible detail, but it was there waiting to be exploited and perhaps made visible. Now it's gone, never to return.

CMYK to Lab

The conversion from CMYK to Lab (and vice versa) loses a little more information than from RGB to Lab, and the pattern is a little different (see Figure 7-2). You're likely to get subtle color shifts, in addition to losing tonal distinctions. Basically, you get more rounding errors switching between a three-channel and a four-channel color space than you do switching between two three-channel color spaces.

Figure 7-2
Data loss when going
from CMYK-to-Lab-to-
CMYK

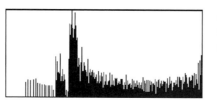

*A gray wedge histogram looks like
this after CMYK-to-Lab-to-CMYK
conversion.*

RGB to CMYK

Converting an image from RGB to CMYK in Photoshop—the most common and necessary of conversions—loses a lot of image information (see Figure 7-3). It has to. The RGB color space contains 16.7 million colors, of which a few thousand (at most) are printable using four-color process printing. When the conversion is done right, the printed CMYK piece will bear a reasonably close resemblance to the RGB image on the screen, even though it contains far fewer colors, a smaller dynamic range, and a much narrower color gamut (see the sidebar "CMYK Myths," later in this chapter).

The best you can hope for in the RGB-to-CMYK conversion is a per-

Figure 7-3
Data loss in RGB-to-
CMYK conversion

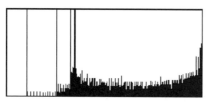

fect translation of the RGB original squeezed into the smaller gamut of press-ready CMYK. You lose differences between colors, and as we keep repeating, difference is detail.

RGB to RGB

The only real drawback to using an RGB working space is that you need to convert images into your chosen working space. Like other color space conversions, this one too involves some data loss. In the vast majority of cases, we think the benefits of a gray-balanced, perceptually uniform working space outweigh the data loss, and on high-bit files it just isn't an issue, but you should know that RGB-to-RGB conversions aren't lossless.

How much data loss are we talking about? It depends on the specific RGB spaces you're converting from and to. Figure 7-4 shows the histograms of some typical conversions. Some of the histograms in Figure 7-4 look scarier than others, and some don't look scary at all. The loss occurs when there's a mismatch between the gammas or gamuts of the two RGB spaces involved—converting between two gamma 1.8 spaces, such as Apple RGB and ColorMatch RGB, or between two gamma 2.2 spaces, such as Adobe RGB (1998) and sRGB, is relatively lossless, particularly when going from a larger gamut to a smaller one.

We generally advocate the use of gamma 2.2 for editing spaces, because it's more perceptually uniform than gamma 1.8, and it devotes more bits to the shadows, which is usually where we need them. But there's no getting around the fact that converting a gamma 1.8 image into a gamma 2.2 working space loses some data, though not nearly as much as an actual

Figure 7-4
Data loss in RGB-to-RGB
conversions

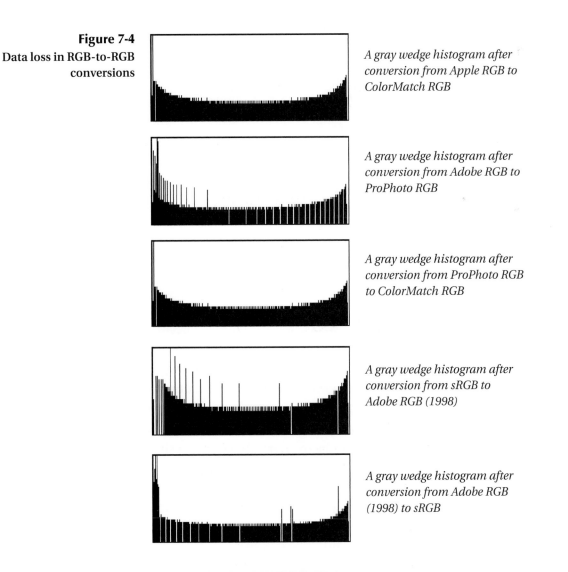

A gray wedge histogram after conversion from Apple RGB to ColorMatch RGB

A gray wedge histogram after conversion from Adobe RGB to ProPhoto RGB

A gray wedge histogram after conversion from ProPhoto RGB to ColorMatch RGB

A gray wedge histogram after conversion from sRGB to Adobe RGB (1998)

A gray wedge histogram after conversion from Adobe RGB (1998) to sRGB

mode change. Most Windows users' legacy images are already in a gamma 2.2 space, so they don't have a problem.

Converting legacy gamma 1.8 images into a gamma 2.2 working space can sometimes help if you need to edit the shadows, but it can also make the image fall apart if it has already had heavy edits applied. The one conversion we *do* strongly advocate is the one that converts high-bit data from your capture device into your working space of choice.

RGB vs. CMYK

The debate over whether to work in RGB or CMYK has been the subject of countless magazine articles, several online flame wars, and even a few books. Of course, if your work is destined for a film recorder, the computer screen, or videotape, then CMYK is quite irrelevant; but if you're working in the print medium, it's very important indeed.

There are still people who continue to maintain that if your work is destined for print, you should work exclusively in CMYK. When confronted, they usually give four reasons for this.

▶ It's the only color space that matters.

▶ RGB is meaningless.

▶ Monitor calibration is inherently impossible.

▶ All that matters are the CMYK dot percentages.

While all these points have some validity, we beg to differ with the philosophy as a whole. As we've noted before, when all you have is a hammer, everything starts to look like a nail. People who tell you to do everything in CMYK may have excellent traditional prepress skills and a deep understanding of process-color printing, but they just don't realize how much image information Photoshop loses during the conversion, and they probably are not comfortable working in RGB.

As a result, they convert raw scans (or even worse, JPEGs from consumer digital cameras) to CMYK immediately, damaging the image irretrievably. Then they make huge corrections in CMYK, trying to salvage a printable image from what's left. Once they're done, they congratulate themselves

CMYK Myths

One of the reasons we wrote this book was to dispel a number of the myths that have cropped up during the short life of desktop prepress (and some others that have been around even longer)—especially those regarding CMYK and RGB issues. Here are our answers to two areas that people often find confusing.

CMYK has more colors (false). We've heard experts deride the notion that CMYK contains fewer colors than RGB. "Do the math, stupid," they say. "CMYK has 256⁴, or more than 4 *billion* colors." We wish that were the case. CMYK has more than 4 billion color *specifications*, but a large number of them are simply alternate ways of specifying the *same* color using a different balance of black to CMY inks. And many of them (for example, 90C 90M 90Y 100K) are "illegal" specifications that would turn the paper into a soggy mess scattered all over the pressroom floor. When you also take into account the constraints imposed by the black-generation curve and the total ink limit, you end up with far fewer colors than RGB.

CMYK is more accurate (true, sort of). Other experts say, "CMYK may have a narrower gamut, but the data points in CMYK are packed much closer together than they are in RGB, so CMYK specifies colors *more accurately* than RGB."

Here they have a point. You *can* specify smaller differences between colors in CMYK than you can in RGB, because the same number of bits is being used to describe a smaller color gamut. (Whether these smaller color differences are detectable by the human eye is a question we'll leave to someone willing to carry out the empirical research.)

But this is relevant only if your RGB original is being converted to CMYK from high-bit RGB. The CMYK conversion can't be any more accurate than the RGB scan, and even in high-bit mode your image will still suffer from rounding errors. You can and very likely should fine-tune your CMYK after conversion, but you're *much* better off doing the heavy lifting on source RGB, preferably high-bit RGB.

on their exquisite skills while pointing out the limited quality you can attain with desktop color.

These limits are self-imposed and largely illusory. If you follow these people's recommendations, you too will throw away about a third of your image right off the bat; then you'll be able to labor mightily, use all sorts of nifty tricks, and be rewarded with mediocre results for your efforts.

We have a very simple rule: *Don't change color modes unless or until you have to, and do as much of your correction as possible in the image's original color mode. The ideal number of color-mode conversions is one or none.*

All images ultimately come from an RGB source, so even if the desired end result is a set of CMYK separations, you should do as much of your image correction as possible in the RGB file. This is not a universally accepted view, but we believe that the arguments in its favor are compelling. When you prematurely convert to CMYK, you restrict yourself in at least four ways.

► You lose a great deal of image information, making quality tonal and color correction much more difficult.

► You optimize the image for a particular set of press conditions (paper, press, inks, and so on). If press conditions change, or if you want to print the image under various press conditions, you're in a hole that's difficult to climb out of.

► You increase your file size by a third, slowing most operations by that same amount.

► You lose some convenient Photoshop features that work only in RGB, like the Levels clipping display (see "Levels," later in this chapter).

More important, correcting images in RGB prior to CMYK conversion just plain works.

For the vast majority of Photoshop users, that means working in RGB for as long as possible, and converting your image to CMYK only after you're finished with your other corrections and you know the printing conditions. It's useful to keep an eye on the CMYK dot percentages while you work, but you don't need to work in CMYK to do that—they're always available in the Info palette, even when you're working in RGB.

We're not saying that you should never make corrections in CMYK—far from it. Your CMYK separations will often benefit from fine-tuning. Editing the black plate is a particularly powerful technique, but it's most effective as a fine-tuner, making small moves. Similarly, Hue/Saturation changes in CMYK are generally more delicate than in RGB. If you work in print, you must learn to edit in CMYK. But it isn't the only game in town.

When to Use CMYK

If your images come from a traditional drum scanner in CMYK form, it makes no sense to convert them to RGB for correction. You should stay in CMYK. If you find that you have to make major corrections, though, you'll almost certainly get better results by rescanning the image instead of editing it in Photoshop. In high-end prepress shops, it's not unusual to scan an image three times before the client signs off on it.

Tip: Ask for RGB. Color houses are so used to providing CMYK scans that they sometimes forget that their high-end drum scanners actually create RGB values, which an internal color computer then converts to

CMYK on the fly. These color computers use essentially the same kinds of conversion algorithms as Photoshop, so productivity, not quality, is the main reason color houses use them.

But if you plan to manipulate the image yourself in Photoshop, or need an image that can be repurposed for multiple devices or press conditions, ask the shop to save the image in RGB format. They may tell you it can't be done, but most color houses are now RGB-capable. Of course, you're then responsible for the conversion to CMYK.

Certain kinds of fine-tuning, such as black-plate editing, can *only* be done on the separated CMYK file. But if you find you need to make large moves in CMYK after a mode change, it's time to look at your CMYK settings in Color Settings, because the problem probably lies there—a wrong profile, incorrect settings in Custom CMYK, or color management policies that weren't set the way you thought they were (see Chapter 5, *Color Settings*). In that case, it makes more sense to go back to the RGB original and reseparate it using new settings that get you closer to the desired result.

If all you have is a CMYK file, work in CMYK if at all possible. In dire emergencies, such as when you have a CMYK file separated for newsprint and you need to reproduce it on glossy stock, you *may* want to take the desperate step of converting it back to RGB, correcting, and reseparating to CMYK; but in general, treat RGB to CMYK as strictly a one-way trip.

Tip: CMYK to RGB. We can think of two reasons to convert a CMYK image to RGB: you need an image for the Web or multimedia, and a CMYK scan is all you have, or you need to repurpose the CMYK image for a larger-gamut output process. In either case, you need to expand the tonal range and color gamut—if you just do a mode change from CMYK to RGB, you'll get a flat, lifeless image with washed-out color, because the tonal range and color gamut of the original were compressed in the initial RGB-to-CMYK conversion, and the mode change reproduces the compressed gamut and squashed tonal range faithfully in RGB.

Instead, use the Convert to Profile command to do the transformation, using perceptual intent, with black point compensation and dither turned on. Then, open Levels, and click Auto. If this makes the image *too* saturated, back the black and white point sliders off a few levels. You'll find it works surprisingly well (see Figure 7-5). That said, this is a last-resort technique. Work on a copy of the file, and watch for color shifts and posterization.

Figure 7-5 Repurposing an image that's been prepared for reproduction on newsprint

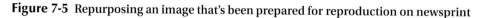

The image above left was separated for newsprint. The separation settings resulted in a flat image that would reproduce well in that medium, but that had lost a great deal of its tonal and color range.

For the image above, we started with the news-print-targeted CMYK file, pulled it back into RGB, made a Levels tweak, then reseparated for this book's wider gamut. The results aren't great, but as we said, it's a last-resort technique.

The image at left was created from the original RGB file, and separated using the proper settings for these printing conditions.

When to Use RGB

If your image comes from an RGB source, such as a desktop scanner or a digital camera, you should do as much of your work as possible in RGB. The files are smaller, so your work goes faster, and you have the entire tonal range and color gamut of the original at your disposal, allowing you to take full advantage of the small differences between pixels that you want to emphasize in the image. It's also much easier to repurpose RGB images for different kinds of output than it is to do so with CMYK.

RGB has less-obvious advantages, as well. Some features (such as the clipping display in Levels) are available only in RGB, not in CMYK. And when you work in RGB, you have a built-in safeguard: It's impossible to violate the ink limits specified by your CMYK profile or Custom CMYK settings (because they'll always be imposed when you convert to CMYK).

When you edit CMYK files directly, you have no such constraint—you can build up so much density in the shadows using Levels or Curves that you're calling for 400-percent ink coverage. On a sheetfed press, this will create a mess. On a web press, it will create a potentially life-threatening situation! In any case, it's something to avoid unless you're printing to the rare desktop color printer that can handle 400-percent total ink.

Image Correction and Optimization

In Chapter 6, *Tonal Correction Fundamentals,* we alluded to the distinction between correction and optimization. *Correction* is the process of compensating for flaws in the original and for distortions introduced during the image-capture process. *Optimization,* on the other hand, compensates for the shortcomings of the output process.

The distinction is less important than it used to be. Photoshop can handle optimization of grayscale images for press output the same way it handles optimization of color images—automatically. If you're using accurate dot gain curves or a good ICC profile, Photoshop will do a pretty good job of setting the endpoints to the print process's minimum and maximum dot. This can be both a blessing and a curse, as you'll see.

Correcting Color Images

Correcting color images is very much like correcting grayscale images, but with a catch. You're still stretching and squeezing the bits, but you're doing so on three (RGB) or four (CMYK) channels instead of only one, so it's nine or sixteen times more complicated!

The classic order for preparing color images for print is as follows.

► Spotting, retouching, dust and scratch removal

► Global tonal correction

► Global color correction

► Selective tonal and/or color correction

► Optimization (resizing, sharpening, handling out-of-gamut colors, compressing tonal range, converting to CMYK)

We generally adhere to this, but it depends on the image and on the quality of the image capture. For instance, you often have to lighten an image before you can even consider retouching it.

And sometimes it's impossible to separate tonal correction and color correction. Changes to the color balance affect tonal values, too, because you're manipulating the tone of the individual color channels. For example, if you add red to neutralize a cyan cast, you'll also brighten the image because you're adding light. If you reduce the green to neutralize a green cast, you'll darken the image because you're subtracting light. In any case, we try whenever possible to make a single set of curve adjustments that take care of all the global problems.

Fix the biggest problem first. The rule of thumb we've developed over the years is simple: Fix the biggest problem first. This is partly plain common sense. You often have to fix the biggest problem before you can even see what the other problems are. But it's usually also the most effective approach, the one requiring the least work, and the one that degrades the image the least.

With many desktop flatbed scanners—especially 8-bit scanners—the biggest problem is usually that the midtones and shadows are too dark, so we start with global tonal correction. If, on the other hand, we're faced with a badly acquired Photo CD image, the overall tone may be fine, but the image will have a global color cast which we go after first. With a purely synthetic image bound for a printing press, such as one created by a 3D rendering program, we might first desaturate the whole image a little.

Tip: Look at the Image Before You Start. This may seem obvious, but stop for a moment. Look at the image carefully. Zoom to 100 percent and look at every pixel. Have you missed dust or scratches? Are there particularly noisy areas that might cause problems? Look at each channel individually. Are there details (or defects) lurking in one channel that are absent from others? Is noise concentrated in one channel? (It's usually most prevalent in the blue.) Look at the histogram. Is the image using the full tonal range? If not, should it? A few minutes spent critically evaluating the image can save hours later on. Develop a plan, and stick to it unless it obviously isn't working (in which case, see below).

Tip: Leave Yourself an Escape Route. The great Scots poet Robert Burns pointed out that the best-laid schemes o' mice and men gang aft agley. He didn't have the benefit of the History palette, or the Undo and Revert commands, but you do. History is a great feature, but it's a RAM-hog, and eventually it starts dropping states, so foster good habits. If a particular move doesn't work, just undo (Command-Z)—you can reload Levels, Curves, Brightness/Contrast, Color Balance, and Hue/Saturation with the last-used settings by holding down the Option key while selecting them either from the menu or with a keyboard shortcut. If a whole train of moves has led you down a blind alley, revert to the original version.

If you're working on a complex or critical problem, work on a copy of the image. When you apply a move using Levels, Curves, or Hue/Saturation, save the image before you apply it. That way, you can always retrace your steps up to the point where things started to go wrong.

Photoshop's Adjustment Layers feature lets you avoid many of the pitfalls we've just discussed. You don't need to get your edits right the first time because you can go back and change them at will. You automatically leave yourself an escape route because your edits float above the original image rather than being burned into it, and it really doesn't matter what order you choose to make the edits in, because they'll all be applied simultaneously when you flatten the image.

But sometimes it's impractical to use adjustment layers because of file size constraints, particularly with high-bit files, and to use adjustment layers effectively, you need to know how the various controls operate on a flat file. So even if you plan to use adjustment layers for as much of your editing as possible—and we encourage you to do so—you still need to master the techniques we discuss in this chapter, and the pitfalls they entail. For a much deeper discussion of adjustment layers, see Chapter 9, *The Digital Darkroom*.

Optimizing Color Images

As with grayscale images, you can choose to separate the process of correcting color images from that of optimizing them for a specific output, or you can do both at once. The trade-off is speed versus flexibility. When you optimize an image for one output process, it's often difficult to reproduce it satisfactorily using a different output process.

You may be able to convert a magazine separation for newsprint, but going the other way is likely to be a nightmare, because you've compressed the image into the small gamut of newsprint. And repurposing a newsprint separation for output to a wide-gamut inkjet printer is pretty much impossible. If you try to stretch the tonal range back to the gamut of film, it will probably fall apart; and if you don't try, it'll be flat and lifeless (see Figure 7-5 and "Tip: CMYK to RGB," earlier in this chapter).

So if you think you may want to use the image for multiple outputs, you should treat correction and optimization as two separate processes: You can save the corrected image while still in RGB, and then use it to create versions targeted for the specific output conditions. If you just want to get it on the page and out the door, you can make all your corrections with the final output in mind, optimizing as you correct, and save yourself some time.

Automatic versus manual optimization. When you convert an RGB image to CMYK using ICC profiles or a Custom CMYK setting, it automatically compensates for dot gain and for the reduced color gamut of CMYK. The results that you get depend—critically—on the quality of the CMYK profile or the choices you make in the Custom CMYK settings, so it's important to get these right (see Chapter 5, *Color Settings*). But even with the great profiles, you may still want to adjust some things by hand before doing the conversion. One of the trickier issues is handling out-of-gamut colors.

Gamut compression and gamut clipping. As we discussed back in Chapter 4, *Color Essentials*, RGB colors that can't be reproduced on output are called *out-of-gamut* colors. There are two fundamentally different ways to handle these colors, and Photoshop offers both.

▶ Reduce the color gamut of the entire image proportionally, so that differences in color saturation are preserved (*gamut compression*). Most ICC output profiles support perceptual rendering, which fits the source gamut into that of the output in such a way that the overall color relationships are maintained.

▶ Clip the out-of-gamut colors to their nearest printable equivalents, while leaving the in-gamut colors unchanged (*gamut clipping*). Photoshop's Custom CMYK always works this way, as do ICC profiles when you set the Intent to relative or absolute colorimetric.

Each approach has its strengths and weaknesses. The disadvantage of the former approach is that, if your image contains no out-of-gamut colors, you'll lose saturation unnecessarily. The disadvantage of the latter approach is that differences in saturation between out-of-gamut colors are lost, and so detail in highly saturated areas goes away. For example, if you have a pixel that's really hot pink and another one that's even hotter, they'll both get clipped to the same dull pink color; the difference between them is gone.

Photoshop CS uses ICC-based color management for all its color conversions, but the old "Photoshop Classic" separations method lingers on in the Custom CMYK feature. You can build ICC profiles from Custom CMYK, but profiles built this way can't do perceptual rendering, only relative and absolute colorimetric. We only recommend using the classic separation engine if you already have separation settings that you know will work on your output process. Otherwise, you're much better off using real profiles.

Unless you take care of the out-of-gamut colors yourself, Photoshop will take care of them for you during separation, and it may not give you the results you want. This is true even if you use ICC profiles with perceptual rendering, but with Custom CMYK settings, you need to be particularly careful.

The issue isn't really one of rendering intent. Rather, it's that all the rendering intents have absolutely no knowledge of the image content. They only know about the space in which the image lives, not how much of that space the image actually occupies. So they'll perform exactly the same conversion on a pastel misty-morning landscape and a saturated plastic product shot, a black cat in a coal cellar and a polar bear in the snow.

Fortunately, Photoshop lets you preview any color conversions, and even work inside a live simulation of the color conversion using Proof Setup (see "Soft Proofing Controls" in Chapter 5, *Color Settings*). You can see the effect the conversion will have on your image, and take any necessary remedial action *before* the conversion to control the way your out-of-gamut colors are mapped into the output space. Figure 7-6 shows conversions from the RGB original to this book's CMYK using straight conversions compared with the results of hand-tuning the RGB original inside a soft proof. Note the huge difference in detail on the saturated reds between the straight conversions and the hand-tuned versions.

You can't change the gamut of your output process—it's determined by the actual inks or other colorants used. But careful editing of colors near the gamut boundary can make a huge difference to the image, so don't feel you have to accept conversions as-is.

Tip: Optimizing Color Images for RGB Output. Some output processes—notably film recorders, computer screens, and many inexpensive inkjet printers—use RGB data. Photoshop CS lets you work with multiple RGB spaces at the same time, so if you really want to, you can edit images in an RGB output space; but we advise against it, because most RGB output spaces aren't even close to being gray-balanced or perceptually uniform.

Instead, keep your image in your RGB working space, and use a Custom Proof Setup to simulate your print space (see Chapter 5, *Color Settings*). For optimizations for RGB output, Bruce usually uses adjustment layers grouped in a layer set and saved in the working space RGB image. This technique lets you store optimizations for different RGB output processes in the same master RGB file. You can turn on the layer set for the print process you're aiming at when it's time to print, and either make a duplicate to convert to the printer space, or just let Photoshop do the conversion at print time. (For more on using adjustment layers for non-destructive editing, see Chapter 9, *The Digital Darkroom*.)

Figure 7-6 Out-of-gamut color handling

Note the detail differences in the saturated gloves and water bottle.

Separated with perceptual rendering

Hand-tuned, then separated with perceptual rendering

Color-Correction Tools

For color correction, we rely heavily on the same four tools that we use for grayscale correction—the Histogram and Info palettes, and the Levels and Curves dialog boxes (and the eyedropper tools they contain). They operate in the same way as they do in grayscale, but their effects are sometimes significantly different because we're dealing with three or four channels instead of one.

With Levels, Curves, and the Histogram palette, you can operate on the color channels individually or on a composite of them all. The Info palette shows what's happening in each of the channels, and warns you when RGB colors are outside the CMYK gamut. We also use the Proof Colors command for a visual check of our predicted CMYK (or RGB output) values while we're still working in an RGB working space.

In addition to these four tools, we use the Hue/Saturation command for both global and selective corrections, and its close relative, the Replace Colors command, for selective corrections. The Selective Color command, despite its name, is as useful for global corrections to the entire image as it

Figure 7-6 Out-of-gamut color handling, *continued*

With relative colorimetric rendering, you have to map out-of-gamut colors manually to avoid clipping.

Separated with relative colorimetric rendering

Hand-tuned, then separated with relative colorimetric rendering

is for selective corrections to parts of the image, but we generally reserve it for fine-tuning CMYK files.

Let's look at each of these tools in more detail.

Histogram Palette

As we noted in the last chapter, the Histogram palette is a simple bar chart that plots the levels from 0 to 255 along the horizontal axis, and the number of pixels at each level along the vertical axis. But it works a little differently with color images than it does with grayscale ones. In a grayscale image you have only one histogram, but in color images, you have a histogram for each channel (three for RGB and Lab, four for CMYK), plus composite histograms for the combined channels.

In fact, the Histogram palette offers not one, but three different composite histograms: One (the default) named for the current color mode—RGB or CMYK—one labelled Luminosity, and a third labelled Colors.

The histograms of the individual channels, and the composite RGB or CMYK, are identical to those shown in Levels. The composite Luminosity histogram, however, is different, and usefully so. The composite Luminosity histogram shows the overall tonal range of the image—it's analogous to the histogram for a grayscale image or for a single channel. Hence, it's useful for determining how bright your highlights and how dark your shadows are. For reasons we'll cover in "Levels," later in this chapter, the RGB composite histogram (which is the only composite in Levels) doesn't do this. The Colors histogram simply shows the RGB histogram in color.

Info Palette

The Info palette is a vital tool for working in color, particularly when you work in RGB. It lets you read the RGB values under the cursor, and equally important, it can show you the approximate CMYK values that you'll get when you do a mode change to CMYK.

We say "approximate" because if you examine the CMYK values for an RGB file, then convert to CMYK and examine the values again, they may differ very slightly. With rare exceptions, the CMYK values match to within a percentage point, which is a closer match than any imagesetter operator will promise you.

So, you can work on RGB images in their native color space, and still keep an eye on the CMYK values Photoshop will produce when you make color separations. You get the best of both worlds (see Figure 7-7).

When you're working on an RGB file, the CMYK values displayed by the Info palette are governed by the settings in the Color Settings dialog box. If these preferences are set correctly, you should have to do little or no work on the CMYK file after you've converted from RGB to CMYK. See Chapter 5, *Color Settings*, for strategies for setting up these key preferences.

We prefer working visually—relying on a well-calibrated monitor—rather than going strictly by the numbers, but even the best monitor and the best calibration have inherent limitations. Some things are hard to detect visually. For example, without looking at some kind of printed reference under controlled lighting, it's difficult to tell from the monitor whether or not a gray is really neutral. But the numbers in the Info palette

Figure 7-7 Histograms, Levels, saturation, and brightness

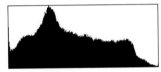

The Luminosity channel in the Histogram palette depicts the overall brightness distribution of the image—how the histogram would look if you converted the image to grayscale.

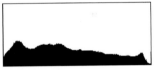

The RGB histogram in Levels shows how many pixels are at a given value in any of the channels. Note the spike at the right (255), even though there are no pure whites in the image.

The Levels highlight clipping display (here set to level 220) shows more about saturation levels. The green areas are fully saturated (255G) at this clipping level, the cyan areas are at 255G 255B, and so on. The white areas are truly white—255R 255G 255B.

The Gamut Warning display—here set to display in red—shows the saturated areas of the image that can't be reproduced with the current separation settings.

The Info palette's gamut alarm shows that the fully saturated blue-green sleeve colors can't be printed, along with the CMYK values that will result.

provide an infallible guide. Without a well-calibrated monitor, they're your only real guide to what's going on.

Likewise, it's very hard to see differences of one or two levels between adjacent pixels, but the Info palette lets you find these differences, and as we've pointed out, difference is detail. Overly macho prepress guys will tell you that you can do color correction using a black and white monitor. This is true only if you have a good sense of the target values you're aiming for, which comes only with experience. But a big part of gaining that experience comes from examining the values on the Info palette for key areas of your images.

Info palette setup. For color work, we use the same Info palette setup more than 90 percent of the time. We set the first color readout to RGB, the second color readout to CMYK, and the mouse coordinates to pixels. You can set all these options with the Palette Options menu on the Info palette, or you can set individual readouts using the individual popup menus.

Setting eyedropper options. You can set the Info palette to show the values of the individual pixels under the cursor, a 3-by-3-pixel average, or a 5-by-5-pixel average, by setting the options for the Eyedropper tool to Point Sample, 3-by-3 Average, or 5-by-5 Average from the Sample Size menu in the Options bar. David generally chooses 3-by-3 Average unless he's working with a very high-resolution image (destined for high-screen-frequency or continuous-tone output), in which case he might go to 5-by-5. Bruce sticks with point sample, but double-checks the values by zooming in at 100-percent view. Checking at 100-percent view is necessary because the zoomed-out displays are antialiased, so sampled values at less than 100 percent view may be misleading.

Tip: Use the Average Filter for Bigger Eyedropper Apertures. If you need a sample bigger than 5-by-5 pixels, make a marquee selection of the required size, choose Filter>Blur>Average, and read the result from the Info palette. Just don't forget to undo the filter once you've read the values!

Color samplers. An alternate eyedropper tool, the Color Sampler tool, lets you place up to four locked eyedropper probes, or color samplers, each of which has its own Info palette readout (see Figure 7-8). The color samplers are saved with the image, so they'll still be there even if you close and reopen the image. With the Color Sampler tool selected, you can move a sampler by dragging, and you can delete a sampler by Option-clicking it.

When you're using one of the editing or painting tools, you can always get the eyedropper by holding down Option. If you add the Shift key, you get the Color Sampler tool instead. However, to delete color samplers, you must either choose the Color Sampler tool from the tool palette using the mouse or the keyboard shortcut (I or Shift-I, depending on whether the tool was set to the eyedropper or the color sampler), then Option-click to delete the color sampler, or drag the color sampler out of the image area. Or choose the Eyedropper tool, and Command-drag the color sampler out of the image area.

Each color sampler has its own readout on the Info palette. These behave just like the other Info palette readouts. You can change the color space each sampler displays by clicking its individual popout menu, and you can hide or show all the color samplers by choosing Show/Hide Color Samplers from the Info palette's popout menu.

We use the color samplers to track what's happening to critical areas in the image when we edit. Typically, we'll place one color sampler for the highlight, a second for a neutral midtone, a third for a neutral three-

Figure 7-8 Color samplers and the Info palette

You can place up to four color samplers in an image, each of which has its own Info palette readout.

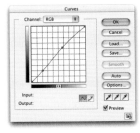

When you work with any of the adjustment tools, the samplers show before-and-after values.

quarter-tone, and the fourth on any critical color we're trying to adjust, or, just as often, to maintain.

Using the Info palette with other controls. While you're editing an image using any of the controls on the Adjust submenu under the Image menu (Levels, Curves, Hue/Saturation, Replace Colors, and so on), the Info palette provides a before-and-after reading (see Figures 7-8 and 7-9). This allows you to see numerically what is happening while you are making the adjustments.

Tip: Add Swatches for Critical Colors. The Color Sampler tool lets you lock down up to four samplers, which you can then read from the Info palette. But if you need to track more than four colors, you can use the following workaround.

1. Before opening the Levels or Curves dialog box (or whatever adjustment you're making), increase the image canvas size by 50 or 100 pixels.

2. For each pixel that you want to track, pick up its color with the Eyedropper tool.

3. Fill a part of the new white space with the picked-up color—drag out a selection and press Option-Delete to fill it with the foreground color (see Figure 7-9).

Now, while you make color corrections, you can always place the cursor over that color swatch to see how it's changing. When you're finished, crop out the swatches and you're back to normal.

Proof Colors

If you've gone through the process described in Chapter 5, *Color Settings*, for calibrating your monitor's display of CMYK files to the printed output, you can get a good visual idea of what will happen to your image once it's been converted to CMYK by choosing Proof Colors from the Mode menu. This doesn't change the file itself—it just changes the way it displays on the screen. (This simulation is based on the CMYK setting in Color Settings, but you can change it by choosing Custom from the Proof Setup submenu on the View menu.)

Figure 7-9 Adding color swatches

Since it's hard to find exactly the same pixel to examine values as you make corrections, add some color swatches to your image, picked up from key areas.

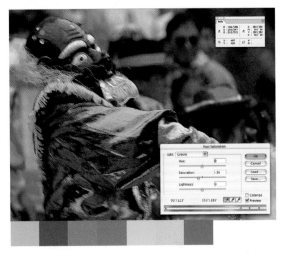

This allows you to see, measure, and evaluate the changes you're making in key color ranges.

We often work with Proof Colors turned on, especially when we're fine-tuning out-of-gamut colors before we convert to output CMYK or output RGB.

Tip: Use Proof Colors for Before-and-Afters. Photoshop lets you open more than one window for an image. This is particularly useful in conjunction with Proof Colors. When you choose Proof Colors, it only applies to the currently active window, so you can open two windows for the image—use one to view it in working RGB, and the other in simulated output CMYK or RGB.

Gamut Alarm

When you're working in RGB mode, Photoshop displays an exclamation point next to color specifications (in the Info palette and the Color Picker) to warn you when an RGB color is outside the printable CMYK gamut (see Figure 7-7, earlier in the chapter).

This gamut alarm is telling you that when you convert the image from RGB to CMYK, Photoshop will clip the RGB color to the closest available CMYK equivalent.

Gamut Warning

Photoshop's Gamut Warning shows you which colors in the image are out of gamut by displaying them with the color you choose in the Gamut Warning Preferences. We don't find this particularly useful—we'd rather just *see* what's going to happen to our colors using Proof Colors and the Info palette, but we thought we'd mention it for the sake of completeness.

Occasionally we'll turn on Gamut Warning just to see if we've overlooked a trouble spot (such as a highly saturated color in an important area of the image), but nine times out of ten, it just tells us that most of our deep shadows are out of gamut.

Unless we see a glaring problem with the shadows when we turn on Proof Colors, we just leave them alone and accept the CMYK values that Photoshop produces when we do the conversion. Doing a lot of work to bring very dark colors into gamut manually is just a waste of time. Instead, let Photoshop do it when it converts to CMYK; it's unlikely that you'll be able to see the difference in print.

Tip: Don't Sponge Saturated Colors. The fact that you can load the out-of-gamut colors as a selection using Color Range may tempt you to use the Sponge tool to desaturate them and hence bring them into gamut. Don't, because if you do, you're simply doing manually what Photoshop does automatically during RGB-to-CMYK conversion—clipping out-of-gamut colors. Besides requiring a lot of handwork, it can distort the relationship between the in-gamut and out-of-gamut colors, changing the appearance of the image in odd ways.

Levels

The Levels command operates on color images exactly as it does on grayscale images. The only difference is that, unless you tell it otherwise, it operates simultaneously on all the color channels in the image. We usually find Levels too coarse a tool to use for correcting problems with color balance (though we know people who've developed incredible skills doing so), but we still use it in three ways on color images.

▶ As an image-evaluation tool, using both the histograms and clipping display.

► When we have a color image that has no problems with color balance, but needs some lightening (or much more rarely, darkening) in the midtones. Often, a move with the gamma slider is all that's needed.

► As an image-targeting tool. If the image doesn't contain specular highlights that we want to blow out to white, we use the black and white Output sliders to limit the minimum highlight and maximum shadow dots. If there are specular highlights, we use the eyedropper techniques (outlined later in the chapter) instead.

The Levels composite histogram. Like the Histogram palette, Levels displays the histogram for an individual channel when you're viewing a single channel, and offers a Channels menu when you're viewing the composite image. The composite histogram it displays (labeled RGB or CMYK, depending on the image's color space) is the same as the default composite histogram in the Histogram palette, but different from the Histogram palette's Luminosity histogram (see Figure 7-7, earlier).

In the Luminosity histogram, a level of 255 represents a white pixel. In the RGB and CMYK histograms in Levels, however, a level of 255 *may* represent a white pixel, but it could equally well represent a saturated color pixel—the histogram simply shows the maximum of the individual channels. This means that you have to be careful with the black and white Input Levels sliders, because you can easily drive colors to saturation in a misguided attempt to clip highlights.

Figure 7-7, earlier in this chapter, shows the Luminosity histogram and the RGB Levels histogram for the same image. As you can see, they're very different. The image has no pure whites, and the Luminosity histogram shows this. The RGB histogram, in contrast, shows a distinct spike at level 255. In this particular image, rather than indicating clipped highlights, the spike shows the presence of saturated colors—a saturated color always has at least one of the primaries at level 255.

A look at the Levels clipping display shows this quite clearly. If we press Option and hold down the mouse button on the white Input Levels slider, we don't see any white areas, but we do see areas of saturated red, green, and blue.

How Levels works on color images. As the composite histogram implies, any moves you make to the Levels sliders when you're working in the composite channels apply equally to each individual color channel. In other words, you get identical results applying the same move individually to each color channel as you would applying the move once to the composite channel.

However, since the contents of the individual channels are quite different, applying the same moves to each can sometimes have unexpected results. The gamma slider and the black and white Output sliders operate straightforwardly, but the black and white Input sliders can be dangerous.

The white Input slider clips the highlights *in each channel* to level 255. This brightens the image overall, and neutral colors stay neutral. But it usually has an undesirable effect on non-neutral colors, ranging from oversaturation to pronounced color shifts. The same applies to the black Input slider, although the effects are usually less obvious. The black Input slider clips the values in each channel to level zero, so when you apply it to a non-neutral color, you can end up removing all trace of one primary from the color, which also increases its saturation.

Because of this behavior, we use the black and white Input sliders primarily as image-evaluation tools in conjunction with the Option-key clipping display. They let you see exactly where your saturated colors are in relation to your neutral highlights and shadows. If the image is free of dangerously saturated colors, you can make small moves with the black and white Input sliders; but always try to avoid clipping, staying well outside of the significant areas of the histogram. And keep a very close eye on what's happening to the saturation—it's particularly easy to create out-of-gamut saturated colors in the shadows.

The image shown in Figure 7-10 is a good candidate for correction using Levels. It has no real color problems, and no dangerously saturated colors, but it's dark and flat. The Levels clipping displays reveal that the only data above level 128 is a tiny specular highlight, and all that exists below level 26 is noise. A midtone adjustment with the gamma slider completes the job—three quick moves make an immense difference to the image. Whenever possible, it's better to make large corrections like this on high-bit data. They're doable in 8-bit-per-channel mode, but you run a much higher risk of posterization or color-banding.

Figure 7-10 Image correction using Levels

Note the absence of combing in the histogram because we opened and edited the image as a high-bit file.

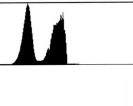

The raw scan, and the tone-distribution histogram

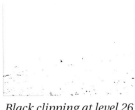

Black clipping at level 26   *White clipping at level 124*

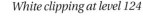

Input Levels: 26   1.80   128

The Levels move above yields the image at left and the histogram below.

Auto Levels, Auto Contrast, and Auto Color

In the past, we've always recommended avoiding the auto-adjustments that appear on the Adjust submenu (under the Image menu). Auto Levels generally wrecks color images, causing huge color shifts; and its younger sibling, Auto Contrast, while less of a blunt instrument than Auto Levels, still leaves a great deal to be desired. But we find the third option, Auto Color, very useful indeed for making major initial corrections, particularly on scans of color negatives or on images that need major adjustments in color balance and contrast.

If you simply use the default settings, you'll typically get a less-than-desirable result, as shown in Figure 7-11. (This is the same result you'd get if you simply chose Auto Color from the Adjust submenu.)

With very little help, though, Auto Color can quickly get you a lot closer to where you need to be. Here's how we use it.

Figure 7-11
Auto Color defaults

▶ We always launch it by choosing Levels and clicking the Options button.

▶ We click the "Find Dark and Light Colors" button to get Auto Color rather than Auto Contrast, which for some annoying reason is the default.

▶ We check the "Snap Neutral Midtones" checkbox.

▶ We adjust the clipping percentages from the ridiculously high default value of 0.50 percent to a much lower value, typically in the range of 0.00 to 0.05 percent, depending on the image content.

▶ When necessary (that is, more often than not), we click the Midtones swatch to open the color picker, and adjust the midtone target value.

In the example shown in Figure 7-12, we reduced the default clipping percentages to a lower value to avoid blowing out the highlights in the sky and plugging up the shadows. The default midtone color setting produced too little red and too much blue—we took the gray clouds as a guide, attempting to make them approximately neutral—so we raised the red and lowered the blue target values. The image updates as you change the target values, so the process is quick and interactive.

You can adjust the midtone swatch color by changing the numbers in the Color Picker, or simply by dragging the target indicator in the color swatch. Neither method is better than the other—use whichever you find more convenient.

Tip: Save as Defaults. When you dismiss the Levels dialog box, you're prompted to save the new settings as defaults. You may be tempted not to do so since the corrections are almost always image-specific. Save them anyway, because that way, the next time you click the Options button in Levels, it should be set to "Find Light and Dark Colors" with "Snap Neutral Midtones" checked. You'll still probably want to adjust the clipping percentages and midtone target color, but you'll save yourself some time.

Tip: If Things Aren't Working Right. For some strange reason, the Options button in Levels sometimes defaults to "Enhance Per Channel Contrast" (Auto Contrast), and when you switch it to "Find Light and Dark Colors" (Auto Color), the "Snap Neutral Midtones" checkbox is unchecked. If you're like us, you'll find yourself diving right in and adjusting the midtone target value, then wondering why nothing's happening. Don't forget to check the checkbox!

Other than in the situations covered by the two preceding tips, we don't usually bother saving the settings as defaults when prompted unless we're processing a bunch of images that need the same correction. More often than not, the settings are image-dependent. But we find that simply adjusting three values—the highlight clipping percentage, the shadow clipping percentage, and the midtone target color—lets us carry out powerful initial corrections with a minimum of fuss. We don't aim for perfection; rather, we use Auto Color to get the image into the ballpark, and preferring to fine-tune the results using Curves.

Figure 7-12
Auto Color tweaked

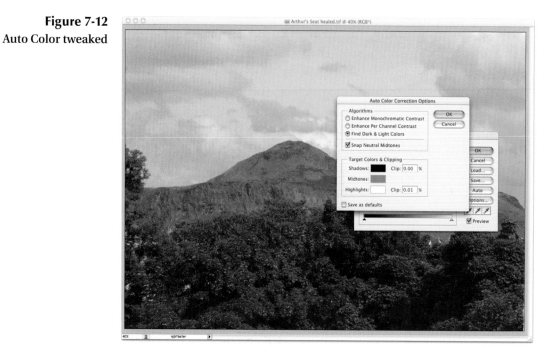

We start by reducing the default highlight and shadow percentages to prevent the blown highlights and plugged shadows produced by the defaults.

We click the midtone swatch to open the Color Picker, then we increase the red and reduce the blue until the gray clouds are approximately neutral.

Curves

The Curves command is probably the single most useful tool Photoshop offers for making corrections to tone and color, both globally and locally, and mastering it is an essential Photoshop skill. Almost every color image we work with gets some treatment with Curves; if we're in a hurry, a single round of curve adjustments may be the only correction we make.

In Chapter 6, *Tonal Correction Fundamentals,* we likened Levels to an automatic transmission and Curves to a stick shift. When you work in color, the difference is more like that between a chain saw and a scalpel.

The Curves command works the same way with color images as it does with grayscale ones, save that you can operate on all channels simultaneously (useful for tonal corrections) or on individual channels (useful for changing the color balance).

Curves tips for color images. All the options that exist for Curves in grayscale apply to working in color, too (see "Tip: Customizing the Curves Dialog Box" in Chapter 6, *Tonal Correction Fundamentals*). We always use the fine grid (Option-click on the grid area), and we generally use the Levels values with RGB files and the Percentage values with CMYK files—we're used to thinking of RGB in terms of levels and CMYK in terms of dot percentages.

To adjust the shape of the curve, we almost always use the point tool instead of the freehand (pencil) tool. The freehand tool is useful in some special situations that we discuss in Chapter 6, *Tonal Correction Fundamentals*, but the point tool keeps the curve as smooth as possible, and hence avoids sudden unnatural shifts in tone and color.

We use two distinct methods of placing curve points: one when we're going by the numbers, and the other when we're working visually.

▶ **By the numbers.** If we're going by the numbers, we use the fields at the bottom of the dialog box to type in the input and output coordinates we want. This places the point and automatically bends the curve so that it passes through that point.

▶ **By eye.** If we're operating visually, we Command-click in the image to place the point on the curve, then nudge it with the arrow keys to where we want it to be.

Tip: Channel Menu Shortcut. When you're working in either Curves or Levels, the "display channel" shortcuts—pressing Command-1 through Command-4 for individual channels, and Command-~(tilde) for the composite channel—operate the Channel menu in the dialog box. However, this only changes the popup menu; if you want to view an individual channel, you must cancel out of Levels or Curves, make the desired channel visible, then reopen Levels or Curves.

You've seen how you can use Levels to make a straightforward tonal adjustment. Figure 7-13 shows the same image adjusted a little more precisely with a master RGB curve instead.

Maintaining tone when correcting. Whether you're working in RGB or in CMYK, the individual channel curves often offer the easiest way to take care of color-balance problems. Remember that cyan is the inverse of red, magenta is the inverse of green, and blue is the inverse of yellow. To remove a red cast, for example, you'd pull down on the red curve in an RGB file, or pull up on the cyan curve in a CMYK file.

However, in cases where the image has a severe color cast, working on a single channel may have too drastic an effect on the overall tone of the image, because each curve adds or subtracts light (in the case of RGB) or ink (in the case of CMYK). In the case of a severe red cast, for example, rather than eliminating it using the red or cyan curve exclusively, you may need to adjust the other curves as well. That way, the overall tone of the image is preserved.

Editing the black plate. If we do our work with Curves correctly in RGB, we rarely have to make curve-based adjustments to the C, M, and Y plates (unless we're starting with a CMYK image), but the black plate is a different matter. Small changes to the black plate can have a profound effect on both the contrast and the apparent purity of the colors in the image, so we often use curves to fine-tune the black in CMYK.

We trust our monitors for most color issues, but for black-plate editing we go by the numbers, or, ideally, a proof, because it's quite difficult to judge the effect of a black plate tweak on the monitor. If the colors in the proof appear muddy, it's usually a sign that the black plate is too heavy. In extreme cases, we'll go back and reseparate the RGB image using a lighter

Figure 7-13 Image correction using Curves

The adjustment with Curves provides more control for fine-tuning particular tonal ranges. The highlights are slightly brighter, and the shadows have more contrast, than in the image corrected with Levels.

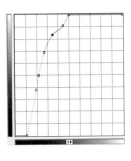

black, but often a small tweak that brightens the quartertones in the black plate can do wonders.

Likewise, small adjustments to the black plate can fix contrast problems, without having to go back to the original and reseparate. But if you're running into color-balance problems, it's a sign that your CMYK profile or your monitor profile needs further refinement. You can fix the image at hand by working the CMY curves, but you'll have to fix every other image you produce using these settings, too. It's much more efficient to go back and fix the fundamental problem (see Chapter 5, *Color Settings*, for a detailed discussion of these all-important settings).

Fix the neutrals, and the rest will follow. When you're wrestling with a global color cast, a very easy way to fix it is to find spots in the image that should be neutral, and make them so. If you do that, the rest of the color will generally fall into place. If you're working in RGB, equal amounts of red, green, and blue produce a neutral tone. If you're working in CMYK, it's a little more challenging. You'll have to determine by experience what combination of C, M, Y, and K produces a neutral tone.

Each combination of ink limits and black generation will give you different numbers; but if your Separation settings are based on SWOP inks, your neutrals will always contain more cyan than magenta and yellow, because you need more of the relatively impure cyan than the other inks to produce a neutral. When you work in RGB, Photoshop automatically figures the correct percentages of CMYK to produce a neutral. When you work in CMYK, you have to determine the neutral combinations yourself.

Finding neutrals isn't always easy—a great many images simply don't contain any. Sometimes you can find neutrals hiding in the shadows or lurking in the highlights—the Info palette is invaluable for hunting them down (see "Info Palette," earlier in this chapter).

Figure 7-14 shows an example of correcting a color cast using Curves. In this case it's a pretty simple correction, mainly adjusting for a yellow cast by tweaking the blue curve (remember that blue and yellow are complementary colors). If we had to make the same correction to a CMYK file, we'd apply the inverse curve to the yellow channel. Then we'd increase the cyan slightly in the midtones.

Figure 7-14 Correcting a color cast with Curves

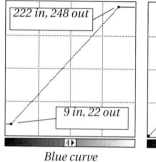

Blue curve

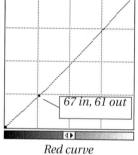

Red curve

To remove the yellow cast in this image, we start with the shadow inside the lower-left window, adjusting the dark end of the blue curve to make it neutral. Then we neutralize the highlight below the upper-left window by adjusting the highlight end of the blue curve.

These two moves kill the color cast but leave the midtones slightly red. We check the values in the lighter shadows, and adjust the red curve to make them neutral.

Black, White, and Gray Eyedroppers

The eyedropper tools in Levels and Curves function identically in both places, and they operate quite differently from the main controls in those dialog boxes, so it's worth looking at them separately.

We don't always use these tools. Besides an understanding of how they work, it takes experience to decide whether or not an image would benefit from using them. We encourage you to experiment with them while thinking about what they do. That way, you'll gain a much better understanding of both their possibilities and their pitfalls.

The black and white eyedroppers operate on color images in the same way they do on grayscale images, except that you set a target and source value for each channel in the color image. (See "White Points and Black Points and Grays, Oh My!" in Chapter 6, *Tonal Correction Fundamentals*, for a full discussion of how these tools work.)

The biggest difference between using the black and white eyedroppers in color and in grayscale is that in color images, the relationship between the source and target colors becomes much more critical, because it affects color balance as well as tone. If you set a neutral target color and click on a non-neutral source pixel, the color balance of the whole image changes. To get a feel for this, it's worth experimenting by clicking the eyedroppers on a few different pixels in the image.

The gray eyedropper. Back in Chapter 6, *Tonal Correction Fundamentals*, we described how the black and white eyedroppers work. We put off our discussion of the gray eyedropper until now, however, as it is only available with color images. The gray eyedropper does something similar to the other two eyedroppers, but it's different in one major way.

Where the other two eyedroppers always set the color you click on in the image to the target color you specify, the gray eyedropper does not. Instead, it adjusts the gamma values for each channel in an attempt to map the source color you click on in the image to a color with the same *hue and saturation* as the target color, but with the *luminance* of the source color. It's trying to adjust the color without affecting the tone.

Using the Eyedroppers

Now that you understand a little more about what the eyedroppers do, let's look at how you can use them. You can use the eyedropper tools in (at least) three ways.

▶ As highlight/shadow limit tools for optimization

▶ As color-balancing tools

▶ As arbitrary color-matching tools

However you use them, be careful with the relationship between your target color and your source color. You may get dramatic (read: "incredibly ugly") shifts in the color balance when you set a neutral target color and click on a non-neutral source color. Basically, the tools work better for making small moves than for making large ones.

Setting the highlight dot. We use the white eyedropper primarily as an optimization tool, for setting the minimum highlight dot after sharpening and immediately prior to converting the image to CMYK. But we do so only when we have an image that has clearly defined neutral highlights and contains specular highlights that we want to blow out to white.

Unless both of these apply, it's easier to limit the highlight and shadow dots using Curves, or using the black and white Output sliders in Levels.

Here's the procedure to set the minimum highlight dot.

1. **Determine the highlight point.** We work with the Levels command clipping display. We Option-drag the white Input slider to identify where we want to set the minimum highlight dot (the lightest area where there is actual detail), then return it to a setting of 255.

2. **Set the target color.** We set the target color according to our printing conditions, but since we're usually working in RGB we specify it using RGB values. The Color Settings preferences, when correctly set, give us the desired CMYK values. For example, using our preferred setup for sheetfed printing, a 243R 243G 243B highlight translates to 6C 3M 4Y 0K. If we're working on a CMYK file, we just specify the CMYK values directly.

3. **Select the source pixel/color.** We use the white eyedropper to click on a pixel that has the values we want to set to the minimum highlight dot. Typically, it'll have a value somewhere in the 247–251 range. Pixels brighter than that are allowed to blow out softly to white paper, so we preserve the highlight detail with a printable dot but still get the sparkle from the true specular highlights.

Setting the shadow dot. We use the black eyedropper to set the maximum shadow dot in a different situation. Photoshop's Custom CMYK feature seems to produce the best results when the Black Ink Limit is set to 100 percent, but most presses plug up the black long before it reaches 100 percent. Rather than change the Custom CMYK settings, we use the black eyedropper to back off the maximum black in the image to the maximum value the press can hold, without changing the percentages of CMY. Most ICC profiles built using third-party profiling software have a lower black ink limit set already, so in the majority of these cases we don't need to use the black eyedropper.

The procedure for setting the maximum shadow dot is essentially the same as it is for setting the minimum highlight dot. We identify the darkest pixels in the image that still contain useful detail, and use them as the source pixels for the black eyedropper. We set the target color to the maximum dot the press can hold without plugging up; the difference is that we specify the target color as CMYK, as follows.

1. Double-click the black eyedropper to set the target color.

2. Click on the pixel you've identified as the source pixel to load its color as the target color. With a typical setup for a sheetfed press, it might read something like 73C 62M 65Y 100K.

3. Reduce *only* the K component of the target color to your desired maximum black value. This can range from 97 percent for very high-quality sheetfed presses with coated stock to 75 percent for newsprint.

4. Click OK to set the new target color.

5. Click the black eyedropper on the source pixel in the image to map it to the new target color.

When you convert the image to CMYK, your maximum shadow dot will have the values you set for the target color, and your black plate won't have plugged-up shadows.

Color balancing. We generally use Curves to fix color-balance problems, but if we're in a hurry and the problem isn't too severe, the eyedroppers can be used for a quick fix. Again, this technique works best in images with clearly defined neutrals.

We set the target colors for the black, white, and gray eyedroppers to neutral RGB values. The exact values depend on the image and press conditions, but generally the white eyedropper works best in the range from 200 to 255, the gray eyedropper works best in the range from 100 to 156, and the black eyedropper works best in the range from 0 to 64. All these numbers are approximate, but they're good general guidelines.

The trick is to match the source pixel and the target color so that you make a transformation that changes the source pixel to a neutral color without greatly affecting its brightness (remember, adding or removing color changes tone). The gray eyedropper does this as a matter of course, but you have to do some figuring with the black and white eyedroppers. For example, if your source pixel is 242R 234G 241B, try a target color that's a loose average of the three, perhaps 239R 239G 239B.

In the example shown in Figure 7-22, later in the chapter, we eliminated most of the red cast by applying the white eyedropper to the water inside the glass, the gray eyedropper to the light shadow under the sugar bowl, and the black eyedropper to the deep shadows.

Arbitrary color matching. In some cases, you can use the eyedroppers to match colors between images. For example, a classic problem comes up when you shoot an event like a daytime football match, where the light changes over the course of the game. If you're going to run several shots of the game, you want the uniforms to be a consistent color in all the images. The eyedroppers can (sometimes) help you do this.

Note that this technique is *not* what the designers of these tools had in mind. When we mentioned it to a senior engineer on the Photoshop team, he commented that the technique "will work in many cases; but as the algorithms get stressed with larger moves, it will fail, sometimes dramatically, so don't come crying to me if it doesn't work."

Use the white eyedropper to match highlights, the gray eyedropper to match midtones, and the black eyedropper to match shadows. You need to have both images that you're trying to match open on the screen.

1. Double-click the appropriate eyedropper tool to bring up the Color Picker to choose the target color.

2. Pick up the target color from the "correct" image (the one you aren't changing) by clicking the cursor on the color you want to match. Then click OK to confirm the new target color, and close the Color Picker.

The Color Balance Command

We'd be remiss if we didn't at least mention Photoshop's Color Balance command (see Figure 7-15), which lets you make separate color adjustments to the shadows, midtones, and highlights. While we'll mention it, we don't use it—for two reasons.

▶ It doesn't do anything we can't do with Curves.

▶ The things it does are more difficult to control than they are with Curves, because there are some hidden moves happening that are hard to understand.

The command works by warping three preset gamma curves that cover the highlight, midtone, and shadow ranges. Problems can crop up in the areas where the curves overlap—it's easy to get unnatural color shifts, particularly when you shift one range in one direction and another in the opposite direction. You can get the same effect with Curves, but you aren't limited to the preset ranges of the Color Balance tool, and you know exactly what's going on.

Figure 7-15 (Not) using Color Balance

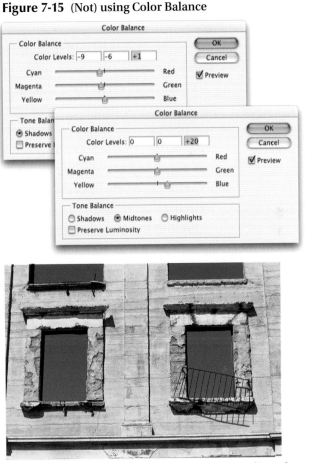

While it's possible to use Color Balance to neutralize color casts (as its name implies), it's more difficult than using Curves, because you can't target particular tonal ranges—only the generalized Shadows, Midtones, and Highlights.

3. In the image you want to change, find the color you want to change, and click the eyedropper on it to convert it to the target color.

   If it works, great! If it doesn't work, give it one more try, being a little more careful when choosing target and source colors. The technique works well with small moves, but if it isn't working it will quickly become obvious. In that case, use Curves or the new Match Colors command instead. They're more work, but you'll get more predictable and controllable results.

Hue/Saturation

The Hue/Saturation command allows you to address saturation problems much more easily than you can using Curves, and also lets you make changes to the hue of specific colors. We use it both for correction and for optimizing our images. One of the most powerful features of Hue/Saturation is that you can tailor the range you're adjusting to fit the image.

Hue/Saturation lets you make tweaks to the hue, the saturation, and the lightness of the entire image using the Master setting. This is mainly useful for controlling saturation—desaturating oversaturated scans or (more rarely) beefing up washed-out scans. The Hue control may seem like a useful tool for dealing with global color casts, but in practice we've found we get much better results using Curves or the eyedroppers in either Levels or Curves.

Besides the Master setting, Hue/Saturation lets you adjust the hue, saturation, and lightness of the individual primary and secondary colors (R, G, B, C, M, and Y). You can accept the preset ranges, but you can also fine-tune the range of color you're adjusting using the slider at the bottom of the dialog box. The center bar in the slider lets you adjust the color range, while the lighter bars on each end let you control the fall-off. This is basically like feathering a selection (see Figure 7-16).

Tip: Use Hue to Refine Your Color Range. Hue/Saturation lets you adjust the range of color that's being affected quite precisely, but it doesn't offer any obvious visual feedback. If you drag the Hue slider all the way to the left or right, it suddenly becomes very obvious exactly which pixels are being affected by the move because they change color drastically. With this whacked-out display, you can fine-tune the color range precisely, and then return the Hue slider to the zero position and start editing.

Hue/Saturation is useful but also dangerous. The effects you'll get depend very much on the original image, but when you're working in RGB, it's easy to oversaturate colors. If you're trying to increase the saturation of a color, keep a watchful eye on the gamut warnings in the Info palette—you can create colors that look wonderful on the screen but simply aren't reproducible in print. Remember that those out-of-gamut colors get clipped when you go to CMYK, so detail in those areas will vanish. You can always turn on Proof Colors for a more realistic view. For delicate saturation adjustments, we usually work on the CMYK file—in CMYK mode,

Figure 7-16
Hue/Saturation dialog
box

The numbers show the position of the selection controls.

Drag the ends of the slider to change the fall-off. This is like feathering a color range selection.

We clicked this point in the image to customize the range of greens the adjustment will affect. Doing so sets the position of the color range slider in the dialog box.

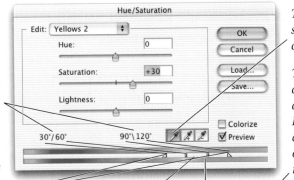

The eyedroppers let you select a color range by clicking in the image.

The slider lets you control the range of colors you're affecting. Drag the center bar to change the hue; widen or narrow it to change the range.

Hue/Saturation is changing the amounts of ink, and the adjustments tend to be much more subtle than in RGB.

Hue/Saturation vs. Levels and Curves. It's a great deal easier to manipulate saturation or to make slight hue changes with this tool than with Levels or Curves. To change a color's saturation with those tools, you have to manipulate each channel separately. In the simplest case—desaturating a saturated primary color such as red (255R 0G 0B)—you have to reduce the amount of red and add equal amounts of blue and green, which is quite hard to do with Levels or Curves.

With a saturated orange (255R 160G 0B), you have to reduce the amounts of red and green proportionally, and add an amount of blue proportional to the amount by which you reduced the red and green. This would be insanely difficult with Curves, and just about impossible with Levels! Hue/ Saturation lets you do it with one move.

Creative uses. Hue/Saturation is often particularly effective when it's used in nonobvious ways. The image in Figure 7-17 has screaming reds that almost overwhelm the rest of the image. The obvious solution would be to desaturate the reds, but they give the image much of its impact.

Instead, we go after the colors that aren't readily apparent in the image. We pump up the greens, increasing the green saturation to 43, and increasing the cyan saturation slightly to 11. Finally, since the reds in the RGB original tend to go slightly yellow when we convert to CMYK, we shift the hue of the reds by -3, making them a hair more magenta. For each move, we selected the range of color we wanted to affect by clicking in the image, and then fine-tuning with the slider in the Hue/Saturation dialog box. The effect is subtle, but we think it improves the image considerably.

Tip: Colorizing Grayscale Images. You can also use Hue/Saturation to colorize grayscale images, or to make a color image look like a hand-toned black-and-white print. Convert the grayscale to RGB, choose Hue/Saturation, and turn on the Colorize checkbox. For a warm sepia-tone look, try setting Hue to around 50, Saturation to between 25 and 30, and Lightness to 0. For normal color work, you *must* leave the Colorize checkbox unchecked.

Hue/Saturation in CMYK. Hue/Saturation is also a powerful tool when working in CMYK, but unless you have a very clear idea of exactly what you're doing, it's best used as a fine-tuning tool after you've seen a proof. When we got the proof of the drummers image in Figure 7-17, it was still a little flat. Boosting the yellow saturation, and shifting and saturating the reds, produced the result shown in the last image in Figure 7-17.

Unlike Curves, Hue/Saturation won't let you violate the ink limits specified in your CMYK Color Settings when you work on a CMYK file. If you want to override the ink limits in a CMYK file, use Curves instead. Just remember that you're playing with fire when you do so.

Figure 7-17 Hue/Saturation enhancements in RGB and CMYK

The reds in the image at left overwhelm the rest of the image, but desaturating them would weaken the image; so instead we go after the other colors.

Working in RGB, we use Hue/Saturation to increase the green and cyan saturation—pumping up the background and boosting contrast in the shirts.

Switching to Proof Colors, we see the reds are too orange, so we shift them toward magenta, producing the result below.

Brings out the greens

Cyan creates contrast in the shirts.

Makes the shirts less orange, more red

The reds are still too heavy and too orange, so we edit the CMYK file.

Brings out background splashes of yellow

Counteracts the extra yellow, turning the shirts magenta instead of orange

Replace Color

The Replace Color command (see Figure 7-18) takes the features of Hue/Saturation even closer to those of the Color Range selection command (see "Color Range" in Chapter 8, *Selections and Channels*). It offers a quick, easy way to make local (as opposed to global) color corrections. As with all local color corrections, the biggest problem is in blending the corrected area seamlessly into the image as a whole. With small moves this isn't a huge concern; but if you're trying to turn a red shirt green, you may have to do some handwork to get the edges right, no matter how careful you are in setting up the initial selection.

Figure 7-18 Replacing out-of-gamut colors

The uncorrected image

The RGB version of the image shown at left contains screaming greens (we wish we could show them to you) that are impossible to reproduce in print. When they're converted to CMYK, they turn a bluish gray.

Rather than desaturating the greens and weakening the image, we replace the unprintable colors with printable ones using the Replace Color command. The result, seen below, may be less accurate than Photoshop's interpretation of the color, but it looks a lot better.

We use a low Fuzziness setting and Shift-click several points in the problem area to select the bluish gray colors on the sleeve.

This replaces the problem colors with a plausible-looking substitute.

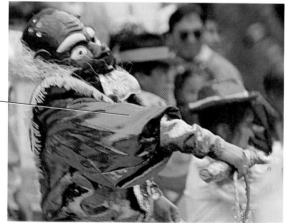

The image after replacing unprintable greens

For more detailed work, you're better off using the full range of selection and painting tools to make a detailed mask in an alpha channel, and using the Hue/Saturation command (see Chapter 8, *Selections and Channels*).

Replace Color does exactly what its name implies. It lets you select a range of colors and replace them with different colors by changing the hue, saturation, and lightness. We use it to make small changes to color areas that we can easily blend into their surroundings.

For example, the limitations of our output gamut render the high-lights on the green sleeve in the image in Figure 7-18 as a fairly unattractive blue-gray. One approach is to select the out-of-gamut colors using the Color Range command, then use the Sponge tool to desaturate them. As we've already said, we think this approach is *meshugge*: Photoshop will desaturate (clip) these colors when you convert them to CMYK, so you're just doing manually what's going to happen anyway.

Instead, we use Replace Color. First we turn on Proof Colors, so that we can see how the image will be rendered. Then we use Replace Color to select the problem area, and make tweaks to the Hue, Saturation, and Lightness. We feel the result is more pleasing, though it's arguably less accurate. The bottom line here is that our output process isn't capable of reproducing the color in the original, and something has to give. (See the

Interpreting RGB and CMYK Values

As we noted back in Chapter 4, *Color Essentials*, RGB and CMYK are both device-dependent—the color that you get from a given set of values varies dramatically depending on the device to which those values are sent. But working in RGB is considerably more predictable than in CMYK. If a sampled color has equal amounts of R, G, and B, you can be sure it's a neutral gray, although if your monitor isn't properly calibrated, it may not look that way. (And of course you're relying on your separation preferences to render a

neutral CMYK gray on press from those neutral RGB values.)

Likewise, you can tell if a color is overly saturated for the CMYK gamut if it contains a large amount of one or two RGB primaries and almost none of another.

CMYK numbers need a lot more interpretation—they only make sense in the context of a specific printing process. Every expert has their own set of magic numbers. They're all correct, but only for the situation in which they're being used.

Recommendations such as 5C 2M 2Y 0K for a neutral highlight, 60C 46M 45Y 11K for a neutral 50-percent gray, and 15C 24M 25Y 0K for Caucasian flesh tones (for instance) are good starting points, but they aren't sacrosanct. After proofing, you may find that you get better results with slightly different values. The same caveat applies to process-color swatch books. The CMYK values they contain were the ones used to print the swatch book. You'll get different results printing on a different press and paper.

sidebar "Truth in Imaging" for a discussion of a controversy surrounding this practice.)

Selective Color

Photoshop's Selective Color command attempts to reproduce the kind of color-within-color correction features found on drum scanners. We find that it's only useful for fine-tuning already-proofed CMYK files. It lets you adjust color ranges—you can, for example, pull some yellow out of the greens without affecting the yellow component of the other colors. Its major shortcoming is that it offers no control over the color range you select—you simply have to accept Photoshop's idea of "green" or "cyan."

Absolute vs. Relative mode. When we use Selective Color, we always use the Absolute mode, never the Relative. The Absolute mode simply looks to see how much of the color you're changing is present in the color you've selected, and removes the specified percentage of it. For example, if a red contains 93-percent yellow and you remove 11-percent yellow, you get 83 percent, not 82—it removes 11 percent of 93 percent, not an absolute 11 percent, despite its name.

In Relative mode, Photoshop tries to evaluate how red the red is, and then tries to make it 11 percent less yellow by adjusting all four color plates. This makes us crazy, because we never know what it's going to do.

Truth in Imaging

We often have to make decisions as to whether we should try to reproduce an image as accurately as possible and perhaps settle for some flaws, or adjust it to make it less accurate but also more pleasing. This is a subjective decision, and it leads us to a tricky area.

Photographers often lament that prepress people screw up their color. Prepress people often lament that photographers shoot images that can never hope to be reproduced in print. Both viewpoints contain some truth.

We don't believe that prepress people should simply override the intentions of the image creator—if you want to make stuff up, just paint a picture and leave the poor photographer's work alone—but we also realize that image creators sometimes have unrealistic expectations of the printing process.

We don't have a magic answer here, but we'd like to suggest that this is a situation where clear communication can prevent engendering a good deal of ill-will. In a

commercial situation, the person who signs the check has the final say, but unless the job is done as work for hire, the photographer has an interest in how the image is reproduced.

In the case of the image in Figure 7-18, we're working on our own photograph, so we can do whatever we like with it and no controversy arises. But we ask you to at least give some thought to the intentions of the image creator when you're faced with a situation like this.

Tip: Use a New Window to See Selective Color in Action. When we use Selective Color, we like to see what it's actually doing to the individual color plates, but unless you're viewing the composite color image, the command is dimmed. The easy workaround is to open new windows for the image, and set each one to view a different channel. Then you can make the composite color window active, choose Selective Color, and turn on the Preview checkbox. That way, you can see the effect on each plate as you make adjustments, though it's a little slow on older machines.

Channel Mixer

We debated whether to mention the Channel Mixer as a color-correction tool. We find it useful for getting grayscale images out of color ones (see "The Color of Grayscale" in Chapter 15, *Essential Image Techniques*), but its usefulness as a color-correction tool is less obvious.

We've been known to use Channel Mixer on an RGB image, but we're more likely to use it on CMYK files for which no RGB version is available. We show one such scenario in Figure 7-19. The original separation setup put black into the skin tones, making them muddy. We'd rather fix this by going back to the RGB original, changing the separation parameters, and reseparating the image, but that's not always possible. Lightening the

Figure 7-19 Removing black from skin tones

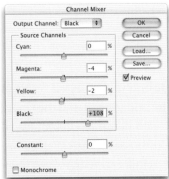

The image at left has black in the skin tones. We subtract some yellow and rather less magenta (the pink background relies on magenta), and boost the black slightly to produce the result at right.

Are All Color Casts Bad?

Some images simply don't (and shouldn't) contain neutrals. An image shot half an hour before sunset will have a reddish-yellow cast, and removing it almost certainly isn't a good idea, particularly if the photographer spent several hours up a tree waiting for that magical golden light.

Determine the origin. Think about where the color cast originated. Scanners often introduce color casts—sometimes they even introduce color crossovers, where the highlights have a cast in one direction and the shadows have a cast in the opposite direction. Some film stocks have crossovers too (photographers call them *cross-curves*).

Scanner-induced color casts can and should be corrected. Some color casts are more ambiguous. Distant shadows in landscapes actually appear blue to our eyes, and if you make them neutral, you'll produce an unnatural-looking image. But on a tabletop product shot, you probably want neutral shadows.

Look at the original. The best recourse is (obviously) to look at the original. The usual request is to match the original image, which is impossible—film has a wider tonal range and color gamut than you can hope to achieve in print. Instead, you can attempt to provide the illusion of matching the original within the limits of the output process.

Preserve relationships. The trick here is to preserve the relationships between the important colors in the image. Our eyes are very good at detecting color relationships, but they're easily fooled when it comes to detecting absolute color values—to judge color, they rely a great deal on context.

If the original is not available, you just have to guess. We almost hesitate to call this "color correction," because it's unlikely that you'll produce anything that resembles the intentions of the photographer—you're essentially making things up. But you can at least make educated guesses.

Look for memory colors. If the image doesn't contain neutrals, it may contain some *memory colors*. Memory colors are so called because we have an automatic expectation of how they should look. Blue skies, green grass, red fire engines, and foods like apples, oranges, green peppers, and carrots are good examples. When these colors look wrong, the whole image looks wrong. If they look plausible (not necessarily accurate), so will the image.

black plate in Levels or Curves would destroy the contrast—we only want to change the skin tones—and the Channel Mixer provides an easy means of doing so, with better feedback and, arguably, finer control than Selective Color. In the Channel Mixer dialog box, we set black as the output channel; then, while sampling values from the image and checking them on the Info palette, we subtract some of the magenta and yellow channels from the black. We also boost the black so that the black values in the shadows remain unchanged.

Color Correction in Practice

Let's look at some practical examples of how we put all the tools to work on images, from start to finish. Here is a representative sampling of originals, each with its own set of problems, and our proposed solutions.

Fixing a Bad Scan

In Figure 7-20 we have a bad original, captured on consumer film with a consumer point-and-shoot camera, printed at a one-hour photo store, then made worse by a scan from an ancient 8-bit flatbed scanner—a Hewlett-Packard ScanJet IIc that probably only captured six good bits with a tailwind. The Levels clipping display and histogram show no data above level 225, and there's heavy posterization in the shadows. In short, we're faced with quite a challenge!

Given the option, we'd reject this scan as unsuitable for reproduction, but clients typically don't go for that argument. We've debated dropping this example every time we write a new edition of the book, but we always decide to leave it in, because it really does represent a worst-case scenario. We endorse all the old caveats about Garbage In, Garbage Out and the impossibility of making silk purses from sows' ears, but we still see people receiving one-hour prints shot from disposable cameras and "scanned" using a video frame grabber from clients. Our fervent hope is that you never run into an image quite this bad, but if you do, realize that with care and skill, you can produce a usable image even from an original as degraded as this one.

We hear a good many prepress operators grumbling about how terrible digital photography is. When we press the subject, we usually find that they're talking about JPEGs from consumer-level digital cameras with nowhere near the required resolution for the job for which they were submitted. There's little you can do about insufficient resolution with JPEGs (digital images captured as TIFF or Camera Raw are a somewhat different story), and we don't recommend using amateur equipment for pro work. But this example shows that, in a pinch, you can produce acceptable results from the most unpromising source material if you take the time and energy to learn how.

Figure 7-20 Fixing a really bad scan

We obey our own admonition to fix the biggest problem first. The scan is far too dark.

Original scan

Shadow clipping (level 3). The shadows are heavily posterized, with huge tonal jumps between levels 0, 1, 2, and 3.

Highlight clipping (level 210). The deck is the brightest part of the image, and the red channel is brighter than the others.

The histogram shows that the highlights are completely empty and the shadows are clipped.

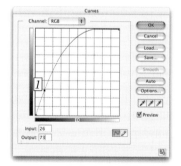

Working with Curves, we drag the cursor over the image and find that the values in the face lie around level 26, so we place point 1 to make the face visible. This blows out the highlights, so we place point 2 to bring them back into a reasonable range.

Point 3 clips the empty values in the extreme highlights. Point 4 brings down the brighter areas of the deck, and point 5 flattens the curve slightly to bring back detail in the sweater. We prefer to make all of our curve adjustments at once, but in this case we need to fix the color before we can go much further.

Point 1. 26 in, 73 out. Makes the face visible, but it blows out the highlights.

Figure 7-20   Fixing a really bad scan, *continued*

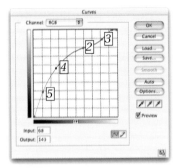

Point 2. 209 in, 228 out. Brings the highlights under control.

Point 3. 240 in, 255 out. Clips the unused highlight values.

Point 4. 152 in, 203 out. Controls posterization on the deck.

Point 5. 68 in, 143 out. Puts detail back into the sweater.

The red is heavily oversaturated, so we need to desaturate it before we can apply a final curve. Using the Hue/Saturation command to desaturate the red by 48 points produces the image seen at right.

The color looks more natural, but the contrast on the face is still too harsh and the spotless white outfit doesn't snap. We fix this with a second set of curve moves.

Normally we would have done any necessary spotting—fixing blemishes, dust, and scratches—before starting our tone and color moves, but in this case we couldn't because we couldn't see them! So we spotted the image before applying the final curve.

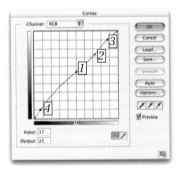

The image is still a little dark, and there simply is no detail in the shadows to be pulled out, so we limit our moves to avoid obvious posterization in the shadows.

Point 1 lightens the image overall, and points 2 and 3 bring back some detail to the bright areas of the sweater. Point 4 simulates a little fill-flash on the shadowed side of the face without posterizing it too much. After sharpening, we get the image at right. It isn't wonderful—there's some unavoidable posterization in the face, and there's no shadow detail at all—but it's much better than the original scan.

Fixing Contrast and Color

The preceding example was an extreme case. The next example (Figure 7-21) may seem similar at first glance, but a more detailed examination tells a different story. The image looks dark, but it contains good image data throughout the tonal range—it just needs to be redistributed. We can work more precisely with this image than with the previous one because we have much more information to work with. We use the same tools as before—Curves and Hue/Saturation.

Figure 7-21 Fixing a dark image

The clipping display and histogram show that there's detail in both the highlights and the shadows. There are a few white pixels at level 255, but the true whites lie around a more comfortable level 236. In the shadows, most of the darker pixels represent the saturated flowers in the foreground.

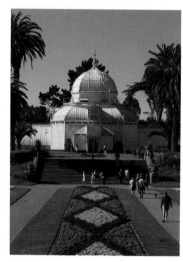

Shadow clipping (15)   *Highlight clipping (238)*

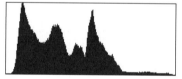

We need to make the midtones and three-quarter tones brighter, compress the highlights, and reduce the harsh contrast on the sunlit side of the building.

We start with tonal adjustment. Point 1 opens up the midtones, point 2 pulls back the highlights, and point 3 opens up the shadows. Point 4 fine-tunes the sky, and point 5 has a surprisingly large impact on the apparent overall contrast, even though it flattens the curve only slightly.

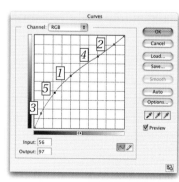

Point 3. 18 in, 39 out. Opens up the shadows.

Point 1. 102 in, 144 out. Brightens the midtones.

Point 4. 179 in, 199 out. Fine-tunes the sky and the detail in the quartertones.

Point 2. 226 in, 232 out. Controls the highlights.

Point 5. 56 in, 97 out. Deepens the three-quarter tones to improve overall contrast.

Figure 7-21 Fixing a dark image, *continued*

Color correction next. The image has a slight magenta cast—eyedropper sampling shows us that neutral areas are deficient in green—so we adjust the green curve.

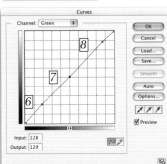

We increase green in the shadows (point 6), midtones (point 7), and highlights (point 8). Very small moves have a surprisingly noticeable effect.

Point 7. 128 in, 129 out. Adds green to midtones.

Point 8. 222 in, 226 out. Adds green to the highlights.

Point 6. 47 in, 52 out. Adds green to shadows.

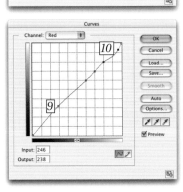

After placing a few anchor points on the red curve, we add warmth to the three-quarter tones (point 9) and pull some red out of the highlights (point 10).

Point 9. 74 in, 82 out. Adds warmth to the shadows.

Point 10. 246 in, 238 out. Neutralizes the highlights.

The image is usable as is, but it can be further improved by the saturation moves shown below, which bring out the green in the grass.

We sharpen the image with the Unsharp Mask filter, set the output limits in Levels to 249 for highlights and to 14 for shadows, and convert to CMYK, producing the final image at right.

Correcting Color Balance with Eyedroppers

The eyedropper tools in Levels and Curves can be difficult to control, but they can make short work of fixing color balance, particularly in images with well-defined neutrals (see Figures 7-22 and 7-23). The key to successful use of the eyedroppers is careful matching of the target color to the source color that you click on in the image. The eyedroppers don't work well for large moves, but they're very effective with small ones.

Figure 7-22 Cast removal with eyedroppers

The image at right was scanned on a midrange desktop flatbed scanner at default settings. It has handled the tonal range quite well, but the neutrals are magenta in the highlights and green in the shadows. Removing slight casts like this is one of our main uses of the eyedroppers.

We look for areas in the image that we think should be neutral, and sample their values using the Info palette. The background viewed through the water in the glass reads 242R 231G 237B—too magenta.

To make the color neutral, we set the target color for the white eyedropper to 237R 237G 237B (237 is the approximate average of the three source pixels' values), and click the white eyedropper on the source pixel. This makes the highlights a lot more neutral.

We still have a greenish tinge in the midtones. The fringes of the shadows provide our source pixels—we use a pixel under the sugar bowl that reads 124R 134G 130B. We set the gray eyedropper target color to 127R 127G 127B, and click it on the source pixel.

The deepest shadow, 4R 2G 4B, is under the teapot. We set our maximum shadow dot at the same time that we neutralize the cast. We set the black eyedropper target color to 13R 13G 13B, and click it on the source pixel in the shadows.

Figure 7-23 Partial cast removal with eyedroppers

You don't have to limit yourself to neutral target values with the eyedroppers. You can set any target color and click on any source color, although large differences between source and target colors can produce unpredictable results. Curves let you control color casts very precisely, but they can be a lot of work, and you can only manipulate one channel at a time. The gray eyedropper can be both faster and more flexible.

The image has a yellow cast but no obvious neutrals to use as a reference for correction by the numbers. When we make the background neutral using the curves shown below, the result is the rather ugly and austere rendition shown here.

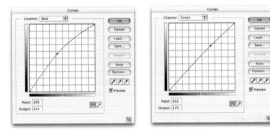

The gray eyedropper provides a more flexible solution. We decide to try removing half of the yellow cast instead of neutralizing it completely.

   We sample the background and see that it has about 25 points less blue than red or green. Halving the difference, we set the gray eyedropper target color to 127R 132G 122B, then try clicking various source pixels in the background.

   Clicking a source pixel of 111R 107G 80B produces the result at right, which looks much more natural than the strictly neutral one above.

Figure 7-24 Correcting a Photo CD image of unknown origin

The Universal Negative 3.0 profile worked better than others in acquiring this image, but the resulting image, top left, is flat, with a cyan cast. Not a bad starting point, though.

We apply the curves at right to get the result above, which represents our best guess.

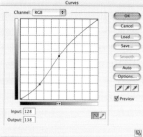

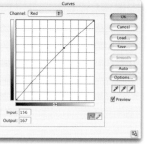

Correcting an Old Photo CD Image

Photo CD got a bad rap when it first appeared, and you still hear people saying that scans from Photo CD are usually flat, with a color cast. This isn't true; a properly made and properly acquired Photo CD scan usually looks great right off the bat. But we understand how Photo CD got its reputation, as this exercise illustrates.

Color management has always been at the heart of Photo CD—when you open a Photo CD image, you're always asked to choose a source and destination profile. But when Photo CD first appeared, parts of the system were still under construction. With modern Photo CDs, you can use the Image Info button in the Photo CD Open dialog box to find out which profile to use as the source profile for the image.

But most early Photo CDs don't have this information embedded, and they were often scanned using early film profiles (or film *terms*, in Kodak jargon) that provided less accurate results than today's. You have to guess which source profile to use (or try them all), and the images often need tweaking for color balance and contrast. This is the case with the image in Figure 7-24, from Kodak's first Photo CD Sampler.

A little experimentation suggested that the best profile for this image was the Universal Negative 3.0 profile—it gave us a better starting point than either the Kodachrome or Ektachrome profiles. So we took a first pass at the image using that profile and a few curve corrections.

But we were guessing, so we cheated and asked a friend at Kodak for a print made from the original negative. As it turns out, our guess wasn't too far off—it was a little on the conservative side. The image did indeed come from a negative. It has the characteristic orangey fleshtones and strong saturation of the Ektar 25 stock on which it was shot.

With the print as a reference, we created the curves shown at left, and then sharpened the image using the techniques described in Chapter 10, *Sharpening*.

The result is the final image at upper right on the facing page, which is about as close a match to the color and appearance of the original print as our output process will allow.

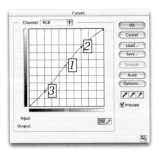

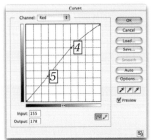

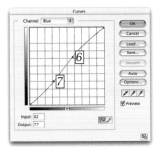

We created the tone curve at left and the color curves below to match the print we used as a reference. We used them to create the upper-right image on the facing page. We also desaturated the reds (see Chapter 9, The Digital Darkroom*), and emphasized the eyes with some sharpening tricks (see Chapter 10,* Sharpening*).*

The RGB curve improves the overall contrast, concentrating on the midtones and quartertones. Point 1 lightens the hair slightly, point 2 brightens the highlights on the face, and point 3 pulls back the curve to prevent the shadows from washing out.

The red curve kills the cyan cast. Point 4 puts red back into the fleshtones, and point 5 pulls back the red curve to avoid making the whole image too red.

The blue curve is the fine-tuner. Point 6 takes a little yellow out of the fleshtones, and point 7 pulls back on the blue curve to avoid a blue cast.

Working with High-Bit Images

At long last, high-bit images are first-class citizens. In Photoshop CS, all the convoluted workarounds we've taught for years to overcome the limited support for high-bit imagery simply go away. You can use layers, layer styles, adjustment layers, masks, and many of the most useful filters (including Blurs, Sharpens, and Noise).

In some ways, the high-bit support in Photoshop CS falls into the "be careful what you wish for" category. We used to think that 500 MB files were on the large size—now we're getting used to thinking in terms of gigabytes! (File size is still limited to 4 GB by the 32-bit operating systems Photoshop CS supports, but the underlying architecture of Photoshop CS will allow future versions of Photoshop to support terabyte-sized files once the OS and the hardware are available to do so.)

We used to ask, "When do we downsample to 8 bits per channel?" Now, the more pressing question is "when and how do we get rid of some of these layers?" We'll discuss these questions in detail in Chapter 14, *Building a Digital Workflow*.

The great benefit of high-bit images is that you have vastly more editing headroom, as shown in Figure 7-25.

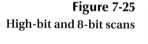

Figure 7-25
High-bit and 8-bit scans

The raw scan has a very compressed dynamic range, and the contrast is a little flat. Two simple moves can make a huge improvement.

Figure 7-25
High-bit and 8-bit scans,
continued

*We use Auto Color, accessed
through the Options button
in Levels, to tweak the
dynamic range and color
balance.*

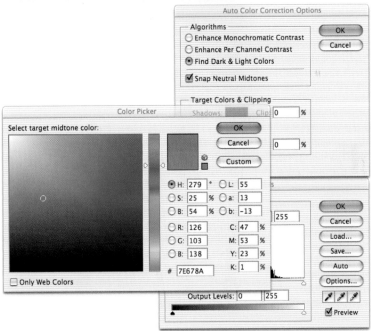

*We set the clipping percentages for both highlight and shadow to 0 (zero).
Setting the target midtone color to a neutral gray removes all traces of the
warm, one-minute-after-sunset light. Instead, we opted for a midtone target
color a long way from neutral, preserving the original color balance while
extending the dynamic range of the original.*

Figure 7-25
High-bit and 8-bit scans,
continued

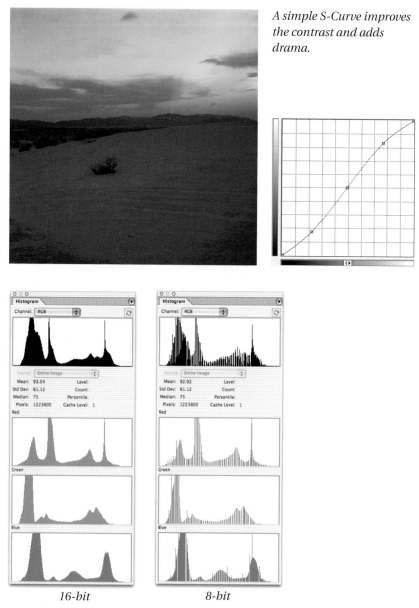

*A simple S-Curve improves
the contrast and adds
drama.*

16-bit   8-bit

The Histogram palette above left shows the histograms of the edited 16-bit-per-channel image. They are smooth, with no gaps. The Histogram palette above right shows the results of identical edits performed on an 8-bit-per-channel version of the image. It shows potential posterization around the quarter- and three-quarter-tones, as well as a considerable loss of levels in all three channels. At this point in the editing process, the difference is unlikely to be visually significant, but the 8-bit version won't tolerate much more editing.

Interpreting a Color Negative

Dealing with color negatives presents a challenge. With reversal (slide) film, you have a relatively unambiguous entity to deal with: You can throw the film on a light table and see what the image looks like. Color negatives are a different story. You *don't* want to reproduce what's on the film (unless you like your images inverted and orange). Instead, you need to interpret the image.

There is no single correct way to do this. Negatives permit many different, equally valid interpretations, because they capture a much wider dynamic range than we can render in a print. A look at the history of Ansel Adams's "Moonrise over Hernandez, New Mexico" illustrates this point dramatically—over the course of his career Adams created many different interpretations from the same negative.

Negative film captures a wider dynamic range from the scene than does slide film, but it also compresses that scene information into a much smaller density range on film than does slide film. This makes color negative quite friendly to desktop scanners with a limited dynamic range. The problem is getting a decent image—most desktop scanners will do the negative-to-positive conversion, but there's usually a global color cast. Correcting the image in the scanner software is often an exercise in frustration—the tools tend to be limited, and you're often forced to work on a postage-stamp-sized prescan.

The technique we show in Figure 7-26 certainly isn't the only way to get decent images from color negative, but we've been using variants of it for years, and we've found it reliable and relatively quick—even more so thanks to Auto Color, which does an amazing job (with some help) of making initial corrections on negatives. We use Kodak's very large-gamut ProPhoto RGB as our working space for color negative, and we deliberately scan the image flat and unsaturated. When we correct the image in Pro-Photo RGB, we increase saturation by increasing contrast. Any RGB space tends to increase saturation as you increase contrast, simply because you're driving the levels in the color channels closer to 0 and 255, but ProPhoto RGB is so large that the effect is much more pronounced than in smaller spaces.

In a pinch, you can obtain acceptable results using a 24-bit file, but anytime you work in a large-gamut space you'll find that you can really benefit from a high-bit capture, and this example is no exception.

342   **Real World Adobe Photoshop CS**

Figure 7-26   Interpreting a color negative

We start with the raw scan. We did no editing in the scanner software, so the scan is flat and unsaturated. Normally this might present a problem, but for rendering a color negative in ProPhoto RGB, it's exactly what we want.

If your scanner allows you to scan into a profiled working space, you can set it to scan directly into ProPhoto RGB. Failing that, you can just scan raw high-bit data, open the image with no conversion, and use Assign Profile to assign the ProPhoto RGB profile, which is what we did here.

We start by using the new Auto Color feature, which we access from Levels. We adjust the clipping percentages from the default setting of 0.50 percent to a much gentler 0.01 percent for the highlights, and no clipping at all in the shadows. This kills the color cast without losing any highlight or shadow detail.

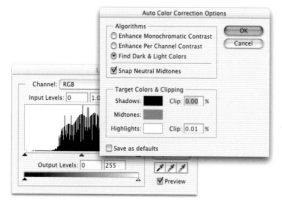

Figure 7-26 Interpreting a color negative, *continued*

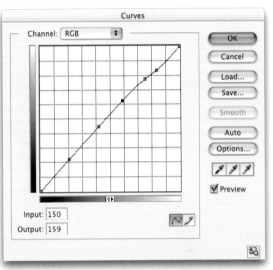

We use Curves to brighten the image in the shadows, holding the highlights unchanged, to produce the result shown at left.

To increase the saturation of the red rocks, we first fine-tune the range, moving the Hue slider all the way to the left to make the affected range obvious.

Once we've perfected the range, we increase the saturation, as shown at right, to produce the result shown at the far right.

Figure 7-26 Interpreting a color negative, *continued*

We use the same
procedure to refine
the color range for a
tweak to the greens.
This time, we made
a small hue tweak
in addition to the
saturation boost,
producing the result
shown at the right.

Next, we make a local correction, increasing
contrast in the shadows, midtones, and
quartertones while masking the highlights.
We use Color Range and QuickMask to make
a selection that excludes the highlights. Then
we apply the curve at lower right to produce
the result shown at lower left.

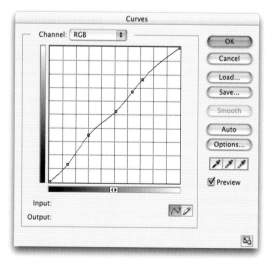

Figure 7-26 Interpreting a color negative, *continued*

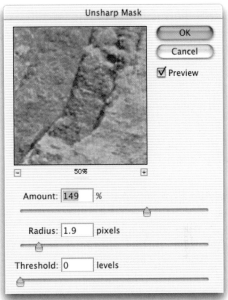

Our final step applies gentle Unsharp Masking to create a master archive image that we can repurpose for different output processes.

Color Is Personal

It's been argued that no two people see the same color. Experience has taught us that we see the same color differently on different occasions or in different contexts. We don't pretend to have all the answers, and you may disagree with some of our decisions. That's fine. Our aim isn't to wow you with our color expertise, but to show you how to evaluate images, how to see problems, and how to use Photoshop's tools to address them.

8

Selections
and Channels

Paths, Masks, and Shapes

You love the painting and retouching tools that Photoshop offers; you love layers; you even love all the options it gives you for saving files. But as soon as someone says "alpha channel" or "mask," your eyes glaze over. And when someone strings together a sentence like, "Edit your selection in Quick Mask mode and then intersect it with the eighth alpha channel," you drop your mouse and head for the door.

It doesn't have to be this way. Masks, channels, and selections are actually really easy once you get past their bad reputation. Making a good selection is obviously important when silhouetting and compositing images—two of the most common production tasks. But perhaps even more important, selections are also a key ingredient for nondestructive tonal corrections, color corrections, sharpening, and even retouching. We'll discuss these in the coming chapters, but before we get there, we must first make you a mask maven and a channel champion!

The first part of this chapter covers all the tools used in Photoshop for working with selections, channels, and masks, along with a lot of tips for using the tools the smart way. Next, we cover Photoshop's vector (bézier curve) drawing tools, including the "shape" tools and layer-based clipping paths. Then, at the end of the chapter, we run through some step-by-step selection techniques to show how you can use all these tools together to handle both simple and complex situations.

Masking-Tape Selections

The key to understanding selections, masks, and channels is to realize that they're all basically the same thing down deep. No matter what kind of selection you make—whether you draw out a rectangular marquee, draw a path with the Lasso, or use the Magic Wand to select a colored area—Photoshop internally sees the selection as a grayscale channel (see Figure 8-1). Note that in this section we're only talking about raster (bitmapped) selections; we'll discuss sharp-edged vector clipping paths and masks in "Paths," much later in this chapter.

If you've ever carefully painted around a window (the kind in the wall of your house), you've probably used masking tape to mask out the areas you didn't want to paint. If you apply the masking tape to the window, you can paint right over it, knowing that the window remains untouched. Selections, masks, and channels are electronic forms of masking tape.

In Photoshop, the masking tape is typically colored black. Let's say you use the elliptical marquee to select a circle. Behind the scenes, Photoshop sees this circle as a grayscale channel. In this selection channel, the areas that you selected (the parts with no masking tape over them) are white, and the unselected areas (the parts with masking tape over them) are black. As our friend and colleague Katrin Eismann likes to say, "Black conceals, white reveals."

Why Digital Tape Is Better

However, like everything else in life, there's also a spectrum of gray area between the two extremes. In real life, you can't have partially opaque masking tape. The wood or window or whatever is either covered and

Figure 8-1
Selections are
channels, too

 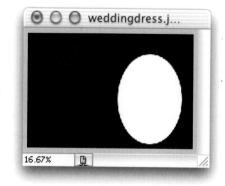

This selection is the same...   *...as this mask/channel.*

no paint touches it, or it's not (all the paint touches it). Fortunately, we're not dealing with real life; we're dealing with computers, and they're much more flexible than normal ol' tape.

If you look carefully around the edges of that circle we selected, you'll notice that there are gray areas between the black and the white. The gray parts of a selection channel are areas that are partially selected. If an area in a selection channel is 25-percent gray, then that area is 75-percent selected. Remember, the lighter the gray, the more selected the area is.

Benefits of Partial Selection

There were gray areas in that circle we selected because the elliptical marquee was anti-aliased (see Figure 8-2). If you turned off the Anti-aliased checkbox in the Marquee Options bar, the selection you'd get would have no gray, partially-selected pixels.

Smooth transitions between selected (white) and unselected (black) areas are incredibly important for compositing images, painting, cor-

Figure 8-2
Anti-aliased
edges

Aliased edges make for poor masks because they're too jaggy.

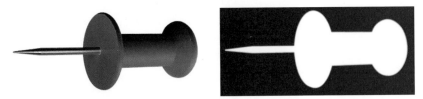

Smooth, anti-aliased masks create nicer, smoother edges appropriate for compositing one image on top of another.

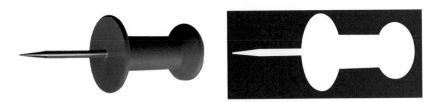

Vector-based masks (like clipping paths) create mathematically smooth edges but are often so sharp that they look unnatural.

recting areas within an image—in fact, just about everything you'd want to do in Photoshop.

When you paint over an area that is fully selected (no black masking tape), 100 percent of the paint is applied to each pixel. When you paint over an area that isn't selected (fully covered with black masking tape), no paint is applied. And when you paint over an area that's partially selected, only a percentage of the paint is applied to the underlying image.

The same thing goes for deleting, smudging, applying a filter, or any other action you can take on a pixel in Photoshop. The more selected the pixel is, the more the effect is applied (see Figure 8-3).

Figure 8-3
Partially selected pixels

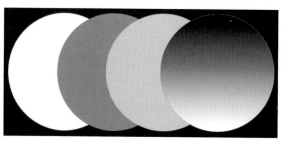

This is the selection mask; the circles are selected by varying amounts (the one on the left is fully selected; the one on the right has a gradient selection).

Delete key pressed

Gaussian Blur filter applied

Paint brush zigzagged up and down

Various effects applied to an image while the above selection is active.

Tip: You Can Always Move Your Selection. One of the most frequent changes you'll make to a selection is moving it without moving its contents. For instance, you might make a rectangular selection, then realize it's not positioned correctly. Don't redraw it! Just click and drag the selection using one of the selection tools. The selection moves, but the pixels underneath it don't. Or, press the arrow keys to move the selection by one pixel. Add the Shift key to move the selection ten pixels for each press of an arrow key.

Tip: Moving a Selection While Dragging. One of the coolest (and least known) selection features is the ability to move a marquee selection (either rectangular or oval) while you're still dragging out the selection.

The trick: hold down the Spacebar key while the mouse button is still held down. This also works when dragging shapes with the Shapes tool (which we cover in "Paths," later in this chapter) and even when dragging frames and lines in Adobe InDesign and Adobe Illustrator.

Selection Tools

Although there are a mess o' ways to make a selection in Photoshop (we'll look at them all in this chapter), there are three basic selection tools in the Tool palette: the Marquee tool, the Lasso tool, and the Magic Wand (see Figure 8-4). While some people eschew these tools for the more high-falutin' selection techniques, we find them invaluable for much of our day-to-day work.

Figure 8-4
Selection
tools

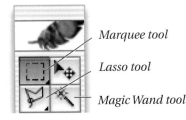

Marquee tool

Lasso tool

Magic Wand tool

The important thing to remember about these selection tools (and, in fact, every selection technique in Photoshop) is that they can all work in tandem. Don't get too hung up on getting one tool to work just the way you want it to; you can always modify the selection using a different technique (this idea of modifying selections is very important, and we'll touch on it throughout the chapter).

Tip: Adding to and Subtracting from Selections. No matter which selection tool you're using, you can always add to the current selection by holding down the Shift key while selecting. Conversely, you can subtract from the current selection by holding down the Option key. Or, if you want the intersection of two selections, hold down the Option and the Shift keys

Figure 8-5

Adding, subtracting, and intersecting selections

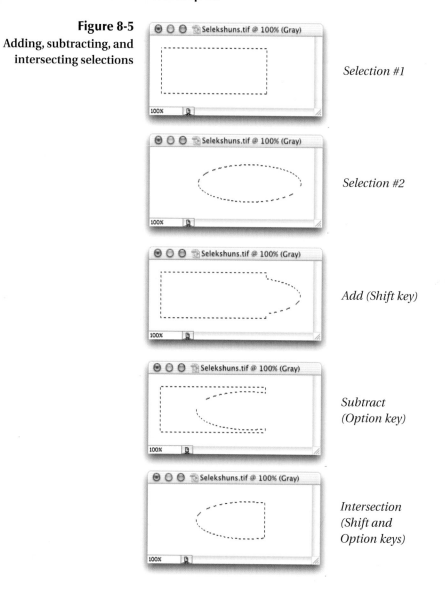

Selection #1

Selection #2

Add (Shift key)

Subtract
(Option key)

Intersection
(Shift and
Option keys)

while selecting (see Figure 8-5). If you don't feel like remembering these keyboard modifiers, you can click on the Add, Subtract, and Intersect buttons on the far-left side of the Options bar instead.

Tip: Select It Again. While Bruce is the steady-and-sure type, David tends to rush through Photoshop like a madman. One result is that David often deselects a selection without having thought through the implications (like "will I need this again?"). Fortunately, when he finds he does need that old selection again, he can recall it by pressing Command-Shift-D (or choosing Reselect from the Select menu).

Tip: Transforming Selections. Getting a selection right the first time you make it is a rarity (we keep a bottle of '96 Côtes du Rhône ready for those few occurrences). For instance, an object might look rectangular, but once you try to select it with the Marquee tool, you find that the selection needs to be rotated, stretched, and skewed slightly. In the past, we found ourselves succumbing to all sorts of horrible workarounds to tweak our selections. Now we just use the Transform Selection feature in the Select menu (sorry, we don't know of any keyboard shortcut here, but you can add one yourself by selecting Keyboard Shortcuts in the Edit menu).

When you choose Transform Selection, Photoshop places the Free Transform handles around your selection and lets you rotate, resize, skew, move, or distort the selection however you please. When you're done, press Enter or click the Checkmark button in the Options bar.

Less obvious is that after you choose Transform Selection, you can pick options from the Transform submenu (under the Edit menu) or type transform values into the fields in the Options bar. For example, if you want to mirror your selection, turn on Transform Selection, drag the center point of the transformation rectangle to the place around which you want the selection to flip, then choose Flip Vertical or Flip Horizontal from the Transform submenu (see Figure 8-6).

Marquee

The Marquee tool is the most basic of all the selection tools. It lets you draw a rectangle or oval selection by clicking and dragging. If you hold down the Shift key, the marquee is constrained to a square or a circle, depending on whether you have chosen Rectangle or Ellipse in the Marquee Options bar. (Note that if you've already made a selection, the Shift key adds to the selection instead.) If you hold down the Option key, the selection is centered on where you clicked.

Tip: Toggle Between Tools. You can switch between the rectangular and elliptical selection tools on the Shape popup menu under the Marquee in the tool palette, but it's faster to press M once to select the tool, then press Shift-M to toggle between the tools (Option-clicking on the Marquee tool in the Tool palette also toggles between them).

Figure 8-6
Transforming a selection

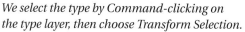

We select the type by Command-clicking on the type layer, then choose Transform Selection.

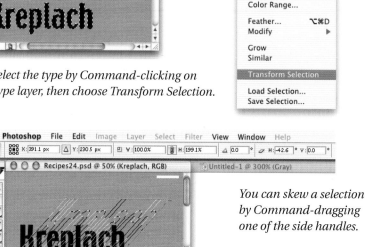

You can skew a selection by Command-dragging one of the side handles.

By dragging the center point to here, the transformation is centered at this location.

We skewed and scaled the selection by dragging and typing in the Options bar. You can also select items from the Transform submenu (under the Edit menu).

After pressing Enter (to set the transform), we added a Levels adjustment layer and moved the midpoint slider to darken the "shadow."

Tip: Pull Out a Single Line. If you've ever tried to select a single row of pixels in an image by dragging the marquee, you know that it can drive you batty faster than Mrs. Gulch's chalk scraping. The Single Row and Single Column selection tools (click and hold the mouse button down on the Marquee tool to get them) are designed for just this purpose. These are godsends when a low-end scanner glitches and slightly (or severely) throws off a row or column of pixels. We use them to clean up screen captures, or to delete thin borders around an image. They're also useful with video captures, because each pixel row often equals a video scan line.

Tip: Selecting Thicker Columns and Rows. If you want a column or row that's more than one pixel wide/tall, you need to use a different method. Set the selection style to Fixed Size on the Options bar, and type the thickness of the selection into the Height or Width field (note that you have to type a measurement value, like "px" for pixels, or "cm" for centimeters). In the other field, type some number that's obviously larger than the image, like 10,000px. When you click on the image, the row or column is selected at the thickness you want.

Tip: Selecting that Two-by-Three. You've laid out a page with a hole for a photo that's 2 by 3 inches. Now you want to make a 2-by-3 selection in Photoshop. Ordinarily, trying to select that with the Marquee tool would be nigh-on impossible without patience and a scratch pad full of math. However, when you choose Constrained Aspect Ratio from the Style popup menu, Photoshop lets you type in that 2-by-3 ratio on the Options bar (when you have the Marquee tool selected).

If you're looking to select a particular-sized area, you can select Fixed Size from the Style popup menu. In earlier versions of Photoshop, you had to type this value in pixels; fortunately, you can now type any measurement you want ("in" for inches, "px" for pixels, and so on).

Lasso

The Lasso tool lets you create a freeform outline of a selection. Wherever you drag the mouse, the selection follows until you finally let go of the mouse button and the selection is automatically closed for you (there's no such thing as an open-ended selection in Photoshop; see Figure 8-7).

Tip: Let Go of the Lasso. Two of the most annoying attributes of selecting with the Lasso are that you can't lift the mouse button while drawing, and you can't draw straight lines easily (unless you've got hands as steady as a brain surgeon's). The Option/Alt key overcomes both these problems.

Figure 8-7 Lasso selections

Beginning the selection   *End of (very rough) selection*   *Closed on mouse release*

When you hold down the Option key, you can release the mouse button, and the Lasso tool won't automatically close the selection. Instead, as long as the Option key is held down, Photoshop lets you draw a straight line to wherever you want to go. This solves both problems in a single stroke (as it were).

The folks at Adobe saw that people were using this trick all the time and decided to make it easier on them. Photoshop includes a Straight-line Lasso tool that works just the opposite from the normal Lasso tool—when you hold down the Option key, you can draw non-straight lines. If you press the L key once, Photoshop gives you the Lasso tool; then press Shift-L, and you get the Straight-line Lasso tool. (Of course, the Shift key trick won't work if you've turned off the Use Shift Key for Tool Switch option in the Preferences dialog box.)

In order to close a selection when you're using the Straight-line Lasso tool, you have to either click at the beginning of the selection or double-click anywhere.

Tip: Select Outside the Canvas. You may or may not remember at this point in the book that Photoshop saves image data on a layer even when it extends past the edge of the canvas (out into that gray area that surrounds your picture). Just because it's hidden doesn't mean you can't select it. If you zoom back far enough, and enlarge your window enough (or switch to full-screen mode) that you can see the gray area around the image canvas, you can hold down the Option key while using the Lasso tool to select into the gray area. (Ordinarily, without the modifier key, the selections stop at the edge of the image.)

Magnetic Lasso. The Magnetic Lasso tool (it, too, is hiding in the Tool palette behind the Lasso tool) lets you draw out selections faster than the regular Lasso tool. This tool can seem like magic or it can seem like a complete waste of time—it all depends on three things: the image, your technique, and your attitude.

To use the Magnetic Lasso tool, click once along the edge of the object you're trying to select, then drag the mouse along the edge of the selection (you don't have to—and shouldn't—hold down the mouse button while moving the mouse). As you move the mouse, Photoshop "snaps" the selection to the object's edge. When you're done, click on the first point in the selection again (or triple-click to close the path with a final straight line).

So the first rule is: Only use this tool when you're selecting something in your image that has a distinct edge. In fact, the more distinct the better, because the program is really following the contrast between pixels. The lower the contrast, the more the tool gets confused and loses the path.

Here's a few more rules that will help your technique.

▶ **Be picky with your paths.** If you don't like how the selection path looks, you can always move the mouse backward over the path to erase part of it. If Photoshop has already dropped an anchor point along the path (it does this every now and again), you can remove the last point by pressing the Delete key. Then just start moving the mouse again to start the new selection path.

▶ **Click to drop your own anchor points.** For instance, the Magnetic Lasso tool has trouble following sharp corners; they usually get rounded off. If you click at the vertex of the corner, the path is forced to pass through that point.

▶ **Vary the Lasso Width as you go.** The Lasso Width (in the Options bar) determines how close to an edge the Magnetic Lasso tool must be to select it. In some respects it determines how sloppy you can be while dragging the tool, but it becomes very important when selecting within tight spots, like the middle of a "V". In general, you should use a large width for smooth areas, and a small width for more detailed areas.

Fortunately, you can increase or decrease this setting while you move the mouse by pressing the square bracket keys on your keyboard. (For extra credit, set Other Cursors to Precise in the General Preferences dialog box; that way you can see the size of the Lasso Width.) Also, Shift-[and Shift-] set the Lasso Width to the lowest or highest value (one or 40). If you use a pressure-sensitive tablet, turn on the Stylus Pressure checkbox on the Options bar; the pressure then relates directly to Lasso Width.

▶ **Sometimes you want a straight line.** You can get a straight line with the Magnetic Lasso tool by Option-clicking once (at the beginning of the segment) and then clicking again (at the end of the segment).

▶ **Occasionally, customize your Frequency and Edge Contrast settings.** These settings (on the Options bar) control how often Photoshop drops an anchor point and how much contrast between pixels it's looking for along the edge. In theory, a more detailed edge requires more anchor points (a higher frequency setting), and selecting an object in a low-contrast image requires a lower contrast threshold. To be honest, we're much more likely to switch to a different selection tool or technique before messing with these settings.

The last rule is patience. Nobody ever gets a perfect selection with the Magnetic Lasso tool. It's not designed to make perfect selections; it's designed to make a reasonably good approximation that you can edit. We cover editing selections in "Quick Masks," later in this chapter.

Tip: Scrolling While Selecting. It's natural to zoom in close when you're dragging the Magnetic Lasso tool around. Nothing wrong with that. But unless you have an obscenely large monitor, you won't be able to see the whole of the object you're selecting. No problem; the Grabber Hand works just fine while you're selecting—just hold down the Spacebar and drag the image around. You can also press the + and - (plus and minus) keys to zoom in and out while you make the selection.

Magic Wand

The last selection tool in the Tool palette is the Magic Wand, so-called more for its icon than for its prestidigitation. When you click on an image

Figure 8-8
Magic Wand
selections

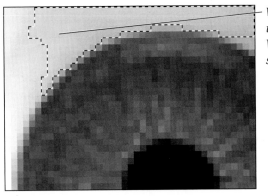

We clicked here with the Magic Wand tolerance set to 18.

with the Magic Wand (dragging has no effect), Photoshop selects every neighboring pixel with the same or similar gray level or color. "Neighboring" means that the pixels must be touching on at least one side (see Figure 8-8). If you want to select all the similar-toned pixels in the image, whether they're touching or not, turn off the Contiguous checkbox in the Options bar before clicking.

How similar can the pixels be before Photoshop pulls them into the selection? It's entirely up to you. You can set the Tolerance setting on the Options bar from 0 to 255.

In a grayscale image, this tolerance value refers to the number of gray levels from the sample point's gray level. If you click on a pixel with a gray level of 120 and your Tolerance is set to 10, Photoshop selects any and all neighboring pixels that have values between 110 and 130.

Tip: Sample Small, Sample Often. The Magic Wand tool can be frustrating when it doesn't select everything you want it to. When this happens, novice users often set the tolerance value higher and try again. Instead, try keeping the tolerance low (between 12 and 32) and Shift-click to add more parts (or Option-click to take parts away).

Tip: Sample Points in the Magic Wand. Note that when you select a pixel with the Magic Wand, you may not get the pixel value you expect. It all depends on the Sample Size popup menu on the Options bar (when you have the Eyedropper tool selected). If you select 3 by 3 Average or 5 by 5 Average in that popup menu, Photoshop averages the pixels around the one you click on with the Magic Wand. On the other hand, if you select Point Sample, Photoshop uses exactly the one you click on.

Bruce prefers Point Sample because he always knows what he's going to end up with. David only uses Point Sample when using the eyedropper tools in Levels or Curves (see Chapter 6, *Tonal Correction Fundamentals*); when he's just trying to pick up a color, he uses 3 by 3 Average.

In RGB and CMYK images, however, the Magic Wand's tolerance value is slightly more complex. The tolerance refers to each and every channel value, instead of just the gray level.

For instance, let's say your Tolerance is set to 10 and you click on a pixel with a value of 60R 100G 200B. Photoshop selects all neighbors that have red values from 50 to 70, and green values from 90 to 110, and blue values from 190 to 210. All three conditions must be met, or the pixel isn't included in the selection (see "Grow," later in the chapter for more info).

Bruce almost never uses the Magic Wand; he finds it too limiting, so he uses Color Range instead (which we talk about later in this chapter; see Figure 8-27). David finds himself using the Magic Wand frequently. However, he almost never gets the selection he wants out of it, so he uses other tools to fine-tune the selection.

Tip: Select on a Channel, Not Composite. Because it's often difficult to predict how the Magic Wand tool is going to work in a color image, we typically like to make selections on a single channel of the image. The Magic Wand is more intuitive on this grayscale image, and when you switch back to the composite channel (by pressing Command-~ (tilde, to the left of the 1 key on your keyboard) or clicking on the RGB or CMYK tile in the Channels palette), the selection's flashing border is still there.

Tip: Reverse Selecting. One simple but nonobvious method that we often use to select an area is to select a larger area with the Lasso or Marquee tool and then Option-click with the Magic Wand tool on the area we don't want selected (see Figure 8-9).

Floating Selections

We need to take a quick diversion off the road of making selections and into the world of what happens when you move a selection. Photoshop has traditionally had a feature called floating selections. A floating selection is a temporary layer just above the currently selected layer; as soon as you deselect the floating selection, it "drops down" into the layer, replac-

Figure 8-9
Reverse selecting

In order to select the green leaf, we first draw a marquee around the whole area.

By Option-clicking with the Magic Wand tool twice (once on the background and once on the yellow), our selection is almost complete.

Now the rough selection can be cleaned up with the Lasso tool or in Quick Mask mode.

ing whatever pixels were below it. When you move a selection of pixels within an image, Photoshop acts as though those pixels were on a layer. Unfortunately, while these floating selections act like layers, they don't show up in the Layers palette.

The Photoshop engineering team has been trying to get rid of floating selections for years, but there are still a few instances where they appear. In general, however, we prefer to avoid floating selections and instead move pixels to a real layer for accurate positioning.

Tip: Forcing a Float. If you want to cut out the pixels and float them (so that a blank spot remains where the pixels were), you can drag the selection with the Move tool. Remember that you can get the Move tool temporarily by holding down the Command key. If you'd rather copy the pixels into a floating selection, you can hold down the Option/Alt key while dragging.

Selections from Channels

Why would you go through all the trouble of creating a selection if the selection was already made for you? More often than not, the selection you're looking to make is already hidden within the image; to unlock it you only have to look at the color channels that make up the image (see "Channels," later in this chapter).

Here's one good way to tease a selection mask out of an image (see Figure 8-10). We demonstrate these techniques in more detail in the step-by-step examples at the end of this chapter.

1. Switch through the color channels until you find the one that gives the best contrast between the element you're trying to select and its background.

2. Duplicate that channel by dragging the channel tile onto the New Channel icon in the Channels palette.

3. Use Levels or Curves to adjust the contrast between the elements you want to select and the rest of the image.

4. Clean up the mask manually. We typically use the Lasso tool to select and delete areas, or the Brush tool with one finger on the X key (so you can paint with black, then press X to "erase" with white, and so on).

Using Levels and Curves. The real key to this tip is step number 3: using Levels or Curves. With Levels, concentrate on the three Input sliders to isolate the areas you're after.

In the Curves dialog box, use the Eyedropper tool to see where the pixels sit on the curve (click and drag around the image while the Curves dialog box is open, and watch the white circle bounce around on the curve). Then use the Pencil tool in the dialog box to push those pixels to white or black. The higher the contrast, the easier it is to extract a selection from it. Some people use the Smooth button after making these sorts of "hard" curve maps. But in this case, we often run a small-value Gaussian Blur after applying the curve, so we just don't bother with smoothing the curve.

Using RGB. It's usually easier to grab selection masks from RGB images than from CMYK images. However, if you're going to switch from CMYK to RGB, make sure you do it on a duplicate of the image, because all that mode switching damages the image too much.

Figure 8-10   Starting with a channel

Red channel

Green channel

Blue channel (best contrast)

Quick and dirty Levels adjustment to blue channel

Fine-tuned version of blue channel

Tip: Floating Selections Are Layers, Too. You can change the mode of a floating selection to Multiply, Screen, Overlay, or any of the others. You can even change its opacity. But if the floating selection doesn't appear in the Layers palette, how are you to make these changes? After floating the pixels, select Fade from the Edit menu. (Non-intuitive, but true.) However, as soon as you try to paint on it, or run a filter, or do almost anything else interesting to the floating selection, Photoshop deselects it and drops it back down to the layer below it. That's one reason we would rather just float pixels onto a real layer before messing with them.

Quick Masks

When you select a portion of your image, you see the flashing dotted lines—they're fondly known as *marching ants* to most Photoshop folks. But what are these ants really showing you? In a typical selection, the marching ants outline the boundary of pixels that are selected 50 percent or more. There are often loads of other pixels that are selected 49 percent or less that you can't see at all from the marching ants display. Very frustrating.

Tip: Hide the Marching Ants. The human eye is a marvelous thing. Scientists have shown us that one of the things the eye (and the optical cortex in the brain) is great at is detecting motion (probably developed through centuries of hunting and gathering in the forests). However, evolution sometimes works against us. In Photoshop, the motion of a selection's marching ants is so annoying and distracting that it can bring production to a halt.

Fortunately, you can hide those little ants by turning off Show Extras from the Select menu (or pressing Command-H). We do this constantly. In fact, we almost never apply a filter or do much of anything in Photoshop while the ants are marching.

The only problem is that you actually have to use your short-term memory to remember where the selection is on screen. With complex operations, you also have to remember that you have a selection—we've lost count of the number of times we've wondered why our filter or curve was having no visible effect on the image, only to remember belatedly that we had a 6-pixel area selected, usually one that wasn't currently visible.

But seeing cut-and-dried marching ant boundaries is often not helpful. So Photoshop includes a Quick Mask mode to show you exactly what's selected and how much each pixel is selected. When you enter Quick Mask mode (select the Quick Mask icon in the Tool palette or type Q), you see the underlying selection channel in all its glory. However, because the quick mask is overlaying the image, the black areas of the mask are 50-percent-opaque red and the white (selected) areas are even more transparent than that (see Figure 8-11). The red is supposed to remind you of rubylith, for those of you who remember rubylith.

You can change both the color and the transparency of the quick mask in the Quick Mask Options dialog box (see Figure 8-12)—the fast way to get there is to double-click on the Quick Mask icon. If the image you're working on has a lot of red in it, you'll probably want to change the quick mask color to green or some other contrasting color. Either way, we almost always increase the opacity of the color to about 75 percent, so it displays more prominently against the background image.

Note that these changes aren't document-specific. That is, they stick around in Photoshop until you change them.

Tip: How Selected Is Selected? Even when you're in Quick Mask mode it's difficult to see partially selected pixels (especially those that are less than 50-percent selected). Note that the Info palette shows grayscale values when you're in this mode; those gray values represent the "percentage

Figure 8-11
Quick Mask mode

The marching ants show some of the selected areas of the image.

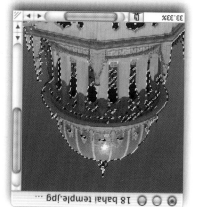

The quick mask shows all the selected pixels (fully and partially selected).

selected" for each pixel. It's just another reason always to keep one eye on that palette.

Editing Quick Masks

The powerful thing about quick masks isn't just that you can see a selection you've made, but rather that you can edit that selection with precision. When you're working in Quick Mask mode, you can paint using any of Photoshop's painting or editing tools, though you're limited to painting in grayscale. Painting with black is like adding "digital masking tape" (it subtracts from your selection), and painting with white (which appears transparent in this mode) adds to the selection.

If the element in your image is any more complicated than a rectangle, you can use Quick Mask to select it quickly and precisely. (We do this for almost every selection we make.)

1. Select the area as carefully as you can, using any of the selection tools (but don't spend too much time on it).

2. Switch to Quick Mask mode (press Q).

3. Paint or edit using the Brush tool (or any other painting or editing tool) to refine the selection you've made. Remember that partially transparent pixels will be partially selected (we often run a Gaussian Blur filter on the quick mask to smooth out sharp edges in the selection).

4. Switch out of Quick Mask mode by pressing Q again. The marching ants update to reflect the changes you've made (see Figure 8-13).

Note that if you switch to Quick Mask mode with nothing selected, the quick mask will be empty (fully transparent). This would imply that the whole document is selected, but it doesn't work that way.

Figure 8-12
Quick Mask
Options dialog box

Figure 8-13 Editing quick masks

Original, quick-and-dirty
selection with the Lasso tool

In Quick Mask mode, you can
clean up the selection using any
tool, including the brushes.

When you leave Quick Mask
mode, the selection is updated.

Tip: Filtering Quick Masks. The Quick Mask mode is also a great place to apply filters or special effects. Any filter you run affects only the selection, not the entire image (see Figure 8-14). For instance, you could make a rectangular selection, switch to Quick Mask mode, and then run the Twirl filter. When you leave Quick Mask mode, you can fill, paint, or adjust the altered selection.

Tip: Reversal of Color. Some people are just contrary. Give it to them one way, and they want it the other. If you're the kind of person who likes the selected areas to be black (or red, or whatever other color you choose in Quick Mask Options) and the unselected areas to be fully transparent, you can change this in Quick Mask Options. Even faster, you can Option-click on the Quick Mask icon in the Tool palette. Note that when you do this, the icon actually changes to reflect your choice.

If you do change the way that Quick Mask works, you'll probably want to reverse the way that channels and layer masks work, too (double-click on the channel in the Channels palette). Otherwise, you'll have a hard time remembering whether black means selected or unselected. Bruce doesn't worry about keeping these things straight—he just uses Inverse

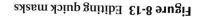

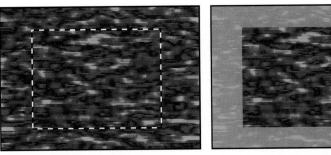

Original selection

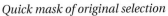

Quick mask of original selection

Quick mask after Twirl filter applied

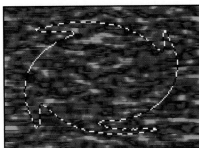

Post-Twirl selection

(from the Select menu, or press Command-Shift-I) when the selection winds up being the opposite of what he wants.

Anti-Aliasing and Feathering

If you've ever been in a minor car accident and later talked to an insurance adjuster, you've probably been confronted with their idea that you may not be fully blameless or at fault in the accident. And, just as you can be 25-percent or 50-percent at fault, you can partially select pixels in Photoshop. One of the most common partial selections is around the edges of a selection. And the two most common ways of partially selecting the edges are anti-aliasing and feathering.

Anti-Aliasing

If you use the Marquee tool to select a rectangle, the edges of the selection are nice and crisp, which is probably how you want them. Crisp edges around an oval or nonregular shape, however, are rarely a desired effect. That's because of the stair-stepping required to make a diagonal or curve out of square pixels. What you really want (usually) is partially selected pixels in the notches between the fully selected pixels. This technique is called *anti-aliasing*.

Every selection in Photoshop is automatically anti-aliased for you, unless you turn this feature off in the selection tool's Options bar. Unfortunately, you can't see the anti-aliased nature of the selection unless you're in Quick Mask mode, because anti-aliased (partially selected) pixels are often less than 50-percent selected. Note that once you've made a selection with Anti-aliased turned off on the Options bar, you can't anti-alias it—though there are ways to fake it (see below).

Feathering

Anti-aliasing simply smooths out the edges of a selection, adjusting the amounts that the edge pixels are selected in order to appear smooth. But it's often (too often) the case that you need a larger transition area between what is and isn't selected. That's where feathering comes in. *Feathering* is a way to expand the border area around the edges of a selection. The border isn't just extended out; it's also extended in (see Figure 8-15).

To understand what feathering does, it's important to understand the concept of the selection channel that we talked about earlier in the chapter. That is, when you make a selection, Photoshop is really "seeing" the selection as a grayscale channel behind the scenes. The black areas are totally unselected, the white areas are fully selected, and the gray areas are partially selected.

When you feather a selection, Photoshop is essentially applying a Gaussian Blur to the grayscale selection channel. (We say "essentially" because in some circumstances—like when you set a feather radius of over 120 pixels—you get a slightly different effect; however, there's usually so little difference that it's not worth bothering with. For those technoids out there who really care, Adobe tells us that a Gaussian Blur of the quick mask channel is a tiny bit more accurate and "true" than a feather.)

There are three ways to feather a selection.

▶ Before selecting, specify a feather amount in the Options bar.

▶ After selecting, choose Feather from the Select menu (or press Command-Option-D).

▶ Apply a Gaussian Blur to the selection's quick mask.

Figure 8-15
Feathering

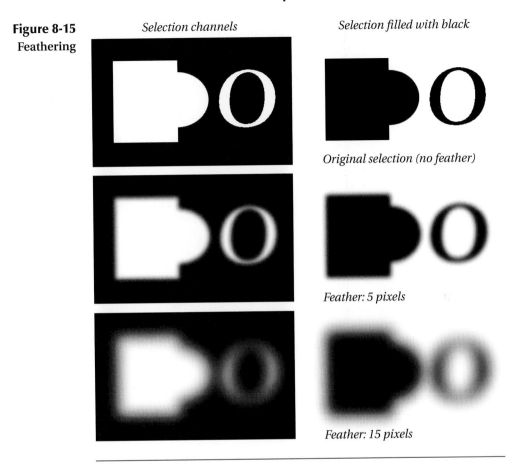

Selection channels

Selection filled with black

Original selection (no feather)

Feather: 5 pixels

Feather: 15 pixels

Tip: Tiny Feathers. You don't need to use whole numbers when feathering. We find we often need a value of only .5 or .7 to get the effect we're looking for (a nice, subtle blend from what is selected to what's not). Let's say that after you've spent five minutes making a complicated selection, you realize that Anti-aliased was turned off on the Options bar. You can fake the anti-aliasing by feathering the selection by a small amount, like .5. This blurs the selection slightly (the edges contain partially selected pixels), giving an anti-aliased look.

Tip: Feathering a Portion of a Selection. When you choose Feather from the Select menu, your entire selection is feathered. Sometimes, however, you want to feather only a portion of the selection. Maybe you want a hard edge on one half of the selection and a soft edge on the other. You can do this by switching to Quick Mask mode, selecting what you want feathered with any of the selection tools, and applying a Gaussian Blur to it. When you flip out of Quick Mask mode, the "feathering" is included in the selection.

Note that if you want a nice, soft feather between what is feathered and what isn't, you first have to feather the selection you make while you're in Quick Mask mode (see Figure 8-16).

Figure 8-16 Feathering part of a selection

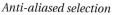

Original image   *Anti-aliased selection*   *After Gaussian Blur*   *Mustache and neck "feathered"*

Channels

Back in "Masking-Tape Selections," we told you that selections, masks, and channels are all the same thing down deep: grayscale images. This is not intuitive, nor is it easy to grasp at first. But once you really understand this point, you've taken the first step toward really surfing the Photoshop tsunami.

A *channel* is a solitary grayscale image—each pixel described using either 8 bits or 16 bits of data, depending on whether or not it's a high-bit image. You can have up to 56 channels in a document—that includes the three in an RGB or four in a CMYK image. (Actually, there are two exceptions: First, images in Bitmap mode can only contain a single 1-bit channel; second, Photoshop allows one additional channel per layer to accommodate layer masks, which we'll talk about later in this chapter.)

But in the eyes of the program, not all channels are created equal. There are three types of channels: alpha, color, and spot-color channels (see Figure 8-17). We discuss the first two here, and the third in Chapter 11, *Spot Colors and Duotones.*

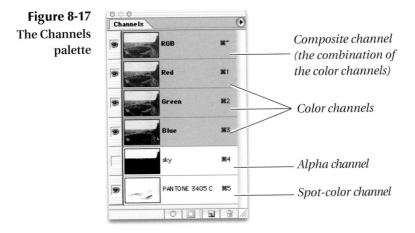

Figure 8-17
The Channels
palette

Composite channel
(the combination of
the color channels)

Color channels

Alpha channel

Spot-color channel

Alpha Channels

People get very nervous when they hear the term "alpha channel," because they figure that with such an exotic name, it has to be a complex feature. Not so. An *alpha channel* is simply a grayscale picture. Alpha channels let you save selections, but a solid understanding of these beasts is also crucial to tackling layer masks. Note that in Photsoshop CS, 16-bit images are finally first-class citizens: You can make, save, and load any sort of selection or channel in high-bit images!

Saving selections. Selections and channels are really the same thing down deep (even though they have different outward appearances), so you can turn one into the other very quickly. Earlier in this chapter we discussed how you can see and edit a selection by switching to Quick Mask mode. But quick masks are ephemeral things, and aren't much use if you want to hold on to that selection and use it later.

When you turn a selection into an alpha channel, you're saving that selection in the document. Then you can go back later and edit the channel, or turn it back into a selection.

The slow way to save a selection is to choose Save Selection from the Select menu. It's a nice place for beginners because Photoshop provides you with a dialog box (see Figure 8-18). But pros don't bother with menu selections when they can avoid them. Instead, click the Save Selection icon in the Channels palette. Or, if you want to see the Channel Options dialog box first (for instance, if you want to name the channel), hold down the Option key while clicking the icon (see Figure 8-19). Of course, you

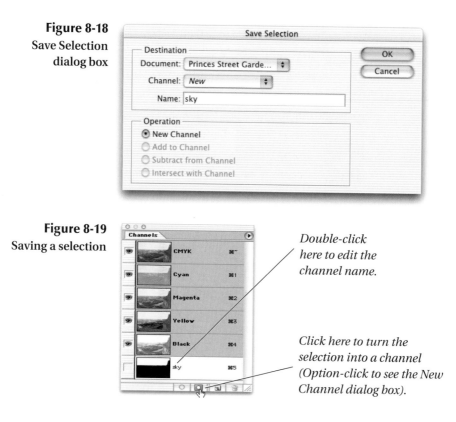

Figure 8-18
Save Selection
dialog box

Figure 8-19
Saving a selection

Double-click here to edit the channel name.

Click here to turn the selection into a channel (Option-click to see the New Channel dialog box).

can also assign a keyboard shortcut to the New Channel feature if you use this a lot.

Tip: Loading Selections. Saving a selection as an alpha channel doesn't do you much good unless you can retrieve it. Again, the slowest method is to use the Load Selection item from the Select menu (though there are benefits to this method; see "Tip: Saving Channels in Other Documents," later in this chapter).

One step better is to Command-click on the channel that you want to turn into a selection. Even better, press Command-Option-#, where the number is the channel you want. For instance, if you want to load channel six as a selection, press Command-Option-6.

Note that if you press Command-Option-~ (tilde), you load the luminosity mask. This isn't really the "lightness" of the image; rather, it's like getting a grayscale version of your image. (In fact, David sometimes uses this method—saving the result to a separate file—to convert a color image to grayscale.)

Tip: Be a Packrat! Every time it takes you more than 20 seconds to make a selection in your image, you should be thinking: Save This Selection. We try to save every complex selection as a channel or a path until the end of the project (and sometimes we even archive them, just in case). The reason? You never know when you'll need them again. Photoshop doesn't let you go back and change what you've done too often, and we've just been burned too many times by having to re-create selections from scratch (of course, the new selection never matches the old one exactly).

Tip: Channels in TIFFs. If you're saving a mess of channels along with the image you're working on, and you want to save the file as a TIFF, you should probably turn on LZW compression in the Save as TIFF dialog box. Zip compression is even better, though QuarkXPress and most other programs can't read Zip-compressed TIFFs yet. However, Adobe InDesign can, and of course you can always re-open Zip-compressed TIFFs in Adobe Photoshop. Whatever the case, use some kind of compression—otherwise, the TIFF will be enormous. Of course, you could save in the native Photoshop format, but we find that a Zip-compressed TIFF file is almost always smaller on disk.

Tip: Adding, Subtracting, and Intersecting Selections. Let's say you have an image with three distinct elements in it. You've spent an hour carefully selecting each of the elements, and you've saved each one in its own channel (see Figure 8-20). Now you want to select all three objects at the same time.

In the good old days, you would have sat around trying to figure out the appropriate channel operations (using Calculations) to get exactly what you wanted. But it's a kinder, gentler Photoshop now. After you load one channel as a selection, you can use Load Selection from the Select menu to add another channel to the current selection, subtract another channel, or find the intersection between the two selections.

Even easier, use the key-click combinations in Table 8-1. Confused? Don't forget to watch Photoshop's cursor icons; as you hold down the various key combinations, Photoshop indicates what will happen when you click.

Figure 8-20 Adding, subtracting, and intersecting selections

Original image

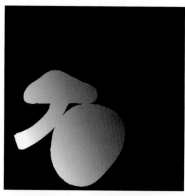

Mushroom channel

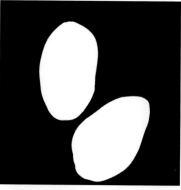

Potato channel

Radish channel

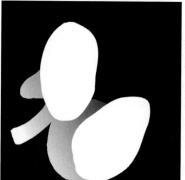

Potato channel added to mushroom channels

Potato channel intersected with mushroom and radish channels

Table 8-1 Working with selections	Do this to the channel tile...	...to get this result
	Command-Shift-click	Add channel to current selection
	Command-Option-click	Subtract channel from selection
	Command-Shift-Option-click	Intersect current selection and channel

Multidocument Channels

As we said earlier, your alpha channels don't all have to be in the same document. In fact, if you've got more than 56 channels, you have to have them in multiple documents. But even if you have fewer than 56, you may want to save off channels in order to reduce the current file's size. Here are a bunch of tips we've found helpful in moving channels back and forth between documents.

Tip: Saving Channels in Other Documents. From what we've said earlier in this chapter, you might infer that we think only a dolt trying to waste time would use the Load or Save Selection items on the Select menu. Not true! Taking the extra time to use the menu items can pay off in certain circumstances. Here's one: You can save selections to or load selections from other documents.

As long as another file is currently open, you can save a selection into it using Save Selection, or load a selection (from a channel) from the file using the menu items. You can even save selections into a new document by selecting New from the Document popup menu in the Save Selection dialog box.

If you have two similar documents open and you've carefully made and saved a selection in one image, you might want to use it in the other image. Instead of copying and pasting the selection channel, take a short-cut route and use the Load Selection dialog box (see Figure 8-21). You can load the selection channel directly by choosing it from the Document and Channel popup menus.

Figure 8-21
Load Selection
dialog box

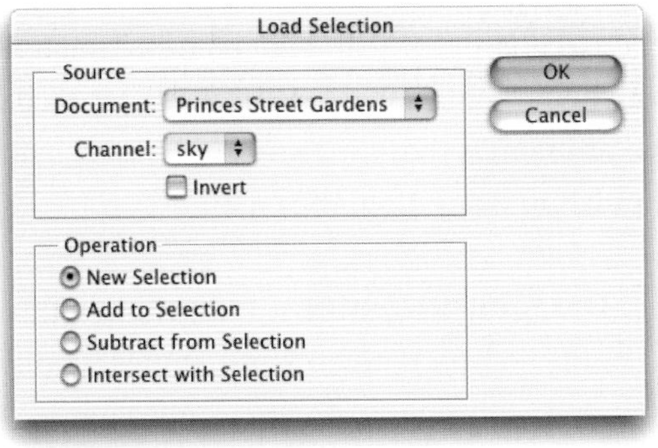

The catch here is that both documents have to have exactly the same pixel dimensions (otherwise, Photoshop wouldn't know how to place the selection properly).

Tip: More Saving Off Channels. If you've already saved your selection into a channel in document A, how can you then get that channel into document B? One method is to select the channel and choose Duplicate Channel from the Channel palette's popout menu (see Figure 8-22). Here you can

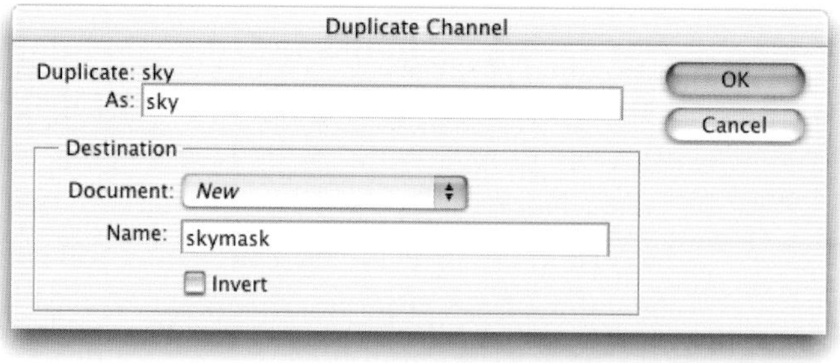

Figure 8-22
Duplicating a channel to
another document

Duplicate Channel

Duplicate: sky
As: sky

— Destination —
Document: *New*
Name: skymask
☐ Invert

OK
Cancel

choose to duplicate the channel into a new document or any other open
document (as long as the documents have the same pixel dimensions).

Tip: Saving Off Channels Using Copy and Paste. We hear you asking, "Why not just copy and paste the channel from one document into
another?" The answer is that copy and paste can really bog down in large
files. ("Large" means different things to different people; Bruce counts in
gigabytes!) In smaller files, however, copy and paste works just as well.

Tip: Copying Channels the Fast Way. However, when it comes right
down to it, the fastest way to copy a channel from document A to document B is simply by dragging the channel's tile (in the Channels palette)
from document A onto document B. It's nice, quick, simple, and elegant.
The problem is that the two documents have to be the same size, or else
Photoshop won't align the channels properly.

Tip: Dragging Selections. Photoshop is full of little, subtle features that
make life so much nicer. For instance, you can now drag any selection
from one document into another document using one of the selection
tools. (The Move tool actually moves the pixels inside the selection; the
selection tools move the selection itself.)

Normally, the selection "drops" wherever you let go of the mouse button.
However, if the two documents have the same pixel dimensions, you can
hold down the Shift key to pin-register the selection (it lands in the same
location as it was in the first document). If the images aren't the same pixel
dimension, the Shift key centers the selection.

Color Channels

When a color image is in RGB mode (under the Mode menu), the image is
made up of three channels: red, green, and blue. Each of these channels

is exactly the same as an alpha channel, except that they're designated as color channels. You can edit each color channel separately from the others. You can independently make a single color channel visible or invisible. But you can't delete or add a color channel without changing the image mode.

The first tile in the Channels palette (above the color channels) is the composite channel. Actually, this isn't really a channel at all. Rather, the composite channel is the full-color representation of all the individual color channels mixed together. It gives you a convenient way to select or deselect all the color channels at once, and also lets you view the composite color image even while you're editing a single channel.

Tip: Selecting and Seeing Channels. The tricky thing about working with channels is figuring out which channel(s) you're editing and which channel(s) you're seeing on the screen. They're not always the same thing!

The Channels palette has two columns. The left column contains little eyeball checkboxes that you can turn on and off to show or hide individual channels. Clicking on one of the tiles in the right column not only displays that channel, but lets you edit it, too. The channels that are selected for editing are highlighted (see Figure 8-23). The two columns are independent of each other because editing and seeing the channels are not the same thing.

When you're jumping from one channel to another, skip the clicking altogether and use a keystroke instead. Command-# displays the channel number you press; for instance, Command-1 shows the red channel (or

Figure 8-23
Selecting multiple channels

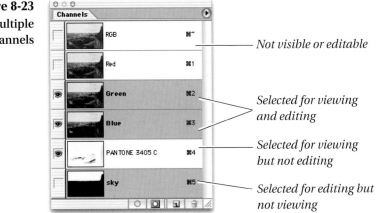

Not visible or editable

Selected for viewing and editing

Selected for viewing but not editing

Selected for editing but not viewing

whatever the first channel is), and Command-4 shows the fourth channel (the first alpha channel in an RGB image or Black in a CMYK image).

In earlier versions of Photoshop, Command-0 would select the color composite channel (deselecting all other channels in the process). Now, the keystroke is Command-~ (tilde). Sorry, there's no way (that we know of) to select channels above number nine with keystrokes.

You can see as many channels at once as you want by clicking in the channel's eyeball checkboxes. To edit more than one channel at a time, Shift-click on the channel tiles.

Note that when you display more than one channel at a time, the alpha channels automatically switch from their standard black and white to their channel color (you can specify what color each channel uses in Channel Options—double-click on the channel tile).

The Select Menu

If making selections using lassos and marquees, then saving or loading them, were all there was to selecting in Photoshop, life would be simpler but duller. Fortunately for us, there are many more things you can do with selections, and they all—well, almost all—help immeasurably in the production process.

You can find each additional selection feature under the Select menu: Grow, Similar, Color Range, and Modify. Let's explore each of these and how they can speed up your work.

Grow

Earlier in the chapter, when we were talking about the Magic Wand tool, we discussed the concept of tolerance. This value tells Photoshop how much brighter or darker a pixel (or each color channel that defines a pixel) can be and still be included in the selection.

Let's say you're trying to select an apple using the Magic Wand tool with a tolerance of 24. After clicking once, perhaps only half of the apple is selected; the other half is slightly shaded and falls outside the tolerance range. You could deselect, change the tolerance, and click again. However, it's much faster to select Grow from the Select menu.

When you choose Grow, Photoshop selects additional pixels according to the following criteria. (By the way, the last time we checked, the Photoshop manuals were wrong about how Grow works . . . it's weird but we figured it out.)

1. First, it finds the highest and lowest gray values of every channel of every pixel selected—the highest red, green, and blue, and the lowest red, green, and blue of the bunch of already-selected pixels (or the highest cyan, magenta, yellow, and black, and so on).

2. Next, it adds the tolerance value to the highest values and subtracts it from the lowest values in each channel. Therefore, the highest values get a little higher and the lowest values get a little lower (of course, it never goes above 255 or below 0).

3. Finally, Photoshop selects every adjacent pixel that falls between all those values (see Figure 8-24).

In other words, Photoshop tries its hardest to spread your selection in every direction, but only in similar colors. However, it doesn't always work the way you'd want. In fact, sometimes it works very oddly indeed.

For instance, if you select a pure red area (made of 255 red, and no blue or green), and a pure green area (made of 255 green, and no red or blue), then select Grow, Photoshop selects every adjacent pixel that has any red or green in it, as long as the blue channel is not out of tolerance's range.

Figure 8-24
The Grow
command

After Magic Wand click   *After Grow*

That means that it'll pick out dark browns, lime greens, oranges, and so on—even if you set a really small tolerance level (see Figure 8-25).

Tip: Controlled Growing. If you switch to a color channel (like red or cyan) before selecting Grow, Photoshop grows the selection based on that channel only. This can be helpful because it's much easier to predict how the Magic Wand and Grow features will work on one channel.

Tip: Instead of the Magic Wand. While the Magic Wand tool is pretty cool and provides a friendly point-and-click interface, it's often not very useful because colors in a natural image (like a scan) are typically varied. Even if you click in what looks like a representative spot, you might not get the full range you expect.

Instead, try selecting a larger representative area with the Lasso or Marquee tool. Then, select Grow or Similar from the Select menu (see below for a discussion of Similar). Bruce maintains that the best method is just to use Color Range instead (see "Color Range," later in this chapter).

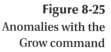

Figure 8-25
Anomalies with the
Grow command

When the two center squares are selected, Grow selects all the bottom squares and none of the top squares. Why? Because of slight blue "contamination" in the top squares.

Many of these colors are selected unexpectedly with Grow.

Similar

The Grow feature only selects contiguous areas of your image. If you're trying to select the same color throughout an image, you may click and drag and grow yourself into a frenzy before you're done. Choosing Similar from the Select menu does the same thing as choosing Grow, but it chooses pixels from throughout the entire image (see Figure 8-26).

Note that Similar and Grow are both attached to the settings on the Options bar when you have the Magic Wand selected; Photoshop applies both the Wand's tolerance and its anti-alias values to these commands. We can't think of any reason to turn off anti-aliasing, but it's nice to know you have the option.

Figure 8-26
The Similar
command

Selection made with Magic Wand.
A Tolerance setting of 24 manages to
avoid the shadows and green areas.

After Similar is selected. Some
brighter areas of the apples
are still not selected.

Color Range

One of the problems with Similar and Grow is that you rarely know what you're going to end up with. On the other hand, Color Range lets you make color-based selections interactively, and shows you exactly which pixels will be selected. But there's one other advantage of Color Range over the Magic Wand features (we think of Similar and Grow as extensions of the Magic Wand).

The Magic Wand–based features either select a pixel or they don't (the exception is anti-aliasing around the edges of selections, which only partially selects pixels there). Color Range, however, fully selects only a few pixels and partially selects a lot of pixels (see Figure 8-27). This can be incredibly helpful when you're trying to tease a good selection mask out of the contents of an image.

We rarely use Color Range to create a final selection mask. Rather, we find it great as a first or second step in building the mask, and then we follow it up with other tools (including Levels or Curves), adding and removing pixels. There are four areas you should be aware of in the Color Range dialog box: selection eyedroppers, the Fuzziness slider, canned sets of colors, and Selection Preview.

Adding and deleting colors. When you open Color Range, Photoshop creates a selection based on your foreground color. Then you can use the eyedropper tools to add or delete colors in the image (or, better yet, hold down the Shift key to get the Add Color to Mask eyedropper, or the Option key to get the Remove Color from Mask eyedropper). Note that you can

Figure 8-27   Magic Wand versus Color Range

While you can make similar selections with the Magic Wand and Color Range, each is more efficient in particular situations. Magic Wand is faster for big, consistent areas, while Color Range excels for finer details.

The original image. It is photographed on a good, uniform white background, and includes an area of relatively solid color (the reds) that is an obvious target for change.

Three quick Shift-clicks with the Magic Wand yield a very serviceable silhouette mask. A bit of feathering or a Gaussian Blur on the mask (combined with a Levels tweak to adjust the blur) deals with the hard edges.

Because the object is hard-edged to begin with, the Magic Wand's inability to partially select pixels doesn't pose much of a problem in compositing.

A mask created with Color Range (here with few sample points and a high Fuzziness setting) is more appropriate for subtle selections.

A detail of the mask shows that there are partially-selected pixels (the gray areas).

This more subtle mask is just the ticket for a Hue/Saturation tweak, changing the red areas to blue without an artificial look.

always scroll or magnify an area in the image. You can even select colors from any other open image.

The Fuzziness factor. Every Photoshop book we've seen (including Photoshop's manuals) says that the Fuzziness slider in the Color Range dialog box is more or less the same as the Tolerance field on the Magic Wand Options bar. That's sort of like saying that Republicans are more or less the same as Democrats. Yes, they're both in the business of running the country, but . . . .

As we said earlier, pixels that fall within the tolerance value are either fully selected or not; pixels that fall on the border between the selected and unselected areas may be partially selected, but those are only border pixels. Color Range uses the Fuzziness value to determine not only whether a pixel should be included, but also how selected it should be. We're not going to get into the hard-core math (you don't need to know it, and we're not entirely sure of it ourselves), but Figure 8-28 should give you a pretty good idea of how fuzziness works.

Tip: Avoid Sample Merged. Color Range is always in Sample Merged mode. It sees your image as though all the visible layers were merged together. If you've got an object on a layer that you don't want included in the selection mask, hide that layer before opening Color Range.

Tip: Sampling vs. Fuzziness. Should you use lots of sample points or a high Fuzziness setting? It depends on the type of image. To select large areas of similar color, tend toward a lower Fuzziness (10–15) to avoid selecting stray pixels. For fine detail, you need to use higher Fuzziness settings, because the fine areas are generally more polluted with colors spilling from adjacent pixels.

Either way, try adding sample points to increase the selection range before you increase fuzziness.

Tip: Return to Settings. If you want to return to the Color Range dialog box with exactly the same settings as you last used, hold down the Option key when selecting Color Range from the Select menu.

Canned Colors

Instead of creating a selection mask with the eyedroppers, you can let Photoshop select all the reds, or all the blues, or yellows, or any other primary color, by choosing the color in the Select popup menu (see Figure 8-29). If you choose one of these, Photoshop selects only a pixel if it contains more of that color than any other. For instance, if you choose Reds, Photoshop selects a pixel with an RGB value of 128R 115G 60B; but it won't even partially select a pixel that has an RGB value of 128R 130G 60B.

The greater the difference between the color you choose (in this example, red) and the other primaries (e.g., blue and green), the more the pixel is selected. (To get really tweaky for a moment: The percentage the pixel is selected is the percentage difference between the color you choose and the primary color with the next highest value.)

Figure 8-28   Fuzziness versus sample points for Color Range

Four selections created with Color Range. At right is the result of a Hue/Saturation move on the selection.

*Few sample points,
low fuzziness*

*Few sample points,
high fuzziness*

*Many sample points,
low fuzziness*

*Many sample points,
high fuzziness*

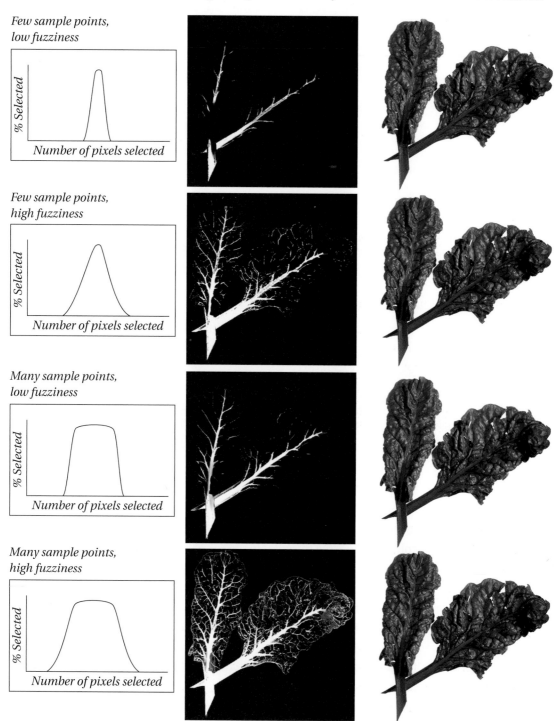

Figure 8-29
Color Range
dialog box

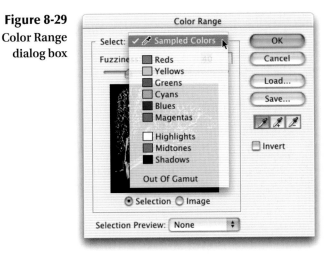

Do you really need to know any of this? No. Probably the best way to use these features is just not to use them at all (we almost never do).

On the other hand, you can also choose Highlights, Midtones, or Shadows, which we find a bit more useful. When you choose one of these, Photoshop decides whether to select a pixel (or how much to select it) based on its Lab luminance value (see Table 8-2 and Chapter 5, *Color Settings*, for more information on Lab mode).

We find selecting Highlights, Midtones, and Shadows most useful when selecting a subset of a color we've already selected (see "Tip: Color Range Subsets," next).

Table 8-2
Ranges for Color Range
(L value in Lab mode)

Select name	Fully selected pixels	Partially selected pixels
Shadows	1–40	40–55
Midtones	55–75	40–55 and 75–85
Highlights	80–100	75–85

Tip: Color Range Subsets. If you're trying to select all the green buttons on a blouse using Color Range, you're going to pick up every other green object throughout the image, too. However, you can tell the Color Range feature to only select green items within a particular area—the blouse, for instance—by making a selection first. Draw a quick outline of the area of interest with the Lasso tool, then choose Color Range. Photoshop ignores the rest of the image.

Similarly, you could select all the green items in the image, then go back to Color Range again and select only those greens that are in Highlight areas.

Tip: Invert the Color Range Selection. Do you often find yourself following up a Color Range selection with an Invert from the Select menu? If you are trying to select the opposite of what's selected in the Color Range dialog box, you can remove that extra step by turning on the Invert checkbox in the Color Range dialog box; Photoshop automatically inverts the selection for you.

If you already have a selection made when you invert the Color Range selection, Photoshop deselects the Color Range pixels from your selection.

Selection Preview. The last area to pay attention to in the Color Range dialog box is the Selection Preview popup menu. When you select anything other than None (the default) from this menu, Photoshop previews the Color Range selection mask.

The first choice, Grayscale, shows you what the selection mask would look like if you saved it as a separate channel. The second and third choices, Black Matte and White Matte, are the equivalent of copying the selected pixels out and pasting them on a black or white background. This is great for seeing how well you're capturing edge pixels. The last choice, Quick Mask, is the same thing as clicking OK and immediately switching into Quick Mask mode.

Because the Selection Preview can slow you down, we recommend turning it on only when you need to, then turning around and switching back to None. It can be really helpful in making sure you're selecting everything you want, but it can also be a drag on productivity.

Tip: Changing Quick Mask Options. If you're a hard-core Color Range user, you may one day have the strange desire to change your Quick Mask options settings while the Color Range dialog box is open. You can do it (believe it or not). Hold down the Option key while selecting Quick Mask from the Selection Preview popup menu. Don't say we don't strive to give you every last tip!

Tip: Forget the Color Range Radio Buttons. Here's another little tip that can speed up production by a moment or two: If you frequently use the Image and Selection radio buttons in the Color Range dialog box, stop! Instead, press the Command or Control key—either one works on the Mac—on your keyboard. This toggles between the Selection and Image Previews much faster than you can click buttons. This is sometimes helpful if you need a quick reality check as to what's selected and what's not.

Modify

When you think of the most important part of your selection, what do you think of? If you answer, "what's selected," you're wrong. No matter what you have selected in your image, the most important part of the selection is the boundary or edge. This is where the tire hits the road, where the money slaps the table, where the gavel slams the podium, where the invoice smacks the client. No matter what you do with the selection—whether you copy and paste it, paint within it, or whatever—the quality of your edge determines how effective your effect will be.

When making a precise selection, you often need to make subtle adjustments to the boundaries of the selection. The four menu items on the Modify submenu under the Select menu—Border, Smooth, Expand, and Contract—focus entirely on this task.

Border. Police officers of the world take note: There's a faster way to get a doughnut than driving down to the local Circle K. Draw a circle using the Marquee tool, then select Border from the Modify submenu under the Select menu. You can even specify how thick you want your doughnut (in pixels, of course). Border transforms the single line (the circle) into two lines (see Figure 8-30).

The problem with Border is that it only creates soft-edged borders. If you draw a square and give it a border, you get a soft-edged shape that looks more like an octagon than a square. In many cases, this is exactly what you want and need. But other times it can ruin the mood faster than jackhammers outside the bedroom window.

Tip: Level Borders. If selecting Border gives you a super-soft edge when what you want is a harder, fatter edge, try this quick-mask trick. Switch to Quick Mask mode (press Q), then use the Levels or Curves dialog box

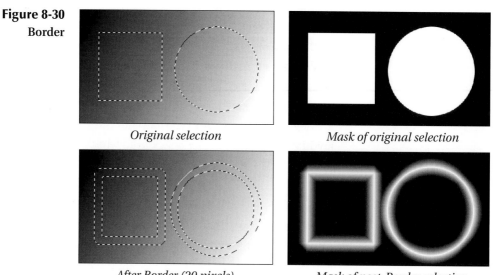

Original selection

Mask of original selection

After Border (20 pixels)

Mask of post-Border selection

Figure 8-30
Border

to adjust the edge of the selection (see "Tip: Finer Spreads and Chokes," later in this chapter). If you find that the edge of the selection becomes too jaggy, you can always apply a .5-pixel Gaussian Blur to smooth it out. Remember that when you're in Quick Mask mode, you can select the area to which you want to apply the levels or blur.

Tip: More Border Options. Here's one other way to make a border with a sharper, more distinct edge.

1. Save your selection as an alpha channel.

2. While the area is still selected, choose Expand from the Modify submenu under the Select menu (we discuss this command later in the chapter).

3. Save this new selection as an alpha channel.

4. Load the original selection from the alpha channel you saved it in.

5. Choose Contract from the Modify submenu.

6. Mix the two selections (expanded and contracted) together by Command-Option-clicking on the other channel.

You can save this selection and delete one or both of the other alpha channels you saved. Note that you don't have to expand *and* contract the selection; this method also lets you choose to only contract or expand.

Tip: Using Borders When Compositing. One of the positive aspects of Photoshop giving you a soft-edged border when you select Border from the Modify submenu is that you can use it to touch up the edges of objects you're placing over a background. For instance, if an object on a layer is not feathered or anti-aliased enough, you can use Border to blur its edges into the background. Or, if the edge of a composited object has some edge spill from the previous background, you can touch it up with Border.

1. Paste the object and place it exactly where you want it (this creates a new layer).

2. Make sure the edges around the object are selected. One fast way to do this is to select the layer's transparency mask by Command-clicking on the layer in the Layers palette (see "Selections and Layers," later in this chapter).

3. Select Border from the Modify submenu.

4. Feather the border selection slightly (with a radius like .5).

5. Hide the marching ants (Command-H).

6. If you want to get rid of aliasing, apply a Gaussian Blur to the area. If you're trying to rid yourself of some background color spill, you can use the Rubber Stamp tool to clone some of the object's color into the border selection (we'll discuss this in more depth in "Step-by-Step Silhouettes," later in this chapter). Or you can just press Delete to remove the edge pixels, blending the foreground and the background images together.

Finally, you may want to apply some unsharp masking to sharpen the edge a little. Therein lies the art: blurring enough and sharpening enough to get a smooth but clean edge.

Smooth. The problem with making selections with the Lasso tool is that you often get very jaggy selection lines; the corners are too sharp, the curves are too bumpy. You can smooth these out by selecting Smooth from the Modify submenu under the Select menu. Like most selection operations in Photoshop, this actually runs a convolution filter over the selection mask—in this case, the Median filter. That is, selecting Smooth is exactly the same thing as switching to Quick Mask mode and choosing the Median filter.

Smooth has little or no effect on straight lines or smooth curves. But it has a drastic effect on corners and jaggy lines (see Figure 8-31). Smooth (or the Median filter, depending on which way you look at it) looks at each pixel in your selection, then looks at the pixels surrounding it (the number of pixels it looks at depends on the Radius value you choose in the Smooth dialog box). If more than half the pixels around it are selected, then the pixel remains selected. If fewer than half are selected, the pixel becomes deselected.

If you enter a small Radius value, only corner tips and other sharp edges are rounded out. Larger values make sweeping changes. It's rare that we use a radius over 5 or 6, but it depends entirely on what you're doing (and how smooth your hand is!).

Figure 8-31
Smooth

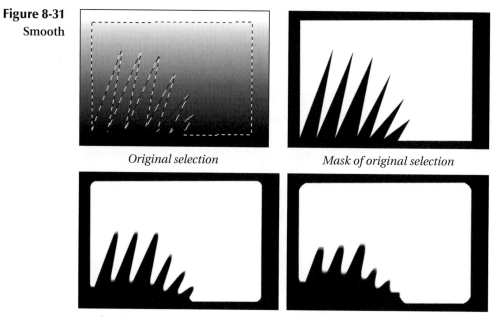

Original selection   *Mask of original selection*

After Smooth with 10-pixel radius   *After Smooth with 16-pixel radius*

Expand/Contract. The Expand and Contract features are two of the most useful selection modifiers. They let you enlarge or reduce the size of the selection. This is just like spreading or choking colors in trapping (if you don't know about trapping, don't worry; it's not relevant here).

Once again, these modifiers are simply applying filters to the black-and-white mask equivalent of your selection. Choosing Expand is the same as applying the Maximum filter to the mask; choosing Contract is the same as applying the Minimum filter (see Figure 8-32).

Note that if you enter 5 as the Radius value in the Maximum or Minimum dialog box (or in the Expand or Contract dialog box), it's exactly the same as running the filter or selection modifier five times. The Radius value here is more of an "iteration" value; how many times do you want the filter applied at a one-pixel radius?

While we frequently find these selection modifiers useful, they aren't very precise. You can only specify the radius in one-pixel increments (see "Tip: Finer Spreads and Chokes," next).

Figure 8-32
Expand and Contract

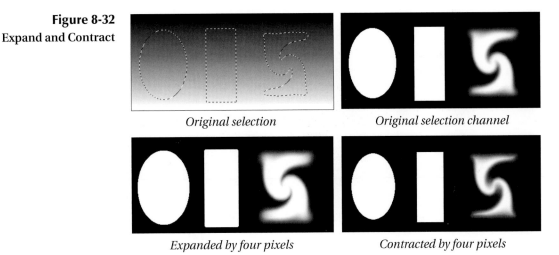

Original selection   *Original selection channel*

Expanded by four pixels   *Contracted by four pixels*

Tip: Finer Spreads and Chokes. You can make much finer adjustments to the size of a selection by using Levels rather than Expand or Contract from the Select menu. Here's how.

1. Once you have your selection, switch to Quick Mask mode.

2. Apply a Gaussian Blur to the area you want to expand or contract (if it's the whole selection, then blur the whole quick mask). We usually use a low Radius value, such as .5 or 1.

3. In Levels (Command-L), adjust the middle (gamma) slider control to make the area darker or lighter. Making it darker contracts the

selection; lighter expands the selection (see Figure 8-33 and, later in the chapter, Figure 8-48).

What's nice about this tip is that it's a very gentle method of expanding or contracting the selection. Instead of "Wham! Move one pixel over," you can say, "Make this selection slightly bigger or smaller."

Figure 8-33
Precision control
over expanding
and contracting

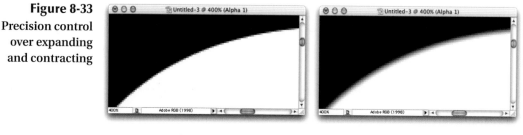

Original selection channel

Selection channel after
Gaussian Blur and Levels

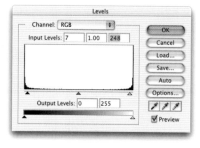

The gamma slider controls the
expansion or contraction of
the mask channel's gray levels—hence
the abruptness of the blur.

Selections and Layers

It's almost impossible not to use multiple layers in a Photoshop document. There's very little difference between painting or editing on a background or on a layer. There is, however, a big difference in making a selection on a layer. Plus, Layers opens up three new features that are related to selections: transparency masks, layer masks, and using layers as a mask.

When reading about these new features, don't forget that masks are just channels, which are 8-bit (or 16-bit) grayscale images, just like we talked about earlier in this chapter. (Photoshop also lets you build a hard, vector-edged mask that is *not* based on a channel, called a *layer clipping path*; we'll discuss this in "Paths," later in this chapter.)

Transparency Masks

Most of the time when you create a new layer, the background is transparent. When you paint on it or paste in a selection, you're making pixels opaque. Photoshop is always keeping track of how transparent each pixel is—fully transparent, partially transparent, or totally opaque. This information about pixel transparency is called the *transparency mask* (see Figure 8-34).

Remember the analogy we made to masking tape earlier in the chapter? The selection/channel/mask (they're all the same) acts like tape over or around your image. In this case, however, the mask doesn't represent how selected a pixel is; it's how transparent (or, conversely, how visible) it is. You can have a pixel that's fully selected but only 10-percent opaque (90-percent transparent).

Tip: Load the Transparency Mask. You can load the transparency mask for a layer as a selection in the Load Selection dialog box, but it's much faster to Command-click on the layer's tile in the Layers palette. For instance, if you have some text on a type layer and you want to make a selection that looks exactly like the type, Command-click on the type layer's tile. This loads the selection, and you're ready to roll.

Figure 8-34
Transparency masks

This area is transparent.

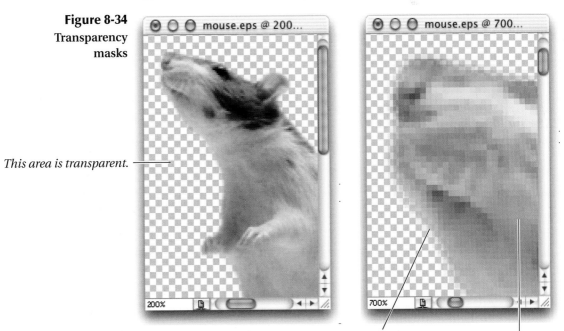

This area is partially opaque.   *This area is opaque.*

Layer Masks

It's hard to emphasize in print just how important non-destructive editing is in our workflow. (A future MTV adaptation of this book will show us jumping up and down, rapping, "Yo, this is life-changing!") Perhaps you're compositing several images on a background, or you're retouching an image, or you're adjusting the hue and brightness of a photograph. Whatever the case, you know that after hours of sweat and mouse-burn, when you show the result to your art director, she's going to say, "Move this over a little, and we need a little more of this showing here, and you shouldn't have changed the color of this part . . . ."

Fortunately, you can use layer masks to avoid this sort of nightmare in your work. Layer masks are just like transparency masks—they determine how transparent the layer's pixels are—but you can see layer masks and, more important, edit them (see Figure 8-35). If you had used non-destructive layer masks in the example above instead of erasing or editing your

Figure 8-35 Layer masks

The earth is on a separate layer above the background image of the car.

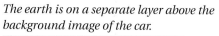

The layer mask

After the layer mask is applied to the Earth layer

original pixels, you would have smiled at your art director and made the changes quickly and painlessly. Here's how you do it.

Creating and editing layer masks. You can apply a layer mask to a layer by selecting Add Layer Mask from the Layer menu. When a layer has a mask, it can have only one (or two, if you include layer clipping paths)—the Layers palette displays a thumbnail of the mask (see Figure 8-36).

Figure 8-36

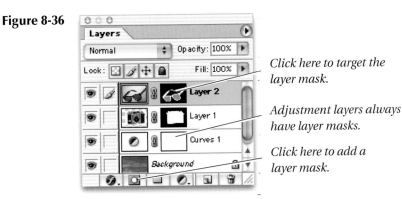

Click here to target the layer mask.

Adjustment layers always have layer masks.

Click here to add a layer mask.

At first, it's difficult to tell whether you're editing the layer or the layer mask. But there are three differences: The layer mask thumbnail has a dark border around it (on a high-resolution screen, the two borders look about the same), the second column of the Layers palette changes to a mask icon (a white circle on a gray background), and the document title bar says "Layer *x* Mask." We typically glance at the title bar about as often as we look in our car's rear-view mirror; it's a good way to keep a constant eye on what's going on around us.

Once you have a layer mask, you can edit it by clicking on its icon in the Layers palette (see "Tip: Layer Mask Keystroke," below).

We may be breaking a record for redundancy here, but it's important to remember that a mask is the same as a selection, which is the same as a channel. Underneath, they're all grayscale images. Editing a mask is as simple as painting with grays. Painting with black is like adding masking tape; it covers up part of the adjoining layer (making those pixels transparent). Painting with white takes away the tape and uncovers the layer's image. Gray, of course, partially covers the image.

Tip: Faster Layer Masks. While there's no built-in keyboard shortcut to add a layer mask (you can assign one if you want), it is a little faster to click on the Add Layer Mask icon in the Layers palette. If you Option/Alt-click on the Add Layer Mask icon, Photoshop inverts the layer mask (so that it automatically hides everything on the layer).

Note that you can make a selection before clicking on the icon. In this case, the program "paints in" the non-selected areas with black for you (on the layer mask). This is usually much easier than adding a layer mask, then using the paint tools to paint away areas. (Of course, Option-clicking on the icon with a selection paints the selected areas with black, so that whatever was selected "disappears.")

Tip: Paint It In Using Masks. Layer masks let you paint in any kind of effect you want. For example, duplicate the Background layer of an image in the Layers palette, apply a filter to the new layer (like Unsharp Mask), then Option/Alt-click on the Add Layer Mask icon to mask out the entire effect. Now you can paint the effect back in using the Brush tool and non-black pixels. If you change your mind, you can paint away the effect with black pixels. This flexibility is addictive and you'll soon find yourself using this technique over and over, whether it's painting in texture or sharpening or blurring or whatever.

Tip: Use Gradients for Masks. Another trick you'll find us using daily is placing gradients on a layer mask. Whether you use a linear or radial blend, adding a gradient is a great way to affect just part of an image. For example, on a partially-cloudy day, the lighting of a scene may be uneven. You can apply a global tonal adjustment on a separate layer and then draw a gradient across the layer's mask to affect just the part of the image that needs it (we discuss this in detail in the next chapter). If the gradient isn't quite right, open the Levels or Curves dialog box and make adjustments to the layer mask itself—these tonal adjustments to the mask give you almost infinite control over how your effect is applied.

Tip: Getting Rid of the Mask. As soon as you start editing layer masks, you're going to find that you want to turn the mask on and off, so you can get before-and-after views of your work. You can make the mask disappear temporarily by selecting Disable Layer Mask from the Layer menu. Or, if you need to get your work done quickly, do it the fast way: Shift-click on the Layer Mask icon.

If you want to hide the mask with extreme prejudice—that is, if you want to delete it forever—select Remove Layer Mask from the Layer menu (or, faster, drag the Layer Mask icon to the Trash icon). Photoshop gives you a last chance to apply the mask to the layer. Note that if you do apply the mask, the masked (hidden) portions of the layer are actually deleted.

One last way to get rid of a mask: All layer masks go away when you merge or flatten layers.

Tip: Layer Mask Keystroke. When you're working on a layer, you can jump to the layer mask (making it active, so all your edits are to the mask rather than the image) by pressing Command-\ (backslash). When you're ready to leave the layer mask, press Command-~ (tilde) to switch back to the layer itself.

Displaying layer masks. The second tricky thing about layer masks is that when you create one, you can't see it, so editing the mask can seem difficult. The trick is to Option-Shift-click on the Layer Mask icon in the Layers palette. This displays the mask *and* the layer, as if you're in Quick-Mask mode. If you don't like the color or opacity of the layer mask, you can Option-Shift-double-click on the icon to change the mask's color and opacity. Then, when you're ready to see the effects of your mask editing, Option-Shift-click on the icon again to "hide" it.

If you want to see only the layer mask (as its own grayscale channel), Option-click on its icon. This is most helpful when touching up areas of the layer mask (it's sometimes hard to see the details in the mask when there's a background image visible).

Tip: When Masks Move. As we explained back in Chapter 2, *Essential Photoshop Tips and Tricks*, the best way to move an image on a layer is to use the Move tool. However, note that the layer mask is tied to its layer, so when you move the layer with the Move tool, the layer mask moves, too.

While this is usually what you'd want, you can stop it from happening by clicking on the Link icon that sits between the layer and layer mask previews in the Layers palette. When the Link icon is on, the layer and layer mask move together; when it's off, the layer and layer mask can be moved independently.

Layers as Masks

Layers not only have masks, but they can act as masks for other layers. The trick is to use *clipping groups*. For instance, if you place a circle on a layer with a transparent background, then make a new layer and fill it entirely with some bizarre fractal design, the strange texture totally obliterates the circle. However, if you group the two layers together, the lower one acts as a mask for the higher one, and the fractal design only appears within the circle.

You can group layers together in one of two ways.

▶ Select Create Clipping Mask from the Layer menu (or, even faster, press Command-G).

▶ Option-click between their tiles in the Layers palette (the layers have to be next to one another in any of these cases; see Figure 8-37).

You don't have to stop with grouping two layers. You can group together as many as you want, though the bottommost layer always acts as the mask for the entire group (see Figure 8-38). No, you can't group a layer with a layer set—only individual layers.

Figure 8-37
Grouping layers together
to make a layer mask

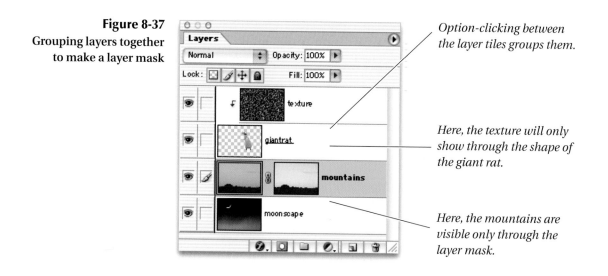

Option-clicking between the layer tiles groups them.

Here, the texture will only show through the shape of the giant rat.

Here, the mountains are visible only through the layer mask.

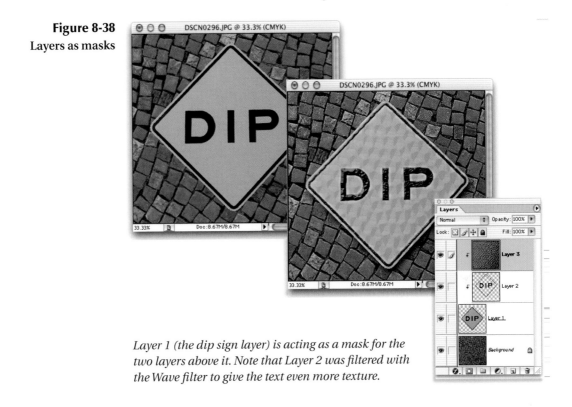

Figure 8-38
Layers as masks

Layer 1 (the dip sign layer) is acting as a mask for the two layers above it. Note that Layer 2 was filtered with the Wave filter to give the text even more texture.

Paths

After we explored the differences between bitmapped graphics (made of pixels) and object-oriented, vector graphics (made of lines, curves, and other objects) back in Chapter 3, *Image Essentials*, we pretty much ignored the latter. If you're a typical Photoshop user, you, too, have likely focused most of your attention on pixels and let those wacky Illustrator users deal with the vectors. But Photoshop now lets you perform many of the tasks for which you might use an illustration or page-layout program. Plus, Photoshop's drawing tools can be very helpful even if you're a photographer or Web designer who usually ignores vector artwork, because vectors are infinitely modifiable, and they can easily be converted to bitmaps at the drop of a hat.

Photoshop CS offers a wide array of vector tools.

▶ Draw, edit, delete, and save paths

▶ Copy and paste paths between Photoshop and Adobe Illustrator or Macromedia FreeHand

▶ Convert paths into selections and *vice versa*

▶ Rasterize paths into pixels (stroking and filling)

▶ Create layer clipping paths

▶ Draw shapes that remain vectors through print time

▶ Convert text to shapes (so you can edit the outlines)

▶ Save EPS images with a path applied as a clipping path

Photoshop CS also has very powerful tools for handling text (which by default are vectors), including placing text along a path. We cover the text features in Chapter 15, *Essential Image Techniques*.

Strengths and Weaknesses. Curiously, the primary strength and weakness of paths stem from the same attribute: Paths have no connection to the pixels below them; they live on a separate mathematical plane in Photoshop, forever floating above those lowly bitmapped images.

The strength of this is that you can create, edit, and save paths without regard for the resolution of the image, or even for the image itself. You can create a path in the shape of a logo (or better yet, import the path from Illustrator or FreeHand) and drop it into any image. Then you can save it as a path in Photoshop, ask the program to rasterize the path (turn it into a bitmapped image), drop it down into the pixel layers, convert the path to a selection, or just leave it as a path so that it prints with sharp edges (as high resolution as the PostScript device you print on).

The weakness of paths' separateness is that paths used as selections can't capture the subtlety and nuance found in most bitmapped images. A path can't, for instance, have any partially-selected pixels or blurry parts; you can only achieve hard-edged selections (see Figure 8-39).

While we occasionally use paths for selections, we more typically use them for clipping images (or layers in images) that will be placed in other programs (read: PageMaker, InDesign, or QuarkXPress) for output. We discuss the use of clipping paths in some detail in Chapter 16, *Storing Images*. In this section, we'll focus on *layer* clipping paths.

Tip: The Space-Saving Paths Myth. There's a myth that you can save a lot of disk space if you convert your channels into paths before saving your document. Sorry, not true. True, paths take up almost no space at all

Figure 8-39 Paths versus channels

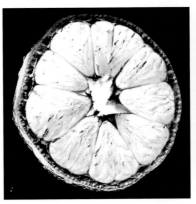

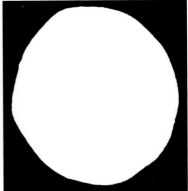

The original image

Selection masks can partially select pixels (here only selecting orange).

Paths are good at clean, sharp outlines, but they can't select image detail.

in a document (they're just tiny mathematical descriptions of lines and curves). However, Photoshop compresses simple alpha channels—ones that are mostly black and white—down to almost nothing, anyway. And any channel that you can successfully convert into a path (that is, without ruining essential elements of the channel) will most certainly have to be one of these types. A simple channel may take up between 40 and 100 K in a 6 MB document, while a path may only take 1 or 2 K. But if you're worried about saving 100 K, you might reconsider working with Photoshop in the first place.

Creating and Editing Paths

If you've ever used Adobe Illustrator or Macromedia FreeHand, you're already familiar with drawing and editing paths in Photoshop. In fact, the paths interface is most similar to Adobe Illustrator's (no surprise there; see Figure 8-40).

Whether you're drawing a layer clipping path, a path to clip the entire document, a path to help you select pixels, or one of Photoshop's new Shape layers, you have to use the same basic tools. Remember that paths are visible only when the path is selected in the Paths palette (or, for layer clipping paths, when its tile is selected in the Layers palette). The Paths palette displays all the paths in your document, and gives you some control over what to do with them. To draw a path, you must select one of the

Figure 8-40
Paths

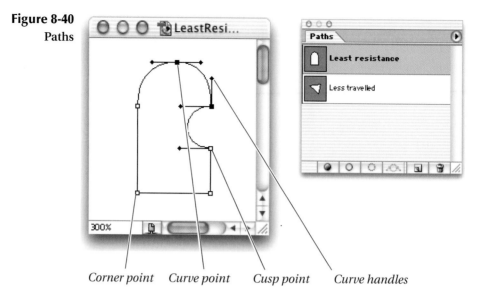

Corner point   *Curve point*   *Cusp point*   *Curve handles*

Pen tools or Shape tools in the Tools palette. There are seven Pen tools and six Shape tools, but we tend to use only two or three of the Pen tools, using modifier keys to get to the rest.

Pen tool. The Pen tool (press P) is the only tool we ever select to draw paths. Without modifier keys, you can draw straight-line paths by clicking, or curved paths by clicking and dragging. You can also easily access any of the other tools. For instance, if you move this tool over a point on a line, it automatically changes to the "delete point" tool. If you move the Pen tool over a segment, it lets you add a point (click or click-and-drag). If you're forever adding or deleting points when you don't mean to, just turn off the Auto Add/Delete checkbox on the Options bar.

Selection tools. As in Illustrator and InDesign, Photoshop has both a Selection tool and a Direct Select tool. You can press A (for "arrow") to jump to the selection tool in the Tool palette, and then press Shift-A if you want the other selection tool. However, if you want the Direct Select tool, it's much easier to hold down the Command key when any Pen tool or the Selection tool is active. These tools let you select a point or points on the path. For example, you can select points on a curve with the Direct Select tool by clicking on them or by dragging a marquee around them. To select all the points on a curve, use the Selection tool or hold down the Option key when you click on the path with the Direct Select tool (or, Command-Option-click with the Pen tool).

Once you've selected a point or a path, you can move it. As in most other programs, if you hold down the Shift key, Photoshop only lets you move the points in 90- or 45-degree angles. If you hold down the Option key when you click and drag, Photoshop moves a copy of the entire path.

Convert Point tool. When you're working with the Pen tool, you can create a sharp corner by clicking, or a rounded corner by dragging. When you have two round corners on either side of a corner point, that corner point is called a *cusp* point. But what if you change your mind and want to make a corner into a curve, or a curve into a cusp?

The Convert Point tool lets you add or remove curve *handles* (those levers that stick out from the sides of curve or cusp points). If you click once on a point that has curve handles, the curve handles disappear (they get sucked all the way into the point), and the point becomes a corner. If you click and drag with the Convert Point tool, you can pull those handles out of the point, making the corner a curve.

Similarly, you can make a cusp by clicking and dragging on one of the control handles on either side of the point. If you select the Pen tool, you can get the Convert Point tool by holding down the Option key.

Tip: Use Cusp Points. Many folks tell us that they make all points cusp points while drawing paths. Here's how: To create the first point of the path, just click and drag to set the angle of the first curve. All subsequent points on the path are created by clicking, dragging to set the angle of the previous curve, and then Option-dragging from the point to set the launch angle of the next curve. Finally, to close the path (if you want it closed), Option-click—if you want the final segment to be a straight line— or Option-drag—if you want the final segment to be a curve—on the first point of the path. While it takes some getting used to and takes a bit more work, this technique gives you much more control over the angle and curve of each segment in the path because each point is independent of the ones on either side.

Freeform Pen tool. David got into this business because he can't draw worth beans, but if you've got a steady hand and a sure heart—and a graphics tablet wouldn't hurt, either—you might find yourself wanting to draw paths with the Freeform Pen tool. When you let up on the mouse button,

Photoshop converts your loose path to a smooth path full of corner, curve, and cusp points. (Exactly how closely Photoshop follows your lead is up to the Curve Fit setting on the Options bar.)

Note that, like the Lasso tool, you can draw a straight line with the Freeform Pen tool by holding down the Option key and lifting the mouse button. Then you can either click to "connect the dots" or release the Option key to return to freeform drawing.

Magnetic Pen tool. Once the engineers at Adobe figured out how to make the Magnetic Lasso tool, it was a snap for them to add the functionality to the Pen tool, too. Thus, the Magnetic Pen tool was born. (Well, it's not really a separate tool; you get it by turning on the checkbox labeled Magnetic on the Options bar.) The Magnetic Lasso and the Magnetic Pen work so similarly that it's hardly worth discussing twice; instead go read that section earlier in this chapter (if you haven't already). Their similarity extends to producing a result that you will almost certainly have to finesse; the magnetic tools are not known for their precision.

Tip: Paths vs. Shapes vs. Pixels. Important note: Each time you use the Pen tools, you need to specify in the Options bar whether you want the Pen tools to create a path or a vector shape. When you select one of the Shape tools, you can choose path, vectors, or pixels (see Figure 8-41).

Tip: Hide the Path. When you have a path selected in the Paths palette or a layer clipping path selected in the Layers palette, Photoshop displays the path on screen as a thin gray line. When you have a non-painting tool selected in the Tool palette (like the selection tools or the Move tool), you can deselect the path (make the line go away) by pressing the Enter key.

Tip: Multiple Path Segments in the Path. You don't have to limit yourself to one path per path tile (in the Paths palette) or one shape per layer clipping path. You can have two or more path segments in a single path tile. To some, this is obvious, but others just never think of it.

Tip: Paths as Guides. Photoshop makes it easy to get guides on your image (see "Guides and Grids" in Chapter 15, *Essential Image Techniques*). But Photoshop only offers horizontal and vertical guides. If you want a diagonal or curved guideline, you can fake it using paths. Make a path

Figure 8-41 The Path and Shape tool's Options bar

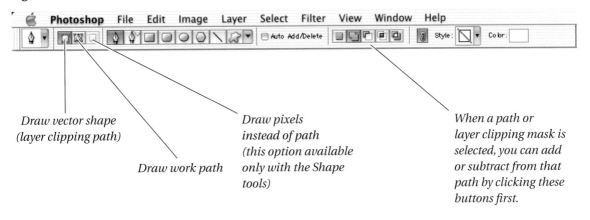

Draw vector shape
(layer clipping path)

Draw work path

Draw pixels
instead of path
(this option available
only with the Shape
tools)

When a path or
layer clipping mask is
selected, you can add
or subtract from that
path by clicking these
buttons first.

using the Pen tools. When you're done making the path, save it by double-clicking on the Working Path tile in the Paths palette and giving it a name.

When you want to hide the guidelines, click off the path's tile in the Paths palette, Shift-click on the tile, or press Enter or Return.

Tip: Arrow Keys and Paths. If you have one or more points on a path selected, you can move them one pixel at a time using the arrow keys—but only when the Pen or one of the Selection tools is selected in the Tool palette. Or, if you hold down the Shift key, the arrow keys move the path ten image pixels (*not* screen pixels). At 100-percent view, image pixels and screen pixels are the same thing, of course.

Tip: Drag Segments, Too. When editing your paths, don't get too caught up with having to move the paths' points and the curve handles around. As in FreeHand and Illustrator, you can also drag the path segment itself. If it's a curved segment, Photoshop adjusts the curve handles on either side of it automatically. If it's a straight-line segment (hence there are no curve handles to adjust), Photoshop actually moves the corner or cusp points on either side of the segment.

Tip: Connecting Paths. You've got two paths you want to connect? It's not as hard as you think.

1. Use the Path Selection tool to select one of the path's endpoints.

2. Switch to the Pen tool.

3. If you want that point to be a cusp, Option-drag out a handle.

4. Click and drag on the other path's endpoint. (Or alternatively, Option-drag to make it a cusp point.)

Tip: Flipping, Rotating, and Modifying Paths. For years, we were frustrated that Adobe Systems, creators of PostScript and Illustrator, hadn't gotten around to putting basic path transformation tools into Photoshop. The only way to rotate or scale a path was to drag it into Illustrator, transform it, and then drag it back. Fortunately, Photoshop now lets you transform paths without leaving the program—just select the path you want to edit in the Paths palette and choose Free Transform from the Edit menu (or press Command-T). Similarly, you can select from the many options in the Transform submenu (under the Edit menu).

You don't have to transform the entire path, either. If the path has several subpaths, you can select one of them (by Option-clicking on the subpath) before transforming. You can even select one or more points on the path; in this case, Photoshop only changes those points and the segments around them.

Tip: Paths Outside Image Boundaries. Paths are like floating selections in that they live on their own layer above the mundane world of pixels. They're also like floating selections in that you can drag them off the side of the image boundary and they don't get clipped.

Paths to Selections

Once you have a path, you can convert it into a selection, rasterize it (turn it into pixels), or fill it with a color or adjustment. Let's look at converting to selections first. Photoshop makes this process easy for you: You can convert a path into a selection in one of four ways.

▶ Select Make Selection from the Paths palette's popout menu (or drag the path's tile on top of this button).

▶ Click on the Convert Path to Selection icon (see Figure 8-42).

▶ Command-click on the path's tile in the Paths palette.

▶ Press Command-Enter (in ancient versions, this was simply Enter).

If you hold down the Option key while dragging a path on top of, or clicking on, the Convert Path to Selection icon, Photoshop displays the Make Selection dialog box. This dialog box lets you add, subtract, or intersect selections with selections you've already made (if there is no selection, these options are grayed out). It also lets you feather and anti-alias the selections. The default for selections (if you don't go in and change this dialog box) is to include anti-aliasing, but not feathering.

Figure 8-42
Converting a path
to a selection

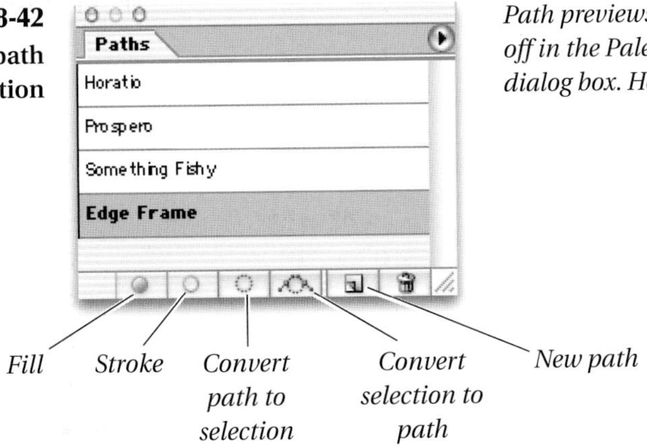

Path previews are turned off in the Palette Options dialog box. Here, they're off.

Fill   Stroke   Convert   Convert   New path
path to   selection to
selection   path

Tip: Avoiding the Make Selection Dialog Box. You know we avoid dialog boxes and menu items whenever we can get away with it. So it should be no surprise at all that we tend to avoid the Make Selection dialog box.

If you're using the Make Selection dialog box to add, subtract, or intersect paths, you can use these keystrokes instead.

▸ Command-Shift-Enter adds the path's selection to the current selection (if there is one).

▸ Command-Option-Enter subtracts the selection.

▸ Command-Shift-Option-Enter intersects the two selections.

Each of these works when clicking on the Make Selection icon or dragging the tile over the icon, too. It's just that the Enter key is so much easier. We still haven't found keystrokes for adding or removing feathering or anti-aliasing, though.

Selections to Paths

To turn a selection into a path, choose Make Work Path from the popout menu in the Paths palette. When you ask Photoshop to do this, you're basically asking it to turn a soft-edged selection into a hard-edged one. Therefore, the program has to make some decisions about where the edges of the selection are.

Fortunately, the program gives you a choice about how hard it should work at this: the Tolerance field in the Make Work Path dialog box. The higher the value you enter, the shabbier the path's representation of the original selection. Values above 2 or 3 typically make nice abstract designs, but aren't otherwise very useful.

Tip: Making Paths with Icons. There's one more way to convert a selection into a new path: Click on the Make Path icon in the Paths palette. Note that this uses whatever tolerance value you last specified in the Make Work Path dialog box, unless you hold down the Option key while clicking on the icon, in which case it brings up the dialog box.

Rasterizing Paths

The second thing you can do with a path is rasterize it into pixels. As we said back in Chapter 3, *Image Essentials*, rasterizing is the process of turning an outline into pixels. Photoshop lets you rasterize paths in two ways: You can fill the path area and you can stroke the path.

Filling. To fill the path area with the foreground color, drag the path's tile to the Fill Path icon, or click on the Fill Path icon in the Paths palette. Or, better yet, Option-click the icon, and the Fill Path dialog box appears (this is the same dialog box you get if you choose Fill Path from the Paths palette's popout menu). The dialog box gives you options for fill color, opacity, mode, and so on.

Stroking. Stroking the path works just the same as filling: You can drag the path's tile to the Stroke Path icon, or simply click on the Stroke Path icon in the Paths palette (while a path is visible). When you do this, Photoshop strokes the path with the Pencil tool. That's pretty lame, so instead, change the tool it uses by Option-clicking on the Stroke Path icon (or select Stroke Path from the popout menu in the Paths palette).

Tip: Stroking on Enter. When you have a painting tool selected in the Tool palette (like the Brush, Dodge, or Rubber Stamp tool), pressing Enter strokes the path with that tool (using the current brush size and blending mode). We like this because we almost always want a different painting tool than the one we used last time. (See "Retouching" in Chapter 15, *Essential Image Techniques*, for a powerful retouching technique that uses the Rubber Stamp tool and this "path stroking" tip.)

Tip: Working with Multiple Paths. As we said earlier, you can have more than one path within a path "layer." For instance, you can have three circular paths together, and save them all under one path name. If you want to stroke or fill just one of those three, select it with the Direct Select tool (Option-click on the path to select the entire path) before stroking or filling.

Tip: Rasterizing Paths Inside Selections. If you make a selection before filling or stroking your path, Photoshop fills or strokes only within that selection. This has tripped up more than one advanced user, but if you're aware of the feature, it can really come in handy.

Layer Clipping Paths and Shapes

Photoshop lets you create *layer clipping paths*—that is, vector paths that define the boundary of a layer, as though someone had snipped around that layer with a pair of scissors. Basically, these are exactly the same as layer masks, except that instead of an 8- or 16-bit channel defining a layer's transparency, Photoshop uses a sharp-edged line. What's cool is that the line always matches the resolution of your PostScript printer—just like text from QuarkXPress or InDesign might look blocky on screen but is perfectly smooth from a laser printer or imagesetter.

(Notice that we snuck the word "PostScript" in there. While we'll discuss a couple of good reasons to use layer clipping paths for Web or fine-art images, they're really designed for printing to a PostScript printer either from Photoshop itself or from a page-layout program like QuarkXPress or Adobe InDesign.)

You may hear people talking about Photoshop's "Shapes" feature, but in reality the Shape tool is just a way to create a layer clipping path quickly. Drawing something with the Shape tool is the same thing as creating a Solid Color Fill layer, adding a layer clipping path, and drawing on it. We use the terms *layer clipping path* and *layer clipping mask* interchangeably.

Making a layer clipping path. There are three ways to make a layer clipping path (well, we can only think of three; see Figure 8-43).

▶ **Shape tool.** When you draw any shape with the Shape tool (press U to select this tool, then choose a shape from the Options bar), Photoshop automatically creates a Solid Color layer with a layer clipping path. If you want to create a working path (in the Paths palette) instead, you can click on the Working Path button in the Options bar. Note that you can set various options—Opacity, Layer Style, and so on—in the Options bar before drawing the shape, but if you forget to set them, you can always apply these afterward in the Layers and Styles palettes.

▶ **Adjustment layer.** If you add an adjustment layer while a path is selected in the Paths palette (if it's visible on screen, it's selected), Photoshop automatically uses that path as a layer clipping path for the new layer. (We discuss adjustment layers in Chapter 9, *The Digital Darkroom*.)

▶ **Add layer clipping path.** You can add a layer clipping path to any layer (except the Background layer) by selecting either Reveal All or Hide All from the Add Layer Clipping Path submenu (under the Layer menu). But that's slow; instead, just Command-click on the Add Layer Mask button in the Layers palette. (Command-Option-click adds a layer clipping path that "hides all.") If a path is already selected in the Paths palette, Photoshop automatically assigns it to the layer clipping path; otherwise, you can just start drawing a path with the Pen tool.

Tip: Adding and Subtracting Paths. If you use the Shape tool while a layer clipping path is selected in the Paths palette (if it's visible on screen), then Photoshop adds your shape to that layer clipping path. Before you draw the shape, you can tell the program how you want this new path to interact with the path already there by clicking on the Add, Subtract, Intersect, or Exclude Intersection button in the Options bar. If you forget to select one, don't fret: Command-click with the Shape tool on the shape you just drew (to select all its points), and *then* click the button in the Options bar.

Figure 8-43
Three ways to make a
layer clipping path

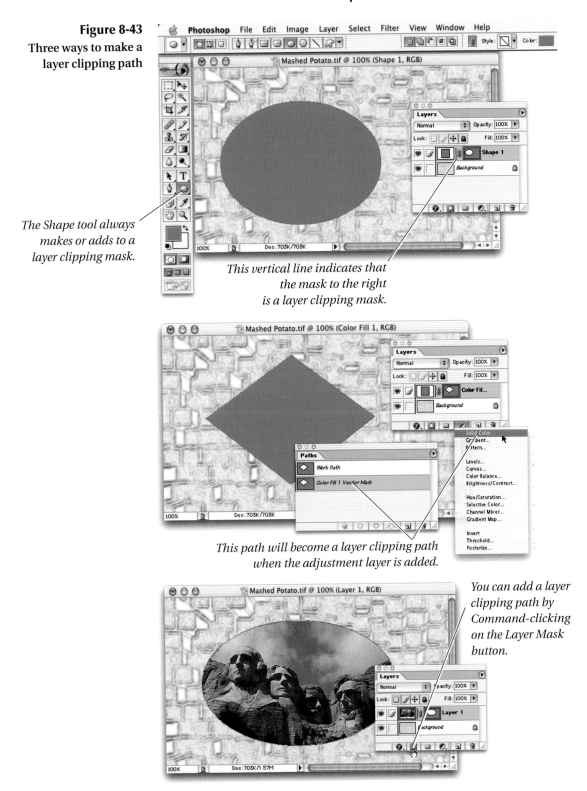

*The Shape tool always
makes or adds to a
layer clipping mask.*

*This vertical line indicates that
the mask to the right
is a layer clipping mask.*

*This path will become a layer clipping path
when the adjustment layer is added.*

*You can add a layer
clipping path by
Command-clicking
on the Layer Mask
button.*

Tip: Vectors for Web and Fine Art. Even if you don't print to a Post-Script printer, vector art (in the form of layer clipping paths) can be useful. For instance, let's say you want a grid of buttons for your Web page. You can make the buttons by painting pixels on a layer and then applying layer effects (such as Emboss) to them; but if you later need to change the buttons—perhaps make them all slightly smaller—it's going to be a real hassle because you need to actually edit the pixels. Instead, if you make each button with the Shape tool (or with the Pen tool on a layer clipping mask), the edits are simple: Just use the Path Selection tool or the Transform Path feature to reshape the paths on the layer clipping path (see Figure 8-44).

Tip: Invert the Path. One of the most annoying parts of making layer clipping paths is that there's no easy way to invert the path (making the clipped-out parts fall inside the path and *vice versa*). But there is *a* way.

1. Make sure the layer clipping path is visible (select the layer and then select the clipping path's tile in the Paths palette).

2. Select the path itself by either Command-clicking inside of it with the Shape tool or Option-clicking on its boundary with the Path Selection tool.

3. With either the Shape or Pen tool selected, click on either the Add or Subtract buttons in the Options bar (see Figure 8-45). If one doesn't invert the path, then the other will.

Tip: Turn Off the Clipping Path. You can disable a layer clipping path (turning it off, so the whole layer is visible) the same way you turn off a regular layer mask: Shift-click on the layer clipping path's thumbnail on the Layers palette. (Or, the slow way: Select "Disable Layer Clipping Path" from the Layer menu.)

Making vectors and pixels interact. Putting vector artwork on a layer on top of pixels is no great feat; if that's all you want to do, you can do the same thing in Illustrator, FreeHand, QuarkXPress, InDesign, or whatever. The real value to Photoshop's layer clipping paths is in how pixels can blend together and still retain a sharp edge. For example, you can use the

Figure 8-44
Quick edits with shapes

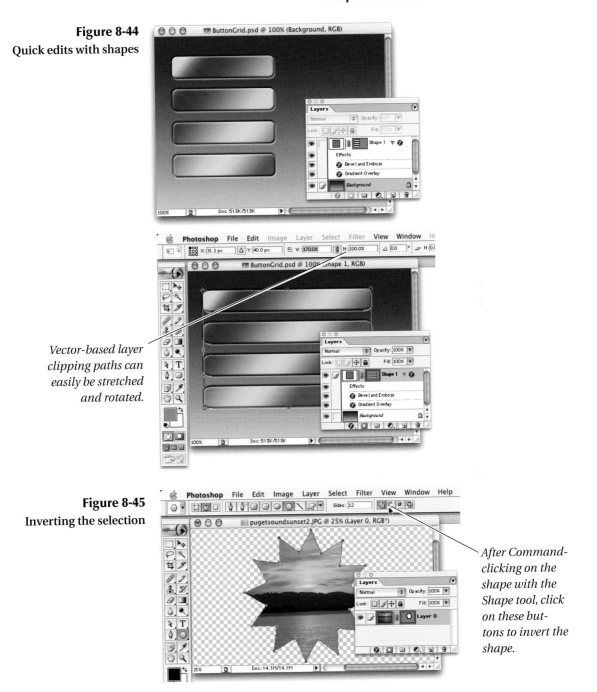

Vector-based layer clipping paths can easily be stretched and rotated.

Figure 8-45
Inverting the selection

After Command-clicking on the shape with the Shape tool, click on these buttons to invert the shape.

Shape tool to draw a solid black oval on top of your Background layer, and then change the opacity of that layer to 50 percent. Now, you can see the background image through your semi-transparent black oval. Of course, the vector artwork isn't really blending with the pixels beneath it. Rather,

Photoshop is mixing the pixels on one layer with the pixels on another layer and then using the layer clipping path to define the edge between the two layers.

If you zoom in to magnify the edge of the oval, it appears as though the edge is anti-aliased with the background; however, when you print from Photoshop (or save the image as an EPS and print it from a page-layout program; see "Tip: Saving Vectors," below), you'll see that the edge is sharp (see Figure 8-46). Remember that what Photoshop is showing you on screen is what the image would look like if you flattened it (losing the vector paths).

Any layer can have a layer clipping path (even text layers), and you can change the opacity, blending mode, or layer effect of a clipped layer just the way you would ordinarily. So, if you want your shape layer to have a drop shadow, use the Overlay mode, and have a 75-percent opacity, you can change all that in the Layers palette.

Figure 8-46
Vectors fool the eye

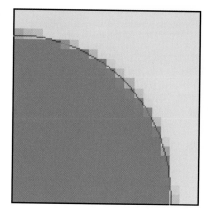

What the vector-based "shape" looks like on screen.

When you print to a PostScript printer, it's much sharper.

Tip: Blending Into Vectors. David has been trying to figure out how to do a *Sports Illustrated* cover for literally ten years. You know the type: a photo of some sports star partially over and partially under the title of the magazine. It has always been very difficult to achieve this sort of look without a high-end system (like Scitex), because where the photograph overlaps the sharp, vector masthead, the pixels have to anti-alias into the text. Photoshop lets you create this kind of effect easily: Just put the text on one layer, and the cutout image on a different one (see Figure 8-47).

Figure 8-47
Vectors and pixels
together at last

Note that this vector text sits both behind and in front of the bitmapped image.

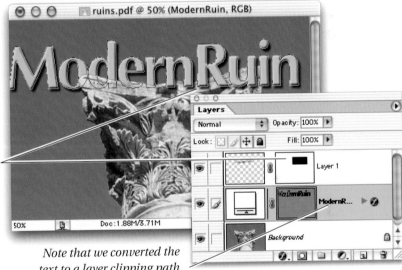

To achieve the effect, we copied some of the image onto a new layer, added a layer mask (which is invisible here), and put the text in between the two layers.

Note that we converted the text to a layer clipping path ("shape") so that we didn't have to send the font to the printer.

Once again, the screen can't be trusted. Here, the text is vector, but it appears to be soft-edged.

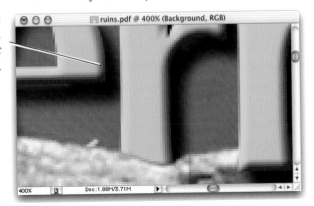

Tip: Don't Fill, Adjust! When you use a Shape tool, Photoshop automatically creates a Solid Color Fill layer and applies the shape to the layer clipping path. But you can change this from a Solid Color Fill layer to any other kind of adjustment layer in the Change Layer Content submenu (under the Layer menu). For example, you could change it to a Gradient Map, a Curves adjustment layer, or a Pattern layer. Then you can adjust the layer's opacity and blending mode to change how it interacts with the shapes and pixels on layers beneath it.

Tip: Saving Vectors. We cover how to save images in Chapter 16, *Storing Images*, but in case you're in a rush, we'll let you in on a secret now: If you have used layer clipping paths, and you want to retain those sharp edges when you print your image from your page-layout application, you should probably save your file as either a PDF or an EPS file. If you are using a spot color, you'll have to use the DCS 2.0 format. Note that while the EPS format saves and prints the layers and clipping paths properly, when you re-open your EPS file in Photoshop, it automatically gets flattened. Very annoying. So, make sure you save the EPS as a copy, and archive your layered Photoshop file just in case you need to go back to edit it. PDF files don't have this problem.

Step-by-Step Silhouettes

Now that we've gone through all of Photoshop's tools for working with selections, channels, and masks, it's time to bring all those tools to bear. And the best place to demonstrate these tools in practice is in the process of creating silhouettes—that oh-so-common and (sometimes) oh-so-difficult of production techniques.

We'll start by showing how to create a simple silhouette, and work our way up to difficult image masks. In the next chapter, we cover even more real-world techniques involving selections and masks.

If there's one thing that makes silhouettes difficult, it's the edge detail. In most cases (especially when you're trying to select fine details), some of the color from the image background spills over into the image you want. So when you drop the silhouetted image onto a different background (even white), the spill trips you up, making the image look artificial and out of place.

A Simple, Hard-Edged Silhouette

When the image you're trying to select has been photographed on a white background with good studio lighting (so the background's free of colors that contaminate the edges), your selection is relatively easy. We typically jump in with several clicks of the Magic Wand along with Grow or Similar. We almost never get a perfect fit, however, so we usually clean up the edges in Quick Mask mode. In Figure 8-48, we use Gaussian Blur and Levels to choke the edges of the selection mask. That way, we can be sure no background color spills over in our final composited image.

Pulling Selections from Channels

Trying to build a selection mask for the tree in Figure 8-49 with the basic selection tools would drive you to distraction faster than having to watch

Figure 8-48 Silhouetting a hard-edged element

The original image. Our goal: to select the object from its background.

The Magic Wand, Grow, and Similar get us most of the way there.

We switch to Quick Mask mode and lasso the areas that should be excluded from the selection.

After fixing the edge detail, we incorporate a new background into the image (see below).

The original selection left some edge pixels unselected, causing edge spill.

We apply a small-radius Gaussian Blur to the quick mask, which appears to worsen the edge spill.

Channel: Quick Mask

Input Levels: 0   0.21   255

A radical Levels gamma shift on the mask makes the edge pixels darker.

When the mask is partially transparent, the dark areas around the edge tell us that there will be no edge spill.

Figure 8-49 Creating subtle masks from multiple channels

The original. Our goal: to select the tree and make it more green.

The blue channel has the best contrast between sky and tree.

The green channel has the best contrast between tree and grass.

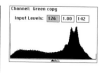

We copy the blue channel, and force the sky to white and the tree to black with the Levels dialog box.

A similar move on the green channel creates a mask for the lower part of the tree.

We delete the "garbage" areas from each mask with the Brush and Lasso. To edit the channels better, we make the mask and the color channels visible at the same time.

We use Calculate (Add) to merge the two channels into one, providing the final mask.

After loading the selection mask, we use Curves to brighten and saturate the greens in the tree, and we pull back the reds and blues slightly.

Barney reruns with your four-year-old. Instead, we found the essence of a great selection hiding in the color channels of the image. While you can often pull a selection mask from a single channel, in this case we made duplicates of both the blue and green channels. Then, using Levels, we pushed the tree to black and the background to white. After combining the two channels, it took only a little touch-up to complete the mask.

Removing Spill from Fine Edges

The finer the pixel selection, the harder it is to remove edge spill. It doesn't get much tougher than the detail in Figure 8-50, so we used a variation of a trick Greg Vander Houwen taught us: Replacing the border pixels with pixels from the background. In this case, once we realized how bad the edge spill was in the composited image, we built a border mask for the

Figure 8-50 Removing edge spill in detailed areas by filling from a background

The original image. The goal: to composite the dandelion onto another background.

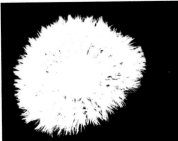

A selection mask created using Color Range with many sample points and a low Fuzziness level.

The edge spill is obvious. We select the transparency mask by Command-clicking on the foreground layer.

We use Border with a large radius, then feather the resulting selection.

We copy pixels from the background to a new layer, and set it to Lighten.

The green fringe disappears, without sacrificing edge detail.

dandelion with the Border command and cleaned it up in Quick Mask mode.

Finally, we chose the new background image's layer, and—using our border selection—copied pixels to a new layer using Command-J. Then, to get rid of dark green pixels at the edges, we placed the new layer above our foreground object and set its blending mode to Lighten. This doesn't touch the lighter pixels in the dandelion. In other images we might have used Normal, Darken, Hue, or Color; it depends on the relationship between the foreground and the background colors.

Removing Spill with Preserve Transparency

Edge spill is insidious, and—as you saw in the last example—it can be a disaster when compositing images. Here's one more method of removing spill that we like a lot. If you place the pixels on a transparent layer, you can make use of the Preserve Transparency feature in the Layers palette to "paint away" the edge spill.

In the example in Figure 8-51, the color from the blue sky is much too noticeable around the composited trees. So we place the trees on a layer and build a selection that encompasses just their edges. This step is really just a convenience—it makes our job of painting out the edge spill easier. With Preserve Transparency turned on, we select the Rubber Stamp tool and clone interior colors over the blue edge pixels. In some areas, we also use Curves to pull the blue out (because our border selection is feathered, these moves affect only the pixels we're after).

This is a trick you can use with all sorts of variations. If the edge color is relatively flat, you might be able to use the Brush tool (we usually add a little noise after painting in order to match the background texture); this is also an area where it behooves you to test out different Apply modes (Lighten, Multiply, and so on).

Tip: Enhancing Edges with Filters. We're naturally wary when it comes to using Photoshop filters; while very powerful, they're almost always used to create funky effects. However, every now and again we see how we can use the same filters to increase our productivity and enhance our work life. Deke McClelland taught us about one such application: Using filters to get better selections.

Figure 8-51 Painting out edge spill using layers, a border mask, and Preserve Transparency

The original image

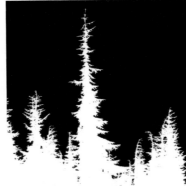

A mask created using Color Range

The trees are copied onto a layer above the sunset image. The blue spill ruins the compositing effect.

A closeup of the composited image shows the blue edge spill from the original sky.

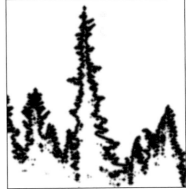

We create a border mask by using Border on the transparency mask, then running a Gaussian Blur.

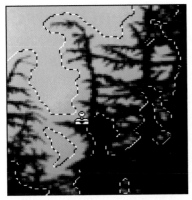

With the border mask selection loaded and Preserve Transparency turned on, we rubber stamp dark interior pixels over the blue pixels.

The final image after the blue edge spill has been removed

A closeup of the final image

The two filters that we use most often for this sort of thing are the High Pass and the Find Edges filters (usually one or the other; not both at the same time). We typically duplicate the image we're working on, then use one or more filters on the copy to extract the selection we want.

Find Edges is a very blunt instrument when it comes to making selections, but it can often draw out edges that are very hard to see on screen.

The trick to using High Pass is to use very small values in the High Pass dialog box, usually under 1 or 2 pixels. Then, you can use the Levels or Curves dialog box to enhance the edges in the mostly gray image.

Tip: Complex Masks with Plug-Ins. After working with Photoshop's selection tools for a while, you begin to know instinctively when you're up against a difficult task. For instance, trying to create a selection mask for a woman in a gauzy dress, with her long, wispy hair blowing in the wind, could be a nightmare. And if you have to perform 20 of these in a day . . . well . . . 'nuf said. It's time to plunk down some cash for one of the several masking programs on the market—for instance, Mask Pro from Extensis or KnockOut from Procreate.

We're not saying that these plug-ins are perfect. In fact, far from it. But they can often get you 90 percent of the way to a great selection in 10 percent of the time it would take you with Photoshop's own tools. From there, you'll still have to tweak using the various methods throughout this chapter.

Enhancing Edges with Adjustment Layers

Adjustment layers are almost always used for tonal or color adjustments (we talk about adjustment layers in quite some detail in Chapter 9, *The Digital Darkroom*). But here's a method that Greg Vander Houwen showed us that uses adjustment layers to help make selections. This is particularly useful when you're trying to select a foreground image out of a background, and the two are too similar in color (see Figure 8-52).

First, add an adjustment layer above the image (Command-click on the New Layer icon in the Layers palette). The type of adjustment layer you choose depends on what you're trying to achieve. You can make a radical adjustment in this layer, knowing that you're not actually hurting your original image data. Use the adjustment layer to boost the contrast between the foreground and background, so that you can make a better selection.

Figure 8-52 Using adjustment layers to emphasize elements and build masks

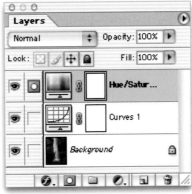

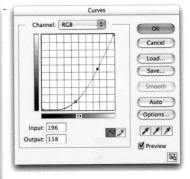

The original image

We add two adjustment layers: a Curves layer that drastically increases the image contrast, and a Hue/Saturation layer that desaturates the image slightly.

The Curves dialog box of the Curves adjustment layer. Note that the shadows have been completely blown out to black. The curve has also been tweaked on the red, blue, and green channels.

After these extreme adjustment layers are applied, the image looks almost unrecognizable.

We duplicate one of the channels of this "extreme" image and clean it up for our water mask. Now we can throw away the adjustment layers (they've done their job).

Finally, we load our new mask into the layer mask of a new, more subtle Hue/Saturation adjustment layer. This way, the effect only affects the water.

Masks, Channels, and Life

While you can get by with performing global manipulations on images, the vast majority of images you'll work with require making a selection. We hope that after almost 80 pages we've done more to allay your fears than to cause you panic when selecting pixels in your image. Remember the two golden rules of selections:

▶ Masks, channels, and selections are all the same thing.

▶ You can (and often should) edit a selection after you've made it.

With those firmly planted in your mind, you'll have no problems as you enter the next chapter, in which we discuss some of the most common Photoshop production tasks, most of which require selecting and building masks.

9

The Digital Darkroom

Photographic Techniques in Photoshop

What would you say if we told you that you could perform color correction, use dodging and burning, build up density in overexposed areas, open up underexposed areas, and more—all with a minimum of image degradation and with an unlimited number of undos? You'd probably just laugh at us. But in this chapter we'll show you how.

You can do a lot using the controls we've already covered, but you can go much further, with more freedom to experiment, when you apply them as adjustment layers rather than simply burning the changes into your image. The controls in adjustment layers behave just as they do on a flat file, but with far more freedom and flexibility. You can change your adjustment settings at any time, vary their strength globally by changing the adjustment layer's opacity, and vary it locally by painting on the adjustment layer's layer mask. In effect, you have not just unlimited undo, but selective, partial undo. And in the "be careful what you wish for" department, adjustment layers are now available in high-bit mode, which allows a virtually lossless workflow—at the expense of some very large files.

The techniques in this chapter can help you get a better image with little or no degradation and unprecedented control. But much more important, they're designed to give you maximum flexibility so that you can experiment and play with your images more. While we'll give you some places to jump off from, it's really in this playing around that you'll see the myriad of options that these techniques make possible.

Why Use Adjustment Layers?

Whenever you apply a Curves or Levels tweak (or even a Hue/Saturation adjustment) to an image, you're degrading it a little by throwing away some image data. Once that data is gone, you can't get it back. In the digital darkroom, this degradation is no longer an issue because you make edits to layers above the image rather than to the image itself.

If you're a photographer, think of it this way: Your raw image is like a negative that you can print through many different filter pack combinations on many different contrast grades of paper. You can make huge changes from print to print, but the negative itself doesn't change. If the raw image is analogous to a negative, adjustment layers are like enlarger filter packs on steroids. You can change the color balance as you would with a filter pack, but you can also change the contrast and do local, selective editing akin to dodging and burning. However, unlike their analog counterparts, you can always undo digital dodging and burning.

There are several other reasons why we love working in the digital darkroom.

▶ **Changing your mind.** Adjustment layers give you the freedom to change your mind. If you make successive edits with Curves or Levels on a flat file, your image will quickly degrade. With adjustment layers, you can go back and change your edits at any time without further degrading the image. This gives you endless freedom to experiment, and because you can fine-tune your edits with no penalty, you're more likely to get the results you want.

▶ **Instant before-and-afters.** You can always tell exactly what you're doing when you use adjustment layers. Because all your edits are on layers, you can easily see "before and after" views by turning off the visibility for the layer you're working on, and then turning it back on again (by clicking on the eyeball in the left column of the Layers palette).

▶ **Variable-strength edits.** The Opacity slider in the Layers palette acts as a volume control for your edits (this is similar to using the Fade Filter feature; see Chapter 2, *Essential Photoshop Tips and Tricks)*.

▶ **Applying the same edits to multiple images.** You can use the same adjustment layer on a number of different images, and even script the layer with actions to batch-apply to a folder full of images.

▶ **Brushable edits.** You can make selective, local edits to a particular area of an adjustment layer. This means you not only have essentially unlimited undo, but also *selective, partial* undo.

▶ **Doing the impossible.** You can use adjustment layers in conjunction with blending modes to do things that are usually extremely difficult, if not impossible—such as building density in highlights or opening up shadows without posterizing the image.

You can use adjustment layers as effectively on CMYK or Lab images as on RGB (though we still typically work with RGB images when we can). If you prefer to work by the numbers, the Info palette shows before-and-after values while you're working an adjustment layer's controls, and you can place color samplers to track key values just as you can on a flat file. If you'd rather work visually, you can use Proof Colors to see how your edits will work on the printed result. In fact, Photoshop CS even lets you preview the individual CMYK plates while working in RGB.

Why Not Use Adjustment Layers?

With all these advantages, why not use adjustment layers for all your edits? We think the only good reasons not to use this powerful feature for making tonal or color adjustments are when you're in a severely RAM-impaired environment, or when you're working on a high-bit image and the file size simply gets out of hand.

Adjustment Layers and RAM. The only downside to using adjustment layers is that they use more RAM and hard drive scratch space than simply burning edits into a flat file. Adjustment layers themselves add very little to the RAM requirements because they contain almost no data, but painting on the Layer mask adds pixels that take up space.

But even if using an adjustment layer exceeds your available RAM, you may not see any slowdown because of the way Photoshop handles its image cache and scratch space. As Photoshop keeps getting smarter about the way it handles memory, it becomes more and more possible to do the seemingly impossible; so don't assume that you don't have enough horsepower to use adjustment layers—try it and see. (See Chapter 1, *Building a Photoshop System,* for more information on memory and scratch space, and Chapter 2, *Essential Photoshop Tips and Tricks,* for a much more detailed discussion of the image cache).

All things considered, the disadvantages to using adjustment layers are minimal. We believe that most people will get better results faster using them.

Adjustment layers and high-bit images. One of the biggest changes in Photoshop CS is the ability to use layers, including adjustment layers, on high-bit files. We love this capability and use it extensively, but we'd be remiss if we didn't point out that doing so can create extremely large files—think gigabytes rather than megabytes.

In Chapter 14, *Building a Digital Workflow*, we'll discuss strategies for dealing with ballooning file sizes in much more detail. For now, a relatively simple rule of thumb is to make your biggest corrections on the high-bit data. After that, we suggest staying in high-bit mode until it hurts, or until you need to do something that you still can't do in high-bit mode, such as running Extract, or Liquify, or some of the more esoteric filters.

The techniques we discuss in this chapter work in both high-bit and 8-bit modes. You need to make your own call on when to downsample to 8 bits per channel based on the quality needs of the job at hand, how much time you're willing to spend on an image, and the capabilities of your hardware. You may elect to downsample to 8 bits right in the camera by shooting JPEG, or you may decide to preserve your high-bit data all the way to the output process. However, unless you're shooting JPEG (in which case, you have no high-bit data to start from), we strongly recommend that you make your big initial edits in high-bit mode, and save the high-bit file. That way, if you run into the wall in 8-bit mode, you'll still have a fallback position.

Adjustment Layer Basics

Before adjustment layers, our digital darkroom techniques involved duplicating the Background layer to use as an editing layer. Since all the edits were made to the duplicate, the original image was never damaged. Adjustment layers do the same thing, but they do it automatically, and with a much smaller RAM footprint. We mention this because it's much easier to get your head around what happens with an adjustment layer if you think of it as a copy of the base image, particularly when you start using adjustment layers in conjunction with blending modes.

The controls in adjustment layers work exactly as they do in flat files. You can apply Levels, Curves, Color Balance, Brightness/Contrast, Hue/Saturation, Selective Color, Channel Mixer, Gradient Map, Photo Filter, Invert, Threshold, and Posterize as adjustment layers. We use Levels, Curves, Hue/Saturation, and Photo Filter far more often than the others, but we encourage you to experiment. You *can't* do any harm, because your original image stays intact on the Background layer until you flatten it.

Creating Adjustment Layers

The first step in working with adjustment layers is (obviously) to create one. Photoshop offers two different methods for creating an adjustment layer.

▶ **The Layer menu.** You can create an adjustment layer by choosing an adjustment layer type from the New Adjustment Layer submenu (under the Layer menu; see Figure 9-1).

▶ **The Layers palette icon.** You can choose an adjustment layer type from the popup menu on the Layers palette's New Content Layer icon. One method isn't better than the other—we use whichever one is closest to the mouse. Most often, though, we rely on the following tip.

Tip: Adjustment Layer Actions. If you're going to be making a number of adjustment layers, you'll do yourself a favor by creating a "Make Adjustment Layers" action in the Actions palette (see "Actions and Automating Photoshop" in Chapter 15, *Essential Image Techniques*). Bruce runs raw images through a Batch action that adds Levels, Curves, and Hue/Saturation layers so that he can get to work quickly as soon as the image opens.

Figure 9-1
Creating an adjustment layer

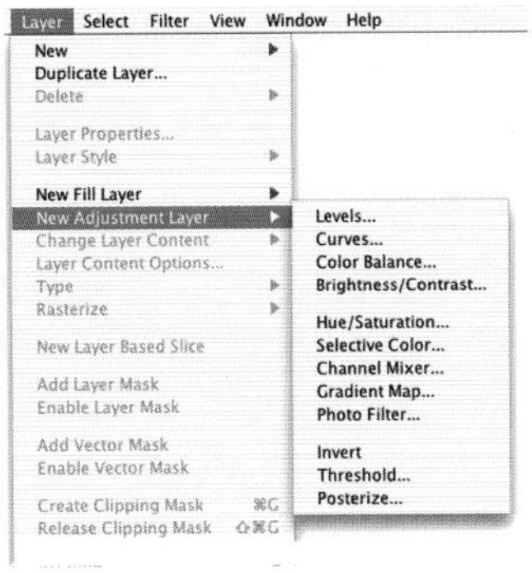

Photoshop offers two different methods for creating an adjustment layer.

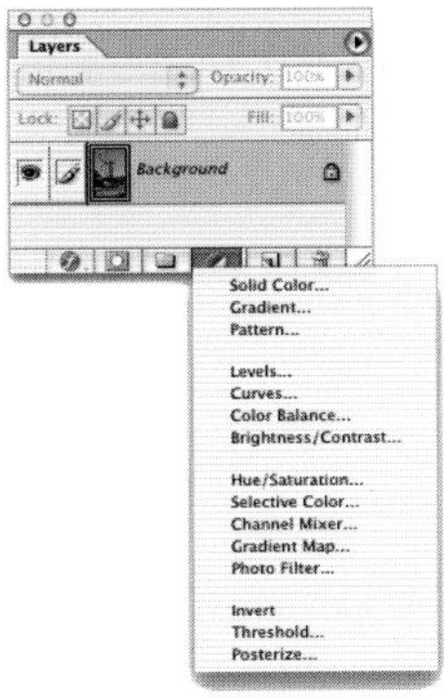

Controlling Adjustment Layers

The big difference between using adjustment layers and editing a flat file is that adjustment layers give you much more freedom to control and refine your edits. You have four ways to control your editing when using an adjustment layer that you don't have with a flat file.

Variable strength. You can control the opacity of the adjustment layer by changing the Opacity slider in the Layers palette. This lets you change the intensity of the adjustment globally. We often make edits that are slightly more extreme than we really want, then back off the opacity of the editing layer to reduce the effect to just where we want it. We find this faster than trying to fine-tune the adjustment in the adjustment layer's dialog box.

Fine-tuning. Whenever you want to make a change to the adjustment layer, you can edit it (changing the curve or choosing other options) by double-clicking on the adjustment layer thumbnail in the Layers palette (see Figure 9-2). When you do this, Photoshop displays the settings you last used in the adjustment layer's dialog box. Not to beat a dead papaya, but you can do this as often as you want without degrading the image, because the edits aren't actually applied until you flatten the file.

Multiple edits. You don't have to limit yourself to a single adjustment layer. You can have as many as you want, each stacked on top of the next to make successive edits without degrading the image. This technique is particularly useful when you want one curve to correct the image globally while another curve edits the image in selective places.

Note that adjustment layers apply to all visible layers beneath them. When you stack two or more adjustment layers of the same type—all Curves, or all Hue/Saturation, for example—you'll get the same results

Figure 9-2
Editing an
adjustment layer

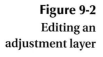

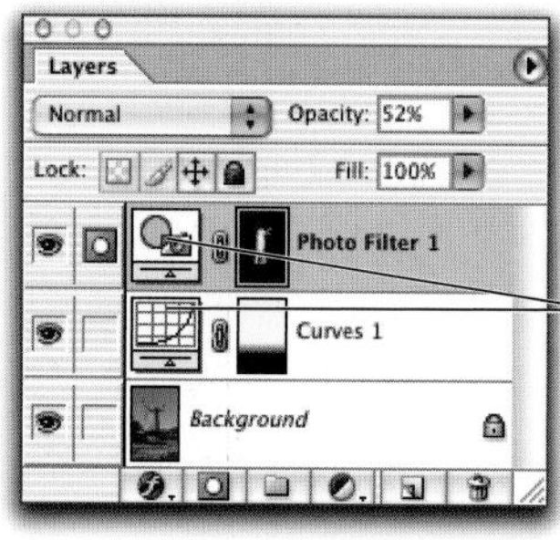

Double-click the adjustment layer thumbnail to change the adjustment layer's settings.

no matter what order they're stacked in. But when you mix adjustment layers of different types, you'll get different results depending on the stacking order. Usually the differences are fairly subtle—you may need to check the numbers in the Info palette to see them—but occasionally the difference can be significant, especially when working with Hue/Saturation and Color Balance.

While you can't merge adjustment layers together, you can merge them into regular, raster layers. If you want only one layer, you can flatten the whole image or select Merge Visible from the Layer menu (Merge Visible retains any transparency in the image). We don't recommend doing this unless it's necessary, since you lose all the advantages of adjustment layers, and they take up very little space. Instead, keep all your adjustment layers live until you're finished with the project. Then, to save a flattened version of the image, choose Save As, and in the Save As dialog box turn on the As a Copy checkbox, and turn off the Layers checkbox.

Selective editing. While the Opacity slider applies to the entire adjustment layer, you can vary the opacity of the layer locally by painting on the adjustment layer's layer mask. To paint on the layer mask, simply click on the adjustment layer tile in the Layers palette and paint; the paint automatically goes on the layer mask. Black paint hides the effect of the adjustment layer; white paint reveals it; gray paint applies the effect partially (25-percent black ink applies 75 percent of the adjustment layer's effect). By varying the brush opacity in the Options bar, you can achieve precise control over the adjustment layer's opacity in specific areas.

Note that a new channel is automatically added to the Channels palette whenever you select an adjustment layer in the Layers palette. This is the channel that you're actually drawing on. You can use all the usual layer mask tricks, like Shift-clicking on the layer mask (in the Layers palette) to turn the mask on or off, and Option-clicking to view or hide the layer mask (see "Selections and Layers" in Chapter 8, *Selections and Channels).*

Tip: Use Painting Shortcuts. There are some little shortcuts that we use so often, we need to mention them again here. When painting on the layer mask, don't forget that you can press X to switch the foreground and background colors. Press the number keys (0–9) to set the opacity of the paintbrush—for instance, 0 sets the opacity to 100 percent, 9 sets it to 90 percent, 45 to 45 percent, and so on.

Saving adjustment layers. You can save an adjustment layer separately from an image. We find this most useful when we want to apply the same color- and tonal-correction edits to multiple images.

Here's how to save an adjustment layer into either a new or a different document.

1. Select the adjustment layer you want to save.

2. Choose Duplicate Layer from either the Layer menu or the Layers palette popout menu.

3. Pick a file in the Duplicate Layers dialog box to save the adjustment layer into. If you choose New for the destination, Photoshop creates a new document for you; if you choose an existing document, Photoshop copies the adjustment layer into that image.

4. Click OK.

The ability to copy adjustment layers also opens up some new workflow possibilities. Before we had adjustment layers, we always took care of retouching our image (dust and scratches, and so on) before we did any editing for tone or color. However, with adjustment layers, the order of these tasks doesn't matter. Two people can even work on the same image at the same time—one doing the retouching while the other edits tone and color—then later, you can apply the adjustment layer(s) to the retouched image.

Another workflow option is to make your color- and tonal-correction edits on a low-resolution version of a large image. The edits may go faster on the low-resolution version, and when you're done you can apply the adjustment layers to the monster 500 MB high-resolution version of the image. Of course, if you've done any painting on the layer mask, that won't translate properly when placed into the high-resolution file (see "Tip: Making Masks Meet," below).

Tip: Copying Adjustment Layers Quickly. The Duplicate Layer feature is useful, but we find it faster to copy an adjustment layer simply by dragging it from the Layers palette in one image on top of another image. Again, if the two images have different pixel dimensions, any layer mask will probably transfer incorrectly (see the next tip).

Even better, you can use actions to script the creation of adjustment layers, and then apply exactly the same edits to a whole folder of images using Photoshop's batch processing features (see "Actions" in Chapter 15, *Essential Image Techniques).* The only limitation is that you can't script edits that you've made by brushing on the layer mask.

Tip: Making Masks Meet. Trying to match an adjustment layer's layer mask in one image to its layer mask in another image is easy, as long as the pixel dimensions of the two images are the same. When you use the Duplicate Layer command to move an adjustment layer to a different document, Photoshop centers the layer mask in the new document. If the two documents have the same pixel dimensions, this works great; if they don't, you'll have problems.

When you drag an adjustment layer from one document into another, any pixels on the layer mask are placed exactly where you drop the layer (where you let go of the mouse button). This is almost never where you want them to be. Instead, as long as the two images have the same pixel dimensions, you can hold down the Shift key while dragging the layer; this way, Photoshop pin-registers the layer to the target image.

Remember, to match the pixel dimensions of an image, open the Image Size dialog box in the target image (the one you want to change), then select the source image (the one you're copying) from the Window menu.

Tip: Adjustment Layers and Disk Space. At first glance, adding one or more adjustment layers to your image seems to double its size when you save it to disk in the Photoshop format (one of the three formats that let you save layers; see Chapter 16, *Storing Images),* even though the adjustment layer is essentially an empty layer. The key is to turn off "Always Maximize Compatibility for Photoshop (PSD) Files" in the Saving Files Preferences dialog box (under the Edit menu). As we noted in Chapter 2, *Essential Photoshop Tips and Tricks,* few workflows need this feature turned on. Turn it off, and your Photoshop files get much, much smaller.

Photoshop also lets you save layered files as TIFFs, which are readable by other applications, up to a point. What they're really reading is the flattened composite that's saved in every TIFF. We haven't seen any credible reports of other applications or RIPs having trouble with layered TIFFs, but the tradeoff you make when you use them is that you get to keep a single, rountrippable file that contains all your edits, at the expense of slinging more data around over your network. If a single-file workflow appeals to you, by all means go for it, but make sure your network and servers can handle the traffic.

Otherwise, you can save a flat version of the image using Flatten Image (from the Layer menu). Or, to save a flattened file without damaging your original layered document, choose Save As, and then in the Save As dialog box, turn on the As a Copy checkbox and turn off the Layers checkbox.

Using Adjustment Layers

In many ways, these tools are more difficult to explain than they are to use, so let's look at some examples. We'll start off with relatively simple examples and work up to more complex ones.

Simple Adjustment Layers

The image in Figure 9-3 is a well-exposed original, but it's a little flat. We'll fix it with a curve, but instead of burning the curve permanently into the image, we'll use a Curves adjustment layer.

A single adjustment layer. We first create a new adjustment layer, and choose Curves in the New Adjustment Layer dialog box. We leave Opacity at 100 percent and the blending mode set to Normal.

Working with a curve on an adjustment layer is very much like working with a curve on a flat file. But this time we'll deliberately make the curve a little more extreme than we would for a flat file.

This curve makes the subject pop, but it's a little too much—the blues of the boat are starting to wash out, and the white trim is perilously close to blowing out. We reduce the opacity of the adjustment layer to 65 percent, using the Opacity slider in the Layers palette. In this case, we deliberately exaggerate the curve and the opacity change to make the difference obvious (see Figure 9-4). Normally, we'd push the curve just slightly past the result we wanted and make far smaller moves with the Opacity slider.

For a last touch, we add a gradient to the layer mask to darken the water at the top of the image, so that the subject "pops" a little more, producing the final result shown in Figure 9-5. The original pixels are still untouched, living on the Background layer, and we can continue to tweak and refine to our heart's content.

Figure 9-3
The raw image

This image is well exposed, holding detail in both shadows and highlights, but it's a little flat.

Figure 9-4
Applying a Curves
adjustment layer

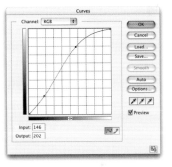

We deliberately exaggerated the curve because we plan to fine-tune it by reducing the adjustment layer's opacity, which in turn lessens the curve's intensity.

Figure 9-5
The final result

Reducing the adjustment layer's opacity to 65 percent, then adding a gradient to the layer mask, produces this result.

Multiple adjustment layers. Figure 9-6 shows a second, slightly more complex example. Again, the image is well exposed, but it has a greenish color cast and it's dark. In the past, we would have tried to construct a single set of curves that took care of both the color and the tone, but with adjustment layers we can use multiple sets of curves, each aimed at a single problem. The curves are easier to construct, and the results are better. We usually try to fix the biggest problem first (though again, when you use adjustment layers, the order in which you correct an image is less important). In this case, the worst offender is the color cast, which we'll correct using a Curves adjustment layer. We could probably achieve similar results using a Levels or Color Balance adjustment layer, but for reasons we've explained elsewhere, we generally use Curves for problems like this.

At this point in the process we don't worry about getting the color exactly right, because we can go back and fine-tune the curve later. We just want to tame the color cast sufficiently to let us make good judgments about the contrast without being distracted by the color balance problems. Then by breaking the contrast adjustments out into a different adjustment layer, we can control the color balance globally, and adjust contrast locally (in specific areas of the image). Here, our second Curves adjustment layer brightens and improves the contrast of the image (see Figure 9-7).

Figure 9-6
Killing the color cast

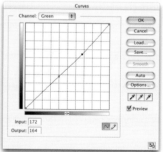

We create a Curves adjustment layer, then bring the green curve down to get rid of the green color cast. Note that a relatively small change to the green curve has a big effect on the water and on the grays of the hull.

Figure 9-7
Fixing the contrast

We create another Curves adjustment layer and apply an S-shaped curve that brightens the image and increases the contrast, making the subject pop.

Now we can return to the first adjustment layer to fine-tune the color balance. We take the water as our starting point. Sampling the pixel values in the water shows us that it's a little orange—the red channel is high, and the blue channel is low. We'd like the water to be fairly neutral, so we adjust the color balance by double-clicking on the adjustment layer's tile in the Layers palette. Then, we check for any other color balance problems and fix them. At this stage, small changes to the curves have a relatively large impact on the color balance (see Figure 9-8).

The image looks much better now, but we've lost almost all the detail in the sky. To bring it back, we target our second Curves layer, the one we used to brighten the image. Using a fairly large soft-edged brush with an opacity of around 40 percent, we paint on the adjustment layer's layer

Figure 9-8
Fine-tuning the color

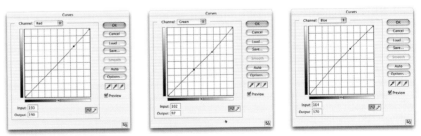

We make the water appear neutral by making very small alterations to the red and blue channels. This in turn makes some of the grays on the hull of the boat look a little magenta. A second point on the green curve neutralizes them.

mask with black paint; this "erases" the effect, returning the detail to the image. If we darken the sky too much, we can simply press X to switch foreground and background colors, and then paint with white to build back the opacity of the layer (see Figure 9-9). If you find that you need to see exactly where you're painting, remember that you can turn on visibility for the layer mask by Shift-clicking on the layer mask or by clicking on the layer mask's eyeball in the left column of the Channels palette—however, we rarely find this necessary.

Figure 9-9
Brushing the layer mask

We brush detail back into the sky by targeting our second Curves layer and using a soft brush at a medium opacity to apply black paint to the layer mask.

This image is destined for print, so we turn on Proof Colors to get an idea of how it will look in CMYK mode. Here, we find the image looks a little unsaturated, so we create one more adjustment layer, this time choosing Hue/Saturation as the adjustment type. Increasing the global saturation by 18 points produces the final result shown in Figure 9-10.

At this point, we save the file with the adjustment layers. Finally, we choose Flatten Image from the Layer menu, then use Save As to save a flattened version of the edited image. We sharpen the copy, set our highlight and shadow points, convert it to CMYK, and send it off for proofing.

Figure 9-10
Adding a
Hue/Saturation layer

We add a Hue/ Saturation layer to increase the saturation by about 18 points.

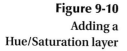

Layer Blending Modes

The previous examples were relatively simple, using straightforward adjustment layers for global editing, with some painting on the layer mask for local corrections. However, when you combine adjustment layers with the power of blending modes, you open up a whole new world of possibilities.

One advantage of using blending modes rather than simply stretching and squeezing the bits with Levels and Curves is that blending interpolates tonal values, producing smoother results. We'll show you some examples of how we use some of the blendng modes, but we encourage you to experiment—there are plenty of new techniques waiting to be discovered.

The blending modes are arranged in logical groups, according to the way they function.

▶ **The Independent modes.** Normal and Dissolve both replace the underlying pixels with the overlying pixels (in the Normal or Dissolve layer) when the layer is at 100-percent opacity. At lower opacities, Normal blends the overlying pixels with the underlying ones according to opacity, while Dissolve replaces pixels randomly (see Figure 9-11).

Figure 9-11
Normal and Dissolve

Underlying layer

Overlying layer

Normal 100% opacity

Normal 50% opacity

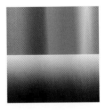
Normal 15% opacity

Dissolve 100% opacity

Dissolve 50% opacity

Dissolve 15% opacity

▶ **The Darken modes.** The neutral color for the Darken modes is white—white pixels on a layer set to a Darken mode leave the underlying pixels unchanged. Non-white pixels darken the result by varying amounts, depending on the blend mode and opacity (see Figure 9-12).

Figure 9-12
The Darken modes

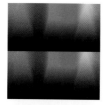  

Darken 100% opacity   *Darken 50% opacity*   *Darken 15% opacity*

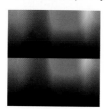 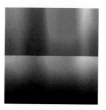 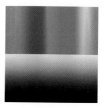

Multiply 100% opacity   *Multiply 50% opacity*   *Multiply 15% opacity*

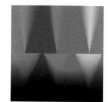  

Color Burn 100% opacity   *Color Burn 50% opacity*   *Color Burn 15% opacity*

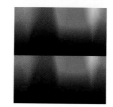  

Linear Burn 100% opacity   *Linear Burn 50% opacity*   *Linear Burn 15% opacity*

▶ **The Lighten modes.** The Lighten modes are the inverse of the Darken modes. The neutral color for the Lighten modes is black—black pixels on a layer set to a Lighten mode leave the underlying pixels unchanged. Non-black pixels lighten the result by varying amounts, depending on the blend mode and opacity (see Figure 9-13).

Figure 9-13
The Lighten modes

Lighten 100% opacity   *Lighten 50% opacity*   *Lighten 15% opacity*

Screen 100% opacity   *Screen 50% opacity*   *Screen 15% opacity*

Color Dodge 100% opacity   *Color Dodge 50% opacity*   *Color Dodge 15% opacity*

Linear Dodge 100% opacity   *Linear Dodge 50% opacity*   *Linear Dodge 15% opacity*

▶ **The Contrast modes.** The contrast modes combine corresponding Darken and Lighten modes. The neutral color for the Contrast modes is 50-percent gray—50-percent gray pixels on a layer set to a Contrast mode leave the underlying pixels unchanged. Lighter pixels lighten the result, and darker pixels darken the result, by varying amounts, depending on the blend mode and opacity (see Figure 9-14).

The odd man out is the new Hard Mix blend, which has no neutral color—but it doesn't really fit anywhere else either. It reduces the image to 8 colors—red, cyan, green, magenta, blue, yellow, white, or black—based on the mix of the underlying and blend colors, with a strrength related to 50-percent gray.

Figure 9-14
The Contrast modes

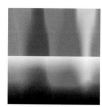  

Overlay 100% opacity   *Overlay 50% opacity*   *Overlay 15% opacity*

 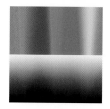 

Soft Light 100% opacity   *Soft Light 50% opacity*   *Soft Light 15% opacity*

Hard Light 100% opacity   *Hard Light 50% opacity*   *Hard Light 15% opacity*

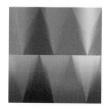 

Vivid Light 100% opacity   *Vivid Light 50% opacity*   *Vivid Light 15% opacity*

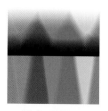  

Linear Light 100% opacity   *Linear Light 50% opacity*   *Linear Light 15% opacity*

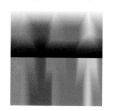  

Pin Light 100% opacity   *Pin Light 50% opacity*   *Pin Light 15% opacity*

Figure 9-14
The Contrast modes,
continued

Hard Mix 100% opacity   *Hard Mix 50% opacity*   *Hard Mix 15% opacity*

▶ **The Comparative modes.** The neutral color for the Comparative modes is black. The Comparative modes look at each channel and subtract the underlying color from the overlying color or the overlying color from the underlying color, choosing whichever returns a result with higher brightness. Blending with white inverts the underlying color values (see Figure 9-15).

Figure 9-15
The Comparative modes

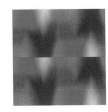

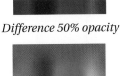

Difference 100% opacity   *Difference 50% opacity*   *Difference15% opacity*

Exclusion 100% opacity   *Exclusion 50% opacity*   *Exclusion 15% opacity*

▶ **The HSL modes.** While the members of the other groups do basically the same things in different strengths, the members of the HSL group each do something rather different, though they all operate on hue, saturation, and luminosity. Hence it makes sense to discuss them individually (see Figure 9-16).

Hue. Hue creates a result color with the brightness and saturation of the underlying color and the hue of the overlying color.

Saturation. Saturation creates a result color with the brightness and hue of the underlying color and the saturation of the overlying color.

Color. Color creates a result color with the luminosity of the underlying color and the hue and saturation of the overlying color.

Luminosity. Luminosity is the inverse of Color. It creates a result color with the hue and saturation of the underlying color and the luminosity of the overlying color.

Figure 9-16
The HSL modes

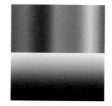

Hue 100% opacity   *Hue 50% opacity*   *Hue 15% opacity*

Saturation 100% opacity   *Saturation 50% opacity*   *Saturation 15% opacity*

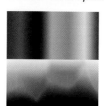
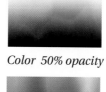

Color 100% opacity   *Color 50% opacity*   *Color 15% opacity*

Luminosity 100% opacity   *Luminosity 50% opacity*   *Luminosity 15% opacity*

Layer Blending in Practice

If the preceding discussion has rendered you crosseyed, some less-abstract examples may be helpful. The blending modes we tend to use most are Multiply to build density, Screen to reduce it, Color to change color balance without affecting luminosity, and Luminosity to sharpen images without introducing color fringes (we discuss sharpening layers in much greater detail in Chapter 10, *Sharpening*). We often apply blending using an adjustment layer—any adjustment layer—with a null adjustment. This is equivalent to merging the visible pixels into a new layer, then applying the blending mode, with the major advantage that an empty adjustment layer takes up much less storage space than a pixel layer—a Big Deal when you're working with layered high-bit images. But if we need to edit the actual pixels, as in the case of a sharpening layer, for example, we apply the blending mode to an actual pixel layer instead.

Tip: Stop-Based Corrections with Multiply and Screen. If you're more comfortable thinking in terms of f-stops than in levels or percentages, thank our friend and colleague Jeff Schewe for this insight. You can lighten and darken by 1 stop by applying Screen and Multiply, respectively, at an opacity of 38 percent.

For a half-stop adjustment, use 19 percent. For a one-third stop, 13 percent seems to be slightly closer than 12, and for a quarter stop, 9 percent is the magic number.

The practical examples that follow don't pretend to exhaust the power of blending modes. They're simply illustrative examples that we hope will fire your imagination and pique your curiosity. Remember—one of the huge benefits of working with layers is that you can't do any harm until you flatten the image, so feel free to experiment. Photoshop offers many ways to produce similar if not identical results, and we each find methods that work for us.

Building density with Multiply. The best analogy we've found for Multiply mode is that it's like sandwiching two negatives in an enlarger. Mathematically, Multiply takes two values, multiplies them by each other, and divides by 255. Practically speaking, this means the result is always darker than either of the sources.

If a pixel is black in the base image, the result after applying an adjustment layer with Multiply is also black. If a pixel is white in the base image, the adjustment layer has no effect (white is the neutral color for Multiply). We use Multiply with Curves adjustment layers to build density, particularly in the highlights and midtones of washed-out images like the one in Figure 9-17.

Figure 9-17
A washed-out image

This scene contains a huge range of contrast from the rising sun to the backlit boat. The image holds detail at both extremes, but the contrast is flat.

This image represents a scene with a huge dynamic range—a backlit boat against the sun rising over the Ganges—and thanks partly to the wonders of modern color negative film, partly to the filtration effect of the omnipresent smoke from the burning ghats, we were able to capture it. Our scan has detail in both the brightest part of the sun and in the darkest part of the boat, but the distribution of the midtones is quite wrong—they're much too light, rendering a potentially dramatic image merely pleasant. We can fix it very quickly with a single Curves adjustment layer, using the Multiply mode.

We create a new Curves adjustment layer, but this time we set the mode to Multiply. If we make no changes to the curve, and instead just click OK, the difference is dramatic. This is equivalent to duplicating the Background layer on top of itself and changing the new layer's blending mode to Multiply (see Figure 9-18).

All that remains is to eliminate the green cast and fine-tune the contrast, which we do by adjusting the green and composite curves, respectively. Now the edited image does a much better job of conveying the oppressive heat, the omnipresent smoke and dust, and the languor of the millennia-old ritual that takes place at dawn on the Ganges.

Figure 9-18
Applying a Curves adjustment layer with Multiply

Applying a Curves layer set to Multiply results in a dramatic increase in contrast.

We could leave more detail on the boat by eliminating the black clipping move on the RGB curve, but after trying it, we decide that the image works better when we leave the boat as a near-silhouette (see Figure 9-19).

Figure 9-19
Adjusting the curve

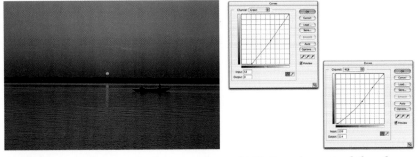

A simple two-point curve in the green channel kills the color cast, while a three-point curve on the composite pulls the midtones and shadows down a little further, to produce this final result.

Opening shadows with Screen. Screen is literally the inverse of Multiply. The best real-world analogy we've heard comes from Adobe's Russell Brown. Screen is like projecting two slides on the same screen. The result is always lighter than either of the two sources.

If a pixel is white in the base image, the result is white, and if it's black in the base image, the result is also black (black is the neutral color for Screen). Intermediate tones get lighter. We use Screen mostly to open up dark shadows.

If you're a techno-dweeb like we are, you probably want to know what Screen does behind the scenes. Photoshop inverts the two numbers (subtracts them from 255) before doing a Multiply calculation (multiplies them by each other and divides by 255); then the program subtracts the result from 255. That's it. Now, don't you feel better knowing that?

Bruce shot the image in Figure 9-20 from his deck, using a Canon EOS 1Ds, on a typically foggy San Francisco late afternoon. The image holds detail in both highlight and shadow, but the foreground is dark and muddy, an ideal candidate for opening up with Screen blending. This time, we'll simply use an adjustment layer—we used Curves, but any adjustment layer type would work equally well—as a shortcut for duplicating the image to a new layer and applying a blending mode. We won't make any adjustments to the curve itself; we'll just use it as an easy way to apply Screen blending to lighten the foreground.

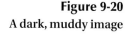
A dark, muddy image

This image holds detail in both the highlights and the shadows, but the foreground is approximately one stop too dark.

We add a Curves adjustment layer with the blending mode set to Screen. Then, we paint on the layer mask to confine the adjustment to the foreground—we want to preserve the dark sky, so a global adjustment won't work. Finally, we reduce the curve layer's opacity to 38 percent (see Figure 9-21). That's it.

Figure 9-21
A Curves adjustment
layer with Screen

The layer mask at right confines the effect of the blend mode to the foreground. Reducing the curve layer's opacity to 38 percent provides about one stop of lightening to the foreground.

Complex blending. Photoshop's Lens Flare filter does a great job of simulating lens flare, but it's no help in removing it. The image in Figure 9-22 has been a crowd-pleaser in previous editions of this book (Bruce is fifth from the left, in case you were wondering), but we've never been totally happy with it. So here's a new treatment that exploits both the power of Photoshop CS and the tricks we've learned over the last couple of years.

Figure 9-22
A problem with lens flare

Although the sky was overcast, the sun shining through the clouds created enough lens flare to wash out the contrast in the center of the image, and the uncorrected negative scan is sickly green.

We always try to fix the biggest problem first, but in this case, it's a toss-up between the color cast and the washed-out area in the center. We decide to fix the color cast by applying a solid color layer using a purplish-magenta to counteract the yellow-green cast, set to Color blending with an opacity of 19 percent.

We refine the adjustment by applying a gradient in the layer mask, from white at the right to 50 percent gray at the left, to even out the color cast across the image. We fine-tune the layer mask using Curves, applied directly to the layer mask, to achieve the exact blend needed to produce even color across the image.

Then we balance the lighting across the image by applying a Curves adjustment layer set to Multiply, with an opacity of 45 percent. We use a radial gradient on the layer mask to control the effect of the Multiply layer, confining it to the washed-out area in the center (see Figure 9-23).

Figure 9-23
Balancing color and tone

*A solid color layer set to Color and a Curves
layer set to Multiply, with layer masks
controlling each, balance the tone and
color across the image.*

Continuing to operate on the governing principle of fixing the most
obvious problem, our next step is to add contrast, which we do with a
Curves adjustment layer set to Overlay at 50 percent opacity, this time
actually containing a Curves adjustment in the composite curve. The combination of relatively low opacity and Overlay blending makes it possible
to use curves that we would never dream of applying in Normal mode, let
alone burning into a flat file! It produces the result shown in Figure 9-24.

Next, we add a Curves layer to fix the pink cast in the sky and to add
detail. First, we set the blend mode to Multiply to add density, and tweak
the opacity, settling on an opacity of 59 percent. Next, we add a simple
gradient to the layer mask to confine the edit to the top of the image. Then
we go in and tweak the individual channel curves to remove the pink cast,
producing the result shown in Figure 9-25.

By now, you'll have seen that we often use gradients, rather than complex selections, in layer masks. Applying a gradient to a layer mask is much
less work than building a painstaking selection, and often produces more
natural-looking results. Sometimes it takes us three or four attempts to get
the gradient right, but it's still much faster than building a selection.

Figure 9-24
Adding contrast

In Normal mode, a curve like the one at right would wreck the image; but with the blend mode set to Overlay, it simply adds contrast. We masked the sky to preserve detail.

Figure 9-25
Fixing the sky

A Curves layer set to Multiply, with a 59 percent opacity and a simple gradient mask, combine with the curves shown here to add density and kill the color cast in the sky.

Our next move fine-tunes the local contrast on the figures. We make a new Adjustment Layer set to Multiply (we used Curves, but any adjustment layer type will work since we're only using it to apply Multiply blending), reduce the opacity to 75 percent (which is still too strong), then fill the layer mask with black to hide effect. Then, using a soft brush with an opacity of around 30 percent, we paint contrast into the areas we want to accentuate, producing the result shown in Figure 9-26.

The percentages we used here are pretty arbitrary—you can achieve the same effect using many different combinations of layer opacity and brush opacity—but we like to use brush opacities of around 30 percent because that way we have plenty of headroom to strengthen or weaken the effect. With a pressure-sensitive stylus, setting the pressure-sensitivity to control opacity lets you simply paint on the mask without worrying about the opacity setting at any given moment.

We have one remaining problem. The noon sunlight was actually quite warm, but the gray overcast sky in the background tells our eyes otherwise, so something just doesn't look right. The new Photo Filter adjustment in Photoshop CS lets us fix this very easily.

We add a Photo Filter layer using the Cooling Filter (80) setting, with a Density of 15 percent, then fine-tune the effect by pulling back the layer opacity to 82 percent. The default Density setting of 25 percent in Photo Filter is almost invariably too strong; but when it's applied on an adjustment layer, you have the whole range of layer opacity from 0 to 100 percent to play with. So we almost always use a setting in the Photo Filter dialog that produces a stronger effect than we want, then dial back the layer opacity to get it just right.

We finish up with a simple white input slider tweak in Levels to brighten the whole image—throughout the editing process we left plenty of headroom to make sure that we didn't blow out highlights. At this stage, we don't need the headroom any more. Figure 9-27 shows the final result and the Layers palette with the layers that produced it.

The key lesson here isn't efficiency, but rather the freedom to experiment. We can always get back to the original image, because it's still lying untouched on the Background layer. We learned from this image that the fundamental problem was that it was too warm, but the other problems didn't allow us to see that until fairly late in the game. When you know exactly what an image needs, you can go ahead and do it; but when the issues are less obvious, it pays to experiment.

Figure 9-26
Painting local contrast

An adjustment layer set to Multiply, with a layer mask set to Hide All, lets us paint extra density into arbitrary areas with much greater flexibility than the Burn tool offers, and allows us to do so non-destructively.

Figure 9-27
Cool it with Photo Filter, lighten it with Levels

All the edits we made to this image are non-destructive, and tweakable, since they're all on layers. You may think this is a recipe for creating monster files, but the layers and accompanying layer masks resulted in a file that was slightly more than double the size of the original flat file, because the layers don't contain any pixels. The size increase is mostly from the masks.

Extracting invisible detail. The Channel Mixer isn't a terribly intuitive color-correction tool, but Figure 9-28 shows a situation where it comes in handy. The shadows appear completely blocked, but there's a lot more detail in the blue channel than in the other two. We can pull out that detail by feeding the blue channel into the other two channels, working on an adjustment layer through a layer mask to confine the effect to the shadows.

We create a Channel Mixer adjustment layer, and create a layer mask to constrain its effect to the shadow areas. In this case, we simply brushed the layer mask, but you could also use Color Range to create it. We replaced 90 percent of the red and green channels with blue, producing the image in Figure 9-29.

Figure 9-28
Blocked-up shadows

Red   *Green*

Blue

The shadows in this image appear completely blocked, but when we look at the individual channels, we see that there's much more detail in the blue than in the red or green.

To produce the final image in Figure 9-30, we create a Hue/Saturation layer, copy the layer mask from the Channel Mixer layer, and then bump up the saturation. Since the three color channels are now almost identical, there's very little color left, so we can make a fairly extreme 68 percent saturation boost to bring back some color and prevent the shadows from looking flat.

Figure 9-29
Mixing the channels

Applying the Channel Mixer through a layer mask, we replace 90 percent of the red and green channels with blue, bringing out the hidden detail.

Figure 9-30
Returning color to the
shadows

Using the same layer mask as for the Channel Mixer layer, we create a Hue/Saturation Layer and bump up the saturation to bring back a little color into the shadows, which would otherwise be very neutral indeed.

Sharing a layer mask. Sometimes we need to use multiple layers on an image to achieve an effect in a particular area, using the same layer mask on each layer. A case in point is the image shown in Figure 9-31. What provoked Bruce to shoot the image in the first place was the brilliant patch of sunlight on the hillside contrasting with the diffuse light from the foggy afternoon. The RGB version of the image shows it quite well, but soft-proofing for a CMYK rendition indicated that the image needs help to make it work in print.

Figure 9-31
The unedited image

The sunlit patches that are the real subject of this image are only hinted at in this raw version.

We can improve this rendition by adding three layers, all using the same layer mask, to make those sunlit patches much more obvious. We start by creating the layer mask, which we then apply to each layer as it's added, by Command-clicking the original layer mask tile to load it as a selection. Each adjustment layer automatically uses that selection as a layer mask.

Once we've added the layers, we can create a more efficient file by creating a layer set, adding the mask to the set, and deleting it from the individual layers. That way, the only pixels added to the image are a single layer mask, so the file size stays relatively small.

You may be tempted to start by creating the layer set, adding the mask, then creating the layers inside the set. You can certainly do so, but you won't get the same effect—the mask is applied to the individual layers before they're created, so you'll have much less of a range in which to correct.

Figure 9-32 shows the creation of the layer mask, the three layers we used to build the effect, the creation of the layer set, and the transfer of the mask from the individual layers to the layer set, along with the final result. The edits take longer to explain than they do to execute!

Figure 9-32
Using a layer set to share
a mask across layers

We add an adjustment layer with a null adjustment, set to Color Dodge blending with an opacity of 50 percent.

We press Command-I to invert the layer mask, filling it with black to hide the effect, then we paint the effect into the image using a low-opacity brush with white paint.

The Color Dodge layer applied through the new layer mask

We load the mask as a selection and add a Photo Filter layer using Warming Filter (85) with a Density of 90 percent and a layer opacity of 40 percent. Then we load the mask as a selection again and add a null adjustment layer set to Screen, with an opacity of 50 percent.

Command-click the layer mask tile to load the mask as a selection before adding each layer.

Figure 9-32
Using a layer set to share
a mask across layers,
continued

The final image

We load the mask as a selection, click the
Layer Set button to add a layer set, which
automatically inherits the selection as a layer
mask, and drag the individual layers into
the set. Then, we select each layer in turn and
Option-click on the Trash icon to delete each
layer's individual mask, thereby reducing the
file size considerably.

Beyond Adjustment Layers

In many cases, you can achieve the desired result by simply adding null adjustment layers that use blending modes and the opacity controls. But sometimes, you may need to duplicate the image to a new layer, then edit the duplicate pixels themselves.

The image shown in Figure 9-33 lends itself to several different techniques. Our online friend Alan Womack asked for help with it on one of the many lists we frequent, so we cut a deal: If we could fix the image to his satisfaction, he'd let us use it in this book. We could, and he did. The image was shot using some fill flash, but the subject is dark, and the shade from the canola plants turned her a little blue too. For this edition of the book, we reworked the image taking advantage of some of the new capabilities in Photoshop CS.

Obeying our general maxim of fixing the biggest problem first, we lighten the skin tones. This situation is a strong candidate for the new Shadow/Highlight command. Shadow/Highlight is designed to address

Figure 9-33
The raw image

exposure problems such as dark backlit subjects, and it does a great job; but because it corrects each pixel adaptively, it isn't available as a layer adjustment. Of course, we have a workaround for that!

We duplicate the background layer, and run Shadow/Highlight on the duplicate. That way, we can make a slightly stronger correction than we want, and use the layer's opacity to fine-tune it after the fact. We apply the adjustment to the whole image, paying attention only to the areas we want to affect, then add a layer mask set to Hide All, and paint the adjustment into the areas where we want it. This is much easier than first making a selection, then making the edit, because we can see the effect on the areas we brush in, so it's easier to decide where the mask edges should lie.

Shadow/Highlight has three main controls for both shadow and highlight adjustments. The Amount is the "volume control" that dictates the strength of the edit. The Tonal Width slider controls how far toward the highlights a shadow adjustment goes and how far towards the shadows a highlight adjustment goes. The Radius slider is a little trickier. It controls the area over which the surround luminance is calculated, which in turn controls the degree of correction. A good rule of thumb is to set the Radius to around half the width of the feature—in this case, Lexxie's face—that you're trying to correct. Running Shadow/Highlight, then brushing on the layer mask, produced the result shown in Figure 9-34.

Figure 9-34
Applying Shadow/
Highlight on a
duplicate layer

*We make a strong
correction using
Shadow/Highlight,
apply a layer mask set to
Hide All, then brush the
effect in where we want
it. Making a stronger
correction than we
ultimately want lets
us control it using
brush opacity and
layer opacity.*

*After creating the mask, we settle on a
layer opacity of 88 percent.*

Next, we Command-click the layer mask tile to load the mask as a selection, then we add a Photo Filter layer using Warming Filter (85) to get rid of the blue cast on the figure. The Photo Filter layer automatically uses the selection as a mask. Figure 9-35 shows the result.

The highlight on the hair is almost, but not quite, blown out, so we try to rescue it by selecting the hair highlight, then using the selection as a mask for a Multiply layer. This technique often works, but this time there's a problem—the highlights become heavily oversaturated.

When we look at the individual channels, we can see that there's much more detail in the blue channel than there is in the red and green. So we duplicate the highlight pixels to a new layer, set it to Multiply, then use the Channel Mixer to edit the actual pixels on the duplicate layer, feeding the blue channel into both the red and the green, to create an essentially neutral copy. One round isn't quite enough, so we duplicate the layer, pull back the opacity, and put both layers into a layer set, producing the result shown in Figure 9-36.

Figure 9-35
Warming the subject

A Photo Filter layer using Warming Filter (85) warms the subject. We make a strong correction in the filter dialog so that we can control it using the layer opacity.

Figure 9-36
Taming the hair highlight

The desaturated, darkened hair pixels

We darken the hair pixels by duplicating them to a new layer set to Multiply, then extract hidden detail by running the Channel Mixer to feed the detail in the blue channel into the red and green. We do this twice and put the results in a layer set.

Two quick fixes add snap to the eyes and brighten the smile. We use Quick Mask to paint a selection of the eyes, then we add a null adjustment layer set to Overlay at 50 percent. We repeat the process for the teeth, this time using a null adjustment layer set to Screen at 48 percent, producing the result shown in Figure 9-37.

The image is still a little flat, so we add two more null adjustment layers set to Overlay—one with an empty layer mask to control global contrast, the other using the same mask we used for the Shadow/Highlight layer and the Photo Filter layer (again, we Command-click on the mask's tile to load it as a selection prior to creating the second adjustment layer so that the layer automatically uses it as a layer mask). Adding two layers rather than one lets us fine-tune the contrast on the subject separately from the overall contrast, which we almost always find useful.

Figure 9-38 shows the final result. Of course, we can always go back and fine-tune the various different aspects of the image simply by tweaking the opacities of the individual layers—one question we have as yet been unable to answer convincingly is, "When is a digital image really finished?" But breaking up the edits into layers that address specific problem areas makes fine-tuning much easier than when you make lots of global moves, each depending on the ones that preceded it.

Figure 9-37
Local enhancements

A masked layer set to Overlay adds snap to the eyes, while another set to Screen brightens the smile.

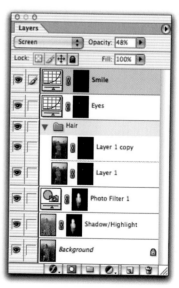

Figure 9-38
The final image

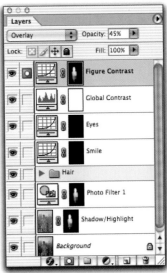

*An unmasked layer set
to Overlay controls the
overall contrast, while a
second, masked layer set to
Overlay allows us to fine-
tune the subject contrast.*

Making Prints

The digital darkroom wouldn't be worthy of the name if it didn't let you make prints. Fortunately, it not only does so, but also offers a key advantage over its analog counterpart: Thanks to the wonders of color management, it lets you see what will happen in the print before you make it.

The naive view of color management is that it will make your prints match your monitor. If you've read this far, you've probably realized that this is an impossible goal—printers simply cannot print the range of color a good display can display. Instead, color management tries to reproduce the image as faithfully as the limitations of the output process will allow.

But color management knows nothing about images, it only knows about the color spaces in which images reside. So no output profile, however good it is, does equal justice to all images. When you convert an image from a working space to the gamut and dynamic range of a composite printer, the profile treats all images identically, using the same gamut and dynamic range compression for all. But thanks to the soft-proofing features in Photoshop, you can see ahead of time exactly how the profile will render your images, which gives you a good basis for taking the necessary corrective action. If you want great, rather than just good, you need to optimize images for different output processes, because something always has to give, and each image demands its own compromises.

Adjustment layers provide a very convenient method for targeting images for a specific output process. You can use adjustment layers grouped in layer sets to optimize the same master image for printing to different printers, or to the same printer on different paper stocks. The following technique uses three basic elements.

▶ **A reference image.** Create a duplicate of the image, with Proof Colors turned off, to serve as a reference for the image appearance you're trying to achieve.

▶ **A soft proof.** Use the Proof Setup command to provide a soft proof that shows how the output profile will render the image.

▶ **A layer set containing adjustment layers.** Group each set of optimizations for a specific output condition (printer, paper, ink) into a layer set, so that you can turn them on and off conveniently when you print to one or another device.

Making the reference image. Choose Duplicate from the Image menu to make a duplicate of the image. The duplicate will serve as a reference for the appearance you're trying to achieve on the print.

You need to make a duplicate rather than simply open a new view because you'll be editing the master image to optimize it for the print, and the edits would show up in a new view. The duplicate isn't affected by the edits you make to the master file, so it can serve as a reference—a reminder of what you want to achieve in the print.

Setting the soft proof. Choose Custom from the Proof Setup submenu on the View menu to open the Proof Setup dialog box. Load the profile for your printer, and check Paper White to make Photoshop use absolute colorimetric rendering to the monitor (see Figure 9-39). We find that all the soft-proof views (using the different combinations of Paper White and Ink Black) tell us something useful, but the absolute colorimetric rendering produced by checking Paper White is, in theory at least, the most accurate.

However, the first thing you'll notice is that checking Paper White makes the image look much worse. Sometimes it seems to die before your eyes. At this point, a good many people think Photoshop's soft proof must be inherently unreliable and give up on the whole enterprise. What's really

Figure 9-39
Setting the soft proof

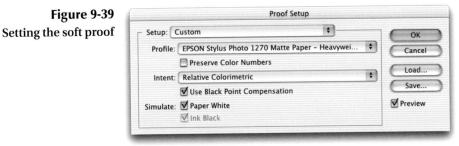

Load the profile for your output device, and check Paper White.

going on is that Photoshop is trying to show you the dynamic range compression and gamut compression that will take place on printing.

The reason the soft proof looks bad at first glance is that Photoshop can only show you the gamut and dynamic range compression within the confines of your monitor space, and it can only do so by turning things down, so white in the image is always dimmer than your monitor white.

A second problem is that the vast majority of monitor profiles have a "black hole" black point (a black with a Lightness of zero in Lab), while real monitor black typically has a Lightness of 3 to 5. As a result, the soft proof typically shows black as slightly lighter than it will actually appear on the print. Typically, in the soft proof you'll see washed-out shadows, compressed highlights, and an overall color shift caused by the difference between the white of your working space and the white of your paper. Some images are only slightly affected by the conversion to print space, while with others the change can be dramatic, as shown in Figures 9-40a and 9-40b. As with just about any proofing method we've encountered, you need to learn to interpret Photoshop's soft proofs. You may find the following tips helpful in doing so.

Tip: Look Away When You Turn On Paper White. Much of the shock you feel when you see Photoshop's absolute colorimetric rendering to the monitor stems from seeing the image change. If you look away from the monitor when you turn on Paper White, your eyes will be able to adapt to the new white point more easily.

Tip: Use Full-Screen View to Evaluate Soft Proofs. Your eyes can't adapt to the soft-proof white point unless you hide Photoshop's user interface elements, a good few of which are still pure white. Press F to switch to full-screen view with a neutral gray background, then press Shift-F to

Figure 9-40a
The soft proof and the
reference image

*The soft proof, left, shows
reduced contrast and a
slight blue shift when
compared to the reference
image, below.*

hide the menu bar. Press Tab to hide all the palettes. Now you can see the soft-proofed image on a neutral background with no distracting elements to bias your vision.

A further problem, one we hope proves to be temporary, is that many output profiles weren't built with soft-proofing in mind. They do a good job of converting the source to the output, but they don't do nearly as good a job of "round-tripping"—converting the output back to a viewing profile. All the profiles we've built with current third-party profiling tools make the round trip very well. The problem seems confined to older profiles, and to some, but by no means all, of the canned profiles that printer vendors include with their printers.

If all this seems discouraging, take heart. Soft-proofing for RGB output may have passed its infancy, but it hasn't yet reached adolescence. And problems with profiles aside, the soft proofs offered by Photoshop are not, in our experience, any less accurate than those offered by traditional proofing systems. You simply need to learn to "read" them.

Figure 9-40b
The soft proof and
the reference image,
continued

The soft proof, left, shows a dramatic color shift in addition to the reduced dynamic range when compared with the reference image, right.

Make your edits. We suggest starting out viewing the soft proof and the reference image side-by-side. Once you've edited the soft-proofed image to get it back to where you want it to be, fine-tune your edits looking at the soft-proofed image in full-screen view.

Some images need minimal editing, others may require significant reworking. We start by applying adjustment layers to get the soft-proofed image to match the reference (the duplicate) as closely as possible. We group these adjustment layers in a layer set named for the print process it addresses. That way, we can easily optimize the master image for different print processes by turning the layer sets on and off. Figure 9-41 shows the edited and reference images with their accompanying layer sets.

Once we've edited the soft-proofed image to match the reference image, we use full-screen view to take a final look at the soft-proofed image prior to printing. (We prefer the gray background, with the menu bar hidden—the black background makes the shadows look too light.) In the majority of cases we find that no further editing is necessary, but occasionally we'll fine-tune highlight and shadow detail.

The final step is, of course, to print the image. See "Imaging from Photoshop" in Chapter 17, *Output Methods*.

Figure 9-41

The edited image and
the reference image

*We edited the soft-proofed
image, above, to match the
reference image, below.*

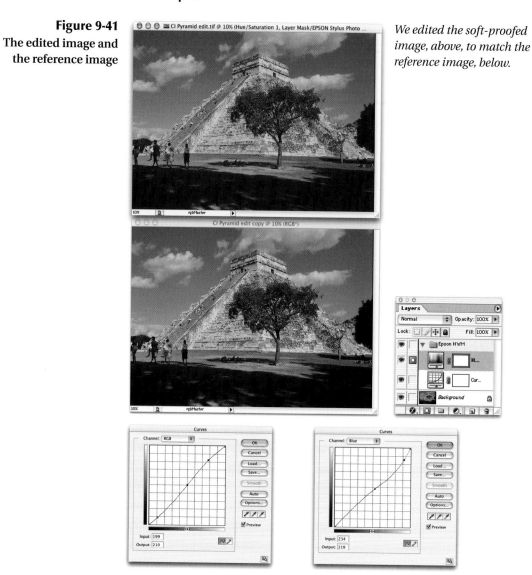

The RGB curve restores contrast.   *The blue curve removes the blue cast.*

*The Hue/Saturation layer shifts the
blue of the sky slightly toward magenta.*

Figure 9-41
The edited image and
the reference image,
continued

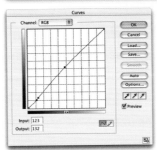

The Curves adjustment
layer adds contrast
using the RGB curve.

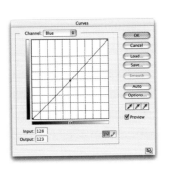

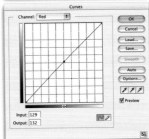

We added small
amounts of red and
green, and reduced
blue, to remove the
color cast in the sky and
on the building.

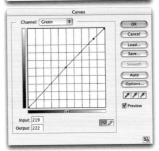

History and Virtual Layers

Before we became blessed with 16-bit layers in Photoshop CS, we tended to use History mostly as a workaround for their absence. With 16-bit layers, we find our need for History has lessened, but it hasn't disappeared entirely.

Layer-based edits offer great freedom and flexibility, but they have one major disadvantage—they make large files that can also be dauntingly complex. It's often a sobering exercise to return to a layered file you created months or years ago and try to figure out what each layer was supposed to do. Layer naming helps, but only up to a point.

We confess that when the History feature first appeared in Photoshop, we saw it as little more than a massively-overengineered multiple undo. But our friend and colleague Jeff Schewe, who has probably had more influence on the History feature's development than anyone outside of Adobe, dropped some hints that made us realize the error of our ways.

History certainly gives you many levels of Undo—up to 1,000—but it does much more besides. When you use History in conjunction with blending modes and the History Brush, you have something that lets you apply very similar effects to those you can achieve with layers and masks.

Virtual Layers

We like to think of History as providing "virtual layers" because it lets us do many of the things we can also do with layers. But let's look at the important ways in which History's virtual layers differ from real ones.

▶ History is ephemeral. It's only around as long as your file is open. Once you close the file, its history is gone forever, giving a whole new twist to the old adage that those who can't remember history are doomed to repeat it. You can't save History with the file, so you have to get your edits right before you close. (You can save a history log, either in the file's metadata or in a text file, but the log doesn't let you re-create previous states of the image.)

▶ History is easier than layers when you know exactly what you're doing and can get things right on the first (or possibly second) try, but if you're less decisive than that, it quickly becomes more work than using layers to achieve the same effects.

▶ History is more demanding on your hardware than adjustment layers. It requires plenty of scratch space, and the faster the disk, the better.

Nevertheless, History is a powerful feature for making quick, effective, dare we say gonzo, edits.

History Tools

History works using just a handful of tools. The History palette lets you set the source for your History-based edits—the pixels that you'll apply to the image (see Figure 9-42).

Figure 9-42
The History palette

Click this column to set the History source.

This icon indicates the current History source.

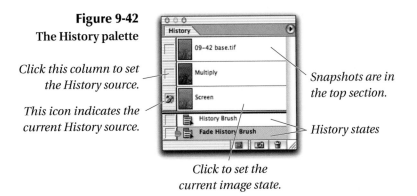

Snapshots are in the top section.

History states

Click to set the current image state.

The History palette. The History palette lets you click in the left column to set the History source to a History state or snapshot (the paintbrush icon indicates the current History source), or click on a snapshot or History state's tile to set the current state of the image.

The three icons at the bottom of the palette let you create a new document from the current History state, create a new snapshot, and delete the current History state, respectively. Snapshots are a convenience feature—they're usually easier to track than History states, and unlike History states, you can name them.

Applying History. You can apply History using either the History brush tool or the Fill command from the Edit menu. Fill is easier when you have a selection or you want to affect the entire image. The History brush is useful for actually brushing in edits. When you use either one, you can immediately use the Fade command (on the Edit menu) to adjust the edit's opacity.

Figures 9-43 and 9-44 show a quick set of edits performed entirely with History. We don't recommend this approach for all, or even most, edits, but it's one more useful set of techniques to get under your belt. The raw image is flat, so we want to add contrast. Specifically, we want to darken the sky, then add contrast to the sagebrush while brightening the highlights. First, we set up a series of snapshots, as shown in Figure 9-43.

Figure 9-43
Setting up Snapshots

Set the initial snapshot as source...

...then choose Fill, with History, Multiply, and 60 percent opacity, and save the result as a new snapshot.

Keeping the initial snapshot as the source, repeat the process, this time using Screen instead of Multiply as the blending mode for the Fill.

Save the result as a new snapshot, so that you now have a darkened version using Multiply and a lightened version using Screen, in addition to the original image.

Next, we apply the edits. We make a selection of the sky and fill it from the Multiply snapshot. Then we invert the selection, and use the History brush to paint the Screen snapshot into the sagebrush, using Overlay blending to increase contrast, as shown in Figure 9-44.

Figure 9-44
Applying the edits

We make a quick Color Range selection of the sky and save it as a snapshot in case something goes wrong. Then we set the History source to the Multiply snapshot.

With the selection active, we Fill from History, using the Multiply layer as source, with Normal blending.

We invert the selection, then...

...we choose the History brush with a large brush size, 60 percent opacity, and Overlay blending...

...we set the History source to the Screen snapshot...

...and use it to brush increased contrast into the sagebrush, as shown in the final image, right.

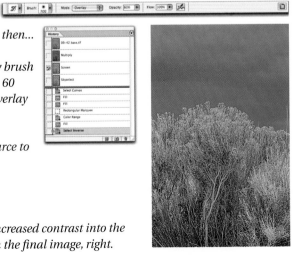

Darkroom Experiments

Don't get the idea that you have to work exclusively using adjustment layers, layer masks, blending modes, and the History brush. Photoshop always offers multiple methods of doing just about anything, so we present these as interesting and often useful approaches—it's up to you to decide whether and when to use them. You can mix and match the techniques in this chapter with more conventional curve-based editing.

Nonetheless, working with these techniques offers a huge amount of freedom to experiment. You can take chances, drive your images to extremes, and generally do things you couldn't do using more conventional techniques.

10 Sharpening

Getting an Edge on Your Image

The human visual system depends to a great degree on edges. Simply put, our eyes pass information to our brain, where every detail is quickly broken down into "edge" or "not edge." An image may have great contrast and color balance, but without good edge definition, we simply see it as less lifelike.

As it turns out, no matter how good your scanner and how crisp your original may be, you always lose some sharpness when the image is digitized. Images from low-end flatbed scanners and digital cameras always need a considerable amount of sharpening. High-end scanners sharpen as part of the scanning process. Even a high-resolution digital camera back mounted on a finely focused view camera produces images that will benefit from sharpening. You *cannot* solve the problem of blurry scans by scanning at a higher resolution. It just doesn't work that way.

Your images also lose sharpness in the output process. Halftoned images (almost anything on a printing press) and dithered ones (such as those printed on thermal-wax and inkjet printers) are by far the worst offenders. But even continuous-tone devices such as film recorders and dye-sublimation printers lose a little sharpness.

To counteract the blurries in both the input and output stages, you need to sharpen your images. Photoshop offers several sharpening filters, but Unsharp Mask is the only one that really works as a production tool. The

Sharpening tool and the other sharpening filters may be useful for creative effects (and even then, we prefer other approaches), but they'll wreck your images very quickly if you use them to compensate for softness introduced during either acquisition or output.

Unsharp Masking

Unsharp masking (often abbreviated as USM) may sound like the last thing you'd want to do if you're trying to make an image appear sharper, but the term actually makes some sense; it has its origins in a traditional photographic technique for enhancing sharpness.

The things we see as edges are areas of high contrast between adjacent pixels. The higher the contrast, the sharper the edges appear. So to increase sharpness, you need to increase the contrast along the edges.

In the traditional process, the photographic negative is sandwiched in the enlarger along with a slightly out-of-focus duplicate negative—an unsharp mask—and the exposure time for printing is approximately doubled. Because the unsharp mask is slightly out of focus and the exposure time has been increased, the light side of the edges prints lighter and the dark side of the edges prints darker, creating a "halo" around objects in the image (see Figure 10-1).

As you'll see throughout this chapter, this halo effect is both the secret of good sharpening, and its Achilles' heel—depending on the size and intensity of the halo, and where it appears in the image. Photoshop lets you control the halo very precisely, but there's no single magic setting that works for all images; so you need to know not only how the controls work, but also what you're trying to achieve in the image.

How the Unsharp Mask Filter Works

The Unsharp Mask filter operates pixel by pixel, which explains why it takes so long, even on a very fast machine. It compares each pixel to its neighbors, looking for a certain amount of contrast between adjacent pixels—which it assumes is an edge. It then increases the contrast between those pixels according to the parameters you set. This creates a halo that, at normal viewing distances, increases apparent sharpness.

But Photoshop can't actually detect edges—it just looks at contrast differences (zeros and ones again). So unsharp masking can also have the

Figure 10-1 Edge transitions and sharpening

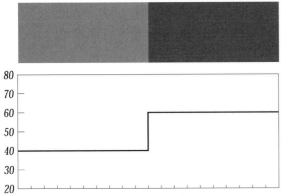

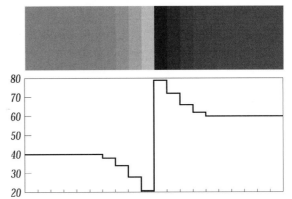

This image and graph depict an edge transition— from 40 to 60 percent. Each tick mark across the bottom of the graph represents a column of pixels.

After sharpening, the transition is accentuated— it's darker on the dark side, and lighter on the light side, creating a halo around the edge.

Unsharpened   Sharpened

The effect on images ranges from subtle to impressive to destructive. This image is somewhat oversharpened to make the effect clear.

   *These samples are darker after sharpening.*

These samples are lighter after sharpening.

The net result is a sharper-looking image.

undesired effect of exaggerating texture in flat areas and skin tones, and emphasizing any noise introduced by the scanner in the shadow areas.

You need to walk a fine line, sharpening only where your image needs it. The filter itself has few controls to adjust what gets sharpened (see Figure 10-2). So, we much prefer running sharpening through a mask. But to do so, you still need to understand how Unsharp Mask works; so here's a rundown of the settings you can control in Photoshop's Unsharp Mask filter, what they do, and how they interact.

Figure 10-2
The Unsharp
Mask filter

Amount

We think of Amount as the volume control of unsharp masking. It adjusts the intensity of the sharpening halo (see Figure 10-3). High Amount settings—you can enter up to 500 percent—produce very intense halos (with lots of pixels driven to pure white or solid black); low Amount settings produce less intense ones. Amount has no effect on the width of the halos—just on the amount of contrast they contain.

As you increase the Amount setting, the blips around big tonal shifts (edges) can be pushed all the way to white and black. At that point, increasing Amount has no effect whatsoever—you can't get more white than white! Worse, the all-white halos often stand out as artifacts and can look really dumb.

We almost always start out by setting Amount much higher than we'll eventually want it—between 400 and 500—until we set the Radius. Then we adjust downward from there, depending on the image (see "Working the Controls," later in this chapter).

Figure 10-3
Varying the USM
Amount setting

Image resolution: 225 ppi
Radius: 1.2
Threshold: 4

Amount: 50   *Amount: 200*   *Amount: 350*

Radius

Radius is the first thing to consider when you're setting up sharpening; it sets the width of the halo that the filter creates around edges (see Figure 10-4). The wider the halo, the more obvious the sharpening effect. Choosing the correct Radius value is probably the most important choice in avoiding an unnaturally oversharpened look, and there are several factors to take into account when you choose, starting with the content of the image itself, the output method, and the intended size of the reproduction (see "Image Detail and Sharpening Radius," later in this chapter).

Note that a Radius value of 1.0 does not result in a single-pixel radius. In fact, the halo is often between four and six pixels wide for the whole light and dark cycle—two or three pixels on each side of the tonal shift. However, it varies in width depending on the content of the image.

Figure 10-4
Varying the USM
Radius setting

Image resolution: 225 ppi
Amount: 200
Threshold: 4

Radius: 0.6   *Radius: 1.2*   *Radius: 2.4*

Threshold

Unsharp Mask only evaluates contrast differences: it doesn't know whether those differences represent real edges you want to sharpen, or areas of texture (or, even worse, scanner noise) that you don't want to sharpen. The Threshold control lets you specify how far apart two pixels' tonal values have to be (on a scale of 0 to 255) before the filter affects them (see Figure 10-5). For example, if Threshold is set to 3, and two adjacent pixels have values of 122 and 124 (a difference of two), they're unaffected.

You can use Threshold to make the filter ignore the relatively slight differences between pixels in smooth, low-contrast areas while still creating a halo around details that have high-contrast edges. And, to some extent at least, you can use it to avoid exaggerating noisy pixels in shadow areas.

Figure 10-5
Varying the USM
Threshold setting

Image resolution: 225 ppi
Amount: 300
Radius: 2

Threshold: 12   *Threshold: 6*   *Threshold: 0*

Low Threshold values (1 to 4) result in a sharper-looking image overall (because fewer areas are excluded). High values (above 10) result in less sharpening, but often produce unnatural-looking transitions between the sharpened and unsharpened areas. We typically start out with a zero Threshold value, and then increase it if necessary.

Tip: The Preview Checkbox. The Preview checkbox applies the Unsharp Mask filter to the entire image or selection on the fly, but we often keep this turned off. Even on fast machines, the preview can take a long time on large files, and every time you change the filter settings, Photoshop has to recalculate and redraw the entire screen. Of course, the larger the image, the longer it takes.

We use Preview for quick before-and-afters, and when we want to check the final settings on the whole of the visible image.

Tip: Select a Critical Area to Preview. When you're working interactively with the Unsharp Mask settings, you may want to strike a happy medium between relying on the tiny proxy and previewing the whole image. You can do this with an additional step or two.

1. Select a critical area in the image, then select Unsharp Mask and turn on the Preview checkbox.

2. When you've arrived at the correct settings, click OK.

3. Press Command-Z (to undo the change you just made), Command-D (to deselect the area), and Command-F (to reapply the filter with the last-used settings).

This is one of those tips that takes longer to explain than it does to do!

Tip: Look at Every Pixel Before You Proceed. Just like any other Photoshop effect, you can undo Unsharp Mask as long as you don't do any further editing. After we've applied Unsharp Mask, and before we do anything else, we make a point of looking at the entire image at a 100-percent view to make sure that we haven't created any problems. If we find a stray noisy pixel, we may just spot it out with the Healing Brush tool, or we may decide to redo the sharpening to avoid the problem.

Tip: Recalling the Filter. If you don't like the results of the filter after seeing them, you can press Command-Z to undo, then Command-Option-F to reopen the filter's dialog box with the last-used settings. (This works with all filters that have user-settable parameters, but we use it more with Unsharp Mask than with any other filter.)

Tip: Fade Filter. If your sharpening is a little too strong, you can reduce the effect of the Unsharp Mask (or any other) filter using the Fade command from the Edit menu (see "Filters and Effects" in Chapter 15, *Essential Image Techniques*). This is one of the best uses of Fade we've come across.

Tip: Fade Luminosity Instead of Convert to Lab. Some people like to sharpen images by converting them to Lab and sharpening only the Lightness channel. You can get an almost identical result by sharpening the RGB file, then using the Fade command from the Edit menu, with the Mode set to Luminosity. It's faster, and kinder and gentler on the image.

Everything's Relative

One of the most important concepts to understand about sharpening is that the three values you can set in the Unsharp Mask dialog box are all interrelated. For instance, as you increase the Radius setting, you generally need to decrease Amount to keep the apparent sharpness constant. Similarly, at higher Radius settings, you can use much higher Threshold values; this smooths out unwanted sharpening of fine texture, while still applying a good deal of sharpness to well-defined edges.

Working the Controls

When we're trying to determine the right sharpening settings for an image, we start by setting the Radius. We usually start out with exaggerated Amount and Threshold settings (400 percent and 0), then we experiment with the Radius value. The exaggerated Amount and Threshold make it easy to see what's happening as we adjust the Radius (see Figure 10-6).

As you increase the Radius, the apparent sharpness also increases—often to an undesirable extent. This is where the aesthetic considerations come in. Some people like more sharpening than others. We find over-sharpened images more disturbing than slightly soft ones, but that's a matter of taste. It's up to you to decide how much sharpening you want.

However much sharpening you decide to apply, you'll find that as you increase the Radius setting, you need to decrease the Amount to keep the apparent sharpness constant. You can work these controls in opposition to achieve a wide range of sharpening effects.

Threshold is the third part of the equation. You can think of it as a selective smoothing function. At small (less than 1 pixel) Radius settings, a Threshold value as low as 15 or so will probably wipe out most of the sharpening effect. At higher Radius settings, you can use much higher Threshold values to smooth out unwanted sharpening of fine texture, while still applying a good deal of sharpness to well-defined edges.

There are dangers lurking here, though. As you use higher Amount and Threshold settings, you run an increased risk of driving pixels to solid black or solid white. The solid black ones aren't usually too much of a problem, but the blown-out white ones can appear as noticeable artifacts, especially when they're large due to higher Radius settings.

Figure 10-6 **Radius versus Amount versus Threshold**

Very different USM settings can combine to provide equivalent apparent sharpness.
We've sharpened this 225 ppi image with four different settings for Amount, Radius, and Threshold.

230 / 0.6 / 12   *390 / 0.6 / 33*   *79 / 4 / 19*   *300 / 5 / 113*

With very high Threshold settings, you get dramatic unnatural sharpening of high-contrast edges, while leaving smaller details soft. This makes the image look quite disturbing—it's hard for the eye to reconcile the sharp edges and the soft detail, so the image looks like there's something wrong with the focus.

In short, the three parameters provided by Unsharp Mask give you a lot of control over the sharpening effect, but it takes a while to get your head around the way they interact.

Sharpening—Why, How, and When?

If we got a nickel for each time we've been asked what sharpening settings someone should use, we'd probably be sipping wine on a tropical island rather than writing books on Photoshop. Of course, we couldn't really come up with a short answer any less lame than "it depends."

The longer answer, of course, involves explaining the various factors on which it depends, which we'll now proceed to do. First, a necessary disclaimer: Bruce and his colleagues at PixelGenius publish a sharpening plug-in, called PhotoKit SHARPENER. While we'd be pleased as punch if you considered purchasing PhotoKit SHARPENER, you should know that a lot of what it does is based on the information in this chapter. The plug-in just does it a lot faster than you can do it manually.

Why We Sharpen

We—that's a collective "we," which we hope includes you, too—sharpen images for several reasons, including the inevitable loss of sharpness from the capturing process. Every reason to sharpen imposes its own demands. Fairly often, though, these demands contradict one another.

Sharpening the capture. Whenever you turn photons into pixels, you lose some sharpness, because no matter how high the resolution of your capture devices, they sample a fixed grid of pixels, turning the continuous gradations of tone and color that exist in the real world into discrete pixels. Each capture device imposes its own noise pattern on the image, whether it's from film grain, from digital noise, or, as is common in many film scans, from a combination of the two.

Image Detail and Sharpening Radius

You can achieve the same apparent sharpness with many different combinations of Amount, Radius, and Threshold settings, but the difference between good and bad sharpening lies largely in matching the Radius setting to the image content.

Look closely at the image at hand. How big, in pixels, are the details that you want to sharpen? You need to match the size and intensity of the sharpening halo to the size of the details in the image.

High-frequency images contain a lot of detail, with sharp transitions between tonal values, while *low-frequency* images have smoother transitions and fewer small details. Whether a given image is high frequency or low frequency depends on the content of the image and on its pixel density. High-frequency images, where the edges of objects are reproduced using only one or two pixels, need a smaller Radius setting than low-frequency images, where the edges may be a dozen or so pixels wide.

An image containing fine detail, such as a picture of trees, is likely to have many more high-frequency transitions than a head shot, for example. But if you scan the trees at a high enough resolution, even the edges on the tiniest leaves will be reproduced several pixels wide in the scan. So it isn't *just* the content that dictates the sharpening, it's the relationship between content and resolution.

Unpleasant settings. Too large a Radius is the prime cause of over-sharpened images. Moreover, an overly large Radius can actually wipe out the detail it's supposed to be accentuating. Too small a Radius can result in too little apparent sharpening. This might in turn seduce you into cranking up the Amount setting so far that you create spurious specular highlights, and over-emphasize textures such as skin in undesirable ways. With very extreme settings, you can change the overall image contrast—which in most cases isn't what you want.

Figure 10-7 shows two images that need quite different sharpening settings. The trees image contains a lot of fine detail that needs a low Radius setting and a fairly high Amount setting to bring it out. If we apply the same sharpening to the pumpkin, it fails to bring out the necessary detail (while threatening to create unpleasant mottling).

Conversely, sharpening settings that work well on the pumpkin don't work at all well on the trees. The larger Radius sharpens the larger elements well, but the more delicate elements are lost. It cre-

You need to sharpen the image content to restore what was lost in the conversion to pixels, but you don't want to also sharpen—and hence emphasize—the noise and grain. So effective sharpening must take into account the source of the image.

Sharpening the image. People often sharpen for creative reasons: to tell a story, to make a point, to emphasize an area of interest, or to sell a product. To do this successfully, you need to match your sharpening to the content of the image. A busy, high-frequency image with lots of tiny details, like a forest full of trees, has much narrower edges than a close subject with soft detail like a head shot or pumpkin (see Figure 10-7).

Figure 10-7 Unsharp Mask settings for high- and low-frequency images

Settings that work for one image can be ineffective or destructive on another. Resolution: 266 ppi

| *Unsharpened* | *High-frequency settings: Amount 275, Radius .6, Threshold 3* | *Low-frequency settings: Amount 200, Radius 2, Threshold 9* |

ates a very confused appearance, where the same element in the image appears sharp in some places and soft in others.

If you get the Radius correct first, it's easy to set the Amount to achieve the degree of sharpness you want. Then you can adjust the

Threshold to suppress noise, and to avoid oversharpening patterns, film grain, and the like.

When sharpening image content, you want to emphasize the edges without overemphasizing textures—like skin tones—and without introducing spurious texture into flat areas like skies. So effective sharpening must take into account the image content.

Sharpening the output. When you turn pixels into marks on a substrate—in other words, when you print—you lose sharpness again. In most cases, individual pixels aren't translated into individual dots of ink or dye, and even in those cases where they are (such as photographic printers like the Durst Lambda or Fuji Pictrography) the printed "pixels" tend to be round rather than square. In either case, the output loses some sharpness.

Because you want to make the print as sharp as the output device can render it, effective sharpening must take into account the output process.

When We Sharpen

Needless to say (but we'll say it anyway), the chances are exceedingly slim that you can satisfy all these different sharpening criteria with a single round of Unsharp Mask, applied globally to the image. Of course, if one pass of Unsharp Masking is all you have time for in your workflow, it's better than not sharpening at all. But for the highest quality, we recommend using a two- or three-stage approach to sharpening. Rather than try to satisfy all the criteria simultaneously, this workflow approach to sharpening addresses them separately.

First, apply a gentle round of sharpening very soon after image capture to take care of the source-sensitive aspects. After you make your major tone and color corrections, apply some localized creative sharpening (we skip this step in automated workflows). Then, once the image is at final output resolution, apply sharpening tailored to the chosen output.

At the risk of drawing an analogy from one incomprehensible subject to another, we liken the sharpening workflow to the color management workflow.

▶ Capture sharpening is like converting from the source profile to the working space—it compensates for the quirks of the source and puts the image in a good state for editing.

▶ Creative sharpening is like doing color correction, using creative skills to make the image do what you want it to.

▶ Output sharpening is like converting to an output profile, creating a device-specific version of the image that is designed to work only for the designated output process.

Essentially, the capture and creative sharpens make a file that is repurposable (our mothers always taught us to keep our options open as long as possible), and responds well to resizing and final output sharpening.

Of course, if approached carelessly, this workflow can create some very ugly images. Just hitting the image with three rounds of Unsharp Mask using different radii is a recipe for certain disaster. Instead, retaining optimum quality requires finesse and some fairly advanced sharpening techniques. We look at individual sharpening techniques in detail later in this chapter, but here's the 30,000-foot overview.

Capture sharpening. The first round of sharpening in the workflow must be done very gently indeed; otherwise the result is likely to be a hideously oversharpened mess. It's often helpful to sharpen through an edge mask—so that only the high-contrast edges get sharpened—and to focus the sharpening on the midtones, protecting highlights and shadows so that they don't get driven to solid black and solid white.

With very grainy or noisy originals such as high-ISO digital capture or fast color negative, you may first want to apply some noise reduction (essentially *un*sharpening) by despeckling each channel individually. However, you should use an edge mask to protect the edges, which you're going to want to sharpen.

Creative sharpening. For creative sharpening, you can build "sharpening brushes" to paint your sharpening just where you want it. As you'll see, you do this by creating a new merged layer, setting the layer's blending mode to Luminosity (to avoid color-fringing), applying a global Unsharp Mask to the layer, then adding a layer mask set to Hide All. As you paint on the layer mask, Photoshop adds or removes the sharpening.

Creative sharpening effects are really only limited by your imagination. For example, one way to make an object appear sharper is to blur its surroundings— you can create "smoothing brushes" using essentially the same techniques as sharpening brushes, substituting a blur for the sharpen.

Output sharpening. Since the image-specific and source-specific concerns have already been addressed in the capture and creative sharpening phases, output sharpening can concentrate solely on the output process.

Note that you can only sharpen the image's pixels—Photoshop has no control over how those pixels are rendered to ink on paper (or any other output process). So the key factor in output sharpening is the relationship between the pixels and the resulting hard copy. Hence output sharpening must be done at the final size and resolution, often as the last step before converting an RGB file to CMYK and saving the file to disk. Note that unlike capture and creative sharpening, output sharpening is something we always apply globally. Here are a few other considerations.

▶ A rule of thumb that has served us well is to aim for a sharpening halo of approximately $\frac{1}{50}$- to $\frac{1}{100}$-inch (.5 to .25 mm) in width, the thinking being that at normal viewing distances, a halo this size falls below the threshold of human visual acuity, so you don't see the halo as a separate feature—you just get the illusion of sharpness that it produces.

   A good starting point for the Unsharp Mask filter's Radius setting is image resolution ÷ 200. (Remember: we're talking about final image resolution, after it has been placed on a page and scaled to fit.) Thus, for a 300-ppi image, you'd use a Radius of 1.5 (300 ÷ 200). For a 200-ppi image, you'd use a Radius setting of 1. This is a suggested starting point, not a golden rule. As you gain experience, you'll find situations where the rule has to be bent. When sharpening using methods that don't involve Unsharp Mask, you'll have to look closely and do some math yourself.

▶ Of course, there's really no way to get an accurate on-screen representation of how a sharpened halftone output will look—the continuous-tone monitor display is simply too different from the halftone. An image well-sharpened for halftone output will typically look "crunchy" on screen. And the monitor resolution and view percentage can help or hinder your appraisal of an image's sharpness. See the sidebar "Sharpening and the Display" for more on the subject.

▶ On very large prints, you may have to use a slightly larger sharpening halo—if the resolution is below 100 ppi, the halo will be larger than $\frac{1}{50}$-inch because it takes at least two pixels, one light, one dark, to create the halo. But large prints are generally viewed from further away, so the longer viewing distance tends to compensate for the larger halo.

Someday, RIPs and printers may even be able to apply output sharpening on the fly, particularly if things like color conversions and trapping are also going to occur there. But for such an approach to succeed, the device will somehow need to know the state of the incoming images (what kind of sharpening has already been performed, and so on).

Sharpening and the Display

Back in the days when all our monitors were CRTs, we thought we had a good idea of how to judge sharpness from the screen. But the vast differences in apparent sharpness between LCD and CRT monitors, and the research we've undertaken in applying output sharpening, have caused us to re-evaluate that position.

LCD monitors are much, much sharper than CRTs at any given display resolution. Moreover, an image will appear quite different in terms of sharpening at a lower display resolution than it will at a higher one.

So where color management lets us compensate for a huge range of different display behaviors, we have no such solution for sharpening.

What we do have is a new set of very general rules of thumb. Use these with caution: You need to learn the relationship between what you see on your particular display at your preferred resolution and the resulting output (just as you had to do with color in the days before color management). With that caveat in mind, here are some very general guidelines.

Zoom percentage. We believe it's a good idea to look at the Actual Pixels view to see what's happening to the actual image pixels, but unless your output is to a monitor, Actual Pixels view may give a fairly misleading impression of the actual sharpness on output.

For halftone output, bear in mind that each halftone dot may be comprised of four image pixels. Viewing at 25-percent or 50-percent view may give a truer impression of halftone sharpness. Avoid the "odd" zoom percentages—33.3, 66.6, and so on, because Photoshop applies fairly heavy antialiasing to those views. For inkjet output, the key factor is the resolution you're sending to the printer. Look at the even-divi-sor zoom percentage that comes closest to reproducing the image at actual print size on the display.

How sharp is sharp? For the first two passes of sharpening—capture and localized creative—our general rule of thumb is to apply sharpening that looks good on a CRT display, or very slightly over-sharpened on an LCD display.

For output sharpening, you can really push the sharpening far beyond what looks acceptable on the monitor at Actual Pixels view, particularly when you print at higher resolutions (like 350 ppi for a 175-lpi halftone or 360 ppi for an inkjet print).

The key here is bear in mind the actual size of the pixels on output. At 360 ppi, each pixel is only $\frac{1}{360}$ of an inch, so to produce a $\frac{1}{50}$ of an inch halo, you'd need a dark contour approximately 3.6 pixels wide ($\frac{1}{100}$ of an inch) and a light contour the same size.

The Sharpening Workflow

We'll be the first to admit that taking a workflow approach to sharpening is a fairly radical idea, but the more we use it, the more we find that it makes sense. We've done a great deal of testing—Bruce reckons he sharpened about 5,000 images to build and fine-tune PhotoKit SHARPENER—but plenty of work remains to be done.

The results of two- or three-pass sharpening often justify the extra pains, especially with images we plan to reuse for several different types of output. However, if you're in a hurry, and you're preparing an image for one-off reproduction (particularly with a low screen frequency that can only show a limited amount of detail anyway), one-pass sharpening may make just as much sense.

We don't claim to have solved every conceivable sharpening problem. The techniques that follow are ones that we use every day in our sharpening workflow, and as we describe them, we'll tell you how we use them. But feel free to pick and choose, and to adapt them to your own work.

Sharpening Techniques

We use a host of techniques in the sharpening workflow—some obvious, others less so. Some attempt to avoid accentuating dust and scratches, noise, and film grain by sharpening through a mask. Others seek to make sharpening non-destructive, and editable after the fact, by applying the sharpening on a layer, and still others use localized sharpening applied with a brush, to pick out specific details in the image. In practice, we often mix these techniques into a single sharpening move, and we'll provide some examples. However, it's easier to digest the various techniques separately, so that's how we'll present them.

Sharpening Layers

We prefer to do most of our sharpening on layers, for much the same reasons we prefer using adjustment layers to burning Curves or Levels directly into an image—it's non-destructive, it affords us control after the fact, and it allows us to use masking when we need to. In the first stage of the sharpening workflow, layer-based sharpening also provides an easy way to concentrate the sharpening in the midtones through the Blend If sliders in the Layer Options dialog box.

Figure 10-8 shows the steps for creating a sharpening layer on a flat file, or on a layered one. The layer is set to Luminosity mode to avoid any color shifts or color fringes—it produces essentially the same result as converting the image to Lab and sharpening the Lightness channel. You can then run the Unsharp Mask filter globally on the layer, or apply Unsharp Mask through an edge mask.

Tip: Use Fade to Luminosity. If you really don't want to create a sharpening layer, but you want the benefit of sharpening in Luminosity mode,

Figure 10-8 Creating a sharpening layer

On a flat file, simply duplicate the Background layer.

On a layered file, create a new layer, then choose Option-Merge Visible (or press Command-Option-Shift-E) to merge the visible layers into the new one...

...then, set the new layer's blending mode to luminosity, to avoid color-fringing.

you can run the Unsharp Mask filter, then choose Fade from the Edit menu, and set the blending mode to Luminosity in the Fade dialog box.

Edge Masking

Edge masks are an indispensable tool for both sharpening and noise reduction. When sharpening, we use an edge mask to concentrate the effects of the sharpen on the edges, so that flat areas such as skies, and textured areas such as skin tones, don't get oversharpened. For noise reduction, we use the same kind of mask, but inverted, so that the edges are protected from the noise reduction.

Figure 10-9 shows the steps for building an edge mask. The first step is to create a channel that has good contrast between the edges and the non-edges. Sometimes one of the existing color channels will work—simply duplicate the channel to serve as the basis for the edge mask—but often you can achieve better results by using Channel Mixer or Calculations to create the channel. See "The Color of Grayscale" in Chapter 15, *Essential Image Techniques*, for a slew of methods for creating a grayscale version of the image.

Once you have a grayscale version of the image, you can run the Find Edges filter to locate the edges, then use a combination of blurring and contrast adjustments to control the relationship of the edges and non-

Figure 10-9 Building an edge mask

Add a new channel, either by duplicating an existing color channel, or by using the channel mixer to create a grayscale version of the image. Then run the Find Edges filter to isolate the edges.

The raw image

The new channel

The new channel after Find Edges

A Gaussian Blur softens the transitions and blurs the noise.

Inverting the image creates white edges where we want sharpening.

A Curves move controls the contrast between edges and non-edges.

edges. Once you've created this edge mask, you can use it to make a selection through which you apply the sharpening, or you can add it to the sharpening layer as a layer mask. Each approach has advantages and disadvantages.

Edge mask as selection. To load the edge mask as a selection, Command-click on the channel's tile in the Channels palette. We suggest hiding the selection's marching ants (Command-H). Then, with the sharpening layer targeted, you can run Unsharp Mask. The white areas in the edge mask get fully sharpened, the black areas are fully protected from sharpening, and the gray areas receive sharpening proportional to the gray value.

The disadvantage here is that you have no control over the transition between sharpened and unsharpened areas once you've applied the sharpening.

Edge mask as layer mask. Instead of sharpening through the mask as a selection, you can sharpen the layer globally, then add the edge mask as a layer mask: Load the edge mask as a selection, target the sharpening layer, and then click the Add Layer Mask icon in the layers palette (see Chapter 8, *Selections and Channels*).

Once you've added the layer mask, you can tweak the contrast of the layer mask with Levels or Curves to fine-tune the relationship between the sharpened and unsharpened areas. The downside to using the edge mask as a layer mask (rather than just sharpening the selection) is simply that it creates a larger file. Figure 10-10 shows the steps for applying the edge mask as a selection, or as a layer mask.

Figure 10-10
Applying the edge mask

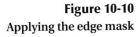

Command-click on the edge mask channel's tile to apply the edge mask as a selection.

To apply the edge mask as a layer mask, first load it as a selection, then target the sharpening layer, and click the Add Layer Mask icon.

Edge mask for noise reduction. You can use the same edge-masking technique to apply noise reduction instead of sharpening. Just invert the mask (or omit the inverting step when creating the mask), leaving the edges black (so that they're protected from the noise reduction), and the non-edges white (so that they receive the full benefit of noise reduction).

We find that the Despeckle filter does a great job of minimizing both film grain and digital noise, but we generally apply it separately to each color channel, because typically one channel will need more applications than another. With film or print scans, the blue channel is almost invariably the noisiest, so we may run Despeckle once on the red channel, twice on the green, and three or more times on the blue. On digital captures, we look at each channel to determine where the noise lies, and Despeckle accordingly.

As with sharpening, we prefer to carry out noise reduction on a layer set to Luminosity blending. Using separate layers for sharpening and noise reduction offers more control, but at the cost of a larger file size.

Controlling the Tonal Range

One of the keys to a successful multipass sharpening workflow is to concentrate the first round of sharpening on the midtones while protecting the extreme highlights and shadows. It's so much easier to do this using a sharpening layer that we don't even try to use a non-layered sharpen. The trick to controlling the tonal range is to use the Blend If sliders in the Layer Style dialog box—choose Layer Style>Blending Options from the Layer menu, or double-click the layer's tile in the Layers palette (see Figure 10-11).

The Blend If sliders let you control which tonal values in the overlying (sharpening) layer get applied to the underlying layer. (And, conversely, which tonal values in the underlying, unsharpened layers are affected by the sharpening layer.) Bruce thinks of the overlying layer as a ton of bricks suspended over a basket of eggs (the underlying layers). The top Blend If slider controls which bricks fall, and the bottom Blend If slider dictates which eggs receive the impact. (If this makes no sense to you, don't worry—Bruce often thinks of things in weird ways.)

Figure 10-11 shows some typical settings for the Blend If sliders for initial midtone sharpening. Depending on the image source (film or digital), and the amount of noise present, you may find that the shadow values need to be set higher or lower, but the basic principle is to set the bottom

Figure 10-11 Controlling the tonal range

The Blend If sliders let us focus sharpening on the midtones.

Unsharpened   *Before blending tweak*   *After blending tweak*

Here, the top sliders fully apply tonal values between level 65 and 200, and gradually feather values from 65–20 and 200–245.

The bottom sliders protect the underlying values below 20 and above 245, and feather the adjustment to values between 20 and 40, and 230 and 245.

The result is that the contrast of the dark and light sharpening halos is reduced, allowing headroom for subsequent creative or output sharpening.

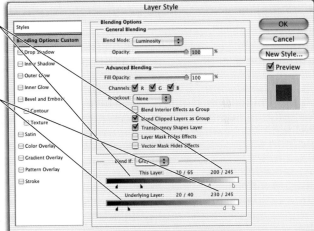

sliders to protect extreme highlights and shadows, and the top sliders to apply most of the sharpening in the midtones.

Sharpening Brushes

For localized creative sharpening, nothing beats painting with a brush. We have two methods that we use to make a "sharpening brush," one using a layer, the other using History. Layer-based brushes offer more control because you can control the local opacity of the layer mask by brushing with different opacities, and you can control the global strength of the sharpen by varying the opacity of the layer itself. However, layers increase your file size. Using the History brush is less controllable (because your only control is through the brush opacity itself) but doesn't add to the size of the file. Keeping your file size down is important when you're working with huge files.

Layer-based sharpening brush. To create a layer-based sharpening brush, first make a sharpening layer as we showed earlier in Figure 10-8. It's usually a good idea to apply slightly more sharpening to the layer than you ultimately desire, because that way you have more control after the fact. Next, add a layer mask set to Hide All. To brush in the sharpening, make sure that the layer mask is targeted, then choose the Brush tool, set the foreground color to white, and simply brush the sharpening in as desired. We prefer to use a brush set to substantially less than 100 percent opacity, because the lower opacity allows us more control. Figure 10-12 shows the results of a sharpening brush.

History Brush sharpening. If you're too lazy to create masks, you're in a RAM-limited situation, or if you just want more interactivity than a mask offers, you can use the History Brush to paint sharpening into the image. This is a particularly handy technique with a pressure-sensitive stylus, because you can set the pressure-sensitivity to Opacity, and achieve fine control over both the strength of the sharpening, and exactly where it's applied.

The basic technique is a simple three-step process.

1. Apply the Unsharp Mask filter.

2. Set the History state to the step before you applied Unsharp Mask, and the source for the History brush to the Unsharp Mask step.

3. Paint the sharpening into the image as desired.

Or, if you prefer, you can *reduce* the sharpening with the History Brush by leaving the History state at the Unsharp Mask step, and then loading the step before it as the History Brush source. We typically choose the method that will require least brushwork on the image at hand.

The unsharpened image in Figure 10-13 is quite soft. (No, this isn't David or Bruce's child!) If we apply enough sharpening to pick up the texture in the fabric, it leaves the skin crunchy, which is bad at the best of times, but particularly so on babies!

In this case, it's much less work to set the History Brush source to the unsharpened state, and brush out the crunchies than it would be to start with the unsharpened state and brush in the sharpness. A few quick strokes with a soft History Brush using opacities between 30 and 80 percent produce the much more pleasing rendition shown in Figure 10-14.

Figure 10-12 A layer-based sharpening brush

The unsharpened image   *The unmasked sharpening layer (before choosing Hide All)*   *The sharpening brushed in locally on the mask*

The unmasked sharpening layer   *The brushed layer mask*

Tip: Luminosity Sharpening with History. Earlier you saw that you can perform luminosity sharpening by selecting Fade from the Edit menu after running the Unsharp Mask filter (and setting the blending mode in the Fade dialog box to Luminosity). If you're brushing sharpening in

Figure 10-13 Global sharpening makes crunchy skin

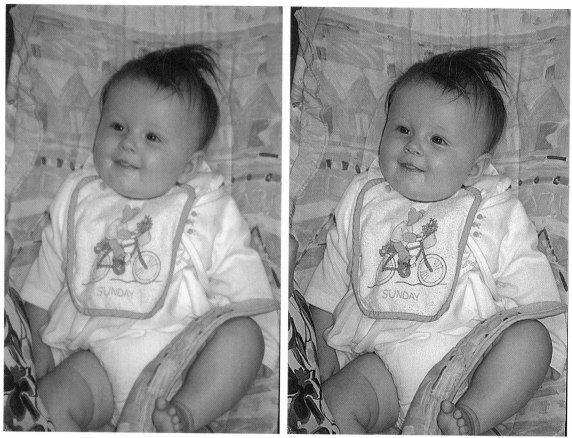

The unsharpened image   *The image sharpened globally*

rather than out, you can do the same thing by setting the blending mode for the History Brush to Luminosity using the Mode popup menu in the Options bar (see Figure 10-15).

Sharpening Without Unsharp Mask

Unsharp Mask is the Swiss Army Knife of sharpening tools, but it's not the only way to sharpen images. One technique that we often use, particularly when sharpening for output, is to make a duplicate layer, using the techniques we described earlier in this chapter under "Sharpening Layers." But rather than setting the blending mode to Luminosity and running Unsharp Mask, we use one of the contrast-increasing blending

Figure 10-14 History Brush sharpening

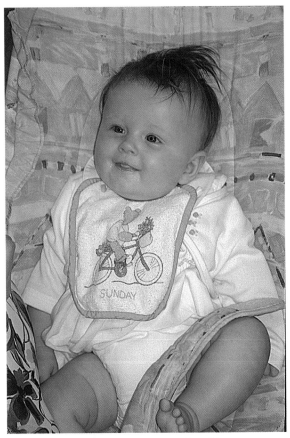

Taking the globally sharpened image as the starting point, we set the source for the History Brush to the unsharpened state, and brush out the crunchies.

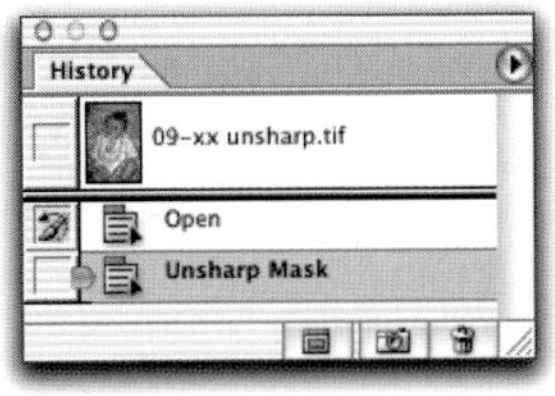

The image after History brushing

Figure 10-15
Luminosity sharpening
with History

You can run Unsharp Mask, then choose Fade Unsharp Mask (from the Edit menu) and set the blending mode to Luminosity...

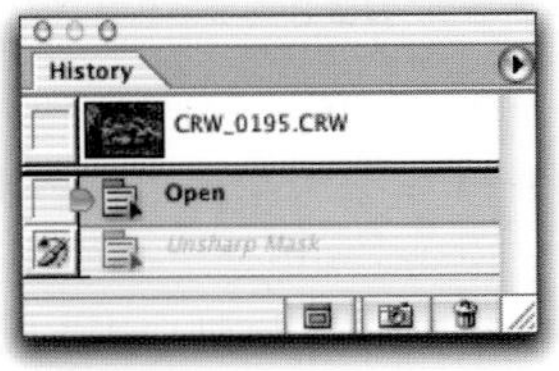

...or you can run Unsharp Mask, set the History state to the unsharpened image, set the History Brush source to the sharpened image, then set the blending mode for the History Brush to Luminosity.

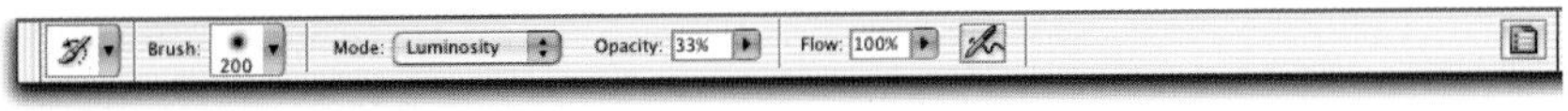

modes such as Soft Light or Hard Light, then we run the High Pass filter on the layer.

High-Pass Sharpening

The High Pass filter (in the Other submenu, under the Filter menu) is a simple way to create an edge mask, but in this case we don't use this as a layer mask. Instead, we simply create a duplicate of the background layer (or create a new merged layer if we have more than one layer in the Layers palette), apply the High Pass filter to it, and then set the layer's blending mode to Soft Light or Hard Light—which increases the contrast around the edges, effectively sharpening the image.

As with the other layer-based sharpening techniques, you can use a whole bag of tricks to refine the sharpening—like blurring noise in the mask, or painting on the layer itself with 50-percent gray (the neutral color for both the Hard Light and Soft Light blending modes) to erase the sharpening in local areas. You can apply a layer mask to confine the sharpening to a specific area, and you can stack multiple sharpening layers to apply selective sharpening to different areas of the image.

The critical parameter in using this technique is the Radius setting for the High Pass filter. If it's too small, you'll get little or no sharpening. If it's too big, grain and noise will appear in the image as if by some evil magic. However, for optimum output sharpening, we often need to produce a result that appears very ugly on screen (see the sidebar, "Sharpening and the Display," earlier in this chapter). Figure 10-16 shows the application of this technique and the resulting image—it looks fine in print, but the onscreen appearance is downright scary!

On soft subjects and skintones, Hard Light can give too strong a sharpening effect. On these types of image, or in any case where we want a more gentle sharpening effect, we often use Soft Light instead of Hard Light to avoid oversharpening the skin texture, as shown in Figure 10-17.

Techniques in the Workflow

In our sharpening workflow, we use combinations of all the techniques covered in the previous section. In this section, we'll describe briefly how we incorporate these techniques into a sharpening workflow.

Figure 10-16 Sharpening with High Pass/Hard Light

We create a sharpening layer and set the blending mode in the Layers palette to Hard Light, then run the High Pass filter.

The filtered layer set to Hard Light creates an unsharp mask very similar to a photographic unsharp mask. You can vary the character of the sharpening by using different radius settings in High Pass, and you can vary the strength of the sharpening by adjusting the layer's opacity.

If we're working on images from scratch—either from a film scan or from a digital capture—we use two or three sharpening passes, as described in "When We Sharpen," earlier in this chapter. When we have to deal with files that already have had some sharpening applied, we deal with them on a case-by-case basis. If we feel that they're adequately sharp, we may do no additional sharpening, or we may apply localized creative sharpening. If we have to resize the image for output, we'll almost certainly do a global sharpen after resize, tailored to the output process.

The First Sharpening Pass

Our first sharpening pass aims to compensate for the shortcomings of the capture in a way that's sensitive to the image content. We do so by creating a sharpening layer, applying an edge mask, sharpening with a radius that matches the image content, then constraining the tonal range to the midtones using the Blend If sliders in Layer Style.

Figure 10-17 **Sharpening with High Pass/Soft Light**

Starting with the unsharpened image, left, we create a sharpening layer, and set the blending mode to Soft Light; then we run the High Pass filter to produce the result shown below.

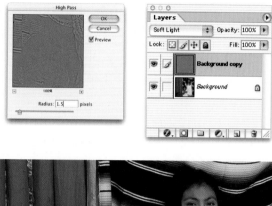

Setting the blending mode before running the High Pass filter lets us see the effect of different Radius settings on the image—the proxy window in the High Pass filter only shows the duplicate layer on which the filter is operating.

The image is now acceptably sharp with no exaggerated noise pixels, but the eyes could benefit from a little extra sparkle.

The result is a subtle sharpen that makes the image behave better through resizing and through the subsequent sharpening phases. If the image has already had sharpening applied, we omit this step. We usually apply this sharpen after we've made our initial global adjustments for tone and contrast, because major contrast moves afterwards may defeat the sharpening. If file size is a concern, we may flatten the image after we've fine-tuned the initial sharpen.

Figure 10-17 Sharpening with High Pass/Soft Light, *continued*

We quickly use the Lasso tool with Feather set to around 5 pixels to select the eyes. Then we target the Background layer, and use Command-J to copy the eyes to a new layer, which we set to Hard Light. We then run High Pass on the new layer to produce the result shown at right.

Creative Sharpening

For localized creative sharpening, we generally use some variant of the sharpening brush techniques. We apply creative sharpening after we've fine-tuned the tone and color both globally and locally, because changes to contrast and color can easily affect the perceived sharpness.

Output Sharpening

We apply output sharpening globally, using a sharpening layer with no layer mask. For halftone and inkjet outputs, we often use the Hard Light/ High Pass sharpening technique. Output sharpening must be done at final output resolution. If you think it's likely the image will be resized after it leaves your hands, we advise omitting the output sharpening step—anyone who resizes the image will probably resharpen anyway, and if you've done a reasonably good job in the capture and creative phases, the final result will be sharp.

The key difference between output sharpening and the earlier phases is that often we produce a result that looks downright scary on the monitor. Keep in mind the physical size of the sharpening halo on output. Light and dark contours that are 3 pixels wide may look hideous on the monitor; but if you're printing at 300 ppi, they'll translate into contours (light and dark parts of the sharpening halo) that are only $\frac{1}{100}$ of an inch wide, so they won't be obvious on the final print.

Attempting to show the apparent on-screen sharpness in print is a very uncertain endeavor. What we've attempted to do in Figure 10-18 is to show the image pixels at 200-percent view through the various phases of sharpening, along with the final printed image at print size, in the hope that doing so will give you some idea of the relationship between what happens to the pixels themselves and the influence on the final printed result.

Obviously, the on-screen appearance at Actual Pixels will vary dramatically over different display types and resolutions, but as you zoom in, the differences between display types become much less significant. We hope that the figure at least demonstrates the dramatic differences in halos created by the capture and creative sharpening phases, and those created by the final output sharpening. To help understand what you're seeing, we've also noted the sharpening settings we used for each step of the sharpening process, from capture through to final output.

Avoiding the Crunchies

The ability to sharpen your images is a powerful tool. Used well, it can give your images the extra snap that makes them jump off the page. Used badly, it gives images the unpleasant "crunchy" look we see in all too many Sunday newspaper color supplements. In overdoses, it can make images look artificial, or even blurry. With that in mind, we leave you with two final pieces of advice.

First, it's better to err on the side of caution. Despite what we've said about output sharpening, an image that's too soft will generally be less disturbing than one that's been oversharpened.

Second, always leave yourself an escape route. One of the great benefits of sharpening on layers is that you can always tweak the layer opacity to strengthen, reduce, or even eliminate the sharpening.

Sharpening is definitely one of those things that improves with experience, and a considerable part of that experience can be gained from revisit-

Figure 10-18 The sharpening workflow

The first pass: Capture sharpening applied on a layer (with an edge layer mask) set to the Luminosity blend mode, at 66-percent opacity. Unsharp Mask applied at Amount 100, Radius 0.8, Threshold 0.

The unsharpened image pixels at 200 percent view

Capture sharpening at 200 percent view

Creative sharpening applied on layer set to Overlay at 50-percent opacity, Unsharp Mask applied at Amount 500, Radius 0.6, Threshold 0, then High Pass filter applied at Radius 5. Sharpening brushed in with a brush at 33-percent opacity.

Creative sharpening at 200 percent view

The image was downsampled from its native 3072 by 2048 pixels to 488 by 732 pixels using Photoshop's Bicubic Sharper interpolation. Then final output sharpening was applied on a layer set to Luminosity at 66-percent opacity, with Unsharp Mask at Amount 187, Radius 1.3, Threshold zero to produce to the result at right. A zoomed detail is shown below.

Downsampled to print size, then sharpened for output, at 200-percent view

The final image

ing your earlier efforts and figuring out what went wrong. If you save an unsharpened copy, or use layers to do your sharpening, you can always go back and refine your sharpening to get closer to the result you want.

11 Spot Colors and Duotones

Special Inks for Special Projects

The fundamental problem with printing presses is that they can only print one color at a time. It's like pixels on a black-and-white screen: The color is either on or off. You may have a gloriously rich full-color image on screen, but you've got to be mighty clever to get that image out the back side of a printing press, and no matter what you do, there will be trade-offs involved.

There are two methods for printing color on a press: spot color and process color. Both can give you a wide variety of colors. But they are hardly interchangeable.

Process color. As we've noted throughout the book, process color is the method of printing a wide range of colors by overlapping halftones (tints) of only four colors: cyan, magenta, yellow, and black. The colors themselves do not mix on paper. Rather, the eye blends these colors together so that ultimately you see the color you're supposed to.

Spot color. If you are printing only a small number of colors (three or fewer), you probably want to use spot colors. The idea behind spot color is that the printing ink is just the right color you want. With spot color, for example, if you want some type colored teal blue, you print it on a plate (often called an *overlay*) that is separate from the black plate. Your commercial printer prints that type using a teal-blue ink—probably a PMS ink—and uses black for the rest of the job.

Because process colors simply cannot simulate some colors—like deep blues, and metallics like gold—spot colors are also used as *bump* plates and varnishes that print alongside or on top of process-color images. For instance, a picture of a fancy car might be printed with the four process colors, plus a spot red to highlight ("bump up") some areas of the car, plus a varnish over the image to make it glossy.

This is relatively easy to print on a six-color press. The hard part has always been building the spot color and varnish plates.

Spot Colors from Photoshop

"How can I print spot colors from Photoshop?" has long been one of the most common questions we hear. Remember that Photoshop was originally designed to do process-color work (or continuous tone RGB output), not spot color overlays. The process of getting spot colors out of Photoshop isn't difficult, though it's not as simple as it should be, even in Photoshop CS. There are three ways to do spot-color work in Photoshop.

▶ Use spot-color channels for all the spot-color image information, and save the file in DCS 2.0 or the native Photoshop (PSD) format. This feature lets you place spot colors in specific areas (like in text or in a logo).

▶ Use the Duotone mode. Duotones (or tritones or quadtones) are used to print neutral grayscale images with two or more colors (we'll discuss why you'd want to do this later in this chapter).

▶ Simulate spot colors in CMYK mode. You can use this technique for either duotones or specific-area spot colors.

Tip: Don't Pick Spot Colors. Note that choosing a Pantone (PMS) color from Photoshop's Color Picker and then painting with that color does *not* provide you with a spot-color ink. Rather, as you apply the "spot" color, it's actually being broken up into RGB or CMYK components. We've always felt that it was a particularly cruel joke by the programmers to offer people the chance to see and pick spot colors without also offering the opportunity to print these colors out on spot-color plates.

Tip: Bézier vs. Raster Spot Color. Photoshop can create vector artwork, but it can't yet apply spot colors to vectors, so any spot color you create here is going to be bitmapped. If you need crisp, high-resolution edges (like for text or a logo), you'll probably get a better result creating the spot-color art in a program like QuarkXPress, Adobe InDesign or Illustrator, or Macromedia FreeHand. (See Chapter 3, *Image Essentials*, for more on the difference between bitmapped and vector artwork.)

Spot-Color Channels

When you print color separations of a CMYK file, you get four plates—one plate per channel. So it's logical that if you want a spot color (or varnish or whatever) to print on its own plate, you have to add another channel to your image. Photoshop has a special kind of channel for spot colors called (you guessed it) a *spot channel*. Spot-color channels are, in most respects, identical to normal channels on the Channels palette. The primary difference is that they display on screen looking like spot colors—more or less. To create one of these beasts, select New Spot Channel from the popout menu on the Channels palette (or, faster, Command-click the New Channel button at the bottom of the palette).

The New Spot Channel dialog box offers you three controls for your new spot color: Name, Color, and Solidity (see Figure 11-1).

Name. You should generally leave the naming of the spot color up to Photoshop (it assigns one when you choose a color). The important thing is this: To ensure that your spot color appears on the correct plate when

Figure 11-1 Making a new spot-color channel

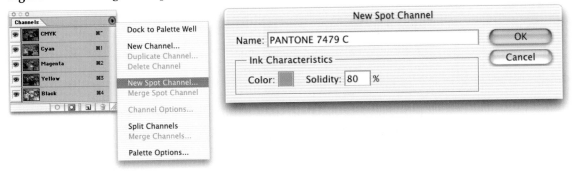

printing from a page-layout program, you must make sure the name of the spot channel matches the name of the same ink in the page-layout program.

Color. You can choose a spot color by clicking on the color swatch and then clicking on a color (if the Color Picker appears, click the Custom button to display the Custom Colors dialog box). The default color model here is Pantone Solid Coated, but you can choose a different swatch book type from the Book popup menu (see Figure 11-2). Curiously, the Book popup menu displays several process-color swatch books (like Trumatch and Focoltone) along with the spot-color swatch books (like Pantone and Toyo), even though the process-color books are meaningless here.

Actually, to be honest, all the colors here are meaningless, because they're used only for screen display. You can pick any color you want (even a regular RGB color, though for technical reasons we strongly encourage you not to spec spot colors using CMYK percentages), and as long as the name is right, it'll print fine. This is handy if you need to create an image even before you know what PMS color you'll be using on press. Just pick a color and name it "My Spot Color" (or whatever). Later, you can either change the name or just tell your printer that this piece of film should be printed with such-and-such a color.

Solidity. The Solidity feature lets you control how opaque the color is on screen (this is similar to the Opacity setting for regular alpha channels).

Figure 11-2
Picking a spot color

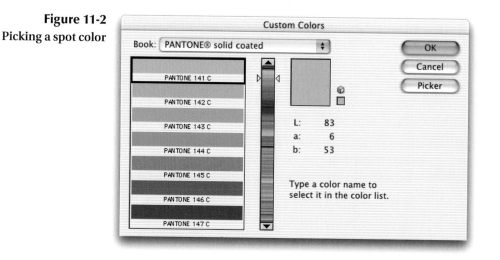

Again, like Color, this only determines your on-screen preview; it has no effect on the final printed image.

Picking the correct Solidity value for a spot color is almost impossible because every spot-color ink has a slightly different opacity, depending on how it was mixed, what colors it's printed over, and so on. In general, metallic inks are almost totally opaque, letterpress inks are usually more opaque than offset inks, and inks that include a good dose of Opaque White in their ingredients are less transparent than those without.

Ultimately, however, you just have to make up a number and move on, knowing that your screen display of the spot color will almost certainly be somewhat inaccurate. We almost always use a value of about 30 percent for spot colors. If we used 100 percent, we might forget that other colors might show through the spot color, causing mottling (see "Building Traps," later in this section). Of course, if the spot color is a varnish, we'd set the Solidity value to zero, because varnishes are almost transparent (here's one place that Solidity is not the same as Opacity—zero-percent Solidity can still be seen).

Applying Spot Colors

Spot-color channels appear on the Channels palette, though some people erroneously look for them on the Layers palette because spot colors always appear on top of the underlying original image. When you first create a spot-color channel, Photoshop automatically selects it for you; so if you start painting, the "ink" appears on this channel and not the RGB or CMYK channels. When you're finished working on the spot-color channel, you must manually switch to the RGB or CMYK channels (the fastest way to do this is to press Command-~(tilde)).

Annoyingly, because spot colors appear on their own special channel, you cannot use the Layers feature with spot colors. In fact, even if you use the Type tool to place text on your spot-color channel, the text is automatically rendered and dropped into the channel, not on a layer. (You can still move it and adjust its mode and opacity by choosing Fade from the Filter menu while it's selected, but once you deselect it, it's rendered onto the layer.)

Remember that when you're painting on a spot-color channel, you're always painting in black, white, or gray, even when it looks like you're painting in color. Black is solid spot color; white is no ink at all; and gray is a tint of the spot color.

By the way, you can always change the spot-color channel's settings by double-clicking on its tile in the Channels palette.

Tip: Converting a Layer to a Spot-Color Channel. David finds the inability to use spot colors on layers frustrating at best (it's like going back to the Photoshop 2.x days). So he'll often lay out his spot colors on one or more layers first, using black rather than a color. Then this trick converts the layers into spot colors.

1. Load the "spot color" layer's transparency mask as a selection by Command-clicking on the layer in the Layers palette.

2. Hide the layer (by turning off the Layer's visibility eyeball), or delete it if you don't think you'll need it again.

3. In the Channels palette, create a new spot channel, or select one you've already made. If you created a new spot channel, you're done; skip the next step.

4. If you picked a pre-made spot channel, fill the selection with black (usually the foreground color is black, so you can just press Option-Delete).

That's it! The information that was on the layer is now on your spot-color channel.

Tip: Converting Alpha Channels to Spots. If you find yourself wanting to convert a regular alpha channel into a spot-color channel, don't panic; just open the Channel Options dialog box by double-clicking the channel's tile (the little thumbnail preview, not the name of the channel). There you can select the Spot Color radio button. When you click OK, the channel is changed.

Tip: Building Bump Plates. Putting text or basic shapes on a spot-color channel is relatively easy. Creating quality bump plates for scanned images is much harder. One method is to use the Color Range feature (under the Select menu) to select the kinds of colors you're trying to enhance. For instance, if you're trying to bump up the color in a shiny red bicycle, you might use Color Range to select the reds in an image. When you create a spot-color channel after making your selection, Photoshop automatically converts the selection into spot color (the fully selected parts become solid spot color, and so on).

If you need to create a lot of bump plates or you need better precision, you might consider using ImagesWare's Color Correction Pro (written by the same folks who wrote the well-known MPC CoCo plug-in), an excellent tool for building high-quality spot-color bump plates. Color Correction Pro's color-range selection is optimized for building bump plates, and it tends to give rather better results than the one built into Photoshop.

Merge Spot Channel. Photoshop also lets you convert your spot-color channel into its RGB or CMYK color equivalents (choose Merge Spot Channel from the popout menu on the Channels palette). Generally, you only need to do this when sending an on-screen comp to a client or putting the image on the Web. (Make sure you save a backup of your file first!) Note that the Photoshop documentation implies that you have to merge spot colors before printing to a color printer, but this isn't necessarily true. Just make sure you choose RGB from the Space popup menu in the Print dialog box; that way, Photoshop simulates the spot colors in the RGB it sends to the printer.

Knocking Out vs. Overprinting

As we said earlier, spot-color inks are rarely fully opaque, so if you try to print a solid PMS ink on top of your CMYK image, it'll probably look mottled. What's more, it may result in too much ink on the page, causing troubles at print time.

To avoid these overprinting problems, you'll need to manually knock out the parts of your image that lie underneath the spot colors. This knocking-out process is taken care of for you in other programs, such as when you place spot-color type over an image in QuarkXPress, Adobe InDesign, or PageMaker. Here's one way to do this in Photoshop. (Of course, if you're using a spot color as a bump plate or a varnish then you *don't* want to knock out the image behind it.)

1. Load the spot-color channel as a selection. (You can use Load Selection if you want, but we find it faster simply to Command-click on the spot-color channel's tile in the Channels palette.) You can now control color

trapping by choking or spreading the selection (see the next section for more on this technique).

2. Create a new layer in the Layers palette.

3. Use the Fill command on the Edit menu to fill the selection on this new layer with white. (It may not look like much has changed, because the spot color is probably still overlapping the area you just filled with white. Try turning off the visibility of the spot-color channel to see the knocked out area below.)

Creating a new layer is optional—you could just fill the background image with white—but we find it more flexible to knock out the portions of the image with a layer, just in case you have to make a change later. Of course, you'll still have to flatten the file before saving it in the DCS 2.0 format.

On the other hand, if you have two spot colors that overlap, and you want one to knock out the other, you won't be able to use this layer trick (because spot colors always sit on top of layers). In this case, you have to fill the selection with white on the lower spot-color channel.

Building Traps

There's only one problem with the knock-out steps outlined above: They don't take trapping into account. Trapping compensates for the slight paper misregistration that is inevitable on a printing press. For instance, if a cyan box abuts a magenta box, but the paper is slightly misregistered when the magenta plate is printed, there'll be a white sliver between the cyan and the magenta (see Figure 11-3).

Scanned images generally don't need trapping because there are gradual transitions between colors. For example, if you scanned a picture of a cyan box and a magenta box, the edge between the two would actually be made up of both cyan and magenta, creating a natural trap. If one plate misregisters, there's still enough overlap to avoid a white gap.

As soon as you knock out the background behind a spot color, however, you'll almost certainly need to think about trapping. There are three methods of trapping spot colors in Photoshop: choking the background, spreading the spot color, and the Trap feature.

Figure 11-3
Trapping colors

The image looks great on screen…   *…but if the press misregisters, an ugly gap appears.*   *A trap ensures that misregistration won't cause problems.*

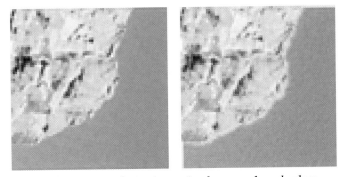

Scanned images rarely need trapping because shared colors usually mask press misregistration.

Choking the background. The general rule of trapping is to spread the lighter color so that it slightly overlaps the darker color. If the spot color is dark, you can effectively spread the background colors "into" the spot color by making the area that you knock out (set to white) smaller. After loading the spot-color channel as a selection in the last step-by-step instruction, choose Contract from the Modify submenu (under the Select menu). A value of 1 pixel chokes the selection (shrinks it) by a single pixel, which is enough for most trapping problems. (A single pixel is about .25 point—.0033 inch—in a 300-ppi image.)

As it turns out, we often find ourselves using this method even when the spot color is lighter, especially when the spot-color channel contains type or other fine detail.

Spreading the spot color. If the spot color is lighter, you can spread it (make it bigger) so that it slightly overlaps the background. One way to do this is to select the channel in the Channels palette and choose the Minimum filter from the Other submenu on the Filters menu. Minimum spreads the image on a channel (makes it bigger), so that it slightly overlaps whatever is behind it. Again, a one-pixel value here should work well for most images. (Some printing processes—such as newsprint—require larger traps.) Watch out for muddying up the fine detail on the spot-color channel with this process, however.

Trap. While the previous technique works pretty well when you're trapping a spot color that is completely surrounded by other colors (because it spreads everything on the spot-color plate), it's not as effective when the spot color only partially overlaps another color. The Trap feature (under the Image menu; see Figure 11-4) lets you build some basic trapping between channels in your image, and traps only where two or more colors intersect.

To trap one spot-color channel, make sure both the background image and the spot-color channel are visible, but select the spot-color channel in the palette. To trap two channels, select them both (you can select multiple channels with the Shift key).

The Trap feature lets you specify a trap in millimeters, points, or pixels. Unfortunately, Photoshop currently seems to have some trouble interpreting these values, so you'll probably need to specify a trap significantly

Figure 11-4
Trap

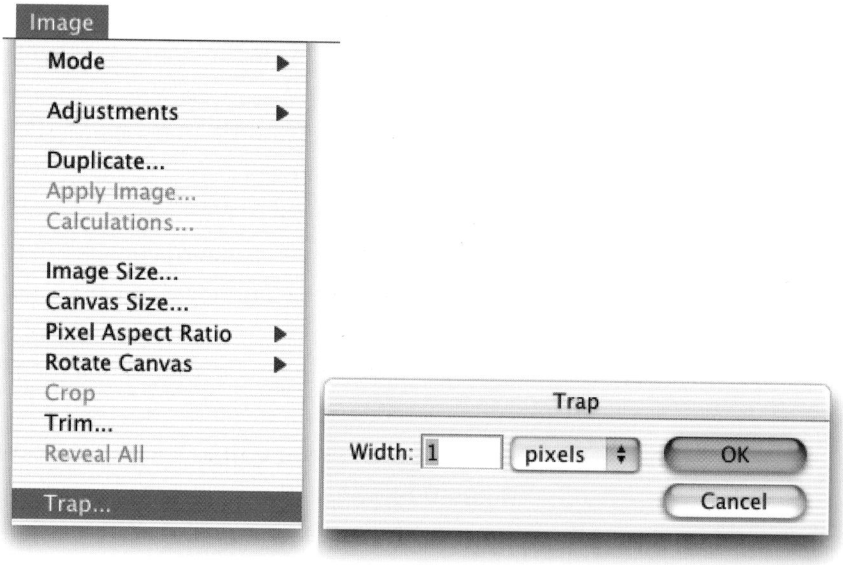

larger than your printer prescribes. For instance, a .25-point trap doesn't have any effect at all on most images; you need to use a value of 1 point to get even a negligible trap. Note that if you enter a value that's too small, Photoshop won't perform any trapping at all (it's as though you didn't even use the feature), so you should always check to make sure some trapping really occurred.

(To be honest, while we find the Trap feature occasionally useful, we use the "choking the background" method the most.)

Saving Images with Spot Colors

While we're going to hold off providing details about the various graphic file formats until Chapter 16, *Storing Images*, when it comes to saving images that contain spot-color channels, the choice is currently pretty simple. If you're going to import the graphic into QuarkXPress, you should save it in the DCS 2.0 format. For Adobe InDesign, you can use DCS 2.0 or—if you're using InDesign CS or later—the native Photoshop file format. In all other cases, you should use Photoshop (.psd), TIFF, or PDF format. In the future, we may have versions of XPress and InDesign that are able to better handle TIFF or PDF files containing spot colors, but at the time of this writing, it's safest to avoid them. We *do* know people who have made these formats work, but we know a greater or equal number who have not. DCS 2.0, however, is a sure thing.

Screen angles. When you print two colors on top of each other, and the colors are tinted, each halftone screen has to have a different angle or else you'll end up with distracting moiré patterns. (See Chapter 17, *Output Methods*, for more on halftone screens and how to set them.) If your spot colors are solid (100 percent), then you don't have to worry about screen angles. If your spot colors are tinted but they don't overlap any other colors, you don't have to worry about it. But you'd better pay attention if you place 50 percent of some Pantone color on top of 20-percent black, or if you're building a spot-color bump plate to enhance a color in your image.

You can set the halftone screen angles in Photoshop (in the Print with Preview dialog box) or in your page-layout program. Generally speaking, halftone angles should sit either 45 or 30 degrees apart. (For more information, see the discussion on screen angles in "Saving and Outputting," later in this chapter.)

In the case of bump plates, all the available angles are typically taken up by the cyan, yellow, magenta, and black inks. You can either print the image with stochastic screens, or match the bump plate to one of the process-color inks. It's generally safe to match it to the closest color. For example, if you're printing a bright-red bump plate over a dull-red process-color image, you can probably get away with matching the bump plate's angle to the magenta screen (often 75 degrees). The two colors are similar enough, and the percentage of tint is high enough (almost solid) that you probably won't have any patterning.

Multitone Images

In the old tale of the four blind men and the elephant, each man describes the animal according to the piece he's experienced. "It's a snake-like creature with wrinkled skin," says one, holding the trunk.

"No, it's a hairy animal with giant wings," says another, feeling the ear.

Printing a grayscale image is similar to this experience. Printing presses are powerful and delicate instruments, but depending on the press, the operator, the ink, and the paper, they're often limited to printing far fewer than the 256 shades of gray you can theoretically achieve with an 8-bit image. So after you've gone through a lot of trouble adjusting tone, those tones are pummeled when the image is slapped onto paper. In other words, the final printed result is only a fraction of the whole image, and the viewer is blind to the richness of the original.

There are ways, however, to coax more gray levels, more detail, and more depth out of a printed image. Printers have traditionally tackled this problem by printing the grayscale image more than once, each time with a different-colored ink. These are called *duotones, tritones,* and *quadtones* (depending on the number of inks you use). When talking about the genre as a whole, we call these *multitones,* because we're too lazy to keep typing "duotones, tritones, and quadtones." Remember, multitones differ from color images in that they almost always represent an underlying neutral, grayscale image.

Expanding the Tonal Range

While they're often used to colorize grayscale images, the original goal of multitones was to expand the tonal range of the image. For instance, a

50-percent tint in gray ink may be lighter than an 11-percent spot of black ink; so an 11-percent spot of the gray ink is far lighter than the tonal range of black ink can achieve. If you print black ink in the shadows and gray ink in the highlights, you can achieve more levels of highlight grays.

On the other end of the spectrum, we usually think of 100-percent black ink as solid—you can't get darker than that. But in reality, printing 100-percent black on top of 100-percent gray results in a darker, richer, denser black. Therefore, by adding the gray in the shadows, you expand the tonal range of the image even further toward real black.

Adding an ink is like listening to two of the blind men instead of just one; you get that much more information and can see the whole of the image that much more clearly.

Colorizing Images

When most designers think about duotones, they don't think about expanding tonal range; they think about colorizing grayscale images. For instance, many newsletters are printed with two inks—black and some Pantone color. When given the opportunity to print with a second ink, many designers immediately think, "Oh, I can give some color to my grayscale images by making them duotones."

There's nothing wrong with colorizing a grayscale image. But colorizing images without thinking about the expanded tonal range usually looks pretty bad. In this chapter we talk about both, and how they relate to one another.

Tip: Dumb, Fast Duotones. If we didn't know how hectic life can get in a production setting, we would hardly believe how many people (printers, especially) still use the flat-tint duotone trick. The idea is that you can fake a duotone by laying a flat tint behind the grayscale image. For example, let's say you want to add some blue to a grayscale image. To fake the duotone look, you could lay down an 11-percent tint of magenta or PMS 485 behind the entire image (see Figure 11-5), and set the image to overprint in your page-layout program.

Note that this really is an old printer's trick, and it doesn't look very good. Since you're making no allowance for the tonal shift, fake duotones are often too dark and muddy. Photoshop makes creating real duotones so easy that faking it is hardly worth the effort. It's faster, but it's not that much faster.

Figure 11-5 Fake versus real duotones

Just dropping a flat magenta tint behind this grayscale image does little to enhance it.
Adjusting the curves for the two inks adds tonal range and depth.

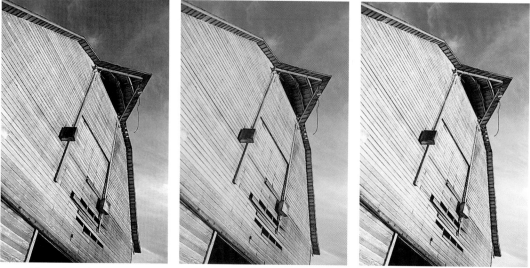

The original grayscale   *Fake duotone*   *Real duotone*

Photoshop's Duotones

There are two ways to create multitone images in Photoshop: Switch from Grayscale to Duotone under the Mode submenu, or create them in CMYK mode. We're focusing our discussion on the Duotone mode, and will cover CMYK mode later in this chapter.

In every other color mode in Photoshop, the color is made of multiple channels—CMYK color is made of four channels, RGB is made of three. Multitones are different. In a multitone image, Photoshop saves a single grayscale image along with two curves—one for each color plate. These curves are just like those in the Curves or Transfer Function dialog boxes (see Figure 11-6). Note that you can only create a duotone from a grayscale image. (If you've got a color image, see "The Color of Grayscale" in Chapter 15, *Essential Image Techniques.)*

Because you're typically replacing a single gray level with two or more tints of ink, you almost always need to adjust the amounts of ink used by each channel. Otherwise, the image appears too dark and muddy (see Figure 11-7). For instance, if you replace a 50-percent black pixel with 50-percent black and 50-percent purple, it appears much darker. Instead, replacing that 50-percent black with something like 30-percent black and 25-percent purple maintains the tone of that pixel. On the other hand, if the second color were much lighter, like yellow, you'd need much more ink to maintain the tone. You might, for example, use 35-percent black and 55-percent yellow.

The duotone curves give you the ability to make these sorts of tonal adjustments quickly and with a minimum of image degradation because

Figure 11-6
Duotone curves

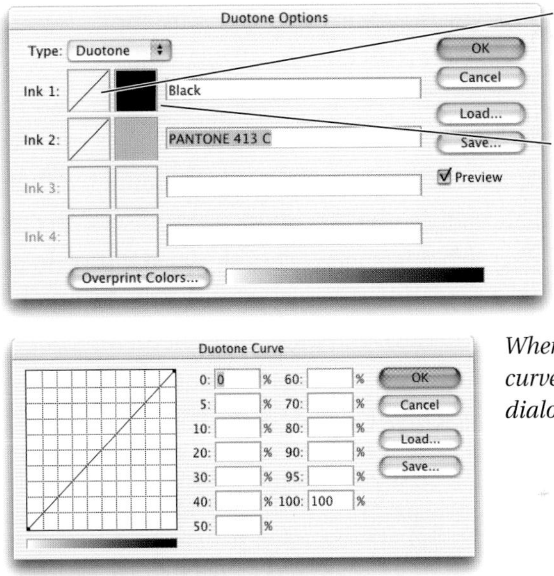

Click here to change the curve.

Click here to change the color.

When you click on the curve, you get this dialog box.

Figure 11-7 Adjusting multitone curves

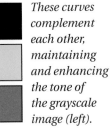

The three inks are way too heavy, darkening the image considerably and obscuring shadow detail (far left).

These curves complement each other, maintaining and enhancing the tone of the grayscale image (left).

applying a duotone curve *never* affects the underlying grayscale image data. You can make 40 changes to the duotone colors or the curves and never lose the underlying image quality.

Note that we say the "underlying image quality" won't suffer. We're not saying that you can go hog-wild with the curves, and your final image will always look good. Far from it. In fact, duotones, tritones, and quadtones are often very sensitive and can quickly succumb to "lookus badus maximus." But the image data saved on disk is unchanged by adjusting these curves; they're like filters that are applied to the image data, but only when you view it on screen or print it out.

Tip: Use Stephen's Curves. Unless you really know what you're doing, just use the duotone curve sets built by photographer Stephen Johnson that ship with Photoshop. We almost never create a multitone image from scratch. Instead, we click the Load button in the Duotone dialog box, navigate to the Duotones folder (inside the Presets folder in the Adobe Photoshop folder), and pick one from there. Then we make small tweaks to the curves, depending on the image.

Most of the curves come in sets of four.

▶ The first and second colorize the image (the first does so more than the second).

▶ The third curve of the set affects the midtones and three-quarter tones primarily, and does very little to the highlights. The effect is to warm or cool the image significantly without colorizing it much.

▶ The final duotone curve makes the image slightly warmer or cooler (still mostly neutral), primarily affecting the three-quarter tones.

If we're using a Pantone color that's not included in the canned presets, we usually pick a canned set for a color that has similar brightness to the one we're using, and replace the color with ours. Then, depending on the two colors' tones, we adjust the curves accordingly.

Tip: Checking Each Duotone Channel. The biggest hassle with images in Duotone mode is that you can't see each channel by itself. If you make a tonal adjustment to an RGB or CMYK image, you can always go and see what that did to each channel. With a duotone, however, you're in the dark. Here's one way out: Convert the image to Multichannel mode.

While you're in Multichannel mode, you can view each channel of the multitone image. The first channel corresponds to the first ink, the second to the second ink, and so on. When you're done playing voyeur, select Undo (Command-Z), and you're back where you started.

Adjusting Screen Colors

No one is more aware than Adobe that colors on screen may not match colors on paper. Adobe tech support gets calls all the time from people screaming that they followed the manual's directions, but their images are always different from what they see on the screen.

Calibrating your system and adjusting your monitor is one way to get results that more closely match your display. But the Color Settings dialog box is really only designed to handle process-color printing and RGB monitors. Duotones, on the other hand, are often printed with spot-color inks such as Pantone or Toyo.

Fortunately, Photoshop not only lets you pick custom spot colors in the Color Picker (click the Custom button), it also lets you adjust how they appear on screen. This is crucial for duotone work, where you want your monitor display to be as accurate as possible.

Note that your monitor simply cannot display many spot colors (including metallic and fluorescent inks) accurately, or even closely. If you want to produce metallic duotones, you have to use a great deal of imagination. A custom proof such as DuPont's Cromalin is a good idea, too.

Adjusting Colors

While Photoshop does a reasonably good job of representing spot colors on screen, we find that we occasionally want to make adjustments so that what we see on screen is closer to what we see in our swatch book. Once you've selected a spot color from the Color Picker's Custom dialog box, click the Picker button (see Figure 11-8). You can now adjust the RGB, HSB, or Lab values for that color to make it appear closer to your printed swatch.

If you use a spectrophotometer, such as X-Rite's Digital Swatchbook, you can read the Lab values directly from your printed swatch and type those into the Picker's Lab fields. However, if your screen isn't calibrated, then this representation may look even worse than Photoshop's.

Don't adjust the color's CMYK values, however. As soon as you change one value here, Photoshop assumes you want to adhere to the process-color gamut (not necessary for spot colors). For instance, if you adjust the color of a rich blue such as PMS 2738, making even a one-percent change to the CMYK values makes Photoshop snap the color to a pale imitation of the blue. (It's in gamut, but who cares? This is for screen representation only; the real color will appear only when ink hits paper.)

Then, if you switch back to the Custom Color dialog box, Photoshop finds the closest match to this new, blah color: PMS 653. Again, it's just for on-screen display, but we're trying to get as close as we can.

Figure 11-8 The Color Picker and Custom Color dialog boxes

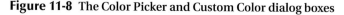

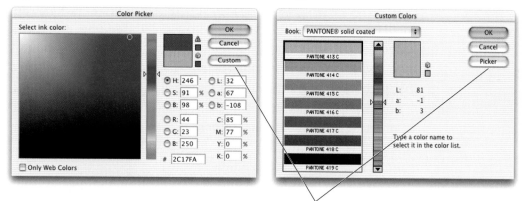

You can toggle between these two dialog boxes by clicking here.

Overprint Colors

Once you've told Photoshop how you want each of your colors to display individually in the multitone, you need to tell it how you want the colors to look when printed on top of each other. Duotones are easy, because most duotones are printed with black and another color. Overprinting these two colors results in a darker, richer black, but it's black nonetheless. Unfortunately, Photoshop won't distinguish between the two blacks.

However, when you add more colors to the image (as in a tritone or a quadtone), or don't use black in the mix, telling Photoshop how to display the overprinted colors becomes significantly more important. To set the overprint color, click the Overprint button in the Duotone dialog box (see Figure 11-9).

Figure 11-9
Setting the
overprint color

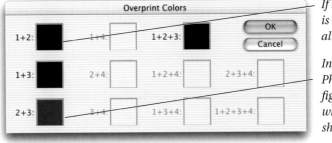

*If the first color
is black, this will
always be black.*

*In a tritone,
Photoshop
figures out
what this color
should be.*

The basic advice for the Overprint dialog box is to leave it alone unless you have a printed sample of what the overprinted colors *should* look like, or you're really certain that Photoshop has built it wrong.

On the other hand, with some cajoling (and perhaps a pint of Häagen-Dazs sorbet or, for really big favors, Laphroiag), you can often get your printer to "draw down" a sample of the two colors overprinting. Place that under a 5,000-degree Kelvin light, and adjust away. Or, if you're using Pantone inks, you may want to purchase the Pantone Tint Effects Color Suite, which shows various tint builds of Pantone inks, including 100-percent overprints (which is the relevant swatch here).

Changing the overprint colors has no effect on your printed output. It only affects how the colors appear on screen. It does affect mode changes, however; if you switch from Duotone mode directly to CMYK, RGB, or Lab, the overprint colors are taken into consideration. However, this conversion would be a silly thing to do unless you're printing to a color printer (see "Printing Proofs of Spot-Color Images," later in this chapter).

Setting Curves

Once you've specified the colors you want in your multitone image and adjusted the tonal range of the grayscale image, it's time to start adjusting your multitone curves. If you followed our advice in "Tip: Use Stephen's Curves," you may have already loaded a curve set that's somewhat appropriate for your image. However, we'd like to emphasize that every image (and every spot-color ink) is different, so your curves probably need some kind of tweaking. Whether or not you go through the trouble is up to you, but here are some things to think about if you want to give it a go.

Expanding Highlights and Shadows

There are two ways in which you can expand your tonal range with multi-tones: focusing inks and using ink tones.

Focusing inks. You can focus an ink plate on a particular area of the tonal scale by increasing the contrast in that area. Let's say you want to increase the detail in the shadows. From Chapter 6, *Tonal Correction Fundamentals*, you know that you need to increase the slope of the tonal curve in the shadow areas. However, that means you have to decrease the slope (and therefore the contrast) in the highlights, so you lose detail there.

With one ink, that could be an unacceptable trade-off. But with two or more inks, you can use one to focus on the shadows—increasing the contrast there and bringing out detail—and use another to focus on the highlight detail (see Figure 11-10). When the page comes off press, you have greater detail in both areas. This is one methodology behind double-black duotones (where you print with black ink twice).

Tip: Save and Load Curves. As we said earlier, it's a hassle not being able to see how each "channel" of the image changes as you adjust its curve. This is especially frustrating to new users who have a difficult time picturing what the curves are doing without the visual feedback. Whether you're a beginner or a seasoned pro, you may find this technique useful.

1. Duplicate the image. (Remember that if you hold down the Option key while selecting Duplicate from the Image menu, Photoshop won't bother you with a superfluous dialog box.)

2. If the duplicate image isn't already in Grayscale mode, select Grayscale from the Mode menu. This simply throws away the duotone curves. It doesn't affect the image data.

3. Use Curves (Command-M) to create the curve you're trying to achieve for the duotone ink. You can use Preview or any of the other curve tricks we talk about in Chapter 6, *Tonal Correction Fundamentals*. You cannot, however, use arbitrary maps (curves made with the Pencil tool). Duotones don't understand those at all.

4. Save the curve to disk, then click OK or Cancel in the Curves dialog box. (It doesn't matter at this point; we usually cancel to save time.)

Figure 11-10 Focusing inks on different tonal ranges

Grayscale

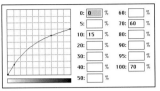

Cyan plate. Steep in the highlights, emphasizing
detail at the top of the
ripples.

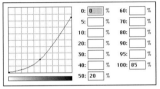

Magenta plate. Provides
warmth, particularly in
the shadows.

Tritone

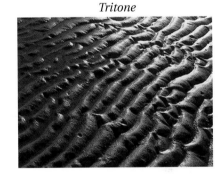

Black plate. S-curve brings
out detail in the quartertones
and shadows.

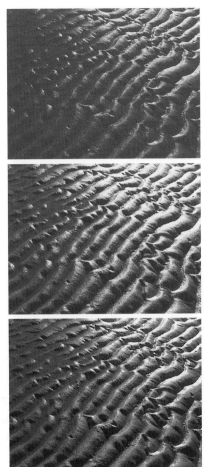

5. Switch back to the duotone image, open the Duotone dialog box (by
   selecting Duotone from the Mode menu again), and load the curve
   you've made into the ink's Curves dialog box.

   If the curve you've made isn't quite right, you can always adjust it in the
   duotone image; or if you want to get visual about it, go back and load the
   curve into the grayscale image's Curves dialog box again.

Ink tones. The second method of expanding your image's tonal range, ink
tones, is almost always performed in conjunction with the first method,
focusing inks. As we said earlier in the chapter, by printing with a gray

Curves Is Curves

If you're wondering about the difference between Duotone curves and regular curves (and transfer curves), the answer is: There's hardly any difference at all. It's mostly a matter of when the corrections are applied to the image.

When you use the Curves dialog box, the image data is affected immediately; you're actually changing the image. Curves also lets you use arbitrary maps (a fancy way of saying that you can draw a line with the Pencil tool).

Curves that you create in Duotone mode, on the other hand, don't get applied until you print the image. In fact, Photoshop just saves the grayscale image plus the curves. When you print, each curve is sent down along with the image data in the form of a transfer function. So you can always go back and change the curves without degrading the image.

Duotone curves have their pros and cons, though. You can't preview how a single channel changes as you move the curve; you can't even see how the mix of curves and inks looks on your image until you click OK in the Duotone dialog box. On the other hand, the Duotone Curves dialog box has an excellent feature: You can type in values instead of simply clicking on the curve. This is especially handy when it comes to targeting by compressing the tonal range.

Because a curve is a curve, you can save a curve from one dialog box and load it into another (see "Save the Curves" in Chapter 6, *Tonal Correction Fundamentals*). But you can't load curves with arbitrary maps into the Duotone or Transfer dialog box.

ink along with black you immediately expand the tonal range, because a tint of gray is lighter than a tint of black; plus, gray printed over black is darker than black alone. Therefore, you can affect the tone of your image by picking appropriate second, third, and fourth colors.

For instance, printing with two dark colors may make less sense than printing with a dark and a light color. If you're printing with three colors, you may want to use black plus a lighter gray (to extend the highlights) plus a darker color (to enrich the shadows).

Creating the Curves

To ensure tonal consistency throughout the image, you need to think carefully about adjusting curves for each ink, depending on their relative tones. For example, let's say you're printing with black plus a PMS ink, Warm Gray 6 (which we can't show you, since we only have process inks to work with).

▶ The black is going to make up the skeleton of the image, with a lot of contrast in the shadows. To do this, we pull the black entirely out of the extreme highlights by setting the 5-percent field to zero. Then we compress the tonal range of the image slightly by setting the 100-percent black to 94 (that way, no pixels become totally black). Finally, to add even more contrast, we pull the 70-percent value down to 45.

▶ The warm gray will be the flesh of the image, holding the contrast in the midtones, and especially focusing on the highlights. To do this, we're going to boost the contrast in the highlights by raising the curve from 5 percent up to 9 percent. Next, we'll lower the 100-percent mark to 90 percent, so that the shadows don't get too dark when both inks print on top of each other. Finally, the curve in the highlights and midtones is steep, but we want it even steeper, so we'll raise the 50-percent mark to 75 percent.

While these adjustments flatten out the contrast in the shadows, we don't care, because the details there are handled by the black ink.

Note that this example is only that—an example. Change the ink, and you had better change the curve. Change one curve, and you had better change the other. Most of all, the curves you make and use must be dependent on the image you have, the data that makes up the image, and what you want to do with that data. Again, every image is different; so you should tailor the curves to bring out the detail where you want it most. (Fortunately, you can preview your duotone image as you adjust its colors and curves with the dialog box still open, making it easier to get it right the first time.)

The Info Palette

When we work on multitone images, we like to set up the Info palette so that the First Color Readout is Actual Color. This way, we can always see how much ink is being laid down in an area (see Figure 11-11). Then we set the Second Color Readout to Grayscale, which tells us what the original underlying grayscale data is. Finally, we set the Mouse Coordinates in the Info palette to Pixels (so that we can easily refer back to the same pixel coordinate if we need to).

Figure 11-11
The Info palette
for duotones

The Info palette shows how much ink is in each channel.

Tip: Make Gray Wedges Match. One of the most complicated challenges of creating multitone curves is maintaining the overall tone of the image while attempting to expand its tonal range. One method we use while adjusting multitone curves is to work with a gray wedge.

1. Create a new grayscale document as wide as your duotone image and perhaps an inch or so tall.

2. Turn off the Dither checkbox in the Options bar, then fill this document with a gradient from black to white.

3. Select Posterize from the Adjust submenu under the Image menu, and type "21" in the Posterize dialog box. Press Return.

4. You've now created a 21-step gray wedge, ranging from 0 to 100 percent in 5-percent increments.

5. In the original image (the one that's going to be turned into a duotone), increase the height dimension of the image by a little more than the height of the gray wedge (select Canvas Size from the Image menu, click in the bottom-middle square, then increase the number of pixels in the Height field).

6. Back in the gray-wedge document, Select All (Command-A) and copy the gray wedge into the duotone-to-be by dragging the selection from one document to the other, and then place it in the blank area above the image (see Figure 11-12).

Now, as you make adjustments to the duotone curves, you can watch for two important things. (Ordinarily we'd say, "Watch the Info palette." However, we haven't been able to extract information that's relevant to comparing images. Let us know if you know something we don't!)

▶ Watch the gray wedge in the duotone image to see if some gray levels are blending into their neighbors. This way you can quickly see when the highlights, midtones, or shadows are losing definition.

▶ If you align the two document windows (the duotone image gray wedge and the grayscale gray wedge), you can compare their tones. For instance, if the duotone gray wedge is significantly lighter than the grayscale gray wedge, you know that you probably need to bump one or more of the duotone curves.

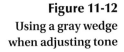

Figure 11-12
Using a gray wedge
when adjusting tone

*By comparing the two
gray wedges, you can get a
feel for how the shades in
your multitone are being
affected by the curves.*

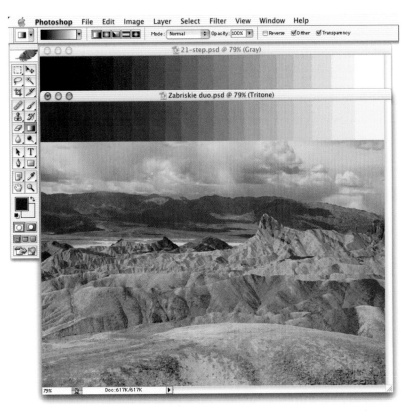

Again, the goal of making a duotone is most often to maintain the overall tonality, so the two gray wedges should be approximately the same in tone (even if one is colorized and the other is not). However, sometimes your goal is to alter the tone—perhaps to make the highlights lighter or darker. In those cases, the grayscale wedge is still useful as a benchmark.

Unthinkable Curves

In the preceding example, we created two curves that we would *never* ordinarily apply to an image, because they can result in severe posterization in some areas and lack of contrast in others. We can get away with these unthinkable curves, however, because the posterization and lack of detail are masked, in part, by the overprinting of the two inks. But these curves are still timid compared to some you might want to create.

For instance, you may want to lay down a heavy solid swath of a light-gray ink under almost the entire image, in order to boost the feeling of depth, or to colorize the image slightly (see Figure 11-13).

Or you may want to hit only a certain highlight area with an ink. In this case, it may be tempting to make the curve return to zero so that this ink won't fall into the shadows. Instead, we suggest you level off the curve so that the ink enriches the midtones and shadows as well (see Figure 11-14). That way, you get extra benefit from the ink, and avoid the hue shift caused when one ink is totally absent from part of the tonal range.

Figure 11-13 **Boosting depth by adding gray**

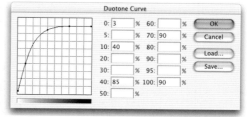

This curve can add depth to, or colorize, the entire image. (Of course, this strange-looking plate would be printed with a light color under black, so it wouldn't look so harsh.)

Original image   *After the curve is applied*

Figure 11-14 **Adding ink in the highlights**

It's usually better to extend an ink through the tonal range (top and left), rather than restricting it (bottom and right).

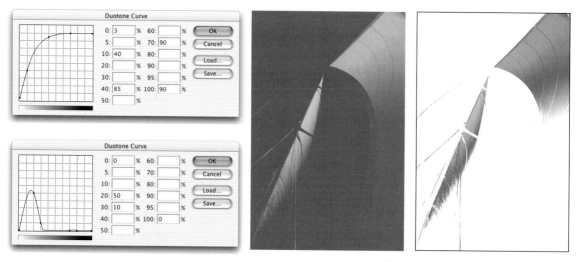

Compressing Tones for Targeting

There's no doubt that printing presses have difficulty printing extreme highlights or shadows—the tiny halftone spots disappear to white, and the white areas in the shadows fill in, resulting in solid ink. This is the reason we're so adamant about compressing the tonal range of your images so that all the gray values and details appear in a range that can successfully print on press (see "White Points and Black Points and Grays, Oh My!" in Chapter 6, *Tonal Correction Fundamentals*).

Nonetheless, one of the goals of multitone images is to expand the tonal range and recapture some of that highlight and shadow detail lost in the horrors of the printing process. If you compress the image data significantly before you start adjusting duotone curves, you've simply lost your chance to bring out those details.

We suggest avoiding the targeting step during tonal correction, and instead using the duotone curves to compress the data (see Figure 11-15 and Figure 11-16).

Turning Grayscale to Color

We've been exploring how to create multitones using the Duotone mode. But just because you want a multitone doesn't mean that you need to use the Duotone mode to get it. In fact, you can often get just as good results by manipulating the grayscale image in either the Multichannel mode or the CMYK mode. There are, however, pros and cons to each technique.

▶ **File size.** An image in Duotone mode, whatever the number of inks, is saved as an 8-bit grayscale image along with curves. CMYK images, then, are four times the size, because each pixel is described with 32 bits of information, even if you're using only two channels. Similarly, a two-channel multichannel file is twice as large as a duotone.

▶ **Single-color areas.** In Duotone mode, there's almost no way to create a single area in which only one color is present. For example, it's a pain to make a 20-percent blue square in the middle of an image, without black also printing in it. However, this is easy to do in any other mode.

▶ **Blends.** There's also no way to create a gradient blend between two spot colors while in Duotone mode. In CMYK mode, it's easy.

Figure 11-15
Examples of curves for
compressing data

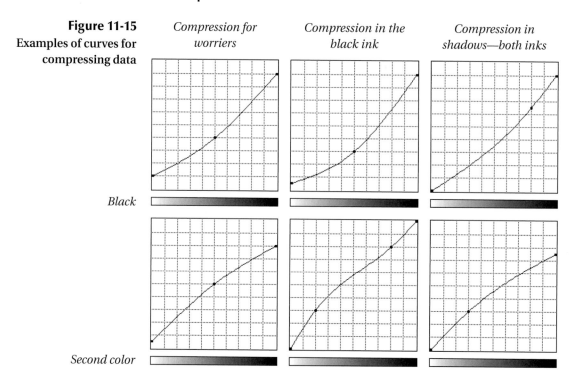

Compression for worriers

Compression in the black ink

Compression in shadows—both inks

Black

Second color

► **Outputting images.** When you output a multitone image, the mode it's in may have an impact on your output process. For instance, you cannot transfer an image in Duotone mode to a high-end imaging system (like Scitex). Also, because duotone images must be saved in an EPS format (see "Saving and Outputting," later in this chapter), you cannot take advantage of any tricks your page-layout software may be able to do with TIFF images (see Chapter 16, *Storing Images*).

► **Adjusting tone.** In Duotone mode, you can always change the duotone curves without affecting the underlying grayscale image data. That means you can quickly repurpose the image to a number of different output devices. Or, if your art director decides to print with green instead of yellow ink, you can quickly change the tonal curve to adjust for the difference in ink density.

On the other hand, if you're creating multitones in CMYK mode, you may be changing the image data in each channel, so you want to minimize the number of adjustments you make to avoid image degradation (or use adjustment layers). Working in CMYK mode, however, gives you the chance to actually see (interactively) how your curves are affecting the image data. And you can use features like the white-and-black-

Figure 11-16 Creating curves for duotone and tritone images
By focusing inks on different tonal ranges, you can colorize a grayscale image, and emphasize otherwise-hidden details. The tables show the values entered in the Duotone Curves dialog box.

Cool neutral, details held with black

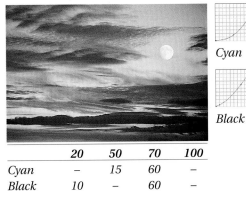

Cyan

Black

	20	50	70	100
Cyan	–	15	60	–
Black	10	–	60	–

Cyan and yellow in the midtones, black elsewhere

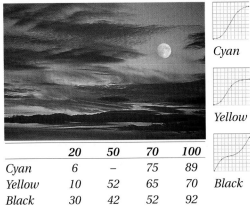

Cyan

Yellow

Black

	20	50	70	100
Cyan	6	–	75	89
Yellow	10	52	65	70
Black	30	42	52	92

Magenta and yellow carry the highlights.

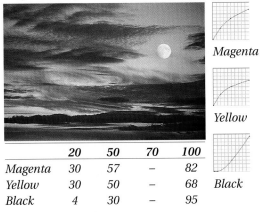

Magenta

Yellow

Black

	20	50	70	100
Magenta	30	57	–	82
Yellow	30	50	–	68
Black	4	30	–	95

Cyan holds highlights, magenta holds shadows.

Cyan

Magenta

	20	50	70	100
Cyan	36	67	–	–
Magenta	–	33	–	90

Magenta and yellow emphasize the shadows.

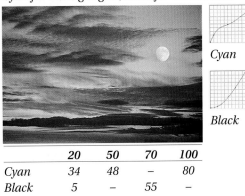

Magenta

Yellow

Black

	20	50	70	100
Magenta	5	15	–	85
Yellow	4	15	35	85
Black	15	40	–	95

Cyan for the highlights, black for the shadows

Cyan

Black

	20	50	70	100
Cyan	34	48	–	80
Black	5	–	55	–

point clipping display in Levels to make decisions about your curves. This can be very helpful, especially when making small tweaks to the curves (see Figure 11-17).

▶ **Screen representation.** Photoshop knows how to represent most spot colors reasonably well on screen when you're in Duotone mode. However, if you're creating spot-color multitones rather than process-color multitones in CMYK mode, you'll either have to ignore the colors you see on the screen (which are RGB representations of CMYK colors) or look ahead in the chapter to "Simulating Spot Colors in CMYK."

Converting Grayscale Images to Color

Because a multitone image typically represents a grayscale image using color, you generally begin with a grayscale image. (If you've got a color image, see "The Color of Grayscale" in Chapter 15, *Essential Image Techniques*, for more on how to convert it to grayscale.) In this section we're discussing using CMYK to create duotones, so you'll want to switch your image from Grayscale mode to CMYK mode. You can use two methods—simple conversion, or copying into a new file.

Simple conversion. You can simply switch your image from grayscale to CMYK using the Mode menu. However, many people seem to think that this simply adds three new channels (cyan, magenta, and yellow), and leaves all the grayscale information in the black channel. Not so. Photoshop uses the color settings preferences (see Chapter 5, *Color Settings*) to convert the neutral grays into colors. The amount of black generation (based on the profile or Custom CMYK setting you've selected in Color Settings for CMYK) determines what appears in the Black channel.

You can use Custom CMYK as an equivalent to creating a quadtone using the Duotone dialog box. We rarely use this method; it's clunky and nigh-on impossible to make adjustments to each plate after the conversion. Plus, Photoshop's separation curves are not designed to expand the tonal range of a grayscale image, so you're losing the opportunity to enhance your image.

Nonetheless, if you *do* use this method, we strongly suggest you set Black Generation to Heavy in the Custom CMYK dialog box first. That way, the black channel contains more information, and small anomalies on press won't result in large color shifts.

Figure 11-17 Grayscale reproduction with the four process inks

The grayscale image

Cyan plate

Yellow plate

Magenta plate

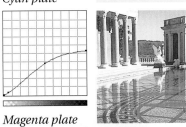 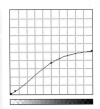

Black plate

Printed using the four process inks

The multichannel step. A second, more reasonable, way to convert your grayscale image into CMYK form is to convert the file to a Multichannel document first.

1.   Duplicate your image (select Duplicate from the Image menu).

2.   Select Multichannel from the Mode submenu (under the Image menu). Notice that the Grayscale channel in the Channels palette has changed to "Black."

3.   Duplicate the Black channel three times by dragging it on top of the New Channel button in the Channels palette. You should end up with four identical channels.

4.   Finally, select CMYK from the Mode submenu. Photoshop assigns each channel to one of the colors (the first channel becomes cyan, the second channel is magenta, and so on).

Now it's time to start adjusting curves for each of the channels. This is a tricky proposition because, as we pointed out back in Chapter 6, *Tonal Correction Fundamentals*, you typically don't want to make tonal adjustments to a channel more than once or twice. You can work around this by using a Curves adjustment layer to tune the curves, and then flattening the image when the curves are the way you want them (see Figure 11-18).

Simulating Spot Colors in CMYK

If you've decided to create or adjust your multitone in CMYK mode, you'll likely want to see a reasonable representation of the image on your screen. If the image is a process-color multitone, this isn't a problem at all. But if you're using one or more spot colors, Photoshop balks at the proposal—it thinks only in cyan, magenta, yellow, and black.

Fortunately, you can change Photoshop's thinking by creating a custom profile with your own definitions of CMYK, by choosing Custom CMYK from the CMYK working space menu in the Color Settings dialog box. As we discussed back in Chapter 5, *Color Settings*, Photoshop knows what color inks you're using by the ink set you've chosen from the Ink Colors menu in the Custom CMYK dialog box.

Here's how you can change these values to simulate spot colors and get a reasonably good on-screen representation of your image.

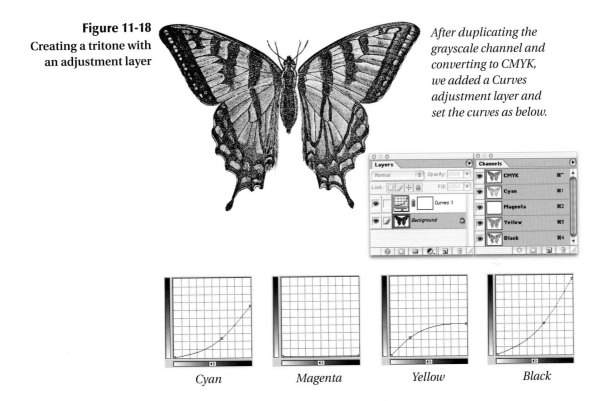

Figure 11-18
Creating a tritone with
an adjustment layer

After duplicating the grayscale channel and converting to CMYK, we added a Curves adjustment layer and set the curves as below.

Cyan   Magenta   Yellow   Black

1. Find the Lab values for the inks you'll be printing with. (If you've already picked a Pantone or other spot color in the Duotone dialog box, click on the color swatch there. If you haven't picked one yet, you can find one by opening the Color Picker, clicking Custom, then clicking the Picker button to go back to the Color Picker.)

2. Note the Lab values for the color. (Yes, you have to write them down.)

3. Open Color Settings (Command-Shift-K) and choose Custom CMYK from the CMYK working space popup menu. Next, choose Custom from the Ink Colors popup menu (see Figure 11-19).

4. Click on the cyan color swatch and type in the Lab values for the spot color you chose. (If you have precise Lab or xyY values from a spectrophotometer, you can skip clicking on the color swatch and simply turn on the Lab Coordinates checkbox.) We suggest turning on the Estimate Overprints checkbox so you don't have to specify values for C+Y, C+M, and so on; this won't guarantee that the screen color will be any better,

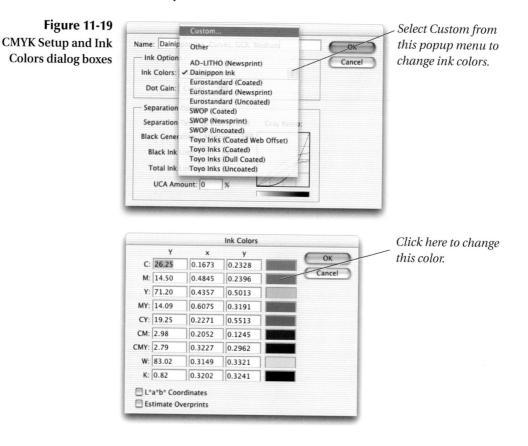

Figure 11-19
CMYK Setup and Ink
Colors dialog boxes

*Select Custom from
this popup menu to
change ink colors.*

*Click here to change
this color.*

but other than using a spectrophotometer on an ink drawdown, it's about as good as it's going to get.

Click OK to save the ink settings (or, if your image is a tritone or quadtone, change those inks first), then click OK again to close the Custom CMYK dialog box. If you want to save your custom settings as an ICC profile, see "Tip: Creating ICC Profiles from Custom CMYK Settings" in Chapter 5, *Color Settings*.

Photoshop now thinks of cyan as the spot color. However, if your image already has an embedded profile, you'll have to select Assign Profile (from the Mode submenu under the Image menu) and choose either "Don't Color Manage This Document" or the CMYK working space you just built. When you save this CMYK working space, your multitone images should appear correctly—more or less—on the screen.

Note that making changes in Color Settings has no effect on CMYK image data. *It has a radical effect,* however, on any image that you convert *to* CMYK mode, and on the way Photoshop displays CMYK images.

Therefore, we strongly suggest you give the custom profile a name that clearly indicates that it's for use with a non-standard ink set, and switch back to a standard SWOP ink set (or whatever you usually use) whenever you're not working on your spot-color image.

Saving and Outputting

While we explore printing and saving from Photoshop in depth in Chapter 16, *Storing Images,* and Chapter 17, *Output Methods,* multitones have some specific requirements that we can better discuss in the privacy of this chapter. The two most relevant issues in getting a duotone out of Photoshop and onto paper or film are saving and screen angles.

The file format that you use when saving a multitone document depends entirely on the mode the image is in: Duotone or CMYK.

Duotone mode. You can save Duotone-mode images in four formats—Photoshop, EPS, PDF, and Raw. QuarkXPress users may use only the EPS file format; InDesign users can use EPS files, native PSD files, or PDF files (only InDesign CS or later).

To make the duotone separate properly from the page-layout program, however, you have to make sure that the color names in the duotone exactly match the names in your page-layout program's color list. For instance, if you used "Pantone 286 CVC" in your duotone, you should also have a color named "Pantone 286 CVC" in QuarkXPress, Adobe PageMaker, or InDesign. Fortunately, if you haven't defined the color name when you import the multitone, the latest versions of these programs add the name to the color list automatically on import.

CMYK mode. If you've created your multitone image in CMYK mode, you have a choice, just as with any other CMYK image, to save in either EPS or TIFF (or PDF or whatever other file format you normally use). However, if you need to specify particular halftone screen angles in your duotone—and you often do—you have to use EPS (TIFFs don't let you save that sort of information). Plus, if you've built custom ink colors, you may have to save as EPS in order to see the proper preview in your page-layout program. (If the program is smart enough to read and interpret an embedded ICC profile, TIFF files may work properly.)

Converting from Duotone to CMYK Mode

While we wouldn't do this with most multitone images, we have occasionally found it helpful to convert our files from Duotone mode to either CMYK or Multichannel mode to take advantage of capabilities like solid color tints, blends, grayscale representations of each plate, and output benefits (see "Turning Grayscale to Color," earlier in this chapter). Of course the trade-off is that the file's size becomes much larger.

As in the conversion from Grayscale to CMYK mode, there are two methods for converting from Duotone mode to CMYK. The easiest method is simply to select CMYK from the Mode menu. Unfortunately, it's also the least useful, unless your art director just told you that you can only use process colors and have to do away with all spot colors. You're out of luck, however, if you want to change any of the multitone curves further.

If you're planning on converting the image in order to make further adjustments to it (add areas of solid color, and so on), it's much better to convert the image to Multichannel mode first. When you convert to Multichannel mode, Photoshop gives you two, three, or four spot color channels (depending on the number of inks you're using), each with the proper curve automatically applied to the original grayscale image. You can save multichannel images as DCS 2.0 files (see "DCS" in Chapter 16, *Storing Images*).

You can also convert your file from Multichannel mode to CMYK mode, with two changes.

▶ If there are only two or three channels (if the image is a duotone or a tritone), add channels until you have four. We suggest naming them (double-click on the channel tile in the Channels palette) so you know which is which.

▶ Make sure the channels are in the correct order in the Channels palette. When you convert to CMYK mode, the first channel tile in the palette is always read as the cyan plate, the second as magenta, and so on. However, when you convert a quadtone into Multichannel mode, Photoshop makes black the first tile in the list. You have to drag it into its correct place, or the image will turn out incorrectly.

This, by the way, is how you can convert a duotone image into a CMYK format that Scitex (and other CMYK-only systems) can read and use. Of course, unless you've changed the definitions of cyan, yellow, magenta, and black, the image may look very different than when it was in Duotone or Multichannel mode.

The most important thing to remember when creating duotones, tritones, or quadtones in CMYK mode is this: If you're not intending to use process-color inks, be very careful at separation time. If you import a CMYK image into a page-layout program and print color separations, the cyan channel ends up on the cyan plate, the yellow channel ends up on the yellow plate, and so on. This is what you'd expect and want if you were using process-color inks in your image; but if you're using spot-color inks (as in the earlier section, "Simulating Spot Colors in CMYK"), this could be a disaster.

Screen Angles

Every topic in digital imaging must have at least one controversy. One of the controversies surrounding duotones is what screen angles you should use when printing them. People fall into two camps: those who favor 30 degrees between inks, and those who favor 45. We are in the latter camp—45 degrees between the halftone screens results in the least obvious patterns. (You always get *some* patterning when you overlap screens; the trick is to minimize it.) The angles you pick, however, may vary.

We typically print black ink at 45 degrees because people tend to "blur out" this angle the most (important for a dark color). But that leaves only zero degrees for the second ink. If that ink is very light, like yellow or a light gray, you can print it at zero degrees. With a darker color like burnt sienna, cyan, or dark gray, however, a zero-degree screen may appear too obvious. Our second choice is printing the inks at 30 and 75 degrees.

With these screen combinations, be aware that the RIP might think it knows better and substitute "optimized" process-color angles. Ask your service bureau to turn off Balanced Screens, HQS, or whatever halftone substitution algorithms it may use.

The more traditional among us usually print with 30-degree offsets. We suspect there may be an element of superstition in this, but many people who've built more duotones than we've had hot dinners use angles 30 degrees apart. However, when pressed, most confess that they do so because that's what they were taught to do.

Conventional wisdom puts the strong color at 45 degrees and the weak one at 75 degrees. But this can have the effect of making one screen more obvious than the other, so in many cases, angles of 15 and 75 degrees are used instead.

In a tritone image, of course, we always revert to the second opinion: 30-degree offsets, usually using 15, 45, and 75 degrees (with 45 used for the ink/curve combination that is dominant—that has the greatest density). Finally, for quadtones, we use the four standard process-color angles: 0, 15, 45, and 75. (Note that many people state these angles as 45, 90, 105, and 165; they're the same thing, but three of them are rotated 90 degrees.) The lightest ink is always printed at zero degrees.

Printing Order

In order for the inks to match their proper halftone screen angles automatically, arrange them from darkest to lightest in the Duotone dialog box (bearing in mind the curves you've set up for each ink; a dark ink with a very light curve may not be terribly dominant on press).

If you want to specify angles manually, however, you can use the Screens button in the Print with Preview dialog box (see Figure 11-20 and "Imaging from Photoshop" in Chapter 17, *Output Methods*).

You usually can't do much about the order in which the inks are laid down, though, even though it may significantly affect the image. Discuss the topic with your printer, and rely on their experience with inks.

Figure 11-20
Setting screens
for duotones

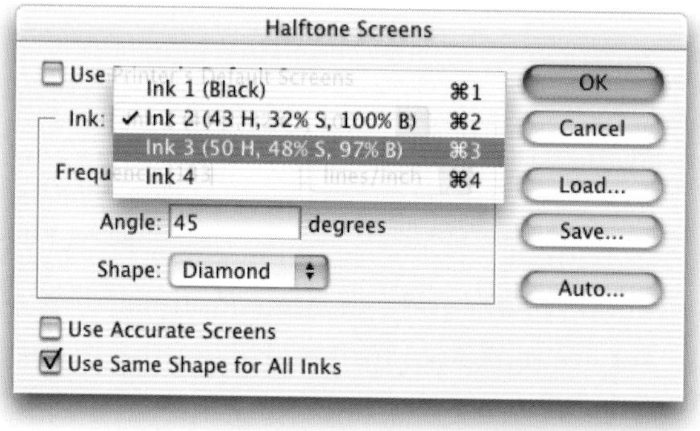

Printing Proofs of Spot-Color Images

Seeing spot colors on screen is one thing. Proofing them on paper is quite another. You really have only two choices when trying to proof your multitone images: custom inks and converting to process colors.

Custom inks. Some service bureaus provide proofing systems that attempt to match Pantone and other spot colors. For instance, the Cromalin system lets you build proofs using Pantone's spot colors (Matchprints cannot do this, by the way). This is certainly an expensive proposition, but it's the closest approximation you can get this side of a press check.

For this type of proofing, it doesn't matter whether you've used Duotone or CMYK mode to create your multitones, or what type of inks you'll finally be printing with. You're dumping a piece of black film for each ink color; the color (spot or process) appears only when the proofs are made.

Process colors. An alternative is to print proofs on a color printer with CMYK colorants. Most spot inks just can't be reproduced faithfully with

CMYK, but with skill, luck, and a good dose of experience, you can get something meaningful out of these devices.

There are two ways to print a multitone image on a color printer.

▶ **Just print it.** If your image is in Duotone mode and you select Print from the File menu, Photoshop sends the grayscale image to the printer along with four transfer curves (one for each process color). Grayscale printers discard the transfer curves and just print the grayscale image. Color printers render the image as best they can.

The big problem with this approach is that Photoshop assumes that your multitone colors are spot colors—even if they're specced as process colors—so it pushes them through its color engine (see Chapter 5, *Color Settings*). This is more or less the same as converting to CMYK mode yourself and printing. If you have assigned the correct profiles and your system is well calibrated, there's a fair chance you'll get a nice-looking image. Otherwise, your image may look bizarre.

▶ **Convert to RGB.** A second method of printing multitone images is to convert them to RGB mode first (whether they're in Duotone or CMYK mode), and then tell Photoshop to send the RGB data to the printer (select RGB in the Print dialog box). Most desktop inkjet printers prefer to get RGB data like this, and as long as you apply the proper printer profile in the Print dialog box (see Chapter 17, *Output Methods*), the image will probably come out okay. Remember though, that the inkjet is still just simulating your spot colors with its own inks.

Note that no matter which method you use, the color you see from a color printer is almost certainly going to be different from your final image, and no sane printer would take something like this as a contract proof. But it may be helpful in the process of creating good curves.

Tip: Be There During the Print Run. Stephen Johnson has made more duotones than anyone we know, and he maintains that even after printing hundreds of multitone images, he still doesn't know *exactly* what he's going to get until he shows up for the press run. Take his advice. If you're doing critical duotones, *be there* during the press run—the way the press operator controls the inks can make or break the final printed piece.

Billions of Shades of Gray

If the real world would simply perform as all the theories tell us, grayscale images would fly off the printing press with deep, rich tones and an incredible dynamic range, and CMYK images would simulate every color in the rainbow. But the real world doesn't pay much attention to theories, so we need to help the process along. Spot colors—whether in the form of bump plates, solid spot areas, or duotones—are great ways to do this. After all, if you're trying to faithfully reproduce an elephant, you want to listen to (or see) as many different perspectives as you can.

12 Line Art

Dreaming in Black and White

With all the frenzy on the Photoshop scene that surrounds cool effects like fractalization, motion blurs, and drop shadows, it's easy to lose sight of the basics. And there are few scanned images more basic than line art.

Line art—those black-and-white images (or *bitmap images*, in Photoshop terminology) with no halftoning, dithering, or anything else—are as simple as can be. Each pixel is either on or off, black or white, and you aren't concerned with levels of gray or halftones. Scanning, manipulating, and printing these things should be easy. And it is—at least compared to the vagaries that surround grayscale and color images.

Nonetheless, we've found that most people's line art images don't begin to approach the quality of (even mediocre) photographic reproduction. Edges are jaggy, fine lines break up, and dense patterns clog up. Many of you are going to be surprised when we tell you that it doesn't have to be that way.

With line art, you can actually produce an image that matches the original to an extent that just almost never happens with grayscale and color images. With just a few techniques under your belt, you can achieve that ethereal, Platonic state of perfect line art reproduction, and with very little effort. The tricks lie in scanning mode, resolution, sharpening, and thresholding.

Scanning in Grayscale

It's *essential* that you scan in Grayscale mode to take advantage of the techniques covered in this chapter. If you scan in Bitmap mode (line art or 1-bit), you can't do much of anything to improve your image. In Grayscale mode, however, you can sharpen, adjust the black/white threshold to control line widths, and increase your effective line art resolution; each of these techniques helps create a beautiful reproduction.

So avoid the temptation to scan line art *as* line art, and scan it as grayscale instead. Sure, your files are eight times as large, but it's only temporary. You can convert them to Bitmap mode when you're done with your manipulations. And the quality difference with these techniques is like the difference between... well... black and white.

Resolution

When you're printing to an imagesetter, you need very high image resolution to match the quality of photographically reproduced line art. That means 800 ppi minimum image resolution. You *can* see the difference between 800- and 1,200-ppi line art (see Figure 12-1), so you may want to opt for the higher resolution if your printing method can hold it. On the other hand, if you're printing on newsprint, the spread of the ink as it hits the paper will likely blur any jaggies, so a lower resolution of 800 ppi should be fine.

Of course, you never need image resolution higher than your output resolution. If you're printing your final artwork on a 600-dpi laser printer, for instance, you don't need more than 600-ppi image resolution. The additional data just gets thrown away.

Tip: Scan Big for High Resolution. "Great," you're saying. "They say we need 800-ppi images, but all we've got is a 600-ppi scanner. And they said back in the *Image Essentials* chapter that upsampling is useless. What are we supposed to do with this business card the client gave us?"

You've got two ways to get a higher resolution out of a low-resolution scanner. First, you can scan a large original at your scanner's highest optical resolution and scale it down, increasing resolution. If you reduce the image to 50 percent, for instance, you double the resolution.

You can either scale the image in a page-layout program, or adjust the size in Photoshop's Image Size dialog box while the File Size checkbox is turned on (see Chapter 3, *Image Essentials*).

Figure 12-1 Line art resolution

Grayscale scan

144 ppi

300 ppi

600 ppi

800 ppi

1,200 ppi

If you don't have a larger version of the artwork, you can enlarge your small version on a quality photocopier, and scan that. You still get a higher-quality image because the optical enlargement doesn't cause pixelization (there may be some cleanup work involved after the scan, of course).

The second solution (which you can use in combination with this enlargement/reduction technique) is covered in the next tip.

Tip: Doubling Your Scanner's Line Art Resolution. The second method for going beyond your scanner's resolution essentially "steals" information from an 8-bit grayscale scan, converting that information into higher line art resolution.

1. Scan your artwork as a grayscale image at your scanner's maximum optical resolution (let's use 600 ppi for this example).

2. Double the image resolution (thus quadrupling the file size) using the Image Size dialog box (make sure the Resample Image checkbox is turned on with Bicubic as the resampling method). In our example, you'd upsample to 1,200 ppi. Note that if your scanning software can interpolate up to this same resolution, you can use that as you scan, and save yourself a step.

    If you're yelling, "Hey! You said interpolation was useless," you're right—we did. This is an exception; upsampling here adds pixels where you need them, even though it doesn't add any detail.

3. Sharpen and threshold the image as outlined later in this chapter.

4. Switch to Bitmap mode at the same resolution (1,200 ppi in our example), with the 50% Threshold option selected (see Figure 12-2).

Voilà! A 1,200-ppi line art image from a 600-ppi scanner. While it isn't a true 1,200-ppi scan, it's so close that we dare you to find a difference. You may be able to raise the image's resolution above two times optical resolution, but that's pretty much the point of diminishing returns.

Note that you can use this tip alongside the previous one to res up to 1,800 ppi or higher.

If the arithmetic of scaling and resolution is giving you trouble, you might want to take a look at the tip "Figuring Scaling and Resolution" in Chapter 13, *Capturing Images*.

Figure 12-2
Converting to
Bitmap mode

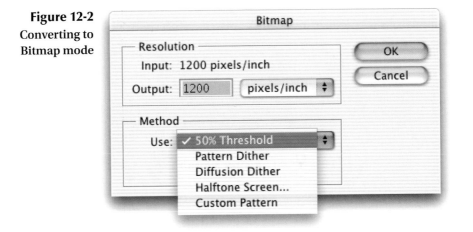

Sharpening

Nothing will do more for the quality of your line art images than sharpening the grayscale scan (see Figure 12-3). 'Nuf said. We recommend running the Unsharp Mask filter twice with the settings 500/1/5. However, if the second USM makes the image look terrible (it often does if you're scanning poorly printed originals), undo it and stick with just one pass of unsharp masking. By the way, if your scanning software can sharpen, you may be able to save yourself a step, though most scanners' drivers don't do as good a job as Photoshop's Unsharp Mask filter.

Thresholding

When you scan line art in Grayscale mode, lines aren't captured as hard lines, but as a collection of pixels with different values (see Figure 12-4). But although you scanned in grayscale, you ultimately want a straight black-and-white image. The way you get there is via the Threshold command (from the Adjust submenu under the Image menu). Threshold turns gray pixels above a certain value to black, and pushes all other pixels to white.

By adjusting the break point in the Threshold dialog box where pixels go to black or white, you can control the widths of lines in your scanned-as-grayscale line art image (see Figure 12-5).

For simple line art images that don't include very detailed and dense shadow areas, just set Threshold to 2 and press Return. With images that do include densely detailed shadows, try values up to about 55. As you move the slider to the left, you can see the fine lines start to break up. As

Figure 12-3
Line art with and
without sharpening

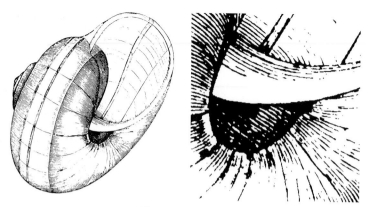

Without sharpening

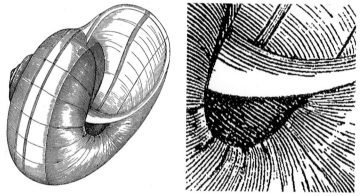

With sharpening

you move right, the shadow areas start to clog. It's a lot like working the trade-off between shadow and highlight detail with the Levels dialog box on a grayscale image.

As we noted earlier, there are no grayscale pixels left in the file after you use Threshold, so you might as well convert the image to Bitmap mode (in the Mode submenu of the Image menu). Bitmap images are one-eighth the size of Grayscale images.

Scanning Prescreened Art

Rescreening—scanning images that have already been halftoned—is one of the toughest quandaries you'll encounter in Photoshop. We cover it in some detail in Chapter 15, *Essential Image Techniques,* but because you're

Figure 12-4
Line art scanned
as grayscale

Scanned as line art   *400%*

Scanned as grayscale   *400%*

Scanned as grayscale with sharpening   *400%*
and thresholding applied

scanning something that is essentially line art (there are no gray values in a printed halftone screen), it's worth a note here, as well.

One way to avoid the screen conflicts (moiré patterns) that you can get by scanning black-and-white halftoned images is to use the line art techniques described in this chapter. In other words, don't try to make Photoshop convert the halftone spots into gray levels; just leave them

Figure 12-5
Threshold
settings for
line art

Threshold: 2

Threshold: 80

Threshold: 185

as halftone spots. This works best with images screened at 85 lpi or less, because you can pick up the detail you need to hold the screen.

However, if you scan a halftone this way (scan as grayscale, use Unsharp Mask, and then use Threshold), you cannot later resize the image in a page-layout program without causing the image to fall apart or create moiré patterns. If your halftone was printed at 100 lpi or higher, it's probably better to convert it into a grayscale image using the techniques in Chapter 15, *Essential Image Techniques.*

Perfect Forms

There are few absolutes in imaging, and it's nice to find something that gets close. Get these line art techniques down pat (or automate them with Photoshop's Actions—see Chapter 15, *Essential Image Techniques*), and you can get great line art every time without hardly trying.

13

Capturing Images

Starting Out Right

Ansel Adams often said that the key to getting a great print was to start with a great negative. Of course, even with great negatives he still did massive amounts of manipulation in the darkroom. It's the same in Photoshop. You may do lots of post-capture tweaking in Photoshop, but if you didn't start with a good image capture in the first place, you're unlikely to get great results from Photoshop.

We have split our discussion of capturing images into two chapters. If you shoot a digital camera using the camera's "raw" format, you may want to skip ahead to Chapter 14, *Building a Digital Workflow*, where we cover the new strategies and tactics made possible by the integration of the Camera Raw plug-in and the File Browser. However, if you shoot film, use a scanner, capture JPEG or TIFF on a digital one-shot camera, or use a three-shot or scanning back digital camera, you need the information in this chapter. And even if you're totally sold on a digital raw workflow, it's probably worth skimming through this chapter before delving into the inner workings of Camera Raw.

What Makes a Good Capture (and Why You Should Care)

If there's a single generalization we're comfortable making about Photoshop work, it's the golden rule of computing: GIGO, or Garbage In, Garbage Out. Photoshop's tools let you make all sorts of corrections to an image after you've opened it, and if push comes to shove, you can sometimes rescue a shot that would otherwise be unusable. But if you start with a good capture, you'll have less work to do, and your final results will be better than if you had to fight the image all the way.

Film Originals

At the risk of pointing out the obvious, the first thing that makes for a good scan is a good original. We've seen scanners blamed for shadow noise when the problem was actually in the print. Flawed originals can sometimes be saved—for instance, if the image has an obvious color cast or is plagued with dust marks and scratches—but only by dint of applying considerable skill and effort.

Tip: Dealing with Scratched Film. Each piece of film has two sides, with different characteristics. The emulsion side (usually the less shiny of the two) is delicate and should never be handled. The base side is more robust. If you have scratches on the emulsion side, about all you can do is to oil-mount the film before scanning—the oil will fill the scratches. Fingerprints on the emulsion are hopeless.

Scratches on the base side can be filled in using either a special compound available from any good photo store, or—a much cheaper alternative—a judicious application with a Q-Tip of some grease from the side of your nose! Fingerprints on the base side can be carefully removed with a Q-Tip and film cleaner. Don't use Windex, 409, or alcohol.

Some scanners feature a nifty technology from Applied Science Fiction called Digital ICE, which does a great job of removing surface defects. It scans using non-visible wavelengths that let the scanner see through the dust, fingerprints, or scratches to what's on the emulsion. It can't help if the scratch runs all the way through the emulsion to the film base—there's no data left to recover—but short of that, it does an amazing job.

Shadow and highlight detail. Look closely at the dark areas in what you're scanning: are they really black, or do they have random speckles of color? Are the highlights blown out? Are the shadows plugged up? None of these problems is easy to correct, and some aren't correctable at all. If you usually get your film processed by Joe's One-Hour Photo and Bait, and you find yourself fighting with the images in Photoshop, you may want to consider using a professional photo lab that monitors its chemistry more carefully.

Lower-contrast originals. In general, most steps in the printing process increase contrast, so it's better to start with an image that's slightly flat than one that's too contrasty. You can boost the contrast of a flat image, but it's harder to decrease contrast without compromising quality.

Digital Camera Captures

If you're capturing images with a digital camera, the scene *is* the original. If you're shooting in the studio, you have a great deal more control over lighting than you do if you're shooting in the field, but in either case, the same principles apply as with scanning. You need to make sure that you're capturing the entire dynamic range, without blowing out highlights or plugging up shadows (though if something has to give, plugged shadows are usually less offensive than blown highlights).

When you shoot JPEG, you need to get everything right in the camera—JPEGs are much like slide film, where over- or underexposure by ⅓ of a stop makes a critical difference. Raw captures, on the other hand, behave more like negative film, with considerably more leeway over post-capture interpretation of exposure and white balance, though correct exposure is still important—see "Camera Raw" in Chapter 14, *Building a Digital Workflow.* In general, raw captures are a great deal more forgiving than JPEG, though they take up much more space on disk and on your camera's storage medium.

The preceding remarks apply to one-shot digital cameras. If you shoot a specialized camera such as a "three-shot" or a scanning back, where the camera captures real data in every color channel for each pixel, there are three key requirements: Gray-balance the camera by shooting a neutral gray card (the ubiquitous Kodak 18-percent gray card is *not* neutral—use something like the 24-patch Macbeth Color Checker instead); set the exposure to make sure that you don't clip highlights or shadows; and if at

Digital Camera Types

The term "digital camera" is really an umbrella that covers several approaches to capturing images. But they all share two common features: they use some kind of lens-and-shutter setup that's recognizable as a camera, and they replace the film plane with some kind of CCD array.

Area array cameras. Area array cameras work more or less like conventional cameras—the image is captured by a flat array that sits behind the lens in the film plane. They can even use flash lighting. But because high-resolution area arrays are expensive, these cameras have lower resolution than scanning backs. Plus, those based on film-camera bodies have another interesting wrinkle.

The array has a smaller area than the film for which the body was designed, so the effective focal length of each lens is increased—a normal lens becomes a telephoto, and a wide-angle lens becomes a normal lens. On most six-mega-pixel cameras, for example, a 28 mm wide-angle lens gives approximately the same field of view as a 50 mm lens on a 35 mm camera. To get true wide-angle coverage, you'd need a (pricey) lens in the 16 mm range!

When it comes to capturing color, area array cameras use one of two approaches: one-shot or three-shot. In the three-shot approach, you make three separate exposures through red, green, and blue filters. You get the full resolution of the CCD,

but you're pretty much limited to static subjects. The one-shot approach is far more common, but it too involves some significant compromises.

One-shot color cameras are often referred to as decal cameras, because the color filters are applied directly onto the CCD elements as decals, so each sensor element is dedicated to capturing a single color. Most one-shot cameras use two green, one red, and one blue element to create each full-color image pixel (in varying arrangements). The captured image is a grayscale file that simply records the amount of light recorded by each element in the array.

Decal camera images need considerable post-processing to

all possible bring the resulting captures into Photoshop as a 16-bits-per-channel image. See the sidebar "Digital Camera Types," for more on the differences between the various technologies labeled "digital camera."

Why Good Captures Are Important

If you're really good at editing images in Photoshop, you can make a bad capture look almost as good as a good capture—at least on easy images with a narrow tonal range and no heavily saturated colors. But doing so can take a long time, and involve a constant battle to avoid posterization, artifacts, and color shifts. With difficult images that are heavily saturated with a wide tonal range, a good capture is indispensable.

High-bit files certainly offer a great deal more editing headroom than do 8-bit-per-channel ones (see "The high-bit advantage," later in this turn the captured grayscale image into RGB. The conversion software interpolates the missing colors for each pixel from its neighbors. One of the great advantages to shooting raw format over JPEG is that you get to control the processing of this grayscale image into RGB, so you have a great deal of latitude in interpreting the white balance and exposure, as well as being able to control the combination of sharpening and smoothing that the interpolation process invariably entails.

A new type of area array, the X3 sensor developed by Foveon, has at time of this writing been embodied by only one vendor, Sigma, in commercially-available cameras. The X3 sensor captures true red, green, and blue infor-

mation for every pixel by using three photosensitive layers in the array, exploiting the fact that longer waves penetrate deeper into the sensor. The top layer detects red, green, and blue, the middle layer detects red and green, and the bottom layer detects only red. By using some sophisticated post-processing, the X3 sensor can provide real RGB information for each pixel. Acceptance of these cameras has almost certainly been slowed by Sigma's proprietary lens mount, but we believe technology has great potential for combining the flexibility of the one-shot decal with the superior quality of the three-shot array.

Linear array cameras. To avoid the problems inherent in decal

cameras, very high-resolution digital cameras generally use linear arrays and a stepper motor that moves the array across the image area. These setups are often called "scanning backs" because they're just like flatbed scanners stuck on the back of a camera.

Scanning backs offer much higher resolutions and wider dynamic range than area array cameras, so you can produce much bigger images and capture a broader tonal range. They're also free of the artifacts that plague the decal approach. The disadvantage is that they require exposure times measured in minutes, which limits their use to static subjects, and prohibits the use of flash or strobe lighting. For more information, see *www.sjphoto.com*.

chapter), but even they have their limits. And while we've been known to use every trick in the book (or at least every trick in *this* book), a good capture simply means less handwork in Photoshop, and hence greater productivity, which in this book is the name of the game.

Getting a Good Scan

You have three primary concerns when you're capturing images: tone, color balance, and resolution. A good capture contains detail (with little noise) in both the highlights and shadows, captures both pastels and saturated colors, and, preferably, contains clean neutrals that are free of obvious color casts. It also contains the right number of pixels for reproduction at the desired size. Without proper resolution, you either lose details in your image or slow down your workflow with files bloated with data you don't need.

Resolution

When you're scanning, you first need to make sure that you're capturing the right number of pixels. If you're unsure of what this is, see "How Much Is Enough?" in Chapter 3, *Image Essentials*. Note that even if you only need a 200- or 266-ppi image, you may want to scan higher than that. Then, later, you can downsample the image to the resolution you need using Photoshop's Image Size dialog box.

Scanning and downsampling. With CCD scanners, we always scan at either the scanner's optical (not interpolated) resolution (see the sidebar "Scanner Resolution") or an integral divisor of that resolution. Then we downsample in Photoshop as necessary. In other words, on a 1600-ppi scanner we may scan at 400 or 200 ppi (the optical resolution divided by four or eight), but not at 250. Then we downsample using Photoshop's Bicubic interpolation to the resolution we actually need.

We have to admit that there are elements of superstition and simplification in this two-step process. We haven't tested how every scanner on the market downsamples from its maximum resolution, but from what we've seen, Photoshop often does a better job than most of them. If you're in a real hurry, and you want to save yourself the extra step of downsampling in Photoshop, try scanning at the resolution you need.

Or test for yourself. Compare the results you get by scanning the same image at full optical resolution, then downsampling in Photoshop, to those you get by scanning at a lower resolution to begin with. If you find that your scanner downsamples just as well as Photoshop, by all means save yourself some time and use its capabilities. If you're using a drum scanner, just scan to the required resolution—drum scanners always scan at the requested resolution, whereas CCD scanners scan at optical resolution, then resample.

If you're shooting digital, you probably don't have much choice over resolution (and often, you're fighting to capture enough pixels). The exceptions to this rule are high-end scanning-back cameras such as the BetterLight and PhaseOne. In terms of resolution, these types of camera behave somewhat more like a drum scanner than a CCD device (specifically, they scan to the requested resolution in the scan element's direction

Scanner Resolution

Scanner resolution is probably the most misunderstood of all scanner specifications, and the lion's share of the blame for this goes to flatbed scanner vendors. Drum scanner resolutions are usually stated unambiguously—most are around 2700 ppi (over res 100; see "Terms of Resolution" in Chapter 3, *Image Essentials*). The same holds true for desktop film scanners, though the resolutions are higher—the Imacon Flextight 848, and the older Nikon LS3510AF and Leafscan 35 and 45 all boast resolutions over 5000 ppi (res 200).

Flatbed resolution. Flatbed scanners are a different story. Two factors determine the optical resolution of a flatbed. The resolution across the bed is determined by the number of elements in the CCD array—typically 600 or 1200 per inch,

although some low-end flatbeds now claim 1600 or even 3200 per inch. The resolution along the bed is determined by the increments in which the stepper motor moves the scanning head.

Stepper motors are cheap and CCD arrays are relatively expensive, and it's easy to produce a scanner that steps in $\frac{1}{2400}$-inch increments. But if the CCD array is only 1200 ppi, it's really a 1200-ppi scanner.

Interpolated resolution. Most flatbeds also offer interpolated resolution. Interpolated resolution is useful for smoothing curves in line art, but it's essentially useless for continuous-tone image scanning. If a flatbed scanner's specs mention more than one number for resolution, the real resolution is always the lowest one. Interpolation only adds pixels—not information. You could

interpolate image resolution up to a million ppi (with your scanning software, with Photoshop, or whatever), and not improve image quality a whit. But while high-resolution scanners that interpolate in only one direction (1200 × 2400 ppi, for example) may not give you as clean a scan as a true 2400-ppi scanner, if you're very careful with sharpening, you may not see the difference in print.

Dual resolution. A few flatbed scanners, such as the Agfa DuoScan, use two sets of lenses to provide two different optical resolutions. The lower resolution covers the entire image area, but you can switch to a higher resolution with a reduced image area to scan transparencies or small reflective originals. However, as higher-resolution CCD arrays are now commonplace, this approach has largely been abandoned.

of travel, and they scan to optical resolution and downsample in the dimension parallel to the scan element). With a scanning back, if you don't need the full resolution, by all means shoot to the required resolution, leaving a little extra for potential cropping and resizing.

Tip: Figuring Scaling and Resolution. The arithmetic of resolution and scaling is always hard to wrap your brain around. Here's a fast way to use Photoshop as a calculator to figure out the numbers, given that you know the final size of the image on the page. (You can get it from PageMaker's Control palette, InDesign's Transform palette, or QuarkXPress's Measurements palette: draw a box where the image goes, and read out the height and width numbers.)

1. Choose New from the File menu, and enter the dimensions and resolution of the image you want. If it's a grayscale or line art image, choose Grayscale from the Mode popup menu. Otherwise, choose RGB.

2. Note the pixel dimensions and file size, then click Cancel to leave the dialog box.

3. Back in your scanning software, select the area you want to scan, then adjust the resolution setting until the resulting pixel dimensions are close to the numbers you got in step two. When they match, you know you've got the right scan size. If your scanner software doesn't report pixel dimensions, you can try to match the file size instead (it's just a little less accurate).

4. Scan the image, manipulate it as necessary in Photoshop, place it on the page, and scale it to fit.

Tip: Lose the Noise. You can often reduce the noise from a CCD scanner considerably by scanning at the scanner's maximum optical resolution, then downsampling to the resolution you need.

This works particularly well if you scan at 200 percent or more of the required resolution, because the noise tends to show up as single pixels. When you downsample, each pixel in the downsampled image is created from four pixels in the original scan, and those four pixels are averaged into one, so the noise is reduced significantly.

Tip: Don't Bother Upsampling Scans. We never scan at a low resolution and sample up in Photoshop (except when we're creating line art; see "Tip: Doubling Your Scanner's Line Art Resolution" in Chapter 12, *Line Art*). Photoshop can interpolate pixels, but it can't add detail through interpolation that wasn't there before you resized it. The result? The resized image usually ends up looking soft or blurry.

Tip: Do Upsample Digital Captures. Digital camera captures respond very differently to upsampling than do scans from film, and you can often get away with upsampling digital camera captures to a surprising degree. We don't pretend to fully understand why this works, but here are two possible factors.

First, digital captures are grainless, unlike film scans. When you scan film, you don't usually resolve the grain unless you're scanning at extremely high resolutions. Instead, you get an interference pattern between the grain of the film and the scanner's sampling grid. With a digital capture, there's no grain, so no interference pattern. Second, with a digital capture, you have at least one fewer set of optics involved than you do with film scans. Whatever the case, we find that we can generally upsample digital captures to at least 200 percent with a single-shot camera, and up to 400 percent with a three-shot camera, and still get very acceptable results.

Tone and Color—Defining Your Goals

In the process of reproducing an image, you need to make two sets of tonal and color corrections.

▶ **Image correction.** This fixes defects in the original and distortions in the image-capture process.

▶ **Image optimization.** This compensates for the output process, and in the case of CMYK output processes, also involves an RGB-to-CMYK conversion.

How and when you make these corrections depend on the capabilities of your image-capture hardware and software, and on your workflow. We discuss this distinction throughout Chapters 6 and 7, *Tonal Correction Fundamentals* and *Color Correction Fundamentals*.

With some capture devices, you can correct and optimize the image at the same time—this is standard operating procedure in prepress houses that use drum scanners. The advantage is productivity: you need to do less to the image in Photoshop once it's been captured. The disadvantage is loss of flexibility: you end up with an image purposed for a particular set of output conditions—it contains only the image data needed for that output process.

Obviously, if you don't know the intended output process when you're capturing the image, you can't optimize the image for it during the capture. If you do know the output process, you may be able to realize some significant productivity gains by combining correction and optimization, but desktop scanners generally don't let you do so very easily, and most digital cameras don't let you do so at all.

Optimization is almost invariably a matter of going from a wider range of tone and color to a narrower one. It's easy to do this in Photoshop without introducing posterization or color shifts (see Chapter 6, *Tonal Correction Fundamentals*). So as a rule, we recommend that you simply try to capture as much good image information as you can, and take care of optimizing the image in Photoshop.

Correcting the image is another story. You have two challenges to face, both involving color management (see Chapter 5, *Color Settings*):

▶ Getting the tone and color correct in the scanner's RGB space

▶ Converting from scanner RGB to Photoshop's working RGB

The question boils down to whether you do your corrections in the scanner software or in Photoshop. The decision on where to make your corrections depends on the capabilities of your capture hardware, and on the software that drives it. Specifically, it depends on the capture device's high-bit capabilities, and the supporting software's color management capabilities.

The high-bit advantage. If your capture device grabs more than 8 bits per color internally (and any scanner on the market today that costs more than $49.95 almost certainly does), you want to get the image as close as possible to its desired state while it's still in high-bit form. If you don't, you're just wasting those extra bits (see Figure 13-1).

A 12-bit scanner, for instance, uses 4,096 levels internally for each color. When you use the scanner's controls, you're performing tonal correction on this high-bit data. Rather than stretching and squeezing eight bits of data, you're choosing which 256 out of the possible 4,096 gray levels will appear in the final output. You can set the tone of the image the way you want it and still have a full 256 gray levels. If you make those same adjustments after scanning instead, operating with eight bits of data, you lose tonal information and end up with substantially fewer than 256 shades of gray.

If your scanner or digital camera can deliver a high-bit file to Photoshop, it doesn't matter, from a quality standpoint, whether you make your corrections in the scanner software, or on the high-bit file in Photoshop. The two are functionally equivalent. Your decision on where to make cor-

Figure 13-1
Using the
extra bits

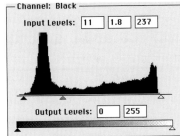
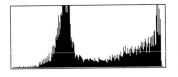

If you apply this kind of big tonal move to an 8-bit scan, you lose a lot of data (see the depopulated histogram below) and create an image that's harder to work with.

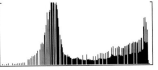

With tonal correction of a high-bit image, you can make big moves and still end up with a full 256 gray levels in the 8-bit file—making further corrections much easier.

rections depends on the driver software's support for image correction and color management, or its lack thereof.

A few capture devices use a high bit depth internally, but can only deliver 8 bits per channel to Photoshop. In those cases, make your basic global edits in the capture software before bringing the file into Photoshop.

Eight-bit capture devices. Almost every scanner being sold today captures at least 10 bits per channel, and 12 is typical. However, some scanners let you pass that high-bit data on to Photoshop and some don't. If your scanner only captures 8 bits internally, or can't save the high-bit data, the first thing to do is to find the "sweet spot," making sure that you capture the best 8 bits the scanner can deliver.

Sometimes, this is just a matter of leaving the software at its default settings, but often it's not. The only way to be sure is through trial and error. With scanners, you can simply tweak the controls. If you're working with an 8-bit digital camera (or shooting JPEG), you also have lighting and exposure to take into consideration, but the same principles apply.

1. Try capturing a range of representative images that have real blacks, real whites, and a good range of tones in between. (If you have access to a gray-step wedge, or to a color target such as the Macbeth Color Checker, the IT8 or Kodak's Q60, use it instead.)

2. Start with the scanner's defaults, and look at the histogram of the resulting scan. Check to see if the scanner is clipping the highlights or shadows (see "The Histogram Palette" in Chapter 6, *Tonal Correction*

Dynamic Range and Bit Depth

A scanner's dynamic range is the range of densities it can see, and the maximum density—or dMax—is the deepest shadow into which it can see. For example, if a scanner has a dynamic range of 3.0 and a dMax of 3.2, then the deepest shadow it can see has an optical density (O.D.) of 3.2. But if you set the black point to capture shadow detail going down to the dMax of 3.2, you'll blow out any highlights lighter than 0.2, because the scanner's total density range is only 3.0.

If you're scanning transparencies, dynamic range is crucial because of the large density range transparencies capture. It's less important when scanning reflective art and color neg, because those media have a much lower dynamic range.

While dMax is important, the value printed in the manuals should be read with a grain of salt, at least with CCD scanners. Scanners work by shining a bright light on or through artwork, and reading how much light gets bounced back (for reflective art) or comes through the film (for transparencies). In the shadow areas, very little light does either, and the CCD has a difficult time seeing the differences between one very dark area and another.

The dMax that vendors quote is typically the point at which the noise inherent in the CCD overwhelms the relatively weak signal produced in the dark areas of the image. Usually you'll see significant amounts of noise in the shadows that are quite a bit lighter than the dMax.

Scanner specs sometimes claim that a higher bit depth gives more dynamic range, but the two are unrelated—dynamic range is an analog limitation of the sensor. But a wider dynamic range needs more bits to describe it adequately, producing smooth tonal gradations.

Very high-contrast prints may have a dynamic range approaching 2.4, although 1.4–1.8 is more typical. Negative film generally has a dynamic range of 2.4 or so, while slide film may approach 3.4 or even 3.6. (Note that if film has a dynamic range of 3.6, it's implicit that the dMax is 3.6, too; dMin, on the other hand, is film plus fog.) But no one has developed a spec that measures how accurately a scanner records all the shades between black and white.

Fundamentals). If it's doing one or the other, reduce or increase the brightness and try again. If it's clipping both, try reducing the contrast in the scanning software.

3. If the image has real blacks and whites, but the scan isn't covering the full tonal range, you might try increasing the contrast. Once you've found settings that work, save them, and use them for all your scans.

Note that these settings may not produce very good-looking images. That doesn't matter—you're just trying to get as much good information (as wide a tonal range) as possible to tweak in Photoshop.

Although you want to capture the entire tonal range of the image without clipping the shadows or blowing out the highlights, sometimes you may find that your scanner or camera can't do this. In that case, you'll have to decide whether you want to sacrifice highlight detail or shadow detail.

The image content is the final arbiter, but when in doubt, remember that blown-out highlights usually look worse than plugged shadows.

With an 8-bit digital camera, your options are limited unless you're shooting in a studio under controlled lighting. In the studio, you can make sure that you're capturing the entire tonal range. If you're shooting outdoors with an 8-bit camera, what you get is what you get, and you simply have to make the best of it in Photoshop.

Color management support. The second problem is in making sure that Photoshop interprets correctly the color that your scanner produces. Many desktop scanners and digital cameras produce uncalibrated "random" RGB. (While a growing number claim that they capture in sRGB, this may or may not actually be the case.)

Some desktop scanners offer varying degrees of support for color management, and a few, including the Heidelberg scanners that use NewColor, the Nikon LS-4000, and the Imacon Flextight scanners, actually allow you to scan into a profiled color space, such as your RGB working space. Similarly, a growing number of digital cameras let you shoot JPEG as Adobe RGB (though some of them promptly misidentify it as sRGB).

Tip: Why Does My Camera Suddenly Produce sRGB? If your digital camera images have suddenly started showing up in Photoshop with an sRGB color profile (see Chapter 5, *Color Settings*), the camera software is probably setting a flag in the EXIF data that claims the camera is producing sRGB (see Chapter 16, *Storing Images,* for more on EXIF). This flag is just an on-off switch—it either says sRGB or Uncalibrated RGB—and in our experience it's not terribly reliable. Early versions of Photoshop ignored it, but Photoshop 7 and CS honor it. Fortunately, a few cameras will embed an ICC profile for the camera, in which case Photoshop uses that profile in preference to the EXIF tag.

There are really only two choices. You can attempt to use color management to make Photoshop understand your scanner or camera RGB, or you can simply bring the image into Photoshop as untagged RGB and correct it there. In the latter case, a high-bit file is vastly preferable to an 8-bit-per-channel one.

Some scanners have implemented color management support by scanning to monitor RGB. This isn't ideal because the monitor gamut clips colors that are attainable on most output devices. In these cases, your best bet is to make sure you aren't clipping highlights or shadows, and make your corrections in Photoshop, ideally on a high-bit file. Many scanners and digital cameras, though, still don't allow capture to a profiled space, and don't use Photoshop's display mechanism to display the image. We've developed several strategies for dealing with this.

Capture Strategies

Your choices will depend on the capabilities of your scanner or camera and its accompanying software, and on your workflow requirements. It's important to make your major edits on the high-bit data. If your capture device lets you export high-bit data to Photoshop, you can do your major corrections either in the capture software or in Photoshop. If it only outputs 8-bit data, you need to do the major corrections in the capture software.

Raw high-bit capture. This approach applies to scanners, three-shot cameras, and scanning back cameras—for one-shot digital cameras, "raw" means something else, which we cover in detail in Chapter 14, *Building a Digital Workflow*. In this approach, you make all your corrections in Photoshop. You turn off all corrections in the capture software, and simply bring all the bits the device captured into Photoshop. The raw image may look really scary, but as long as the capture device had a sufficiently wide dynamic range to capture the shadows and highlights without clipping, you'll be able to fix it in Photoshop relatively easily. If you've profiled the raw behavior of your capture device (easy with scanners, somewhat more difficult with three-shot and scanning back cameras), you can save yourself some work by assigning the capture profile in Photoshop, then converting to a well-chosen working space for editing (see Figure 13-2).

Figure 13-2
Assigning scanner profile, then converting to the working space

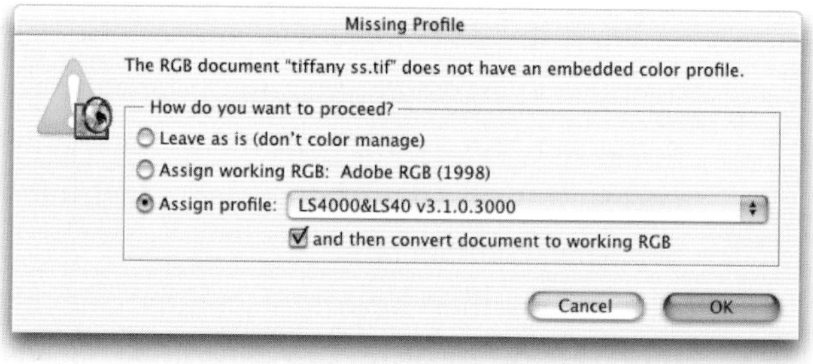

The Missing Profile warning lets you apply your scanner profile and convert to working RGB in a single step.

Almost-raw high-bit capture. If your capture software allows it, there are three useful ways you can modify the raw capture approach to save some work in Photoshop.

▶ **Gamma adjustment.** If your capture device allows you to choose an output gamma (most scanners do, most cameras don't), you can save yourself some heavy lifting by setting it to match the gamma of your Photoshop working space. If you're using Adobe RGB as your working space, you would choose a gamma of 2.2.

▶ **Profile embedding.** If your capture software lets you embed a profile for the capture device, and you have one, by all means embed it. (Note that capture devices driven by Photoshop plug-ins can't embed profiles—the image just appears directly in Photoshop's working space, so you have to assign the profile using Assign Profile, then convert to the working space using Convert to Profile; see Figure 13-3.)

▶ **Convert to working space.** If your capture software lets you export the file to a particular profiled space, you can have the capture software do the conversion from its known profile to the specific profile (like Adobe RGB) during image acquisition. This saves you some time, since the conversion is done as the pixels are being acquired.

Bruce almost always uses high-bit captures, letting the capabilities of the software dictate which of the above approaches he uses. The only

Figure 13-3
Assigning scanner profile, then converting to working space (in two steps)

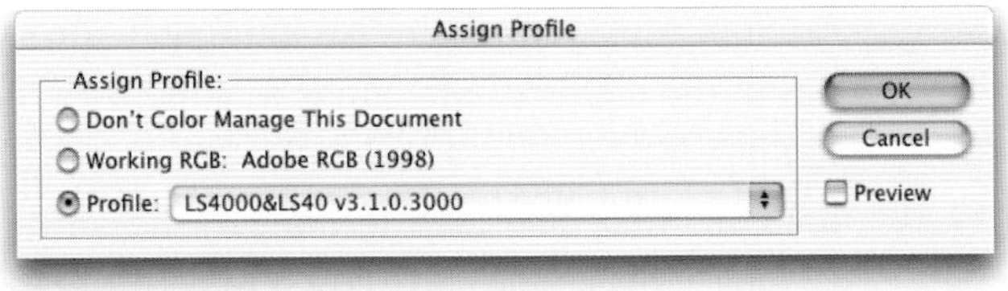

Alternatively, you can first apply the scanner profile using Assign Profile...

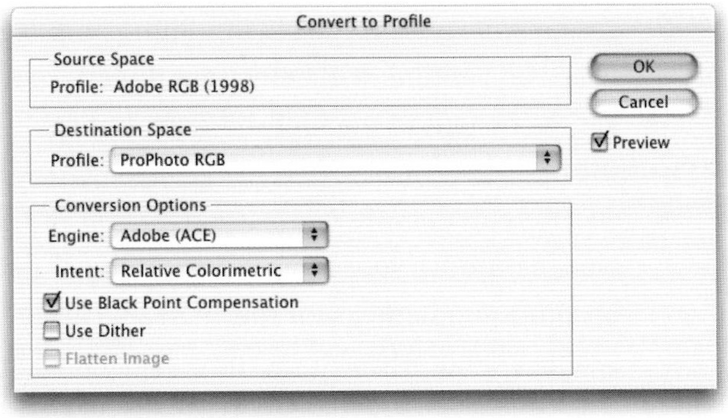

...then convert to working RGB using Convert to Profile.

other adjustment he's likely to make in the capture software is that, with color negatives, he may make a gray-balance correction to get the color approximately correct before bringing it into Photoshop.

Color-managed 8-bit capture. If your 8-bit scanner lets you export images into a profiled space, you can scan directly to a Photoshop working space, making all your major edits for tone and color in the capture software. If your digital camera supports capturing JPEG to more than one space, the choices are almost certainly sRGB and Adobe RGB. Unless you're shooting solely for Web use, we recommend capturing JPEG as Adobe RGB to preserve more of the original captured color.

If color management support is limited to correcting the image for your monitor using your monitor profile, you can make corrections in the scanner software, apply your monitor profile to the image once it's in Photoshop, and then convert it to a working space for further editing. The major downside of this approach is that you limit the gamut of the capture to that of your monitor, which may mean that some colors get clipped, so we recommend it *only* when your capture device uses a high bit depth internally but only outputs 8 bits.

Unmanaged 8-bit capture. If your capture device has no color management support, and doesn't let you capture high-bit files, your options are fairly limited. It may be better to perform all major corrections in Photoshop, where you're working in a calibrated environment, than to work in random capture RGB. In this approach, the only task we advise carrying out in the capture software is making sure that you haven't clipped the highlights or shadows. You do, however, lose all the benefit of any high-bit data that may be used internally by the capture device.

Alternatively, you can make the corrections in the capture software, and assign your monitor profile in Photoshop (since your corrections were based on capture RGB being sent directly to the monitor). That way, you get the benefit of the high-bit data, but again your colors get clipped to the monitor gamut.

If the capture software lets you turn off all auto-corrections, you may be able to improve your images by profiling the capture. The workflow then becomes the same as for raw high-bit captures—you assign the capture profile in Photoshop, then convert to a working space.

Capture profiles. We believe it's not a necessity to create a color management profile for your capture device, but rather a luxury that may be useful in the following two situations.

▶ You can turn off all auto-corrections and get your scanner or camera to deliver raw high-bit RGB.

▶ You have an 8-bit capture device for which you've identified the "sweet spot" settings.

In pretty much all other cases, we believe that profiling a capture device simply isn't worth the trouble for two reasons.

First, if you profile a capture device, you must capture all your images using the same settings you used to create the profile. With some low-end scanners, you can't turn off autoexposure, which effectively makes them impossible to profile. With high-end capture devices, locking everything to a single setting means you're wasting a lot of the device's capabilities, unless you profile the raw high-bit capture.

Second, all a profile can do is to try to reproduce the original as faithfully as possible. Any scanner operator will tell you two things: they're always asked to match the original, and once they've done so, they're always asked to make corrections that make the image more appealing, but less like the original.

If you're using capture software such as LinoColor (or its replacement, NewColor) or LaserSoft's SilverFast, which have profiling capabilities built in, and allow you to scan into any profiled space, by all means use those capabilities. Or, if your scanner supports scanning to a profiled RGB space, you can simply designate your RGB working space as the target profile.

If you're capturing raw high-bit data, profiling the capture can save you a little time in Photoshop, at least on transparency scans and on studio digital captures. With negative scans, creating a profile is pretty much impossible, since the density of the orange mask varies so much with exposure. With field digital captures, we either shoot raw format and acquire the image through the Camera Raw plug-in (see "Camera Raw" in Chapter 14, *Building a Digital Workflow*), or we shoot JPEG in whatever space the camera offers. If the space is unspecified, or simply identified as sRGB by the EXIF tag, we often bring the image into a larger space such as Adobe RGB, and edit the image.

Software Tools

We can't hope to cover every piece of image-acquisition software on the market, but fortunately most of them offer features that are similar to Photoshop's tone- and color-correction tools. We recommend you look at the discussion of those tools in Chapters 6 and 7, *Tonal Correction Fundamentals* and *Color Correction Fundamentals*; the techniques discussed there are equally applicable to scanning.

Six key tools help you get the data you need when you capture images.

▶ Preview

▶ Histograms

▶ On-screen densitometers

▶ Black/white-point settings

▶ Gamma settings

▶ Curve controls

The first three help you evaluate the image, the last three help you fix it. If you're lucky, your image-acquisition software will offer all six, but it's more typical to get two or three out of the six in any given capture software package.

Image-Evaluation Tools

Almost all scanners and most scanning back cameras let you do a quick prescan, a low-resolution capture that you can use to set the cropping rectangle. You can also use it as a basis for tone- and color-balance adjustments. But even with a perfectly-calibrated monitor, there's only so much you can tell from looking at the typical postage-stamp-sized preview.

Instead, you can use two other tools (when available) to evaluate your image before your final scan: the histogram and the densitometer.

Histogram. The histogram is simply a bar chart that shows the number of pixels in the image at each gray level from 0 to 255 (see Figure 13-4). This gives you a quick look at how the information is distributed in the scan. Good capture software lets you see the histogram before and after correction. Photoshop displays a histogram in the Levels dialog box, or when you choose Histogram from the Window menu. In most capture software, the histogram is simply a static display, though a few packages, let you carry out adjustments using something like Photoshop's Levels dialog box.

The histogram is a key tool for evaluating tonal range; it can tell you a lot about your scan at a single glance. A histogram that ends in a "cliff" at the left (shadow) end of the scale indicates a scan where shadow detail is lost. If it ends in a cliff at the right (highlight) end of the scale, you've blown out the highlight detail. A correctly exposed scan produces a histogram with a slope (rather than a cliff) at each end, indicating relatively few pixels at either the darkest value (0) or the lightest value (255).

All this assumes a "normal" image—if you have a picture of a black cat in a coal cellar, or a polar bear in the snow, your histogram will look different; but in each case, you want to try to hold as much detail in both shadows and highlights as possible.

Densitometer. An on-screen densitometer lets you read the value of the pixel under the cursor. Like Photoshop's Info palette, it lets you get a little deeper into analyzing the image, particularly if the tool offers before-and-after readouts. Some scanning software puts the densitometer information on a palette, while others put it in the prescan window itself.

Figure 13-4 Evaluating captures with the histogram

Note that these images have not been through final correction. They represent what comes in from the scanner.

| *An overly dark scan* | *A too-light scan* | *A well-exposed scan* |

Tip: Use the Densitometer to Find Detail. You can use the densitometer to check for detail in the highlight and shadow regions, which can be hard to see on your monitor. Pass the cursor over very bright or very dark areas in the image. If the pixel values change as you move around, there's detail in there, even if you can't see it. As you make gamma moves to brighten the midtones, you emphasize detail in the shadows and suppress it in the highlights. By evaluating the detail with the densitometer, you can play the trade-off between the two.

Image-Adjustment Tools

To capture the tonal range of an image correctly, you have to set the black point and white point properly to avoid plugging up the shadows or blowing out the highlights, and you have to set the gamma to distribute the midtones properly. For a detailed discussion of tonal correction, see Chapter 6, *Tonal Correction Fundamentals*.

Scanning software that comes with 8-bit scanners often limits your adjustments to changing brightness or contrast. But using brightness or contrast is like bungee jumping without a cord—you may live through it, but you'll probably lose something in the process (see the sidebar "The Non-Linear Advantage" in Chapter 6, *Tonal Correction Fundamentals*).

Unfortunately, a few high-bit scanners also limit the controls to brightness and contrast. They're better than nothing, but keep an eye on the histograms for shadow or highlight clipping. Most high-bit scanners offer more sophisticated methods for adjusting the tone and color: black- and white-point settings, gamma settings, and arbitrary curves.

Tip: Make Sure Your Capture Controls Really Work. It's important to determine that the capture device's gamma and/or curves controls are really affecting the high-bit or analog data that the scanner produces, rather than just being applied to 8-bit data as a postscan filter. If they're being applied post-scan, you're better off making the same adjustments in Photoshop after the scan.

How can you tell if your capture software is working on high-bit data? One easy way is to apply a fairly extreme curve or gamma adjustment to a scan—say, a gamma of 2.2 or thereabouts. First, pull an uncorrected capture into Photoshop and make the move using Photoshop's Levels command, then go back and reacquire the image applying the same gamma tweak in the capture software. Compare the histograms of the two images. If the one with the gamma tweak applied during the capture isn't substantially cleaner, with fewer spikes and missing levels, the capture software is almost certainly applying the tweak as a post-process on the 8-bit data. In that case, simply treat the scanner or camera as an 8-bit capture device. (Console yourself with the fact that it's probably at least capturing 8 good bits of data, unlike many 8-bit-only scanners.)

Experimenting in Photoshop is an excellent way to get a feel for how these controls operate. Work in Photoshop with an image captured at default settings. When you've figured out exactly what needs to be done to the scan in Photoshop, try going back to the capture software and reacquire the image using settings that duplicate your Photoshop tweaks as closely as possible. After a while, you'll find that your initial scans are getting much closer to the desired results as you exploit the power of the scanner's controls. But you'll be retaining more image detail than you would if you did the same tonal moves on the 8-bit data in Photoshop.

Setting black and white points. Most high-bit image-capture software offers one or more of the following methods of setting the black point and white point. If in doubt, you're better off leaving the black and white points alone in the capture software, so that you know you're capturing the full dynamic range the device can produce, and setting the gamma, if available, to match your Photoshop working space. Bear in mind that if you're making these critical settings based on a small preview, you're using a pretty blunt instrument, particularly where specular highlights are concerned. If the image has important specular highlights, leave some headroom when you set the white point.

▶ **Autoexposure.** Though they can be a little brain-dead, these features are often a good place to start. They look for the darkest and lightest pixels in the image to set the white and black points.

One problem with these features, particularly with film scanners, is that they're easily fooled by dust or scratches. If the software lets you designate an area of the image to consider when determining the endpoints, you can simply change the area under consideration to avoid the offending spot. If not, you'll have to resort to setting the endpoints manually.

▶ **Black and white input levels.** These work identically to, and usually resemble, the black and white input sliders you find in Photoshop's Levels dialog box. They're almost invariably accompanied by some kind of histogram that lets you see the amount of shadow or highlight clipping taking place.

▶ **Black and white eyedroppers.** Eyedropper tools let you set the black and white points by clicking on specific areas in the image preview. These tools work roughly the same way as do the eyedroppers in Photoshop's Levels and Curves dialog boxes, but they don't always let you choose a target color—they just set the area you clicked to black or white.

   In some cases, if you click a non-neutral pixel in a color image, they'll maintain the color of the pixel while setting its brightness to the maximum or minimum value possible. In other cases, they'll also eliminate the color cast. To use these features effectively, you need an on-screen densitometer. This will also let you determine exactly what the eyedropper is doing.

Gamma controls. Unlike Brightness and Contrast controls, gamma adjustment lets you make large changes to the midtones with (usually) only minimal effects on the shadows and highlights. In Photoshop, you make gamma adjustments using the Levels command (Command-L). The middle (gray) slider in the top bar changes the gamma as you drag it, or you can type a number into the middle field. Many scanner drivers only offer numeric control over gamma—you just type in the gamma value you want. For a full discussion of gamma adjustments and how to use them, see Chapter 6, *Tonal Correction Fundamentals*.

   Almost all scans need a gamma adjustment. Typically, scans come in looking dark. Most scanners have a native gamma of 1.0—the output values are exactly the same as the input values. But neither our eyes nor our monitors have a linear response to changes in brightness. Usually you'll need to scan with a gamma setting somewhere between 1.4 and 2.2. In theory, if you want your on-screen image to match the original, your scanner gamma setting should match that of your RGB working space. But as the EPA says, your mileage may vary. If you're scanning for print, a gamma setting of around 1.8 is a good starting point.

Tip: Determining Optimum Gamma. To figure out what gamma setting on your high-bit scanner will provide an accurate midtone reading, scan a gray target with a known gray value, such as the ubiquitous Kodak 18-percent gray card, which reflects 18 percent of the light striking it. Scan at a variety of gamma settings, and use the one that renders the gray card somewhere around level 100 to 120.

Curves. Curves are by far the most flexible way of controlling both the overall tonal characteristics of the scan and the color balance of the individual channels. Curves appear in various places within scanning software, and often have the same appearance and functionality as the Curves dialog box in Photoshop.

We believe that all high-bit scanners should offer some kind of curves controls. They are essential for correcting color balance while tapping the full capabilities of these scanners. Fortunately, most vendors seem to be coming around to that view. For a full discussion of curve-based adjustments, see Chapters 6 and 7, *Tonal Correction Fundamentals* and *Color Correction Fundamentals*.

Sharpening

Note that even though some scanners and digital cameras allow you to sharpen images on the fly, we almost never do, for two reasons.

▶ Photoshop's Unsharp Mask filter offers far more control than the sharpening in most scanner software.

▶ It's always best to do sharpening after you've made all your tone and color adjustments. This is because sharpening relies on minute adjustments in the contrast of neighboring pixels. If you make tonal adjustments after sharpening, you can wipe out the effect of sharpening or possibly even worse, exaggerate it.

Unless you have a great deal of faith in your scanner's sharpening algorithms and don't plan on doing anything more with the image in Photoshop, we recommend that you simply leave sharpening to Photoshop.

One-shot digital cameras offer a possible exception to this rule. Pretty much all single-shot cameras do a considerable amount of processing to the image, and sharpening is invariably a part of that processing. If you find that using one of the camera's sharpening settings produces good results, by all means use it.

Photo CD

When Photo CD first appeared, it seemed like one of those occasional Kodak aberrations (like the disc camera)—we thought it very unlikely that people would want to view their family snapshots on TV. We were right about the consumer market's indifference to Photo CD, but we came to recognize it as a simple and cost-effective method of acquiring and storing images. Today, we suspect that Photo CD's time has come and gone, but it's still a cost-effective method of digitizing and storing film images, though the availability of inexpensive scanners that can produce similar quality makes it less compelling than it used to be.

Through a highly ingenious compression scheme, Photo CD manages to squeeze about 120 color images, each available at five different resolutions (see Table 13-1), onto a CD-ROM. The exact number of images depends on the content; some images compress more than others.

Don't confuse a Photo CD scan made by a pro lab with Pro Photo CD. While Photo CD is limited to 35 mm format, Pro Photo CD can handle up to 4-by-5-inch transparencies. But the addition of the 64Base resolution reduces the number of images that can fit on the CD (and increases the price per scan).

Bringing Photo CD Images into Photoshop

Photoshop can't simply open Photo CD images, because they're stored in a proprietary color space, called Photo YCC, developed by Kodak. This color space contains only 24 bits of data per pixel, but the data is in a highly compressed form—Kodak claims to encode 12 bits of luminance data plus two 8-bit color channels into the YCC format. To work with Photo CD images in Photoshop, you have to convert them into RGB or Lab.

When you open a Photo CD image, you're always asked to choose a source profile (see Figure 13-5). For the source profile, choose Kodak Photo CD Color Negative V 3.0 for negative scans, either Kodak Photo CD Universal K-14 V 3.2 or Kodak Photo CD 4050 K-14 V 3.4 for scans from Kodachrome, and either Kodak Photo CD Universal E-6 V 3.2 or Kodak Photo CD 4050 E-6 V 3.4 for all other scans from slide film. (The 4050 profiles

	Photo CD resolution	Size in pixels	Size at 225 ppi	File size
Table 13-1	Base/16	192 × 128	.85″ × .57″	72 K
Photo CD resolutions	Base/4	384 × 256	1.7″ × 1.1″	288 K
	Base	768 × 512	3.4″ × 2.3″	1.13 MB
	4Base	1,536 × 1,024	6.8″ × 4.5″	4.5 MB
	16Base	3,072 × 2,048	13.6″ × 9.1″	18 MB
	64Base*	6,144 × 4,096	27.3″ × 18.2″	72 MB

*Pro Photo CD only

are made for Kodak Pro Photo CD, which scans up to 4-by-5 format, but we've found we often get better results using them on regular Photo CD images than we do using the equivalent V 3.2 profiles.)

While the actual file names for the Photo CD profiles are pretty cryptic, there are some subtle mnemonic hints that "pcdnycc" is color neg, "pcdekycc" is E-6, and "pcdkoycc" is Kodachrome. If you don't know the original film type, you can check the Image Info to find out whether the image was scanned from slide or negative film (but you can no longer find out whether it was E6 or Kodachrome slide film—you just have to try both). A few early Photo CDs lacked this information, but just about any Photo CD made in the last seven years should have it.

Photoshop no longer lets you choose a destination profile for Photo CD import. Instead, you now have four choices: 8-bit or 16-bit Lab, and 8-bit or 16-bit RGB. Either of the RGB choices converts the image into

Figure 13-5
Opening a
Photo CD image

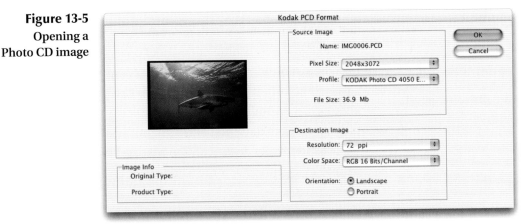

When you open a Photo CD image, you're presented with the dialog box above. You can specify size, source profile, and one of four destinations, as well as getting information about the original film type.

your current RGB working space. We recommend 16-bit if you plan to do significant editing on the image; otherwise the 8-bit option is fine. If you want to adjust the tone with minimal impact on color, use Lab; otherwise you're probably better off with RGB.

From Photons to Pixels

No matter how good a job you do of capturing the image, you'll almost certainly need to massage it some more using Photoshop's own tools. If your scanner has allowed you to capture the image as close as possible to the way you want it, the tweaks you make in Photoshop will be small and subtle, so you'll run far less risk of losing valuable image data, and introducing posterization and artifacts. Plus, you'll preserve the shadow and highlight detail that make the difference between a so-so image and one that leaps off the page and grabs you.

Go back and revisit Chapter 6, *Tonal Correction Fundamentals*, and Chapter 7, *Color Correction Fundamentals*. Given a little ingenuity, almost all the techniques we discuss in those chapters can be applied during the scan itself. You'll get better results, and you'll have less work to do in Photoshop after the scan.

If your scanner is lacking in basic controls or in color management support, as many desktop scanners are, you'll need to do more work in Photoshop. If you treat the scanner as a dumb capture device, you can bring raw high-bit image data into Photoshop's calibrated environment, and use all Photoshop's tools to produce the image you want.

The large variety of different scanner drivers dictates that bringing scans into Photoshop will always entail some complexity. We've long wished for a native Photoshop plug-in that behaved as a universal driver for all scanners. Well, we're unlikely to get it, but now we do have a native Photoshop plug-in, Camera Raw, that acts as a universal driver for digital cameras. This chapter really deals with the past and present. In the next chapter, we look at the image capture workflow of the future.

14

Building a Digital Workflow

Making Quick Work of Raw Images

Digital photography has been around in one form or another for over a decade, but it's only recently that we feel it has truly come of age. Today, the question is not whether, but when digital capture will replace film for the vast majority of uses.

That said, anyone who has made the switch from film to digital can tell you that one major—and usually unanticipated—bottleneck crops up as soon as it's time to choose the "keepers" from a day's shooting. With film, you can pay extra for rush processing, and sort the images on a light table. Digital captures, however, have to be transferred to the computer—and if they're saved in the camera's raw format, they must be converted to RGB images—before you even know what you've captured.

We probably won't win any friends by saying this, but the excellence of most camera vendors' hardware tends be matched equally by the wretchedness of their software. Some photographers despair at the lengthy processing times for raw images, and opt to shoot JPEG instead, sacrificing both quality and flexibility in the interest of getting the work done quickly enough to allow them to have lives. Others rely on third-party conversion tools that complicate the workflow as well as cost extra money.

Recognizing this, the Adobe Photoshop team has delivered a set of powerful solutions in Photoshop CS, from the vastly improved File Browser, to the seamlessly integrated Camera Raw plug-in (which acts as a universal converter for the raw formats from a large and growing variety of cameras). Together, these features provide the essential building blocks for creating a powerful, speedy, and efficient digital workflow right inside Photoshop. But before we get into strategies for this workflow, let's look at what a digital raw capture is.

Digital Raw Formats

Camera Raw appears as a file format in Photoshop's Open dialog box, but it isn't actually a single file format. Rather, it's Photoshop's catch-all name for files that the Camera Raw plug-in can open, including Canon CRW files, Nikon NEF files, and raw files saved as TIFF by various cameras.

A list of officially supported cameras appears on Adobe's Web site, currently at *www.adobe.com/products/photoshop/cameraraw.html*. The URL and the list will likely change during the lifetime of this book, so if you don't find the information there, keep digging. Camera Raw also offers "unofficial" support for many cameras that don't appear on the list, including the Canon 300D, Minolta A1, Olympus E-1, Kodak 720X, 760C, and 14N, and Leaf Valeo 22. "Unofficial support" means that Adobe won't provide tech support and makes no guarantees about the quality of the conversions. We won't make any guarantees either, but we've been happy with the results from the unofficially supported cameras we've tried (in the case of the Canon 300D, downright ecstatic).

What Is a Raw Capture?

As we discussed in the last chapter, one-shot digital cameras use color filters over each sensor in the area array to split the incoming light into its red, green, and blue components. So, each sensor captures only one color, depending on the filter that covers it. The actual capture is essentially a file that records the amount of light recorded by each element in the array.

Considerable processing is required to turn this raw capture into a color image. When your camera is set up to save JPEG files (that's the default for most digital cameras), the conversion is performed by the camera's firmware, using the on-camera settings for white balance, tone, saturation, sharpness, and so on. However, when you tell your camera to save images in its raw format, the processing is deferred until you open the image on the computer using specialized software (like Camera Raw).

Why Shoot Raw?

Shooting raw images is a much more flexible workflow than shooting JPEG. When you shoot raw, the only on-camera settings that affect your capture are the shutter speed, aperture value, and ISO value. All other settings—white balance, tone curve, color space, contrast, saturation—are written into the capture as *metadata*—literally, data about data—that accompanies the raw information. Photoshop's Camera Raw feature may use this metadata as guidance for how to process the capture into an RGB image, but the settings have no effect on the actual capture of the image pixels.

As a result, raw captures allow tremendous flexibility in post-processing, allowing you to reinterpret white balance (and to a considerable extent, exposure) with no degradation to the image. Rather than stretching or squeezing levels, you're simply reinterpreting the way the captured photons get converted into an RGB image.

Raw capture offers other key benefits, too.

► It creates a smaller file on disk than an uncompressed RGB image.

► It allows you to capture a high-bit image from a one-shot camera.

► It allows you to convert the image into RGB spaces other than the ones supported by the camera.

There are several disadvantage to raw, too. Of course, the primary one is the need for processing the images, which takes time. Also, raw files are much larger than JPEG images, so it may take longer to save them to your camera's storage medium (which fills faster, too). However, we've struggled with most of the raw converters out there, and we're convinced that Camera Raw is one of the fastest available—fast enough to make shooting raw worthwhile for all but the most time-critical applications.

Moreover, Camera Raw starts working for you automatically as soon as you point the File Browser at a new folder of raw images, quickly generating thumbnails and previews so you can see the raw images in enough detail to make a quick initial choice between the "hero" shots you plan to keep and the less-successful efforts you plan to discard (or revisit later).

If you want to simply jump in with both feet, take a quick look at Figure 14-1, then get to work. But the combination of the File Browser and Camera Raw really constitutes a mini-application in its own right, so at some point you'll probably want to read the rest of this chapter to get the rest of the juicy details!

The Digital Raw Workflow Quick Start

Figure 14-1 A quick start to a digital raw workflow

Start by copying your raw images to a new folder (we strongly recommend that you never open images directly from the camera storage media). Point the File Browser to the image folder using the File Browser's Folders panel. The File Browser immediately starts generating thumbnails and previews, then it reads the metadata from each image.

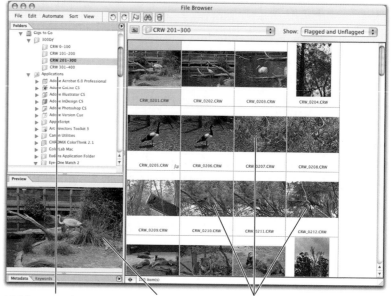

Folders panel   *Preview*   *Thumbnails*

Drag the resizing controls to make the preview area large enough to allow you to see enough detail in your images that you can decide which ones you want to work with.

You can save different File Browser configurations by choosing Save Workspace from the Workspace submenu (under the Window menu). The saved workspaces then appear on the Workspace submenu for easy recall.

Drag to resize

Double-click an image's thumbnail or preview to launch the Camera Raw plug-in, which allows you to control the conversion of the raw file into any of four preset RGB working spaces.

The histogram, preview, and RGB readouts all show the results of the conversion from the raw file to the designated working space.

To apply the settings without opening the image, Option-click on the OK button (it changes to Update). The settings are remembered until you next open the file.

To apply the settings quickly to similar images, choose Apply Camera Raw Settings from the File Browser's Automate menu, then choose Previous Conversion from the Settings menu in the Apply Camera Raw Settings dialog box.

Note that you can apply any or all the settings to the selected images.

The settings get recorded in the image's metadata, and are used when you open the image.

You can now process the images without revisiting the Camera Raw dialog box, either by Shift-double-clicking to open the selected images, or by choosing Batch from the File Browser's Automate menu to process the images automatically using Actions.

Camera Raw

Camera Raw is a fast, full-featured converter for raw digital captures. Originally released as a standalone, $100 plug-in, the new version, Camera Raw 2.0, is built into Photoshop CS. It starts working as soon as you point the file browser at raw images, creating thumbnails and previews, but its real power is in the control and flexibility it offers in converting raw images.

The Camera Raw dialog box opens automatically whenever you open a raw image. It offers two sets of controls, one static set that appears all the time, and another dynamic set that changes depending on which tab is currently selected in the lower-right corner (see Figure 14-2).

The Camera Raw dialog box can drive you to distraction. Not only are there so many settings that it's hard to know where to turn first, but these tools let you achieve so many different results—each great—that it's hard to know when to stop fiddling. We can't help with the latter, but we can describe the options and when you'd want to use them (or not).

Camera Raw Static Controls

The static controls, which are always available in Camera Raw, fall into several groups: the tool palette; the preview controls; the destination controls; the main control buttons; the histogram; the settings menu; and the Camera Raw menu. Let's look at each of these in turn.

Tool palette. Camera Raw's tool palette contains three tools. The Zoom (magnifying glass) and Pan (or Grabber Hand) tools work just like their Photoshop counterparts. They even use the same keyboard shortcuts: press Z or the Command key for the Zoom tool; press H or the spacebar for the Pan tool. The White Balance tool (press I), however, works differently from the white eyedroppers that appear elsewhere in Photoshop.

The White Balance tool lets you set the color temperature by clicking on the image. Unlike the white eyedropper in Levels or Curves, it doesn't allow you to choose a source color, and it doesn't affect the luminance of the image. Instead, it lets you set the white balance—the color temperature and tint—for the capture by clicking on pixels you've determined should be white. It's best used on a white area that still contains detail rather than on a specular highlight—the second-to-lightest gray patch on the old 24-patch Macbeth Color Checker works well. The area you click on isn't pushed to white; it's just made neutral (equal RGB values).

Figure 14-2
Camera Raw
dialog box

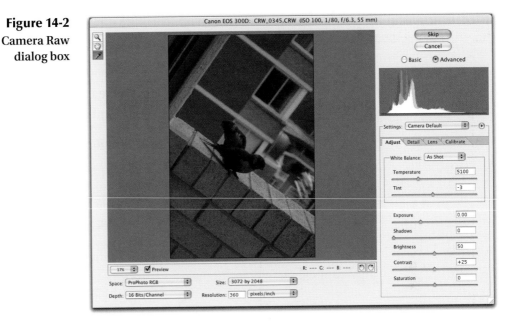

Click-balancing with the White Balance tool provides a very quick way to set color temperature and tint simultaneously. You can always fine-tune the results using the individual Temperature and Tint controls in the Adjust tab, which we cover later in this chapter.

Preview controls. Situated immediately below the image preview, the preview controls are a mishmosh of settings that adjust what you see on screen, provide feedback about the image, and tell Photoshop to rotate the image.

▶ The Zoom Level menu lets you choose a zoom level for the image preview—zoom in to check fine details, zoom out to see the global effects of your adjustments on the image. Of course, you can also use the Zoom tool to zoom in (or, with the Option key, out). Note that Photoshop's View menu is active when the Camera Raw dialog box is open—you can use it (or the associated keyboard shortcuts, like Command-+ and Command--) to adjust the on-screen magnification.

▶ The Preview checkbox toggles between your current settings and those that were in effect when you opened Camera Raw—it provides the same before-and-after functionality as the Preview checkbox in the

Adjustments dialog boxes such as Levels or Curves. Press P to toggle Preview on and off.

▶ The RGB readout is like an RGB "densitometer," displaying the RGB values you'll get when you convert the image at the current settings. If you don't see any values, move the cursor over the image!

▶ The Rotate Left (counterclockwise) and Rotate Right (clockwise) buttons (press L or R) let you rotate the image. Actually, they just rotate the preview, so they're very fast. Photoshop honors this, performing the calculation-intensive rotation when you open the image.

Destination controls. At the bottom of the dialog box, four controls let you set parameters for the converted image.

▶ The Space popup menu lets you choose the destination color space for the conversion. You can choose from four preset working spaces: Adobe RGB, ColorMatch RGB, ProPhoto RGB, or sRGB IEC61966-1 (this is the "standard" flavor of the sRGB "standard"). See the sidebar "Camera Raw and Color" for details on how Camera Raw handles the color management aspect of the conversion.

▶ The Depth popup menu lets you specify whether to convert the raw image to 8-bits-per-channel or 16-bits-per-channel. If you can perform most of your color and tonal correction in this dialog box, then an 8-bit-per-channel image is reasonable. If you're going to be performing significant edits (using Curves, Levels, or whatever), then you should probably import the file in 16-bit mode.

▶ The Size popup menu lets you resample the image on the fly, or open it at the native camera resolution. The sizes displayed here depend on the camera, but they correspond to: the native resolution, downsampled to 66 percent, downsampled to 50 percent, upsampled to 133 percent, upsampled to 166 percent, and upsampled to 200 percent. It makes very little difference whether to resample in the Camera Raw dialog box or in Photoshop. The one possible exception is with cameras that use non-square pixels such as the Nikon D1x and Fuji S2 Pro. Thomas Knoll advises upsampling images from these cameras by one step in Camera Raw when a larger image is needed; we always heed his advice!

▶ The Resolution field lets you specify a resolution for the converted image. Setting the resolution here saves yourself a trip to the Image Size dialog box once the image is converted. Changing this value does not resample your image—it's like setting resolution in the Image Size dialog box while the Resample checkbox is turned off (see Chapter 3, *Image Essentials*).

OK and Cancel buttons. The OK and Cancel buttons both have multiple duties. Simply clicking OK opens the image using the settings specified in the Camera Raw dialog box. Clicking Cancel closes the Camera Raw dialog box, leaving the image unchanged, and no conversion takes place.

However, when you hold down the Shift key, the OK button changes to Skip. There's a subtle difference between Skip and Cancel: If you select multiple images to open with Camera Raw, Cancel aborts the entire process, while Skip simply skips the current image, and loads the next one in the Camera Raw dialog box.

When you hold down the Option key, the OK button changes to Update. Update tells Photoshop to write the dialog box's current settings to the image's metadata without performing the conversion and opening the image. This is helpful when you need to process a bunch of images quickly with similar settings, but you don't need to open them yet. Photoshop applies the settings later, when you do open the files.

The Option key turns the Cancel button into a Reset button. As in other dialog boxes, this resets any changes you've made in Camera Raw without closing the dialog box. Note that you can also perform multiple undos in Camera Raw, stepping back through your changes by pressing Command-Option-Z, and stepping forward with Command-Shift-Z.

Histogram. The Camera Raw dialog box also displays a histogram that reflects your image's red, green, and blue channels—that is, the histogram that will be created by the current conversion settings, *not* the histogram of the raw image. (Raw histogram data would look distinctly strange—as digital cameras capture at linear gamma, all the image data would be scrunched over to the left.) The histogram always appears in color; the white areas are where red, green, and blue pixels overlap equally. See Chapter 6, *Tonal Correction Fundamentals*, for a review of how to read a histogram.

It's important to watch the histogram, as it can tell you if your settings are causing clipping in one or more channels. It also lets you check for clipping caused by colors you've captured that are outside the gamut of your chosen working space (see Figure 14-3). If you find that the chosen working space is clipping some colors, you can select a larger one. (If you choose ProPhoto RGB and you're still seeing clipping, you've captured something other than visible light!)

Figure 14-3
Camera Raw
gamut clipping

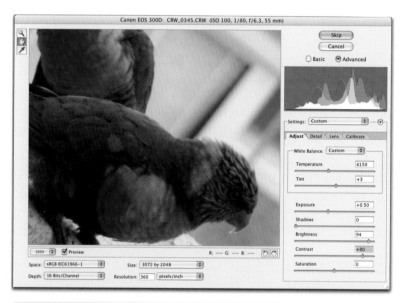

The histogram of the image converted to sRGB shows that the red channel is being clipped.

The histogram of the image converted to ProPhoto RGB shows no clipping.

Settings. The Settings popup menu lets you recall and apply any saved Camera Raw settings. The items that always appear are: Selected Image (like clicking Reset, it reverts to the original settings), Camera Default, and Previous Conversion (whatever settings you used the last time you opened this dialog box). You can also save your own custom settings, which then become available from this popup menu. However, it's easy to overlook the mechanism for saving your settings: the Camera Raw popout menu.

Camera Raw popout menu. Hidden under the small, unlabeled triangle next to the Settings menu is one of the most important controls in this dialog box: the Camera Raw popout menu. This allows you to load, save, and delete settings or subsets of settings, set the default setting for an individual camera, restore Camera Raw's default settings for a Camera, and set up your Camera Raw preferences.

▶ **Save and Load.** The Save Settings command lets you save the setup of this dialog box. If you save settings in the right place (Adobe Photoshop CS/Presets/Camera Raw), they appear in the Settings menu. Otherwise, you can later retrieve your saved settings with the Load Settings command.

▶ **Saving subsets.** In Advanced mode (click the Advanced button), the Save Settings Subset command becomes available (see Figure 14-4). This lets you save a setting that affects only some of the dynamic settings in the dialog box. For example, you can make a subset that only remembers (and affects) the White Balance and Brightness controls. Bruce has created settings that adjust only the Exposure value up or down by ¼-stop increments: +0.25, +0.5, -0.25, -0.5, and so on.

Figure 14-4
Save Settings Subset

Save Settings Subset lets you save settings that adjust one or more parameters while leaving others unchanged.

▶ **Camera Default.** The Camera Raw plug-in knows the factory default settings for each supported camera model, which it uses by default anytime you open an image shot by that model of camera. However, you can also create your own default settings—not merely for one camera model, but for each individual camera body. For example, if you have two Nikon Coolpix 5000 cameras, each saves its serial number in its image's metadata, so you can create a default setting for each one. To make a default setting, specify the settings in the Camera Raw dialog box, then select Set Camera Default from this popout menu. If you find that you've made a mistake, choose Reset Camera Default to revert the default setting back to Camera Raw's original factory default.

▶ **Preferences.** Camera Raw's Preferences command (which is also accessible from the Photoshop menu when Camera Raw is in the foreground) contains two items (see Figure 14-5). First, the "Save image settings in" option lets you choose whether to save the metadata (the settings you choose in the Camera Raw dialog box) for images in the Camera Raw database, or in individual "sidecar XMP" files. Camera Raw treats raw images as read-only (which we think is a Good Thing), so your raw images never get overwritten on disk.

Figure 14-5
Camera Raw Preferences

We generally prefer saving the Camera Raw settings in a sidecar XMP file—a small file saved in the same folder as the raw image itself. If you delete that XMP file, Photoshop resets the Camera Raw controls to the camera's default next time you open it. However, if you find that the file management is onerous, or if you make a practice of renaming your raw files (we never do), you may prefer to save the settings in the Camera Raw database instead. The Camera Raw database indexes your images by file content rather than name, so even if you rename the raw file, the Camera Raw database will still find the correct settings.

The second preference, labeled "Apply sharpening to," lets you choose whether to apply any sharpening you set in Camera Raw to the

Camera Raw and Color

The way Camera Raw handles color has been the subject of a good many online flame wars. On the one side are those Bruce calls "color management fascists," who maintain that a custom camera profile is an absolute necessity and that since Camera Raw has no facility for using one, it's a toy suitable only for weekend warriors who need pleasing color. On the other side are those others who either recognize Camera Raw as a breakthrough or are simply happy with the way it works.

It's pretty obvious from the above paragraph which camp we fall into, so let's just look at how Camera Raw actually handles color, and why we believe this approach makes sense. Our experience with custom profiling has been that a custom profile may be helpful for images shot under the same lighting conditions used when we photographed the profiling target, but it's less than helpful when the lighting conditions

change. Some cameras are better-behaved than others, but we generally find that most cameras' behavior doesn't change in a linear fashion across different color temperatures, so a profile that works well under daylight may fail miserably under tungsten, or *vice versa*.

To address this problem, Camera Raw uses two hard-wired profiles for each supported camera—one that records the spectral sensitivities of the camera under D65 daylight, another that does so under 3200K tungsten light. The White Balance controls—Temperature and Tint—in Camera Raw's Adjust tab let you interpolate between, or even extrapolate beyond, these two profiles. The interpolated result is then used as the source profile for the conversion to your designated working space.

For cameras that provide white balance information in the metadata, the white balance set on-camera is used as the default interpretation in Camera Raw.

When cameras don't provide this information, Camera Raw automatically calculates the white balance settings. In either case, we find that the results are better than anything we've been able to obtain using custom profiles, and the ability to fine-tune the color temperature and tint beyond these defaults is invaluable.

However, it's true that the profiles hardwired into Camera Raw are generic profiles for that camera model. Some cameras seem to have much better unit-to-unit agreement than others, but if your camera behaves differently from the one used to create the profile, the color may not be as good as you'd like. To address this issue, choose the Calibrate tab (available in Advanced mode) to dial in the performance of your specific camera. You can then save the results as the camera default, which will thenceforth be used to tweak the generic profiles' response, giving you more accurate color.

previews and to the converted image, or to the previews only. Bruce prefers to apply his sharpening later, using the techniques we discuss in Chapter 10, *Sharpening*, so he sets this option to "Preview images only"—that way he can enjoy reasonably sharp previews on screen, but apply more nuanced sharpening to the converted images. If you need to process a bunch of images quickly, you might want to set this to "All Images" instead. Note that this preference only affects the Sharpness setting, not the other settings which are found alongside the Sharpness control (see "Detail tab," later in this chapter).

Camera Raw Dynamic Controls

The image-specific settings—the ones you're likely to change with each image—occupy the rest of the Camera Raw dialog box. In Basic mode, the options are split between two tabs: Adjust and Detail. When you click the Advanced button, you get two more tabs, Lens and Calibrate, that provide additional controls for the more advanced user.

These four sets of controls are the meat and potatoes of Camera Raw, offering very precise control over your raw conversions. Some of them let you do things that you simply cannot do to an already-converted file, while others are just included for workflow convenience—that is, you could make the adjustments in Camera Raw or Photoshop with the same results. We'll point out which ones are which as we go.

Adjust tab. The controls in the Adjust tab let you tweak your image's color balance, exposure, tonal behavior, and saturation. The first three controls in this tab are typically the most important: Temperature, Tint, and Exposure (see Figure 14-6). These let you control your image in unprecedented ways because you can alter the color balance dramatically *without introducing any degradation to the image*. You simply can't do that once the image is open in Photoshop. The settings affect the colorimetric interpretation of the image rather than stretching or squeezing levels, so the change is lossless (see Figure 14-7).

▶ **Temperature.** The Temperature control lets you specify the color temperature of the lighting in Kelvins, thereby setting the blue-yellow color balance. Lowering the color temperature makes the image more blue to compensate for yellow light; raising the color temperature makes the

Figure 14-6
The Adjust tab

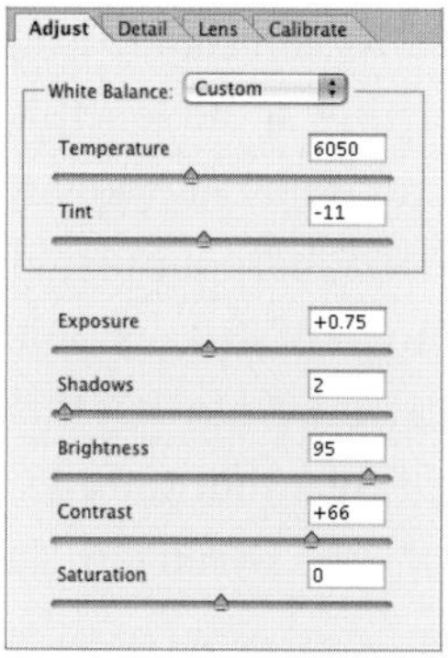

The Adjust tab lets you adjust the color Temperature and Tint, the Exposure and Shadow point, and Brightness, Contrast, and Saturation.

image more yellow, to compensate for the blue light. (Remember that something heating up becomes red, then yellow, then finally—when it's at a very high temperature—blue.) The up and down arrow keys change the color temperature in increments of 50 Kelvins. Adding Shift changes the temperature in increments of 500 Kelvins.

Figure 14-7
Camera Raw adjustments

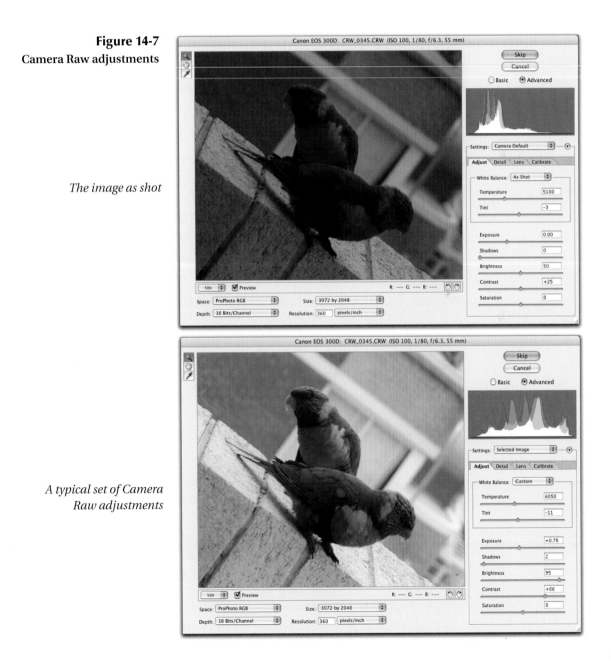

The image as shot

*A typical set of Camera
Raw adjustments*

▶ **Tint.** The Tint control lets you fine-tune the color balance along the magenta-green axis. Negative values add green, positive ones add magenta. (You can remember this by using the slider over and over and over until you dream about it at night.) The up and down arrow keys change the tint in increments of 1. Adding Shift changes the tint in increments of 10.

Tip: Fine-Tuning the White Balance. To get the approximate settings for Temperature and Tint, click the White Balance tool on an area of detail white (some white that isn't a specular highlight). This automatically sets the Temperature and Tint controls to produce as close to a neutral as possible. Then make small moves with Temperature (and, if necessary, Tint) to fine-tune the results

---

▶ **Exposure.** The Exposure slider controls the mapping of the tonal values in the image to those in your designated working space. Theoretically, it's a lossless control (unless you use it to induce shadow or highlight clipping) like the white balance controls, in that it doesn't lose any levels in operation.

However, in practice, large increases in exposure value (more than about 0.75 of a stop) may increase shadow noise, and possibly even make some posterization visible in the shadows. Raw captures have a gamma close to 1 (very linear), so many more bits are devoted to describing the highlights than to describing the shadows. If a 12-bit camera captures five f-stops of dynamic range, half of the values (2,048 levels) are devoted to describing the data in the first stop, half of the remainder (1,024 levels) are devoted to describing the data in the second stop, and so on. This means you only have 128 levels to describe the darkest stop's worth of data. Large exposure corrections may help you get a useful image, but they aren't a substitute for correct exposure in the first place. If you deliberately underexpose to hold highlight detail, your shadows won't be as good as they could be.

The up and down arrows change the exposure in increments of 0.05 of a stop. Adding Shift changes the exposure in increments of 0.5.

▶ **Shadows.** The Shadows slider works very like the black input slider in levels—it lets you darken the shadows to set the black level. Unlike the first three controls, it doesn't do anything you can't do equally well to the converted image, so make the shadow adjustment wherever it's more convenient—either in Camera Raw, or in Photoshop. The up and down arrow keys change the shadows in increments of 1. Adding Shift changes the shadows in increments of 10.

Tip: Use the Clipping Display in Exposure and Shadows. We've long relied on the threshold clipping display in the Levels dialog box to show us exactly what's being clipped in each channel as we adjust the black and white input sliders. Camera Raw offers the same feature for the Exposure and Shadows sliders. (We wish it offered it for Contrast, too.) Hold down the Option key as you move the Exposure or Shadows slider, and you'll see the clipping display. White pixels indicate highlight clipping (pixels blown out to pure white) and black pixels indicate shadow clipping (pixels dropping to black). Colored pixels indicate clipping in one or two channels. For more on this technique, see Figure 7-7 in Chapter 7, *Color Correction Fundamentals.*

▶ **Brightness.** Unlike its image-destroying counterpart on Photoshop's Adjust submenu (under the Image menu), Camera Raw's Brightness control is a non-linear adjustment that works the same as the gray input slider in levels (see "The Non-Linear Advantage" in Chapter 6, *Tonal Correction Fundamentals*). It lets you redistribute the midtone values without clipping the highlights or shadows. Like the Shadows slider, it's here for convenience. The up and down arrow keys change the brightness in increments of 1. Adding Shift changes the brightness in increments of 10.

▶ **Contrast.** The Contrast slider is a somewhat gentler version of the Contrast slider in Photoshop's Brightness/Contrast command. It's possible to drive shadows or highlights to clipping with this slider, so use it carefully and keep an eye on the histogram if you decide to make this adjustment in Camera Raw. The up and down arrow keys change the contrast in increments of 1. Adding Shift changes the contrast in increments of 10.

▶ **Saturation.** The saturation slider acts like a gentler version of the Saturation slider in Photoshop's Hue/Saturation command. It offers somewhat finer adjustments than Hue/Saturation, but a Hue/Saturation Adjustment Layer allows you to fine-tune by varying the layer opacity. So, as with the Shadows, Brightness, and Contrast sliders, it's pretty much a wash whether you make the adjustments in Camera Raw or in Photoshop.

Detail tab. The sliders in the Detail tab let you apply global sharpening, and reduce noise in both luminance and color (see Figure 14-8). To use these controls effectively, you need to zoom the preview to 100 percent, or occasionally even 200 percent.

▶ **Sharpness.** The Sharpness slider lets you apply a variant of Unsharp Mask to the Preview image or to both the Preview and the converted image, depending on how you set Camera Raw Preferences. Unlike the Unsharp Mask filter, Camera Raw's Sharpness only offers a single control that roughly controls both Radius and Amount. The Threshold value is calculated automatically based on the camera model, ISO, and exposure compensation values reported in the image's metadata.

   We find the Sharpness control a bit of a blunt instrument, and for images that will receive more than cursory attention from us, we either set the slider to zero or, more likely, set the Preference so that Sharpness only applies to the preview. But if we're simply trying to get a bunch of images processed for approval, trying to make them good rather than great, we'll apply a quick sharpen here, knowing that we can re-process the "hero" shots from the raw file with no sharpening once we know which ones they are.

Figure 14-8
The Detail tab

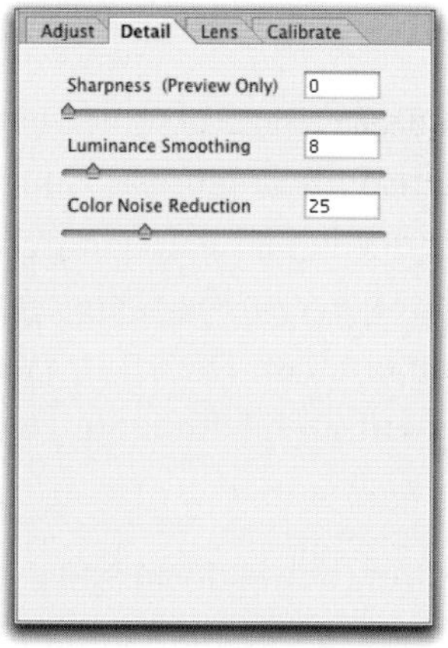

The Detail tab lets you adjust sharpness, and control noise in both luminance and color.

▶ **Luminance Smoothing.** The Luminance Smoothing slider controls grayscale noise that may make the image appear grainy—typically a problem when shooting at high ISO speeds. The default setting is zero, which provides no smoothing, but we find that even at slower speeds most cameras benefit from a modest amount of luminance smoothing (about 5). You may want to experiment to find a good setting for your camera and then incorporate it in your Camera Default settings. At very high settings it can produce images that look like they've been hit with the Median filter, so always check at 100 percent view or above before committing to a setting.

▶ **Color Noise Reduction.** Color noise manifests itself as random speckles of color rather than gray, and again it's a bigger problem on some cameras than on others. The Color Noise Reduction slider replaces the "Moiré Filter" checkbox in Camera Raw 1.0 with a more controllable alternative. We usually leave this control at its default setting of 25 unless we see a need to increase it.

Lens tab. The controls in the Lens tab (see Figure 14-9) let you address two problems that occasionally show up in digital captures, one much more common than the other: chromatic aberration and vignetting.

Chromatic aberration is a phenomenon where the lens fails to focus the red, green, and blue wavelengths of the light to exactly the same spot, causing red and cyan color fringes along high-contrast edges. In severe cases, you may also see some blue and yellow fringing. It typically happens with wide-angle shots, especially with the wide end of zoom lenses.

Figure 14-9
The Lens tab

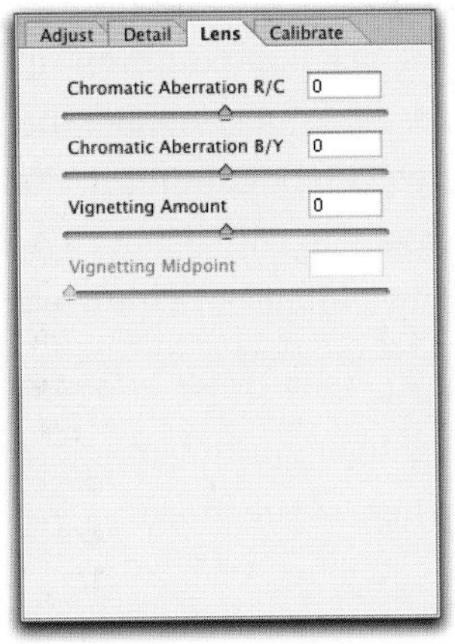

The Lens tab lets you address common shortcomings of camera lenses.

Some pundits claim that chromatic aberration in digital captures is caused by the microlenses some camera vendors place in front of each element in the array, but we're skeptical—we've seen it happen on cameras without microlenses, using wide-angle lenses that don't display chromatic aberration when shooting film. We believe it's simply because digital capture is more demanding on lenses—film scatters the incoming light due to grain and to the presence of the multiple layers in the emulsion, so it's somewhat more forgiving than digital sensors. Whatever the reason, it's entirely likely that you'll encounter chromatic aberration in some wide-angle shots.

▶ **Chromatic Aberration R/C.** This slider lets you reduce or eliminate red/cyan fringes by adjusting the size of the red channel relative to the green channel. While the red/cyan fringes are usually the most visually obvious, chromatic aberration usually has a blue/yellow component too. Holding down the Option key while moving the slider hides the blue/yellow fringe, letting you concentrate on the red/cyan fringe.

▶ **Chromatic Aberration B/Y.** This slider lets you reduce or eliminate blue/yellow fringes by adjusting the size of the blue channel relative to the green channel. Holding down the Option key while moving the slider hides the red/cyan fringe, so you can concentrate on the blue/yellow fringe.

Figure 14-10 shows before-and-after versions of a chromatic aberration correction. As with the controls in the Detail tab, we always zoom the preview to 100 percent or more when making corrections with the chromatic aberration sliders.

Vignetting, where the lens fails to illuminate the entire sensor area, darkening the corners, is a less-common problem with digital captures because the sensor area is usually smaller than the film for which the lens was designed. But if you do encounter it, the vignetting sliders can help compensate. Of course, you can also use these two controls for special effects, such as making a foreground image appear more prominent.

▶ **Vignetting Amount.** This slider controls the amount of lightening or darkening (negative amounts darken, positive amounts lighten) applied to the corners of the image.

Figure 14-10
Chromatic aberration
correction

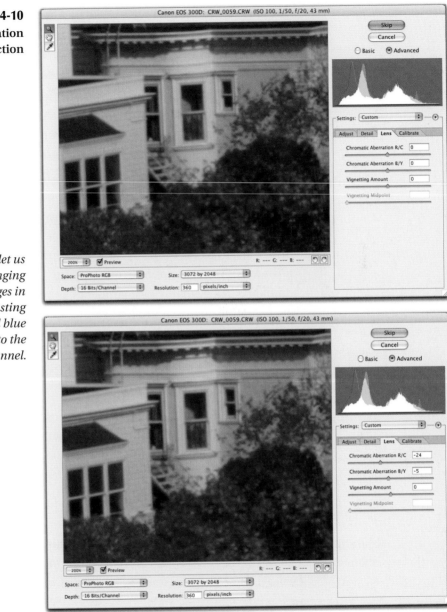

*The Lens controls let us
remove the color fringing
from the window edges in
this image by adjusting
the size of the red and blue
channels relative to the
green channel.*

▶ **Vignetting Midpoint.** This slider controls the area to which the Vignetting Amount adjustment gets applied. Smaller values reduce the area, larger ones increase it.

Calibrate tab. The set of controls on the Calibrate tab lets you fine-tune the behavior of the built-in camera profiles to address unit-to-unit variation (see Figure 14-11). The up and down arrow keys move the sliders in increments of 1. Adding Shift moves the sliders in increments of 10.

Try photographing a 24-patch Macbeth Color Checker and compare it with a Lab version of the target converted to your working space. You can download a Lab image of the Color Checker, made from averaged measurements from several physical targets: *www.colorremedies.com/realworldcolor/downloads.html*. If you're shooting under controlled lighting, do a custom white balance in the camera before capturing the target.

Start by adjusting the controls in the Adjust panel to get approximately the same luminance values for the black and white patches as are in the Lab file, and adjust the contrast to get an approximate visual match to the Lab image. If you're shooting in available light or under changing lighting conditions, it's probably best simply to aim for a good visual match. If you're shooting under controlled lighting, you can use the Calibrate sliders to nudge the RGB numbers closer to the ones in the target image.

▶ **Shadow Tint.** The Shadow Tint slider controls the green-magenta balance in the shadows. Negative values add green, positive values add magenta.

▶ **Red, Green, and Blue Hue.** The Red, Green, and Blue Hue sliders work like the Hue sliders in Photoshop's Hue/Saturation command. Negative values move the hue angle counterclockwise, positive values move it clockwise.

Figure 14-11
The Calibrate tab

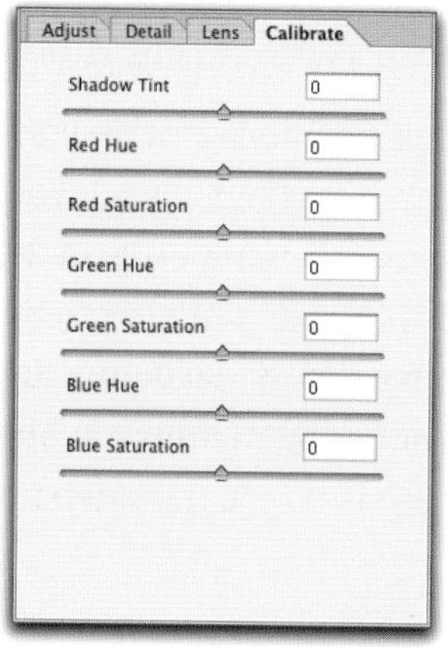

The Calibrate tab lets you dial in the color for your specific camera body, to improve the performance of Camera Raw's built-in camera profiles.

▶ **Red, Green, and Blue Saturation.** These sliders work like gentler versions of the Saturation slider in Photoshop's Hue/Saturation command. Negative values reduce the saturation, positive values increase it.

Once you've dialed in your camera's response, you can save the Calibrate settings as a new Camera Default for that specific camera using the Save Camera Default command on the Camera Raw popout menu.

Camera Raw and the File Browser. Camera Raw is a powerful tool, but if it forced you to make detailed corrections on every image individually, you probably wouldn't make much money unless you were being paid by the hour. Fortunately, thanks to the integration of Camera Raw with the File Browser, you can easily apply Camera Raw settings to multiple images, then either open them while bypassing the Camera Raw dialog box, or set up a batch process to convert the raw images, and optionally rename and save the converted files while applying any Action you can dream up. And if that's not enough, the File Browser can do even more to streamline your workflow. Let's see how.

The File Browser

When the File Browser first appeared in Photoshop 7, we thought of it as a nice alternative to the Open dialog box when dealing with a folder full of files. The File Browser was great because it let us see thumbnails and previews of the images, allowing us to identify the ones we wanted quickly. But working with raw digital captures in Photoshop CS has led us to realize that the File Browser is now a mission-critical tool.

When we make our initial selects from a shoot, we do so using the File Browser as a virtual light table. When we want to convert our images, we apply Camera Raw settings through the File Browser. We also use the File Browser to add and edit metadata—one of the first things we do to a new folder of raw images is to add our copyright notice to each image. And while we confess to being less assiduous than we should be, we're also using the File Browser to add keywords to our images so that we can find them easily years from now (see the sidebar, "All About Metadata," later in this chapter).

Even when we work with scanned images rather than digital captures, we find the File Browser useful in helping us find, open, and manage our images thanks to its quick searching and previewing capabilities. So if you've considered the File Browser as simply an Open dialog box on steroids, allow us to introduce you to the bigger picture. The File Browser is deep, and while we certainly don't have the space to write the definitive File Browser reference, we can and will introduce you to its various parts, explain what they do, and show you how we use them.

Also, you might review the techniques in "The File Browser," in Chapter 2, *Essential Photoshop Tips and Tricks*.

Tip: Open the File Browser. When we work on single-monitor systems we usually keep the File Browser closed when we aren't actually using it. You can open the File Browser by doing any of the following:

▶ Choose Browse from the File menu, or press Command-Shift-O.

▶ Choose File Browser from the Window menu.

▶ Click the File Browser button in the Options bar (it's the icon that looks like a magnifying glass over an open folder).

Anatomy of the File Browser

The File Browser has evolved from being a somewhat oddly behaved palette in Photoshop 7 to being a mini-application in its own right in Photoshop CS (see Figure 14-12). The File Browser window contains seven different areas, three of which—the main window, the menu, and the tool bar—are always visible. The four remaining components are palettes that you can rearrange and resize, as well as combining them just as you can with other Photoshop palettes.

File Browser menu bar. As befits a mini-application, the File Browser has its own menu bar. We won't give a blow-by-blow description of every single menu command. Instead we'll content ourselves with giving you an overview of the menus, and details about the commands we find particularly useful and interesting.

▶ **File menu.** Beyond the usual tasks of opening files, the File menu lets you work with the File Browser's cache for the current folder. The cache

Figure 14-12
The File Browser

Menu bar

Tool bar

Palettes

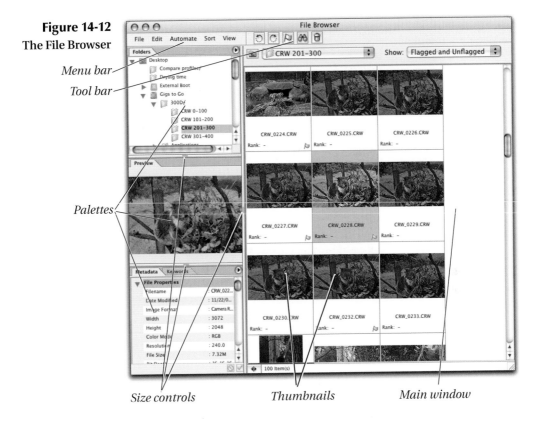

Size controls   Thumbnails   Main window

holds the thumbnail information, as well as any flagging or ranking you apply to the images (see "Selecting and Sorting," later in this chapter). When you burn a CD, or copy the folder to removable media, you can export the cache using the Export Cache command, so that when the folder is opened by Photoshop it doesn't have to spend time rebuilding the cached information. In a dire emergency, you can also use the Purge Cache command to free up hard disk space—depending on just what's in the cache, you may recover anything from about 2 to about 8 megabytes.

The File Info command offers a way to edit an image's IPTC metadata without first opening the image, which is particularly handy if you simply need to add copyright or captioning information to a huge file. It also allows you to save metadata templates for IPTC info, which you can use to apply metadata to multiple files (see Figure 14-13).

▶ **Edit menu.** The Edit menu generally offers somewhat slower ways to do things that you can accomplish faster by other means, such as

Figure 14-13
Save Metadata Template

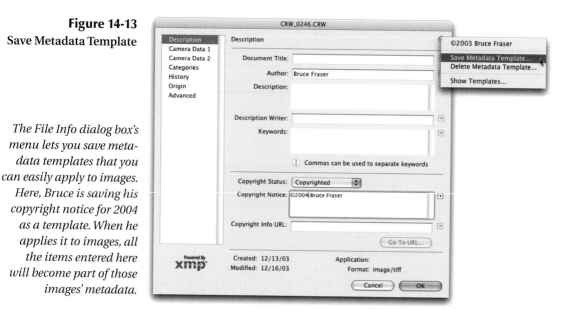

The File Info dialog box's menu lets you save metadata templates that you can easily apply to images. Here, Bruce is saving his copyright notice for 2004 as a template. When he applies it to images, all the items entered here will become part of those images' metadata.

selecting, deleting, rotating, and flagging images, or applying metadata templates. However, three commands are of particular interest.

First, you can apply a ranking to multiple images simultaneously by selecting them in the File Browser, choosing Rank from the Edit menu, then entering a rank in the dialog box. Photoshop's online help shows ranks like "Good" and "Bad," but we suggest using a single number, or, if you really need more than 10 ranks, a single letter, so that you can easily sort images by rank (see "Selecting and Sorting," later in this chapter).

Second, Metadata Display Options lets you specify which metadata fields appear in the metadata palette, and gives you the option to automatically hide fields that are empty for the current image. If you don't have a GPS-enabled camera, for example, you may as well hide all the GPS fields.

Finally, Preferences opens the File Browser Preferences dialog box. (This is the same as the File Browser panel in the normal Preferences dialog box; see Figure 14-14.) Here are a few tips for choosing preferences. If you're primarily concerned with processing raw digital captures, set the limit under "Do Not Process Files Larger Than" to a value a little bigger than your raw files so that the File Browser doesn't spend time churning away on those layered 16-bit monster images.

All About Metadata

Metadata (which literally means "data about data") isn't a new thing. Photoshop's File Info dialog box has allowed you to add metadata such as captions, copyright info, and routing or handling instructions for years. But digital capture brings a much richer set of metadata to the table.

For example, most current cameras adhere to the EXIF (Exchangeable Image File Format) standard, which supplies with each image a great deal of information on how it was captured, including but by no means limited to the camera model, the specific camera body, shutter speed, aperture, focal length, flash setting, and of course the date and time.

IPTC (International Press Telecommunications Council) metadata has long been supported by Photoshop's File Info feature, allowing copyright notices and the like. Other types of metadata supported by Photoshop CS include GPS information from GPS-enabled cameras (we think

it's immensely cool that our good friend Stephen Johnson's stunning landscape images include GPS metadata that will allow people to stand where they were shot ten or a hundred years from now, and note how the landscape has changed). Camera Raw settings can be applied as metadata, so you can instruct Photoshop how you want the image to be processed without actually doing the conversion. You can even record every Photoshop operation applied to the image as metadata using the History Log feature.

Adobe has been assiduous in promoting XMP (eXtensible Metadata Platform), an open, extensible, W3C-compliant standard for storing and exchanging metadata—all the Creative Suite applications use XMP, and because XMP is extensible, it's relatively easy to update existing metadata schemes to be XMP-compliant. However, it will probably take some time before all the other applications that use metadata, such as third-party digital raw converters, get updated to handle XMP.

But let's be very clear: XMP is not some proprietary Adobe initiative. It's an open, XML-based standard. So if you find that another application is failing to read XMP metadata, contact the publisher and tell them you need them to get with the program!

Right now, unless you're a programmer or a very serious scripting wonk, there may not be much you can do with the metadata, at least, not automatically; but it won't be too long before we start seeing things like camera-specific sharpening routines that vary their noise reduction with ISO value and exposure time, to give just one example. The more information we have about an image, the better our chances of being able to do useful things to it automatically, and the more things we can do automatically, the more time we can spend doing those things that only a human can do, like exercising creative judgment.

We set the Custom Thumbnail Size to make the largest thumbnails that will let us see two thumbnails side-by-side on our display. The limit is 1024 pixels wide. The Allow Background Processing option lets the File Browser keep working—generating thumbnails and previews, and reading metadata—while you do something else. While this sounds like a good idea, we don't recommend this option unless you have a fast machine. However, if you do have more processor speed than you need, letting the File Browser update thumbnails and previews in the background can be a time-saver.

Figure 14-14
File Browser Preferences

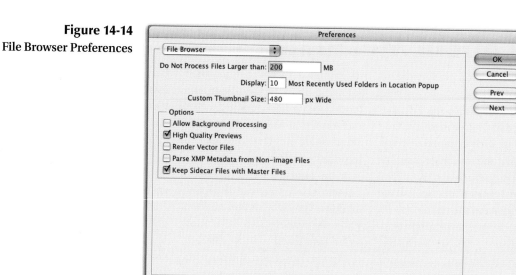

The High Quality Previews checkbox is an option we always leave turned on—we find the ability to view large previews invaluable in making initial selections, and when it's turned off, large previews get very pixelated. We also always leave Keep Sidecar Files with Master Files turned on. That way, whenever we move image files using the File Browser, the files containing the metadata always travel with them.

▶ **Automate menu.** The Automate menu offers many of the options found on Photoshop's Automate submenu (see Chapter 15, *Essential Image Techniques*, for more on this submenu and automation in general). Running a batch process from the File Browser is often easier and faster because you can quickly pick the images you want to affect. The Automate menu has two important additions, too: Batch Rename, and Apply Camera Raw Settings.

Batch Rename lets you replace the less-than-useful names digital cameras typically assign to images—DCS07540.TIF, for example—with ones that are more meaningful to you (see Figure 14-15).

Tip: Don't Forget the Extension. If your raw captures are accompanied by sidecar thumbnail and XMP (metadata) files, you must include the extension in the new file names. Otherwise, the Batch Rename will fail.

Figure 14-15
Batch Rename

Batch Rename lets you
rename your raw files
with names that are more
informative than the ones
most cameras assign.

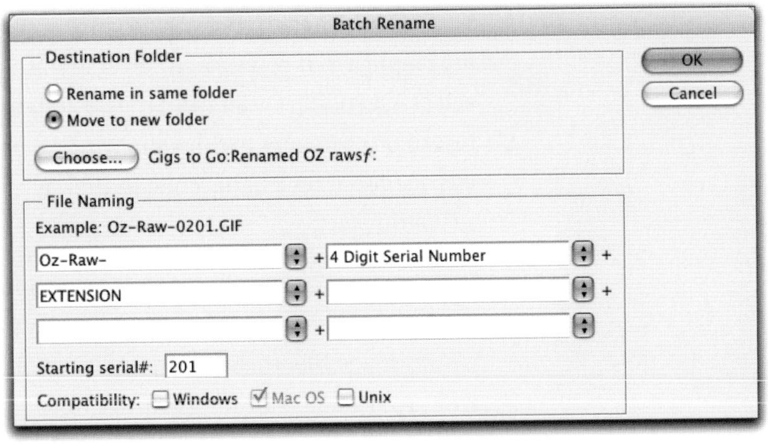

The Apply Camera Raw Settings feature is our favorite command in the File Browser's menus. It lets us quickly apply saved Camera Raw settings, or settings from the previous image, to multiple files we've selected in the File Browser, without opening them or going through the Camera Raw interface (see Figure 14-16). By the way, when you're in Advanced mode, Apply Camera Raw Settings offers even more flexibility by letting you choose subsets of settings to apply. For example, you could leave each image's white balance unchanged, and just adjust the exposure, or any other permutation you find useful.

Figure 14-16
Apply Camera
Raw Settings

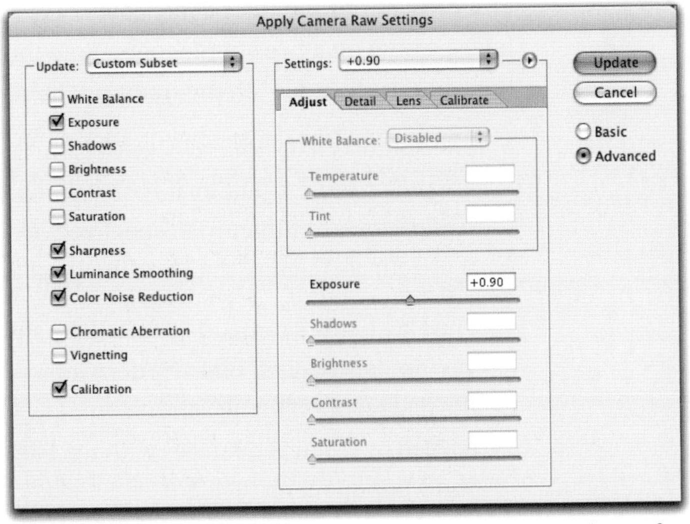

Apply Camera Raw Settings lets you apply settings, or subsets of settings,
to selected raw images without actually opening and converting them.

▶ **Sort menu.** The Sort menu lets you control the order in which images are displayed. If you want to reverse the order (make the last one first), select Ascending Order from the bottom of the Sort menu. You can also re-order the images in the main window by dragging them around, just as you would on a light table. In this case, the Sort menu will indicate a Custom sort.

▶ **View menu.** The View menu lets you control what you see in the File Browser window. If you want to see every file in a folder, whether or not it's an image file, turn on Unreadable Files. We're not sure why you'd want to do that, but it's great to know you can do it in a pinch. The View menu also controls the size of the thumbnails (choose Custom Thumbnail Size to get the one you specified in the File Browser Preferences dialog box), whether to display image rank (if you don't use Rank, turn this off), and whether to show Flagged or Unflagged images (see "Selecting and Sorting," later in this chapter).

If you need to find the file on disk that corresponds to an image, select the image (or images) and choose Reveal Location in Finder from the View menu. If you leave the File Browser open while you add new images to a folder, you'll find yourself scratching your head because the images don't show up. That's what Refresh (press F5) is for: It forces Photoshop to update its list of images for the current folder.

File Browser tool bar. The tool bar is a great deal simpler than the menu bar, sporting only five simple tools. Note that these are actually just buttons, not really "tools," in the traditional sense of the word.

▶ The Rotate Left (Counterclockwise) and Rotate Right (Clockwise) tools are pretty self-explanatory. Faster than clicking, you can press Command-[and Command-], respectively. Don't forget that you can apply these effects to more than one image at a time.

▶ The Flag tool (Command-') provides a simple mechanism for making "yes/no" (also called "binary") decisions—clicking the Flag tool toggles the flag on or off for all selected images. Then you can display all the flagged or unflagged images with the File Browser's View menu or the Show popup menu.

▶ The Search tool (which, sadly, lacks a keyboard shortcut) lets you perform fairly detailed searches for images in any folder (including subfolders, if you want). You can search based on a wide variety of criteria, including file name, creation date, file size, or metadata such as EXIF information or keywords, or other metadata. To use more than one search criteria, click the + button in the Search dialog box. For example, you could find all images that were created during the month of June, 2003, that were saved in a TIFF format, and that have the word "Paris" as a keyword.

▶ The Trash tool (keyboard shortcut is the Delete key) moves selected images to the operating system's Trash (or Recycle Bin)—which won't fully delete them until you empty it.

File Browser main window. The main window within the File Browser is devoted to displaying image thumbnails (see Figure 14-12, earlier in this chapter). You can control the size of these previews using the commands from the File Browser's View menu, and set the order in which they're sorted with the File Browser's Sort menu.

At the top of the main window, the Up One Level button (it looks like an arrow inside a folder) lets you navigate upwards through the folder hierarchy. By default, the Location popup menu displays the current folder, but you can click on this to navigate to its "parent" folder, any other mounted volumes, and recent folders you've looked at (you can choose how many recent folders in the File Browser's Preferences). If you often use a particular folder, add it to your Favorite Folders list by choosing Add Folder to Favorites from the File Browser's File menu—it will then appear in this Location popup menu, too.

The Show popup menu lets you choose whether to display thumbnails for Flagged files, for Unflagged files, or for both Flagged and Unflagged files (see "Selecting and Sorting," later in this chapter). In the lower left corner of the main window sits the Toggle Expanded View button (it looks like a double-headed arrow), which lets you hide or show the File Browser's palettes—when they're hidden, the main window expands to fill the entire File Browser with thumbnail previews.

Folders palette. The Folders palette displays the volume and folder hierarchy, allowing you to navigate among the folders on your computer or network. It also displays two items that aren't really folders, but act like them: Favorites and Search Results. The Favorite Folders folder lists the folders you've designated as favorites, and the Search Results folder holds the results of the last search you performed with the Search tool. Most of the time we don't want to look at our entire hard drive in this palette, so we click on the icon to hide the file structure for our computer (scroll to the top of the palette's list of folders to see this) and then rely solely on the list of Favorites we've set up.

As we noted earlier, the File Browser won't update itself automatically if you mess around with files or folders outside of Photoshop, so you'll need to select Refresh from the Folders palette popout menu (or press F5). Also, like other palettes in Photoshop, you can double-click on the palette's title bar to minimize it, giving more room to the other palettes.

Preview palette. The Preview palette displays a preview for the selected image. It has no menu and no secrets (at least none that we know of). However, like the other palettes, you can minimize ("collapse") it by double-clicking on its tab, or resize it by dragging its size controls. You might want to minimize the Preview and Metadata palettes if you're annoyed by that momentary pause each time you click on an image thumbnail.

Metadata palette. The Metadata palette displays the metadata associated with the currently selected image or images—from its file creation date to its resolution, its current camera raw settings to its color profile. (Of course, when you have more than one image selected, many of the metadata fields read "Multiple Values Exist.")

The only metadata fields that you can manually edit in Photoshop are the IPTC fields. (As we said in a sidebar earlier, IPTC stands for International Press Telecommunications Council; don't worry, you won't be tested on that later.) Editable fields have a pencil icon next to them. To edit these fields, select the images or images whose metadata you wish to edit, then either click the pencil icon, or click directly in the text area, to enter the new metadata. The only IPTC field that isn't editable here is the Keywords field; to edit an image's keywords, you need to use the Keywords palette (see below).

The Metadata palette's popout menu lets you launch a search (it's the same as clicking on the Search tool), as well as increase or decrease the font size used in the palette (are we getting old or is the default size just really tiny?). Plus, if you've used the File Info dialog box to create templates, you can choose Append or Replace from this popout menu to add your template data to your selected images. For example, once you've made a template that has your copyright notice, it's much faster to add it from the template than it is to type the notice manually.

Metadata Display Options has the same functionality as the identically named command in the File Browser's Edit menu, so use whichever one is the more convenient. It's definitely worth taking the few minutes needed to decide which fields you want to display (see Figure 14-17)—very few Photoshop users need to see them all!

Keywords palette. Need to find that photograph of a firetruck you shot last year? Not a problem, as long as you tagged the image with a "firetruck" keyword. There are two ways to add keywords to images: the File Info dialog box and the Keywords palette. These keywords get written into the Keywords field of the IPTC metadata, but while they appear alongside

Figure 14-17
Metadata Display Options

Metadata Display Options lets you control which metadata items will be visible in the Metadata palette. It also offers the option to hide empty fields dynamically.

the other IPTC tags in the Metadata palette, you can't edit or apply them there. Why not? Because.

The benefit to using the Keywords palette is consistency. You can type any keyword you want in the File Info dialog box, so for one image you might type "firetruck" and another image you might type "fire truck." Later, when you do a keyword search for the image, you'll likely only find one or the other. The Keywords palette makes you first create a keyword, like building a color swatch, so you know it'll be the same each time you use it to tag an image.

Photoshop ships with several default keywords, few of which you'll ever use, unless you know people named Julius or Michael. To create your own keyword in the palette, click the New Keyword button at the bottom of the palette or select New Keyword from the palette's popout menu. Or, if you want to put it in one of the listed categories ("sets"), select the category before creating the keyword. Of course, you can also make your own categories by clicking the New Category button or choosing New Keyword Set from the popout menu. Don't worry if you put a new keyword in the wrong category; you can drag keywords from one category to another.

Categories appear as folders—the triangle to the left lets you expand and collapse them. When they're expanded, you can see the list of keywords in the category (see Figure 14-18). Then, to apply a keyword to one or more selected images, double-click on the keyword or click in the column to the left of the keyword—a checkmark appears, indicating that the selected images contain this keyword. To apply all the keywords in a

Figure 14-18
Keywords palette

The Keywords palette lets you create keywords and categories of keywords, then assign them to selected images by clicking in the left column.

category to an image, click to the left of the category name rather than beside the individual keyword.

Note that if you have applied keywords using the File Info dialog box, they appear in a category called "Other Keywords." If you find yourself using one of these keywords a lot, we suggest you drag it up to a category.

To delete an existing category or keyword, select it and click the Delete button in the palette, or choose Delete from the popout menu. However, deleting a keyword only removes it from the list, not from any files tagged with it. (So if you've applied a keyword to an image, deleting it simply moves it down into the Other Keywords category.) You can also rename a keyword by selecting Rename from the popout menu. If you want to search for images with a specific keyword, choose the keyword and select Search from the popout menu (this is the same as clicking the Search tool and typing the keyword in yourself).

By the way, you can also find all these keyword controls (New, Delete, Search, and so on) in the context menu (Control-click on a keyword on the Macintosh; right-button click in Windows).

Configuring the File Browser

The default layout of the File Browser lets you see where all the bits and pieces are, but the layout is highly customizable. You can resize the File Browser itself as well as its individual palettes by dragging the size controls. You can also change the thumbnail size using the commands on the File browser's View menu. As we noted earlier, you can even hide the palettes entirely by clicking the Toggle Expanded View button in the lower-left corner of the thumbnails window (the double-arrow button). We typically use different File Browser layouts for different tasks (see Figure 14-19).

Of course, if we had to reconfigure the File Browser manually every time we wanted to change its layout, we'd be distinctly unhappy campers. Fortunately, Photoshop's Workspace feature applies to File Browser layouts, so we simply save each layout as a workspace (see "Saving Workspaces" in Chapter 2, *Essential Photoshop Tips and Tricks*). We like to create each workspace with all the other palettes hidden, so the File browser can use all the available desktop real estate—that way we don't have to waste time pressing Tab to hide the palettes. Bruce has gone so far as to record actions that switch among the different File Browser layouts using keystrokes. (See Chapter 15, *Essential Image Techniques*, for more on actions.)

Figure 14-19
File Browser layouts

The File Browser window configured for a large preview. We use this layout for evaluating individual images for ranking or flagging.

The File Browser window configured to display custom thumbnails. We use this layout for comparing images.

The File Browser window configured for working with metadata.

File Browser Navigation

Like any decent mini-application that resides inside Photoshop, the File Browser is reasonably well-equipped with keyboard shortcuts. (Unfortunately, you can't edit the File Browser shortcuts using the Edit menu's Keyboard Shortcuts feature. Perhaps in the next version.)

Here's a few shortcuts we use all the time: If you click on a folder in the Folders panel, you can press the Up and Down Arrow keys to move up and down one folder at a time. Adding the Command key moves up one level in the hierarchy, whether the Folders palette or the main window is active.

If you click on a thumbnail preview, the Up, Down, Left, and Right Arrow keys move the selection to the next thumbnail in their respective directions. Adding Shift extends the selection to include the next thumbnail in that direction. (You can't, however, make discontiguous selections from the keyboard—you have to Command-click the thumbnails to add discontiguous images.) The Home key selects the first thumbnail, and the End key selects the last one in the folder. Command-A selects all thumbnails, Command-Shift-A selects all Flagged thumbnails, and Command-D deselects all thumbnails.

Building a Workflow

Camera Raw is a wonderful raw converter, and the File Browser is maturing into a more-than-competent image manager, but what really makes Photoshop CS a compelling solution for a raw digital workflow is the integration between the two. As soon as the File Browser encounters a folder of raw files, Camera Raw kicks in automatically, generating thumbnails and generous-size previews that allow you to make reasonable judgments about each image without actually opening the file, so that you can quickly make your initial selections.

Then, when you've flagged the images you want to work with, you can bypass the Camera Raw dialog box and use the File Browser to apply your conversion settings—increasing exposure, adjusting white balance, and so on—simply by adjusting the image's metadata. This lets you perform the conversions (actually opening the images, which can take time) as a batch process. You can even incorporate other actions to the conversion process. For example, we've set up one batch process to produce high-res JPEGs for client approval, another to produce low-res JPEGs for e-mailing, and still another to prepare images for serious editing. Then, when the computer is busy doing our work for us, we go off and lead our glamorous lives.

Let's look at other workflow possibilities, and the many ways in which Camera Raw and the File Browser help you to be more efficient and more productive.

Selecting and Sorting

As we mentioned at the beginning of this chapter, one of the biggest bottle-necks in a raw digital workflow is in making your initial selections from a day's shoot. The File Browser can be enormously helpful in getting past this bottleneck thanks to the Flag and Rank features.

We start by copying the files from the camera media to our hard drive—we've learned from bitter experience to avoid opening images directly from the camera media in all but the direst emergency. Then we point the File Browser at the folder full of raw images, and wait the few minutes while it builds the thumbnails and previews, and reads the metadata.

At this point, if you shoot for a living (and perhaps even if you don't), we suggest that before doing anything else, you enter your copyright notice on all the images. You can do this quickly by pressing Command-A to Select All, and then either appending a metadata template from the Metadata palette menu, or clicking in the Copyright field in the IPTC section of the Metadata palette and typing in the notice manually.

Yes/No sorting. For the first round of "yes or no" sorting, we set the File Browser to show a large preview, then we use the arrow keys to advance from one image to the next. We rotate images that need it by pressing Command-[or Command-] to rotate them left or right, respectively. For the keepers, we press Command-' (that's the apostrophe key) to apply the Flag attribute. The rest we simply bypass.

When we've gone through all the images, we choose Flagged Files from the main window's Show popup menu. This way, we can commence with processing our "keepers" without being distracted by the rejects. (Of course, we'll later choose Unflagged Files from the Show popup menu to take one last look at the rejects before deleting them.)

Sorting by Rank. For a more nuanced decision, you can use the Rank feature. (David hates this term; it always makes him think Photoshop is telling him that all his shots "stink.") To highlight the Rank field (which by default just has a hyphen in it), you can click on the field or (if the image is already selected), press Option-Enter. We like to type A for "yes," B for "maybe," and C for "no." Then press Enter to confirm the entry. To rank a all the images quickly, rank the first one, then press Tab to advance to the next image (this automatically highlights the next Rank field).

Of course, ranking isn't limited just to three levels. You can enter up to 16 characters in the Rank field—numbers, letters, or symbols. (Theoretically, you could keep track of about 4×10^{26} possible rankings—that's a 4 with 26 zeros after it, far more than the number of grains of sand on every beach on Earth.) For most of us, using either single digits from 0–9 or single letters from A–Z provides more than enough flexibility.

When you're done ranking your images, you can either choose Rank from the Sort menu (to sort by rank), or use Search to find just the yesses, just the nos, or just the maybes. Note that if you change an image's rank while the thumbnails are sorted by rank, nothing changes until you select Refresh from the File Browser's View menu (or press F5).

Sequencing. Last but not least, if you're the type who thinks in terms of sequences of images rather than single images, you can drag the thumbnails into the order you want, just as you did with film on a light table. Once you've sequenced the images, you can use Batch Rename to rename the files. (This even lets you use a numbering scheme that reflects your custom Sort order.)

Processing Images

The slowest possible way to process raw images in Photoshop CS is to open them one by one, make adjustments in Camera Raw, click OK to open the image in Photoshop, then save it. Unless you're working for an hourly rate, we don't recommend this as a workflow.

Instead, we usually apply Camera Raw settings to each image as metadata, then either open them all at once, or open and save them as a batch process. This way, we don't have to wait for Camera Raw to process each image individually. Much of the time, the goal is simply to deal with a lot of images and try to make them all good. After we've whittled the workload down to the few that we'll try to make perfect, we may revisit each one in Camera Raw and apply carefully customized settings to each one to make them perfect, but even then we'll almost certainly run a batch process to convert them and prepare them for final editing in Photoshop.

Applying one image's settings to others. The simplest way to process a bunch of similar images is to edit one in Camera Raw, then apply those edits to the others. With a contiguous series of images, we edit the first one and dismiss the dialog box by Option-clicking on OK. Then we select both the edited image and the other similar candidates—Shift-click on the final image in the series to select them all. Finally, we choose Apply Camera Raw Settings from the File Browser's Edit menu, and select First Selected Image from Camera Raw's Settings menu.

With non-contiguous images, we again edit the first one in the Camera Raw dialog box. Then we select the other images by Command-clicking, choose Apply Camera Raw Settings from the File Browser's Edit menu, and select Previous Conversion from Camera Raw's Settings menu.

Working with saved settings subsets. Sometimes we need to apply more individualized settings to each image, so one of the first things we did when we first started working with Camera Raw was to save subsets of settings that we could apply to images. Bruce has saved settings for exposure adjustments in 0.25-stop increments, and Brightness and Contrast adjustments in increments of 10 units. He's played with saving White Balance adjustments but has thus far found them less useful because the Temperature and Tint controls usually need to be adjusted interactively. However, Bruce almost invariably shoots with available light—if you shoot in the studio under controlled lighting you may find it worthwhile to save White Balance settings too.

Obviously, there's a trade-off between the number of settings you save the ease with which you can find and apply them. If you create hundreds of subsets, your Camera Raw Settings menu will become very long and unmanageable.

The key to being productive when applying subsets is to apply them to all the images that need them simultaneously. We generally start with Exposure adjustments, then Brightness, then Contrast. We look for all the images that need a +0.25-stop exposure boost, then for the ones that need a half-stop, and so on. Then we apply Brightness adjustments, followed by

Contrast. The image thumbnails and previews update to reflect the new settings, so checking the preview at a reasonably large size gives us a good idea of their effect. (This is one situation where it helps to have a machine fast enough to let the File Browser do background processing.)

Opening images. Once you've applied settings to one or more images, you can open them and bypass the Camera Raw dialog box by Shift-double-clicking. (If you're opening multiple images, Shift-double-click on the last one; otherwise you'll just change the selection.) Add Option if you also want to close the File Browser.

Photoshop then processes the images using their assigned Camera Raw settings, and opens the converted images in Photoshop. However, if we're dealing with more than a handful of images, we tend to run a batch process instead, by choosing Batch from the File Browser's Automate menu.

Using Batch. The Batch feature lets you process images with Camera Raw and, optionally, rename them, save them to a different location, or even apply an action. Telling Photoshop to run an action on these images allows for tremendous flexibility in automating your workflow. For example, we use one action to batch process the creation of 1024-pixel JPEGs, and another to save 16-bit-per-channel TIFFs with adjustment layers added ready for editing, saved with Zip compression to save storage space. They save us hours of repetitive grunt work, which is, after all, what computers are supposed to do.

However, there are a few stumbling blocks that can trip you up when you first try to implement this kind of automation.

▶ If you want the batch process to save the images in a specific format, you need to record the saving steps as part of the action you're using.

▶ If you want to bypass the Camera Raw interface when you run the batch, you must turn on the Suppress File Open Options Dialogs checkbox in the Batch dialog box (see Figure 14-20). It's probably a good idea to turn on Suppress Color Profile Warnings, too, just in case your working space isn't set the way you thought it was. (It's always frustrating to start a batch process, go for lunch, then come back to find that the Profile Mismatch warning for the first image is sitting on the screen waiting for input.)

▶ If your action included a save, you must turn on the Override Action "Save As" Commands checkbox. Otherwise, the batch process tries to save each file under the name you used for the save when you recorded the Action, and it will stop on the second image when Photoshop asks you if you want to replace the previous image of the same name.

Figure 14-21 shows the two actions we just discussed—one for creating Web-happy JPEGs after sharpening and resizing have been carried out on the 16-bit-per-channel ProPhoto RGB file; another that prepares images for final editing in Photoshop by adding adjustment layers set to Multiply, Screen, and Overlay, and named Darken, Lighten, and Contrast, respectively. The action turns off the layers' visibility so that when we open the image, we see it with no adjustments—that way it's easy for us to decide what it needs, turn on the appropriate layers, and tweak their opacities to get the desired effect.

Figure 14-20
The Batch dialog box

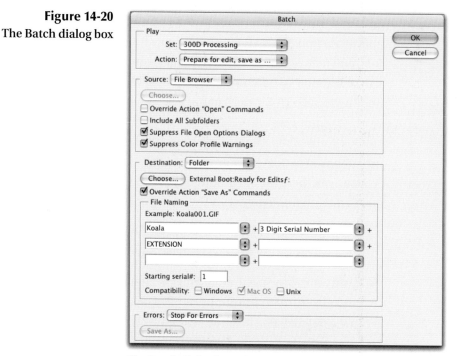

The Batch dialog box allows us to process raw conversions automatically. We incorporate different actions in the batch to perform different tasks, such as creating JPEG versions of the image for emailing, or creating 16-bits-per-channel TIFF versions with adjustment layers already in place for comprehensive editing in Photoshop.

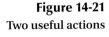

Figure 14-21
Two useful actions

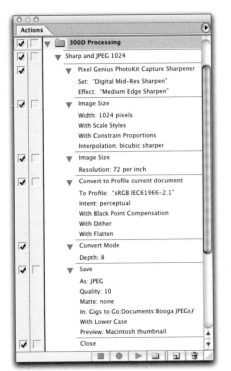

This action, when included in Batch, opens the raw image and converts it to a 16-bits-per-channel RGB image using the assigned Camera Raw settings. It then applies Pixel Genius's PhotoKit Capture Sharpener, downsizes the image to 1024-pixel width, sets the resolution to 72 ppi, converts it to sRGB, downsamples to 8 bits-per-channel, and saves the result as a JPEG with a quality of 10.

This action adds a Curves adjustment layer (with no curve adjustment applied) set to Multiply, renames the layer as "Darken," and hides it. It adds two more such layers, one set to Screen and named "Lighten," another set to Overlay and named "Contrast." Finally, it saves the image as a 16-bit-per-channel TIFF, with ZIP compression applied to both the image and the layers. When we open the file, it's ready for editing without us having to do the grunt work of adding the layers and setting the blending modes.

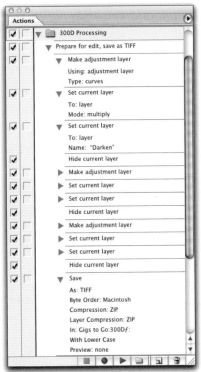

Be Lazy, Be Smart

Any way you slice it, shooting digital virtually guarantees that you'll spend more time in front of the computer and less time behind the lens, because it's really only when you open the images on the computer that you can tell just what you've captured. But the power of automation is there to let you make sure that when you *are* sitting in front of the computer, you're doing so because your critical judgment is required.

Digital capture involves processing masses of data—the files themselves may be smaller than film scans, but you'll almost certainly have to deal with a lot more of them—so if you find yourself doing the same things to images over and over again, teach Photoshop how to do them for you.

Photoshop's Actions feature provides a simple means of automating many repetitive tasks, though it has its limitations. For more complex automation, note that Photoshop is fully scriptable through AppleScript, Visual Basic, or Java.

One of the major differences between working with film scans and working with digital captures is that, thanks to standards like EXIF, digital captures contain a great deal more useful information about the image than do film scans. This opens up exciting new possibilities for more sophisticated automated routines. One of the challenges in automation is to do the right thing to each image automatically, and the more information you have about the image, the better your chances of doing so.

In the next chapter, *Essential Image Techniques*, we'll cover scripting and automation in more detail. For now, we'll leave you with the thought that if you find some operations boring and repetitive, you should almost certainly be able to teach the computer to do them for you so that you can concentrate on the exciting stuff.

15 Essential Image Techniques

Pushing Pixels into Place

The vast majority of Photoshop users stare at this program many hours a day, doing the same sort of image manipulation over and over again. Retouch the background of this photo; convert this color image to grayscale; add a drop shadow behind this car; silhouette this pineapple; put a new background behind this amazing kitchen aid; incorporate this logo into that image.

In this chapter we offer a whole mess of tips and tricks to make your images fly a little faster, and perhaps make them a little more fun to manipulate, as well. The chapter is split up into a hodgepodge of common Photoshop issues: retouching, batch processing images, working with vector graphics and text, and so on. Read 'em and reap!

Taking Care of the Basics

The two most important techniques in image editing are, in many respects, the simplest to accomplish.

- ▶ Look at every pixel.

- ▶ Build base camps.

Look at every pixel. Try to get in the habit of returning to 100-percent (Actual Pixels) view frequently, so you can get a sense of what's going on in your image. People often zoom in closer than this, thinking "the closer the better." Not so. Sure, you can see the pixels, but you're not really seeing the image. (Zen koan or sage advice? You be the judge.)

If you can't fit the image on your screen, start at the upper-left corner (press the Home key) and use the Page Down key to move down until you reach the bottom. Scroll once to the right (press Command-Page Down), and start over. We can't overstress the importance of this procedure.

If you like working zoomed in or out and can't be bothered with getting back to 100-percent view, check out "Tip: Use New Window" in Chapter 2, *Essential Photoshop Tips and Tricks.*

Build base camps. Our friend and colleague Greg Vander Houwen (you've probably read about him elsewhere in this tome) turned us on to the mountaineering phrase "base camp." The concept is simple: while you're working on an image, don't just save every now and again; instead, create an environment that you can return to at any time. That means taking snapshots in the History palette or—better yet—using Save As at strategic moments in your image manipulation. It also means saving your curves before applying them, and sometimes even writing down the various settings you use in dialog boxes (like Unsharp Mask).

When you've built a solid base camp, you can always return to it, get your bearings, and start up the hill again. As Greg noted, "I might build a few base camps along the way, depending on how high the mountain is."

The Color of Grayscale

Photoshop may be just about the most powerful application there is for handling color, but we don't live by color alone. Grayscale images have a magic all of their own, and a growing number of photographers—even those who print exclusively in grayscale—are finding that they can produce much better grayscale images from color captures than they can from black-and-white captures, whether they're shooting with film or digital cameras.

However, if you convert images by selecting Grayscale from the Mode menu, there's a good chance you're not getting the best-quality images you can. Most color images contain a great grayscale version, but you often have to wrestle to find it. Getting a good grayscale out of a CMYK image is particularly challenging, but even with RGB images the obvious method isn't always the best.

Let's first take a look at several ways to get grayscale information out of a color file.

Tip: Scan in Color. Almost every scanner on the market these days is built to scan color images. If your original image is a color picture, you'll often get a better final result by scanning it in color and then converting it to grayscale in Photoshop using one of the techniques below—it's like using color filters when you shoot black-and-white film. If you're scanning a grayscale picture, you may also get a better result scanning in color; it depends on how neutral gray the image really is. For instance, we're more likely than not to scan an ancient yellowed black-and-white photograph as an RGB color image.

Convert to Grayscale. The most obvious way to convert an image to grayscale is simply to choose Grayscale from the Mode submenu (under the Image menu). When you do so, Photoshop mixes the red, green, and blue channels together, weighting the red, green, and blue channels differently (according to a standard formula that purports to account for the varying sensitivity of the eye to different colors). It works (more or less) on some images, but the results are often far from ideal.

For instance, there are many images in which this weighting loses more information than it keeps. Remember, detail is in the differences between pixels, and if the gray pixels are too similar, you can lose important information.

Take a channel, any channel. Look at the individual color channels in the image. Occasionally you'll find the perfect grayscale image sitting in one of them. Then you can copy and paste it, or use Duplicate Channel from the Channel palette's popout menu to save it into a new document. Or you can just delete the other two channels by first displaying the channel you want, and then selecting Grayscale from the Mode menu.

Desaturate. You can select Desaturate from the Adjustments submenu (under the Image menu, or press Command-Shift-U). This is the same as reducing the Saturation setting in the Hue/Saturation dialog box to zero—

it literally pulls the color out of each pixel in the document. The image is still RGB, but if you convert it to grayscale you'll get a different result than if you'd simply converted it to grayscale without desaturating first.

Convert to Lab. For a more literal rendering of the luminance values in an image, you can convert the image to Lab, then discard the color channels (a and b). This gives you yet another different rendering.

Load the luminance mask. One of David's favorite methods for squeezing a grayscale image out of a color photograph is to Command-click on the composite color channel (the RGB or the CMYK tile in the Channels palette), which loads the file's luminance map (this is different than the L channel of a Lab file). You can then tell Photoshop to save this selection as a new file by choosing Save Selection from the Select menu. We find that this often provides a much better grayscale image than simply converting to Grayscale mode.

Devious methods. Sometimes none of the above methods provides the grayscale image you want. Photoshop offers some more devious alternatives. In the past you had to use the dreaded Calculations dialog box to mix channels; we still use Calculations sometimes, because it lets you do things you can't do any other way, but the Channel Mixer feature offers an easier way to blend channels, so we often turn to it first.

The Channel Mixer dialog box is more utilitarian than you'd hope from a program like Photoshop (see Figure 15-1), but it lets you do one thing very well: mix the color channels of your image. You mix channels by percent-

Figure 15-1
Channel Mixer dialog box

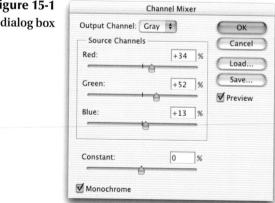

age, and the result is a single channel (you can choose which channel the result will end up on in the Output Channel popup menu).

When converting an RGB image to grayscale, remember two things. First, the percentages in the dialog box should always add up to 100 percent to maintain the same overall tone of the image (though there may be situations where you don't *want* to maintain the overall tone of the image). We wish there were a way to constrain the percentages in this way, but unfortunately, you have to just do the math (in your head, or on a calculator). Second, turn on the Monochrome checkbox; this ensures that the result will be neutral gray (in RGB, the result ends up on all three channels; in CMYK, the result is placed solely on the black channel).

(Note that the Channel Mixer works fine with CMYK images, but it's much harder to maintain the image's tone. We prefer working from an RGB image when building grayscale images with the Channel Mixer, even if it means converting from CMYK to RGB first.)

Tip: Channel Mixer Adjustment Layers. We pretty much always use the Channel Mixer on an adjustment layer rather than applying the effect directly to an image, because the adjustment layer makes it very easy to edit—just double-click on the tile in the Layers palette, and you can change the Channel Mixer settings. Even better, you can combine a Channel Mixer adjustment layer with a Levels or Curves adjustment layer to really bring out your image's most important tones. (See Chapter 9, *The Digital Darkroom*, for more on adjustment layers.)

Calculating images. Like the Channel Mixer, selecting Calculations from the Image menu lets you mix and match a new grayscale image from the existing channels, but with much more power and flexibility (see Figure 15-2). The options in the Blending popup menu are the same as the ones in the Layers palette, and the Opacity field serves the same function as the Layers palette's Opacity slider. Calculations lets you combine the channels in much more complex ways than the simple addition and subtraction offered by the Channel Mixer.

Tip: Use Preview in Calculations. At first glance, the Calculations dialog box seems a lot less interactive than the Layers palette. But it doesn't have to be that way. When you turn on the Preview checkbox, you can

Figure 15-2
The Calculations
dialog box

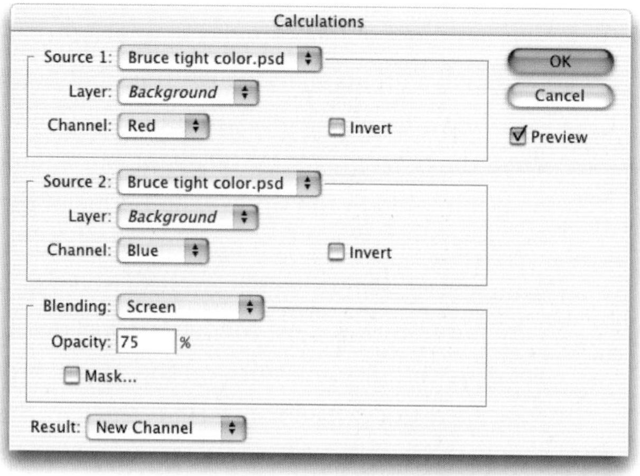

actually watch how the various combinations work in real time (or at least as fast as your machine can compute).

For instance, changing opacity can be a real bear, but when you turn on Preview, you get to see the effect before clicking OK. Then you can type a new Opacity setting almost as quickly as you can move the slider in the Layers palette.

Figure 15-3 shows an image's individual color channels and the results obtained using conventional methods of producing grayscales. Then it shows the result using the process outlined below. (We present this as an example rather than as the "correct" solution—you could achieve similar results using several different methods. Again, we encourage you to experiment.)

1. We start out by screening the blue channel into itself at 70-percent opacity, creating a new channel 4. We choose the blue channel as our starting point because it has closest-to-normal contrast, other than being very dark. The lipstick and hat in the green channel are almost black, and the red channel just looks strange.

2. In a second calculation, we apply the red channel to channel 4, using Hard Light at 40-percent opacity, to create channel 5. This lightens up the midtones, and fixes the unsettling effect created by the eyes being much lighter than the skin.

3. At this point we have a decent image, but the contrast is still too harsh, and the hat and lipstick are still a little dark. We take the red channel

Figure 15-3 Finding the hidden grayscale

Red channel

Blue channel

Green channel

L channel from Lab mode

Converted to Grayscale mode

Calculated channels

(the one with the least contrast) and screen it into channel 5 at 30-percent opacity. Rather than creating a new channel, we select a new document as the destination.

The result is a creditable monochrome rendering of the color original. If the hidden grayscale is hard to find in your color image, experiment with Calculations. You may be surprised at what you can find.

Retouching

Every time we get into an argument (sorry, we mean "discussion") about the ethics of digital imaging, we find that everyone has their own tolerance level of what can or should be changed in an image. We've heard photographers argue convincingly that each time you manipulate an image, especially when you add or remove real objects, it erodes the credibility of photography as a representation of the real. But we also recognize that people have to make a living, and sometimes (for better or worse) that involves improving the purported reality the photograph represents. We don't have an answer to this debate, but we urge you to at least consider the question.

We believe it's also important to make the distinction between "dust-busting" (removing specks of dirt, dust, mold, hair, and so on) and "retouching" (actually changing the content of an image). In this section, we want to relay a few key pointers that we've learned over the years about both dust-busting and retouching images, in the hope that they'll make you more efficient in whatever work you're undertaking.

Tip: Use Feathering. Often, the smallest thing makes the biggest difference—feathering, for example (see Figure 15-4). When you're retouching

Figure 15-4 Feathering as a retouching tool
This trick only works when covering an element with an area of uniform color and texture.

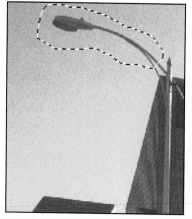 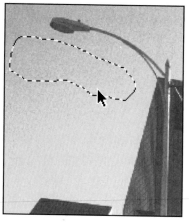 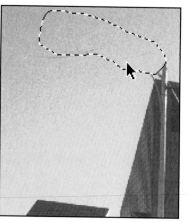

Make a loose selection with the Lasso tool and feather 4 pixels.   *Drag the selection to another location.*   *Command-Option-drag back to cover the original. The feathering ensures a seamless edge.*

a local, selected area—whether you're adjusting tone, painting, using a filter, or editing pixels—it's often important to feather the selection (see "Feathering and Anti-Aliasing" in Chapter 8, *Selections and Channels*).

Feathering is like applying a Gaussian Blur to the edges of a selection: it blends the selected area smoothly into the rest of the image. How much to feather depends entirely upon the image and its resolution, but even a little feathering (two or three pixels) is much better than nothing.

On the other hand, we find that using a soft brush when dust-busting often kills the grain or texture of an image, so we typically use a harder-edged brush or selection for this sort of work.

Tip: A Myriad of Small Spots. Mildew, dust, bugs, corrosives, abrasive surfaces, or even a mediocre scanner can cause hundreds or thousands of tiny white or black spots in an image. And after sharpening, these spots pop out at you like stars on the new moon. If you're like us, you're already cringing at the thought of rubber-stamping all those dots out.

Here's a technique that can stamp out thousands of dust spots in a single move. You still may have to use the Clone Stamp or the Healing Brush tool to get rid of a few artifacts and some of the larger spots, but most of your work is already done (see Figure 15-5).

1. Select the area with the spots, and feather the selection.

2. Copy the selection to a new layer (Command-J).

3. If you're trying to remove white spots, set the blending mode in the Layers palette to Darken. If you're trying to remove black spots, set it to Lighten.

4. Use the Command and arrow keys to move the new layer left, right, up, or down by a few pixels—just enough that you see the dust spots disappear (if the spots are tiny, a one- or two-pixel move does the trick).

5. You can see a "before and after" by turning on and off the visibility of the new layer.

6. If you want, you can press Command-E to merge the new layer back into the original. (However, we often leave these as separate layers, so we don't damage the original image before we have to.)

Figure 15-5
Getting rid
of spots

The raw image

Setting the blending mode

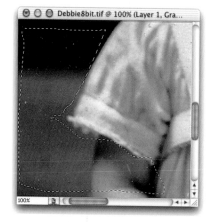

The dust spots copied to a new layer, and moved 4 pixels up and to the left

The final despotted image

At first, this seems like it takes a lot more work; but with experience, you'll find that you can make the right selections very quickly, and the dust spots simply disappear. Note that instead of using the Lighten or Darken blend mode, you can use the layer blending technique outlined in "Tip: Layer Blending Is Fast Blending," later in this chapter. Layer blending takes more time, but offers more control.

The Clone Stamp Tool

The Clone Stamp tool (which was once called the Rubber Stamp tool, though we have no idea why) lets you copy pixels from any place in your image (or even another image) and then paint them someplace else: Option-click to pick up a source point, and then paint away elsewhere to copy those pixels. Remember that you can control the opacity and blending mode of the tool using the Options bar or with keystrokes (see Chapter 2, *Essential Photoshop Tips and Tricks*).

Tip: Retouch on a Layer. However you retouch your image—with the Clone Stamp tool, the Healing Brush, painting, copying pixels from other portions of the image, and so on—try to do the work on a separate layer. When your edits are on a separate layer, it's easy to erase a change, and it's easy to see "before-and-after" views by turning the layer's visibility off and on. Remember that if you're using the Clone Stamp tool when painting on a separate layer, you need to turn on the Use All Layers checkbox in the Options bar.

Tip: Unlimited Cloning Supply. Don't let the boundaries of your image's window restrict you. If you want to clone from another open document, go right ahead and do it. You don't even have to switch documents, as long as you have a large enough monitor.

Tip: Keep Jumping Around. The single biggest mistake people make when using the Clone Stamp tool to clone from one area to another is dragging the mouse in a painting fashion. You should almost never paint when cloning. Instead, dab here and there with a number of clicks.

One exception to this rule is when the area you're cloning is relatively flat and has little texture or detail (like the blurry background behind a portrait). The second exception we make is when we're using the Clone Stamp tool with a blending mode like Darken, Lighten, Soft Light, and so on—and then only when the effect is subtle and doesn't create an obvious clone.

A second mistake people make is continuing to clone from the same area. Keep changing the source point that you're cloning (the point on which you Option-click). For example, if you're erasing some specks of dust on someone's face, don't just clone from one side of the specks. Erase one speck from pixel information to the left; erase the second speck from the right, and so on. That way, you avoid creating repeating patterns, and make the retouch less obvious (see Figure 15-6).

There are times, of course, when both these pieces of advice should be chucked out the window. For example, if you're rebuilding a straight line by cloning another parallel line in the image, you'd be hard-pressed to clone it by any other method than painting in the whole line. The following tip provides a way to do so relatively painlessly.

Tip: Stroking Paths. If you're trying to get rid of long scratches in an image, or to clone out those power lines that are always much more noticeable in a photograph than they were in reality, you can use the Pen tool to define a path, then use the Clone Stamp tool to stroke the path, obliterating the offending pixels in one swell foop (see Figure 15-7).

1. Draw the path using the Pen tool, keeping it as close to the center of the scratch (or powerline, or whatever) as possible. It's a good idea to

Figure 15-6
Changing the
source point

The annoying tree branches in the above left image can be removed by cloning with the Clone Stamp. But simply selecting a source point and painting with the Clone Stamp produces the "hall of mirrors" effect seen in the image above right. Dabbing with the Clone Stamp, choosing a new source point each time, produces the more convincing result shown at left.

Figure 15-7
Stroking a path with the
Clone Stamp tool

Getting rid of the powerlines by hand would take forever.

We draw a path along the powerline. Then, with the Clone Stamp tool set to a small soft-edged brush, we carefully align the source point to the path.

We Shift-click on the path in the Paths palette to hide the path, then drag the path over the Stroke icon at the bottom of the palette.

After repeating the process twice for the remaining powerlines, we arrive at the result shown at right. The critical parts of the operation are choosing the correct brush size, and setting the source point. In some cases, it's best to split the path into sections, choosing a different source for each one.

save it (double-click on the Work Path in the Paths palette and give it a name).

2. Select the Clone Stamp tool, and click the Aligned button in the Options bar. To remove a light-colored scratch, set the mode to Darken; to remove a dark powerline, set the mode to Lighten.

3. Choose a soft-edged brush that's somewhat wider than the widest point of the scratch.

4. Option-click beside the start of the path to set the source point for the cloning operation, just as you would if you were going to clone-stamp the scratch by hand.

5. Shift-click on the path in the Paths palette to hide it, then drag the path over the Stroke button at the bottom of the palette.

Presto, the scratch is gone. The keys to making this technique work are careful selection of the brush size and source point. If the brush is too big (or small), or your source point isn't aligned correctly, you may wind up duplicating the scratch instead of removing it. However, with a little practice you can make this work very quickly and easily.

The Healing Brush and the Patch Tool

Photoshop introduced two new tools that should make even the most hardened retoucher crack a smile: the Healing Brush and the Patch tool. The Healing Brush (press J) is quite a marvel of modern science; you first pick a spot on your image from which you want to clone (like the Clone Stamp tool, you Option- or Alt-click to pick the source), and then you paint in the area you want to change (see Figure 15-8). While the mouse button is down, the screen looks as though you were using the Clone Stamp tool. However, when you let go of the mouse button, Photoshop uses a complicated algorithm to blend the image of the source layer with the tone and texture of the area you're painting. The result is a Clone Stamp tool that blends in better than the Clone Stamp tool ever could.

The Patch tool is like a combination of the Healing Brush and the Lasso tool. Drag the Patch tool around an area you want to fix like you would make a selection with the Lasso tool (Option-click to create straight-line segments). Then click inside this selection and drag it to the part of your image that you want to copy. When you let go of the mouse button, Pho-

Figure 15-8
Painting with the
Healing Brush

The red-eye caused by a camera flash was fixed by selecting the pupils with a feathered edge, copying them to a new layer, and using Hue/ Saturation to alter the hue (to blue), heavily desaturate, and slightly darken them.

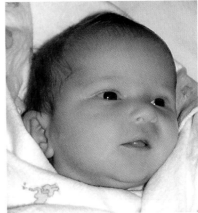

The original image.
Infants often have splotches and scratches that pass in a day or two.

Here, the red marks and other distractions have been removed with the Healing Brush.

The lip, caught by the camera at a bad moment, was selected with a feathered edge and fixed with the Liquify command.

Healing brush paint area ———

Source area (Option/Alt-click) ———

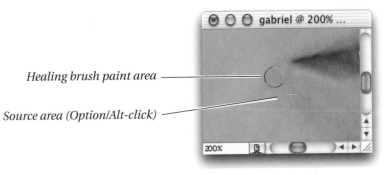

toshop clones that source area over the area you first selected, and then performs its "healing" algorithm to blend the source in properly (see Figure 15-9).

We find that the Patch tool rarely makes a perfect fix, and the results usually need to be cleaned up with the Healing Brush or Clone Stamp tool. But using it and then cleaning up the details is still significantly faster than not using the Patch tool at all.

Tip: Watch Out for Edges. The main problem with the Healing Brush and the Patch tool is that they don't work particularly well along edges in your image. For instance, let's say you have a shot of a dark-haired model against a light backdrop. These tools work beautifully in the model's face, but they can cause a mess when used along the edge where the hair meets the backdrop. The reason? These tools rely on the pixels around the

Figure 15-9
Quick fixes with
the Patch tool

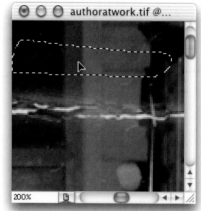

The original photograph has scratches and folds.

After dragging out a selection with the Patch tool, drag it on top of an area you want to copy (above). Here, we hold down the Shift key to constrain the drag vertically, ensuring the door frame will align properly when we let go (below).

The Patch tool fixes most of the heinous problems quickly, but the image still requires help, especially in the newly created anomalies in the window panes.

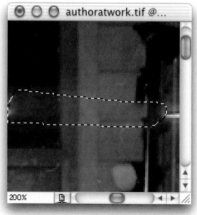

We use the Healing Brush to fix the details, including despotting.

brush stroke to blend in properly. Near high-contrast edges, the algorithm breaks—in this case, the dark pixels of the hair would smear into the lighter background pixels. The solution: make a soft-edged selection around the area you want to change; these tools won't take the areas outside the selection into consideration, so you won't get this smear effect.

Tip: Replace Mode. When you have the Healing Brush selected, you can select something called Replace from the Mode popup menu in the Options bar. The idea is simple: The Clone brush doesn't work particularly well with soft-edged brushes (the edges get too blurry). The Healing Brush set to Replace mode acts just like the Clone Stamp tool, but works much better if you have a hankerin' to use a soft-edged brush.

Dust and Scratches

While the Dust and Scratches filter promises great things ("wow, a filter that dust-busts my image!"), you should be aware that this tool can do significant harm to the rest of your image, too. The Dust and Scratches filter is basically the same as the Median filter, but with a threshold feature (so that you have some control over what gets "median-ized"). That means that it removes all small details in your document, including film grain or other image details that might be important.

If, in fact, you're trying to smooth out a grainy image while dust-busting, Dust and Scratches might be just the ticket. In that case, make sure you set the Radius value as low as possible and the Threshold value as high as possible. (It'll take some trial and error to get it right, so that the dust and scratches are gone, but the image isn't too blurry.) Then, re-sharpen the image with Unsharp Mask to return some edge contrast.

There are other uses for Dust and Scratches, too. For instance, we've had some luck using it to remove halftone patterns when rescreening (see "Rescreens," later in this chapter). Also, you can use it to blur the a and b channels in Lab images to get rid of digital-camera artifacts or film grain (see "Sharpening Channels" in Chapter 10, *Sharpening*, for a discussion of this technique). The Dust and Scratches filter is slower than the Gaussian Blur filter, but the Threshold slider makes it more controllable.

Tip: Maintain the Texture. While the Healing Brush and the Patch tool are designed to maintain the original texture of the image (including film grain), the Clone Stamp tool, Dust and Scratches filter, and other tools tend to destroy texture, and hence appear unnatural. You can sometimes simulate texture that's been lost by running the Add Noise or Grain filter on the affected area at a low setting. However, it's generally better to keep a close eye on what's happening to your texture as you retouch. (Also, see "Tip: Snapshot Patterns," below.)

Tip: Snapshot Patterns. Sometimes it's nice to paint a texture or a pattern with one of the brush tools. For instance, instead of adding noise to a selection, you might want to paint noise selectively. The most flexible way to do this is to create a layer by Option-clicking on the New Layer button in the Layers palette (which brings up the New Layer dialog box). Choose Overlay from the Mode popup menu, and turn on the "Fill with Overlay-neutral color" checkbox. Now, run the Grain filter or Add Noise filter to this layer, and add a layer mask. When you paint on the layer mask with black and white pixels, you paint the effect on and off.

Red-Eye

One of the most common retouching tasks is removing red-eye—that unfortunate, devilish effect that can appear when a camera flash reflects off the eye's retina. Asking your subject not to look directly into the camera lens can help avoid red-eye, as can avoiding the use of a flash, or using the red-eye pre-flash available on many point-and-shoot cameras (these make the pupil constrict so less flash enters the eye). But preventative measures don't help if your photograph already has red-eye. There are many ways to remove the red, but here are a couple of our favorites.

Hue/Saturation. Try selecting the offending pupils with an oval marquee, feathering the selection by a few pixels, copying the selection to a new layer (Command-J), and then using Hue/Saturation to shift the color, brightness, and saturation. Every image requires different Hue/Saturation values, but we usually start with a Hue setting of +40 (for brown eyes) or –120 (for blue eyes), a Saturation setting of –75, and a Lightness value of –50. The key is to remove the glaring color while still maintaining some specular highlights and color that make the eye look alive.

Color Replacement tool. The Color Replacement tool lives "under" the Healing Brush in the Tool palette. It lets you change the color of pixels to the foreground color, but leave the pixels' saturation and brightness alone. In other words, it changes the color but retains the detail. We haven't found it useful for large areas, but it's quite good at fixing things like red-eye. Hold down the Option key and click on the darkest part of the eye (or some other dark area nearby), then let go of the Option key, adjust the brush size to slightly smaller than the pupil, and draw over the red portions. You may need to increase the Tolerance level in the Options bar to 35 or 40 percent.

Compositing Images

As we explained in the last chapter, the number one problem in making selections and compositing images together is edge spill, where some of the background color gets picked up as fringe along the edges of your selection. There are a number of methods for getting rid of edge spill, but most of them involve simply cutting away at the edge pixels rather than removing the background color from the mix.

Now, to the rescue, comes the Extract feature, which is designed to search out edges, erase pixels, and—most important—perform edge-color decontamination, where Photoshop distills out background colors while leaving the foreground colors. It's almost like magic, and would be extraordinary if it really worked for more than a handful of images.

Note that Photoshop also has a Magic Eraser and Background Eraser tools, which erase to transparency. You can think of the Magic Eraser as like clicking with the Magic Wand tool and then pressing Delete. Either way, both of these tools are simply too blunt as instruments for us to consider them particularly helpful, and we just generally ignore them.

Of course, there are a number of other tools in Photoshop for compositing images together, too, from Layer Blending to the Photomerge feature (for creating panoramas). Let's take a look at just a few.

Tip: Layer Blending is Fast Blending. One of our favorite compositing techniques doesn't involve making selections or using Extract. It's the little-known and less-understood Blending Options feature in the Layer Style dialog box. If your image stands out well from its background on any one channel, you may find that layer blending is the fastest way to composite it into a different background (see Figure 15-10).

Figure 15-10
Compositing an image
with layer blending

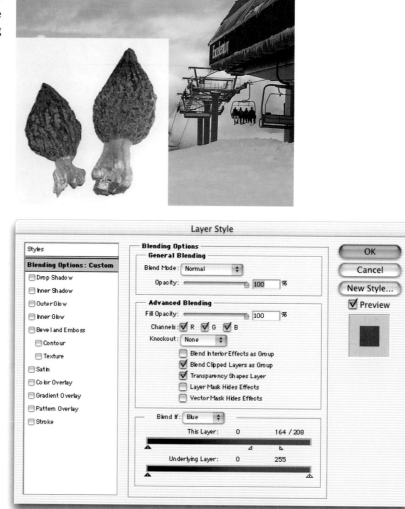

When you set the right "This Layer" slider in the Layer Style dialog box to 20 percent gray, you're telling Photoshop *not* to include any pixels in the layer that are lighter than 20 percent. The problem: this creates a hard edge, so you get a jaggy composite. The solution: Option-click on each of the sliders to break it into two half-triangles. This provides a smooth blend between what is included and what is not. We almost always blur the transitions in Layer Style, even if only a little.

Tip: Alignment via Opacity and Mode. When compositing images together, we prefer to place selected pixels on a separate layer for accurate positioning. You can do this by pressing Command-J (or choosing New Layer via Copy from the Layer menu). As one photographer explains, "I was working on a group portrait of a family where everyone's expressions were great except the teenage son's, whose eyes were closed. There was another shot in the same basic pose where he looked good, so of course I decided to replace the head in image A with the one from image B."

With this kind of massive editing, it's often difficult to align the new image with the old. One way is to change Opacity in the Layers palette to 50 percent or less, so you can see the image underneath. In this example, we align the new head's eyes with the original image's eyes (nudging one pixel at a time with the arrow keys; see Figure 15-11). Finally, we set the Opacity to 100 percent, and retouch the overlying layer's edges.

Note that instead of changing the opacity, you can change the overlying layer's blending mode. When trying to align two objects in an image, we often set the mode to Darken or Lighten. Then we watch the pixels darken and lighten, to give us clues.

Extract: Quick 'n' Dirty Masking

The good news is that Adobe is listening to its customers: The People said that they were tired of buying plug-ins that built high-quality selections and masks, so Adobe created the Extract feature. The bad news is that you'll probably still want to go buy a plug-in.

Don't get us wrong: The Extract feature is reasonably good at what it does, but what it does is not nearly as powerful as most people want. We hope that it's only a first stab at a very tricky problem, and that in the future there will be a better, stronger, cooler Extract feature.

Figure 15-11 Aligning floating selections

The original image

When the new selection is dropped over the original image, it's hard to see where it should be placed.

Opacity set to 60 percent so that positioning is easier

The final image

Nonetheless, Extract is what we've got for now—assuming that you don't have another plug-in, such as Extensis MaskPro—and so Extract is what we're going to talk about.

When to use Extract. There is a temptation to use Extract for any and every selection. Don't. Remember that Color Range or any of the other selection tools may provide a better, faster result. It depends entirely on the image and what you mean to do with it. Extract works best with images that display significant contrast between foreground object and background color, and where the edges aren't too detailed. For instance, your best friend photographed against a bright-blue sky would work well. On the other hand, you're going to have more trouble with an image of the typical blond model, hair shimmering against golden sand.

The best reason to use Extract is its edge-color-decontamination. If you're just trying to make a selection, and you're not planning on compositing an object on top of some other background (one with a very different tonal or color range than its original), then you'll probably find more peace of mind with another selection method.

Tip: Always Work on a Duplicate. Note that the Extract feature does not result in a mask or selection. Instead, it actually changes and deletes pixels in your image (it has to do this because of how it performs color decontamination). Because Extract is a relatively blunt instrument, you almost always have to clean up afterward. Therefore, before using Extract, it behooves you to work on a duplicate layer, or take a snapshot of your document, or save the document, or *something*, so that you don't mess up your original data. We tend to use a duplicate layer; then we can transform the result of Extract into a layer mask by loading the duplicate layer's transparency mask (Command-click on the layer), switching to the original layer, and clicking on the New Layer Mask button in the Layers palette. (Of course, if the original layer is a Background layer, you'll have to turn it into a regular layer first by double-clicking on it.)

Step-by-step Extraction. Once you've identified an appropriate image, open the Extract dialog box by choosing Extract from the Filter menu (in earlier versions, it was in the Image menu). Better yet, just press Command-Option-X to open the Extract dialog box. The Extract interface is still pretty clunky and unlike the rest of Photoshop (see Figure 15-12). But it's not too bad once you know the steps you need to take.

1. Use the Highlighter tool to paint a line along the edge of the foreground object (the thing you're trying to extract). The Highlighter should already be highlighted; if it's not, press B to select it. If you make a mistake, you can erase the "paint" with the Eraser tool (press E).

    When painting, you can press the bracket keys—[and]—to change the size of the highlighter brush. This is important because the brush size has a direct effect on the way Photoshop extracts the image. In general, you want a smaller brush around hard, defined edges, and a larger brush around soft, hairy, difficult edges. Note that you need to completely cover the edge transition with the highlighter, but you want the smallest brush you can get away with (see Figure 15-13). You also want to target the transition area, and stay away from the foreground object (the part you want opaque) as much as possible.

Figure 15-12
The Extract dialog box

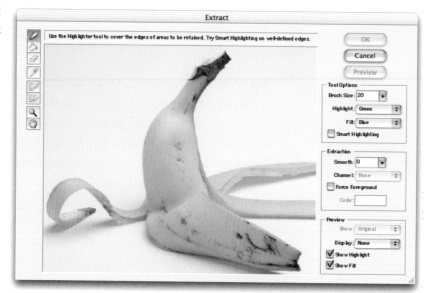

2. Now select the Paintbucket tool (press G) from the Extract dialog box, and click on the foreground object (inside the line you just drew). This tells Photoshop which side of the line is the stuff you want to keep. If the Paintbucket fills past the boundaries of your highlighter line, then there's a break in the line somewhere. In that case, simply select the Highlighter tool again, fill in the break, and then re-click with the Paintbucket tool.

3. Once you've specified what constitutes the edge (with the Highlighter) and what constitutes the inside of the object (with the Paintbucket), you must click the Preview button to see the result. If you don't like what you see, you can tweak the highlighter edge… but first turn on the Show Highlight checkbox, and set the View popup menu to Original.

4. Finally, when you have the effect you want, you can click OK. Photoshop deletes the background pixels, leaves the inside pixels, and "decontaminates" the pixels covered by the highlighter. The result is hardly ever perfect, so you must now use the History brush, the Clone Stamp tool, or any number of other methods to finalize the image.

Tip: Draw Faster Edges. Neither of us has particularly steady hands, so when it comes to drawing out the edge of the image with the Highlighter tool, we tend to use the Shift-click approach: Click once on the edge, then

Figure 15-13
Extracting the
foreground object

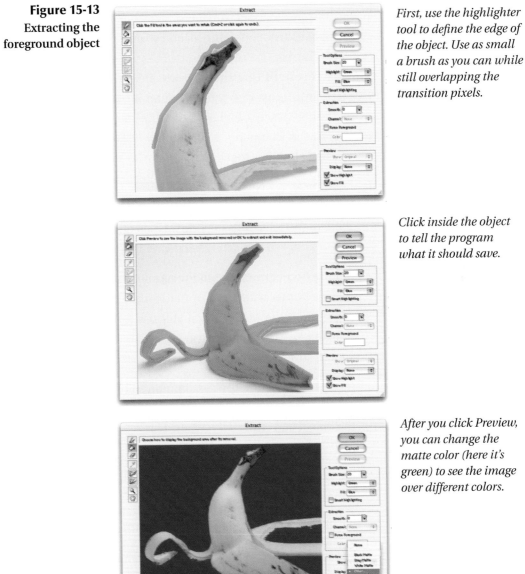

First, use the highlighter tool to define the edge of the object. Use as small a brush as you can while still overlapping the transition pixels.

Click inside the object to tell the program what it should save.

After you click Preview, you can change the matte color (here it's green) to see the image over different colors.

Shift-click someplace else, and Photoshop draws a straight line between the two points. These straight lines are often perfect for tracing the edge of an image.

Tip: Extraction Navigation. When you're flailing around in the Extract dialog box and your image is too big or too small, don't forget that the navigation shortcuts all work here: Spacebar for the Grabber Hand, Command-Spacebar-for zooming in, and so on.

Tip: Use Prebuilt Channels. As we said earlier, the best thing about the Extract feature is its edge-color decontamination. Sometimes it's easier to select the object with other methods (the Magic Wand, the Channels trick we describe in Chapter 8, *Selections and Channels*, and so on). You can use these techniques together to get the best of both worlds.

1. First, make a selection around the foreground object. The selection should be relatively clean and well-defined. (Of course, if you spent more than 15 seconds making this selection, it's a good idea to save it as a channel so you can recall it later if necessary.)

2. Choose Border from the Modify submenu (under the Select menu) and select a border width appropriate for the resolution of the image. For a low-res image, you can probably use 4 or 5 pixels; for higher-resolution images, you'll need to use a larger amount. The resulting selection should straddle the edge of the object (see Figure 15-14).

3. Invert this selection (press Command-Shift-I) and then save it in the Channels palette. The channel should appear black along the edge of the object and white everywhere else.

4. Now, when you open the Extract dialog box, choose this channel from the Load Highlight popup menu. This loads your "selection," so you don't have to draw one manually.

5. Finally, click on the inside with the Paintbucket tool and click Preview.

    This still isn't a perfect system, but it's sometimes easier than drawing the outline yourself.

In our opinion, the Extract feature earns an "A" for effort, a "B" for final results, and a "C" for interface. Ultimately, however, no one ever said extracting images was going to be easy. Just easier.

Photomerge

Even the widest-angle lens can't capture every scene you'll ever want to capture; sometimes you need to shoot several photographs and attempt to match them up for a panorama. Enter the Photomerge feature. Technically

Figure 15-14
Making a border
selection

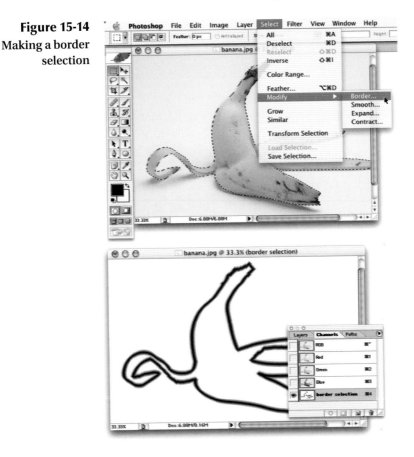

this is an automation tool, but it has both brains and brawn behind it. To merge two or more images together, select Photomerge from the Automate submenu (under the File menu). You can choose which images to merge by picking from the Use popup menu: Open Files (if your images are already open), Files (to pick the files from disk), or Folder (to pick a whole folder of images). Note that after adding files to the list in the Photomerge dialog box, you can remove any of them by clicking the Remove button. You can also select two or more images in the File Browser and select Photomerge from the File Browser's Automate menu.

When you click OK, Photoshop goes to work: It opens both images, resamples them if necessary to make them match, merges them as layers in a single file, and then opens the Photomerge dialog box (see Figure 15-15). Photoshop compares the edge detail to find matches, and then attempts to stitch the images together by blending from one into the next. Adobe's marketing team likes using the term "seamless," when describing Photomerge's results, but unless you were mighty careful about the light-

Figure 15-15
Photomerge

Vanishing Point tool

*Dragging an image
from the staging
area down into the
layout area*

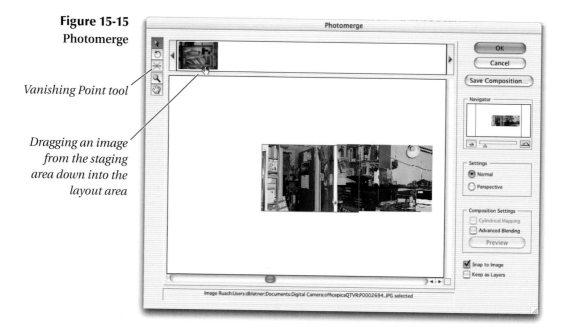

ing when you shot the images you'll almost certainly be able to find the
seams where one image blends into the next. The seams are often at an
angle, so they're less obvious to the eye. You can usually get a slightly better effect by turning on the Advanced Blending option in the Photomerge
dialog box. Click the Preview button to see the difference between regular
and advanced blending.

Tip: Shooting Panoramas. When shooting images destined for Photomerge, try to capture each using the same exposure and the same lighting, using a tripod when possible to keep the camera level. With some
point-and-shoot cameras, you may have to work a bit to ensure you're
getting the same exposure.

Keep as Layers. The Keep as Layers checkbox tells Photoshop not to flatten the image when it's done compositing, so each image remains on its
own layer. Unfortunately, it also removes all the blending from one image
into the next, so you're forced to do that part yourself. That's pretty silly, in
our opinion, so we never turn this on for panoramas. (However, see "Tip:
Fast Image Compositing," below.) With luck, perhaps the next version of
Photomerge will retain layers and include the blending as layer masks.

Manually compositing. Photomerge can analyze and automatically composite most images we've attempted, but not infrequently it fails to figure out how images should be stitched together. In these cases, you can drag the images from the panel at the top of the Photomerge dialog box down into the main compositing area. Drag the images around in this window until you get a reasonably good overlap. If you need to, use Photomerge's Rotate tool to rotate each selected image for a better fit. We recommend leaving the Snap to Images checkbox turned on so that Photoshop will try to snap one image to the other. When you turn this off, Photoshop acts just as though you moved images around using the Move tool in a Photoshop document.

Tip: Fast Image Compositing. Photomerge is designed to build panoramas, but you can use it to composite any group of pictures together into a collage. For example, you might have head shots of ten different sports teams that you want to merge into a collage. In this case, you would turn off the Snap to Images option, and then drag the images around the Photomerge window until you get more or less the effect you want. This is often faster because you're working with the small low-resolution images. When you click OK, Photoshop performs all the annoying grunt work of moving the high resolution data around, increasing canvas size, and so on. If you think you're going to want to tweak and finesse the image, you may want to turn on Save as Layers, too.

Perspective. The problem with panoramas is that they typically ignore perspective. For a more life-like panorama, click the Perspective button. By default, Photoshop designates the middle image as the vanishing point and the images to the left and right (or above and below) splay out, as though the edges were closer to you, the viewer. You can override this by clicking on any other image with Photomerge's Vanishing Point tool (that's the third tool down; see Figure 15-16). Note that the vanishing point image has a blue outline when you click on it with the Select Image tool; non-vanishing point images have red outlines.

Saving Compositions. If it took you more than a minute or so to build your photomontage, it's probably worth saving the composition to disk by clicking (you guessed it) the Save Composition button. Compositions

Figure 15-16
Photomerge
perspective

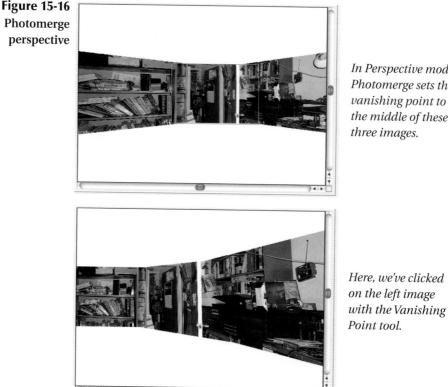

In Perspective mode, Photomerge sets the vanishing point to the middle of these three images.

Here, we've clicked on the left image with the Vanishing Point tool.

are very small files that reference the full-resolution files and how they're blended together. Later, if you decide to make changes, select Photomerge from the Automate submenu and click the Load Composition button instead of selecting files.

Vectors vs. Pixels

Wasn't it Robert Frost who said, "Pixels are pixels, and vectors are vectors, and never the twain shall meet"? They may not meet, but Photoshop brings them awfully close together. In ancient versions of Photoshop, vector information was limited to paths that you could convert to selections or clipping paths. Now, Photoshop offers layer clipping paths (which we discussed in Chapter 8, *Selections and Channels*) and text based on vector outlines. Additionally, paths can affect the pixels around and inside them, especially when you use layer effects.

In this section, we want to look at how you can convert images between pixels and objects (such as paths or Illustrator documents), and why you'd want to. Then, in the next section, we'll look at the vastly improved world of vector text in Photoshop.

Open vs. Place

We all know that clients are notorious for asking the impossible. They want Pantone colors in the middle of a process-color image (without paying for another ink). They want a tiny photograph blown up to poster size (retaining the sharpness, of course). Or they want their crisp, clean logos added to a product shot. Wait—that last one isn't so hard, after all.

Fortunately, you can open *any* EPS or PDF file in Photoshop, no matter the program or the platform, because Photoshop has a built-in RIP that interprets the PostScript in the EPS or PDF and converts it to pixels.

There are two ways to import EPS and PDF files: Open and Place.

Open. When you select an EPS or PDF file in the Open dialog box, Photoshop recognizes it as such and gives you additional options (see Figure 15-17). The additional options you get with an EPS or PDF file let you specify the resolution and size of the final bitmap image. When you click OK, Photoshop creates a new document and rasterizes the EPS or PDF (turns it into a bitmap). Any areas of the EPS or PDF that don't have a fill specified come in transparent.

Tip: Forcing the EPS Point. If you can't see the EPS or PDF file in Photoshop's Open dialog box, it probably means that the file type, creator, or suffix is missing (depending on whether you're on a Macintosh or a PC). Your best bet is to try changing the file's name so that it ends in ".eps" or ".pdf". If this still doesn't work, the file may have become corrupted, and

Figure 15-17
Opening a generic
EPS or PDF file

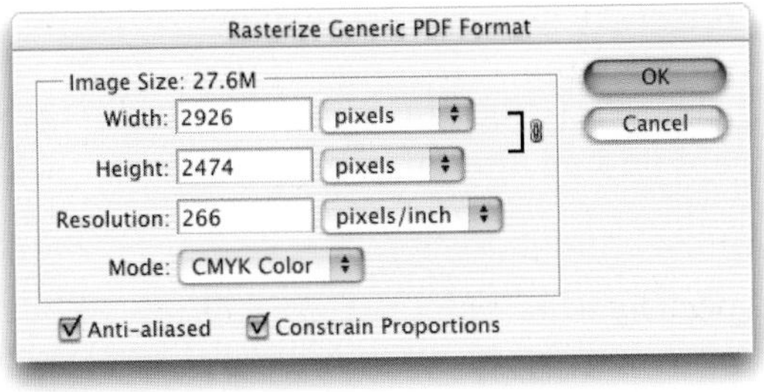

Photoshop will only let you open the PICT or TIFF preview of the EPS file (usually only a 72-dpi representation of the image).

Tip: Opening Previews. You can, if you want, open the PICT or TIFF preview of an EPS file instead of rasterizing the EPS itself. This might come in handy if the whole EPS file is enormous and takes too long to rasterize. For example, if you want a thumbnail of your magazine's cover for your Web site, you could save the cover as an EPS, open it in Photoshop, and reduce it in size. However, you don't need all that high-resolution data, so you could just open the low-resolution preview and shrink that down instead.

The trick is to choose EPS PICT Preview or EPS TIFF Preview from the Format popup menu in the Open dialog box. (In Windows, this is the Open As dialog box.) Now when you open the file, you only get the low-resolution preview.

Place. When you select Place rather than Open, Photoshop drops the EPS or PDF file into your current document and then lets you scale and rotate it to fit your needs (you can scale it by dragging a handle, rotate it by dragging outside the rectangle, and move it by dragging inside the rectangle). When you have finished scaling the image, press Return or Enter. Photoshop doesn't rasterize the image into pixels until you do this, so scaling won't degrade the final image. (Note that you can always press Command-period—Escape on Windows—to cancel the Place command.) Like Paste, Place almost always creates a new layer for your incoming image (although it won't if you place an EPS or PDF on a spot color channel, for instance).

Tip: Proportional Scaling. While QuarkXPress constrains the width/height ratio of a box (so it stays proportional) when you hold down the Option and Shift keys, you only need to hold down Shift in Photoshop.

Tip: Colorizing Black and White Images. For some reason, David keeps finding himself in the position of opening a black-and-white EPS file (like a logo) in Photoshop and needing to colorize it. However, the Colorize feature in Hue/Saturation—the tool he'd usually use for this sort of thing—doesn't work, because it doesn't colorize any pixels that are fully black or fully white. Turns out there are many different ways to get around this, but our favorite is to add a Solid Color adjustment layer just above the logo's layer, set the adjustment layer's color to Screen, and then group it with the logo layer (Option-click between the layers in the Layers palette). Then, if you want to change the color, just double-click on the adjustment layer to edit it.

Tip: Maintaining Objects. What we'd really like is for Photoshop to let us open or place an EPS or PDF file, and give us paths instead of bitmaps. Unfortunately, we can't figure out how to do that. You can, however, *paste* or drag a path from Adobe Illustrator or Macromedia FreeHand into Photoshop (see "Paths" in Chapter 8, *Selections and Channels*). If you paste the path in, Photoshop asks if you want to rasterize the path into pixels, leave it as a path, or turn it into a layer clipping path (see Figure 15-18). If you drag objects across from FreeHand or Illustrator, Photoshop automatically rasterizes… unless you hold down the Command key, in which case you get paths instead. (Note that since Illustrator 10, you must now open the Preferences dialog box and tell Illustrator to copy AICB data as well as PDF data in order for this to work properly.)

Figure 15-18
Pasting Illustrator or
FreeHand paths

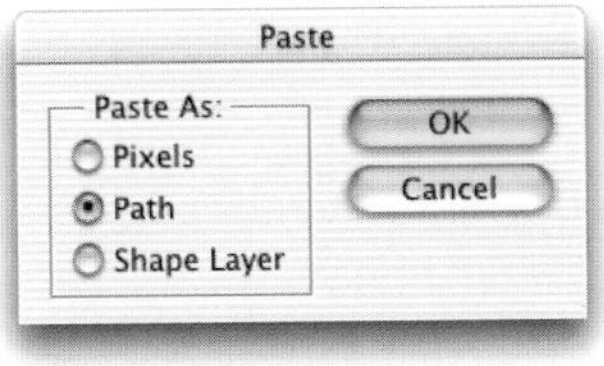

Of course, once you have your image in paths, you can easily convert it to a layer clipping path to create vector-based "shapes" (see "Layer Clipping Paths and Shapes" in Chapter 8, *Selections and Channels*). Beware, though: if your vectors are very complex and you save the file as an EPS (maintaining the vectors), it may take a very long time to print.

If you're creating images for multimedia or the Web, check out "Tip: Maintaining Colors" in Chapter 18, *Multimedia and the Web*, for more information on transferring objects from Illustrator or FreeHand into Photoshop.

Tip: Opening Non-Illustrator EPSes. In theory, Photoshop lets you import and rasterize any EPS file, but it occasionally fails and sometimes it's helpful to use some other program to rasterize the images for you. In these cases, you might take a look at Transverter Pro, from TechPool. This utility rasterizes PostScript images, is relatively inexpensive, and almost always works. Transverter Pro also has the added benefit of converting between a number of other formats. For instance, you can convert Corel-Draw EPS files to Illustrator files, and so forth.

Tip: Add Your Page Layout to Images. Photoshop can help you build photorealistic comps of ads. The client can see their ad in place—on a billboard or a bus, or wherever—before the ad is even created (see Figure 15-19). Create the ad in InDesign or QuarkXPress as usual, then save it as an EPS or PDF file. Once you rasterize it and import it into Photoshop, you can rotate it, scale it, and so on, so that it fits the ad space (don't forget to add a little noise so that it looks more realistic in the photograph).

Figure 15-19
Add your page
layout to images

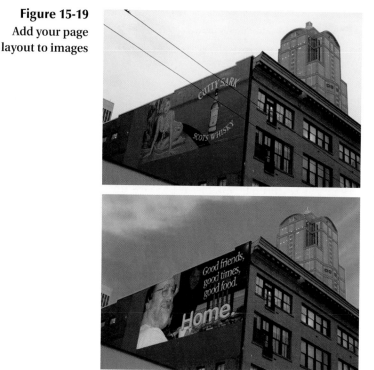

The original image

The ad incorporated into the street scene, ready to show to the client

Text and Typography

Photoshop gained typographic prowess late in its career; in fact, for a long time it was downright painful to get good-looking type out of it. But that's all changed now. It's like the folks on the Photoshop team took a look at the typography in InDesign and suddenly said, "Hey, we can do that!" Photoshop lets you tweak kerning, leading, color, hyphenation, and more to your heart's content. You can set beautiful type in Photoshop… but that doesn't mean you should.

People who want to overlay text on top of pictures often ask us, "Should we use the Type tool in Photoshop, or the features in our page-layout or illustration program?" The answer, as always, is "it depends."

▶ If your final output is to a color printer such as an ink-jet or dye-sub printer, anti-aliased type within Photoshop's bitmapped image often looks better. The hard-edged type from a program such as QuarkXPress looks too jaggy off these low-resolution devices.

▶ If the text is integrated into your image—you want to apply a wacky filter to it, you want it to sit partially behind part of your image, or something like that—instead of being a separate element overlaying the image, there's a good chance that you'll need to create it in Photoshop. While QuarkXPress cannot create transparent text, Adobe InDesign can.

▶ If the text is filtered or textured, you'll probably have to create it in Photoshop (though both QuarkXPress and InDesign let you convert text to outlines, into which you can put bitmapped textures or images saved from Photoshop).

▶ If you save your images in the TIFF format and print from a different program, then the text in your Photoshop document becomes bitmapped. This also happens if you save the file as an EPS or PDF and turn off "Include Vector Data." So if you're working with a 225-ppi image, any text you add to that image in Photoshop is similarly 225 ppi. That's high enough for most images, but it looks crummy for hard-edged type. Sure, you can anti-alias the text in Photoshop; that looks great on screen, but it just looks fuzzy in final output. If you use TIFF files and need hard-edged type, type it in the page-layout program.

(While in theory you can add vector type to TIFF images—see Chapter 16, *Storing Images*—no software other than Photoshop can currently read it, so it still comes out rasterized.)

▶ In order to maintain the hard-edged, vector, outlined text, you have to save the file in the EPS or PDF format (see Chapter, 16, *Storing Images*). However, if you use EPS, Photoshop converts all the text into outlines. This prints more slowly than the same text printed from a page-layout or illustration program. If it's just a few words, then the difference is negligible, but printing a page full of text in a Photoshop EPS is painfully slow (PDF files with text are better, but there are sometimes other problems importing and printing PDF files).

For the same reason, EPS files containing vector type mushroom in size. A paragraph of text in a Photoshop EPS might add over a megabyte to the file size, compared to only 10 or 20 K in QuarkXPress. We've also seen some weird text bugs when we use more than one or two sentences of text in a single text block.

▶ Photoshop's text controls are cool, but they're not exactly speedy. Even on a reasonably fast machine, laying out a column of several paragraphs can force Photoshop to a crawl. Again, the more text you have, the more you should set it in some other program.

So, if you're setting more than a few words, you should probably set them in QuarkXPress, InDesign, PageMaker, Illustrator, FreeHand, or some other program. But if you're hell-bent on using Photoshop to lay out text, here are some tips and tricks to help you do so more efficiently.

Tip: Making Text Blocks. Most people who have used Photoshop for years use the Text tool by simply clicking on their image. That works, but if you're going to type more than one line's worth of text, the click-and-type procedure is a pain because you have to manually break lines by hitting Return. Instead, drag out a text *frame* with the Text tool before typing. Photoshop automatically wraps the text to fit that frame. Plus, you can always reshape the frame by dragging its corner or edge handles, or rotate the text block by dragging outside of the frame.

By the way, keep your eye on the lower-right corner handle; when there's too much text to fit the frame, Photoshop places a little + sign there. It's subtle, so you have to look carefully.

If you want to create a new text block near or on top of another bit of text, you might have trouble because Photoshop will think you're trying to select the existing text. No problem: Shift-click or Shift-drag with the Text tool to force Photoshop to create a new text layer.

When you're done creating or editing text, press Enter on the keypad, or Control-Enter (Windows) or Command-Return (Macintosh).

Tip: Setting the Column Width. Do you need a text block exactly 144 points wide? No problem: Just Option-click with the Text tool, and Photoshop offers you a way to type in an exact size.

Tip: Resizing Text Blocks. It can be incredibly frustrating to make a text block bigger or smaller by dragging a corner or edge handle, because Photoshop often doesn't recognize that your cursor is over a handle. The trick is patience: hover the cursor over the handle for about one or two seconds; as soon as you see it change to a little arrow, you can drag the handle.

Tip: Editing Type Layers. There are several ways to edit text on a type layer.

▶ You can double-click on the type layer's thumbnail icon in the Layers palette. (Double-clicking on the tile instead opens the Layer Style dialog box or lets you edit the layer name.)

▶ You can click on top of the text with the Type tool. You know your cursor is in the right place when the Type tool's cursor changes to an "I-beam." However, if you click in the wrong place, Photoshop will create a new type layer; in this case, press the Escape key to cancel the new layer.

▶ Best yet, when you have both the Type tool selected in the Tool palette and the type layer selected in the Layers palette, you can choose Edit Type from the context-sensitive menu. On the Mac, Control-click anywhere on the image, or right-mouse-button click in Windows.

You can also format various aspects of a layer by selecting the layer in the Layers palette and changing values in the Options bar (when the Text tool is selected), Character palette, or Paragraph palette (see "Text Formatting," later in this chapter, for more on this).

Tip: Rendering Type Layers. Type layers are special; you can't paint or run filters on them, or do anything else that relies on pixel-editing. If you need to do something like that, you have to render them (turn them into proper bitmaps) by selecting Type from the Rasterize submenu (under the Layers menu) or from the context-sensitive menu you get with the Type tool (Control-click on Mac, right-click in Windows).

However, note that in general, it's best to do all the transformations (rotating, scaling, positioning, skewing), and layer effects (drop shadows, and so on) that you need before rendering the type layer. That way, you can be assured of the highest-quality type.

Tip: Making Text Masks. There are two tools in the Tool palette that create text masks rather than text (that is, as you type, Photoshop makes a selection in the shape of text rather than text itself). However, when it comes to making selections in the shape of text, we would rather create a normal type layer and then Command-click on it in the Layers palette. By actually creating a type layer, we can preview it in the image before clicking OK, we can edit the text later, or use the type someplace else (even in another image). If we had simply used a Type Selection tool, we'd have nothing but an ephemeral group of marching ants.

By the way, if you already have a selection made, don't forget that you can add to that selection by Command-Shift-clicking on the type layer in the Layers palette. Conversely, you can remove from the selection by Command-Option-clicking.

Tip: Check Your Spells. No, the Check Spelling feature won't help you with your spells if you end up at Hogwarts School of Magic, but it might help if your Photoshop document has a lot of text in it. To check the spelling of a single word, select the word with the Text tool and choose Check Spelling from the Edit menu or the context-sensitive menu. If no word is selected, Photoshop checks the spelling of every text layer in your file.

We find this feature especially helpful with foreign words, which we often have no idea how to spell correctly. Photoshop ships with a number of different language dictionaries, such as Spanish and Swedish. However, in order for the Check Spelling feature to work correctly with foreign words, you must first select the words and choose the appropriate language from the Language popup menu in the Character palette.

Tip: Find and Replace Text. For those of you who use Photoshop to create advertisements or other materials more appropriate for page-layout applications, note that Photoshop now has a Find and Replace Text feature that lets you search for simple text strings. This feature isn't nearly as powerful as those in other programs (for instance, there's no way to search for text formatting or special characters such as tabs). But if you're trying to find a word or phrase that has gone missing, it does the trick.

Tip: Converting Text to Paths and Shapes. David recently designed and built a business card for a client entirely in Photoshop. However, he knew that his printer (the company that would burn the film and print the card) didn't have the proper font. He might have sent the font along with the file, but there are too many things that could have gone wrong. So instead, he simply converted the text to a layer clipping path (see Figure 15-20). It's easy to do: select the text layer in the Layers palette and choose Convert to Shape from the Type submenu (in the Layer menu). This is a shortcut for selecting Create Work Path (from the same place), adding a Solid Color adjustment layer, and then deleting the text layer.

Once you convert text to a layer clipping path, there's no reason to have the font anymore. Of course, you also can no longer edit the text. Note that this is dangerous if you have a lot of text, because highly complex clipping paths can take forever to print (or not print at all). If you have a lot of text, it's probably better to try exporting the file as a PDF file; in this case, you can actually embed the font in the file so you don't need to convert to outlines.

Tip: Text on a Path. Need to run text along a path? No problem. Simply draw a path with the Pen tools (see Chapter 8, *Selections and Channels*) and then click on it with the Text tool. Note that the Text tool's cursor icon changes when it's on top of a path, and when you click and then start typing, the text begins from the point you clicked. To adjust the starting and ending points for the text on the path, switch to the Path Selection tool (press A); as you hover the cursor over the start or end point, the cursor changes to a vertical line with a thick black arrow. If you click and drag with this cursor, you adjust where the text begins or ends on the line.

The direction you draw your path determines how Photoshop draws the text. If you draw a path from left to right, the text flows on the top of the line; if you draw from right to left, the text flows from right to left—upside

Figure 15-20
Converting text to paths

When you convert text to a shape, it changes to a layer clipping path on a Solid Color adjustment layer.

down. To flip the text over, use the Path Selection tool and drag the beginning or ending endpoint to the other side of the line.

Photoshop doesn't offer a lot of control over how the text flows along the line, but you can rotate the text so that it flows "vertically" along the line by clicking the "Change the text orientation" button on the far left of the Options bar.

Text Formatting

Placing text in your image is all very well and good, but you won't win design awards until you've figured out how to format your text. (Well, there might be a few other steps before you win awards, too. We make no guarantees.) There are two types of formatting: Character (which can apply to one or more characters) and Paragraph (which always applies to one or more paragraphs). You can find these settings in the Options bar (when the Text tool is selected in the Tool palette) or in the Character and Paragraph palettes (see Figure 15-21).

Tip: Hide the Selection. Formatting text is difficult when you have text selected, especially when you're trying to change the text's color. Don't forget you can press Command-H to hide the text selection; the text remains selected, but you can see the changes more easily as you make them.

Tip: Beware of Leading. Leading ("ledding") determines the amount of space between lines in a paragraph. Bruce, who is accustomed to Page-Maker and InDesign, finds Photoshop's leading feature intuitive because in all three programs, leading is considered (Bruce would say "correctly considered") a character attribute. In QuarkXPress, however, leading is a paragraph attribute. If you're used to XPress (like David), you need to be extra careful when changing leading. If you want the leading to be consistent throughout a paragraph, you should either select every character in the paragraph *before* you set the leading in the Character palette, or you should apply the leading while the text layer is selected in the Layers palette (but no text on the layer is selected).

By the way, while the Auto leading (in the Character palette's Leading popup menu) is tempting, we rarely use this. Auto leading sets the leading at 120-percent of the text size (you can change this percentage by choos-

Figure 15-21
Formatting text

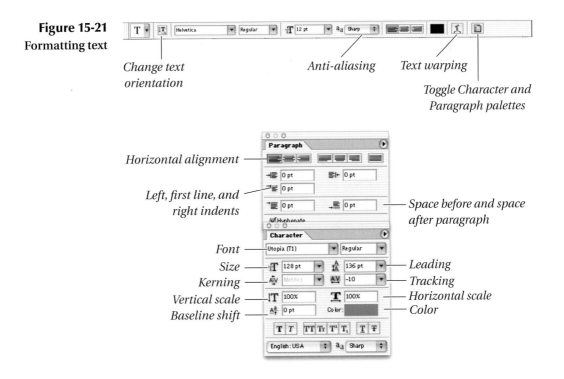

Change text orientation

Anti-aliasing

Text warping

Toggle Character and Paragraph palettes

Horizontal alignment

Left, first line, and right indents

Space before and space after paragraph

Font

Size

Kerning

Vertical scale

Baseline shift

Leading

Tracking

Horizontal scale

Color

ing Justification from the popout menu in the Paragraph palette). If every character is the same size, this is okay, but if you make a single character even one point larger on a line, the leading for that whole line changes, causing inconsistency within the paragraph (read: "ugly"). We much prefer to set the leading manually, to an absolute value.

Kerning and tracking. Kerning determines the amount of space between each character. Tracking is the same thing, but over a range of text (which is why some folks more accurately call it "range kerning"). Photoshop lets you do both in the Character palette—if your cursor is placed between two characters, you can kern them; if you've selected more than one character, then you can track them. (Or, if the type layer is selected in the Layers palette but no text is selected, then tracking applies to every character on that layer.) Note that the kerning and tracking values in Photoshop are based on $\frac{1}{1000}$ em (one em in a 24-point font is 24 points wide; in a 50-point font, it's 50 points wide, and so on). To convert QuarkXPress tracking values into Photoshop tracking values, multiply the XPress value by five.

The default kerning value for text is Metrics, which is reasonable—*metrics* are the kerning pairs built into most fonts. But we almost always select the type layer (with no text selected on it) and change the kerning to Optical in the Character palette, which tells Photoshop to use its very cool method of analyzing the shape of each character and adjusting the kerning accordingly. If it's small text, this sometimes makes it look really ugly, so we change it back to Metrics, or even possibly change it to 0 (zero).

Anti-alias settings. Photoshop has long let you turn text anti-aliasing on and off. While some people recommend turning off anti-aliasing for very small text, we find that anti-aliasing almost always helps on-screen readability, so we generally leave it on. The problem is that in small text sizes, anti-aliasing sometimes leaves fonts looking a bit anemic. Fortunately, Photoshop lets you change the anti-aliasing style.

We usually set the Anti-alias popup menu (in the Options bar or the context-sensitive menu when the Text tool is selected) to Crisp or Smooth (there's too little difference between the two to notice most of the time). However, when working with small text, we sometimes use the Strong option. It's entirely a judgment call—if Strong is too bold, then we'll switch back to Smooth.

Fractional Widths. Text characters rarely fit perfectly on a 72-dpi grid—for instance, a letter "A" might be 18.1 pixels wide. Photoshop now gives you the choice of how to deal with these "fractional widths." When the Fractional Widths feature is turned on in the popout menu in the Character palette, Photoshop rounds the character widths to the nearest pixel, which usually results in some characters moving slightly closer together. In large point sizes, this is usually a good thing, but in small text sizes, the characters often run into each other and it looks dorky.

Generally, if your text looks mushed together, go ahead and turn this feature off. Note that Fractional Widths affects the entire text block, not just selected characters. (Again, you can turn this feature on and off for all linked text layers by holding down the Shift key while selecting the menu item.)

Tip: What's That Font? You might notice fonts in your Font menu (in both the Options bar and the Character palette) that don't appear in other programs. That's because Adobe has instituted a system in which any font placed in a special Fonts folder shows up in Adobe applications only. On the Macintosh, that folder is inside the Library>Application Support>Adobe folder. In Windows, it's inside the Program Files>Common Files>Adobe directory. We find it annoying to find fonts in one program that don't appear in others, but that's life.

Also, note that if you have more than one font installed with the same name, Photoshop kindly informs you by placing a "(TT)" next to the True-Type version, a "(T1)" next to the PostScript version, and an "(OT)" next to the OpenType version.

Tip: Changing Text Color. The fastest way to change the color of one or more characters in a text block is by selecting them with the Text tool and then simply picking a color in the Options bar, or the Tool, Character, Swatches, or Color palette. Or, if you already have the color chosen as your foreground or background color, you can select the text and press Option-Delete (to apply the foreground color) or Command-Delete (for the background color). If you want to apply the same color to every character on a type layer, then select the layer in the Layers palette and press these same keystrokes. (Photoshop acts as though Preserve Transparency—what's now called Lock Pixels—is always turned on for text layers.)

Tip: Keyboard Type Shortcuts. There are a number of keyboard short-cuts that can help you speed up your text formatting (see Table 15-1). Remember that the extra time you take to learn these now will come back as time saved later.

Tip: Linking Text Layers. Do you want to change the font and size of six different text layers in your document? No problem: Link them together (select one of them, then click in the Link column of the other layers in the Layers palette), and then hold down the Shift key while making changes in the Options bar. This also works in the Character and Paragraph palettes, but we've found it to be a little buggy. Note that if you change the track-ing, indent, or any other numeric settings in the Character or Paragraph palettes, you have to press Shift-Return to make it apply to all linked layers. To change the color or Warp Effects for all the linked layers, you have to Shift-click on the button or swatch.

Other character styles. Photoshop offers a number of other charac-ter styles to help make your award-winning text. Here's a few others you should know about.

▶ **Faux styles.** Want Hobo Bold? Or Zapf Dingbats Italic? Sorry, they don't exist (there are no outlines that describe them), so Photoshop won't let you use them. On the other hand, the program is ready and willing to fake them (see Figure 15-22). When you turn on Faux Italic in the popout menu of the Character palette, Photoshop simply obliques (skews) the font slightly. Faux Bold simply makes the font heavier. The effect is generally pretty good, and even lets you make a bolder bold and a more slanted italic face than might otherwise be available. (Note that you can't embed Faux Bold fonts in PDF files.)

The Character palette's popout menu also offers the Underline and Strikethrough styles, which—true to their names—place a line under or through the selected text. No, you can't adjust the size, shape, color, or anything else of the underline or strikethrough line. Yes, we know you can do that in InDesign CS. Personally, we find these faux features particularly silly.

▶ **Scaling and moving.** You can scale individual characters (or all the words on a text layer) vertically or horizontally in the Character palette, though we find that many designers overuse this and create really far-

	To do this...	...press this
Table 15-1	Show/Hide type selection	Command-H
Type tool keyboard shortcuts	Move right one word	Command-Right arrow
	Move left one word	Command-Left arrow
	Select right one word	Command-Shift-Right arrow
	Select left one word	Command-Shift-Left arrow
	Move to next paragraph	Command-Down arrow
	Move to previous paragraph	Command-Up arrow
	Increase size 2 points	Command-Shift-. (period)
	Decrease size 2 points	Command-Shift-, (comma)
	Increase leading 2 points	Option-Down arrow
	Increase leading 10 points	Command-Option-Down arrow
	Decrease leading 2 points	Option-Up arrow
	Decrease leading 10 points	Command-Option-Up arrow
	Increase kerning 2/100 em	Option-Right arrow
	Increase kerning 1/10 em	Command-Option-Right arrow
	Decrease kerning 2/100 em	Option-Left arrow
	Decrease kerning 1/10 em	Command-Option-Left arrow
	Increase baseline shift 2 points	Option-Shift-Up arrow
	Increase baseline shift 10 points	Command-Option-Shift-Up arrow
	Decrease baseline shift 2 points	Option-Shift-Down arrow
	Decrease baseline shift 10 points	Command-Option-Shift-Down arrow

Figure 15-22

Faux Italic

out, stretched typefaces that are simply unreadable. Use with discretion. The Character palette also offers a Baseline Shift feature, which you can use if you want to move individual characters up or down (like in a math equation, the little ® symbol, and so on).

By the way, on a similar topic, you might notice the Rotate Characters feature in the Character palette's popout menu, and you might also notice that it's almost always grayed out. What's the deal? It's only available when you have vertically oriented text, and it simply rotates each character 90 degrees so that it reads sideways. We ignore it; if we want text to read sideways, we use the Transform tool.

▶ **Case and caps.** Want to make your text REALLY SCREAM? Then turn on All Caps in the Character palette's popout menu. (Personally, we find All Caps rather annoying to look at.) There are other features in this menu, too: Small Caps, Super Script, and Subscript. Each of these applies to selected text unless no text is selected on a type layer. You can turn them off again by reselecting them from the popout menu. Note that unless you're using Open Type fonts, the Small Caps feature fakes the small caps (if you have an Expert font that contains the real small caps, you'll get better quality using that instead).

Hyphenation and justification. Hyphenation and justification (usually just called "H&J") are two methods of making text fit into a given space by controlling the amount of space between letters and words, and by breaking certain words at line endings with hyphens. Photoshop can also stretch text in order to help it fit a particular column width. If any one of these methods is used in excess, the results are awful. So it's important to find a good balance among them.

The H&J settings are only relevant when you have a paragraph or more of text—that is, when you've dragged out a text frame, rather then just clicked and typed (see "Tip: Converting Point Type to Paragraph Type," later in this chapter). And the H&Js are always paragraph-wide formats; you can't apply them to a single character or line within a paragraph. Let's look at the several features in Photoshop that relate to H&Js.

▶ **Hyphenation.** By default, Photoshop hyphenates words that fall near the end of a line of text if it thinks it will make the imaginary line down the right side of the text (sometimes called "the rag") look better. If you don't want a paragraph to have any hyphenated words, then turn off the Hyphenate checkbox in the Paragraph palette.

You have a significant amount of control over what sort of words get hyphenated in the Hyphenation dialog box (choose Hyphenation from the popout menu in the Paragraph palette; see Figure 15-23). Alas, there is no way to save these settings so you can later apply them to other paragraphs. If you want a whole text block to have the same hyphenation settings (rather than just the currently selected paragraph), then make sure the cursor isn't in the text block, but the text layer is selected in the Layers palette when you make the change.

Figure 15-23
Hyphenation and
Justification

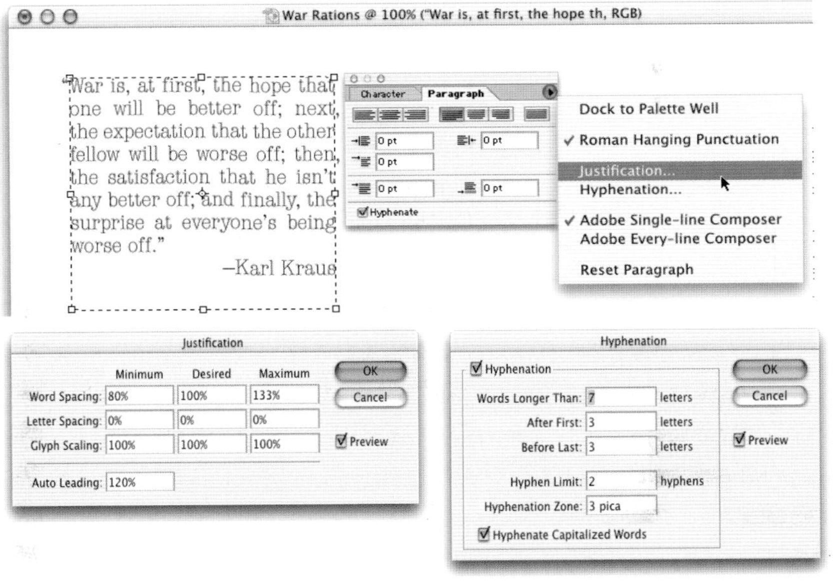

▶ **No Break.** Sometimes Photoshop will hyphenate a word that you really don't want hyphenated. No problem: select the word in the text block and choose No Break from the popout menu in the Character palette.

▶ **Justification.** The paragraphs in this book are "justified," meaning that the right margin is carefully aligned in a straight line (this is sometimes called "flush left and right"). As we said earlier, this is pulled off by adding or removing space between characters and words. Photoshop offers one other control: stretching or compressing text. You can justify a paragraph by selecting it and clicking one of the Justified Text buttons in the Paragraph palette. (There are four, each of which handles the last line of the paragraph differently.)

If you don't like the way that Photoshop justifies your text, you can alter its built-in settings by choosing Justification from the popout menu in the Paragraph palette. Most typographers agree that justified text should have little character spacing, a reasonable amount of word spacing, and no character ("glyph") scaling. However, in a pinch, you may need to bump up the character spacing and glyph scaling by one or two percent; just be careful that it doesn't make the text look too unnatural.

▶ **Composer.** Adobe InDesign shook the publishing world by packaging an old idea into new software: calculating the justification settings based on more than one line of text in a paragraph rather than just setting each line individually (like QuarkXPress and PageMaker have always done). You can now do this in Photoshop, too, by selecting Adobe Every-line Composer from the popout menu in the Paragraph palette. This almost always gives you tighter, better-looking paragraphs with more consistent spacing. However, it's at a price: it can take much longer to reflow the text. If you had pages and pages of text (like in InDesign), that could be a problem. But here in Photoshop, we're not setting much text, so we turn this on and leave it on.

▶ **Hanging punctuation.** Photoshop hangs small punctuation—such as periods, hyphens, quotation marks, commas, and so on—outside the text block, because the human eye tends to ignore these little extrusions and the text usually looks better. This is especially obvious in justified text. If you don't care for the look, you can turn it off in the popout menu in the Paragraph palette.

Ultimately, while it's cool that Adobe included all these typography features in Photoshop, we do find it a little absurd because it's so rare that you would ever want to set more than one or two lines of text in Photoshop. The one exception is creating images for a PDF workflow. In fact, unless you save your files in the PDF format, the text will either be rasterized (antialiased into the background pixels) or it'll take forever to print and create enormous EPS files.

Tip: Converting Point Type to Paragraph Type. As we said earlier, you can create text in Photoshop by either clicking or dragging with the Text tool. If you drag, you get "Paragraph Type," which is a text block with text handles, that can reflow. If you click, you get "Point Type" which is text that starts at a point; all line breaks have to be made by hand, and you can't apply justification or hyphenation. You can change Paragraph Type to Point Type (and *vice versa*) by making sure no text or text blocks are selected (clicking on the text layer in the Layers palette will do this), then choosing Convert to Point Text or Convert to Paragraph Text from the Type submenu (under the Layer menu). You can also select this from the context-sensitive menu you get when Control- or right-button-clicking with the Type tool.

Drop Shadows

Is there any single image technique more ubiquitous than the drop shadow? Every catalog and ad seems to require at least one (and often many) of the little beasts. Because early versions of Photoshop offered no simple, built-in method for building drop shadows, everyone developed their own special techniques, some of which used dozens of steps to achieve the effect. Fortunately, Photoshop's Layer Effects feature makes the process significantly simpler. (While David rejoiced upon seeing this feature, Bruce, a latter-day John Henry, still does drop shadows the hard way, partly because he refuses to admit that an automatic routine could do as good a job, and partly because drop shadows generated by layer effects usually wind up as a rich black rather than as black-plate-only, which is often what he wants.)

Tip: Use a Plug-In for Drop Shadows. Even David agrees that Photoshop's Layer Effects feature is definitely not the end-all and be-all of drop shadow creation. For anything but the most basic drop shadow, you need to either create the effect yourself, spend time tweaking what Photoshop creates, or use a third-party plug-in. For instance, Andromeda Software's Shadow Filter lets you create incredibly complex shadows, with multiple light sources, even projecting them onto a different 3-D plane. EyeCandy from Alien Skin, too, offers some fascinating drop shadow effects.

Photoshop Effects

While we tend to shy away from anything resembling a special effect in Photoshop, the drop shadow effect is so great from a productivity standpoint that we need to cover it, if only briefly. While Photoshop's other automatic effects are kind of fun (glows, bevels, and so on), we'll let those of you with spare time play with them yourselves.

There are several key reasons why you should use Photoshop's drop shadow effect rather than trying to build your own.

▶ You can apply a drop shadow to any layer by simply selecting Drop Shadow from the Layer Style submenu (under the Layer menu) and changing the settings in the Layer Style dialog box (see Figure 15-24). Similarly, you can choose Drop Shadow from the Layer Effects button-menu at the bottom of the Layers palette.

▶ Drop shadows transform along with their layer, so you can move or rotate a layer's pixels and the shadow follows along.

▶ You can edit an effect (change its color, blend mode, position, intensity, and so on) by double-clicking on the layer's tile in the Layers palette.

▶ You can turn off the effect by Option-double-clicking on the "*f*" symbol. To turn it back on again, press Command-Z, or reselect Drop Shadow from the Layer Style submenu. You can also temporarily turn off all the effects in your image by choosing Hide All Effects from the Layer Style submenu, or from the context-sensitive menu you get when Control-clicking (Mac) or right-clicking (Windows) on a layer's tile in the Layers palette.

But perhaps the best thing about automatic drop shadows is that once you get them looking just the way you want 'em, you can convert them into a regular layer by selecting Create Layer from the Layer Style submenu. Once they're a regular layer, you can tweak them to your heart's content using any of the pixel editing, transformation, and filter features in Photoshop. In the next section we'll explore why you might want to save these drop shadow layers out as their own files, too.

Tip: Buggy Create Layer? You may notice a marked shift in tone when using the Create Layer feature. For instance, a drop shadow may become significantly lighter when it sits on its own layer. At first, we thought this

Figure 15-24
Automatic drop shadows

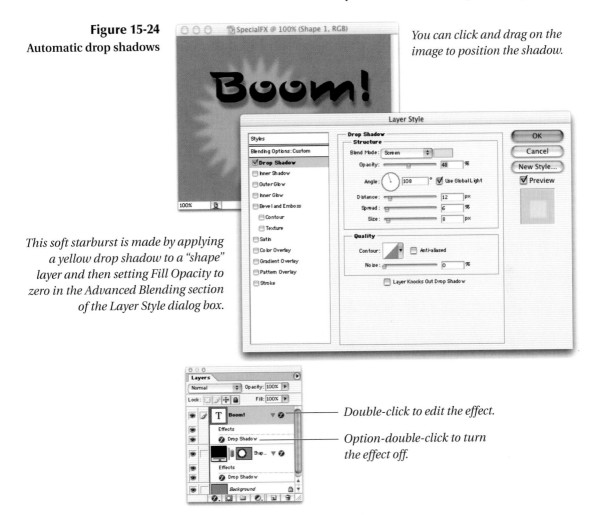

You can click and drag on the image to position the shadow.

This soft starburst is made by applying a yellow drop shadow to a "shape" layer and then setting Fill Opacity to zero in the Advanced Blending section of the Layer Style dialog box.

Double-click to edit the effect.

Option-double-click to turn the effect off.

was a bug, but it's not. It happens when you have the Blend RGB Colors Using Gamma checkbox turned on in the Advanced Settings field of the Color Settings dialog box. Just turn that off (we don't recommend people use it anyway), and Create Layer should work as expected.

Tip: Consistent Drop Shadows. After years of hunting and gathering, the human eye and brain (for it's actually difficult to tell where one ends and the next begins) have developed into an astonishingly good pattern recognition device. In the midst of chaos, we can slowly see patterns emerging. More importantly, in the midst of pattern, we very quickly see anything that breaks the pattern, even by a hair. This, then, brings us to drop shadows.

Inconsistent drop shadows are one of the most common problems with digital imaging. Our eye/brain expects all the shadows in an image to follow a pattern; inconsistency causes confusion, making the viewer say, "something is wrong with this image, though it's hard to say what," (see Figure 15-25).

We could write a whole chapter on getting drop shadows to look right, but instead we'll just point out a few important things to think about when building digital shadows.

▶ **Angle.** Generally, all the drop shadows in an image should cast to the same angle. You can ensure that you get the same angle for all your drop shadows by turning on the Use Global Angle option in the Drop Shadow tab of the Layer Style dialog box. This tells Photoshop to set all the drop shadows in the image to the same angle (so when you change the angle of one, they all change).

Of course, you should turn this off if you're building a three-dimensional scene in which you have multiple light sources, or a single source

Figure 15-25
Consistency in
drop shadows

This image confuses the eye. It's hard to know where the light source is or how far the images are floating from the background.

Here, the shadows are consistent, so you can quickly tell how far away from the background each object is.

that is coming from somewhere in the image itself (so that the angles would be different). At that point, you're on your own to figure out what the proper shadow angles should be.

▶ **Distance, intensity, and blur.** Put your hand one-half inch over your desk. See the shadow? It's dark, focused, and close to your hand. Now raise your hand six inches. The shadow becomes light, diffuse, and probably moves farther away. These are exactly the same rules you want to use when building shadows. If you want something to appear higher (farther from its shadow), increase the Distance and Size values, and decrease the Opacity and Spread settings in the Layer Style dialog box.

If you want the object lower, decrease the Distance and Size, and increase the Opacity and Spread. (Think of the Spread setting as a way of fine-tuning the Size and Opacity settings or "focusing" the shadow. We find it works best in small doses, between zero and 15 percent.)

▶ **Plane.** Remember that you don't use drop shadows to make an object stand out (which is how most people think of them); you use them to create a three-dimensional effect in your image. Thinking in 3-D requires considering the plane on which the shadow falls. If you want your shadow to fall on a wall or a table or anything other than straight back, you'll need to use Create Layer, then use the Transform feature to twist, scale, and turn the shadow until it looks right. If you have several layers, you can either use Transform Again (Command-Shift-T), or just link them together before transforming the first one.

One of the best techniques for ensuring consistency among shadows in your image is to select one layer, choose Copy Layer Style from the Layer Style submenu (under the Layers menu), and then select another layer and choose Paste Layer Style. Or, if you have a number of layers, you can link them together (select one, then click in the second column in the Layers palette for each of the others) and select Paste Layer Style to Linked. Of course, these features are also found in the context-sensitive menus (Control-click or right-click on the layer tile in the Layers menu).

Tip: Drag and Drop Shadows. While the Copy and Paste Layer Style features are cool, if you really want to impress your boss, try dragging the layer style information (the description of the drop shadow or other layer effect that you get under the layer's tile in the Layers palette) from one layer on top of the other. When you let go, the layer effect is copied over automatically.

Tip: Use Light Drop Shadows. Another common mistake people make when building drop shadows is making them too dark. It's easy to control this in the Layer Style dialog box; just change the Opacity setting. (A 30- or 40-percent shadow is usually sufficient.) When building drop shadows manually, or when tweaking shadows on their own layer, we typically use Levels to constrain the gray values in a drop shadow to under 30 percent. You can do this by setting the black Output Level to 180 (either drag the lower-left triangle, or type this value into the first Output field). Often, you can get by with even less; even an 8- or 10-percent drop shadow can appear quite dark enough.

Tip: Add Noise to Your Drop Shadows. A friend of ours kept claiming that Scitex drop shadows always printed better than Photoshop's, but he didn't know why. Finally, after comparing the two carefully, he realized the difference: Scitex drop shadows are slightly noisier, and therefore more lifelike. The solution: increase the Noise setting (in the Drop Shadow tab of the Layer Style dialog box) to between 2 and 10 percent. Or, if you've already made a shadow on a layer, use the Add Noise filter with a low setting on the shadow.

Troubles in Page-Layout Land

The trouble, then, isn't in creating a drop shadow so much as getting that drop shadow into (and back out of) a page-layout program such as InDesign, PageMaker, or QuarkXPress. InDesign can make drop shadows for you, of course, but it can't add noise to its drop shadows (so they look too mathematically pure), and it can't do special effect drop shadows (like shadows at an angle). If the drop shadow blends into the background of the image, there's no problem (the drop shadow is simply part of the image itself). But when the drop shadow must sit on top of a colored background or another graphic in the page-layout program, or even on top of text, life gets… well… interesting.

The essential problem is giving the appearance of transparency, so that the background looks like it's showing through the drop shadow. Here are several workarounds we use, depending on the image, the background, the program, and the time of day.

Separate the shadow. Putting your drop shadow in a separate file can be very handy if you're trying to print a black drop shadow over solid black text, and not over a background color or another image in QuarkXPress. In Figure 15-26, although the drop shadow appears to be over the text, it's really printing beneath it. The image is brought in as an EPS with a clipping path.

Of course, this tip is pretty limited, but the idea of separating the drop shadow from the image is the starting point for several techniques. For example, in InDesign, you can adjust the opacity of this image separately from the object that is casting the shadow, so you can create cool effects.

Tip: Lower Shadow Resolution. Remember we said that the resolution of your images should always be at least 1.2 times your halftone screen frequency? Here's an exception: if you're creating a separate drop-shadow image, you can lower its resolution a lot (there's no detail in a drop shadow, so there's no detail to lose). We rarely use more than a 1:1 ratio (where resolution equals screen frequency), and sometimes we'll go even lower.

Figure 15-26
Separate shadows

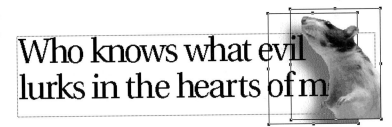

The drop shadow is on the bottom level, then the text above it, then the image of the mouse on top (with a clipping path). This example is from XPress.

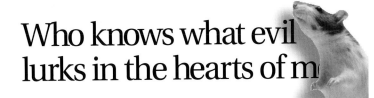

The final image

For instance, a colleague of ours printed a catalog at 150 lpi, and every one of his drop shadows (there were a *lot*) was set to 120 ppi.

Overprinting grayscales. If your drop shadow is a separate file (as above), you can import the TIFF as a grayscale, and make sure that it overprints whatever is beneath it. For instance, you can bring a grayscale drop shadow into QuarkXPress and set it to Overprint (in the Trap Information palette). Or in PageMaker, apply an overprinting black color to the shadow (define a new black, and turn on the Overprint checkbox in the Edit Color dialog box).

There are two problems with this method, however. First, it only works when there's no black in the color beneath it. If the background color is 30C 20M, the grayscale image will overprint fine. However, if the shadow is overprinting a colored background of 50C 30M 10K, the drop shadow image (the whole square) overprints the magenta and cyan, but *knocks out* the black. This happens because in PostScript, whatever tint is printed last wins (if a lighter shade is printed over a darker shade, the lighter one is printed). Of course, this means that if the drop shadow were set to print in cyan, then the background could have black... but no cyan.

The second problem is that when it comes to PageMaker or QuarkXPress, these overprinting grayscale images don't look right on screen or in most color printer output. (It works just fine in InDesign when you turn on the Overprint Preview features.) Nonetheless, this is a handy technique when printing over colors that don't contain any black.

Incorporating background. The very best way to make a drop shadow integrate with a color, a texture, or an image is to use InDesign's transparency features. The second best method is to integrate the shadow into the background image in Photoshop first. That way, you have full control over how the shadow blends in (we usually like using Multiply mode), and it will work in programs other than just InDesign. Plus, you can easily color the drop shadow, so it's not just black (which often looks a little lifeless).

There are two potential problems with this technique.

▶ If your drop shadow hangs partially off a colored box, you face the problem of aligning the box edges both in Photoshop and in the page-layout program. We can only suggest careful measurement and proofing.

▶ You have to be working in CMYK mode when you define the background color in Photoshop, so you're *sure* that the CMYK background values match those in the page-layout program. The colors probably won't *look* like they match on screen when you bring this incorporated image into InDesign, PageMaker, or XPress, because every program has its own way of displaying CMYK colors on your RGB screen. For instance, 30-percent cyan in Photoshop looks different from 30-percent cyan in XPress. But they'll print the same.

Drop Shadows of Text and Objects

The above techniques are all well and good if your drop shadow is of a Photoshop image. But what if you're trying to create a drop shadow of some text, or a shape in QuarkXPress or PageMaker? The key to bringing elements from XPress, InDesign, or PageMaker into Photoshop is first saving the page as an EPS or PDF file. Then you've got two choices for bringing this file into Photoshop. (You InDesign users are laughing because you think InDesign solves all your problems. But there are still instances when you want to create drop shadows this old way, especially when you want to add noise to the shadow or give it a special effect, like ripples or perspective.)

▶ **RIP the EPS/PDF.** Remember, Photoshop can open almost any EPS or PDF file. If you want a drop shadow behind some text, place that text in a separate document and save this new document as an EPS or PDF file. Now, open that image in Photoshop. For a drop shadow, we recommend using Grayscale mode at 120 ppi. Make sure you don't change the size of the image in inches or picas, though!

▶ **Use the PICT resource.** The truth of the matter is that rasterizing an entire EPS in order to build a drop shadow is often major overkill. If it's going to take too long to rasterize, you can open the low-res PICT (Macintosh) or .tif (Windows) preview in the EPS file instead (see "Tip: Opening Previews," earlier in this chapter). Then you can build the drop shadow from that. Note that in Windows, only XPress can save an EPS file with a preview suitable for opening.

The reason you can use the low-resolution preview for this purpose is that you're blurring it so much that you'd never know the difference. Note that this only works reliably for grayscale drop shadows. You can do it with color, but you have to be mighty careful to avoid color shifts.

Once you've opened the text or object in Photoshop, you can quickly turn it into a drop shadow (see Figure 15-27).

1. Crop out everything but the text or object you want to create a drop shadow for.

2. Select Threshold from the Adjustments submenu (under the Image menu), and crank the setting up to 255 so that everything in your image turns black.

3. Blur the entire image with the Gaussian Blur filter, and add a little noise (see "Tip: Add Noise to Your Drop Shadows," earlier in this chapter),

Figure 15-27
The original artwork in the page-layout application

The drop shadow, after Threshold and Gaussian Blur have been applied

When you rasterize the image in Photoshop, make sure the dimensions are set to a measurement, not to Pixels.

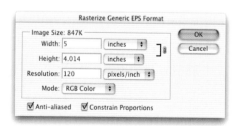

The final artwork back in the page-layout program

but make sure the noise is limited to just the shadow and doesn't run into the white background.

4. Use Levels, Brightness/Contrast, or Curves to make the entire image lighter (we often set the black point to about 40- or 50-percent gray).

5. Save the file as a TIFF, then import it back into your page-layout application, offset slightly from the type.

Tip: Use an XTension/Plug-in. One more tip for XPress and InDesign users. If you find yourself building your own shadows from QuarkXPress and InDesign elements (like type, or boxes, or lines, or whatever) more than once a week, go buy an XTension or plug-in. There are several out there that are very good at making drop shadows, including ShadowCaster from a lowly apprentice production (available for both XPress and InDesign). You can simply select a text box (or anything else) and tell it to make a drop shadow. If the text partially (or fully) overlays a TIFF image, these add-ons are even able to "burn" the drop shadow into the underlying image. (This tip has nothing to do with Photoshop, but it might make your life much, much easier.)

Filters and Effects

Sure, you can paint and retouch and composite within Photoshop, but you know as well as we do that the most fun comes from playing with filters. But if you're like most people, you could make filter-fooling a lot more fun. Here are some methods we've found useful.

Tip: Float Before Filtering. Standard protocol leads people to make a selection, then choose a filter from one of the Filter submenus. We suggest adding one step to the process: copy the selection to a new layer first (Command-J). Doing so gives you much more flexibility in how the filter is applied. For instance, once the filter is applied on the new layer, you can move it, change its blending mode, run an additional filter, soften the effect by lowering the layer's opacity, and so on. Best of all, you don't damage your original pixels until you're sure you've got the effect exactly right. If you don't like what you've done, you can undo, or just delete the entire layer.

Similarly, if you're going to run a filter on a whole layer, consider duplicating the layer first. It's safer, and much more flexible.

Tip: Filter Keystrokes. Like many other features of Photoshop, working with filters can be sped up with a couple of little keyboard shortcuts. You can tell Photoshop to run a filter again by pressing Command-F. However, this doesn't let you change the dialog box settings. As Bill Niffenegger (the king of filters) says, "Never leave a filter alone… always change it!"

If you want to follow this advice, press Command-Option-F; this reopens the dialog box of the last-run filter, so you can change the settings before applying it.

Tip: Fading Filter Effects. Most folks figure that once they run a filter, the choice is to either move forward or select Undo. But the Fade feature (in the Edit menu) allows you to take a middle path by reducing the opacity of a filter, or even changing the blending mode, immediately after running it. (As soon as you do anything else—even make a selection—the Fade feature is no longer available.) You can get to the Fade dialog box quickly by pressing Command-Shift-F (see Figure 15-28).

The Fade feature works not only with filters, but also with any of the features in the Adjustments submenu (under the Image menu) and almost every paint stroke. For example, you can run Hue/Saturation on an image, then reduce the intensity of the effect with Fade. We almost never use this, because we prefer to use adjustment layers, which are even more powerful (see Chapter 9, *The Digital Darkroom*).

Tip: Build Textures on Neutral Layers. Instead of burning filter effects directly into an image, you can filter a neutral-colored layer. Using filters in conjunction with neutral layers gives you much more freedom to change your mind later. When you select New Layer from the Layer menu or the Layers palette, Photoshop gives you the choice of filling that layer with the neutral color for the mode you choose for the layer. For instance, if you set the layer to Screen mode, Photoshop can fill the layer with black—screening with black has no effect on the image below, so it's "neutral." If you choose Overlay mode, then the neutral fill would be 50-percent gray.

Figure 15-28 Opacity changes how much a filter is applied

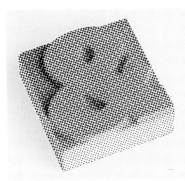  

Filter applied with 100-percent opacity   *Fade set to 60-percent opacity*   *Fade set to 40-percent opacity, and Mode set to Luminosity*

Now, when you apply a filter to that layer, the parts that get changed are no longer "neutral." They change the appearance of the pixels below. Then you can run filters on this layer and they begin to affect the image below (see Figure 15-29). Of course, this primarily works with filters that add texture to an image, like the Texturizer feature. It typically won't have any effect at all with the Distort or Artistic filters.

Figure 15-29
Filtering on a layer

Original image   *Texturizer filter applied to a neutral layer*   *Background image and neutral layer visible at the same time*

Tip: Filtering Layer Masks. Katrin Eismann taught us that running a filter on a layer mask can offer powerful flexibility and cool effects, too.

1. Add a new layer and fill it with a solid color.

2. Select Add Layer Mask from the Layer menu, choosing Hide All.

3. Run the Add Noise filter on the layer mask. The more noise you add, the more the solid color layer shows. Try other filters for other effects.

Rescreens

The problem with printed photos is that they've already been halftoned. That is, the grays or colors of the image are simulated with little dots, and while our eyes are easily fooled, scanners are not. If you scan these images in Grayscale or Color mode and print them, the PostScript printer rescreens them. The conflict between the original halftone screen and the output screen results in a real mess (see Figure 15-30).

The other problem is that in the original screening, a lot of the image detail is lost (the coarser the screen, the less detail remains). So when you scan the screened image, there's not a lot of detail there for the scanner to grab. The goal is to capture (and maintain) as much of that detail as possible, while avoiding the problems of overlapping screens. Don't expect miracles, though. Remember: garbage in, garbage out.

There are two basic approaches to working with screened images.

▶ **Line art.** Reproduce the image as black-and-white line art. This only works well for us with low-frequency images, under about 80 lpi. See "Scanning Prescreened Art," in Chapter 12, *Line Art*, for more on this.

▶ **Grayscale.** Scan in grayscale or color, then use filters to remove the halftone pattern while maintaining detail. The essential concept is "blur, then sharpen." We'll discuss these techniques in the rest of this section.

Tip: Make Rescreens Smaller. Since there's not much detail in screened images, you should generally plan on reproducing them at a smaller size than the original. You can use the techniques described here to break up

Figure 15-30
The problem
with rescreens

The original halftoned image   *A halftoned halftone*

the halftone pattern, and not suffer the loss of detail as much; because the image is smaller, less detail is needed.

Tip: Get Permissions First. This should be obvious, but all too often it is not: if the printed image isn't yours, you should always get permission to use it *before* you scan it in. Ethics aside, there are certainly copyright issues involved here. Many copyright violations in digital imaging occur when people scan pictures from magazines or books without thinking.

Frequency Considerations

One of the first things to consider when working with rescreens is the screen frequency of the printed images. Our techniques vary, depending on whether we're working with low-, mid-, or high-frequency halftones.

Low-frequency halftones. Low-frequency images are both hard and easy. They can be easy because you can reproduce them as line art, as mentioned above. But they're frustrating because there's so little detail; scanning as grayscale is almost always futile. If the line-art techniques aren't working for you, however, you can try using the methods for medium-frequency images described in the next section.

Medium-frequency halftones. Capturing medium-frequency halftones—80 lpi to 120 lpi—is perhaps the hardest of all. These halftone spots are too small to re-create in line art, but they're too large and coarse to blend together as a grayscale without blurring the image unacceptably (see "High-frequency halftones," later in this chapter). You know a halftone falls into this category if you can see the halftone dots when the paper is six inches away from your face, but you can't see them (at least, not clearly) when the paper is two feet away.

There are six techniques that we commonly use when scanning mid-frequency halftones (there are other techniques, but we usually find these ones effective). All five attempt to capture grayscale information and remove the moiré patterns that typically occur (see Figure 15-31).

▶ **Median, Despeckle, and Dust and Scratches.** The Median and Dust and Scratches filters are probably the most effective methods for removing dot patterning, but they work at a cost. Both filters average several pixels together to get a median value for the group. That means your image gets blurry quickly. Often you can retrieve some of the edges with Unsharp Mask, but sometimes you have to apply the filters so much that the image is damaged. Nonetheless, even a one-pixel Dust and Scratches filter can smooth out many of the problem areas in an image.

Figure 15-31 Rescreening mid-frequency halftones often causes moirés.

A 400-ppi scan of the screened image printed with a 75-lpi screen   *After using the Despeckle, Median, and Unsharp Mask filters (75 lpi)*   *After downsampling (133 lpi)*

If the resolution of the printed image is above 100 lpi, the Despeckle filter might work better than Median. We often try Despeckle first, and if it doesn't work well enough (or it damages the image in ways we don't like), we undo it and revert to Median.

▶ **Downsampling.** Downsampling using bicubic interpolation (see Chapter 3, *Image Essentials*) is one of the best ways we know to get rid of patterning, because Photoshop groups together a number of pixels and takes their average gray value. The problem, of course, is that you can also lose detail. Your goal is to downsample just enough to average out the halftone dot pattern, but not so much that you lose details in the image.

▶ **Upsampling.** After you downsample, you might need to upsample again to regain image resolution. You never get lost details back, of course, but sometimes sharpening the higher-resolution image can make it appear as though you did.

▶ **Rotating.** When you rotate an image in Photoshop, the program has to do some heavy-duty calculation work, and those calculations typically soften the image somewhat, breaking up the halftone pattern. If you have a very slight patterning effect after scanning a pre-halftoned image, you might try rotating the entire image 10 or 20 degrees, and then rotate the same amount back again. This double rotation can average out some patterning.

Once you've managed to break up the halftone pattern, you'll need to go after the image with the Unsharp Mask filter to give the impression of sharpness for the detail that remains. Since the image will probably be fairly blurry, you'll have to make the more extreme sharpening moves that we suggest in Chapter 10, *Sharpening*, while being careful to avoid bringing the halftone pattern back out.

High-frequency halftones. Scanning pre-halftoned images with high screen frequencies—over 133 lpi—is often easier, because the dot patterns blur into gray levels while maintaining detail. You often need to use the techniques listed above, but you don't have to work as hard at salvaging the image. In fact, we often find that just scanning at the full optical resolution of the scanner and downsampling to the resolution you need (see Chapter 13, *Capturing Images*) is enough to get rid of patterning. Or, try placing the artwork at an angle on the scanner, then downsampling and rotating in Photoshop (the Cropping tool lets you do both at once).

Tip: Pay Attention to Actual Pixels. Remember that the most important magnification view in Photoshop is Actual Pixels (100-percent view). If you scan an image and you see horrible moiré patterns at 33-percent view, don't panic. Zoom in to 100-percent view and see what's really going on. The damage is often much less than you first thought. Even if you don't see patterning in the Actual Pixels view, you still may opt to do a little smoothing work (especially if you see patterning when zoomed in to 200- or 400-percent), but it's not essential.

Actions, Automate, and Scripting

The trick to being really productive and efficient with computer technology is being lazy. Yes, it's a paradox, but it's true—the lazier you are, the more likely you are to find the really efficient ways of doing things so you can get out of work faster and go to the beach. If you have an overzealous work ethic, you probably don't mind repeating the same mind-numbing tasks 400 times, but you won't be exploiting the power of the computer in front of you.

For example, Bruce works with a lot of digital cameras, and each digital camera's images need a particular kind of tweaking. Rotate the image 90 degrees, run this filter, use that Curves setting, resize the image to such-and-such…. Instead of performing each task one at a time, he can run through them all with a keystroke. Even better, Photoshop's automation features let you batch process all the images in a folder, so you don't even have to open them in Photoshop.

As Photoshop gets smarter with each new version, we can offload more busywork onto it while we take longer trips to the fridge for artichoke dip. (We're just hoping that Photoshop doesn't get too smart and starts making us do the work while it gets the dip.)

Photoshop offers three automation features: actions, Automate, and scripting. Actions are "macros" that live in the Actions palette and let you repeat a series of steps. Photoshop ships with a number of premade actions, and you can easily build your own (we'll show you how). Automate refers to the built-in tools in the Automate submenu (under the File menu). Scripting is a way to automate Photoshop from behind the scenes using AppleScript, JavaScript, or Visual Basic. Let's take a look at each of these techniques in turn.

Actions

Photoshop comes with a number of premade actions that are not only useful, but educational, too, because you can look at them to see how they produce their magic. (You can load additional sets of actions by selecting Load Actions from the Actions palette's popout menu, or by choosing the presets that appear at the bottom the popout menu.) The key is that you can only make an action for something you can do methodically, with no feedback from the program, and with little or no brain activity. For example, you can't record an action that says, "if the pixels in the upper-left corner of the image are sort of reddish, then do such-and-such." That would require Photoshop to be able to see and respond. No can do.

However, you can easily create an action that runs a particular set of Curves, adds a text layer, adds a layer effect, sharpens the background layer, and so on, because all these things are methodical.

Tip: Exporting Actions as Text. Trying to decode how other people made actions can be a hassle because the Actions palette is hard to read. Fortunately, you can export all the actions currently visible in the palette as a text file that you can open in a word processor: just hold down Command and Option while selecting Save Action from the Actions palette's popout menu.

Action limitations. Before you get too heady with your newfound actions power, you should know that Photoshop doesn't let you record everything you might want. While Photoshop can record blend modes, opacity, shapes, brush selections, and even pixel selections, you still cannot record paint strokes (like those made with the Brush, Airbrush, and Clone tools), zooms, switching windows, and scrolls. And there are many features that aren't necessarily recordable, but you can force them into an action (see "Editing Actions," later in this chapter).

Keep in Mind

Besides the limits of what you can and cannot record in the Actions palette, there are a few more things to keep in mind.

Difficulty. While recording and playing simple actions (those with only two or three steps) may be easy, trying to build complicated actions can be damaging to your head (and the wall you're banging it against).

Modularity. Rather than trying to make one big action that does everything you want, break it down into smaller steps that you can debug individually, then chain together to reuse in more complex actions.

Think it through. You should always think the action through completely before you start recording it. You might even write down each step on paper, and then record it after you're pretty sure everything will work out the way you think.

Generic actions. Try to make your actions as generic as possible. That means they should be able to run on any image at any time. Or, barring that, provide the user with a message at the beginning of the action noting what kind of image is required (as well as other requirements, such as "needs text on a layer" or "must have something selected"). This is a good idea even if you're the only one using your actions, because (believe us) after you've made a bunch of actions, you'll forget which action requires what (see "Tip: Talk to Your Users," later in this chapter).

There are a number of things to think about when making your actions generic. The following is a good place to start, but isn't necessarily a complete list.

▶ Never assume image mode. The image may be in RGB, CMYK, Grayscale, or even Indexed Color mode. This is very important when running filters, because some filters don't run in certain modes.

▶ Don't assume the image has layers (or doesn't have layers). Also, don't assume that if the image does have layers, the Background layer is selected (or even that there is a layer called Background). If you need the lowest layer selected, press Option-Shift-[.

▶ Avoid using commands that pick layers by name. For example, if you record clicking on a layer in the Layers palette, Photoshop records the click by layer name, not position. Instead, record pressing Option-[or Option-] to target the next layer down or the next layer up, respectively. Command-[and Command-] move layers up or down.

▶ If you're saving and loading channels, you'll almost certainly have to name the channels. Make sure you give them names that are unlikely to already be present in the image. *Do* name them, though, rather than leaving them set to the default names like "#4". If a document has two channels with the same name when you run an action, Photoshop always uses the first channel with that name.

Clean up. It's a good idea to make your actions clean up after themselves. In other words, if your action creates three extra channels along the way to building some other cool effect, the action should also probably delete them before ending. If the action hasn't cleaned up after itself and you run it a second time, those channels (or layers, or whatever) are still hanging around and will probably trip up the action.

Get more info. This section offers a quick overview of actions, but if you have Web access, check out one or more of the actions-oriented sites on the Internet like *www.actionxchange.com* (which is now owned by Adobe). From there, you can also link to several other great sites.

Actions Basics

Making an action is pretty straightforward.

1. Open the Actions palette (see Figure 15-32).

2. Click the New Action button (or select New Action from the palette's popout menu). Give the action a name (and a keyboard shortcut, if you want). If you have more than one set (see "Sets," later in this chapter), choose which set this new action will be part of. When you click OK, Adobe Photoshop begins recording automatically.

3. Perform the steps that you want the action to do.

4. Click the Stop button in the Actions palette (or select Stop Recording from the popout menu).

Figure 15-32
The Actions palette

New Action or step

Stop   *Record*   *New Action Set*   *Delete Action or step*

Then, to run the action, select the action's tile in the Actions palette and click the Run button (or, better yet, just Command-double click on the action). If the action is relatively simple, it may perform perfectly the first time. But in most of the actions we make, we find that something goes wrong somewhere along the line, usually due to our performing a step that Photoshop can't record into an action (see "Troubleshooting Actions," later in this section).

Tip: Save Your Work First. If you run an action and then decide that you don't like what it did, you're in trouble because you cannot undo a full action, only the last step of an action. If the action used only a few steps, you might be able to use the History palette to return to a pre-action state, but this isn't always possible either, particularly if you ran the action as a batch process on multiple files. To guarantee an "undo" option, we're in the habit of saving a snapshot of our document in the History palette before running any action. That way, if something goes wrong or we don't like the effect, we can revert back to this snapshot. Another option is to simply save your document first, and then use the Revert command (in the File menu) to undo the action. Of course, neither of these techniques works with actions that save and close the file—we recommend always making actions that use Save As, rather than saving over the original.

Tip: Making Buttons. You can change the Actions palette into a palette full of buttons by choosing Button Mode in the palette's popout menu. When it's in Button mode, you only have to click once on a button to run it. Switch out of Button mode to create new actions or edit existing ones.

Sets. Photoshop lets you create sets of actions, a godsend to anyone who works with dozens of actions. Sets are pretty self-explanatory.

▶ You can create a new action set by choosing New Set from the Action palette's popout menu (or by clicking the New Set button in the palette). You can delete a set by selecting it and choosing Delete from the same popout menu.

▶ You can move actions between sets by dragging them.

▶ You can rename a set by double-clicking on its tile in the Actions palette.

▶ You can show or hide the actions within a set by clicking on the triangle to the left of the set's name.

▶ You can also save sets (see "Saving actions," below).

▶ You can play all the actions in a set (in order) by selecting the set and clicking the Play button.

Editing actions. Once you've built an action, you can edit it (in fact, you'll almost certainly want to edit it unless it worked perfectly the first time). If you want to record additional steps somewhere in the middle of the action (or at the end of the action), select a step in the action and click the Record button. When you're done recording actions, click the Stop button. All the new actions fall after the step you first selected.

If you want to add a step that cannot be recorded for some reason (perhaps it's an item in the View menu), you can select Insert Menu Item from the Action palette's popout menu. This lets you choose any one feature from the menus, and then inserts it into the action (after whatever step is currently selected).

To change the parameters of a step, double-click on it in the Actions palette. For example, if a step applies a curve to the image (using the Curves dialog box), but you want to change the curve, double-click on the step and choose a different curve. Note that when you do this, you may actually change the current image; just press Command-Z to undo the change (to the image, not to the action).

Annoyingly, some steps cannot be re-recorded. For instance, a step that sets the foreground color to red should be able to change so that it sets it to blue… but it can't. Instead, you have to record a new step, then delete the original.

If you want to change the action's name, its tile or button color, or its keyboard shortcut, just double-click on the action's name.

Tip: Duplicating Actions. Option-dragging a step within an action duplicates it. For instance, if you want to use the same Numeric Transform step in two scripts, you can Option-drag that step from one action into the proper place in the second action.

Tip: Stop Where You Are. Normally, Photoshop won't display any of the usual dialog boxes when you run an action. For instance, if you include a Numeric Transform step in an action, Photoshop will just perform the transform without displaying the dialog box. However, you can force Photoshop to display the dialog box, stop, and wait for the user to input different settings before continuing. To do this, click once in the second column of the Actions palette, next to the step. A black icon indicating a dialog box appears next to the step, and a red icon appears next to the action's name.

Don't click on a red dialog box icon! If you do, it turns black *and* Photoshop adds a black "stop here" icon next to every step in the action that can have one. There's no Undo here, so the only way to reset the little black icons to their original state is to turn them on or off one at a time. (You can, however, turn them *all* off by clicking the black icon next to the action's name.)

Note that if you insert a step using the Insert Menu Item command, Photoshop always opens the appropriate dialog box and doesn't even offer you the chance to turn this icon on or off (because steps inserted in this way are meant to simulate the user actually selecting the item).

Tip: Talk to Your Users. You can insert a command at any point in your action that stops the action and displays a dialog box with a message in it. This message might be a warning like, "Make sure you have saved your image first," or instructions such as, "You should have a selection made on a layer above the Background." To add a message, select Insert Stop from the Actions palette's popout menu. Photoshop asks you what message you want to appear and whether the message dialog box should allow people to continue with the action (see Figure 15-33).

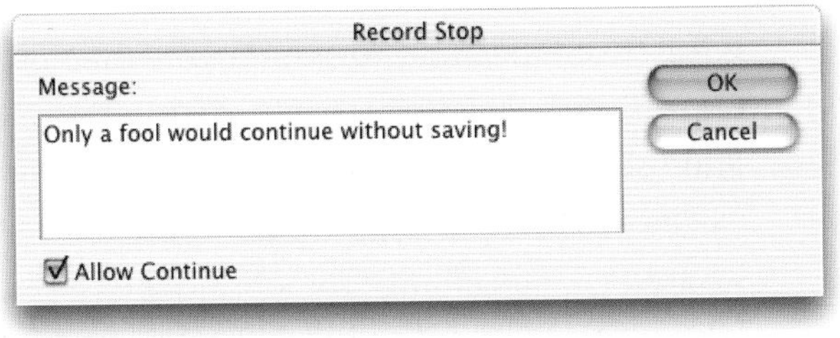

Figure 15-33
Adding a message

If the message is a warning, you should turn on the Allow Continue option, but if the message consists of instructions, you may want to leave this checkbox off. When Allow Continue is turned off, Photoshop stops the action entirely. After the user clicks the OK button in the message dialog box, Photoshop automatically selects the next step in the Actions palette, so the user can continue running the action by clicking the Run button again (this works even if the Actions palette is in Button mode).

Saving actions. After you've created the world's most amazing action, you may want to share it with someone else. You can get actions out of your Actions palette and on to your hard drive by selecting Save Actions from the Actions palette's popout menu. Unfortunately, you cannot save a single action; the Save Actions feature only saves sets of actions. Fortunately, the workaround isn't too painful.

1. Create a new set (click on the New Set button at the bottom of the Actions palette), and name it something logical.

2. Either move or duplicate the action you want to save by dragging it or Option-dragging it into the new set.

3. Select the new set and choose Save Actions from the palette's popout menu.

4. If you want, delete the set you just created.

Of course, you can load sets of actions just as easily with the Load Actions and Replace Actions features in the palette's popout menu. Watch out for Replace Actions and its cousin Clear Actions; these replace or clear *all* the actions in the palette; not just the selected one.

Tip: Curves and Adjustments. We love the fact that Photoshop can record the exact settings of the Curves, Levels, and Hue/Saturation dialog boxes. Nonetheless, you should note that if you record loading a Curves file from disk (or a Levels or Hue/Saturation file, or any other adjustment), Photoshop records the name of the file rather than the curve itself.

The workaround: record loading the setting in the Curves dialog box (or whatever), then change the settings just a tiny bit before clicking OK. As long as there is a difference, Photoshop records the settings in the dialog box rather than the file's name. Remember that you can always go back and change the settings back to the way you want them.

Troubleshooting Actions

Sometime, somewhere, something will go wrong when you're building actions. That's where troubleshooting comes in. When troubleshooting (or debugging, as it's often called), the most important thing to keep in mind is that there *must* be a logical solution to the problem. (This isn't always true, but it's good to keep a positive attitude....)

Dummy files. The first thing you should do after building an action is not test it on some mission-critical image. Rather, try it on a dummy image. Even better, try it on several dummy images, each in a different mode (RGB, CMYK, Grayscale, Indexed Color), some with layers, some without, some with selections made, others without, and so on. If it doesn't operate correctly on any one of these, you can decide whether to work at making it work or to add a message at the beginning of the action that says "don't try it on such-and-such-type of images" (see "Tip: Talk to Your Users," earlier in this section).

Step-By-step. You can force Photoshop to pause between each step and redraw the screen by selecting Step-By-Step in the Playback Options dialog box (you can choose this from the popout menu in the Actions dialog box). This is often useful, but the best troubleshooting technique in the Actions palette (in fact, probably the only troubleshooting technique) is to select the first item in the action and click the Run button while holding down the Command key. This plays only the first step. Now go check out all the relevant palettes. Is the Channels palette the way you expect it? What about the Layers palette? What are the foreground and background colors?

When you're convinced that all is well, press Command-Run again to check the second step in the action. And so on, and so on....

If at any time you find the palettes or colors set up improperly, now is the time to replace the last step or double-click on it to change its settings. If something is really messed up, then don't forget the Revert feature.

Use History. The History palette, when suitably configured, lets you step backwards through all the steps in an action, making it a great deal easier to figure out just where things went awry. So much so, in fact, that we wouldn't dream of trying to debug complex actions without it. The key is simply to make sure that you set Photoshop's Preferences to record a large enough number of History states to cover all the steps in the action. Then, after you've run the action, you can use the History palette to step back to any of the intermediate steps in the action.

Tip: Use QuicKeys. Let's just get one thing perfectly clear: If you don't own and use a copy of QuicKeys, you're just not being efficient in your work. QuicKeys (there are versions for both the Macintosh and Windows) lets you create macros to tell Photoshop—and any other program or utility you use, including the operating system—what to do. Any menu item you can select, any key you can press, any printer or server you can choose on the network, any event you can cause to happen can be assigned a macro keystroke or be built in to a sequence macro. It can be triggered by a keystroke, by the time of day, or by selecting it from a menu. These macros are incredibly helpful and can speed up work enormously because they're easy to create and use.

While we like QuicKeys, there are several other utilities that do the same or similar things, including Westcode's OneClick for the Macintosh and Wilson WindowWare's WinBatch for Windows

---

Automated Workflows

Earlier we said that actions cannot perform any task that requires brain activity. However, Adobe's engineers have built some automation tools that do have some "smarts" and placed them in two places: in the Automate submenu (under the File menu) and in the File Browser's Automate menu. The Automate menu and submenu are also home to the Batch feature, which lets you run an action on an entire folder of images. Let's take a quick look at some of these options.

(Note that we discuss one automation feature—Photomerge—in "Compositing," earlier in this chapter, and we cover a second automation feature—Web Photo Gallery—in Chapter 18, *Multimedia and the Web*. We also explore the File Browser's Automate menu in Chapter 14, *Building a Digital Workflow*.)

Batching files. If you've gone through the trouble to make an action, you probably want to apply it to a bunch of different files. You can automate an action by selecting Batch from the Automate submenu under the File menu (or selecting the images in the File Browser and choosing Batch from the File Browser's Automate menu). The Batch dialog box is pretty utilitarian; you need to step through it carefully or a whole lot of images could be messed up (see Figure 15-34).

▶ **Play.** Choose which action in which set you want to run. If you don't see the action you're looking for, try choosing a different set from the Set popup menu. These popup menus only display actions that are visible in the Actions palette.

▶ **Source.** When you choose File Browser from the Source popup menu, Photoshop applies the action to whatever files are selected in the File Browser (even if the File Browser window isn't currently open). If no files are selected, the action is applied to every image in the current

Figure 15-34
The Batch dialog box

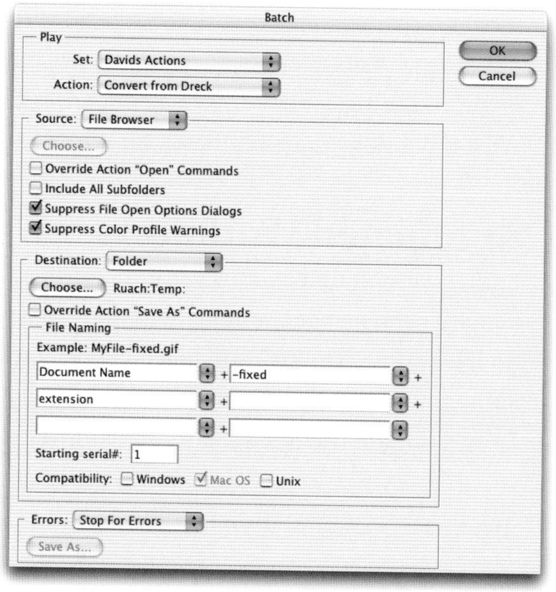

File Browser folder. If your files are on disk (and not selected in the File Browser), set the popup menu to Folder (and then choose a folder).

In either case, you probably want to turn on two checkboxes: Suppress File Open Options Dialogs and Suppress Color Profile Warnings. These two help Photoshop process your files without your further intervention. (When Suppress File Open Options Dialogs is on, Photoshop uses the last-used set of options—for instance, with Camera Raw files, it uses the last-used Camera Raw settings.) We generally leave the Override Action "Open" Commands checkbox off unless the action specifically calls for an Open command and we want it to refer to the batched file rather than the file specified in the action. Turn on a fourth option, Include All Subfolders, if you want Photoshop to process every image inside your folder, even if it's inside another folder.

If the files are coming from a device such as a digital camera (via an Import filter plug-in), then choose Import. If the files are already open in Photoshop, select Opened Files, which simply runs the action on all currently open images.

▶ **Destination.** There are three settings in the Destination popup menu: None, Save and Close, and Folder. None simply leaves the files open after processing them (not very helpful, and takes up too much RAM). Save and Close saves over the original files (we never use this). Folder lets you choose where the final images will be saved (this is just right). Once you choose Folder, Photoshop lets you specify which folder, and how you want it to name the files. If you have recorded a Save As command in your action, you should probably turn on the Override Action "Save As" Commands checkbox—though we try hard to avoid using Save As in our actions.

It's really important to test this on a small number of images before attempting a larger batch process. For instance, if the action has added layers or channels, Photoshop may have to save the file in a different format, forcing the Save As dialog box to appear and stopping the batch process short. It'd be good to know this sooner rather than later.

Tip: Batching Multiple Folders. If you've got several folders worth of images that need processing, you can speed up your work by creating aliases (on the Mac) or shortcuts (on Windows) for each image folder, and then placing them into one folder. Finally, in the Batch dialog box, turn on the Include All Subfolders checkbox. Photoshop sees the aliases as subfolders, and acts on all the images.

Tip: Making Droplets. We're not sure why the Make Droplet feature is hiding in the Automate submenu instead of the Actions palette, but that's where you can find this really awesome feature. You can use Make Droplet to save any Photoshop action to disk as a file. Then, when you want to process an image (or a folder full of images) with that action, you can simply drag the image (or folder) on top of the droplet file.

Bonus tip: If you work on both Macs and PCs, you can copy droplets from one platform to the other. On the PC you simply have to make sure the droplet has a *.exe* extension. When you bring a PC droplet to the Mac, you have to initialize it once by dragging it on top of Photoshop.

Picture Package. Picture Package is a boon to any photographer tired of duplicating, rotating, and scaling photos to fit pictures on one sheet of film. You can use Picture Package to lay out different versions of the same picture (like school photos, where you want so-many wallet-sized, and so on). Or you can use it to lay out different images together onto one page. The interface is simple enough to understand quickly (see Figure 15-35), though there are a few things to watch out for.

Figure 15-35
Picture Package

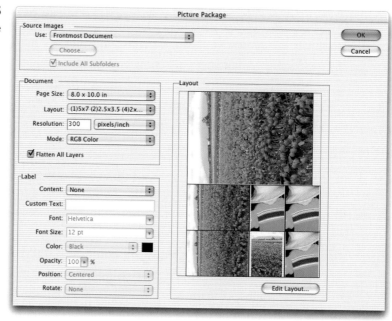

► First off, make sure you pay attention to the final resolution and final image mode setting. The default resolution, 72 dpi, leaves something to be desired if you're planning to print your page out.

► If you want all the images on the page to be the same, just select File from the Use popup menu and then click the Choose button to select your file. If you want different images, you can click on one or more of the preview images in the lower-right area of the dialog box.

► Photoshop lets you choose a label to add to the images. However, the choices are pretty slim. For instance, the label is always added on top of the image (there's no way to get it in a margin), the fonts are limited, and there's no options for styles (like drop shadows or glow around the label to make it stand out better).

► If you choose more than one image (either by selecting Folder from the Use popup menu, or by selecting more than one image in the File Browser and setting the Use popup menu to Selected Images in File Browser), Picture Package doesn't lay them out on the same page; it prepares one page for each image. Unfortunately, there doesn't appear to be any way to preview more than one page at a time, so we generally avoid selecting more than one image when using this feature.

► Note that the final result is not a flattened file, but rather all the images on a single floating layer. This means you can easily change the color behind the images, but it also means that you may need to flatten the file before printing or exporting the document.

Tip: Customized Package Pages. Photoshop offers 16 different Picture Package layouts, but in case you just gotta' be you, you're welcome to create your own customized layouts, too. In Photoshop 7, custom layouts required editing a cryptic text file and ingesting Tylenol. Fortunately, someone at Adobe came to their senses and Photoshop now sports a nifty layout editor (select an example template from the Layout popup menu and then click the Edit Layout button in the lower-right corner of the Picture Package).

The Edit Layout dialog box (see Figure 15-36) works like a basic drawing program: First choose a page size that corresponds to your printed paper size in the Layout area. Then, click on a box (a "zone") to move it or

Figure 15-36
Customizing Picture
Package

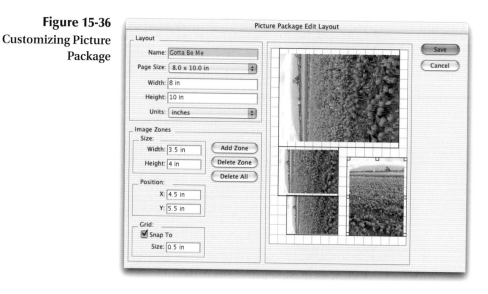

change its size. You can remove a zone by clicking the Delete Zone button, or add one by clicking Add Zone. Unless you're really going wacky and wild, do yourself and everyone around you a favor and turn on the Snap To checkbox so that as you drag or resize a zone it snaps to a grid line; the grid is based on the value in the Size field.

When you're done, give your layout a name and click Save. Photoshop knows just where to save these files (in the Photoshop>Presets>Layouts folder), so you just need to name your file (probably something similar to your layout name) and click Save. The layout name is what appears in the Layout popup menu; the file name is just the on-disk file name.

Contact Sheet II. Contact Sheet builds pages of thumbnails from a folder full of images (see Figure 15-37). In ancient versions of Photoshop, Contact Sheet wouldn't actually label any of the images, making the contact sheet somewhat unusable. That has changed; on the other hand, Photoshop doesn't know what to make of long file names, and usually truncates them. With any luck, Contact Sheet III will give you even more controls (though who knows when that will show up).

Crop and Straighten Photos. The Automate features are designed to save you from mind-numbing grunt work, and the Crop and Straighten Photos feature fits that bill exactly. If you throw four photos on a flatbed scanner, you can either scan four times (adjusting the scanning area each

Figure 15-37
Contact Sheet II

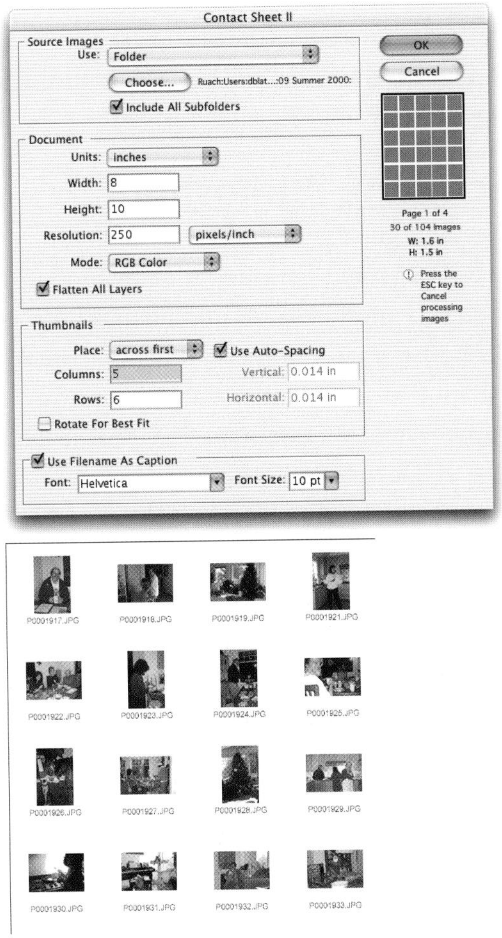

time) or scan once, duplicate the resulting file three times, and crop each one a unique image. Now you've got another choice: Scan once and choose Crop and Straighten Photos from the Automate submenu. This feature does the work for you by analyzing the image, duplicating it, cropping it, and rotating each one so that it sits straight. If you decide you only want a couple of the images on the page, draw selection marquees around the ones you want, and Photoshop will focus on them.

Obviously, the more clear the boundaries are between the images the better the feature works. Crop and Straighten Photos usually works quite well, but we've found we sometimes still need to do a little cropping cleanup on some images (especially old photos that don't have clearly defined boundaries or in contact sheets with black borders). On rare occasions, Photoshop breaks an image into two or more pieces (if the colors in the image have areas that are too similar to the color around the images). In that case, make a selection around the image and then hold down Option/Alt while selecting the feature from the Automate submenu.

Scripting Photoshop

If actions got you all excited about automating Photoshop, you're going to love scripting. Scripting is a way for one application (or your system) to talk to another application behind the scenes. For instance, in Mac OS X 10.3 or later, you can attach a script to a folder, so that as soon as you drop an image into the folder, your system launches Photoshop, performs several operations on it, saves the file, and then closes it again; it's all handled automatically.

Scripting is one of the coolest features in Photoshop, but almost no one knows about it because Adobe doesn't advertise it well. In the past, Photoshop was hardly scriptable at all (you could only tell it to run an action from the Actions palette). Today, Photoshop is *very* scriptable on both Macintosh and Windows platforms.

Scripting vs. actions. There are four basic differences between actions (which are also called macros) and scripts. First, actions are entirely dependent on the user interface—the menus, dialog boxes, keyboard shortcuts, and so on. Scripts, however, let you sneak in the back door of the program and control it from behind the scenes, almost like a puppeteer pulling the strings of a marionette. Second, scripts have flow control. *Flow control* is a programming term that means you can set up decision trees and loops, like "keep doing this until such-and-such happens." Third, scripts often contain variables, so you can save the value of something (like the color of a pixel) to use it later.

Last, scripting lets you control more than one program at time. For example, if you use QuarkXPress (which is also scriptable on the Macintosh) or InDesign (which is scriptable on both Macintosh and Windows), you could write a script that would automatically "see" how you've rotated, sized, and cropped images within your picture boxes. It could then open the images in Photoshop, perform those manipulations on the original images, resave them, and re-import them into the page-layout program. Powerful stuff!

Tip: Hiring a Scripter. Even though scripting is extremely powerful, it's just a fact of life that most people don't want to learn the ins and outs of scripting. Fortunately, there are a number of scripters for hire. In case you're looking for such a beast, we have compiled a small list of freelance scripting consultants—including Ray Robertson of Scripting Matters and the inimitable Shane Stanley—on the Resources page of the *Real World Adobe Photoshop* Web site at *www.peachpit.com/photoshop/*. There are also consultants listed at *www.apple.com/applescript/resources/* if you're scripting for the Macintosh.

Scripting languages. You can script Photoshop using a number of different languages. On the Macintosh, you can use AppleScript or JavaScript. In Windows, you can use JavaScript, Visual Basic, or any other language that is COM aware, such as VBScript, Perl, or Python. Note that only JavaScript scripts can be used cross-platform. That would seem to make it the best option for scripting, but unfortunately, only a few other applications are JavaScript-aware—Adobe InDesign CS is, but QuarkXPress is not.

First steps in scripting. We don't pretend that we can actually teach you how to script Photoshop in this book. Although we believe that almost anyone can learn how to write scripts (especially using AppleScript, which is much easier than other forms of scripting), scripting is still a form of computer programming and as such, it takes time and patience to learn. So where can you learn it?

▶ **Books.** Several good books have been published on scripting. Most are pretty general, such as Matt Neuburg's *AppleScript: The Definitive Guide*, the *AppleScript for Applications Visual QuickStart Guide*, and *Visual Basic Visual QuickStart Guide*—these don't discuss Photoshop's scripting, but they'll get you up to speed so that Adobe's own documentation makes a lot more sense. You might also look at Sal Soghoian's book *AppleScript 1-2-3*—Sal knows everything there is to know about the subject.

▶ **Examples.** The best way to learn how to script Photoshop is by first looking at and deconstructing other people's scripts. If you can find a script that already does what you want, then use it. If the script isn't quite right, then edit it to make it work for you. Adobe has provided a number of scripts to play with, including scripts that add text, warp it, and then convert the text to a selection. You can open AppleScripts in Script Editor (the free AppleScript editor that comes with the Macintosh), and Windows scripts in any Visual Basic editor in Windows to see how they work or edit them to suit your needs. JavaScripts are just text, so you can use any text editor to read or write them.

You can find even more scripts on Web sites, such as the Adobe Studio Exchange at *share.studio.adobe.com*

▶ **Scripting dictionary.** On the Macintosh, all scriptable applications have a built-in scripting dictionary that outlines the various things that can be scripted in that program. One way to see this information is by choosing Open Dictionary in the File menu of the Script Editor utility. The dictionary is often most helpful as a quick reference when your books or documentation isn't around.

▶ **The Web.** The World Wide Web is, of course, one of the best sources for AppleScript, Visual Basic, and JavaScript information. There are a number of great sites out there that offer both tutorials on scripting and scripts that you can download, use, and learn from. If you want AppleScript information, the best place to start, of course, is Apple's own scripting site: *www.apple.com/applescript*. Another excellent place to learn about scripting is the Photoshop Scripting forum on Adobe's own Web site at *www.adobe.com/support/forums/main.html*.

Running scripts. Even if you never find yourself writing scripts, you're missing out if you don't know how to run them—the example scripts that Adobe provides are extremely helpful. AppleScript and Visual Basic scripts must be run from outside of Photoshop, from a program like Script Editor (which ships free with all Macs), or even using QuicKeys.

JavaScript scripts are even more flexible: The easiest way to run a JavaScript from within Photoshop is to place it in the Photoshop>Presets>Scripts folder. Photoshop lists these files in the Scripts submenu, under the File menu (see Figure 15-38). If your script doesn't live in that folder, you can tell Photoshop where to find it by selecting Browse from the Scripts submenu.

Here's a brief description of the four JavaScripts that Adobe ships with Photoshop.

▶ **Export Layers to Files.** This script saves each layer in your document as a separate, flattened file on disk. You get to choose what file format to save in.

▶ **Export Layer Comps to Files.** When you have created one or more layer comps in the Layer Comps palette, this script can save each one as a flattened image on disk. You can choose the file format and output options.

▶ **Export Layer Comps to PDF.** This script saves your layer comps in a single PDF file, one comp per page. We find this is a great way to send multiple comps to a client.

▶ **Export Layer Comps to WPG.** If you want to post your layer comps on a Web site, choose Export Layer Comps to WPG. *WPG* stands for "Web Photo Gallery." We cover these galleries in more detail in Chapter 18, *Multimedia and the Web.*

Tip: Hard-Core Scripting. If you really get into writing scripts, you will find yourself spending a lot of time writing or debugging scripts and you will want to take a look at some of the other scripting applications on the market. For instance, Late Night Software's Script Debugger and Main Event's Scripter are full-featured tools that help you write and debug AppleScripts on the Macintosh, and are better than the rather spartan (but free) Script Editor.

Figure 15-38
Running JavaScripts

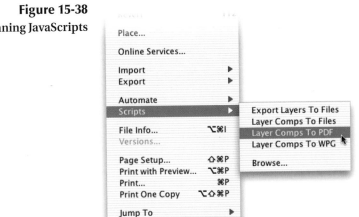

Also, the more complicated a script, the more it requires a way for the user to interact with it—buttons, text fields, dialog boxes, popup menus, and so on. If you're interested in building user interfaces for your AppleScripts, take a look at Apple's own AppleScript Studio or DTI's FaceSpan. In Windows, you can build interfaces using Visual Basic. JavaScript scripts can build user interface elements without additional help; see the *JavaScript Reference Guide* that comes with Photoshop for details.

Tip: Scripting the Unscriptable. Sadly, not everything in Photoshop is scriptable at this time. For instance, there is no way for a script to add an adjustment layer, zoom in, run third-party filters, or create a pattern. Some features are scriptable using JavaScript, but not via AppleScript or Visual Basic. We hope this will change in time, but in the meantime, there are two options to work around any limitations. First, you can create an action in the Actions palette that performs that one step, and then trigger that action inside the script (in AppleScript, you'd use the *do script* command).

The second choice is to use the ScriptingListener plug-in, which comes with the Scripting Support files. When this plug-in is loaded, it can actually write a JavaScript of whatever you do in Photoshop. For instance, you can open a new document, make a selection, fill it with a gradient, and save the file to disk. The ScriptingListener writes the JavaScript for those commands to disk for you (Java Script files are just text files that can be edited in any text editor program). Then you can tell your AppleScript or Visual Basic script to run this little JavaScript code at the appropriate time.

First sample script. Let's take a look at a simple script written in AppleScript which makes a selection, 90-percent of the size of the current file.

```
tell application "Adobe Photoshop CS"
set docwidth to (width of current document as pixels as real)
set docheight to (height of current document as pixels as real)
set docleft to docwidth * 0.1
set doctop to docheight * 0.1
set docright to docwidth * 0.9
set docbottom to docheight * 0.9
select current document region {{docleft, doctop}, ¬
    {docleft, docbottom}, {docright, docbottom}, ¬
```

```
        {docright, doctop}}
end tell
```

The *tell* statement informs the operating system what program you want to talk to, and every *tell* statement must have a corresponding *end tell* (like a closing parenthesis). The next six lines use the *set* statement to define a series of variables with names like *docwidth* and *docleft*. Variables can be named anything you like; they're just holding places for information. In this case, the first two lines get the width and height of the document; the "as pixels as real" part makes sure the information is recorded as the pixel dimensions in numbers that can be part of an equation later. The next four variables are set to percentages of the height and width of the document.

Finally, the *select* command tells Photoshop to make a selection in the current document. This looks complicated at first, but the values of the selection (in curly brackets) are simply the corner points on the rectangle. The ¬ character just means "this command continues on the next line." It's helpful when you have long statements (especially when printing them in a book with a narrow column like this).

Second sample script. Here's a slightly more complex AppleScript that demonstrates how you can move information between QuarkXPress and Photoshop. In this case, the text in the currently selected text box in QuarkXPress is re-created and formatted in Photoshop, then saved as a TIFF file and reimported back into a new picture box in QuarkXPress. (Note that InDesign's scripting architecture is much more robust than scripting in XPress.)

It would take too long to dissect the script fully, but here are a few pointers to keep in mind. The *activate* command brings the application to the front (so you can see what is going on). The word "newDocRef" in the fifth line is just a variable which can be changed to whatever you want. Also, the lines that begin with two dashes are comments, and are ignored by the script. Note that to make this work, you'll need to replace "MacHD: Temp:" with the proper path to the folder you want to use.

```
tell application "QuarkXPress"
set theWord to text of current box of front document
tell application "Adobe Photoshop CS"
    activate
    set newDocRef to make new document with properties ¬
```

```
                {width:6 as inches, height:2 as inches}
        set textLayer to make new art layer in newDocRef ¬
            with properties {kind:text layer, name:theWord}
        set textItemRef to text object of textLayer
        set contents of contents of textItemRef to theWord
        set font of textItemRef to "AGaramondPro-Regular"
        set size of textItemRef to 100 as points
        set position of textItemRef to {0.1, 1.5}
        set warp style of textItemRef to twist
        apply layer style textLayer using "Blue Glass (Button)"
    --NOW SAVE THE DOCUMENT
        set myOptions to {class:TIFF save options, ¬
            save layers:false, image compression:LZW, ¬
            byte order:Mac OS, save alpha ¬
            channels:false, transparency:false, ¬
            save spot colors:false, embed color profile:true}
        save newDocRef in file ("MacHD:Temp:" & theWord) ¬
            as TIFF with options myOptions ¬
            appending lowercase extension
        close newDocRef saving no
    end tell
    --FINISHED WITH THE PHOTOSHOP STUFF
    --NOW LET'S PUT THE PICTURE INTO QUARKXPRESS
        activate
        set boxBounds to bounds of current box
        make new picture box at beginning of front document ¬
            with properties {name:"Bob", bounds:boxBounds}
        set image 1 of picture box "Bob" of front document ¬
            to alias ("MacHD:Temp:" & theWord & ".tif")
    end tell
```

New Techniques

Even though Photoshop is an amazing tool, it still won't do everything for you. Creating drop shadows, silhouettes, special edges, or text in Photoshop can be a chore. But we hope that with these new methods, your work will fly faster and you'll be able to focus on more fun stuff.

16

Storing Images

Managing Files for Fast Production

We've been barking at you for a few hundred pages that what we're really talking about is not images, but rather zeros and ones. But the zeros and ones that one program writes to disk may not be readable by another program. Why? Because the same data can be written to disk in a variety of ways, called *file formats*. Different file formats may be as different as two languages (like Spanish versus Chinese), or as similar as two dialects of the same language (like American versus British English).

The world would be a simpler place if everyone (and all software) spoke the same language, but that's not going to happen. Fortunately, programs such as Photoshop, QuarkXPress, and InDesign can read and sometimes even write in multiple file formats. The important thing, then, is not for us to understand exactly what makes one different from the others, but rather what each file format's strengths and weaknesses are, so that we can use them intelligently. (Wouldn't it be great if we could speak in French to our lovers, German to our bosses, and oh-so-polite Japanese to our acquaintances?)

In this chapter, we're taking an in-depth look at each of the many file formats that Photoshop understands. (Note that we won't cover Photo CD or Camera Raw here, because Photoshop can't write these files—it can only read them; they're discussed in Chapter 13, *Capturing Images*, and Chapter 14, *Building a Digital Workflow.*) More to the point, we'll explore why you'd want to use some of them and avoid others. We also cover saving metadata (textual information about your images) in your files. One of the key issues in storing images is file size, so we also discuss how various file formats handle compression internally. At the end of the chapter we explore the nitty-gritty of compression in file formats: how it works, what it does to your files, and how it's different from archival compression methods.

Tip: Hide Formats You Don't Use. Photoshop itself actually only knows how to read and write about half of the file formats we're discussing in this chapter. But it can read and write the other types because of plug-ins that came with the program. For instance, when the CompuServe GIF and FilmStrip plug-ins are in Photoshop's Plug-ins folder, Photoshop can read and write in these "languages."

However, if you don't use these formats, you don't have to leave them cluttering up your Save As popup menu. Instead, you can move any formats that you don't want out of the File Formats folder (inside the Plug-ins folder in the Photoshop folder) into another folder (outside the Plug-ins folder). Don't just hide them inside another nested folder; Photoshop can still find them there.

Before we get to file formats and compression, however, we need to cover three sets of options that appear in the Save As dialog box: Save, Color, and Image Previews.

Save As Options

Over the years, the Save As dialog box has become pretty complex (see Figure 16-1). It offers a lot of different options, including the important ability to save a copy of your file (see sidebar "Saving and Opening Images"). Depending on the settings in the Preferences dialog box, you may have even more options available to you. Note that the file format you choose (TIFF, PDF, EPS, and so on) determines which of these options are available. If you choose a format that doesn't support something in your file, Photoshop places a warning icon next to the offending option, and forces you to Save As a Copy.

Figure 16-1
The Save As
dialog box

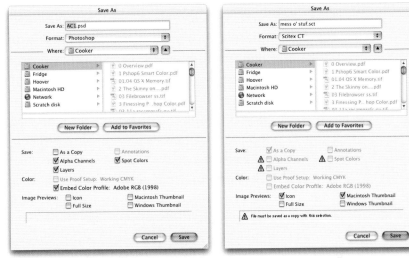

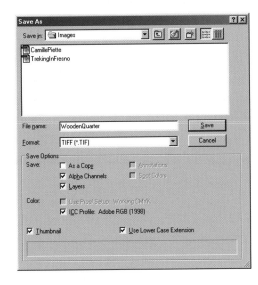

*The Save As dialog box
allows you to decide
which elements to save
in your image. The
Macintosh (upper-left)
and Windows (left)
versions are similar.*

*If you choose a format
that doesn't support
one or more of the types
of data in the image,
Photoshop places a
warning icon beside that
data type and forces you
to save a copy (see above).*

Save Options

The five options in the Save section of the Save As dialog box are relatively self-explanatory, but when you want them turned on or off might not be as obvious.

As a Copy. The "As a Copy" checkbox saves you time. It performs the same tasks as you duplicating the image, changing it (like flattening it or stripping out the annotations, if you want), saving it under a different name, and then closing it. We use this every day—to save proof versions of a document for a client, to make a JPEG copy of a picture without having to visit the Save for Web dialog box (see Chapter 18, *Multimedia and the Web*), or simply to save an archival version of a file in progress to a different hard drive. What you get in that "copy" image depends on the other settings in the dialog box.

Alpha Channels. As we said back in Chapter 8, *Selections and Channels,* we find it prudent to save any selection that takes more than about 15 seconds to make because sooner or later you're sure to need it again. The problem is that this creates files with heaps of alpha channels in the Channels palette. If you want to strip away all those extra channels, turn off the Alpha Channels checkbox.

Layers. If you measure your hard drives in megabytes rather than gigabytes, you may be accustomed to flattening your images before saving them. Do yourself a favor: Buy a bigger hard drive and save your files with layers intact. It's the rare image that doesn't need editing later, and having the layers around makes that much easier. When you need a flattened version (like if you're saving a JPEG or an EPS file), turn off the Layers checkbox in the Save As dialog box—this automatically flattens the file while it saves it. When you turn off the Layers checkbox, Photoshop turns on the As a Copy checkbox—ensuring that you won't write over your original layered file.

Annotations. Photoshop's Annotations feature lets you save comments along with your images, which is a boon for workgroups (see Chapter 2, *Essential Photoshop Tips and Tricks*). However, you may not want your clients to read all the notes you and your design team are writing to each other. No problem: just turn off the Annotations checkbox, and Photoshop strips them away.

Spot Colors. If you've gone through the trouble of making spot color channels in your image (see Chapter 11, *Spot Colors and Duotones*), we're not sure why you'd want to delete them when you save your file. But if you did want to, here's where you would do it. We think the Spot Colors checkbox is most useful as an indicator: When it's grayed out, you can be sure that the file format you've chosen cannot handle spot colors. What we'd like is the ability to automatically merge the spot color channels into our

RGB or CMYK image (for when we want to send a proof to a client)—but this feature doesn't do that.

Color Options

The color options in the Save As dialog box let you control whether or not you embed an ICC profile in the image, and, for some file formats, let you make a color conversion during the save.

Use Proof Setup. This option is only available for EPS and PDF formats, and for EPS DCS when Proof Setup is set to a CMYK profile. When turned on, it tells Photoshop to convert the image from its current space to the Proof Setup space, using the target profile and rendering intent specified there (see "Proof Setup Dialog Box" in Chapter 5, *Color Settings*). When you turn on the Use Proof Setup setting the profile listed under the Embed Color Profile option changes to the one specified in Proof Setup. We don't use this option much—it's not intuitive, and we only use it in those rare cases where we're already in the Save As dialog box and realize that we forgot to convert the image to the correct output space.

Embed Color Profile. The easiest way to get accurate color when you move your image from one machine to another is by sending information about the image's color space with it (see Chapter 5, *Color Settings*). You could write down the color space information on a piece of paper and mail it to the image's recipient, or you could just turn on Embed Color Profile (it's on by default unless you set your Color Management Policy to Off), which embeds the color information in the file itself. That said, there are two instances when you might consider turning off this checkbox.

▶ You might not want to include the color profile when you need to send a file to someone who has siyemesophobia—the irrational fear of color management systems (CMSes). These people, seeing that there's a profile embedded, may get nervous and screw up your image in one way or another.

▶ CMYK profiles are notoriously large (they may add between 700 K and 2.5 MB to the file size). If your file will be further edited on another machine, it's important to include the profile. However, if you've got a tiny 100 K CMYK file that you want to send by modem to a friend for her newsletter, it's ridiculous to add the profile to it. All the color

Saving and Opening Images

Throughout this chapter we discuss "reading" and "writing" various file formats, but we should, just for a moment, explore the mechanisms in Photoshop for performing these acts. The four relevant menu items—Open, Save, Save As, and Save for Web—are all found under the File menu.

Open. You can open, or "read," an image by selecting Open, choosing the file, and clicking OK. Simple enough. The one exception to this (and this is why we mention it at all) is when you have selected All Documents from the Show popup menu. (Note that the Open As feature in Photoshop for Windows is equivalent to selecting All Documents in the Macintosh Open dialog box.) In that case, you can specify what file format ("language") you'd like Photoshop to read in (see Figure 16-2).

This is particularly helpful when trying to open images that were created on a Macintosh without a three-letter file name extension (like .TIF). When you bring the file across to the PC, Photoshop may not recognize it as a TIFF file or

Figure 16-2 Show All Documents

images in this book use the same profile, so we did not save the profile in the images; instead, we brought the untagged images into Adobe InDesign and set the default *document* profile, which works just as well. Of course, if we had to send one of these images to a friend for further editing, they'd be lost unless we sent them our profile, too.

Image Preview Options

When you use Save As with Photoshop's default preferences, Photoshop also creates two miniature preview images within your file: Icon and Thumbnail (in Windows, you just get the Thumbnail; see "Icon," below). You can control this behavior, and—on the Macintosh—add a third type of preview, by selecting Ask When Saving from the Image Previews popup menu in the File Handling Preferences dialog box (select File Handling from the Preferences submenu under the Edit menu, or on Mac OS X, the Photoshop menu; see Figure 16-3). From then on, the Save As dialog box offers you Preview choices: on Windows, you get a Save Thumbnail

EPS file or whatever it may be. In this case, you must use Open As (or turn on Show All Documents), and explicitly tell Photoshop what file format the image is saved in.

Save. Choosing Save in Photoshop works the same as in every other Macintosh or Windows program: it replaces the previously saved image data with the current image data. Photoshop saves in whatever format the original image was saved in. When you select Save (or press Command-S) with a new, unsaved document, Save performs a Save As instead. Similarly, if you open a flattened TIFF file and add a layer or a spot channel, Photoshop prompts you with the Save As dialog box when you save (because the file has fundamentally changed).

Save As. If you want to save the image you're working on but change its name or its file format, or you want to save a flattened version of a layered file, use Save As (or press Command-Shift-S) instead of Save. This doesn't change the original image (the one already on disk). We use Save As all the time as we go through the process of adjusting an image. That way, we can always go back two or three (or more) steps.

While ancient versions of Photoshop offered a Save a Copy feature, it's now built into the Save As dialog box: Turning on the Save a Copy checkbox in the Save As dialog box is like saying, "Save the current image to disk, but let me keep working on the one I have open now." Or, it's like making a photocopy of your artwork, and then continuing to work on the original.

Save for Web. The Save for Web feature lets you save a copy of your image as a JPEG, GIF, or PNG file. We cover this feature in detail in Chapter 18, *Multimedia and the Web*.

checkbox; on the Mac, you get three checkboxes, one each for saving an Icon, a Thumbnail, and a Full Size preview (see Figure 16-1, earlier). Here's a rundown of what the different previews are.

Figure 16-3
Image preview options

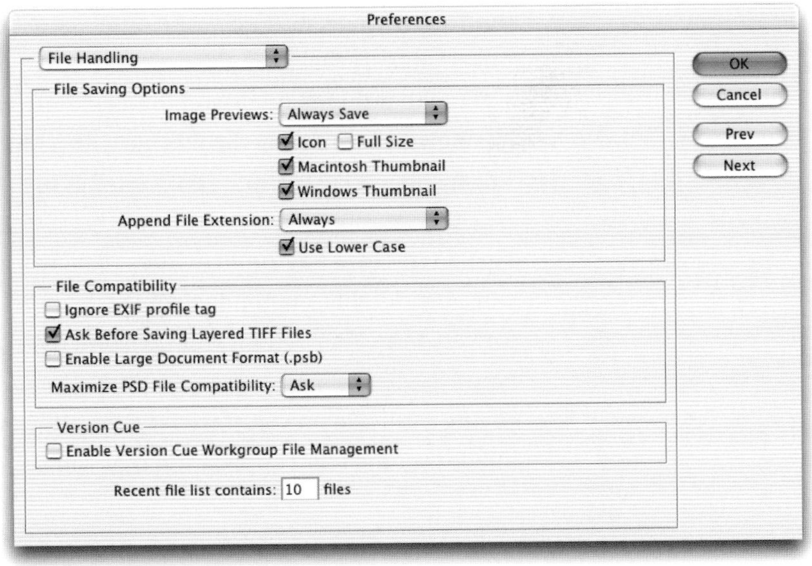

Icon. The first preview, Icon, acts as a desktop picture, so you can see (with a little imagination) what the image is when you're staring at the file on your Macintosh desktop.

Maybe we're missing something really basic, but there doesn't appear to be any reliable way to get Photoshop to save a desktop icon in Windows. JPEG, GIF, and TIFF files almost always show up with desktop icons in Windows (as long as your directory is set to Thumbnails view mode) whether you turn on or off the Thumbnail checkbox. We're told that there's a way to force Windows to generate icons for PSD and other files, but we've never figured it out. Let us know if you can do it.

Thumbnail. The second preview, Thumbnail, is a slightly larger image that QuickTime-savvy applications can display in their Open dialog boxes. This way, you can see just what's in the image before you open it. Photoshop and InDesign don't require this (they'll create a thumbnail on the fly whether you save one or not). There are two choices: Macintosh Thumbnail and Windows Thumbnail. We turn both off.

Full Size. When Ask When Saving is turned on in Saving Files Preferences, Photoshop on the Mac gives you one additional choice: Full Size preview. This one adds a considerably larger JPEG-compressed 24-bit PICT resource to the file; its dimensions are the actual physical output size of the image, downsampled to 72 pixels per inch.

The primary benefit to Full Size preview is that it can be used by many third-party image browsers and databases. Unfortunately, it's ignored by InDesign, PageMaker, and QuarkXPress. We rarely turn on this option.

Note that there's no reason to select Full Size preview with an EPS file; it's equivalent to saving the EPS file with a Macintosh (JPEG) preview (see "Encapsulated PostScript (EPS)," later in this chapter).

Tip: Save Time Saving Previews. Saving an icon or thumbnail preview can considerably lengthen the time it takes to save your image (especially for very large files). But if you save one type of preview, saving the other type as well takes hardly any additional time—one or two seconds at most. Saving a full size preview takes still longer, so you should only do so if the image is going to an application that will benefit from it.

File Formats

You've probably noticed by now that a lot of this book focuses on pre-press; nonetheless, we've done our best to include vital information for those whose output is continuous-tone film or the computer screen. Most people use Photoshop to prepare images that they're going to take elsewhere, be it PageMaker, Adobe InDesign, QuarkXPress, the World Wide Web, or whatever. The file format in which you save your file depends on where it's headed.

In the past, we've always advised that, while you're working on an image in Photoshop, you should save the file in Photoshop's native file format (PSD). But since few other applications besides Adobe's can read these files, you generally need to save your finished images in some other format before transferring them to a page layout, presentation, or multimedia application. Most people have developed the habit of keeping a layered version of the file in Photoshop format, and saving flattened versions in other formats to export to other applications.

You can still do that with Photoshop, but this workflow has become less convenient because Photoshop has made changes to how it handles PSD and TIFF formats. Plus, people are increasingly using Adobe InDesign, which can read PSD files. These changes open up some new workflow possibilities (see the sidebar "One File or Two?" for details).

If your image is destined for a presentation program, a multimedia program, or another screen-based application, PICT and JPEG are probably the best formats to use. But if the image is going to a page-layout program, you should always use PSD (InDesign only), TIFF, EPS, PDF, or DCS.

Photoshop

The Photoshop file format—otherwise known as Photoshop's "native" format—used to be the only way to save everything that Photoshop is capable of producing: multiple layers, adjustment and type layers, layer effects, paths, multiple channels, clipping paths, screening and transfer settings, and so on. (Note that histories and snapshots are not saved in any file format.) We used to recommend it as the format for saving images that were being worked on, and for archiving finished layered images. However, today the Photoshop format is often much less necessary than it used to be. But there are still a few times when it trumps any other format.

The PSD file format is less necessary because almost anything you can save in a Photoshop file, you can now also save in either a TIFF or a PDF file. It's important to note, however, that other applications may not be able to read those formats properly (for instance, you can now save spot colors in a TIFF file, but no other programs currently handle those spot colors properly).

Saving a composite. By default, Photoshop pretty much insists on saving a flattened composite version of the image in every PSD file because it "maximizes file compatibility." As a result, those of us who have become accustomed to using PSD to save files that consist only of a Background layer and some adjustment layers get a rude shock when we find that our Photoshop PSD files are about twice the size of the ones we saved from Photoshop 6 and earlier.

Fortunately, you can prevent Photoshop from saving flattened composites in two ways, each tied to the Maximize PSD File Compatibility popup menu in the File Handling panel of the Preferences dialog box. By default, this popup menu is set to Ask, which means that whenever you try to save a PSD file with layers you get to choose whether or not you want to "maximize file compatibility." Plus, you get a scary-looking warning that suggests turning off Maximize is a course of action that will result in The End Of The Universe As We Know It (see Figure 16-4).

The warning is there for two reasons.

▶ Several other applications claim to be able to read Photoshop files, and while a few can actually read layered files, most just read the flattened composite. Adobe Illustrator, Adobe InDesign, and ALAP's ImagePort QuarkXTension will all attempt to read Photoshop files even if the composite is not present, so if you're using one of these, you can usually proceed without the composite—if your layered files are relatively straightforward. However, if your layers use any of the new blending modes such as Pin Light or Vivid Light, the layers will very likely not be read correctly, so it's safer to include the composite. Plus, while InDesign and Illustrator can read 8-bit layered PSD files without a composite, they can't handle 16-bit PSD files without one.

▶ Future versions of Photoshop may change the layer-blending algorithms, which means that when you opened a layered document it would look slightly different than it does now. Adobe reasons that with

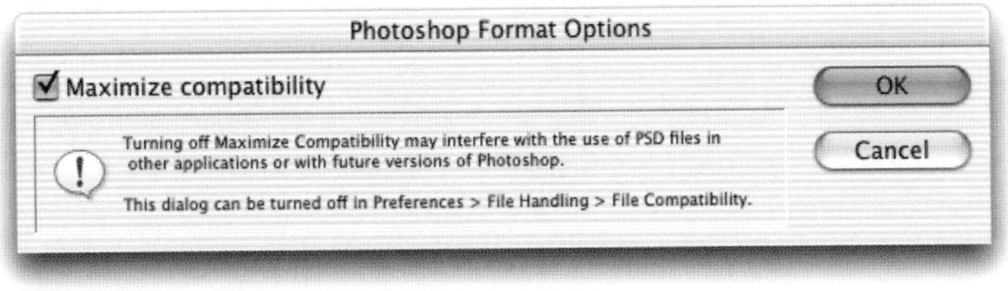

Figure 16-4
The really annoying
"Maximize compatibility"
warning

Figure 16-4
The really annoying
"Maximize compatibility"
warning

Photoshop Format Options

☑ Maximize compatibility

OK

Cancel

Turning off Maximize Compatibility may interfere with the use of PSD files in other applications or with future versions of Photoshop.

This dialog can be turned off in Preferences > File Handling > File Compatibility.

the flattened composite, you'll still be able to retrieve the correct image appearance in future versions. Of course, if you someday open the composite rather than the layered document, you lose all your layers, so the advantage over saving a flattened copy is questionable.

Duotones. Because TIFF and PDF do almost everything that the native Photoshop file format does (and often do it better), we almost never use PSD files anymore. The exception is when using multitone images. Adobe InDesign CS (not InDesign 2) can import PSD files saved in Duotone mode, and these files are more flexible than PDF, EPS, or DCS files. (See Chapter 11, *Spot Colors and Duotones*, for more on spot colors and these file formats.)

Photoshop 2.0 format. No one we associate with still uses Photoshop 2.0. If you need to open your Photoshop documents in some really ancient version, you may be tempted to save your files in the Photoshop 2.0 format. Don't bother. We have not yet found any advantage of saving documents in this format. (Note that this format is not even available in Photoshop for Windows.) Instead, just save the file in Photoshop format, including the flattened composite.

File Formats for Print

If your image is destined for multimedia or the Internet, you may want to use the JPEG or GIF format. But if the image is going to a page-layout program, you should always use TIFF, PDF, EPS, or DCS.

Some page-layout programs will tell you that they can accept and print images in PICT, or BMP, or WMF, or various other weird formats. This may even be true on every third Tuesday of the month, when it coincides with the full moon, and the wind is coming briskly out of the southwest; but in general, using anything other than TIFF, PDF, EPS, or DCS in a print-based

TIFF vs. EPS

As we travel around the world doing seminars and conferences, we are forever hearing people say things like "My service bureau told me to only use EPS files," or "I was told I'd get better images if I used TIFFs," or "Don't EPS files print better?" While we try to appear calm and collected, inside we're just waiting to scream, "Who told you this nonsense? Were they raised by wolves?"

While the confusion is understandable, we want to make a few points about TIFF and EPS that will, we hope, clear the air a tad.

For most images, TIFFs and EPSes contain *exactly the same image data*. The way in which it's written (encoded) may be somewhat different, but that doesn't change the image one iota.

The key differences between TIFFs and EPSes are not what they are or how they're written, but what other programs can do to them and what Photoshop features they can contain.

Encapsulated data. The entire philosophy behind EPS (Encapsulated PostScript) files is that they're little capsules of information. No other program should have to—or even be able to—go in and change anything about the data that's there.

EPS files were designed to be imported into other programs so that those programs wouldn't have to worry about what's in them at all. When it came time to print, that program would simply send the EPS down to the printer, trusting that the PostScript inside would image correctly. EPS files depend on a PostScript interpreter, so if you're using a non-PostScript desktop inkjet, you may have trouble printing them from a program like QuarkXPress.

Open TIFF format. TIFFs, on the other hand, were designed not only to be imported into other programs, but also to be exchanged among image editors.

That is, the program that imports the TIFF can actually access the information inside it and, potentially, change it.

Programs such as QuarkXPress, InDesign, and PageMaker have exploited this property of TIFFs by incorporating features that let you make changes to the TIFF image. On pages, for instance, you can apply a color to a grayscale TIFF image. When you print the page, the program changes the image data on its way to the printer. It almost never changes the data on your disk, but it changes it in the print stream. Other than InDesign's ability to alias one spot color to another, these programs can't really change EPS files at all.

Downsampling and cropping. More important, Adobe PageMaker, Adobe InDesign, and QuarkXPress all have the ability to downsample TIFF data at print time. If you import a 300-ppi TIFF into XPress and print it

application is courting disaster, no matter what the software publisher says. So these are the formats that we'll cover in detail first and foremost; then we'll look at formats appropriate for non-prepress applications.

TIFF

The Tagged Image File Format (TIFF, pronounced just as it reads) is the industry-standard bitmapped file format. Nearly every program that works with bitmaps can handle TIFF files—either placing, printing, correcting, or editing the bitmap. TIFF was once a very straightforward format—the only information it contained beyond the actual pixels themselves was to a desktop laser printer at 60 lpi (see Chapter 17, *Output Methods*, for more on halftone screen frequency), QuarkXPress automatically downsamples the image to 120 ppi (two times the halftone frequency).

QuarkXPress does this because it knows that sending the extra data is wasted time. The result is that your page prints faster. In PageMaker, you can achieve the same result by choosing Optimized in the Print: Options dialog box; in Adobe InDesign, choose Optimized Subsampling from the Send Data popup menu in the Print dialog box. There's no way we know of to downsample an EPS at print time.

Similarly, have you ever tried importing a full-page, 20 MB EPS file into one of these page-layout programs and cropping it down to a 1-by-1-inch square? The program is forced to send the entire 20 megabytes to the printer, even though all you want is a little bit of the image.

With a TIFF image, however, only the data needed to print the page at that screen frequency is sent to the printer, again saving printing time and costs.

Previews and separations. One of the biggest hassles of TIFF images, however, is that they can take a long time to import on slow machines, because the page-layout program has to read the entire file in order to create a screen preview for the image. EPS files can import quickly because Photoshop has already created a preview image.

On the other hand, CMYK TIFF files sometimes print separations much faster than EPS files because the data can be separated into discrete 8-bit chunks (only sending yellow data for the yellow plate, and so on). With EPS files, however, some programs (like PageMaker) have to send all 32 bits (cyan, yellow, magenta, and black) for each plate. This slows down printing considerably. Fortunately, QuarkXPress and InDesign both separate CMYK EPS files properly, so they print about as fast as TIFF files.

Workflow considerations. There are plenty of other differences between EPS and TIFF files—like the fact that you can save transfer functions, duotones, and halftone screening information in EPS files—but we're going to leave them for later in the chapter. Our purpose is simply to show that TIFF and EPS files are equal in stature if not in the goals they were designed to meet.

As for us, when we have a choice, we almost always use TIFF files; we prefer them for their flexibility, and we do a *lot* of page proofing with large grayscale images, so the down-sampling at print time helps a lot. However, if we need fast importing of large files, or a duotone image, we switch to EPS. But don't listen to us. The most important reason why you should use one over the other is not "my consultant/service bureau/guru told me so," but your own workflow. The sorts of images you work with, the kind of network and printers you have, and your proofing needs all play a part in your decision.

the output size and resolution. But that's no longer the case. Photoshop's TIFF files can now contain just about everything you can put in a native Photoshop file, including vector data, clipping paths, content layers, spot color channels, annotations, and adjustment layers. The only exception is that you can't save a duotone as TIFF. But beware. Just because you can save something in a TIFF doesn't mean a program like InDesign or QuarkXPress can open or print it.

A Photoshop TIFF can be any dimension (up to the maximum of 300,000 pixels that applies to all Photoshop images) and any resolution (at least we haven't heard of any limits). You can save it in Grayscale, RGB, CMYK, or

One File or Two?

If you're like us, you probably have the ingrained belief that .psd always means the layered file, and TIFF always means the flat one. For better or for worse, this is no longer a tenable assumption because TIFF files can contain almost everything you can put into a .psd file, including layers. So you have a trade-off.

On the one hand, you can keep a single TIFF file with all your layers, which is fully editable in Photoshop, and place that same layered file in your page layout application. This gives you the convenience of dealing with one file instead of two (no small issue in most people's workflows).

On the other hand, the file is going to be a lot bigger than a flat TIFF would have been, so it takes longer to transmit over e-mail or to download from your server. When your files are 50 MB layered TIFFs instead of 5 MB flat ones, you may have a real job of getting your file to your output provider.

The larger file has a negligible impact on print speed, because the page layout program simply ignores the extra data and sends only the part it can understand to the RIP. In Adobe InDesign and QuarkXPress, it doesn't seem to have any effect on the speed of placing files. PageMaker, however, insists on reading the entire file before concluding that it doesn't understand most of it—so placing layered TIFFs in PageMaker is considerably slower than placing flat ones.

You can continue the practice of saving two files. Nevertheless, it's a sure thing that sooner or later, someone will (deliberately or inadvertently) send you a TIFF that contains layers, so you simply can't assume that TIFF is a print-ready flat file anymore.

Lab color mode with 8 or 16 bits per channel, as 8-bit RGB indexed color, or as a (1-bit) black and white bitmap. Before you get totally carried away, though, bear in mind that TIFF files have a permanent hard-coded size limit of 4 GB.

You can save adjustment layers, content layers, spot color channels, vector data, and screening and transfer-curve information in a TIFF, but they're all mostly ignored by applications other than Photoshop. QuarkXPress can read alpha channel information, but only as a method of building a clipping path (which we don't recommend). Adobe InDesign CS understands spot color channels in TIFF files, though InDesign 2 doesn't. Most applications are also unable to read high-bit TIFFs. So while Photoshop can read everything it saves in a TIFF, the vast majority of applications can't. As a result, just because you can save a vector text layer or a spot channel in a TIFF, and your page layout application can read TIFFs, don't assume that you'll get a spot plate or vector text when you place the TIFF in your page layout app.

Photoshop 6 also let you save all these esoterica in a TIFF file, but you had to turn on the "Enable Advanced TIFF Save" preference to do so. As a result, many users weren't aware that these options existed, and the ones who were generally had good reasons to use them. Photoshop 7 removed the safeguards—you can turn on the "Ask Before Saving Layered TIFF Files" option in File Handling Preferences, but all that it does is give you a somewhat lame warning that adding layers to TIFFs increases the file size, and it only warns you when you add layers to a TIFF that started out flat. If you save your TIFF with ZIP or JPEG compression, you do get a warning that these compression options "are not supported in older TIFF readers"—but a better warning would be that they're hardly supported by any application in existence, except for InDesign and Photoshop. We hope this changes, because ZIP compression is lossless, and highly efficient.

Again, even though you can save spot channels in a TIFF, we know of no application other than Photoshop that can print them properly from a TIFF. And even though you can save your vector data (type and layer clipping paths) in a TIFF, it will print as raster (pixels) from any application other than Photoshop, not vector. So you need to be careful.

Basically, when you save layers and other "advanced" features in a TIFF, Photoshop always saves a flattened version of the image along with the layered version. (David thinks of it as a snail whose body is a flattened TIFF and whose shell is a PSD file; most applications just see the flattened version, but Photoshop can see inside the shell.) QuarkXPress and InDesign import the flattened image, but if you later open the TIFF in Photoshop, it reads the layers.

Some of us wish Adobe had been a little less aggressive in pushing what our friend and colleague Dan Margulis calls, in his inimitable fashion, "exploding TIFFs" on the world; but the toothpaste is out of the tube, the cat is out of the bag, and when it comes to progress, you're either part of the steamroller or part of the road.

Tip: Saving the Image Pyramid. Photoshop's TIFF Options dialog box lets you save something called the Image Pyramid. This option is completely irrelevant for prepress work and was designed looking forward to a time when TIFFs might be used on the Web. The Image Pyramid is basically the contents of the Image Cache (see "Image Cache" in Chapter 2, *Essential Photoshop Tips and Tricks*). With the necessary support from a browser, it lets you download just the resolution you need. But since the necessary browser support is currently rarer than hens' teeth, we don't see any reason to turn on the checkbox.

Previews. When you save an EPS, you almost always ask Photoshop to save a preview image with it. To get a preview for a TIFF file, however, you have to select Full Size Preview in the Save As dialog box. The problem is that no software packages (other than some image databases) currently read those previews, so they're useless.

When you import a TIFF image into a page-layout application, the program reads the entire file and creates a low-resolution preview for you. This is hardly any trouble in a 1 MB image. But you might have to wait while InDesign or QuarkXPress reads and downsamples a 100 MB image. We prefer TIFFs for most of our work, but when we work with larger images, we may switch to EPS files for this reason alone.

Color models. You can save a CMYK image as a TIFF. When you place that file in a page-layout program or the like, no further separation is required. The program can simply pull the cyan channel when it's printing the cyan plate, the magenta channel when it's printing the magenta plate, and so on.

There is a facility in TIFF files to use indexed color, but using indexed color is a prime cause of compatibility problems, in our experience (see "Indexed Color" in Chapter 3, *Image Essentials*). If someone gives us an indexed-color TIFF to work with, we immediately convert it to straight RGB or CMYK and damn the file size. (Of course, if we're resaving it as a PICT or GIF file, we'll leave it in Indexed Color mode.)

IBM vs. Mac. For some reason, the IBM and the Mac have different versions of TIFF. It has something to do with the file's byte order and the processing methods of Motorola versus Intel chips. For whatever reason, you sometimes (though rarely) need to convert TIFFs when you move them between platforms. Happily, programs like Photoshop, PageMaker, InDesign, and QuarkXPress on both Windows and Mac can import either Intel- or Motorola-type TIFFs, so saving in one format or the other is less crucial in the prepress world.

Compression. Photoshop lets you save the composite (flattened) information in TIFF files with LZW or ZIP (lossless), or JPEG (lossy) compression. Unlike the Photoshop or PICT format, if you want compression in a TIFF file, you have to ask for it when you save the image (see Figure 16-5). LZW may still give a few antediluvian applications some problems, but is generally well-supported. However, the only program we know of that can read TIFF files with ZIP or JPEG compression is Adobe InDesign.

LZW compression is quite slow, and storage is getting cheaper every day, so when we're preparing flat TIFFs for placement in a page layout application, we generally don't use any compression, unless we need to transmit the image electronically. In that situation we'll use LZW compression (and we send along a note informing the recipient that we've done so).

Photoshop also always compresses the layers in a layered TIFF files, using either RLE or ZIP. If we're saving layered TIFFs for placement in a page layout application, we almost always leave the composite uncompressed, and we choose ZIP compression on the layers, since Photoshop is the only thing that can understand the layers anyway. ZIP takes a bit longer to save, but it's a much more efficient compression algorithm than RLE so it results in significantly smaller files.

When we're saving layered TIFFs for further work in Photoshop (Bruce has started using TIFF instead of PSD as his archive format), we use ZIP compression on both the layers and the background. We do this only for TIFFs that we only ever plan to open in Photoshop (they work in InDesign too, but not everyone knows that, and it seems too early to start pushing layered ZIP-compressed TIFFs into production workflows). ZIP-compressed TIFFs aren't readable by XPress, PageMaker, or any version of Photoshop earlier than 6.

We've met people who claim that they always save their files in PICT format because it gives them the best compression. Not so. LZW- or ZIP-

Figure 16-5
Saving TIFF files

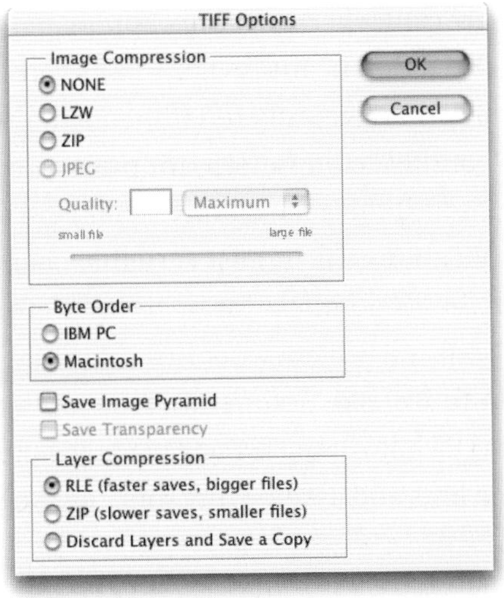

compressed TIFFs are almost always more compact. They're also much more reliable than PICT images for page-layout work. On the other hand, they often take longer to save and open than non-compressed TIFFs, sometimes considerably longer (isn't that always the trade-off, though?).

Compatibility. TIFF is in many ways the ideal bitmapped file format, but it's become increasingly flexible over the years, and that flexibility comes at the price of compatibility. Prepress users tend to believe that there used to be something called a "standard TIFF" that contained pixels and resolution information. But TIFF has always had to serve the needs of communities as diverse as video (where RGB TIFF with alpha channels is a standard), digital camera vendors (where the raw capture is stored as a grayscale TIFF with all sorts of metadata, some of which pertains to converting the raw capture to color), and fax (where compressed bitmapped TIFFs have long been an international standard). JPEG compression and transparency, for example, have been part of the published TIFF specification since 1992, so while prepress folks may blame Adobe for screwing up the TIFF format, an equal number of people have been yelling at Adobe for the past 10 years to implement the features in Adobe's own published specification.

But whatever the politics of the situation, the bottom line is that in Photoshop it's very easy to save TIFFs that are either unreadable by other applications, or may not print as expected from other applications. Photoshop can read anything it can save in a TIFF, so TIFF is great as a work file format for Photoshop. But other applications generally ignore alpha channels (except when building clipping paths) and spot color channels (except for InDesign), and will print any vector data included in the TIFF as raster. The vast majority of TIFF-consuming applications don't understand ZIP or JPEG compression, or transparency.

Since Photoshop is the 800-lb gorilla, the TIFF-reading capabilities of other applications will almost certainly change during the useful life of this book, so it's pointless for us to try to provide chapter and verse on just what will and will not work when you place Photoshop TIFFs in other applications. Instead, we offer this rule of thumb: assume that anything consuming a Photoshop TIFF will read the flattened composite and ignore everything else, and assume that the only widely supported compression option is LZW.

Tip: Color Management Systems. If you're relying on a color management system to control your color, it's generally a great deal easier to do so using TIFF than it is using EPS files, because as yet there's no widespread support for embedded profiles in EPS files, whereas there is for TIFFs. It's possible to build a color-managed workflow around EPS using commercial XTensions and utilities such as Color Solution's Parachute (which intercepts all the color elements in a PostScript stream and applies color transformations based on rules that you set in advance), or PraxiSoft's ColorSyncXT for QuarkXPress (which allows you to apply profiles to imported EPS files). But InDesign, QuarkXPress, and PageMaker all include support for color-managing TIFF files with no additional software.

Encapsulated PostScript (EPS)

As we said back in Chapter 3, *Image Essentials*, Encapsulated PostScript (EPS) is really an object-oriented file format, but Photoshop can save bitmapped and vector (like text) image data in the EPS format. Note that the only time you should use an EPS file is when you're saving an image that you're about to import into a page-layout program. That's what EPS is made for.

While many people prefer working with EPS files over everything else, all too often, that preference is based more on superstition than on knowledge (see sidebar "TIFF vs. EPS," earlier in this chapter). An image saved as TIFF contains exactly the same pixel information as the same image saved as EPS. The difference is in the wrapping that contains the pixels. While TIFF images are open and accessible to all sorts of editing, EPS images are basically TIFFs inside a sealed Postscript box. Once you've saved a file as EPS, it's set in mud, and is generally resistant to any downstream tampering. So receiving applications are limited in what they can do with EPS files besides passing them on to a PostScript RIP.

Of course, you can only print EPS files on a PostScript printer (or with software that acts as a software PostScript interpreter, like Acrobat Distiller). That means those low-cost inkjets are usually ruled out—they'll just print the low-res screen preview instead (see "Previews," below). But we often *do* want to make some changes to images while on pages—colorizing the image, or applying a special halftone screen—and in those cases we switch to a different file format, such as TIFF.

When you save an image as an EPS, Photoshop lets you set the file's preview style and encoding, and it gives you a choice as to whether or not you want to include halftone screening, transfer curves, PostScript Color Management, and vector data (see Figure 16-6). Let's look at each of these. (Ancient versions of Photoshop let you choose a clipping path here, too; see "Clipping Paths," later in this chapter.)

Figure 16-6
Encoding options
in EPS files

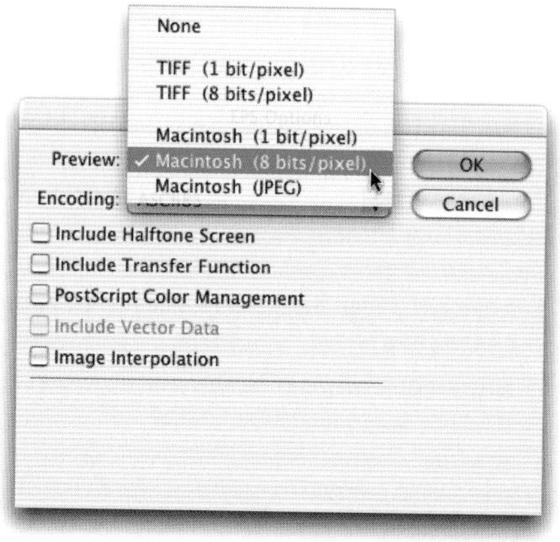

Previews. EPS files typically have two parts: the high-resolution Post-Script data and a low-resolution screen preview. When you import an EPS file into a page-layout program (or a word processor or whatever), the computer usually displays the low-res image on the screen, and when you print the page to a PostScript printer, the computer usually uses the high-res PostScript code.

(Of course, there are always exceptions. If your page-layout program can't find the EPS file on disk, it'll send the low-resolution data to the printer. And Adobe InDesign generally rasterizes the high-resolution data as soon as it notices it's printing to a non-PostScript printer—so you get the best quality possible.)

On the Macintosh, Photoshop lets you save EPS files with five different types of previews, or no preview at all, via the Preview popup menu in the EPS Options dialog box. In Windows, you have only two preview choices. As we said earlier in "Preview Options," with EPSes there's no reason to turn on the Thumbnail and Full Size preview options in the Save As dialog box, because the EPS preview options do the same thing, and give you more control.

▶ **TIFF.** In Windows, Photoshop only offers 1-bit or 8-bit TIFF from the Preview popup menu. The default is 1-bit, which seems strange to us; we always change this to 8-bit. On the Macintosh, the only time you should select one of these is when your image needs to be imported into a page-layout program on a PC. If you choose one of the PICT formats, the preview is lost when the file is moved to the PC (an EPS without a preview just looks like a gray box on pages, though it prints correctly). Some programs on the Macintosh, such as InDesign, Page-Maker, and QuarkXPress, can import PC EPS files with the preview image intact; but no programs that we know of on the PC can read Mac PICT previews. (However, InDesign on either platform can generate a preview on the fly for an EPS file that has lost its preview.)

▶ **PICT.** Files that will stay on the Mac should be saved with a PICT pre-view. Photoshop gives you three choices: 1-bit, 8-bit, and JPEG. Until recently, David always used the 8-bit Macintosh preview when creating EPS files that were destined to stay on the Mac. Somehow it just seemed safer than using JPEG. Then Bruce showed him the light, and David hasn't gone back to 8-bit since.

   When you save an EPS file with a Macintosh JPEG preview, Photoshop has to take the time to build a JPEG preview. However, we gladly take the minor performance hit to get the benefits. JPEG previews are better looking, and take up less space on disk, than their 8-bit brethren. (A JPEG preview for a 300-dpi tabloid-sized image is only about 90 K.) Plus, they occasionally even redraw faster in a page-layout program.

If you're concerned about disk space, you may choose to have no preview (None) or a black-and-white preview (1-bit, either TIFF or PICT). Personally, we'd rather suffer thumbscrews than use either of these when hard drive prices are so low.

ASCII vs. Binary. When you save an image in Photoshop, you have the choice of how to encode the data (see Figure 16-7). Encoding is simply a fancy-schmancy way of saying, "the way the data is written to disk." The first three items in the Encoding popup menu—ASCII, ASCII85, and Binary—are like choosing between long and short words. If you always said "feline" instead of "cat," it would take twice as long to communicate, right? If you choose ASCII, the image takes up twice as much space on

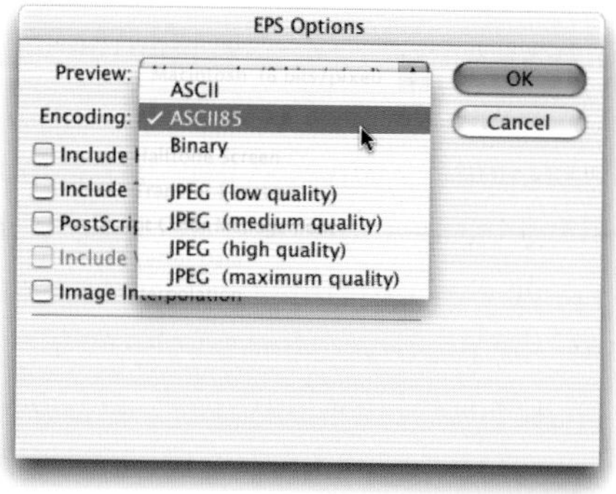

Figure 16-7
Encoding options
in EPS files

your hard drive and takes twice as long to send to the printer than if you choose Binary. ASCII85 is about half way between the two.

You almost never need to use ASCII, and you only need to use ASCII85 when you're printing PostScript over a PC or UNIX serial port, or passing files through some esoteric networks or gateways. Binary images can confuse these pipelines (and PostScript devices that are connected to them), because some of the binary data is interpreted as control characters that say things like, "End of File!" (For the propeller-heads in the audience, this doubling effect occurs because ASCII data is saved in hexadecimal, which uses two 8-bit characters— 0 to 9 and A to F—to describe the same information as 8 bits of binary data.)

JPEG compression. Instead of saving the EPS file with binary or ASCII encoding, you can choose some level of JPEG compression, which we describe in more detail in "Compressing Images," later in this chapter. (Nope, sorry, there's no way to save an EPS file with lossless compression from Photoshop, even though PostScript Level 2 and 3 interpreters can decompress several lossless compression methods.)

Photoshop offers four choices for JPEG quality—Maximum, High, Medium, and Low. The better the quality, the less compression you can achieve. The great benefit of JPEG compression in EPS files is that you not only keep the image small on your hard drive, but you also can send a (much) smaller file down the network lines to your printer, reducing transmission time.

There are two downsides to creating JPEG EPS files, though. The first is that you can *only* print them on a printer that has PostScript Level 2 or 3, because only they know how to decompress JPEG. Older desktop laser printers and imagesetters may not be able to handle JPEG images.

The second problem with JPEG EPS files is a showstopper: they typically won't separate properly when printed from QuarkXPress. They *should*, but for some reason the entire image comes out on the black plate. However, if you save the file as a DCS file (see "DCS," later in this chapter), the separation works like a charm! So, while DCS files can be a hassle in their own right, if your workflow can handle them, the JPEG DCS option can really save a lot of time.

Tip: Removing the JPEG Compression. When you need to print a JPEG-compressed EPS on a non-Level 2 printer, open the file in Photoshop and save it in an uncompressed format. Or you might try the DeBabelizer utility if you have a lot of files to decompress.

Halftone screens and transfer functions. If you want to save halftone-screening or transfer-curve information in the image, you must save it as an EPS file. You can set the halftone screens and transfer functions in the Print with Preview dialog box (see Chapter 17, *Output Methods*, for details). Our basic opinion is that it's extremely rare that you need to save an EPS with a transfer curve; best just to leave that checkbox turned off.

Saving halftone screens in an EPS file, however, is sometimes useful. For instance, when saving duotone, tritone, or quadtone images, you almost always want to set specific screen frequencies and angles for each ink. If you want to import that image into a page-layout program, you have to save it as an EPS (that's the only non-native format you can save duotones in), and to maintain your angles, you have to turn on the Include Halftone Screen checkbox. (Note that InDesign, PageMaker, and QuarkXPress let you specify angles, too, though they cannot override the settings you make in an EPS.)

PostScript Color Management. Some years ago, the folks at Adobe had the clever idea that color management could be made simpler if output devices themselves could do the conversions from one color space into their own color space. They built a basic color management engine into PostScript Level 2 (and made it a bit more robust in Level 3), and waited for the world to get excited. They're still waiting.

It appears that the Photoshop team added the PostScript Color Management checkbox in the EPS Options dialog box in order to drum up some interest in their technology. When this is turned on, Photoshop includes an ICC profile in the EPS file. If you've got a PostScript output device that knows about profiles, it can manage the data "appropriately." Otherwise, the printer should ignore it.

There are so many problems with this workflow (and with the technology itself) that we don't know where to begin. Instead, we recommend you leave this checkbox turned off and handle your color management on the software side of life.

Include Vector Data. If your image includes vector data—vector text or vector clipping shapes that haven't been rasterized into pixels—then you must turn on the Include Vector Data checkbox. (If you turn it off, all that vector data gets left out. Like spot colors, we wish there were a way to "rasterize vector data" upon saving, but that's not an option. If you want to rasterize the vector data, you have to do it before saving the file.) For more on vector data, see Chapters 3, *Image Essentials*, and 15, *Essential Image Techniques*. Note that generally, when you have vector data in your file and you want to import the picture into a page-layout application, EPS is the best format to use.

Image Interpolation. If you have a PostScript 3 printer, you might find the Image Interpolation feature intriguing: It smooths out low-resolution images, like Web graphics or screen captures, on the fly (in the printer). It also works when distilling PostScript files into PDF (so it's helpful for online documentation). It's not fabulous, but it's nice that Adobe gives us the option, just in case. We always leave this turned off for normal images (files with enough resolution so that you can't see the actual pixels).

DCS

In early versions of Photoshop, the DCS (Desktop Color Separation) format was an option inside the Save as EPS dialog box. It made sense: DCS is really just a special case of the EPS file format. However, it's weird (and important) enough that Adobe added it as two separate file formats in the Save As dialog box: Photoshop DCS 1.0 and Photoshop DCS 2.0.

Originally, DCS was designed to separate the high-resolution image data from a low-resolution "preview" version. In version 1.0, the DCS format always resulted in five files. The first four held the high-resolution data for each color place (cyan, magenta, yellow, and black). The fifth file, also called the *master file*, was the one that you actually imported into a page-layout program, and it contained three things: a low-resolution screen preview of the image, a low-resolution composite CMYK version, and pointers to the other four files.

There were (and are) two problems with DCS 1.0. First, some people didn't like to keep track of five files for each image (though to be fair, many other people thought this was great because they could leave the high-resolution data on a server and just use the master file on their own systems). Second, there was no way to include spot colors.

DCS 2.0 solves both problems. If you've already preseparated your image (converted to CMYK mode), you have the choice of saving the image in either a DCS 1.0 or DCS 2.0 format (see Figure 16-8). However, we know of no good reason to use DCS 1.0, so we'll focus on version 2.0, which does everything that 1.0 does and more.

Of the various options in the DCS 2.0 Format dialog box, most of them are equivalent to the ones in the EPS Options dialog box (which we discussed in the last section). For instance, Preview lets you determine the quality and kind of RGB screen preview; Encoding determines the format of the data within the file; and so on. The only new feature here is the DCS popup menu, in which you can choose whether you want one single file or multiple files on disk, and what sort of composite image you want.

Figure 16-8
Saving Desktop Color Separation (DCS) files

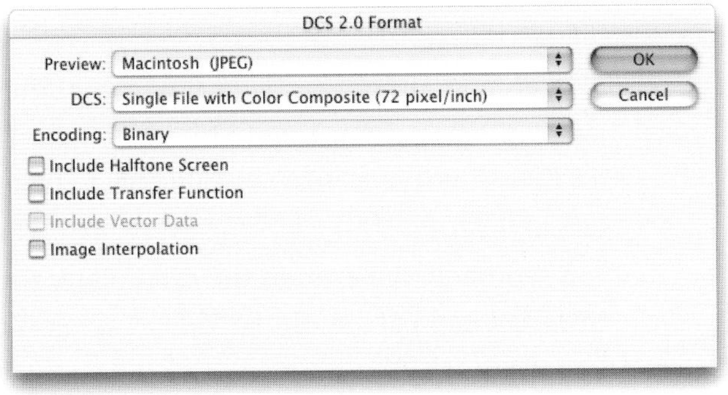

DCS 2.0 Format

Preview: Macintosh (JPEG)

DCS: Single File with Color Composite (72 pixel/inch)

Encoding: Binary

☐ Include Halftone Screen
☐ Include Transfer Function
☐ Include Vector Data
☐ Image Interpolation

OK

Cancel

DCS composites. Many people confuse the EPS's composite image with the preview image. This is understandable, because they're almost exactly the same thing. Both are low-resolution (72-ppi) representations of the original image; and both can be used instead of the high-res image for proofing.

The real difference is in their uses. The preview image is always in RGB mode and is designed for screen use only. The composite image is saved in CMYK mode (literally, it's the same as downsampling the high-res CMYK image to 72 ppi using Nearest Neighbor interpolation), and is meant for sending to a low-resolution color printer for use as a comp or a proof.

For color-proofing devices that require color separations, you can force XPress to send the high-resolution data with an XTension, such as Total Integration's SmartXT. Adobe InDesign CS can do this automatically (though InDesign 2 cannot). We don't know of any way to do this in Page-Maker other than trying to get the color printer to recombine the separations. Honestly, though, we tend to think it's better to proof images before you save them as DCS files; once they're encapsulated like this, it's hard to get any really accurate proofs from them.

Multi-file or single file. Whether you tell Photoshop to write a single file or multiple files is up to you and your workflow. Probably the best reason to use multiple files is if you need or want to keep your high-resolution data in a separate place (like on a server or at your imaging bureau). This is especially helpful with very large files (we leave the definition of "very large" up to you).

On the other hand, keeping track of a number of files can be a pain in the left buttock, and the links to the high-res images can be "broken" if you rename or move those files (see "Tip: Recovering Lost Links in DCS," below).

Note that either way, DCS files sometimes print faster from a page-layout program than either TIFF or EPS files. For instance, with a single-file EPS, some programs (like PageMaker) typically have to send the entire EPS to the printer for each and every plate. However, with DCS files, they can send only the cyan to the cyan plate, and so on. (QuarkXPress and InDesign can usually "break down" single-file EPS files, so this isn't as important.)

Tip: Naming Spot Colors. As we explain in Chapter 17, *Output Methods*, if your DCS file includes spot colors, your page-layout software must also have colors named exactly the same way (yes, PageMaker, InDesign, and XPress import these names automatically when you import a DCS 2.0 file).

Tip: JPEG Compression in DCS. Using JPEG encoding in CMYK EPS files can be a disaster because some programs (notably QuarkXPress) can't separate them properly at print time. However, DCS files are stored in a preseparated state, so XPress has no trouble with them. If your PostScript printer can handle JPEG encoding (PostScript Level 2 and 3 can), JPEG encoding can save you file size and hence network transmission time in exchange for a slight degradation of image quality (see "Compressing Images," later in this chapter).

Tip: Recovering Lost Links in DCS. Occasionally, when working with multi-file DCS files, the master file gets lost or the link between the master file and the high-res color files is broken (this can happen if you move or rename the high-res files). Fixing broken pointers is often easy: Just open the master file in a text editor like BBEdit and edit the file names in the lines that begin with "%%PlateFile".

However, don't fear if you lose the master file entirely; you can always reassemble the separate DCS files in Photoshop.

1. Open each of the high-res images in Photoshop. They're all EPS files, and they're all in Grayscale mode.

2. When all four of the files are open, select Merge Channels from the Channels palette's popout menu.

3. Make sure the mode is set to CMYK and the Channels field is set to 4 (see Figure 16-9); click OK.

4. Photoshop is pretty good at guessing which file should be set to which color channel in the Merge CMYK Channels dialog box, but if it guesses wrong, set the popup menus to the proper files.

Figure 16-9
Merging channels

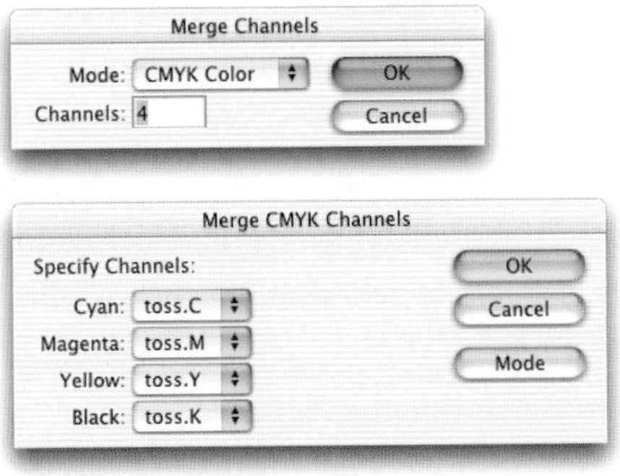

Merge Channels

Mode: CMYK Color   OK
Channels: 4   Cancel

Merge CMYK Channels

Specify Channels: OK
Cyan: toss.C   Cancel
Magenta: toss.M
Yellow: toss.Y   Mode
Black: toss.K

When you click OK, Photoshop merges the four grayscale files into a single, high-resolution CMYK file. You can now create the five DCS files again, if you want. (Note that if you have spot colors in your DCS file, you'll have to add the additional channels manually, after you merge the CMYK channels.)

PDF (Portable Document Format)

Early editions of this book listed Adobe's Acrobat Portable Document Format (PDF) in the "niche file format" section (later in this chapter). However, even though we still find that Photoshop's PDF files are the exception and not the rule, they are robust and common enough now that it's time to move this section up to here. Note that when it comes to importing an image into a page-layout program, we still usually consider TIFF, EPS, and DCS to be safer options (and, occasionally, native Photoshop file, with InDesign). Similarly, if you want to put an image on the Web, use GIF or JPEG, not PDF.

The exception, however, is when the image contains a significant amount of text (even a paragraph's worth) that you want to maintain as sharp-edged vector text in the final output. While text is rasterized in TIFF files (making the edges pixelated) and converted to outlines in EPS files (making them slow to print), PDF files handle text beautifully. Best of all, you can embed a font into your PDF file, so it will display and print correctly wherever it goes (see Figure 16-10).

However, Photoshop writes PDF files using the PDF 1.4 specification. InDesign 2 and CS, and QuarkXPress 5 and 6 can read this; but XPress 4 and PageMaker 6.5 cannot. If you're using an older page-layout program, you'd be better off sticking with TIFF and EPS files. Spot colors can be separated using InDesign or Acrobat 6, but we currently don't fully trust spot color separations from PDF files in XPress so we generally just stick to DCS 2 files when it comes to spot colors. Here's another reason not to use PDF: Photoshop can save transparency in a PDF or spot colors in a PDF, but it can't yet handle both.

Nevertheless, PDF is an excellent format for sending proofs or samples to clients, especially now that Photoshop allows you to include password protection in its PDF files.

It's pretty clear that the PDF file format will replace EPS in the future; but not until Adobe has ironed out all the wrinkles (like supporting both transparency and spot colors) and it's as well-supported as EPS (in QuarkXPress, PageMaker, and so on).

Round-tripping. If you turn on the Layers checkbox in the Save As dialog box, Photoshop places the layered data in the PDF file, too. This means you can re-open the layered image in Photoshop again ("round-tripping"). And, if you use JPEG compression in the PDF, the PDF image degrades, but the layered data does not. So when you open it in Photoshop and resave as PDF, you don't re-compress (and further degrade) your data. Very spiffy. PDF files can now even contain 16-bit, "high-bit" data.

When you turn off the Layers checkbox, the PDF file is smaller; and if you try to reopen it in Photoshop, the program rasterizes the whole thing, even if you had saved your vector data. (Note that Photoshop can open and rasterize PDF files from other sources, too.)

Figure 16-10
Saving a file as
an Acrobat PDF

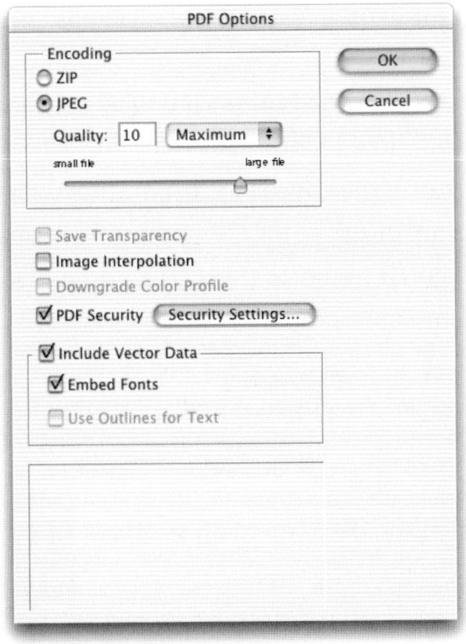

PDF Presentation. Quick, you need to send 15 images from your portfolio to a prospective client! If you send them a bunch of files on disk, they'll need to open each one individually, which means they'll open one or maybe two before getting tired. What if you could send them a single file with all your images? That's what PDF Presentation is for. You won't find PDF Presentation in the Save As dialog box. Rather, it's lurking in the

Automate submenu (under the File menu). But we discuss it here because you end up with a single PDF file full of images.

Click the Browse button in the PDF Presentation dialog box to choose which files you want included, or turn on the Add Open Files checkbox if the pictures are already open in Photoshop (see Figure 16-11). The file path is inevitably too wide to fit in the narrow window, so you'll probably need to drag the dialog box's horizontal scroll bar to see which image is which. Then you can drag each file name up or down to order them. (The order here reflects the order in the final PDF, of course.)

You have a choice between creating a Multi-Page Document or a Presentation. The former is a normal PDF file. The latter tells Acrobat to take over the whole screen and step through the pages automatically, based on the settings you choose at the bottom of this dialog box. When you click Save, Photoshop displays the PDF Options dialog box, where you can choose the file's security settings (whether to allow printing, exporting images, and so on), compression settings, and font embedding.

Tip: Watch Out for Notes. If you've used the Notes tool to add annotations to your images, be aware that Photoshop exports those annotations with your PDF files or PDF Presentations. This is very helpful when you want to send along notes about your files, but it could also prove embarrassing if you have notes there that you didn't intend to send.

Figure 16-11
PDF Presentation

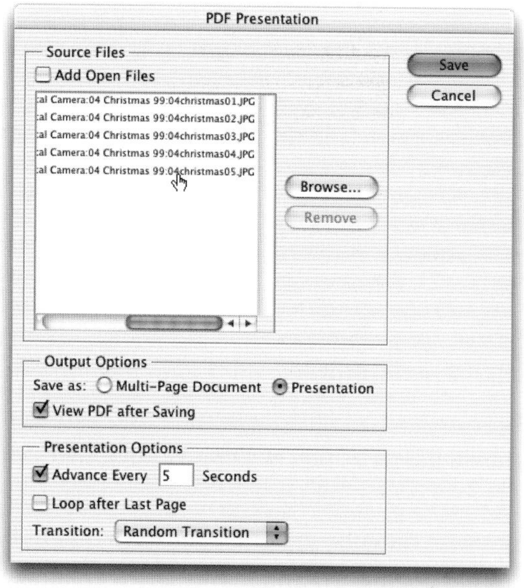

If the recipient decides to further annotate your PDF file using Acrobat's review tools, those notes are also retained when you open the PDF back in Photoshop. However, Photoshop can only open one page at a time, and it always re-rasterizes the image. If you need to convert a bunch of pages to PSD format, you can choose Multi-Page PDF to PSD from the Automate submenu.

File Metadata

Remember the good old days, when you could jot down notes on the back of a photograph with a soft pencil? Storing information about your pictures is essential for a robust workflow, but where's the pencil in an all-digital world? It's called *metadata*—data about data—and in Photoshop it lives hidden inside or alongside image files in a format called XMP (eXtensible Metadata Platform).

(By the way, the word "Metadata" was coined and trademarked by Jack Myers in the early 1970s, back when the word didn't mean anything. However, many people argue that the word has since become part of common language, and is therefore no longer enforceable as a trademark. But if Jack ever prevails, we suggest people use the word "datad'data"—which is more fun to say anyway.)

File Info. Photoshop offers two paths to an image's metadata: the File Info dialog box (choose File Info from the File menu, or press Command-Option-I) and the File Browser's Metadata palette. Bruce likes the Metadata palette because it lets him see and edit information about his images without first opening them (we cover this palette in Chapter 14, *Building a Digital Workflow*). This makes it very easy to perform tasks like adding a copyright notice to 50 images in one fell swoop. David likes the File Info dialog box because he likes the layout better (see Figure 16-12) and he tends to have images open while editing their metadata anyway.

By default, the File Info dialog box has seven panels of metadata, including two that display camera data, one that can capture the file's history, and some general information about the image (title, copyright information, keywords, and so on). The metadata in the Camera Data panels isn't editable (it's captured by the camera itself). Most of the other fields are editable.

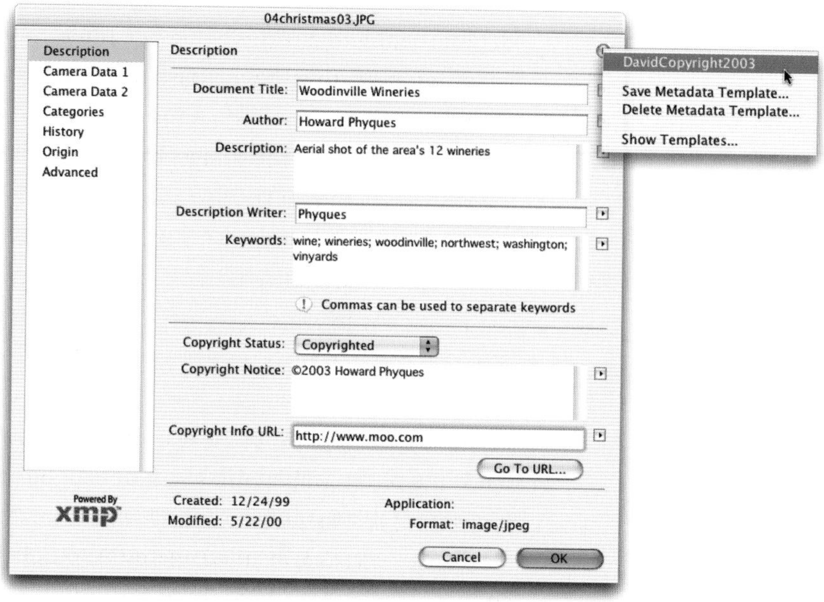

Figure 16-12
File Info dialog box

If you need to store other sorts of specialized data (perhaps you want to store GPS data or model release information for each image), you can create custom File Info panels relatively easily by editing XML files. (There's instructions on how to do this in the Goodies folder on the Photoshop install disc.)

Tip: Move Data to the Page. If you use other Adobe products, you may notice that InDesign CS and Illustrator CS each have an identical File Info dialog box. InDesign CS also has a Info palette that can read the XMP data inside imported images. This means you can use Photoshop to insert metadata such as copyright, image description, and photographer, and then later retrieve that information from within InDesign. You know you're in a digital workflow when you no long receive e-mails or phone calls saying, "Hey, don't forget that the copyright notice for that picture of the girl on a bicycle should be . . . ."

Metadata templates. Generally, much of the metadata you'll want to store in your images is repeated information—data that is the same for lots of different images. Fortunately, you don't have to type that stuff repeatedly. Photoshop remembers recently typed metadata for each field in the

File Info dialog box. To recall something you typed recently, click on the little triangle to the right of the metadata field.

You can also save metadata templates that include a collection of metadata entries. (These aren't really "templates"; they're just a way to fill out a bunch of metadata fields automatically.) The most common example is a template for your copyright information where you want to change three fields: Copyright Status, Copyright Notice, and Copyright Info URL. To do this, set just these fields (leave the others in the dialog box blank), choose Save Metadata Template from the dialog box's popout menu, and give the template a name.

Later, when you want to apply these metadata to another image, just select the template's name from the top of the popout menu. Photoshop appends the metadata template to whatever is already in the File Info palette; it won't delete any data that is already there but it will replace data with the data from the template. (That is, if there was already copyright information saved in the file, the metadata template would replace it with the new data.)

History. Imagine if you took a picture with your digital camera and later had to admit the image as evidence in court. A lawyer might jump up and ask, "How do we know this file hasn't been digitally altered?" If you really care about recording everything that was done to your images, you can turn on the History Log checkbox in the General panel of the Preferences dialog box. You can tell Photoshop where to save the information (Metadata saves it in each file's metadata; Text File saves it to disk). You can also tell Photoshop what to remember.

▶ Sessions just saves when the image was opened and closed. We have no idea how this would be helpful for anyone.

▶ Concise saves the names of basic steps. So it records "Crop" or "Levels" but not how much was cropped or what got a levels tweak.

▶ Detailed records specific actions, such as "Levels Adjustment, Blue Channel, Gamma 0.82".

Generally, if you're going to turn on the History Log, we think it makes the most sense to set it to Detailed. However, if you're going to do a lot of work on a file, it could increase the file size a bit; so you might want to save the history in a log file rather than metadata. (On the other hand, if you're saving it for legal purposes, it probably makes much more sense to save it in the file's metadata.)

Metadata in PDF files. Earlier in this chapter we mentioned that when you save your image as a PDF file, you can give it password protection. If you choose Acrobat 6-level protection, you can choose whether or not you want the metadata to be secure. For example, you might want your PDF files to be password protected, but want to be able to search for them based on keywords or description from within the File Browser.

Clipping Paths

The old art of cutting silhouettes out of paper is mostly gone now, though it lives on at street fairs and tourist spots. If you've ever seen someone cutting one of these, you know how painstaking a process it can be. We wonder why, then, people expect creating a silhouette in Photoshop to be as easy as snapping their fingers. Far from it: masking out the background of an image—leaving only the foreground object—is a difficult proposition. Unfortunately, it's something that many of us in production work have to do every day (see Figure 16-13).

The biggest problem is often not making a selection to silhouette (we cover a lot of selection and silhouetting techniques in Chapter 8, *Selections and Channels*). Rather, it's bringing that selection into a page-layout program without unnaturally harsh edges resulting. In this section we'll discuss getting silhouettes to print properly from PageMaker, InDesign, or QuarkXPress.

The secret to clean silhouettes is Photoshop's paths feature. Remember that Bézier paths are generally smoother than raster (bitmap) data, because

Figure 16-13
The effect of
a clipping path

they're always imaged at the resolution of your output device, whereas bitmapped images print at whatever resolution they're set to, or at the coarseness of your halftone screen. Once you use the Pen tools to create a path in Photoshop (and then save that path in the Paths palette by double-clicking on the Working Path tile), you can specify that your path be used as a clipping path upon output.

1. Select Clipping Path from the popout menu in the Paths palette.

2. Choose the path that you want as a clipping path (see Figure 16-14).

3. Give it a flatness value (see "Tip: Bump Up Your Flatness," later in this chapter) and click OK. The name of the path (in the Paths palette) should now be in outline style, indicating it's a clipping path.

4. Save the image as a TIFF or EPS, and then import it into InDesign, PageMaker, or QuarkXPress.

(Note that earlier versions of Photoshop allowed you to choose a clipping path from within the EPS Options dialog box, but no longer.)

Figure 16-14
Creating a
clipping path

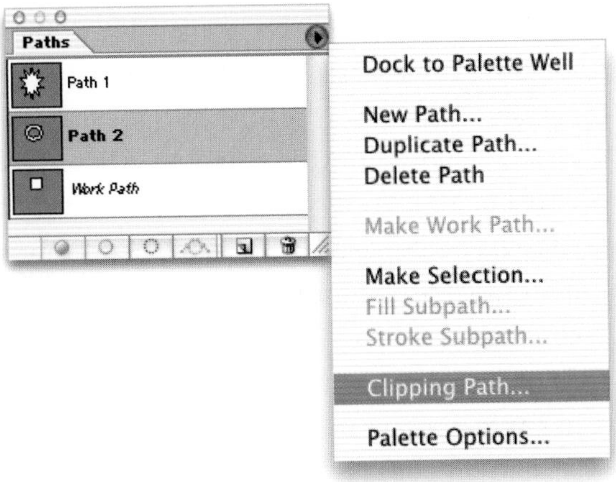

Designate the path as a clipping path.

Assign a Flatness value.

TIFF vs. EPS. Photoshop is able to save—and QuarkXPress, InDesign, and PageMaker can read—clipping paths in either TIFF or EPS files. Because we tend to use TIFF files, this is great news. Remember that clipping paths don't really delete the data itself; the entire image gets sent to the printer along with the instructions on how to clip it down.

Why use paths. People use paths most often when they want to place a silhouette of an object over a colored background in a page-layout program. For instance, many catalogs have a colored tint over the entire page, with irregularly shaped objects—shoes, toaster ovens, cars—floating as if in mid-air. If you try to achieve this effect in QuarkXPress by simply making the background transparent (white) rather than using a clipping path, you'll get an object surrounded by a white box.

Adobe InDesign, on the other hand, can read the transparency in TIFF or native Photoshop files, so you don't need clipping paths at all. If you bring one of these images into InDesign, it will appear as though it had a clipping path, even if it doesn't. In our opinion, this is one of the greatest reasons to use InDesign over QuarkXPress.

Soft edges. The main problem with clipping paths is that you cannot clip a soft or semitransparent edge. Because paths are mathematical lines and curves, they're always as sharp as the printer you print on. That's almost always sharper than the resolution of your image, so be prepared for your edges to look overly crisp. No, you can't make a soft, fuzzy edge with a clipping path—so, no drop shadows or clouds! (See Chapter 15, *Essential Image Techniques*, for more information on these sorts of effects.) Similarly, clipping around a gauzy dress is out. If your subject is having a bad hair day, clipping around the head is going to make it look even worse.

There are several ways of making soft edges interact with your background on pages (see "Drop Shadows," in Chapter 15, *Essential Image Techniques*). The best one, however, is simply to design your page so that the image doesn't have to overlap any other colors in your page-layout application. (Actually, the best one is to just erase to transparency—easier than making a sharp-edged clipping path—and then using InDesign.)

Alternatively, if you have to use XPress or PageMaker, you can forget about clipping paths and composite the image with the background in Photoshop, using the techniques in Chapter 8, *Selections and Channels*.

Tip: Bump Up Your Flatness. You can often speed up print times dramatically and/or avoid PostScript "limitcheck" errors by raising the PostScript flatness value in the Clipping Path dialog box. The flatness value determines how hard the PostScript interpreter works to give you smooth curves. The higher the flatness value, the faster the graphic prints, but the more choppy the curve gets. If you raise your flatness too high, the curve turns into a set of straight lines. However, you can almost always raise your flatness to between 3 and 5, never see the difference, and speed your printing times considerably.

Of course, flatness only applies to PostScript curves, so if you're not using clipping paths on a PostScript printer, there's no need for a flatness value.

Tip: Inset Paths Slightly. When you're drawing paths around objects to silhouette them in Photoshop, make sure you draw the path very slightly inside the object's border—we typically place the path one or two pixels inside the edge. This usually avoids most of the spillover from the background color. If spillover is a significant problem with an image, you should be thinking about building a Photoshop composite instead of using a clipping path.

Tip: Pick Your Clipping Path. Not only can QuarkXPress and InDesign see (and use) a clipping path in your Photoshop TIFF image, they can see (and use) any other path saved with the file, too. You can control the clipping path behavior of TIFFs in QuarkXPress on the Clipping tab of the Modify dialog box. In InDesign, select Clipping Path from the Object menu. This is useful for two reasons.

▶ You don't have to specify that a path be a clipping path within Photoshop. Just save the TIFF file with a regular path, and QuarkXPress or InDesign can use it.

▶ If you have more than one path saved with your TIFF file, you can choose which path you want to use from within XPress or InDesign. This is great if you won't decide which portions of a picture you want to use until you see it alongside the rest of your page layout.

File Formats for Multimedia and the Web

Where TIFF and EPS (and the DCS variant) file formats are designed for print, there are plenty of other formats that you can use for multimedia and Web publishing, including PICT, JPEG, and GIF. Again, the file format is like the envelope that holds the image data; there is usually no inherent difference in the image itself, just how it's presented to whatever program you're trying to view the image with.

PICT

The PICT format (pronounced just as it looks) is a Mac-standard object-oriented file format. A PICT graphic can contain a bitmap as one of the objects in the file, or as its only object ("bitmap-only PICT"). Bitmap-only PICTs can be any size, resolution, and bit depth. While Photoshop for Windows can open a PICT (.pct) image, few other programs on the PC can. If the PC is your final destination, you'd be well advised to use some other file format.

You should especially not use PICTs in a page-layout package; Adobe InDesign, PageMaker, and QuarkXPress are all prone to produce unpredictable results from PICTs.

PICT files can't handle multiple layers, CMYK data, or more than four channels (that's RGB plus one channel total). Nonetheless, PICT is the primary format when you're printing to non-PostScript devices (like most film recorders) or for multimedia work (like working with Macromedia Director); in these cases, you rarely need to move out of RGB mode. The PICT file format is not appropriate for Web publishing.

When you save a file in the PICT format, Photoshop asks whether you want to use JPEG (and if so, how lossy you want it) or no compression at all (see Figure 16-15). However, if you pick None, Photoshop still uses lossless RLE compression.

CompuServe GIF

The Graphics Interchange Format (commonly known as GIF, pronounced "jiff" or "giff," depending on your upbringing), was once the "house-brand" image file format of the CompuServe online information service. That's

Figure 16-15
Saving PICTs

why this file format is listed as "Compuserve GIF" in Photoshop's Save As dialog box, even though GIF images have long since broken free of CompuServe's corporate walls and are now the industry standard on almost every online service, including the Internet (notably for Web pages).

GIF files are designed for on-screen viewing, especially for images where file size is more important than quality, and for screens that only display 8-bit color (256 colors). Photoshop GIFs are always 8-bit indexed color images, making them quite reasonable for on-screen viewing, but totally unreasonable for printing.

GIFs are automatically compressed using lossless LZW compression (see "Compressing Images," later in this chapter). We discuss GIF images and how to make them in Chapter 18, *Multimedia and the Web*.

JPEG

Earlier in the chapter we talked about JPEG as a compression method within another file format—like JPEG DCS—but these days when most people say "JPEG" they're referring to the JPEG file format itself. While plenty of people use JPEG images for prepress work, the vast majority of JPEG images are found on the World Wide Web. The only problem with using the JPEG format for printing is that it's lossy; see "Compressing Images," later in this chapter. We recommend only using JPEG files in a prepress workflow if its essential that you drastically limit your file sizes (perhaps you have limited RAM or hard drive space, or your weekly rag has 800 images). Note that if you do save your files in a JPEG format, it's important not to open them and save them repeatedly—each time you save a JPEG file it further degrades.

Note that neither XPress nor PageMaker nor InDesign actually sends the JPEG information to the printer for decompression (as they do with JPEG-encoded EPSes). Instead, they decompress it and send it down just as they would a TIFF file. So you get the hard disk savings, but it actually takes longer every time you print the file because the printing program has to decompress the JPEG image each time.

JPEGs on the Web are a different matter. JPEGs are ubiquitous on the Internet because they're the only good way to display full color (24-bit) images in a Web page. We discuss JPEG images and how to make them in Chapter 18, *Multimedia and the Web*.

Niche File Formats

As we noted back in the Preface, this book only covers a fraction of the potential uses of Photoshop—those centered around production. People use this program for so many different things that we couldn't hope to cover them all here. In the last two sections, we discussed each of the file formats that are relevant for professionals who are putting images on paper, film, or the Web. You, however, might be doing something interesting, different, or just plain odd. Don't worry; Photoshop can probably still accommodate you.

Reasonable Niche File Formats

In this section, we'll explore several file formats that Photoshop can read and write, and why you might have cause to use them. And even then, you should save the original image in Photoshop or TIFF format as well for archival purposes.

JPEG 2000. In the twilight years of the twentieth century, a bunch of smart folks got together to discuss the future of the JPEG file format. They came up with a new specification for JPEG—labeled JPEG 2000—that does a better job of compressing images (more compression, less image degradation). Plus, unlike JPEG, JPEG 2000 can handle 16-bit-per-channel files, grayscale files, full 8-bit transparency, and even an option for lossless compression.

Unfortunately, just because there's a better format available doesn't mean people will rush to use it. As we go to press, no page-layout application can import JPEG 2000 files (though we assume the next version of InDesign will), nor can any Web browser display them without a specialized plug-in.

Nevertheless, always ahead of the curve, Photoshop can read and write JPEG 2000 files. Actually, it can read and write a flavor of JPEG 2000 it calls JPF. But it can only do so when you have installed the plug-in, found in the Optional Plug-ins folder, inside the Goodies folder on the Photoshop install disc. JPF files aren't compatible with most other JPEG 2000 software (which usually reads a flavor called JP2), but JPF offers more compression options than JP2, including the ability to JPF files compatible with JP2 readers—at the expense of a slightly larger file size.

Once JPEG 2000 support is more widespread, we think this file format should replace the use of JPEG images in the prepress industry, where quality is key. (Note that we said it "should," as in "it ought to, if there's anyone out there who needs compressed files but still cares about quality.")

PSB (Large Document format). While earlier versions of Photoshop limited your images to 30,000 pixels per side (2.5 GB), Photoshop CS lifted this to 300,000 pixels per side (a whopping 251 GB file). We only know of a handful of people who need this, including our friends in the intelligence community (who are reading this book over your shoulder right now), and our friend Stephen Johnson, who is using a scanning back camera to make hyper-resolution panoramas at 7,500 × 75,000 pixels each. While the native Photoshop file format still tops out at 30,000 pixels per side, you can save these truly huge files as TIFF files (up to 4 GB), Photoshop Raw files (not to be confused with Camera Raw), or—the best option—in the Large Document (PSB) format, new in Photoshop CS.

To save a PSB file, turn on the Enable Large Document Format checkbox in the File Handling panel of the Preferences dialog box. (Perhaps PSB stands for "Photoshop Behemoth"?) Then, choose Large Document Format from the Format popup menu in the Save As dialog box. PSB files support layers, effects, and any other Photoshop feature. However, they can only be opened in Photoshop CS or later.

Scitex CT. Whether to use the Scitex CT file format is a no-brainer: if you own a Creo Scitex system or are trying to output via a Scitex system, you may want to save your document in this format as the last stage before printing. If you don't have any contact with a Creo Scitex system, ignore this one.

It may be important to note that the Scitex CT format is not actually the CT ("continuous tone") format that Scitex folks usually talk about. It's actually the Handshake format, which is less proprietary and more common (even QuarkXPress can import these files).

Scitex CT files are always CMYK or grayscale; however, Photoshop lets you save RGB images in this format, too. We don't know why. If you can figure out a good use for them, let us know. By the way, if you're trying to get Photoshop duotones through a Scitex system, you should sprint directly to "Converting Duotones to CMYK" in Chapter 11, *Spot Colors and Duotones*.

PNG (Portable Network Graphic). For a while there it looked like the GIF file format would take over the Internet, and therefore the world. Then, in early 1995, CompuServe and Unisys shocked the world by demanding that developers whose software wrote or read GIF files pay a royalty fee for the right to use the format. Legally, they were entitled; but no one had had to pay before, and it jarred the electronic publishing community enough that a group of dedicated individuals decided to come up with a new file format for Web graphics.

The result of their work is the PNG format (which is pronounced "ping," and officially stands for "Portable Network Graphic," though it unofficially stands for "PNG's Not GIF"). Not only is it a free format that any developer can use, but it does much more than GIF.

For instance, PNG can support both 8-bit indexed color and full 24-bit color. Where GIF can include 1-bit transparency (where each pixel is either transparent or not), PNG has full 8-bit transparency with alpha channels, so a graphic could be partially opaque in some areas. PNG also includes some limited ability to handle color management on the Internet, by recording monitor gamma and chromaticity. There are many other features, too (among which is the significant bonus of, unlike GIF, having a relatively unambiguous pronunciation).

Unfortunately, PNG has never been widely accepted by users or Web browsers, and the patents on GIF (which were based on GIF's LZW compression scheme) will expire by June, 2004. Our prediction is that PNG will slowly fade away over the next couple of years.

PICT Resource. Are you authoring multimedia or developing software on the Macintosh? If so, you may find yourself needing to save an image into the resource fork of a file. Here's where the PICT Resource file format comes in. To be honest, it's not really a different file format; the Macintosh lets you place PICT information in the data or resource fork of a file. Photoshop, however, is a convenient way to move the image from one to the other. (Windows programs don't have a resource fork, so PC users can ignore this file format.)

Note that Photoshop lets you open PICT resources in two different ways. First, if the file has a PICT resource numbered 256, Photoshop lets you open that particular resource directly from the Open dialog box. If there are multiple PICT resources, you can access them only by selecting PICT Resource from the Import submenu (under the File menu).

Filmstrip. Video, film, and animation all have a similar popular appeal, and the tools that let mere mortals create this sort of stuff (like Adobe Premiere) have finally begun to find a market. But that doesn't mean that programs that create or edit still images will go away. For what is video but a bunch of still images strung together over time?

Adobe Premiere and AfterEffects let you save movies in a file format that Photoshop can open, called Filmstrip. You can then edit each frame individually in Photoshop, save the file out again, and import the clip in the video/animation program. This technique not only lets you make small retouching changes, but even perform rotoscoping (a form of animation), colorizing, or any number of other special effects.

When you open a Filmstrip file in Photoshop, it looks like a tall and narrow noodle. But when you double-click on the Zoom tool to scroll in to 100-percent view, you can see each image frame clearly, along with its time and frame code. Note that changing the file's size, resolution, or pixel dimensions may be disastrous, or at least unpredictable. Instead, constrain your edits to the pixels that are already there.

WBMP. Photoshop pictures go everywhere these days, as big as billboards and as small as little icons on cell phone screens. If you're trying to make pictures for cell phones and wireless PDAs, we've got just the file format for you: WBMP. You can save files that are already in Bitmap mode as WBMP format from the Save As dialog box, or any file as WBMP from the Save for Web dialog box (see Chapter 18, *Multimedia and the Web*).

ZoomView. Sure, you can save a 5 MB image as a 200 K JPEG file and put it on a Web site, but when someone views it in a Web browser they'll spend all day scrolling left, right, up, and down to see it all! Instead, if you need to put high-resolution images on a Web site, consider exporting the file in ZoomView (.mtx) format. ZoomView was developed by a company called ViewPoint. You can save ZoomView files by selecting ZoomView from the Export submenu (under Photoshop's File menu). You end up with a bunch of files: the .mtx file, an HTML file, a folder of images that are tiles of the exported image, and a folder of Visual Basic and JavaScript scripts that the HTML file calls. Plus, you must sign up for a license with ViewPoint to use it. (Licenses are free for hobbyists and individuals who are posting their images on their Web site in order to drum up business.) And, your audience has to download the Viewpoint Media Player plug-in to view these images.

It's complex stuff, to be sure, but the benefit is pretty cool: the ability to zoom in and out and pan around the high-resolution image, without forcing someone to download the whole image (you probably don't want them to have your high-resolution file anyway). To be honest, when we need someone to see an image, we'd rather save it as an EPS file, use Acrobat Distiller to convert the EPS to a PDF using JPEG 2000 encoding, and then use Acrobat Professional to save the file with security settings (like "don't allow exporting or printing").

Raw. The last file format that we can even remotely recommend using is the file format of last resort: the Raw format. (Don't confuse this with the Camera Raw format, which Photoshop can read but not write. See Chapter 14, *Building a Digital Workflow,* for more on Camera Raw.) If you've ever traveled in a foreign country, you've probably found yourself in situations where you and the person in front of you share no common language. The answer? Reduce communication to gestures and sounds.

The Raw format is a way to read or write image data in a "language" that Photoshop doesn't know. It relies on the basics of bitmapped images (see Figure 16-16).

▶ All bitmapped images are rectangular grids of pixels.

▶ Some bitmapped images have header information at the beginning of the data.

▶ Color data is usually either interleaved (such as alternating red, green, blue, red, green, blue, and so on) or noninterleaved (such as all the red information, then all the green, and finally all the blue).

If you're trying to import from or export to some strange computer system, you may have to rely on the Raw format because that system might not know from TIFF, EPS, or any other normal, everyday file format. This is becoming less of a problem as most mainframe systems (especially the imaging systems that are used for scientific or medical imaging) learn the newer, better file formats we've been discussing up until now.

Note that Photoshop can only read data using the Raw data format if it's saved as binary data; hexadecimal is out.

Tip: Make Photoshop Guess for Raw Data. Okay, someone gives you a file and you find you can't open it using any of Photoshop's standard file format options. You decide to take a leap and attempt the Raw format. But when you ask your so-called friend about the file's vital signs—"What are the pixel dimensions? Interleaved or noninterleaved color? Is there a header?"—he just stares at you blankly.

Fortunately, Photoshop can do a little guessing for you. If you click the Guess button in the Open as Raw dialog box when the Width and Height fields are blank, Photoshop figures out a likely height/width combination for the image. If it's a color image, you need to know if it's RGB (three channels) or CMYK (four channels).

If there's a header and your friend doesn't know how big it is (in bytes), then it's probably a lost cause. On the other hand, if your friend knows the pixel dimensions but not the header, you can click the Guess button while the Header field is blank.

Figure 16-16
Opening Raw data

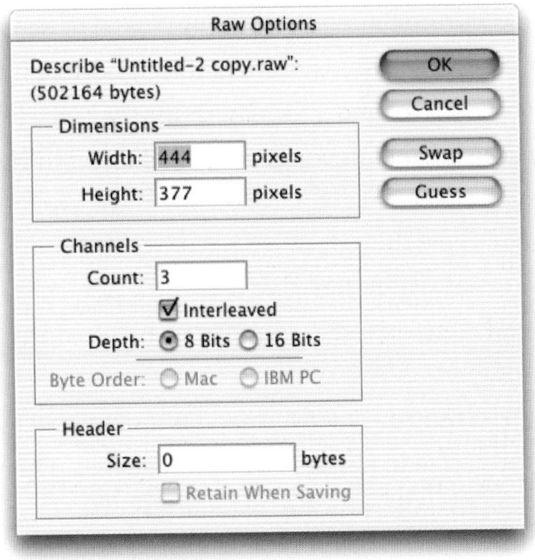

Unreasonable Niche File Formats

We don't mean to be harsh, but there are some file formats that are like putting matches in the hands of small children. The object-oriented PICT format (as opposed to the bitmapped PICT file which we discussed earlier) is completely unreliable and should hence be avoided in professional work. Here are a few file formats that we just ignore most of the time when it comes to bitmapped images. Unless you have a clear, specific, and compelling reason to use them, we strongly recommend that you do likewise.

Alias. Do you use Alias/Wavefront software for 3D rendering? Photoshop can read the Alias .pix file format, but only when you have loaded the Alias plug-in from the Optional Plug-ins folder (inside the Goodies folder on the Photoshop install disc).

Amiga IFF. The Amiga computer story reads like that of the Tucker car or the PublishIt! desktop publishing software. Most people have never heard of these products, much less realized how great they were. Each one of the select group of people who used the Amiga had their own theories about why most of the world shunned the love of their computing life, but when it came right down to it, the computer simply shuffled away in obscurity until it died an ignominious death.

However, perhaps out of a sense of obligation to the would-be contender, or perhaps from a real need in the market (though we don't see it), Photoshop still lets you open and save in the Amiga IFF format. However, unless you really need it, or you want to see a format that features rectangular rather than square pixels, ignore it.

Cineon. Kodak developed the Cineon file format for handling high-bit images (it's actually a 10-bit format). We're told Photoshop can open Cineon files, though we've never tried. Photoshop offers you the Cineon file format when you save a 16-bits-per-channel image. But as far as we can tell, Cineon is a dying format, so we don't bother with it.

ElectricImage. ElectricImage is a powerful 3D rendering program. Photoshop can read native ElectricImage files. This is another optional plug-in you can install from the installation disc.

MacPaint. The MacPaint format is the most basic of all graphic formats on the Macintosh, but it's so outdated that there's almost no reason to use it anymore. Paint files (more rarely called PNTG, or "pee-en-tee-gee," files) are black and white (one bit per pixel), 72 pixels per inch, 8-by-10 inches (576-by-720 pixels). That's it. No more and no less. The MacPaint format is useful for capturing and placing black-and-white Mac screen shots (especially since it's so compatible with every Mac program), but TIFFs are more flexible, so we use those instead.

PCX. Whereas many formats (such as TIFF) are industry standards, the PCX format was developed by ZSoft Corporation, the creators of Publisher's Paintbrush. It's a granddaddy of bitmapped formats, predating Windows 1.0 when it hit the streets as part of PC Paintbrush. The current version of PCX supports adjustable dimensions and resolutions, and 24-bit color, but only a 256-color palette (indexed to 24-bit color), up from earlier 4- and 16-color versions.

Since a variety of palette-color techniques have been applied to PCX files over the ages, files from earlier programs can have serious color-mismatch problems. But if you're satisfied with the results of working with the PCX images you have, then go for it. We typically recommend using TIFF files instead of PCX whenever possible.

Portable Bitmap (PBM). Some Unix tweaks save their images in the Portable Bitmap format (.pbm, .pgm, .ppm, or .pnm). Photoshop can handle them once you install the plug-in from the Optional Plug-Ins folder.

Pixar. To understand why Photoshop still saves and opens Pixar files, you have to understand that Photoshop was born from the minds of Thomas and John Knoll as a way to do some of the low-level grunt work that goes into the cool special effects produced at George Lucas's Industrial Light and Magic (ILM), which is a close cousin of Pixar. As far as we're concerned, someone should put this file format out of our misery.

Pixel Paint. David used Pixel Paint once, a very long time ago. On the odd chance that you have a Pixel Paint file sitting around, it's good to know that Photoshop can read it. This optional plug-in is in the Optional Plug-ins>Photoshop Only folder on the installation disc.

RLA. Wavefront software can also export in the .rla file format, which Photoshop supports. This, too, is an optional plug-in from the installation disc.

SGIRGB. Yes, the SGI in the name SGIRGB is the SGI of the SGI computer company. We just like typing SGI. But we don't use this format. If you do, just make sure your files have one of these file name extensions: .sgi, .rgb, .rgba, or .bw.

SoftImage. Here's one last 3D rendering software format. Photoshop can read SoftImage files, for those who need that sort of thing. Like most of these, it's an optional plug-in on the installation disc.

Targa. The Photoshop manuals maintain that the Targa file format is designed for TrueVision video boards, though other programs (especially DOS programs) also use it. Like Pixel Paint, this format is almost entirely obsolete, as far as we can tell (though it lingers on in some mainframe and minicomputer databases).

Windows Bitmap (BMP). Windows Bitmap (typically called "BMP," pronounced by saying the letters) is the bitmap format native to Windows Paint. It's rarely encountered outside of Windows and OS/2 Presentation Manager, and is hardly a professional's file format. You can store a 1-, 4-, 8-, or 24-bit image of various dimensions and resolutions, but we still prefer TIFF, given its strong support by desktop-publishing applications and compatibility across different computer systems. If you're creating wallpaper for your Windows desktop, this is the format for you!

Compressing Images

One thing that can be said of all bitmapped images is that "they're pigs when it comes to hard disk space." In this day and age, when you can buy a 120 GB hard disk as cheaply as a nice pair of shoes, saving space on disk isn't nearly as important an issue as trying to transfer that data. Whether you have a dial-up connection to the Web or a T1 line in your office, moving massive files around is somewhat painful.

Our aim, then, is to stretch out the scarce resources we have on hand, and keep files that we need to move around reasonably small. And we've got three methods to accomplish this goal: work with smaller images (no, seriously!), archive our images when we're not using them, and work with compressed file formats.

Lossy vs. Lossless

As we keep saying, bitmapped images are made simply of zeros and ones. In an 8-bit grayscale image, each pixel is defined by eight zeros or ones. If images are already reduced to this level of simplicity, how can they be reduced further? By bundling groups of bits together into discrete chunks.

Lossless Compression

Let's take the example of a 1-bit (black-and-white) bitmap, 100 pixels wide and tall. Without any compression, the computer stores the value (zero or one) for each one of the 10,000 pixels in the image. This is like staring into your sock drawer and saying, "I've got one blue sock and one blue sock and one black sock and one black sock," and so on. We can compress our description in half by saying "I've got one blue pair and one black pair."

Run Length Encoding. Similarly, we can group the zeros and ones together by counting up common values in a row (see Figure 16-17). For instance, we could say, "There are 34 zeros, then 3 ones, then 55 zeros," and so on. This is called Run Length Encoding (RLE), and it's automatically used for Macintosh PICT images (fax machines use it, too). We call it "lossless" because there is no loss of data when you compress or decompress the file—what goes in comes out the same.

Figure 16-17
Run Length Encoding
lossless compression

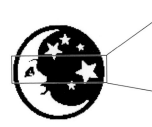

Row 23: 2 zeros, 5 ones, 25 zeros, 43 ones, etc....

LZW, Huffman, and Zip. There are other forms of lossless compression. For instance, RLE compresses simple images (ones that have large solid-colored areas) down to almost nothing, but it can't compress more complex images (like most grayscale images) very much. LZW (Lempel-Ziv-Welch, though you really don't need to know that) and Huffman encoding work by tokenizing common strings of data.

In plain English, that means that instead of just looking for a string of the same color, these methods look for trends. If RLE sees "010101", it can't do any compression. But LZW and Huffman are smart enough algorithms to spot the pattern of alternating characters, and thereby compress that information. Photoshop can also use the Zip compression when it saves PDF, layered TIFF, and PSD files. Zip is a slightly smarter version of LZW (smarter means it compresses better, but it may take slightly longer to do so).

Lossy Compression

The table of contents at the front of most books is a way of compressing information. If you ripped the table of contents out of this book and mailed it to someone else (we're not actually suggesting that you do this!), they would be able to "unpack" it and read what's in this book. But they wouldn't actually be seeing the words you're reading now. Instead, they'd read an "average" of each chapter. The more detailed chapters have more headings, so your friend would see more detail in them than he or she would in a simple-headed chapter like this one.

Bitmapped images can be similarly outlined (compressed), transmitted to someone else, and unpacked. And similarly, when you look at the unpacked version, you don't get all the detail from the original image. For example, if 9 pixels in a 3-by-3 square are similar, you could replace them all with a single averaged value. That's a nine-to-one compression. But the original data, the variances in those 9 pixels, is lost forever.

This sort of compression is called "lossy" compression because you lose data when compressing it. By losing some information, you can increase the compression immensely. Where an LZW-compressed TIFF might be 40 percent of the original size, a lossy-compressed file can be 2 percent or less of the original file size.

Levels of JPEG compression. Lossy compression schemes typically give you a choice of how tight you pack the data. (The primary method is

JPEG, for Joint Photographic Experts Group.) With low compression, you get larger files and higher quality. High compression yields lower quality and smaller files. How much quality do you lose? It depends on the level of the compression, the resolution of the image, and the content of the image.

Different programs implement JPEG differently, and with varying results. Note that JPEG is both a compression method and a file format in its own right (see "File Formats," earlier in this chapter), but both are based on similar algorithms.

JPEG warnings. Here are a few things to remember when working with JPEG. First, note that images with hard edges, high contrast, and angular areas are most susceptible to artifacts from JPEG compression. For example, a yellow square on a green background in a lower-resolution image looks pretty miserable after lossy compression. Similarly, text (rasterized, not vector) almost always looks terrible after JPEG compression because it has such hard edges.

On the other hand, compressing natural, scanned images using JPEG—especially those that are already somewhat grainy or impressionistic—probably won't hurt them much at all, especially if you use the Maximum or High quality setting.

You should only use JPEG on finished images (those on which you've finished all editing and correction). Tone or color correction on a JPEGed image exaggerates the compression artifacts. Sharpening a JPEGed image produces an effect that might one day find its way into Kai's Power Tools, but it's difficult to envisage a use for it in a production setting.

Also, compressing and decompressing images repeatedly can make images worse than just doing it once. But since we just told you that you should only JPEG finished images, the point is moot—you can just open them, look at them, and close them again.

Fractal and wavelet compression. Two other forms of lossy compression—fractal compression and wavelet compression—offer much better compression at the cost of more intense calculation. However, other than JPEG 2000—which is based on wavelet compression—Photoshop doesn't support these compression schemes without a third-party plug-in. For example, the Genuine Fractals family of Photoshop plug-ins, originally developed by Altamira and now sold by Lizardtech, have won a loyal following among the large-format print crowd for their ability to upsample files with noticeably less degradation than other methods. Extensis pxl SmartScale does a similar thing—taking low- to medium-resolution images, compressing them, and then enlarging them with minimum visual degradation.

While these plug-ins' more aggressive compression is lossy, the artifacts that it creates are less objectionable to the eye than those created by JPEG, on the one hand, or overly aggressive upsampling on the other. A lossless compression method is also offered. However, while fractal compression artifacts look natural in images, they look strange on sharp synthetic edges such as type.

Bruce has used Genuine Fractals to upsample 75 MB scans to the 300+ MB required for a 30-by-40-inch print at 300 ppi, and he thinks the result looks more natural than using Photoshop's Bicubic interpolation. But while it can be very useful for this kind of upsampling, the lengthy compression times and relatively low compression ratios of Genuine Fractals make it less appealing as a general compression utility.

To Compress or Not to Compress

Over the years, we've found only a few universal truths. One of those is: "Fast, Cheap, or Good: you can have any two of the three." Compression is certainly no exception to this rule. Compressing files can be a great way to save hard drive space (read: "save money") and sometimes to cut down on printing times (read: "save more money"). But compressing and decompressing files also takes time (read: "lose the money that you just saved").

Optimally, if you have way too much hard drive space and you transfer your files from place to place on DVD discs, you may never need or want to compress your images. Otherwise, you may want to use a lossless compressed file format (like LZW- or Zip-compressed TIFF) for some of your images. If you really need to save space, you might choose a lossy file format (like JPEG).

Bruce almost never compresses files, unless he has to e-mail them, and then he generally just compresses one or more files in an archive (see "Archiving," below). David still has restless dreams about fitting files on 400 K disks in 1985, so he tends to use lossless compression on all but the smallest files. When we absolutely need to save a file in a lossy compressed file format, we use JPEG, but we rarely use anything other than Maximum quality in JPEG—we find the increase in compression at Good, Medium, or Low simply isn't worth the degradation in quality (except for Web images). Ultimately, storage space is getting so inexpensive these days that it's almost silly to worry about compression. Writing 650 MB CDs or 5.2 GB DVDs is now so inexpensive that you might as well buy one and another for your dog. If time equals money, then time spent compressing and decompressing files (whether it's manual or automatic) is money down the big porcelain doughnut.

Archiving

You may have worked with programs such as StuffIt or ZipIt (if you don't already work with one of these, you probably should). They all have the same function: to compress files—any kind of files—and save space on your hard drive. This sort of compression is called *archiving* because people typically use it on files that they're not currently using.

Archiving a file is like folding up a piece of paper and putting it into an envelope. It takes a little time to fold it up (compress it) and a little time to unfold it (decompress it), and while it's in the envelope, you can't read it. The archive file (the "envelope" that contains the compressed file) takes up less room on your hard drive, but to work on the enclosed file, you have to decompress it. Both Mac OS X 10.3 ("Panther") and Windows XP have Zip compression built in.

All archival compression programs use lossless compression methods, so you never have to worry about degrading the image. However, that also means they may not compress down as much as you'd like. Because it often takes a long time to compress very large files, we tend to buy additional removable media and store our files uncompressed. But as we said earlier, if we need to send a number of images to someone via the Internet, we generally zip them first.

From Photoshop to the Future

As you've seen, Photoshop can read and write a number of languages fluently, but they're all based on those ubiquitous zeros and ones. Photoshop can also *sprech* a compressed dialect of many of these languages, saving hard drive space and occasionally printing time, but often slowing down workflow. But perhaps most important, we've learned how to get images out of Photoshop and ready for the rest of the world. In the next chapter, *Output Methods*, we discuss this final process. Then we'll take a quick look at preparing your images for the Web before sending you off to get your work done.

17

Output Methods

Getting It Printed

"The time has come," the Walrus paraphrased, "to speak of many things. Of zeros and ones, pixels and fun, and lastly, imaging." Though Lewis Carroll and his oysters never had to contend with such ephemeral things as pixels, we do. And, as you're probably aware, a pixel's greatest strength is also its greatest weakness: it doesn't really exist, except as electrical current in RAM or as magnetic force on disk. However, sooner or later, we all have to capture those wily devils in a more permanent form, such as paper or film. (We'll discuss multimedia and the Web in the next chapter.)

In the grand tradition of verbing nouns, the term used to include printing, exposing, displaying, or any other process of turning digital images into analog, static ones is *imaging*. In this chapter we focus on the issues specific to imaging your images, whether from Photoshop or another program, such as Adobe InDesign or QuarkXPress. But before we get into the nitty-gritty, we should cover a little background first: the distinction between contone and halftone images.

Contone vs. Halftone

We all live in an illusion (and not just the Buddhist *samsara* that Bruce keeps muttering about): when we see a leaf, our eye makes us think we see a continuous range of colors and tones, continuous lines, and continuous shapes. That's an illusion, because the eye simply doesn't work that way. Without going too far into visual physiology, suffice it to say that the eye works much like an incredibly high-resolution digital camera.

Rods and cones (each a distinct light sensor, like a CCD) cover the back of our eye (the retina), and convert the light that enters our eye into electrical signals. Our brain then—starting with the optic nerve—tries to make sense of all those impulses (you can think of them as zeros and ones). The end effect is that our brains fool us into thinking we're seeing a wash of colors and shapes, when in fact we're simply seeing over a hundred million pixels of information.

And it turns out that because the brain is already so good at fooling us into thinking that we're seeing detail where there is none, or continuous colors where there aren't any, we can fool it even more. The process of imaging data is inherently one of fooling ourselves, and some methods are better than others. The two primary methods of imaging are halftone and contone. Let's take a closer look at each of them.

Halftones

Printing presses, platesetters, inkjet printers, and laser printers all share one thing: they only print on or off, black or white. They can't print shades of gray. To print fifteen different colors, you'd have to run the paper through the machine fifteen times with different colored inks, or toners, or whatever. However, lithographers figured out in the late nineteenth century that they could create a tint of a colored ink by breaking the color down into a whole bunch of little spots. Our brain plays along with the game and tells us that we really are seeing the shade of gray, not just spots (see Figure 17-1). These spots make up the *halftone* of the image.

There are a number of ways to halftone an image, but the most common is to combine printer dots—those tiny square marks that platesetters or laser printers make, sometimes as small as $1/3{,}600$ of an inch—together into larger spots (see Figure 17-2). The darker the gray level, the larger the spot—the more dots are turned on. Each spot sits on a giant grid, so the center of each spot is always the same distance from its neighbors. (The spots don't really get closer or farther from each other, just bigger and smaller; see Figure 17-3.)

Figure 17-1
Halftoning

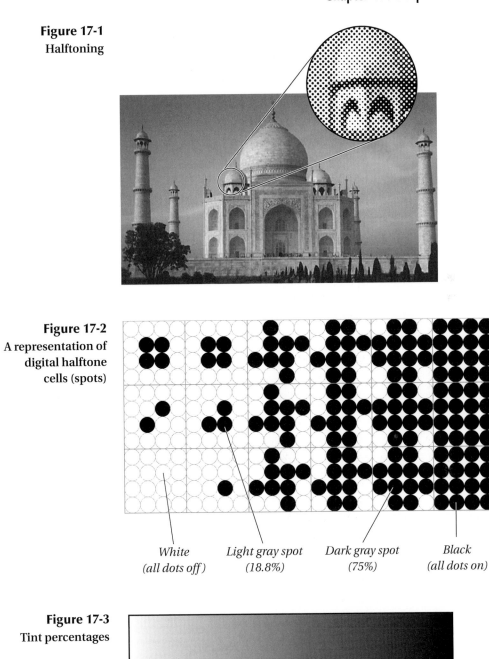

Figure 17-2
A representation of
digital halftone
cells (spots)

*White
(all dots off)*   *Light gray spot
(18.8%)*   *Dark gray spot
(75%)*   *Black
(all dots on)*

Figure 17-3
Tint percentages

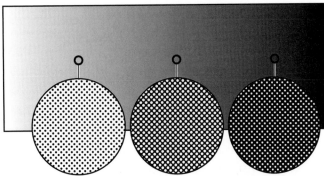

You can print multicolor images by overlaying two or more color halftones (typically cyan, magenta, yellow, and black). Again, our eyes fool us into thinking we're seeing thousands of colors when, in fact, we're only seeing four.

David coauthored a book with Glenn Fleishman, Conrad Chavez, and Steve Roth, called *Real World Scanning and Halftones (3rd edition)*, that covers halftoning in much more detail than we can get into here. However, we should at least cover the basics. Every halftone has three components, or attributes: screen frequency, screen angle, and spot shape.

Screen frequency. Halftone spots on a grid are like bitmapped images; they have resolution, too. The more spots you cram together within an inch, the tighter the grid, the smaller the spots, and so on. The number of halftone spots per inch is called *halftone screen frequency*. Higher frequencies (small spots, tightly packed, like those in glossy magazines) look smoother because the eye isn't distracted as much by the spots. However, because of limits in digital halftoning, you can achieve fewer levels of gray at a given output resolution. Also, higher screen frequencies have much more dot gain on a printing press, so tints clog up and go muddy more quickly (see "Image Differences," later in this chapter).

Lower screen frequencies (as in newspapers) are rough-looking, but they're easier to print, and you can achieve many levels of gray at lower output resolutions. Screen frequencies are specified in lines per inch, or *lpi* (though we're really talking about "rows of spots per inch").

Screen angle. Halftone grids are not like bitmapped images; you can rotate them to any angle you want. (In a bitmapped image, the pixels are always in a horizontal/vertical orientation.) Halftones of grayscale images are typically printed at a 45-degree angle because the spots are least noticeable at this angle. However, color images are more complex.

When you overlap halftone grids, as in color printing, you may get distracting moiré ("mwah-RAY") patterns that ruin the illusion. In order to minimize these patterns, it's important to use specific angles. The greater the angle difference between overlapping screens (you can't get them any farther apart than 45 degrees), the smaller the moiré pattern. With four-color process printing, the screens are typically printed 30 degrees apart at 15, 45, and 75 degrees (yellow, the lightest ink, is generally printed at 0 degrees—15 degrees offset from cyan).

Spot shape. The last attribute of halftones is the shape of each spot. The spot may be circular, square, a straight line, or even little pinwheels (see Figure 17-4). The standard PostScript spot shape is a round black spot in the highlights, square at 50 percent, and an inverted circle (white on black) in the shadows. Changing the shape of the spot is rarely necessary. However, if you're producing cosmetics catalogs, or need to solve tonal shift problems printing on newsprint at coarse screen frequencies (to use two examples), controlling the halftone spot shape can definitely improve the quality of your job.

Figure 17-4
Spot shape

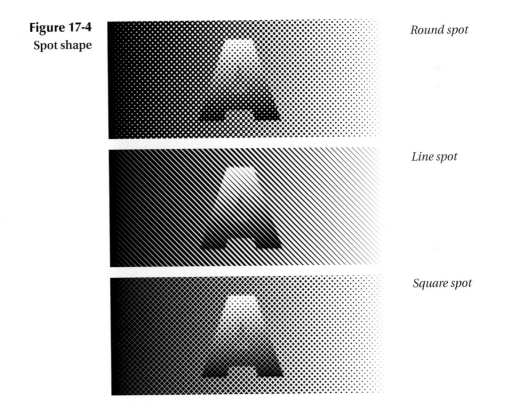

Round spot

Line spot

Square spot

Screen Settings: What Overrides What?

When you send a grayscale or color bitmapped image to a PostScript printer, the computer inside the printer converts the image into a half-tone. That means that the printer sets the halftone screen frequency, angle, and spot shape. However, there are plenty of times when you want to override the printer's default settings to use your own halftone screening information. Fortunately, most programs give you some help in doing this, and Photoshop gives you a *lot* of help.

Figure 17-5 shows, in brief, the order in which screening controls override each other. Let's look at each of them in order.

Device default setting. Every PostScript output device has a built-in default screen setting—what it'll use if nothing else is specified. On many desktop laser printers, it's 53 lpi at 45 degrees. Imagesetters vary widely, but are typically above 100 lpi at 45 degrees.

Driver setting. Printer drivers are the software modules that "drive" printers in the background; PostScript drivers actually write much or all of the PostScript code that gets sent to the printer. Although the Windows PostScript driver lets you control the halftone screen for the print job, most Macintosh drivers do not.

Application setting. Many applications offer control over halftone screen settings for your print jobs. In QuarkXPress 5, PageMaker 7, and InDesign 2 it's in the Print dialog box. In Photoshop CS, you get at it via the Screens button in the Output Options panel of the Print with Preview dialog box. Anytime you set screening information at the application level, it overrides both the device default and the driver settings.

Figure 17-5
What screen settings override what

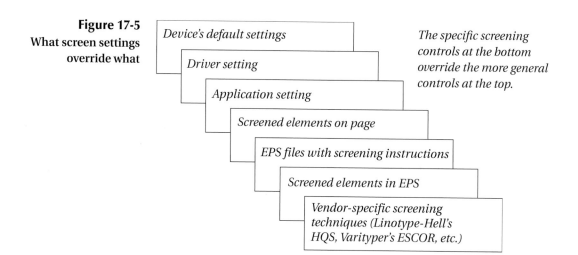

The specific screening controls at the bottom override the more general controls at the top.

The Rule of 16

It's simply a rule of the universe: in digital halftoning, the higher the screen frequency you request at a given output resolution, the fewer levels of gray you can achieve. The problem, in a nutshell, is that higher screen frequencies mean smaller halftone spots; because these halftone spots are made of groups of printer dots, the smaller the spot, the fewer printer dots it contains. The fewer printer dots in a halftone spot, the fewer gray levels that spot can simulate (see Figure 17-6).

There's a simple equation that lets you figure out approximately how many gray levels you can achieve at a given halftone screen frequency on a given printer:

$$(\text{printer resolution} \div \text{screen frequency})^2 + 1$$

However, we can make it even simpler for you. You know that there is a maximum of 256 levels of gray possible on any PostScript printer. Therefore, you can figure out (with a little behind-the-scenes arithmetic) the highest screen frequency you should use on a given printer by dividing the resolution by 16.

Or conversely, if you know you want to print at a given screen frequency, you can figure out what printer resolution you need by multiplying the frequency by 16.

Figure 17-6 Gray levels versus screen frequency

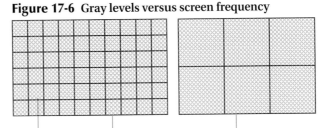

Printer dots   *Halftone cell*   *Halftone cell*
                      4 dots per cell   *12 dots per cell*
                      (17 gray levels)   *(145 gray levels)*

If you break this rule—going to a higher screen frequency than the output device can support—you start losing gray levels. If you lose enough gray levels, you start seeing posterization.

For instance, if you know that you're going to print on a 2400-dpi imagesetter, the highest frequency you should use is 150 (2400 ÷ 16). Or, if you know that you want to print at 133 lpi, you should print on a platesetter with resolution of at least 2100 dpi (133 x 16).

On the other hand, we know that most printing presses can't handle anywhere near 256 levels of gray (especially on uncoated stock). So there's a corollary rule: if you think you don't really need a full range of grays, adjust accordingly. Perhaps use the Rule of 13, which would give you 170 levels of gray, but might save you a little money—it's usually cheaper to run film at a lower resolution because it images faster, saving the service bureau time.

Tip: See Posterization in Action. If you use the Rule of 13, you're going to posterize your image. That's life. But is that so bad? Oftentimes, it's not. You can see approximately what the effect of posterizing your image to 170 levels of gray would be with the Posterize command on the Map submenu under the Image menu. The effect you get by selecting Posterize and typing 170 is more or less what you'd get if you printed your image at 175 lpi on a 2400-dpi imagesetter, or at 110 lpi on a 1270-dpi imagesetter.

If your image is not very posterized to begin with, this level of posterization may have very little effect on it.

Making Halftones in Photoshop

When you print an image from Photoshop or from a page-layout program, the PostScript printer converts your grayscale or color data into halftones. That doesn't mean, though, that you couldn't do it yourself in Photoshop if you really wanted to. In fact, there are a few times when it's advantageous to convert images into halftones in Photoshop.

▶ You are printing to a non-Post-Script printer and you want controllable halftones and smaller image files.

▶ You want a diffusion dither—a stippled screen very similar to the stochastic screening available on many imagesetters,

but useful for lower-resolution output as well (see Figure 17-8, later in the chapter, for an example).

▶ You want to create special halftone-like effects.

▶ You want to learn about how halftones work. Creating halftones in Photoshop is a great way to learn what halftoning is all about. (When we do seminars, it's only when we show people how to do halftoning in Photoshop that they really understand what we've been talking about.)

Here's how to convert a grayscale image into a halftone in Pho-

toshop (yes, this only works with grayscale images; if you're working on a color image, select Grayscale, or duplicate a color channel into a new grayscale document).

1. Select Bitmap from the Mode submenu under the Image menu (see Figure 17-7).

2. In the Bitmap dialog box, choose an output resolution appropriate for your output. All the same rules for line art images that we talked about back in Chapter 12, *Line Art*, apply here.

So if your final output is on a 300-dpi laser printer, you don't need more than 300-ppi image resolution. If your final output

Individual screened elements within publications. Some applications—FreeHand, for example—let you select individual objects (text or graphics) and set a screen for those objects. In others (such as PageMaker and QuarkXPress), you can apply screens to individual bitmapped images (TIFF only). These are called object-level settings, and they override the application-level settings, which still apply to the rest of the job.

EPS files that include screening instructions. When you save a file as EPS from Photoshop, you can tell the program that you want to include screening information. Then, if you import that EPS file into a program such as InDesign or QuarkXPress, the screening information in the EPS overrides the program's settings when you print the whole page—but for that object only.

You almost never need to save screening information with your EPS image. Of course, there are always exceptions; for instance, you often want is on an imagesetter, you may need to raise this to 800 or 1000 ppi.

3. Select Halftone Screen from the Method menu in the Bitmap dialog box, and click OK. (While you're here, you should also check out the Diffusion option; it's a very different look.)

4. In the Halftone Screen dialog box, set the frequency (bearing in mind the Rule of 16), angle, and spot shape, then click OK.

If you don't like the halftone effect that results, you can undo the mode change and start over with different settings.

Note that once you halftone a grayscale image, you can no longer make many edits to it—no tonal adjustments, filters, or the like

(there's nothing there for the tools to work with). Also, you shouldn't scale the image, even a little, or you can expect to get very strange patterning when you print.

We generally let the RIP in the imagesetter take care of the screening for us. We never do this kind of Photoshop halftoning on color images (unless we're trying to create a special effect). But for drop shadows and the like, this is a great technique.

Figure 17-7 Bitmap dialog box

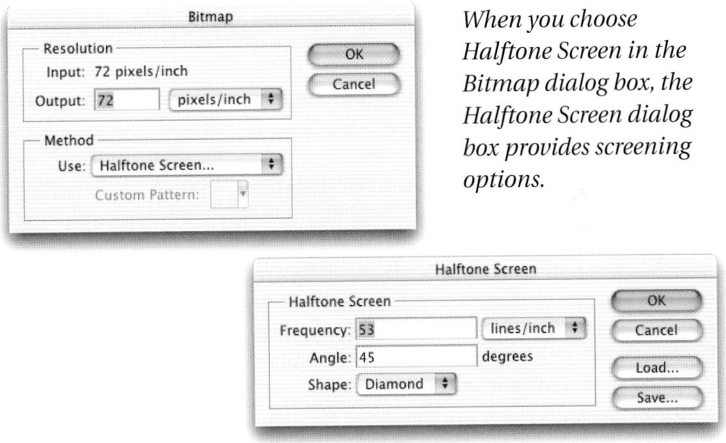

When you choose Halftone Screen in the Bitmap dialog box, the Halftone Screen dialog box provides screening options.

to save particular angles in duotone images (see Chapter 11, *Spot Colors and Duotones*).

Individual screened elements within EPS files. An EPS file that contains screening instructions can also include individual elements within the file that have their own screening instructions. For example, an EPS from FreeHand might have a gray box that has an object-level halftone screen applied to it. That item would be screened as specified, and the rest of the EPS would be screened as it was specified (or if no screen is specified for the whole EPS, using the settings of the printing application— probably InDesign, PageMaker or QuarkXPress).

Vendor-specific screening instructions. If you print to an imagesetter that uses a specialized screening technique such as Linotype-Hell's High-Quality Screening (HQS), Agfa's Balanced Screens Technology (BST), or Prepress Solutions' ESCOR, you may not get the screen settings you expect.

These techniques use screening "filters" that catch *all* screening instructions, and replace the frequency/angle combinations with the closest settings available in their optimized sets. So even if you specify angles in Photoshop and save as an EPS, you still may not get your exact request. This is mostly important if you're after a specialized spot shape. If you are, tell your service bureau to turn off HQS, or BST, or whatever.

Contone Output

With binary devices such as platesetters and printers, you need to use a halftone to fool the eye into seeing shades of gray because you can't create color or gray pixels. With a contone device, you *can* vary the color or gray shade of each pixel. Continuous-tone imaging, usually called *contone*, is different from halftone imaging in two other ways.

▶ The pixels touch each other so that without very close inspection no paper or clear film shows through between marks.

▶ Each pixel is a specific color, made by building up varying densities of primary colors in the same spot.

The most common contone imaging device is your computer monitor. The color of each pixel you see (or don't see, if the screen's resolution is high enough) is made by mixing together varying amounts of red, green, and blue. For example, to make a pixel more red, the monitor must increase the number of electrons that are bombarding the red element of the pixel.

There's no threat of moiré patterns, because there are no grids involved. But then again, there's no chance of mass-reproducing the image, as no printing press can handle continuous-tone images (see "Hybrid Color Screening," below). Aside from the monitor, there are two other types of contone devices that we should mention: film recorders and dye-sub printers.

Film recorders. A film recorder such as a Solitaire or a Fire1000 creates continuous-tone images in one of two ways. Some film recorders place a very high-resolution grayscale monitor in front of a piece of film, and then image the same piece of film three times—the first time with a red filter in front of the monitor, and then with a blue, and finally with a green filter. The same areas of the film are imaged each time, but with varying densities of each color.

Other film recorders color pixels in film by adjusting the amount of three bright light beams—each colored by a red, green, or blue filter—while they focus on a point on the film. Again, unlike halftones, each "pixel" on the film abuts the next, and is set to a specific color.

Film recorders are typically very high resolution devices, ranging from 1,024 (1 K) to 16,384 (16 K) pixels across. High resolutions are necessary because they're often imaging small pieces of film such as 35 mm slides or 4-by-5-inch film, though 16 K film recorders are usually reserved for writing 8-by-10 film.

Dye-sub printers. A second type of contone device is a dye-sub printer, which overlays varying amounts of ink to build a color. Dye-subs are typically 300-dpi devices, but the lack of halftoning or white space between each pixel makes images look surprisingly photorealistic at this seemingly low resolution.

Because of the lack of resolution, hard-edged objects such as type or line art may appear jaggy, but the soft edges and blends found in natural images usually appear nearly indistinguishable from photographs.

Hybrid Color Screening

There is one more method of simulating a "real-world" continuous-tone image: using tiny spots to simulate tints and colors, but making those spots so small and so diffuse that the image appears contone. The three primary examples of this sort of imaging are: high-resolution inkjet, color laser, and stochastic screening, either on a conventional press or on a direct-digital press such as the Indigo E-Print or the Agfa Chromapress.

Inkjet. In inkjet technology, the printer sprays a fine mist of colored inks onto paper. The amount of each ink is varied, much like a contone printer, but it results in tiny spots on paper, often with paper white showing through, more like halftones. While older low-resolution inkjets couldn't be mistaken for contone imaging devices, prints from current high-resolution inkjets are so smooth that for all practical purposes they can be considered contone devices. This holds true for both large-format inkjets like the Epson 9600 and their desktop-size siblings. They use tiny droplet sizes of four, six, or more inks, deployed with very sophisticated error-diffusion screening, to produce results that are indistinguishable to the naked eye from a true continuous-tone print.

Several vendors now supply inkjet cartridges with custom inks for effects such as quadtones built with four gray inks, while others supply third-party color inks either in cartridges or in bulk. But whether you use OEM or third-party inks, a major problem with most inkjet printers is that it's almost impossible to control the ink percentages exactly, so that if (for example) you ask for 50-percent cyan, you get exactly 50-percent cyan. If you send CMYK data to the printer, it typically converts the data to RGB and then back to CMYK at some point in the print stream. Even if you attach a PostScript RIP to the printer, there's little chance you'll get exactly the values you asked for. (Or, if you do, it's at the cost of the high-quality screening, and your image has dots like golf balls.)

Ultimately, CMYK RIPs are occasionally useful for inkjets used as proofing devices; but in our experience, if your goal is to produce final photorealistic output, you're better off using the QuickDraw (Mac) or GDI (Windows) drivers and feeding RGB data to the printer. That said, we have obtained stunning results with some of the RGB RIPs designed for photographic output on inkjets, such as Colorbyte Software's ImagePrint. But we use them as much for workflow reasons—it's easy to gang several images onto the sheet, for example—as for the real but fairly subtle improvement in image quality.

Tip: Printing PostScript to a Non-PostScript Printer. Few inkjets have PostScript RIPs built in to them, and we haven't been particularly happy with the software RIPs that you can buy along with the printers. So when we need to print from QuarkXPress or some other PostScript-dependent program, we create an Acrobat PDF file of our document. Then we print the file from Acrobat (which acts like a PostScript RIP) to the inkjet. However, Adobe InDesign CS prints beautifully through most inkjets' raster drivers, so we just print from InDesign's native application file rather than messing around with this PDF workaround.

Stochastic screening. Earlier in this chapter we discussed how halftones are formed by clumping together groups of printer dots into a regularly spaced grid of spots. However, we oversimplified; this is actually only one way to make a halftone. Remember, a halftone is just a way to simulate tints or colors with tiny spots. Another method of halftoning is a diffusion dither (see Figure 17-8).

Diffusion dithers can create near-contone quality, but they've been avoided until recently because they're often difficult to create and print, especially for full-color work. However, digital imaging has changed all this. Various vendors have created proprietary dithering techniques, usually called *stochastic screening*, that let you mass-reproduce contone-like images from a printing press. Note that proprietary stochastic screening is a type of "frequency modulated" (FM) screen, but it's certainly not the same as Photoshop's diffusion dither feature.

Stochastic screening is very cool for a number of reasons, including:

Figure 17-8
Diffusion dither
as halftone

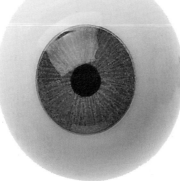

*Grayscale image
screened by PostScript
at 133 lpi*

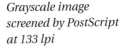

*1000-dpi,
40-lpi halftone
from Photoshop*

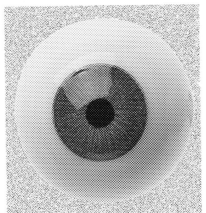

*250-dpi diffusion
dither from Photoshop*

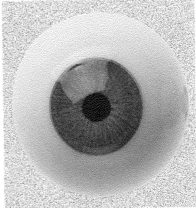

▶ Image content that has been difficult to reproduce using traditional halftoning methods—such as fabric or other fine-detail objects—is much more easily reproduced with stochastic screening because it eliminates *subject moiré*, where the pattern in the subject creates a moiré by interfering with the regular pattern of the halftone screen.

▶ You can print with more than four colored inks without worrying about moiré patterns due to conflicting halftone angles (there are no angles in a diffusion dither).

▶ It's much easier to reproduce near-contone images. Some printers are even getting good results with low-resolution stochastic screens printed on low-quality paper.

▶ You can print more detail at a given image resolution. While the ideal image resolution is around 300 ppi, if all you have is a low-resolution Web graphic, stochastic gives better quality than regular halftones.

On the other hand, stochastic screening, like any new technology, can bring with it a host of new troubles ("challenges," says the ever-optimistic David). For instance, stochastic screening raises the concept of dot gain to new heights, causing many to retreat from printing with it soon after seeing their first printed images appear as big ink blobs. The size of the

Hi-Fi Color

Printers have been simulating thousands of different colors by mixing varying tints of four colors—cyan, magenta, yellow, and black—for many years now, and in theory it should work reasonably well. Unfortunately, we don't live anywhere near the town of "Theory," and so our range (gamut) of printable colors is pretty small. Color scientists, both amateur and professional, have been working at increasing this gamut ever since CMYK became a standard.

One solution is to add "bump" plates, where one or more of the four colors is printed again, expanding the tonal range in one area of the image or another. Another solution is to print with more than four colors: CMYK plus red, green, and blue, for instance; or adding purple and orange to the lineup. But the solutions all have one thing in common: ink gets slapped on the paper more than four times. All told, these gamut-extending solutions are called *Hi-Fi color* (is

quadraphonic color far behind?).

There are all sorts of problems with printing Hi-Fi color, but one stands out from the rest. It's hard enough to print four halftone tints of colors on top of each other while avoiding moiré patterns. Printing more than four is almost impossible unless you resort to extremely high screen frequencies. With the advent of digital stochastic screening, though, Hi-Fi color has become significantly easier to build, separate, and print.

stochastic dot also limits the amount of highlight detail you can reproduce, which is why many inkjet printers add Light Cyan and Light Magenta inks—the dots aren't any smaller, but they appear smaller because they're printed with the lighter inks.

You can create stochastic screens for your images with several pieces of software, including Isis Imaging's IceFields utility. Or you can use any of a number of vendors' built-in imagesetter screening algorithms such as Agfa's CrystalRaster or Linotype-Hell's Diamond Screens.

Color laser printer. Most color laser printers use some kind of diffusion dither to simulate a very high screen frequency. For example, the old Apple Color LaserWriter 12/600PS simulates a 200-lpi screen even though it's only a 600-dpi printer. We've found that it's almost always best to let the laser printer take care of the screening using its own proprietary algorithms, rather than doing it ourselves.

Controlling color on these devices isn't easy—where possible, we prefer to send a calibrated RGB image through a color management system (see Chapter 5, *Color Settings*). If you do want to create your own CMYK separations from Photoshop for a color laser device, the biggest potential pitfalls are specifying too high an ink density and underestimating dot gain. Color laser printers don't have dot gain in the usual sense, and they use dry toner, so you might think that you could go all the way to a 400-percent total ink limit and 100-percent black ink limit. If you do, you'll get very dense shadows and saturated colors that look as though they belong in some other image. As a starting point, try 260-percent total ink with an 85-percent black limit in the CMYK Setup dialog box.

Image Differences

Now that we've explored the various imaging methods, we should recap and highlight some of the different techniques you can use in building images suitable for output on halftone and contone devices. We say "recap," because we've mentioned most (if not all) of these in previous chapters, though never in one place.

Resolution. The first and foremost difference between contone and halftone imaging is the required image resolution. It's quite a bit harder to work out the resolution needed for halftone output than it is for contone, so we'll deal with halftone output first.

▶ **Resolution requirements for halftone output.** The resolution of the output device isn't directly relevant in determining the resolution you need for the image. It's the halftone screen frequency that matters. You never need an image resolution above two times (2×) the halftone screen frequency (and often you can get almost-equivalent results with as little as 1.2× or 1.4×). That means that even if you're printing on a 2400-dpi imagesetter, your image resolution can (and should) be much lower. For instance, printing at 150 lpi, you never need more than a 300-ppi image, and usually no higher than 225 ppi (we generally use the 1.5 multiplier). (See Figure 3-8 in Chapter 3, *Image Essentials*.)

▶ **Resolution requirements for contone output.** The resolution needed for a contone output device is easy to figure, but it can sometimes be hard to deliver. Your output resolution should simply match the resolution of the output device. If you're printing to a 300-dpi dye-sub printer, your image resolution should be 300 ppi. When printing to a 4 K film recorder, your image should have a horizontal measure of 4096 pixels, or about 60 MB for a 4-by-5 print. An 8 K film recorder really wants 240 MB—an 8192-by-10240-pixel image.

In truth, many high-resolution film recorders are more forgiving, and you can halve the resolution. For instance, we know of few people who actually send a 960 MB image to a 16 K film recorder, and we know quite a few who get good results sending a 60 MB file to an 8 K film recorder (about half the amount of data it "requires"). Sending less than a full 60 MB to a 4 K film recorder, however, is a much more marginal proposition. Make sure, though, that you send an integral multiple of the device's resolution. If you send 4095 pixels to a device that wants 4096, it'll either barf when it gets the file, or you'll get some very strange interpolation artifacts.

The appropriate resolution for stochastic screening is less clear, but in general you rarely need over 300-ppi images.

▶ **Resolution requirements for inkjet output.** The necessary resolution for today's photorealistic inkjets is to some extent a guessing game. In part, it depends on the paper stock—matte papers generally require less resolution than glossy ones. Anecdotal evidence suggests that a resolution around 240 ppi is sufficient for most images, but if you're really picky, you may want to determine the ideal resolution for a particular paper stock yourself using good old trial and error. It's certainly possible to send too much data to an inkjet printer, not only increasing print times unconscionably but also degrading the image: you do *not* want to send a 1440-ppi image to a 1440-dpi inkjet!

Synthetic targets composed of black and white line pairs show an improvement when they're printed at an integral divisor of the printer resolution, such as 360 ppi on a 1440-dpi inkjet, but it's uncertain how applicable this is to images with more natural content. Bruce usually prints to 1440-dpi inkjets at 360 ppi if the image contains enough real pixel data to start with. On small prints (8-by-10-inches or less) he may even send 480 ppi and print at the much slower 2880-dpi setting. However, although Bruce insists the benefit is real, it takes careful sharpening to see it. If the image doesn't contain enough pixels to print at these fairly high resolutions, we'll simply send what we have rather than interpolating.

Tonal and color correction. We talk a great deal about compressing tonal range ("targeting") for halftone output in Chapter 6, *Tonal Correction Fundamentals*, and Chapter 7, *Color Correction Fundamentals*, so we won't go into it here. Contone output needs less in the way of tonal and gamut compression than halftone output, because contone devices generally have a greater dynamic range and a wider gamut than do halftone devices. However, this can bring its own problems, particularly when you have a scanner with a tendency to oversaturate some colors, as do many inexpensive scanners (and even some expensive ones). Keep a watchful eye on saturated colors. Some dye-sublimation printers feature a magenta that's almost fluorescent!

Sharpening. As we noted back in Chapter 10, *Sharpening*, contone images need much less sharpening than halftone images. But that doesn't mean they don't need any at all. Halftones, again because of their coarse screens and significant dot gain, mask details and edges in an image; sharpening can help compensate for both the blurriness of the scan and the blurriness of the halftone. And, halftones being what they are, you have a lot of room to play with sharpening before the picture becomes oversharpened (most people end up undersharpening).

In contone images, however, there's a real risk of oversharpening. Not only should you use a lesser Amount setting for unsharp masking, but also a smaller Radius. Where a Radius less than one is often lost in a halftone image, it's usually appropriate in contone images. In this context, inkjet printers tend to behave more like contone devices than halftone devices.

Image mode. This last item, image mode, isn't really dependent on what output method you're using. However, because we still see people confused about image mode, we thought we'd throw in a recap here, too.

Again: if you're printing to a color contone device that outputs to film (or if the image is only seen on a color screen), you should leave your image in RGB mode. Contone and hybrid devices that print on paper use CMYK inks or toners, but in most cases you'll get better results sending RGB and letting Photoshop or the printer handle the conversion. If you have a good profile for the output device, you can preview the output using Proof Setup, and convert the image from your RGB editing space to the device's space at print time (we discuss this in the next section). If you're printing separations, though, you need to send a CMYK file.

We've tried many times to build Photoshop Classic CMYK setups for CMYK dye-sublimation printers, but it simply doesn't work. Photoshop's separation engine is geared toward halftone output, where the ink density remains constant and the dot size varies. It simply can't handle the variable density on dye-sublimation printers. It would work for inkjets if we could control the inks directly, but since we can't, it doesn't.

Imaging from Photoshop

When we started writing the *Real World Photoshop* series back in the days of version 3, it was almost a given that most people who used Photoshop didn't print directly from it; instead, they saved their images in some other format and then imported them into some other program to print later. But the revolution in inkjet printing has changed all that, as legions of photographers discover that the digital darkroom is infinitely more controllable and predictable than the wet one. So we're going to tackle the topic of imaging directly from Photoshop before we move out of Photoshop and into QuarkXPress, InDesign, or other programs.

As in almost every other Macintosh or Windows program, there are two menu items (and accompanying dialog boxes) tied to imaging: Page Setup and Print, both found under the File menu. But Photoshop also offers a third item, Print with Preview, that serves as command central for the two more common ones and adds Photoshop-specific options (in Photoshop 6, this dialog box was called Print Options).

Because Mac OS X and Windows XP currently don't allow applications to add features to the Print and Page Setup dialog boxes, Adobe added the Print with Preview command. Most of the options you need to change when you're printing from Photoshop can be accessed easily in Print with Preview, so when we print from Photoshop, this dialog box is always our first stop (see Figure 17-9).

Figure 17-9
Print with Preview
dialog box

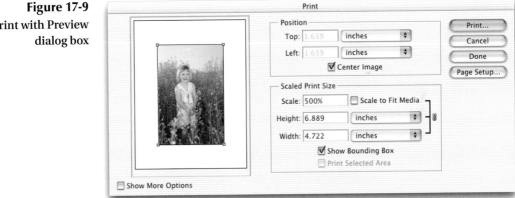

Print with Preview

In its basic form, the Print with Preview dialog box (which is confusingly labeled "Print") lets you control the position and scaling of your image on the page. You can do so either visually, by dragging the image proxy to position it and dragging the bounding box handles to scale it, or numerically, by entering values in the appropriate fields. To scale or position the image by dragging, you must turn on "Show Bounding Box," and if "Center Image" is turned on, you can only scale the image, not position it.

Position. The Position fields let you enter the position of the image's top left corner on the page, in inches, centimeters, points, or picas. If the Center Image checkbox is turned on, the position fields are dimmed.

Scaled Print Size. The Scaled Print Size fields let you enter a scaling percentage, or a height or width in inches, centimeters, points, or picas. The Scale to Fit Media checkbox, when turned on, scales the image to cover as much of the printer's printable area as the image's aspect ratio allows. All three fields are locked together—you can't change the aspect ratio of the image.

The base size that's first reported when you open Print with Preview is based on the settings in the Image Size dialog box. When you change the scaling, be aware that you aren't creating any new pixels—the scaling options are just like changing the size or resolution in Image Size with the Resample Image checkbox turned off.

Tip: Don't Scale in Page Setup. Photoshop lets you apply scaling to the printed image in Print with Preview *or* in Page Setup, but Print with Preview doesn't "know" about scaling applied in Page Setup; so if you apply scaling there, the preview and dimensions in Print with Preview will be incorrect. Since Print with Preview has a much nicer interface for scaling than Page Setup, we recommend you always apply scaling in Print with Preview, and leave the scaling in Page Setup at 100 percent.

Print Selected Area. You'd be surprised how many people wonder how to print just a small portion of their enormous image. They go through all sorts of duplicating and cropping convolutions instead of simply drawing a marquee around the area they want printed, then turning on the Print Selected Area checkbox in the Print with Preview dialog box. If no pixels are selected, or if the selected area isn't a rectangle (like if it's feathered), this checkbox is grayed out.

Show More Options. When you click on the Show More Options checkbox, Print with Preview gives access to even more controls (we never turn this off). The Photoshop-specific items appear when you choose Output from the popup menu, and (surprise!) the various color management output options appear when you choose Color Management from the popup menu (see Figure 17-10).

Output Options

The Output Options (which used to also appear in the Page Setup dialog box) tell Photoshop how to print the document. A couple of these items (screens and transfer curves) also apply when you save files in various formats (see Chapter 16, *Storing Images*).

Some features in the dialog box are determined by which printer driver you currently have selected. Because these are standard system-level features, we're going to skip them and get right to the good stuff: the Photoshop-specific items.

Screen. When you click the Screen button, Photoshop brings up the Halftone Screens dialog box, where you can specify the halftone screen angle, frequency, and spot shape for your image (see Figure 17-11). When the Use Printer's Default Screens checkbox is turned on (it is unless you go and change it), Photoshop won't tell the printer anything about how the image should be screened.

Unless you want to take responsibility for setting your own halftone screens, you should leave Use Printer's Default Screens checked. When

Figure 17-10
Show More Options

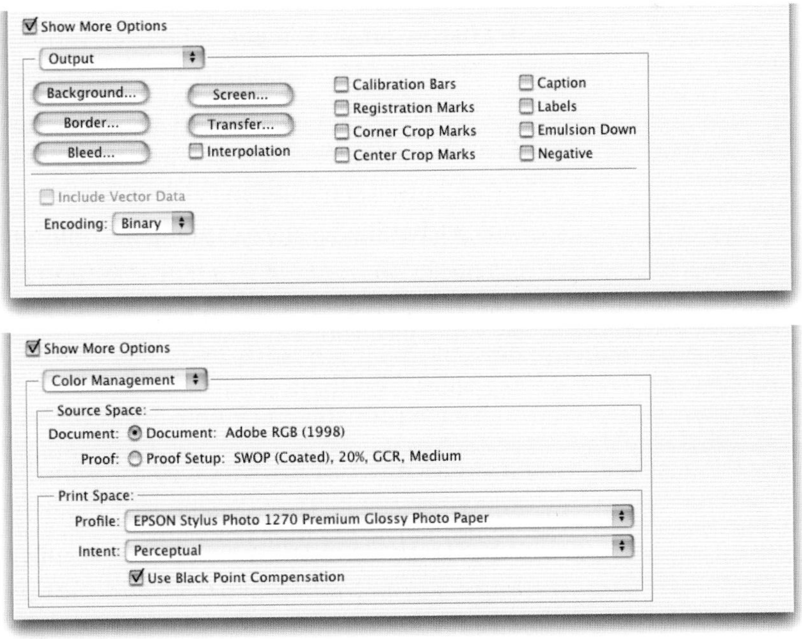

☑ Show More Options

┌─ Output ───┐
│ (Background...)   (Screen...)   ☐ Calibration Bars   ☐ Caption   │
│ (Border...)   (Transfer...) ☐ Registration Marks ☐ Labels   │
│ (Bleed...)   ☐ Interpolation ☐ Corner Crop Marks   ☐ Emulsion Down │
│   ☐ Center Crop Marks   ☐ Negative   │
│ ☐ Include Vector Data   │
│ Encoding: (Binary ▼)   │
└──┘

☑ Show More Options

┌─ Color Management ▼ ──────────────────────────────────────┐
│ ┌─ Source Space: ─────────────────────────────────────┐ │
│ │ Document: ⦿ Document: Adobe RGB (1998)   │ │
│ │   Proof: ○ Proof Setup: SWOP (Coated), 20%, GCR, Medium │ │
│ └───┘ │
│ ┌─ Print Space: ──────────────────────────────────────┐ │
│ │ Profile: [EPSON Stylus Photo 1270 Premium Glossy Photo Paper ▼] │ │
│ │ Intent: [Perceptual ▼]   │ │
│ │   ☑ Use Black Point Compensation   │ │
│ └───┘ │
└──┘

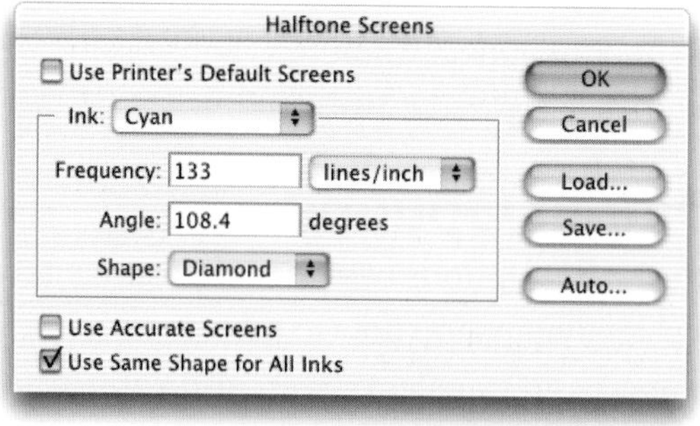

Figure 17-11
Halftone Screens
dialog box

Halftone Screens
☐ Use Printer's Default Screens
Ink: Cyan
Frequency: 133   lines/inch
Angle: 108.4   degrees
Shape: Diamond
☐ Use Accurate Screens
☑ Use Same Shape for All Inks

OK
Cancel
Load...
Save...
Auto...

you do so, you make sure that the file has no halftone screens built in, so unless someone intervenes downstream, the RIP will handle the screening. In the vast majority of cases, it does a better job than you can. Tell your service bureau what screen you want, and then it's their responsibility.

On the other hand, if you want or need to specify your own screens, turn this checkbox off. Photoshop gives you a wide array of possibilities for setting the halftone screen. And when you have a color image, you have even more choices.

▶ **Frequency and Angle.** The frequency and angle are self-explanatory.

▶ **Shape.** When the Use Same Shape for All Inks checkbox is on, the Shape popup menu applies to each process color. We'd only change this for special low-frequency effects.

▶ **Use Accurate Screens.** When you turn on the Use Accurate Screens checkbox, Photoshop includes the PostScript code to activate Accurate Screens in your imagesetter. However, if your imagesetter doesn't have Accurate Screens technology, or if it uses some other screening technology—such as Balanced Screens or HQS—you should just leave this off. (We almost always leave it off, unless our service bureau tells us to turn it on.)

▶ **Auto.** If you don't know what frequency/angle combinations to type in, check with your service bureau. If your service bureau doesn't know, you're probably in trouble. However, as a last resort, you could try clicking the Auto button and telling Photoshop approximately what screen frequency you want and what resolution imagesetter you're using. The program has canned settings that sometimes work. Again, if you're using an imagesetter with HQS or Balanced Screens, you can ignore this feature; those technologies override the screen values. (See "Screen Settings: What Overrides What," earlier in this chapter.)

Note that you can include these screen settings in EPS files (see "Encapsulated PostScript (EPS)" in Chapter 16, *Storing Images*).

Tip: Use Diamond Spot. Peter Fink's PostScript prowess perfected the diamond spot (say that ten times fast). The diamond spot is better in almost every instance than the standard round spot because it greatly reduces the optical tonal jump that is sometimes visible in the mid-to-three-quarter tones—the 50-to-75-percent gray areas. We've also been told that the diamond spot is much better for silkscreening.

Whatever the case, when we print from Photoshop, or save halftone screens in an EPS using our own screening parameters, we use the diamond spot. Again, there's a good chance that this will be overridden or replaced by the imagesetter's specialized screens unless you tell your service bureau to turn them off.

Transfer. Back in Chapter 6, *Tonal Correction Fundamentals*, and in Chapter 11, *Spot Colors and Duotones,* we discussed the idea of input/output contrast curves. Well, here they are once again, in Print with Preview (see Figure 17-12). A transfer curve is like taking a curve that you made in the Curves dialog box and downloading it to your printer. It won't change the image data on your hard drive, but when you print with the transfer curve, it modifies the printed gray levels.

It's a rare occasion that you'd need to use a transfer curve these days. Here are a couple of examples of why you might, however.

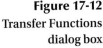
Figure 17-12
Transfer Functions
dialog box

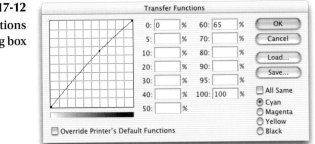

▶ If you're printing from Photoshop to an uncalibrated imagesetter, you can use transfer curves (plus a lot of proof pages and a densitometer) to calibrate the device. We'd rather get calibration software that's made for this sort of thing. (Even better, we'd prefer our service bureau to own this software and calibrate their devices regularly.)

▶ You may have a single grayscale or CMYK image that you want to print on several different presses or paper stocks. Because each type of press or paper requires slightly different targeting (see "White Points and Black Points and Grays, Oh My" in Chapter 6, *Tonal Correction Fundamentals*), in a perfect world you'd want to retarget an "ideally" corrected image for each output method. However, this is often not possible. Transfer curves let you make these sorts of minor adjustments at print time.

Note that while you can save a transfer curve with an image in any format that Photoshop supports, the curve is only recognized when you print directly from Photoshop. To print images with transfer curves from a page-layout application, you need to use EPS files. But there's a danger in using transfer curves with EPS images, because there's no obvious signal to tell anyone working with the image that it contains a transfer curve, except that the values in the file aren't the same as those that print. The only way to tell is to open the image in Photoshop and check to see if there's a transfer curve specified. If you do use a transfer curve, make sure that whoever is responsible for printing the file knows it's lurking there!

Tip: Interchangeable Curves. While Bruce can think about transfer curves in terms of numbers, David needs a more touchy-feely approach. So he tries out his transfer curves in the Curves dialog box first. When he gets a curve just the way he wants it, he saves the curve to disk (using the Save button in the Curves dialog box), then he goes to the Transfer Functions dialog box and loads it in.

You can go the other way, too, setting points by just typing numbers into the Transfer Functions dialog box, saving them to disk, and loading them into the Curves dialog box. But this is less relevant, now that you can key in values numerically in the Curves dialog box. (Also, you can only transfer a "master" curve like this—not the individual color channels.)

Tip: Setting and Retrieving Defaults. There's a hidden feature in the Transfer Functions dialog box. When you hold down the Option key, the Load and Save buttons change into "<-Default" and "->Default" buttons. For some reason it took us a moment before we realized those hyphens and angle brackets were supposed to be arrows. The first, "<-Default", means "replace the current transfer curve with the default curve." The second means just the opposite: "replace the default curve with the current curve" (the one in the dialog box).

The default curve is the curve that all new Photoshop documents are created with. The default curve is also applied when you convert to a new color mode. Note that there are actually two default curves—color and grayscale—so if you set the default for a grayscale image, it won't be applied to color images, and vice versa.

We never change the default curves from their straight, 45-degree settings, because the potential for confusion (and subsequent disaster) is too great. However, if you're using transfer curves as your primary imagesetter-calibration, tonal-correction, or targeting method, this may save you some time.

Note that Photoshop provides you with a checkbox at the bottom of the Transfer Functions dialog box: Override Printer's Default Functions. Don't turn this on unless you really know what you're doing with transfer functions. If your service bureau is using calibration software, turning this checkbox on will override their carefully adjusted settings, and could give you nasty results. While it's nice that Adobe gives us this control, this is one we tend to ignore.

Background. Background and the next 11 features are only relevant when you're printing from Photoshop; you cannot save them in an EPS format (or any other, for that matter) and expect them to carry over to other programs, like you can with Screen and Transfer.

When you print your image from Photoshop to a color printer, the area surrounding the image is typically left white (or clear if you're printing on film). The Background feature lets you change the color that surrounds the image, using the standard Photoshop Color Picker. The background color that you pick acts like a matte frame around the image to the edges of the printable area.

Tip: Make Your Highlights Pop. If you typically make prints with a white border, you can make your highlights appear much snappier if you lay down a *small* amount of ink in the border. Our eyes adapt to the paper-white border: when you print a very light gray or yellow tone in the border, the eye still accepts this as paper white; so, any specular highlights that use the actual paper white appear brighter than they really are, because the viewer's eye is adapted to the white of the surround.

Border. If you specify a border around an image (the border can be up to .15 inches, 10 points, or 3.5 millimeters), Photoshop centers the frame on the edge of the image when you print; that is, half the frame overlaps the image, and half the frame overlaps the background. You cannot, unfortunately, change the color of the frame; it's always black.

Unless we're printing directly from Photoshop *and* we want a print with a black border, we can't think of any reason to use this feature, except perhaps to print an image with a pretrapped frame directly from Photoshop, then strip it in with the rest of the film manually. Yuck. We'd rather import the file into QuarkXPress or InDesign and keyline it there.

Bleed. Setting a Bleed value adjusts where Photoshop places the corner crop marks. You can choose a bleed up to 9.01 points, 3.18 millimeters, or .125 inches (who knows who came up with these values). Again, this is most useful if you're planning on doing manual stripping later. Note that if you specify a 0.125-inch bleed, Photoshop sets the crop marks in by that amount from the image boundary, not out: it effectively says, "cut off the edges of this image."

Interpolation. This item usually does absolutely nothing. In theory, this feature tells your printer to upsample low-resolution images at print time. We've heard various claims that some PostScript Level 2 or greater printers are actually capable of doing this, but we've yet to see evidence of it. But thanks, Adobe, for giving us the choice!

Description. David loves Photoshop's ability to save a description with a file because of the File Info metadata tie-in to InDesign, but it's also helpful when printing a whole mess of images that you need to peruse, file, or send to someone. When you turn on the Description checkbox in

Print with Preview, the program prints whatever caption you have saved in File Info (under the File menu) beneath the image. If you haven't saved a description, this feature doesn't do anything.

You might even include your name or copyright information in the Description field of the File Info dialog box, even though there are other fields for this. At least your name prints out with your images.

Newspapers and stock photo agencies can make much more elaborate use of the File Info feature, including credit lines, handling instructions, and keywords for database searches.

Calibration Bars. When you turn on the Calibration Bars checkbox in Print with Preview, Photoshop prints one (for grayscale images) or several (for color images) series of rectangles around the image (see Figure 17-13). Beneath the image is a ten-step gray wedge; to the left is the same gray wedge, but on each color plate; to the right is a series of colors, listed below. Each color is 100 percent (solid).

▶ Yellow

▶ Yellow and magenta

▶ Magenta

▶ Magenta and cyan

Figure 17-13
Printer marks

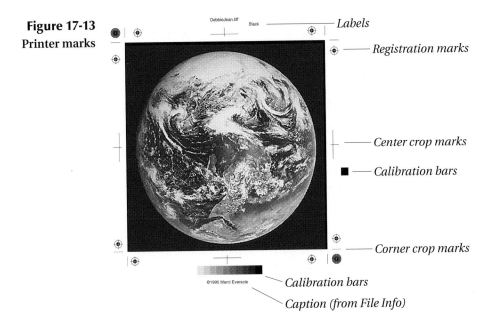

Labels

Registration marks

Center crop marks

Calibration bars

Corner crop marks

Calibration bars

Caption (from File Info)

▶ Cyan

▶ Cyan and yellow

▶ Cyan, magenta, and yellow

▶ Black

Registration Marks. If you're outputting separations, you need to add registration marks so that the printer can align the four colors properly. Turning on the Registration Marks checkbox adds ten registration marks (eight bull's-eyes and two pinpoint types).

Corner Crop Marks. Even if your printer is going to strip your image into another layout, it's helpful to print with corner crop marks, which specify clearly where the edges of the image are. This can help the stripper align the image with a straight edge. In fact, it's essential if the image has a clear white background (like a silhouette); without crop marks, it's impossible to tell where the image boundaries are.

Center Crop Marks. If you need to specify the center point of your image, turn on the Center Crop Marks checkbox. We always turn this on along with Corner Crop Marks as an added bonus, although we aren't always sure why we do so. Note that when you turn this feature on, Photoshop adds two pinpoint registration marks, even on grayscale images, which in theory don't need them.

Labels. When you're printing color separations, turning on the Labels checkbox is a must. This feature adds the file name above the image on each separation, and also adds the color plate name (cyan, magenta, yellow, black, or whatever other channel you're printing). If you're printing a spot color in addition to process colors, it's even more vital that you label the spot separation.

Negative and Emulsion Down. When it comes to the Negative and Emulsion Down options, our best advice is to ignore them. Both of these effects are better performed at the imagesetter rather than in Photoshop. On the other hand, if your service bureau specifically tells you to set these a certain way, or if you're an imagesetter operator and you've developed a workflow that relies on using these options, go right ahead.

Encoding. We mentioned the concept of encoding in Chapter 16, *Storing Images*. Image data can be stored and sent to a PostScript printer as ASCII or binary data. ASCII takes much more space to describe the data than does binary, but it's universally understandable no matter how your PostScript device is connected to the world; so it's often preferable on networks that are administered using DOS or UNIX machines. We recommend saving time and using binary; if it doesn't work, try ASCII85, which is somewhat more compact than ASCII and almost always works.

There's one more option: JPEG. While JPEG is much more compact than either binary or ASCII, and therefore is sent down the wires to the printer faster, the compression is lossy, so image quality degrades slightly. However, when printing with JPEG encoding, Photoshop only compresses the image slightly, so degradation is kept to a minimum. (We'd be surprised if you could see the difference on a scanned image of decent resolution.) JPEG encoding only works when printing to PostScript level 2 or 3 printers, because they know how to decompress JPEG.

Color Management Options

The Color Management options inside the Print with Preview dialog box let you tell Photoshop to do one of three things: perform a color conversion on the data that gets sent to the printer, pass the image data and the profile that describes it to the printer driver for printer driver color management, or simply send the pixels to the printer (see Figure 17-14).

Whether we're making final prints from Photoshop or generating proofs, we find these options invaluable. The only possible pitfall is that if you use

Figure 17-14
Color Management
options

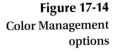

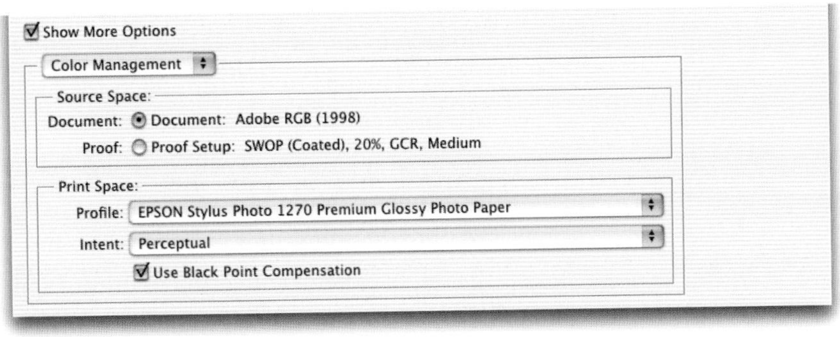

these features to make Photoshop convert the color, you need to make sure that the printer driver isn't also set to make a conversion, because you'll get a double conversion and (probably) hideous results.

Source Space. By default, Source Space is always set to Document, which is either the space represented by the profile embedded in the image or, in the case of untagged images, by the current working space you've set for the document's color mode in the Color Settings dialog box (see Chapter 5, *Color Settings*).

The other option, Proof Setup, tells Photoshop to convert the image from the document space to the profile specified in Proof Setup, using the rendering intent set in Proof Setup, before handing off the data to the printer. We sometimes use this feature when we're trying to make a desktop printer simulate final printed output when we haven't yet converted the file to the final output space. If, for example, we have an Adobe RGB image destined for press output, and we want to print it on an inkjet printer, we set Proof Setup to simulate the press by choosing the press profile there. Then, at print time, we select Proof Setup as the Source Space, and the inkjet's profile as the Print Space. Usually, though, we prefer to convert the file to output space before we print.

Print Space. This option allows you to specify whether or not Photoshop will apply a color conversion before sending the data to the printer, and if so, how the conversion will be made. There are really only three choices: Same As Source, Printer Color Management (or PostScript Color Management in the case of PostScript printers), or one of many ICC profiles.

▶ **Same as Source.** This does what it says—it tells Photoshop to send the data to the printer in the space you specified as the source space. If you chose Document, Photoshop will send the numbers in the image directly to the printer. If you chose Proof Setup, Photoshop will first convert to the Proof Setup space, then send *those* numbers directly to the printer.

The only situations where we use "Same as Source" are when we're printing a calibration target and only care about the numbers in the file, not the colors they represent, or when we're printing an image that has already been converted to output space.

▶ **Printer Color Management/PostScript Color Management.** This option tells Photoshop to send the data to the printer in the space you specified as the source space, with that space's profile embedded. This option is designed for use with printers or printer drivers that perform their own color management.

We almost never use this option. We've yet to see PostScript color management work reliably, though we've heard of a handful of sites that have made it work. The one situation when we do use this option is when we're printing to Epson printers from Windows systems. For reasons known only to themselves, on Windows systems Epson has chosen to bury the quite decent media-specific profiles it distributes inside a single file called "Epson Standard." This isn't really an ICC profile. Rather, when you use Windows ICM inside the Epson printer driver, the driver checks the media settings, then extracts the appropriate media-specific profile from the "Epson Standard" file.

Whenever possible, we prefer to use the individual, media-specific profiles, moving them over from the Mac if necessary, because unlike "Epson Standard," they allow us to soft-proof the image. But if "Epson Standard" is all you have, choosing Printer Color Management as your Print Space, then turning on Windows ICM in the Epson driver, produces decent results.

▶ **ICC profile.** Choosing any ICC profile from the Output Space menu tells Photoshop to convert the image to that profile's space before handing it off to the printer. When you choose a profile, you also are given the opportunity to choose the rendering intent used for the conversion.

This is our preferred method of printing from Photoshop. It lets Photoshop perform all the necessary color conversions, which in our experience is the most reliable workflow. When you use this method, though, you must make sure that any color-management options in the non-Photoshop section of your printer's driver are turned off; otherwise you'll get a double conversion, with results that range from unacceptable to ghastly.

Tip: Don't Downsample High-Bit Files for Printing. If you're printing a high-bit file directly from Photoshop, it's both unnecessary and unwise to downsample it to 8 bits per channel prior to printing. It's unnecessary because Photoshop is smart enough to downsample the data before handing it off to the printer. It's unwise because if you request color space conversions, you'll get better results allowing Photoshop to do the conversion on the high-bit data before it does its automatic downsampling than you will forcing Photoshop to make the conversion on an image that's already been downsampled to 8 bits per channel.

Tip: Printing Separations. Have you been trying to get Photoshop to print color separations of your CMYK and duotone images? The folks at Adobe hid the controls! To print each color on its own plate (rather than a composite color image), you must select Separations from the Profile popup menu in the Print with Preview dialog box. (This option only appears when you're printing an image that's already in CMYK or Duotone mode.)

Tip: Printing Single Colors in Separations. Photoshop doesn't give you an obvious way to print fewer than all four process colors when printing color separations; you only have the option to choose Separations, not "only the cyan and magenta, please." Nonetheless, you can do just this in one of two ways.

▶ Photoshop only prints the color plates that are displayed in the document window. For instance, if you only want to print magenta and black, click on the yellow and cyan eyeballs in the Channels palette to hide them. Now when you print, Photoshop automatically prints separations of the remaining two colors. (The Space popup menu only displays one option, Grayscale, when you do this.)

▶ You can also use the Pages field in the Print dialog box to print fewer than four color separations. For example, when Print Separations is turned on, you can tell Photoshop to print from page two to page two; page two in a CMYK image is the magenta plate. If all the colors are not visible (because you've hidden them, as in the last bullet item), then page two is whatever the second *visible* color is. Note that this doesn't work when Print Selection is turned on in Windows.

Be aware that printing different plates for a separation at different times or from different devices can cause problems with registration and tint (hence color) consistency. If you have to rerun a single plate, it's typically better to rerun all four.

Using an Online Service

Don't own a printer? Prefer photographic prints to inkjet output? Want a poster-sized print? No problem! You can use an online service to print your photographs. When you choose Online Services from the File menu or the File Browser's Automate menu, Photoshop displays a list of available online services. As we go to press, the only available service is Shutterfly prints (click the expand icon next to the company name and then select the service), but in theory you'll see more as Adobe licenses with other companies. These services could offer more than printing, too, but let's not get ahead of ourselves.

If you first select images in the File Browser, they'll appear in the list of files to upload. However, you can add or removes files from this list. When you click Upload, Photoshop sends them to the service, just as you might do manually via the Shutterfly Web site. Of course, if you don't already have a free Shutterfly account, you can create one here, too. You're then given an opportunity to open a Web browser and visit your Shutterfly photo album and (Shutterfly hopes) buy lots of prints.

Note that Shutterfly automatically applies brightness and contrast adjustments to your images unless you turn off the proprietary VividPics feature. If you have carefully tweaked your image in Photoshop, the last thing you want is for those settings to be overridden by a computer that thinks it knows better. Shutterfly says its system assumes that your JPEG images (it only works with JPEG images) are in the sRGB color space. We don't believe for a moment that its system is truly sRGB, but using that is better than shooting blind.

Imaging from a Page-Layout Program

In the prepress world, most people don't print directly from Photoshop—at least for their final output. Instead, they print from separation programs, presentation programs, or page-layout programs. In this section, we're going to focus on the latter item: page-layout programs such as Adobe InDesign, Adobe PageMaker, and QuarkXPress.

Our assumption here is that if you're printing from a page-layout program, you're probably printing to a PostScript imagesetter or platesetter, resulting in paper, film, or plates with black-and-white halftoned images.

QuarkXPress, InDesign, and PageMaker

In the last gasp of the twentieth century, QuarkXPress became the imaging tool of choice for graphic designers, service bureaus, ad agencies, and other heavy color users. Whether or not it deserved this title should be (and is) argued anywhere but here (otherwise Bruce and David would debate themselves into a tizzy). Currently, it appears that Adobe PageMaker is a dead product, and that Adobe InDesign is poised to take the crown from XPress sooner rather than later.

No matter which page-layout tool you use, it's crucial that you consider how your images will transport from Photoshop to the printed page. There are some basic rules you should follow.

File formats. In Chapter 16, *Storing Images*, we cover file formats in some detail, including which ones to use for page layout. To recap quickly: when it comes to printing from page-layout programs, always use TIFF, PDF, DCS, or EPS. With InDesign, you can also use the native Photoshop (PSD) format. Ultimately, we tend toward the TIFF format for almost all our files, though we'll occasionally use EPS or DCS for specialized effects—such as duotones or custom screening. If your image has vector artwork (like text layers) in it, you should use EPS or (preferably) PDF.

CMYK vs. RGB. The choice between importing RGB or CMYK images involves two decisions—when do you want to do your separations, and what program do you want to do them in? You can preseparate all your images with Photoshop (or another program), or you can place RGB images in QuarkXPress, InDesign, or PageMaker, and rely on their color management systems to do the separations for you.

Preseparating has a lot going for it. Images land on pages ready to print; the page-layout program just sends the channels down, with no processing at print time. Note that CMYK EPS files are not color managed in the page-layout program, though CMYK TIFF files may be. That is, if the page-layout program's CMS is turned on, your CMYK values may be altered at print time. To ensure the image data stays the same, choose an output (target) profile that matches the image (source) profile.

Placing unseparated RGB files has advantages as well, though. You can use the page-layout program's color management system to produce better proofs off color printers, and you don't have to target the images until the last minute, when you know all your press conditions and are ready to pull final seps. However, when it comes right down to it, we separate almost all our images in Photoshop first. (But we archive the RGB files, just in case we need to reseparate to some other target.)

Picture linking. Bitmapped images are often big, lumbering creatures that can't be corralled into a single page. That's why page layout applications have picture linking. When you import or place a image on your page, the program typically only places a low-resolution representation image, sort of like a "For Position Only" (FPO) image. When you print, the program ignores this low-res picture and uses the high-res image data on disk instead. That means that the page layout application has to be able to find the high-res data on disk. If you've thrown it away, or moved it to a different folder, the program can't find it and prints with the ugly preview version.

InDesign and PageMaker give you a little more control over linking than XPress does because they let you embed the image right into the document if you choose. This makes some sense; if you've got several 50 K images, it might be more efficient to embed them rather than maintain the links. However, we strongly recommend *not* embedding large, high-resolution images.

The final note on picture linking is that if or when you send your page layout document to a service bureau, make sure you send all the linked graphics, too. We like to think in terms of sending a *folder* to be output, not just a single file. XPress has the Collect for Output feature to help you with this; in PageMaker, use Save As with the Files for Remote Printing option selected; in InDesign, choose Package from the File menu.

Tip: Pasting Images. You can always force InDesign, PageMaker, or QuarkXPress to embed an image by pasting it in rather than using the Place or Get Picture command. However, many people have reported problems with doing this. PageMaker will let you at least try to print separations if you paste in a CMYK image, but not an RGB one. It will even work occasionally, though often what prints is a 72-ppi screen rendition of the image. XPress will try to separate anything that you paste in, but the results are unpredictable at best.

Often, the image you paste is scaled radically differently than the one in Photoshop, or takes much longer to view on screen (which makes scrolling unbearable). Also, if you need to go back and edit that image, you may be lost; for some reason, most people who paste images also delete the original.

Our recommendation? Just don't do it, unless the image you're pasting in is very small, and not in color.

Tip: Relinking Images. Many people get themselves into a bother when XPress all of a sudden can't seem to find their linked images. For instance, if you create a document on the PC, then bring it (and the graphics) to the Mac, XPress can't seem to find the EPS and TIFF files, and lists them as "Missing" in the Picture Usage dialog box.

Here's a little trick you can use to make the program see them all: put the XPress document in the same folder as all of the graphics. Then open the file and select Picture Usage from the Utilities menu. If one or more of the images is listed as "Missing," update one of them; the rest are updated automatically. PageMaker is usually better at cross-platform transfers, but if images do go missing, choose Links from the File menu, navigate to the folder in question, and click Update All.

Rotating. Rotating large bitmapped images is a major pain on anything but the fastest machines. When you import an image into a page layout application and rotate it on the page, it seems to rotate very quickly. But the real math work is done at print time inside your PostScript printer. That means that every time you print (either a proof on a PostScript device or your final piece), your printer has to do the same time-consuming calculations that you could have done once in Photoshop. If you know you're going to rotate an image 15 degrees, do it in Photoshop first, then import it onto your page.

Cropping and clipping. Let's say you've imported a 24 MB photograph of your class of '74 onto your page, but out of 1,400 people, you only want to print the 31 people who were on the lacrosse team. You use the cropping tool (in PageMaker) or the picture box handles (in XPress and InDesign) to crop out everyone else, duplicate the image, recrop, and so on, for 31 people. And then you print the page....

If you saved the image from Photoshop as an EPS, prepare to wait a while for the page to print. In fact, you might want to consider a quick jaunt to the Caribbean. The entire image, no matter how much is showing, has to be sent to the printer for every iteration. Don't laugh. We've seen this plenty of times (usually in the same publications that are littered with gratuitous tabs and space characters).

On the other hand, if you saved the image as a TIFF or a JPEG, the file shouldn't take too long because the layout apps can pull out just the data they need to image your page. However, it does take the program a little extra time at print time to throw away the data it doesn't need.

In either case, the page-layout program has to import and save a low-resolution preview of the *entire* image. That means unnecessary time and file size. The best solution: crop your images in Photoshop before importing them.

Image editing. Both PageMaker and QuarkXPress let you perform some basic tonal manipulation on TIFF files. (InDesign does not.) In PageMaker (with grayscale images only), select Image Control from the Element menu. In XPress, select Other Contrast from the Style menu. However, this is like saying that your kitchen knife lets you perform heart surgery. Sure you can do it, but it's gonna get ugly. Except for special effects (and controlling screen settings on an image-by-image basis), we recommend that people simply not use these features; instead, use Photoshop.

Getting It Out

Photoshop is the best all-around tool we've encountered for working with images, massaging images, and targeting images for specific output devices. However, page-layout programs such as InDesign and Quark-XPress excel at integrating text and graphics into complete pages.

If you keep that distinction clear, you'll use Photoshop to do everything that needs to be done to your images, and give the page-layout program an image file that it can simply pass on to the output device. Your work will proceed more smoothly, and you (or your service bureau) will encounter fewer unpleasant surprises. Sometimes it's nice when life is boring....

18

Multimedia and the Web

Purposing Pixels for the Screen

It's pretty clear that we've spent most of our professional lives focused on preparing images that are destined for a printing press. But the times they are a-changing, and one of the most common uses for Photoshop today is preparing images for screen display, whether in an interactive multimedia presentation or a World Wide Web site. And just as there are techniques for optimizing an image for paper, there are methods you can use to ensure good quality on screen (as well as tips for preparing your on-screen image efficiently).

In this chapter, we take a look at several important issues you need to consider when preparing images for multimedia or the Web, including deciding on a graphic file format and dealing with indexed-color images. Note that we don't discuss all the cool ways you can make funky buttons, rules, bullets, and other page elements; there are other great books on the market that include those techniques.

By the way, one of the most important tools for Web publishers that comes in the Photoshop box is ImageReady, which lets you build or edit dynamic media (animations, rollovers, and so on). Photoshop and Image-Ready work together beautifully via the Jump button at the bottom of the Tool palette (or from the File menu). If your image is open when you switch between the programs, the image automatically opens (or updates) in the other program. Plus, ImageReady and Photoshop can read the same native file format, with layers and so on.

However, the majority of Web graphics never require ImageReady, and Photoshop provides most of the tools you need. Therefore, we won't be discussing ImageReady in this chapter. There are several other programs currently on the market that are expressly designed to build Web graphics, such as Macromedia's Fireworks. However, this is a book on what you can do with Photoshop, so we won't be covering those programs, either.

Preparing Images

No matter whether an image is destined for print or for screen, we always recommend that you do the tonal correction, color correction, and sharpening in Photoshop. But the kind of correction and sharpening you need for on-screen images is almost always different than for printed images.

The one rule that almost always applies to images for the screen is that no matter what the image looks like on your screen, it will look different on everyone else's. Preparing images for multimedia and the Internet is an exercise in frustration for anyone who is used to print production; even the whims of a web press seem trivial compared to the variations from one person's screen to another on the World Wide Web.

Tone

While the display on some computer monitors is darker than on others, monitors connected to a Macintosh tend to display images lighter than those on a PC. While it's not entirely true that the native gamma of Macintosh screens is around 1.8, whereas Windows display systems have a native gamma around 2.3, it's certainly the case that a good many Mac users calibrate their monitors to gamma 1.8, while very few Windows users do so (see Figure 18-1). You can compensate for this to some extent by choosing an appropriate RGB space for your images (see Chapter 5, *Color Settings*); but it's unlikely that the people who view your images will have calibrated monitors, so the above gamma numbers are no more than a general guideline.

There are several strategies for dealing with this mismatch. All involve some compromises. Since the destination monitor is essentially an unknown, you can be fairly certain that until self-calibrating monitors are

Figure 18-1
Monitor gamma
and image tone

*Macintosh screen,
gamma 1.8*

*Windows screen,
gamma 2.2*

ubiquitous and all browsers support system-level color management, your images are going to look much better (or worse) on some systems than on others. Ultimately, it's simply impossible to produce images that will look good to every Web user.

Given the current state of the art, the best you can do is to choose an aim point appropriate for the audience you're trying to reach. We suggest you choose one of the following alternatives.

▶ **Convert to sRGB.** Back in Chapter 5, *Color Settings*, we discussed the sRGB color space, developed by several industry giants to describe the general characteristics of the "typical" Windows monitor. Of course, the sRGB color gamut excludes many of the intense colors that you may want to display. (Ironically, the logo color of one of sRGB's main proponents, Hewlett-Packard, lies outside the sRGB gamut.) Also, we doubt that the majority of monitors on the market actually display sRGB. Still, you can convert your edited images into the sRGB space before saving them, accepting its inherent limitations.

Given the marketing muscle behind sRGB, it's probably the most sensible choice unless you're trying to sell color-critical merchandise or show fine art on the Web. However, there are many good reasons to work in a better RGB workspace and only convert to sRGB just before saving the file (see "Tip: Work in a Big Space," below).

▶ **Prepare two sets of images.** We know some photographers who care so much about color that they've prepared two sets of their images, one at gamma 1.8 and one at gamma 2.2. Then they set up their sites so that Mac users see the gamma 1.8 version while Windows users see the gamma 2.2 version. It's a good idea, except that it still doesn't take into account that out in the real world some Mac monitors actually display more darkly than Windows monitors, and *vice versa*. It is also a lot more work to do this, of course.

▶ **Embed the profile.** The best solution to the color mismatch problem is to embed an ICC profile in each image. Unfortunately, this approach relies on two things: that every person looking at your images has created their own custom monitor profile, and that their browser supports (and corrects for) embedded profiles. But let's get real: Neither of these is likely in the real world, at least not anytime soon. For instance, as far as we know, only Safari and Internet Explorer 4.x and 5.x for the Mac support embedded profiles (and in the latter, only when you turn on the ColorSync checkbox in the Preferences dialog box).

Note that Photoshop does not embed profiles in GIF files because they're always in Indexed Color mode rather than RGB. However, there are ways that you can specify a profile for a GIF file (see the Web site *www.colorsync.com* for more information on specifying an associated profile within your HTML code). Embedding an RGB working space profile usually only adds about 0.5 K to a JPEG image, so file size shouldn't be a consideration.

All three approaches have their strengths and weaknesses, and each of these three strategies optimizes the image for a different set of users.

Tip: Work in a Big Space. Even if every image you create is for the Web, we still suggest setting the RGB popup menu in your Color Settings dialog box to a reasonable color space, like Adobe RGB (if you don't know what we're talking about here, check out Chapter 5, *Color Settings*). Then, if you want to convert your images to the sRGB space before saving them, you can use Convert to Profile (from the Mode submenu, under the Image menu) to convert from your RGB space to sRGB. If you use the smaller sRGB space as your RGB working space, you're limiting your color options unnecessarily when editing your images.

Tip: Color Management Outside of Photoshop. Electronic commerce demands that Web color get more consistent; the number one reason for merchandise returns is, "it wasn't the color I saw in the catalog." Without an easy way for people to characterize their monitor and for images to be compensated on the fly, customers will never be able to tell whether the shirt they're looking at is a dark burgundy or a light red, and e-commerce will flounder. With so much money riding on this, you'd think that there would already be good commercial solutions to ensure accurate color. Unfortunately, the tough part is getting the person-on-the-street to create custom monitor profiles on their machines.

Color

Not only can you rarely predict tonal shifts in images for the screen, you can't assume anything about color. Most graphic arts professionals have 24-bit color ("true color") monitors, but just because you have one doesn't mean that your audience will. In fact, some users of older computers can only view 256 colors at a time, due to the constraints of their video hardware (or the games they like to play on their computer). A very few computer users only have grayscale screens, so they won't see color at all.

What's worse, even two people with the same kind of screen and computer system will probably see the same image differently on each of their monitors. Again, monitor calibration can help considerably, but it's too rare to depend upon. (And a thoughtless quick twist of the brightness or contrast knobs means that the color is even further off.)

However, there are a few rules you can generally trust.

▶ It's usually more important to retain the contrast between colors than the particular colors themselves. Image details that result from subtle changes in color (like the gentle folds in a red silk scarf) are often lost in translation.

▶ Solid areas of color, including text, should be set to one of the 216 "Web-safe" colors (see "Tip: Web-Safe Colors," below) so that they won't dither on old 8-bit screens.

▶ If you built your image on a 24-bit color monitor (which is a good idea, even when making Web graphics), switch your monitor to 8-bit color (256 colors) and 8-bit gray to test how less-well-equipped folks will see your image. (Or, use the Browser Dither feature in the Save For Web dialog box, which we talk about later in this chapter.)

▶ While you're testing, also try looking at your image on both Macintosh and Windows systems. You can also select Windows RGB or Macintosh RGB from the Proof Setup submenu (under the View menu), and then turn on Proof Colors (press Command-Y) to see how they change. This isn't perfect, but it should give you a general idea of how the image may look on a different system.

▶ Images for multimedia and the Web should always be in RGB or Indexed Color mode.

Tip: Web-Safe Colors. Every computer system has a built-in palette of 256 colors that it uses, unless some program tells it to use another palette. The problem is that the palettes that Web browsers use on Macintosh and Windows share only 216 of the 256 colors. These 216 colors are called "Web-safe" or "browser-safe" colors because they appear more or less the same on both platforms (given with the earlier caveats about color and tone rarely being quite the same between the two).

If you use a non-Web-safe color in your image, it—by necessity—gets dithered using the system palette's colors when viewed on an 8-bit color monitor (see Figure 18-2). The dithering is distracting in many images (especially images with text), but is usually unavoidable in pictures that contain anti-aliasing, gradients, or photographic images.

Web-safe colors are less relevant for screens set to display 16-bit ("thousands of colors") or 24-bit ("millions of colors" or "true color") color because little or no dithering is necessary on these monitors.

There are various ways to choose Web-safe colors for a Photoshop image, including buying the ColorWeb swatch book from Pantone that provides the RGB and hexadecimal equivalents of them all. However, the easiest is simply to turn on the Only Web Colors checkbox in Photoshop's Color Picker dialog box. Or, you could open the Swatches palette and choose any of the Web-safe palettes from the palette's popout menu (any palette that begins with the word "Web" or "Visibone").

Figure 18-2
Web-safe colors

On a 24-bit color
monitor, these colors
wouldn't dither.

On an 8-bit color
monitor, however,
these colors simply
aren't available.

If the color is Web-safe, it won't dither on 8-bit color screens.

If you replace the current swatches with a Web-safe palette, the Swatches palette will display only the 216 Web-safe colors. If you choose among them, you can't go wrong.

By the way, if you do the math, you'll find that all the Web-safe colors are in 20-percent steps within the 256-level scale. That is, a typical Web-safe color might be 20-percent red and 60-percent green. You might be tempted with this knowledge to change your Color Picker (in the Preferences dialog box) in order to specify colors by percentage. Don't do it! Photoshop translates these values based on the RGB profile in the Color Settings dialog box, so you won't get the proper values at all. Instead, if you want to type specific numbers into the Color Picker dialog box, use 0, 51, 102, 153, 204, or 255 (these correlate directly with 0, 20, 40, 60, 80, and 100 percent).

Resolution

One of the wonderful advantages to working on images for screen display is that resolution is almost always 72 ppi, making for very small images (relative to prepress sizes, at least). A 4-by-5-inch image at 72 ppi takes up 300 K, where the equivalent prepress image might consume over 4.5 MB of disk space and RAM. With smaller file size come faster processing times and lower RAM requirements. You can actually use any resolution you want, but when it comes time to put the image on screen, each image pixel is mapped to a screen pixel. A 300-ppi image will become enormous on screen!

Of course, similar to the vagaries of color and tone on the Internet, you rarely know what resolution screen your images will be viewed on—your 72-ppi illustration quickly becomes much smaller if someone views it on a high-resolution monitor. Because you cannot assume monitor resolution, it's often a good idea to design your 72-ppi images slightly larger in size so they'll look okay on a higher-resolution screen. The "standard" resolution of most Windows and Macintosh monitors is around 96 ppi. Bruce runs a 22-inch monitor at 1920-by-1440-pixel resolution, which is close to 125 ppi! (This makes all Web images on his screen appear about half the size they were intended.)

Note that when scanning images destined for the screen, we still almost always scan them at a higher resolution (often the full optical resolution of the scanner) and then downsample them in Photoshop (see Chapter 13, *Capturing Images*, for more on this process).

Tip: Pages to Graphics. People spend a lot of time trying to figure out how to get their InDesign or QuarkXPress pages up on the Internet. Converting to HTML is one option, though the page almost never looks the same as it did originally. Saving in the PDF format is another option, but then people need Acrobat Reader to view the page, which is a hassle.

Our favorite method of getting pages from XPress or InDesign (or any other program) up on the 'Net is to make a picture out of each one. Adobe InDesign CS lets you export a document page as a JPEG file (select Export from the File menu). If you're using XPress, an earlier version of InDesign, or some other program, here's what to do:

1. Save a page from the program as an EPS or PDF. InDesign and Quark-XPress have specific features to do this; if your program doesn't, you can print to disk as an EPS file using the LaserWriter PostScript driver.

2. Open this file in Photoshop. When Photoshop opens the Generic EPS or Rasterize PDF dialog box, choose to open the image as an RGB file at 72 dpi. Small type doesn't convert well to bitmap, but you might get a better result by turning on Anti-alias in the Open EPS dialog box.

3. Select Flatten from the Layer menu.

4. Save the file as either a GIF or a JPEG, depending on the content of the page and how much compression you're likely to achieve (see the next section for more on these file formats).

5. Put this picture on your Web site.

By turning the page into a picture, anyone with a Web browser can see it on the Internet. And surprisingly, even a full-page "page image" can be made very small if it's mostly text. (You can see examples of this at *www.pixelboyz.com/pageimage.htm.*)

Tip: Maintaining Colors. If you use Adobe Illustrator or Macromedia FreeHand along with Photoshop, you've probably found that your colors shift when you bring your images from the illustration program to Photoshop. For instance, when you spec a color in FreeHand or Illustrator as 100-percent magenta, it looks really bright on screen; when you bring it to Photoshop (see "Objects vs. Pixels" in Chapter 15, *Essential Image Techniques,* for more information on how to do this), the image appears muddy and dull. The reason is that the illustration programs and Photoshop display CMYK information on screen in completely different ways. If you're creating images for the Web, this is a disaster. Fortunately, you can get consistent color in one of several ways.

From FreeHand, you can export the document (or just particular objects) using the Photoshop RGB EPS file format (select Export from the File menu). This EPS file specifies colors in RGB mode rather than CMYK, so Photoshop displays them properly.

If you're an Illustrator user, you can create your colors in RGB mode, and turn off the CMYK PostScript option when saving your file as an EPS document. This way, when you open the EPS in Photoshop in RGB mode, you get the real RGB values.

While getting RGB colors out of QuarkXPress 5 or 6 is relatively easy (just select RGB from the Color popup menu in the Save as EPS dialog box), RGB colors from XPress 3.x or 4.x is a hassle because these versions always convert colors to CMYK when you save an EPS. The only way around this (that we know of, at least) is to create an EPS file via the Print dialog box.

1. Click the Printer button in QuarkXPress 4's Print dialog box to open the printer driver's settings.

2. Set the Destination popup menu to File (so the program will write the PostScript to disk instead of to the printer).

3. Go to the Save as File tab of the dialog box and change the Format popup menu to "EPS (No Preview)".

4. Click Save and tell the printer driver what to name the file. Then switch to the Setup tab of the QuarkXPress Print dialog box. Here, choose either "Acrobat Distiller" or "Generic Color" from the Printer popup menu.

5. Switch to the Output tab and choose "Composite RGB" from the Print Colors popup menu.

Now when you print, your color information will be saved in the RGB format. When you open this file in Photoshop, you get the same RGB values as you specified in QuarkXPress.

Saving Your Images

It's likely that the majority of images displayed on Web pages today were produced or edited with Photoshop. However, making images for the Web is a study in compromise: You can have either great-looking images or pictures that download quickly. You choose. The problem is that you need to see all the options to make an informed decision about how much to degrade your image in the name of small file sizes. The solution is the Save For Web feature.

Save For Web (select it from the File menu or press Command-Option-Shift-S) lets you see exactly what will happen to your images when you convert them to GIF or JPEG. Better yet, it can display two or four versions at a time and let you tweak each of them until you get just the effect you want (see Figure 18-3).

On-Screen File Formats

We discussed graphic file formats back in Chapter 16, *Storing Images*, but we need to explore two formats—GIF and JPEG—in more depth here, because they're key to the way images appear on the Internet. If your images are destined for a multimedia program such as Microsoft Power-Point or Macromedia Director, you can probably save them in the PICT or

Figure 18-3
Save For Web

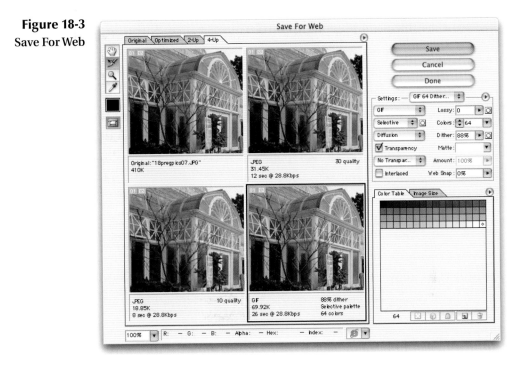

TIFF file format. But for Web use, you almost certainly need to save your images in either GIF or JPEG format.

Tip: Leave Off the Previews. In order to keep your file size to a minimum on the Macintosh, you may want to avoid using Thumbnail or Icon previews (see "Previews" in Chapter 16, *Storing Images*). However, since these previews are stripped away if your server isn't a Macintosh or if you upload your images to the server using the Raw Data format, it may not make much of a difference. In general, though, we avoid the previews altogether for GIF and JPEG images. Note that Photoshop never adds previews to images saved with Save For Web; this tip only applies when you save a GIF or JPEG image using Save As.

Tip: Checking File Size. The file size that Photoshop provides in the lower-left corner of the document window is far from accurate, mostly because it doesn't take into account any form of compression you will achieve with either JPEG or GIF images. The file size you see in the Save For Web dialog box is more accurate, but it's still not perfect. The only way to find an image's true (post-compression) file size is to save it to disk and switch out of Photoshop. If you have a Macintosh, use Get Info in the

Finder (select the file and choose Get Info from the File menu); if you're working on a Windows machine, use Properties on the Desktop (click on the file with the right mouse button and choose Properties from the list of options; see Figure 18-4).

Figure 18-4
Finding file size

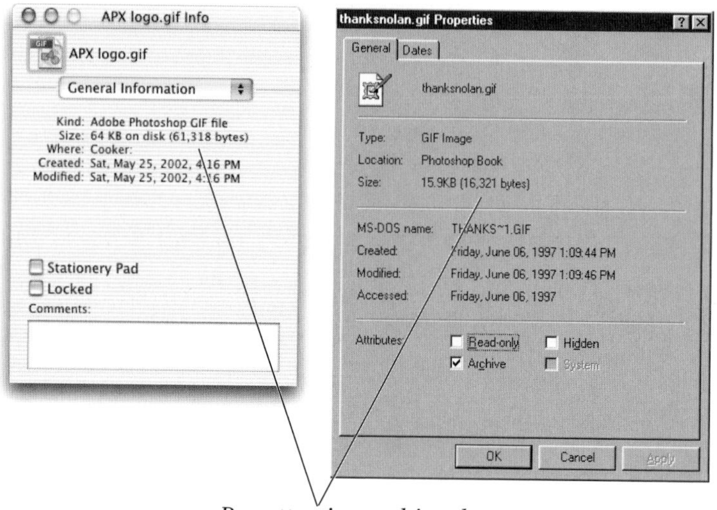

Pay attention to this value.

If the file size is displayed as "27 K on disk (22,045 bytes used)," only pay attention to the second number. The first value is the amount of space the image takes up on your hard disk: this depends on the block size your hard disk uses. If your disk uses 32 K blocks, a 2 K file will occupy 32 K on disk, and a 33 K file will use 64 K of disk space. The second number shows the actual amount of data someone would have to download to see the image, and it's usually smaller than the disk space number.

Save For Web

The trick to the Save For Web feature is to be methodical. Here are the basic steps you should follow once you have the dialog box open.

1. Switch to the 2-Up or 4-Up tab of the window. We like 4-Up except on those rare occasions where we're almost sure what settings we're going to use.

2. Leave the first panel set to Original (so you have something with which to compare your tests). Click on each of the other images and choose

for it a preset configuration from the Settings popup menu. For a good spectrum of results, David usually starts with these three: JPEG Medium, GIF 64 Dither, and GIF 32 No Dither.

3. Check each image's quality (visually) and size, and approximate download time (shown under each image).

4. Pick the one that is closest to what you're trying to achieve, and tweak the settings to minimize the size while maintaining quality. We cover each of the settings and how they work below.

5. When you're ready, click OK (make sure the proper image is highlighted; whichever one is highlighted is the one that gets saved to disk).

The problem is that there are so many settings in the dialog box to tweak, many of them obscure. The Settings and Format popup menus are relevant for any file format you use, so we'll cover them first. Then we'll get into the settings that are specific to GIF, JPEG, WBMP, and PNG.

Settings. The Settings popup menu lets you recall saved sets of settings. There's nothing magic about the settings that are already built-in; they're only there to get you started. If you don't like Adobe's settings, you can delete them by choosing Delete Settings from the popout menu to the right of the Settings popup menu. If you want to add your own group of settings to the list, choose Save Settings instead; make sure the settings are saved in the Optimized Settings folder (inside your Photoshop Presets folder), with an .irs file name extension.

Format. If you prefer to arrange the settings manually, you should start by choosing GIF, JPEG, PNG, or WBMP from the Format popup menu. We discuss these formats in some detail in Chapter 16, *Storing Images,* and in each section below.

JPEG

For best reproduction on the Web, scanned photographic images should almost always be saved in the JPEG file format. This way, people viewing the image on a 24-bit color monitor will see all the colors in the image, and those on 8-bit monitors will see a dithered version. Fortunately, the dithered version is usually pretty good—almost as good as if you had converted the image to 8-bit in Photoshop yourself.

JPEG compresses RGB natural images really well, even if the image does suffer some degradation in the process. On the other hand, JPEG is not suitable for images that have a lot of solid colors, especially computer-generated images, type, and line art. It's also not appropriate for images in which you've used Web-safe colors—because colors often shift in JPEG images—or images that require transparency.

You can save images in the JPEG format from the Save As dialog box (see Chapter 16, *Storing Images*), but you get much more control in the Save For Web dialog box (see Figure 18-5).

Optimized. The only time you want to turn off the Optimized checkbox is if you're sure your image will be displayed on a very old Web browser that may not support the Optimized JPEG format. Almost every browser for the past several years has supported this format, however.

Compression quality. The more compression you apply in Photoshop, the worse the resulting image quality. Where you only have 12 levels of JPEG compression in the Save as JPEG dialog box, the Save For Web dialog box offers you 100 levels. The four settings in the Quality popup menu (Low, Medium, High, and Maximum) are simply presets for values in the Quality field to the right. (The four settings correspond to numerical values of 10, 30, 60, and 80, in case you care.) You can change the value to any number between 1 and 100 (100 being the highest quality and least amount of compression).

If you're a prima donna about your images, and you don't want *any* degradation, you're probably in the wrong business here. Remember that you can usually get away with a lot of degradation. David rarely uses a Quality value over 50 for Web images, though he probably wouldn't use less than 90 (a 9 or 10 setting in the Save As dialog box) for prepress images. Ultimately, it's all trial and error.

Note that if there are particular areas in your image that you don't want as degraded as others by the JPEG compression, you can select those areas, and save the selection as a channel. Then, click the little button next to the Quality field (the one that has a little dotted circle in it), and choose your channel from the Channel popup menu. Here, Photoshop lets you choose compression values for the black and white areas of the channel. Similarly, you can just specify a text or vector layer rather than building a channel. However, watch out: files that have this sort of com-

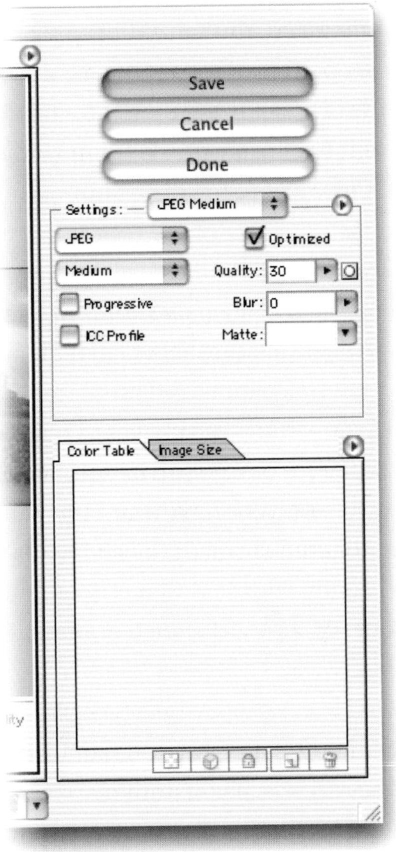

Figure 18-5
Save For Web:
JPEG images

pression-prioritizing area may look slightly better, but are almost always larger than those in which you have a single compression value throughout.

Progressive. Like Optimized, we almost always leave the Progressive feature turned on. When it's on, Web browsers will display a low-resolution version of the image first, then replace it with a high-resolution version. Strangely, progressive JPEG images are even slightly smaller than non-progressive JPEGs, so the only reason not to leave this turned on is for displaying on very old browsers.

Blur. The problem with JPEG images is that the more you compress them, the more blocky they appear. These blocky artifacts are distracting to the eye, and primarily appear around high-contrast edges in your image. One option to combat these artifacts is to blur your image slightly so the edges aren't so pronounced. You can either apply the Gaussian Blur filter to your image before opening the Save For Web dialog box, or you can type a blur value into the Blur field here. Both do exactly the same thing, so if you're going to use it (we rarely do—perhaps only for thumbnails) we recommend just applying it in the dialog box.

ICC Profile. The ICC Profile checkbox lets you tell Photoshop whether to embed your RGB workspace profile in your JPEG image. Currently, the only Web browsers that care about color management assume that images are in sRGB unless an embedded profile tells them otherwise. We generally recommend converting Web images to sRGB, which makes profile embedding moot. But if for one reason or another you don't want to convert the image to sRGB, and you think your target audience will have color management configured correctly, by all means embed your working space profile—it usually adds less than 1 K of data to the file. For more information about ICC profiles and color management, check out Chapter 5, *Color Settings*.

Matte. JPEG images are always opaque and they're always rectangular. That's just the way it is; if you want real transparency, use the GIF or PNG format. So what happens if your image is on a layer that includes transparency? Photoshop fills in all your transparent pixels with whatever color you've chosen in the Matte field. In general, you want the Matte color to be the same color as either the background of the image or the background of your Web page. Note that the color you choose may shift slightly in the conversion to JPEG, especially if you're applying a lot of compression; check the RGB and Hex settings at the bottom of the Save For Web dialog box.

Tip: Keep Your Originals. Remember that if you open a JPEG image in Photoshop and then save it out again as a JPEG, the compression damages the image even more. So remember to always keep the original non-JPEG version of your image. That way, you can go back and make edits on the original and save out the JPEG version fresh again.

Tip: Save Blends as JPEG. Blends (or gradients, vignettes, or whatever you want to call them) look much better when saved as JPEG than when saved as GIFs. This way, people who have 24-bit color monitors will see a smooth blend, and people with 8-bit monitors will see the crummy dithered version (but at least most people will be happy).

GIF

While JPEG is the preferred format for natural ("photographic") scanned images, GIF (don't even get us started on the "how should this be pronounced" argument) is currently *the* format for everything else.

▶ Images that contain areas of solid colors (including most blocks of text and computer-generated pictures)

▶ Animations

▶ Images containing transparency

▶ Images that rely on Web-safe colors

Theoretically, the GIF specification allows for a full 24-bit color image; however, nobody really supports this, so GIF images are always saved in 8-bit indexed color (for more on this mode, see "Indexed Color" in Chapter 3, *Image Essentials,* and "Indexed Color," later in this chapter). That means you can't have more than 256 colors in your image. Fortunately, you can usually specify which 256 colors you want to use.

Tip: Stay in RGB. Some folks convert their RGB images to Indexed Color mode (on the Mode submenu) before saving them as a GIF. There's nothing wrong with doing this, but the Save For Web dialog box makes this workflow obsolete. Just leave the image in RGB and let Photoshop convert to Indexed Color mode on the fly when you save the file. The RGB mode is much more efficient in the long run because it affords the most flexibility in editing the image.

Here are the various options you have when saving a GIF image in the Save For Web dialog box (see Figure 18-6).

Lossy. No, Adobe isn't breaking the rules of GIF images: the GIF file format is still a lossless format (it doesn't degrade your image like JPEG does). Instead, the Lossy feature in the Save For Web dialog box lets you degrade the image before it's saved as a GIF. Photoshop is taking advantage of sev-

Figure 18-6
Save For Web:
GIF images

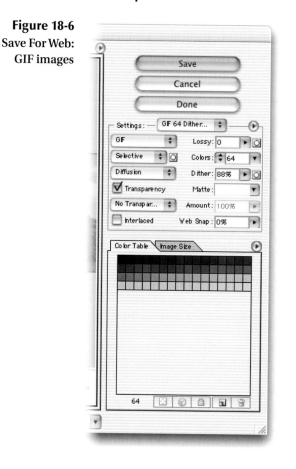

eral characteristics of the compression algorithm that GIF uses; by degrading the image in certain intelligent ways, it can compress the file further.
This is most helpful when you have to save a scanned photographic image
as a GIF instead of a JPEG (for instance, if you want portions of the image
to be transparent). You can often get a significant increase in compression
with hardly any visual noise by increasing the Lossy value to 10 or 20.

Color reduction method. GIF images are saved in the Indexed Color
mode, which means a maximum of 256 colors. If you're converting an
RGB image, or reducing the number of colors in an indexed color image,
you need to tell Photoshop what method of color reduction to use (these
are the same as the reduction methods listed in the Indexed Color dialog box). Photoshop 5.5 introduced two algorithms—Selective and Perceptual—which are like Adaptive but slightly smarter. Where Adaptive
picks colors from your image based on how often they appear in the image,

Perceptual picks a color palette based on how the colors look to the eye; in particular, Perceptual creates much nicer transitions between colors, so it's best for scanned photographic images. The Selective method is slightly better for images that have sharp high-contrast edges, such as synthetic images (like those from Illustrator or FreeHand). We hardly ever use Adaptive anymore.

If you insist on using a Web-safe palette, go ahead and select Web from the popup menu. Or, if you've already built a custom color palette, you can choose it by selecting Load Color Palette from the popout menu next to the Color Table and Image Size tabs (if they labeled these popout menus, it would sure make it easier to describe this stuff to you).

Tip: Giving Preferential Treatment. Do you care about the color in one part of your image more than in other areas? No problem. Make a rough selection of the pixels you care about using the Marquee or Lasso tool, and save the selection in the Channels palette (see Chapter 8, *Selections and Channels*). Then, in the Save For Web dialog box, click the little button next to the Color popup menu (the one where you select Adaptive, Perceptive, and so on). Photoshop lets you pick the saved channel, and re-creates the color palette, giving a weighted preference for colors in that area.

Colors. The fewer colors in an image, the more solid or patterned areas in the image, so the better compression you can get. Very few GIF images need a full 256 colors; in fact, it's rare to find an image that won't look reasonable on screen with only 64. Note that the colors are shown in the Color Table at the bottom-right of the dialog box (see "Color Table," later in this chapter).

Dither. Reducing the number of colors in an image is an imperfect science, and the results are often better if you dither the final colors a little bit. Photoshop has always included the Diffusion and Pattern dithers in the Indexed Color dialog boxes (the first is good, the second is bad). New to the lineup is the Noise option. The results are similar to—though a little "noisier" than—the Diffusion dither; however, you should use the Noise option if you're also slicing the image into smaller pieces (see "Slicing Images," later in this chapter). The reason has to do with the way that diffusion dithers are created (Photoshop looks at each pixel and the pixels around it; if you later slice an image, the pixel values might change and the dither would no longer look right).

If you choose the Diffusion method, you can also pick a Dither amount in the Dither field. Personally, we feel that if you're going to be dithering an image at all, you might as well pick a value in the 70 or 80 percent area. However, the choice is up to you and really is image-specific.

Transparency. If your image contains transparent pixels (that is, it has no opaque Background layer), you can choose whether or not those pixels should be transparent in the final image by turning on or off the Transparency checkbox. When the checkbox is turned off, all transparent pixels are set to the color in the Matte field. If Matte is set to None, then Photoshop sets the colors to white.

On the other hand, if you turn on the Transparency checkbox, Photoshop leaves fully transparent pixels transparent, and blends partially transparent pixels with the color in the Matte setting. This is very useful when you're trying to blend your GIF image into your Web page's background color (see Figure 18-7). If Matte is set to None, then Photoshop simply clips off all partially transparent pixels, and you get a hard, aliased-edged image.

If your image doesn't contain any transparent pixels, you can force particular colors to be transparent in the Save For Web dialog box by selecting them in the Color Table (you can choose more than one by Command-clicking on each color) and clicking the Transparency button. But unless you have very few colors in your image, it's usually just much faster to exit the Save For Web dialog box and create transparency in the image itself.

Photoshop 7 introduced another new transparency feature, too: the ability to create dithered transparency by selecting from the popup menu directly beneath the Transparency checkbox. This only has an effect when there are pixels that are partially transparent in your image (like a drop shadow might be). Unfortunately, the result is typically so extraordinarily ugly that we find it hardly worth the time.

Tip: Finding a Good Matte Color. When choosing a matte color to which Photoshop can blend your semi-transparent pixels, you generally want to pick a color dominant in whatever background you're placing the image over. If you can't remember what that color is, but it appears somewhere on screen (the Photoshop Color Picker, the Swatches palette, or in some image window), you can choose it by clicking once on the Matte color swatch, then clicking on the desired color with the automatically provided eyedropper tool. If the Swatches palette isn't visible (and you want it to be), choose Show Swatches from the Window menu first.

Interlaced. Whereas turning on the Progressive checkbox for JPEGs generally makes the image slightly smaller (a fact which truly confounds us, as the image doesn't appear to change any), turning on the Interlaced checkbox for GIF images actually makes the image very slightly larger.

Figure 18-7
Transparency in
GIF images

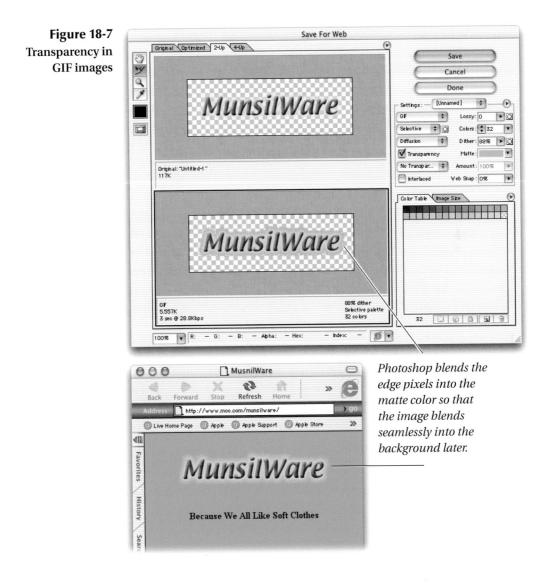

Photoshop blends the edge pixels into the matte color so that the image blends seamlessly into the background later.

Because of this, we only turn this on when having an image appear slowly (like a venetian blind opening) actually benefits the viewer. For instance, we rarely use this for buttons, but we typically do use it for image maps, because the audience might be able to click on an area of the image map before the final image is complete.

Web Snap. Maybe we just don't get it, but the Web Snap feature seems really useless to us. The concept is that as you increase the Web Snap percentage, some number of colors in your image will snap to a Web-safe color palette. Unfortunately, you have no control over what colors are changed. We never use this; if we want to snap colors to a Web-safe palette, we do it manually in the Color Table area.

Color Table. The Color Table not only displays which colors appear in your final image, but also lets you change them or keep them from being changed. While it's rare that you'd need to do so, if you double-click on any color swatch, Photoshop lets you change its color (using the standard Color Picker). More common is tweaking the color to match the nearest Web-safe color. Fortunately, Photoshop makes this really easy: just select the color (or more than one color by holding down the Command key when you click) and click the Snap to Web-safe Color button (that's the one that looks like a little cube). Web-safe swatches appear with a white dot in their centers. The popout menu next to the Color Table lets you add and delete colors, select specific colors, and—best of all—control how Photoshop displays the color swatches. We generally choose to display the swatches by Hue or Luminance, as we find these easiest to comprehend.

Tip: Save That Color! Let's say you've got an image of a banana with a small bit of red text over it. Because the image is composed of mostly yellow colors, the red text might change to a dark yellow color if you lower the number of colors in the image. To save the red pixels, increase the number of colors in the Save For Web dialog box to 128 or so (enough so that the red pixels appear in the Color Table), then select the red swatch and click the Lock button (the one that looks like a little padlock). Now, as you lower the number of colors in the image, that swatch will always remain red. You can unlock it again by selecting it and clicking the button again. Note that locked colors always show a small white square in the bottom-right corner.

Tip: Optimize to File Size. Computers are supposed to figure stuff out for us, right? So if you know that you need an image to be smaller than 10 K, why not let Photoshop figure out the proper settings for you? Click on one of the images in the Save For Web dialog box and select Optimize to File Size from the unlabeled popout menu next to the Settings popup menu. The Optimize To File Size dialog box lets you choose a file format (JPEG or GIF), but we tend simply to choose the Automatic feature and let Photoshop figure out the best solution for us (see Figure 18-8). Whatever you do, though, don't just accept whatever Photoshop gives you: the best images still require some tweaking.

Figure 18-8
Optimize to File Size

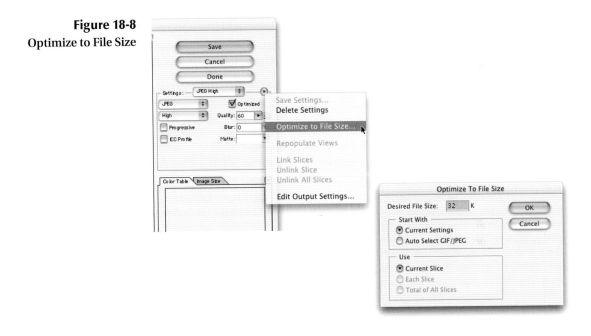

Tip: Layer Animations. Photoshop doesn't let you create GIF animations, but you can use it as a tool to build each frame of an animation and then use ImageReady to piece them together. Often, you can build each frame of an animation on a different layer of an RGB image.

Tip: Eking Out the Bytes. A great many images on the Internet (or "information superhighway," or "Infobahn," or whatever you want to call it) are saved in GIF format, especially those that appear on World Wide Web sites. The reason is simple: they're very compact. But sometimes they're just not compact enough. For instance, on slower modem lines, there's a big difference between watching a 30 K image slowly appear on your screen and a 15 K image appear without trouble.

If you're trying to eke out every little bit of compression in a GIF file, keep in mind how LZW compression works: it looks for repeating patterns of colors. For instance, it can tokenize "red, blue, red, blue, red, blue" into one piece of information. Therefore, the images that get compressed the most contain lots of these repeating patterns.

Here are several ways you can make Photoshop use more repeating patterns when you're converting images from RGB to Indexed Color.

▶ Use solid areas rather than gradations or textures.

▶ If you do use gradations (blends), consider unchecking the Dither option in the Gradient tool's Options palette and making the blend vertical (top to bottom) rather than horizontal (side to side). (This ensures that more pixels of the same color will sit next to each other.)

▶ Using specific color schemes is better than using lots of different colors. The fewer colors you use, the more compression you'll achieve.

▶ Use a smaller bit depth (use 16 or 32 colors instead of 128 or 255). Of course, many images degrade significantly with fewer colors, so you should play around with this.

▶ If you're converting to Indexed Color mode before you export the GIF, choose Pattern dither instead of Diffusion dither (in the Indexed Color dialog box).

▶ Using System palette (or Uniform, if you're using fewer than 8 bits per pixel) instead of Adaptive can save 1 or 2 KB, which is important in some cases. If this doesn't matter as much to you, Adaptive is probably better.

With any of these techniques, the image's dither is almost always slightly more obvious, but you can make the image transfer over phone lines faster.

PNG Images

There are very few settings you can change when saving files in the PNG-24 format (the primary choice is whether or not they should include transparent areas), and the settings for the PNG-8 file format are almost identical to those of the GIF format (see Figure 18-9). As we explained back in Chapter 16, *Storing Images*, we think the PNG format is cool, but it is still isn't widely used or supported fully by Web browsers. Also, note that PNG images are generally larger than their GIF or JPEG counterparts, so there has to be a really good reason to use them (which there isn't yet).

Figure 18-9
Save For Web:
PNG-8 and PNG 24

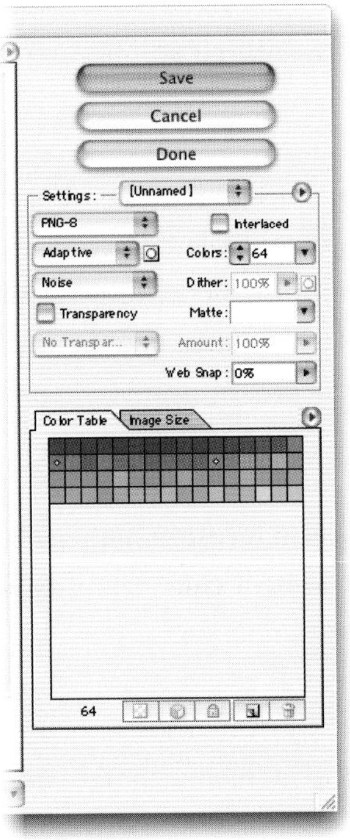

WBMP Images

Web pages are beginning to appear on every sort of device, from cell phones to PDAs to kitchen blenders (well, not yet, but probably soon). However, most of these devices only display black and white pixels—it's like a return to 1984! Standards are shifting, but one file format for displaying these Bitmap images has gained popularity: WBMP (which isn't the same thing as Windows BMP). Photoshop lets you save WBMP files in two ways. If your file is already converted to Bitmap mode from the Image>Mode submenu, you can simply save as WBMP from the Save As dialog box. Otherwise, the Save For Web dialog box lets you save any kind of image in the WBMP format.

The only control you have for WBMP files is the type of dither: None, Diffusion, Pattern, or Noise. Note that Diffusion and None look the same until you increase the dither percentage for the Dither setting. Curiously, the WBMP format doesn't appear to include any compression algorithms, so whatever dither you use creates the same-sized file.

Other Save For Web Controls

Before we move on to other aspects of Photoshop's Web capabilities, we should note just a few other nifty features in the Save For Web dialog box.

Navigating. When you look at the Save For Web dialog box in 4-Up mode, each image window is pretty small. Fortunately, you can (and definitely should) navigate around your graphic to check for image degradation in different areas. First, you can use the Grabber Hand tool (press H) by clicking-and-dragging on any one of the images. As you drag one image, all the other images move, too.

Second, you can zoom in and out on the image by changing the view percentage in the lower-left corner of the Save For Web dialog box (though it's usually faster to Control-click or right-mouse-click on an image and change the scale from the context-sensitive menu). Zooming out rarely helps, but we sometimes zoom in to see the effects of the JPEG or GIF conversion more clearly. Note that you can also resize the Save For Web dialog box by dragging in the lower-right corner of the window.

Image Size. Need your final Web graphic to be smaller than the high-resolution version you've got? You can use the Image Size dialog box to downsample the image before using Save For Web, or you can use the Image Size tab in the Save For Web dialog box. Both do exactly the same thing. The one difference is that the Save For Web dialog box only offers you pixel dimensions, and the result will always be at 72 ppi. This is okay because inches, millimeters, and picas don't mean anything in a Web world where everyone's monitors display at different resolutions.

Browser Dither. Sure, you have a 24-bit color monitor, but your audience might not. A few people still have old 8-bit color monitors, and your glorious color images will get dithered using the 256 colors in their Web browser's color palette. If you care about what those people see, you can turn on the Browser Dither option in the unlabeled popout menu at the top right of the Save For Web dialog box's image area (or, better yet, just select it from the context-sensitive menu). You can turn on (or off) Browser Dither for one image at a time. For best results, try turning it on, then off, then on again to see "before and after" shots of your image.

Download speed. Each image in the Save For Web dialog box lists the approximate time it would take to download this image at 28.8 Kbps. However, if you're pretty sure that most of your audience will be dialing in at 56.6 Kbps, you can change the setting in the popout menu at the top of the dialog box (or in the context-sensitive menu). To be honest, though, we rarely pay attention to this readout, as there are many variables that affect download times (server load, processor speed, cosmic rays…).

Gamma. As we pointed out earlier, Windows boxes typically display images darker than Macintosh boxes. You can simulate this by turning on Standard Windows Color, which simulates a display gamma of 2.2; or Standard Macintosh Color, which simulates a display gamma of 1.8 (either from the popout menu at the top of the dialog box or from the context-sensitive menu). The catch is that many Mac users have their monitors calibrated to a gamma of 2.2, and some Windows users have their monitors calibrated to a gamma of 1.8. So when it comes to color and tone correction for the Web, it's still really hit or miss.

Let Photoshop Write Your HTML

Who wants to write HTML code anymore? Certainly not us. We paid our dues already, and now we just want to let the computer do what it's good at. Fortunately, the Save For Web dialog box will write HTML code that describes our images.

There's two ways to get HTML out of this dialog box. First, you can click on the preview button to open the currently selected image in your Web browser. Not only does the image appear, but so does information about the image and the source code that the Web browser can read. You can then copy the pieces of the HTML that you require (generally the IMG tag).

There's a better way, though: After you select which image you want to save and click OK, Photoshop displays the Save Optimized As dialog box, where you can actually name your file and tell Photoshop where to save it (see Figure 18-10). What's more, you can choose HTML and Images from

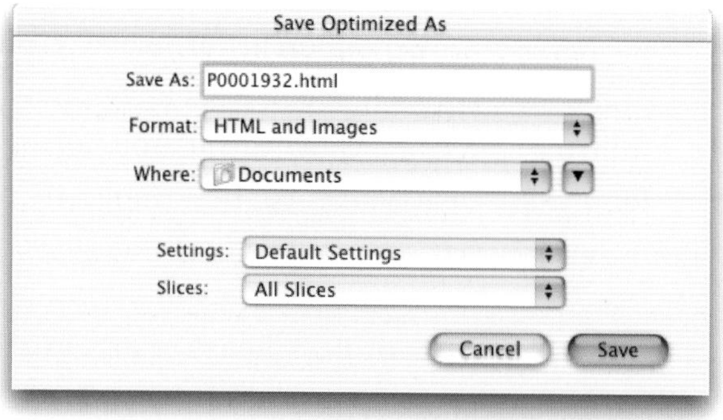

Figure 18-10
Save Optimized As

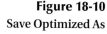

the Format popup menu. (If you're saving Slices, this is really important; see "Slices," in the next section.) You can then open the HTML file in a text editor and copy and paste the relevant information.

More Web Tools

Adobe Photoshop offers many more tools for getting great-looking Web images. In fact, with each new version, we see that the line between Image-Ready and Photoshop becomes less distinct. Where will it ever end?

In this section, we'll explore image slicing, converting images to indexed color, choosing Web-safe colors, and making Web page galleries for browsing your photographs. This certainly doesn't cover every Web feature in Photoshop, but we think it covers the most important ones.

Slices

Not every part of an image is equal, and not all parts deserve equal treatment. Often, some parts of an image can be compressed significantly more (with greater image degradation) than others. Or some parts are destined to be rollovers (areas that change when the cursor rolls over them in the Web browser), animations, or Web links. In any of these instances, you might consider slicing your graphic into smaller pieces with Photoshop's Slice tool. When you do this, and then save the image with the Save For Web feature, Photoshop saves each slice as a separate file to disk with its own compression settings. Or, if you open the sliced image in ImageReady, you can set each slice to be a rollover or other type of dynamic media. (Again, we don't cover ImageReady and dynamic media in this chapter.)

Tip: Slices vs. Image Maps. If your entire image will be optimized the same way, you're not creating rollovers or other dynamic areas in the graphic, but you do want certain areas to be "buttons" or "hot links" (areas that, when clicked, take you to a different URL), then you might want to make the image an "image map" instead of slicing it up. It's easy to make image maps in ImageReady (there's even a special tool for it), and this way you only export a single image rather than one file for each slice. Plus, the "hot" areas in an image map can be rectangular, oval, or even a polygon—whereas slices are always rectangular.

Making (and breaking) slices. Photoshop offers two tools for creating slices: the Slice tool (it looks like a little blade in the Tool palette; press K to select it quickly), and the New Layer Based Slice feature (in the Layer menu).

▶ **Slice tool.** The Slice tool acts much like the Marquee selection tool: just drag it over the area you want to define as a slice. You can constrain the shape or size of the slice by choosing Constrained Aspect Ratio or Fixed Size from the Style popup menu in the Options bar (see Chapter 8, *Selections and Channels*, for more on how to use these options).

▶ **New Layer Based Slice.** Let's say you've got five buttons in your image and you want each one to be a separate slice. If each one is on its own layer, then you can avoid the Slice tool entirely by selecting a layer and choosing New Layer Based Slice from the Layer menu (then repeating this for each layer with a button on it). Photoshop creates slices based on the boundaries of whatever is on each layer. Better yet, if you change a layer, the slices update automatically.

You can't have a single slice of an image; however you make the slice, Photoshop automatically slices the rest of the image up. For example, if you make a square slice in the middle of the picture, Photoshop adds four other "auto-slices" to fill in the area around the square (see Figure 18-11). The slice you make is called a "user slice," and it looks slightly different on screen: user slices have solid boundaries, auto-slices have dotted boundaries. Each time you change or add a user slice, Photoshop reconfigures the auto-slices automatically.

Figure 18-11
Slicing an image

User slice

Auto-slice

How do you change a slice once you've made it? Use the Slice Selection tool. This tool is hiding behind the Slice tool in the Tool palette; you can get it by pressing Shift-K, or, temporarily, by holding down the Command key while the Slice tool is selected. The Slice Selection tool lets you move the slice (click inside the slice and drag) or change the slice boundaries (drag the slice's corner or edge handles). You can only edit or move user slices, though. If you want to change an auto-slice into a user slice, click on it with the Slice Selection tool (you can't use the Command-key trick here) and then click the Promote to User Slice button in the Options bar.

Tip: Minimize Your Slices. The main problem with automatic layer-based slices is that you often get many more slices using this feature than if you use the Slice tool with care. The more slices, the more files you have to keep track of on disk, and the longer it takes to transfer the image to the Web browser. We'll often start our sliced images with layer-based slicing, but then edit the slice boundaries once we're pretty sure the graphic won't change again. To edit the slice boundaries, you have to click on the slice with the Slice Selection tool and then click the Promote to User Slice button in the Options bar. Of course, after you do this, the slices are no longer tied to the layers (see Figure 18-12).

Tip: Overlapping Slices. Slices often overlap each other, especially when you use the New Layer Based Slice feature. In these cases, Photoshop adds "sub-slices" in the overlapping areas, which act just like regular slices, but cannot be selected with the Slice Selection tool. If you don't like the order in which the overlapping slices are arranged, you can change them by selecting the slice and clicking on the Bring to Front or Send to Back buttons in the Options bar (which appear when you have the Slice Selection tool chosen in the Tool palette). In general, you should try to avoid overlapping slices unless you're going to apply the same optimization/compression techniques to each of them.

By the way, once you make your slices, you can lock them in place by selecting Lock Slices from the View menu. That way, you (or some careless colleague) won't accidentally move or resize the slice boundaries.

If you want to delete a single slice, click on it with the Slice Selection tool and press the Delete or Backspace key. If you want to delete all the slices, choose Clear Slices from the View menu. (No, we have no idea why

Figure 18-12
Reducing the
number of slices

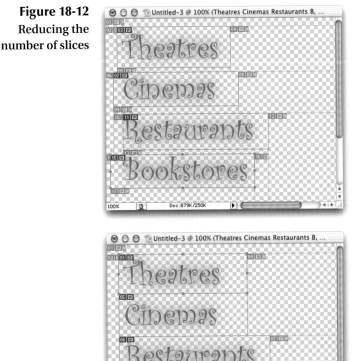

Sloppy slicing creates 17 slices.

By aligning the slice borders, we get only nine slices.

these features are in the View menu; we figure they just couldn't decide where else to put them.)

Slice Options. While you need ImageReady to create dynamic media such as rollovers and animations, you can control each slice and add some basic actions right in Photoshop by selecting the slice with the Slice Selection tool and clicking the Slice Options button in the Options bar. (Even faster, just Command-double click on the slice with the Slice tool.) This opens the Slice Options dialog box (see Figure 18-13). Here's a quick rundown of the options.

▶ **Name.** Photoshop automatically gives your slice a name based on the name of the file itself. When you save the slices to disk, it'll have this name (plus .gif or .jpg, depending on the file type). You can override the name here, if you like. Note that if you're using cascading style sheets (CSS), this is also the object name (see "Saving Slices," below).

▶ **URL.** You can make this slice "hot" (so that you can click on it to jump to a different Web page) by typing a URL into the URL field. If the Web page you're linking to will be in the same folder as the current page's folder, then you can just type the file's name (like "mypage.html"). However, if you're linking to a different site's page, you need the full URL (like "http://www.moo.com").

▶ **Target.** The Target field tells your Web browser where to open the new Web page that you linked to in the URL field. If you leave this blank,

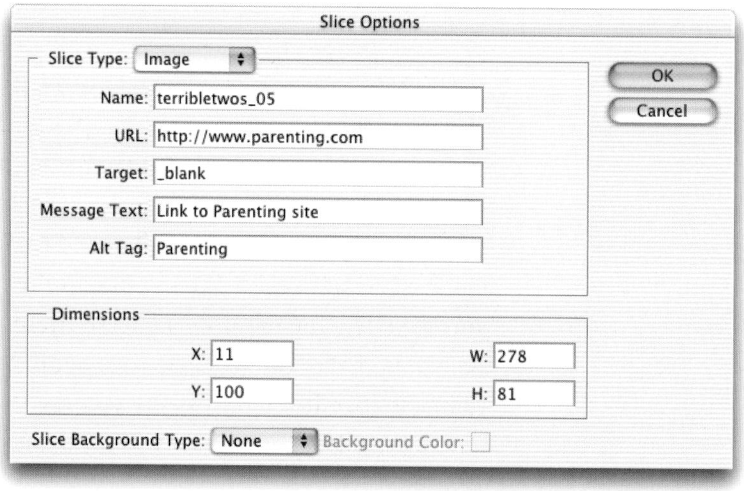

Figure 18-13
Slice Options
dialog box

the Web page replaces the current Web page (if you're using frames, then it replaces the current frame). On the other hand, you can type "_top" in the Target field to force the linked page to replace the entire window (even if there's a frame there), or "_blank" to open the link in a new window. If you're using frames in your HTML, you can also type the target frame name.

▶ **Message Text.** By default, when you move your cursor over a link in a Web browser, the link URL shows up at the bottom of the browser window. You can replace that URL with a specific message by typing in the Message Text field. We usually leave this blank.

▶ **Alt Tag.** If the person viewing your Web page has a slow Internet connection, it might take a while to download an image. While they're waiting, it's often helpful to show them an Alt Tag—some text that describes what the image will be. This is even more important if they've set their browser's preferences so that no images are downloaded at all. The Alt Tag (if you type one in this field) appears in place of the image. For instance, this isn't important in a slice that has no relevant information in it, but it's crucial that you label slices that are buttons with their action. Otherwise, some of your viewers may not be able to navigate your Web site.

▶ **Dimensions.** The Dimensions fields let you specify where the slice is in your image and how wide and tall it is (in pixels). This is most useful when you're trying to align slices along their edges.

▶ **No Image.** If you choose No Image from the Slice Type popup menu, Photoshop won't save this slice to disk. Instead, it includes some custom HTML in its place (whatever you type in the HTML field of the Slice Options dialog box). For example, if you type text here, you'll see that text in place of the slice in the Web browser. If you leave the field blank, it'll leave a hole in the image (the Web page's background will show through, unless you change the Background setting in Output Options, which we'll talk about in a moment). You can type any HTML you want here (up to 255 characters). The important thing to remember here is to make sure whatever you put in the HTML field is no bigger than the slice itself. If it is, and you use the default Table method of writing HTML, then all hell will break loose and your image will fall apart.

The values you set in the Slice Options dialog box are saved with your Photoshop image, and are also transferred to ImageReady if you open the graphic in that program. But you still have to export the picture along with HTML in order for the values to actually be functional.

Saving slices. In the good old days, we used to have to slice up images manually, using the Crop tool, then write down the pixel dimensions for each slice, and then piece them together into a table using hand-coded HTML. And we liked it! (Well, not really, but what choice did we have?) Fortunately, Photoshop can write our HTML for us now, making the whole process pain-free and very quick. The trick is to save the sliced image using Save For Web, as described earlier in the chapter, and make sure that you choose Images and HTML from the Format popup menu in the Save Optimized As dialog box.

However, when you first open the Save For Web dialog box, you must choose the Slice Selection tool (press K), click on each user slice, and specify how you want it to be optimized (GIF versus JPEG, number of colors, and so on). You can also click on one of the auto-slices and choose its optimization settings (all the auto-slices get the same optimization settings).

Before you save the slices to disk (or preview the HTML by clicking on the Preview button at the bottom of the Save For Web dialog box), you may want to click on Output Settings. The Output Settings dialog box (see Figure 18-14) lets you control how Photoshop writes the HTML to disk, including how it names each slice that you haven't already named in Slice Options, whether the slices are arranged in an HTML table or with CSS tags, and a host of other options. Most of the settings aren't that exciting, or they're self-explanatory. Here are a few that we should mention, though.

▶ **Formatting.** There's a certain breed of person who deeply cares about exactly how the HTML is typed—for instance, whether certain words are in all capital letters, in lower-case, or in initial caps. You can specify this sort of thing in the Formatting section of Output Settings. We tend to be more mellow about these things, so we just ignore this section.

▶ **Slice Output.** Photoshop can piece together your slices in one of two ways: as an HTML table or using cascading style sheets (CSS). The default setting is Table, which is probably the way you should go in most instances. The only time we can think of when CSS would make more sense is if you were doing something like animating the pieces of the slice so that they fly around the screen. Otherwise, Table offers easier and smaller HTML. (And you can always position the table on your Web page with CSS later, using something like GoLive or Dreamweaver, if you really want to.) Whichever you choose, we recommend leaving the other settings in this section at their defaults, unless you have a very good reason to change them.

▶ **View As.** If your image is destined to be a background image (a picture that gets tiled so that it covers the whole Web browser window), you should choose View As from the Background tab of the Output Settings dialog box (press Command-2 to jump there quickly). However, you can't make a sliced image a background image, so this is grayed out if you have any slices. Of course, this is only relevant if you're asking Photoshop to write your HTML, which you often don't need if you're just making a background image.

▶ **Background.** The field labeled Background (inside the Background tab of the dialog box) lets you tell Photoshop what to use as a background image in the HTML it writes. For example, if you choose a color from the Color popup menu, Photoshop places your image (even if it's sliced) on top of that color. This isn't really relevant if you're planning on placing the sliced image onto some other Web page using GoLive or Dreamweaver.

▶ **Saving Files.** The Saving Files tab of the Output Settings dialog box (press Command-3 to get there quickly) gives you lots of control over exactly how Photoshop names each file, and where it puts these files. But the file names in this section relate more to dynamic images, such as rollovers created in ImageReady. If we change anything here, it's the name of the folder where the files are saved (the default "images" is fine, but we often use different names, depending on what we're doing; or, if you turn off the Save Images In checkbox, then Photoshop just saves the images and HTML in the same folder).

▶ **Slices.** The place to specify how Photoshop names slices when it saves them to disk is the Slices tab of the Output Settings dialog box (press Command-4 to jump to this tab). Again, we usually just leave this set to the defaults, but you can tweak it if you've got a favorite naming algorithm. Note that we were confused by this setting until we realized

Figure 18-14
Output Settings

*This is actually
four dialog boxes
rolled into one.*

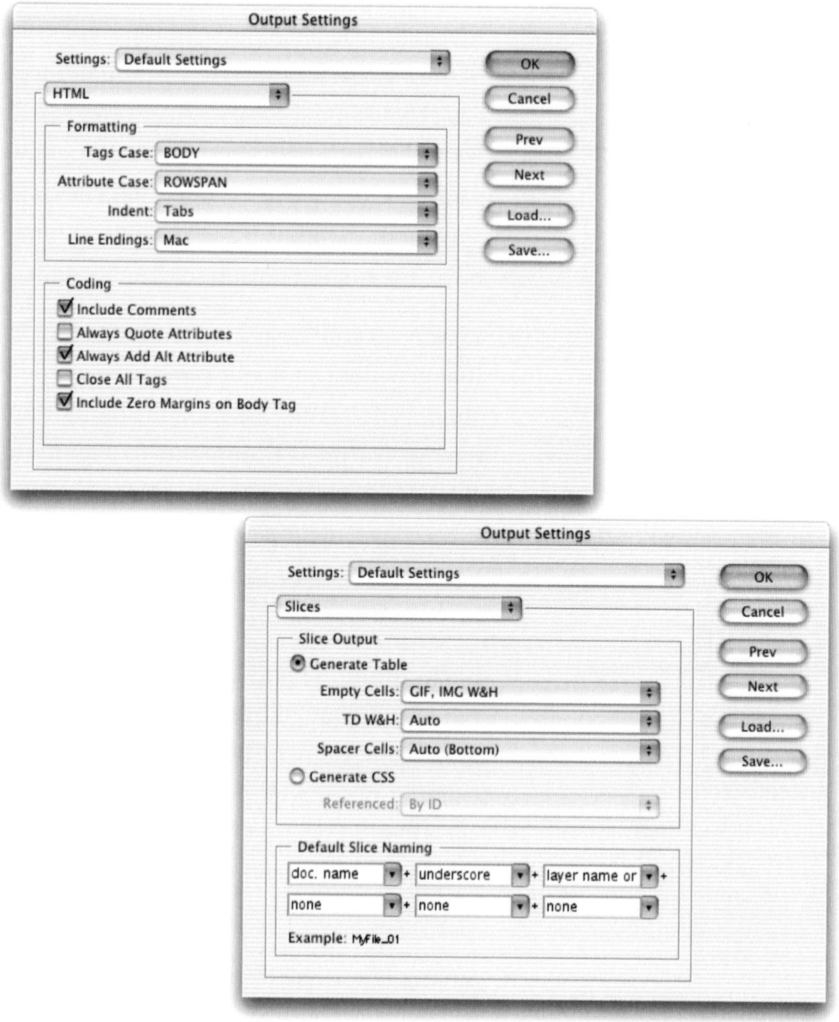

that the second line of popup menus is connected to the first line by the little plus symbol.

You can get to the Output Settings dialog box from either the Save For Web dialog box or the Save Optimized As dialog box (the dialog box that you get once you click OK from Save For Web). Both take you to exactly the same place.

Tip: Saving Output Settings. If you think you'll use a particular configuration of options in the Output Settings dialog box more than once or twice, you might as well save your settings to disk by clicking the Save button in the Output Settings dialog box. (Photoshop saves it in the proper

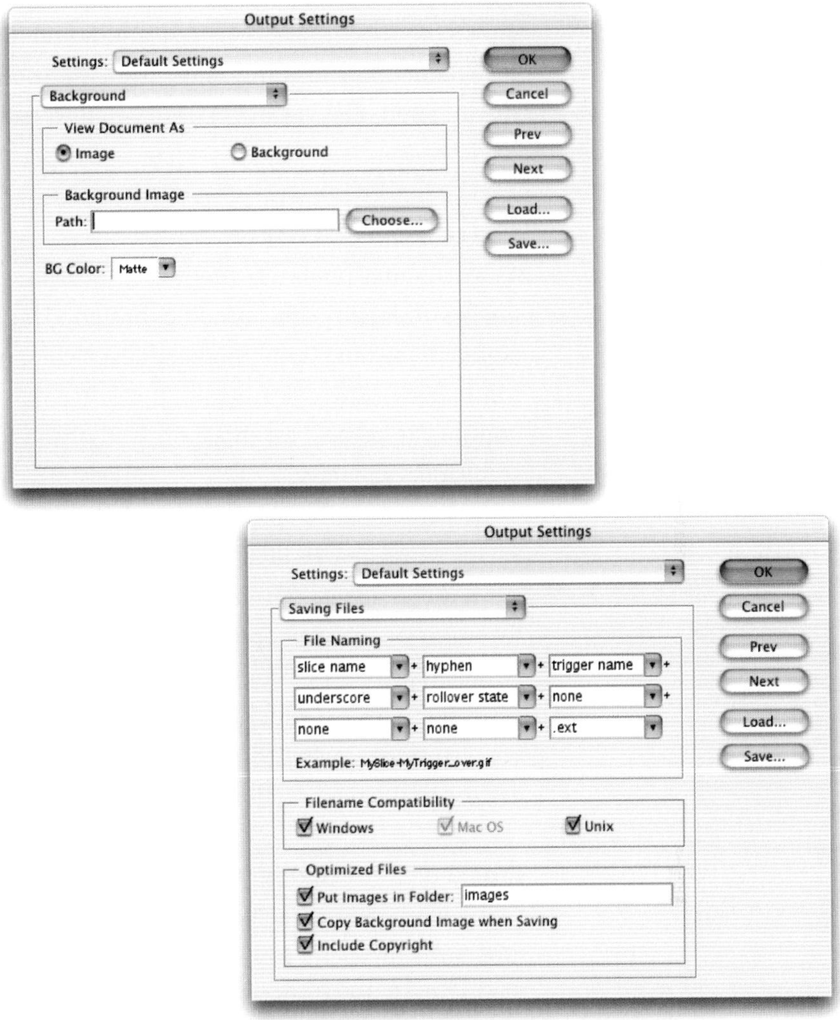

Figure 18-14
More Output Settings,
continued

Output Settings

Settings: Default Settings

OK

Background

Cancel

View Document As

Prev

◉ Image   ○ Background

Next

Background Image

Load...

Path:

Choose...

Save...

BG Color: Matte

Output Settings

Settings: Default Settings

OK

Saving Files

Cancel

File Naming

Prev

slice name + hyphen + trigger name +

Next

underscore + rollover state + none +

Load...

none + none + .ext

Save...

Example: MySlice+MyTrigger_over.gif

Filename Compatibility

☑ Windows   ☑ Mac OS   ☑ Unix

Optimized Files

☑ Put Images in Folder: images

☑ Copy Background Image when Saving

☑ Include Copyright

place by default: the Optimized Output Settings folder, inside the Presets folder, inside the Photoshop folder.) Then, next time you want to use the same configuration, you can simply choose your saved file from the Settings popup menu (or click the Load button). Note, however, that the Save button only appears in the Output Options dialog box when you open it from the Save As Web dialog box; it's missing in action when you open Output Options from the Save Optimized As dialog box.

Tip: Hide Those Slice Marks. As soon as you use the Slice tool, even once, Photoshop starts marking every image you open with slice numbers in the upper-left corner (after all, every image has at least one slice, even

50 MB prepress images). If these annoy you (they sure annoy us), you can turn them off by selecting Slices from the Show submenu, under the View menu. Then, they'll stay off until you next use the Slice tool.

Indexed Colors

As we said in Chapter 3, *Image Essentials*, and earlier in this chapter, GIF images and many other graphics designed for games and multimedia are stored in Indexed Color mode. Indexed color images are small (about the same size as grayscale images), they often compress in file size really well, and they're perfect for those old and obsolete 8-bit color monitors that some folks still have.

Earlier, we said that converting images to Indexed Color mode before saving them as GIF files was obsolete, because it's more convenient to leave the image in RGB mode and use Save For Web to convert it on the fly. However, many people still need to work with indexed color images in Photoshop, and the program offers two features to help manage this process: the Indexed Color dialog box and the Color Table dialog box. There are also several ways to pick and manage Web-safe colors, which we'll discuss in the next section.

Indexed Color dialog box. You can convert an RGB or grayscale image to indexed color by selecting Indexed Color from the Mode submenu (under the Image menu). This brings up the Indexed Color dialog box (see Figure 18-15). Many of the controls here work in exactly the same manner as those we talked about in the Save For Web dialog box (see "GIF," earlier in this chapter). However, there are a few special things to think about.

▶ **Preview.** When Photoshop 5.5 was released, we were pleased to see that Adobe had finally added a Preview checkbox to the Indexed Color dialog box, which lets you see exactly how you're messing up your image. There are few (if any) reasons to turn this off.

▶ **Palettes.** The Palette popup menu offers a number of different options, including Perceptual, Selective, and Adaptive color reduction methods in both "Local" and "Master" flavors. As far as we can tell, there's no reason to use the Master versions in Photoshop; they're errant holdovers from ImageReady. If you want to use master palettes (palettes that are consistent across multiple images), ImageReady is probably

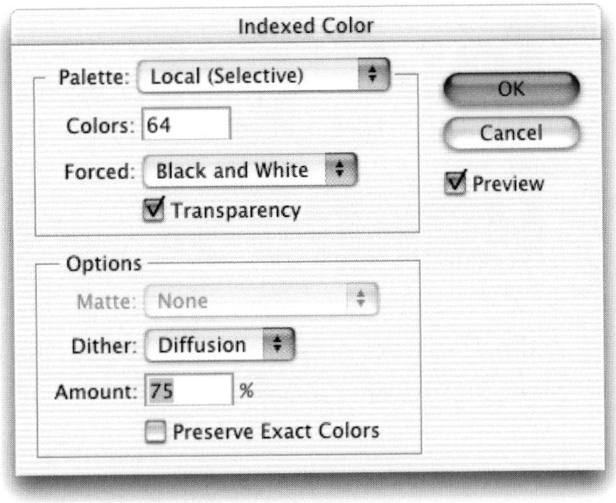

Figure 18-15
Indexed Color
dialog box

a better bet. Again, we generally use Perceptual for scanned photographic images, and Selective for synthetic images with sharp edges.

▶ **Transparency.** Any pixels that are transparent in your image can be
transparent in the final indexed color image, too. However, if you don't
have any transparent pixels, then turn off the Transparency checkbox
in the Indexed Color dialog box; otherwise, Photoshop adds a color
swatch to your color table and specifies that swatch as a transparent
color (taking up a swatch that could better be used for a color).

Of course, indexed color documents cannot contain partially-trans-
parent pixels, so the Matte feature lets you anti-alias these pixels into
some other color (whatever color the image will later sit on). If you set
the Matte popup menu to None, Photoshop gives you a hard-edged
boundary. This sounds bad, and images that have no anti-aliasing
around them often look really jaggy in Photoshop; but when they're
placed over a colored or patterned background, you often don't notice
the jaggies at all (or if you do, they're still better than a halo around the
image; see Figure 18-16).

▶ **Forced.** The Forced popup menu lets you force particular colors into
the image's color palette. For instance, if you choose Black and White
(which is on by default), Photoshop ensures that those two colors are
in the palette. This is especially important when you're using very few
colors or when you need to make sure that a specific color is locked in
and won't change. Besides Black and White, the Forced popup menu
offers you Primaries (which forces red, green, blue, cyan, magenta, yel-

Figure 18-16
Anti-aliasing images

Tempest   *Anti-aliased to white background*

Tempest   *Aliased (jaggy edges)*

The anti-aliased version looks terrible on a colored background.

The aliased version looks good.

low, black, and white into the palette), Web (which ensures that all 216 Web-safe colors are in your palette), and Custom (which lets you specify your own colors that should be in the final palette).

Tip: Prioritizing Colors. Occasionally you and Photoshop might disagree as to what colors in the image are the most important. For instance, if you convert a photographic portrait of someone against a bright blue background, the color palette will include a lot of blues that you might not necessarily care about—you probably want Photoshop to include more skin tones instead. You can force Photoshop to prioritize colors by selecting the area containing the colors you want, then converting to Indexed Color mode. Note that Photoshop may still change the colors slightly, so it's not a wonderful method for ensuring Web-safe colors.

Tip: Saving Palettes. After converting an image to indexed color, you can view the palette by selecting Color Table from the Mode submenu (under the Image menu). More important, from there you can save this palette to disk in order to use it for other conversions (click the Save button). In this way, you can standardize a number of images on the same palette.

Plus, custom color palettes that you've saved to disk from Photoshop can also be used in some multimedia programs. Note that you need to save the palette with an ".aco" extension if you want it to work on Windows or cross-platform machines.

Tip: Finding Dimensions for HTML Tags. If you're writing your own HTML code, it's always a good idea to include height and width values within the image source tag—for instance: <IMG SRC="mooseattack.gif" WIDTH="200" HEIGHT="200">. If you don't include the image's pixel dimensions, the Web browser has to download the entire image before it can lay out the page properly. One of the fastest ways to find these dimensions is by Option-clicking in the Image Size area at the lower-left corner of the document window in Photoshop (see Figure 18-17).

Figure 18-17
Finding pixel dimensions

Editing the color table. In an indexed-color image, each pixel is assigned a number from 0 to 255. The pixel's color comes only by comparing the number with a color lookup table (CLUT). Fortunately, this is all done behind the scenes, so you don't have to think about it much. One reason to convert an image to Indexed Color is so you can edit the particular colors in an image by editing the CLUT. If you choose Color Table from the Mode submenu, you can click on any color in the table to edit it. In color tables that have more than eight or 16 colors, this kind of editing is cumbersome; but in some instances, editing an image's color table can be a very powerful tool.

Tip: Swapping Indexed Colors. Let's say you have a logo on your Web page, which you want to be a different color every week. One way to make this color change would be to edit the GIF image's color lookup table (see Figure 18-18).

1. Open the GIF image and select Color Table from the Mode submenu (under the Image menu).

2. Click on the color you want to change, and when Photoshop asks you to, select a new color from the Color Picker (or type in RGB values). You probably want to make sure that the color you select is Web-safe.

   If the image is anti-aliased and all the intermediary colors are clumped together in the palette (as they often are), you can change them all at once. For example, if you have five different red swatches—from light

Figure 18-18
Swapping indexed colors

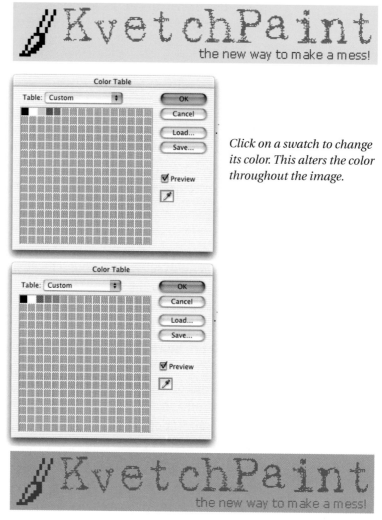

Click on a swatch to change its color. This alters the color throughout the image.

pink to bright red—you can drag the mouse from the first swatch to the last. When you let go of the mouse button, Photoshop asks you for the new first color (to replace the light pink), and then for the new last color (to replace the bright red). It will then build all the intermediary colors for you, based on the two you choose.

3. Click OK and save the image.

Of course, this tip works best when the image has only a few colors.

Tip: Which Swatch to What Color? Trying to figure out exactly which swatch in the color lookup table represents each color in your indexed color image is almost impossible until you notice that the Info palette gives you this information automatically as you move the cursor over each pixel.

Web-Safe Colors

What's a Web color? In Photoshop, this term means two different things, depending on where you find it. Photoshop can display "Web Color" in the Info palette (select Palette Options from the palette's popout menu, or click on one of the little triangles in the Info palette to change the display). In this mode, the Info palette shows you the hexadecimal equivalents of your RGB colors (see Figure 18-19).

(For those of you who care but don't already know: Hexadecimal is simply base-16, which means that after the number 9 comes A, then B, then C, and so on to F, which represents the number 15. So the digits 00 signify zero and FF signifies 255.)

The second use of the term "Web Color" is in Photoshop's Color Picker dialog box, where you can turn on the Only Web Colors checkbox. What this *should* read is Only Web-safe Colors. Or, even more specifically, "Only let me pick colors that won't dither when displayed in a Web browser on archaic 8-bit color monitors."

Tip: Copying Web Colors. The only time you would really need to know the hexadecimal equivalent of a color in your document is if you needed to duplicate it in another program, like GoLive or Dreamweaver. Fortunately, if you select the Eyedropper tool (press I), then hold down the Control key (on the Mac) or the right mouse button (in Windows) while

Figure 18-19

Hexadecimal
equivalents of colors

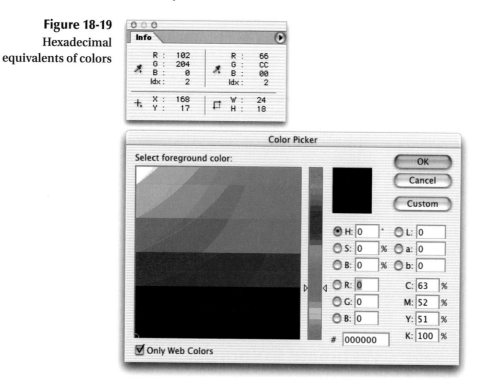

you click, the context-sensitive menu offers to "Copy Color as HTML." The
result: the HTML tag for the color you clicked on. For instance, it might
copy COLOR="#E7ECF6" on to the clipboard. You can then paste this into
some other program.

If you want the hexadecimal equivalent without the HTML tag, you can
simply click once with the Eyedropper tool, then click on the foreground
color swatch in the Tool palette. The Color Picker dialog box now displays
the hexadecimal values, as well as RGB, CMYK, Lab, and HSB.

Tip: Changing Your Jump To Application. If you use Photoshop and
ImageReady together, it's worth noting that Adobe has a Jump To feature
in the File menu and at the bottom of the Tool palette (or you can press
Command-Shift-M). The Jump To feature does just one thing: it switches
to ImageReady. If you have an image open when you invoke this command,
Photoshop prompts you to save it (if it's not already saved), and then it
opens the same picture in ImageReady.

However, the Jump To feature doesn't have to switch to ImageReady. If
there's some other image-editing program that you'd rather use, you can
easily change Photoshop's default behavior. Inside the Photoshop Set-

tings folder there's a folder called Helpers. Inside the Helpers folder there's another folder called Jump To Graphics Editor. Inside this folder are aliases (or shortcuts on Windows). The alias with the curly braces around its name is the application that Photoshop switches to when you click the Jump To button on the Tool palette. We'll leave the rest to your imagination. Of course, whatever application you use must be able to open the file format of the images you're working on.

Web Photo Gallery

The last Web-oriented feature that we'll discuss is the Web Photo Gallery, found in the Automate submenu (under the File menu). This, like the other automated features, performs a task that you could do by hand, but it would be so painful and boring that you might fall out of your chair from the sheer monotony of the chore. In a nutshell, the Web Photo Gallery creates a Web page full of image thumbnails (see Figure 18-20). If you click on one of the thumbnails, it automatically links to a larger-size version of the picture. That's about it.

Figure 18-20
Web Photo Gallery

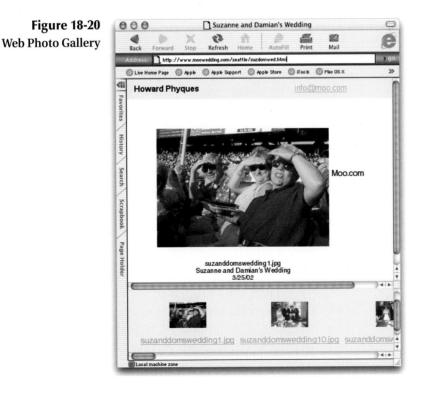

Fortunately, Adobe has come up with some nicer layout templates than earlier versions of Photoshop offered. Some layouts are pretty basic, but any of the layouts are more than adequate when it comes to a quick 'n' dirty display of images from a digital camera that need to be shared among several people on the Web. Some layouts even offer a clever mechanism for your audience to send you e-mail feedback on each image. And if you want to design your own layout, Photoshop lets you (see "Tip: Customize Your Galleries," later in this section).

Using one of these built-in Web photo galleries is pretty easy.

1. After choosing Web Photo Gallery from the Automate submenu, choose a gallery style from the Styles menu: Horizontal Blue & Gray, Horizontal Dark, Horizontal Frame, Horizontal Light, Horizontal Patterned, Simple, Table, Table Blue, Vertical Frame, or Vertical Slide Show 1 or 2. All but Simple, Table, and Table Blue are built using HTML frames, which make them cooler, but some very old Web browsers can't deal with frames.

2. Look at the settings in each tab of the Options popup menu (Banner, Gallery Images, Gallery Thumbnails, Custom Colors, and Security). These choices determine what your final Web gallery will look like (see Figure 18-21). For example, in the Banner tab, you should type the name of the photographer and the date the pictures were taken (or today's date). The Site Name field determines the title of the gallery (it's the Web site name, not usually the site where the photos were taken). Similarly, the two Images tabs let you choose how large and how compressed the final images should be.

   When it comes to image and thumbnail size, the pixel dimension you specify (for instance "Small" means 250 pixels) determines the width or height of the image, whichever side is larger. Unless you have a *lot* of images, we suggest using Large thumbnails—just so you can see them well. But the size of the images should be partly determined by how much data you want your audience to have to download (or how much data you're willing to give them). The only way to find out how large the files will be is by trial and error, though there are some general guidelines. For instance, Large images tend to be around 40–60 K each, while Medium thumbnails tend to be around 25 K each.

   You can assign captions for the thumbnails and/or for the larger images. The captions can just be the file name. Or, if you have filled

Figure 18-21

The five tabs of the
Web Photo Gallery
dialog box

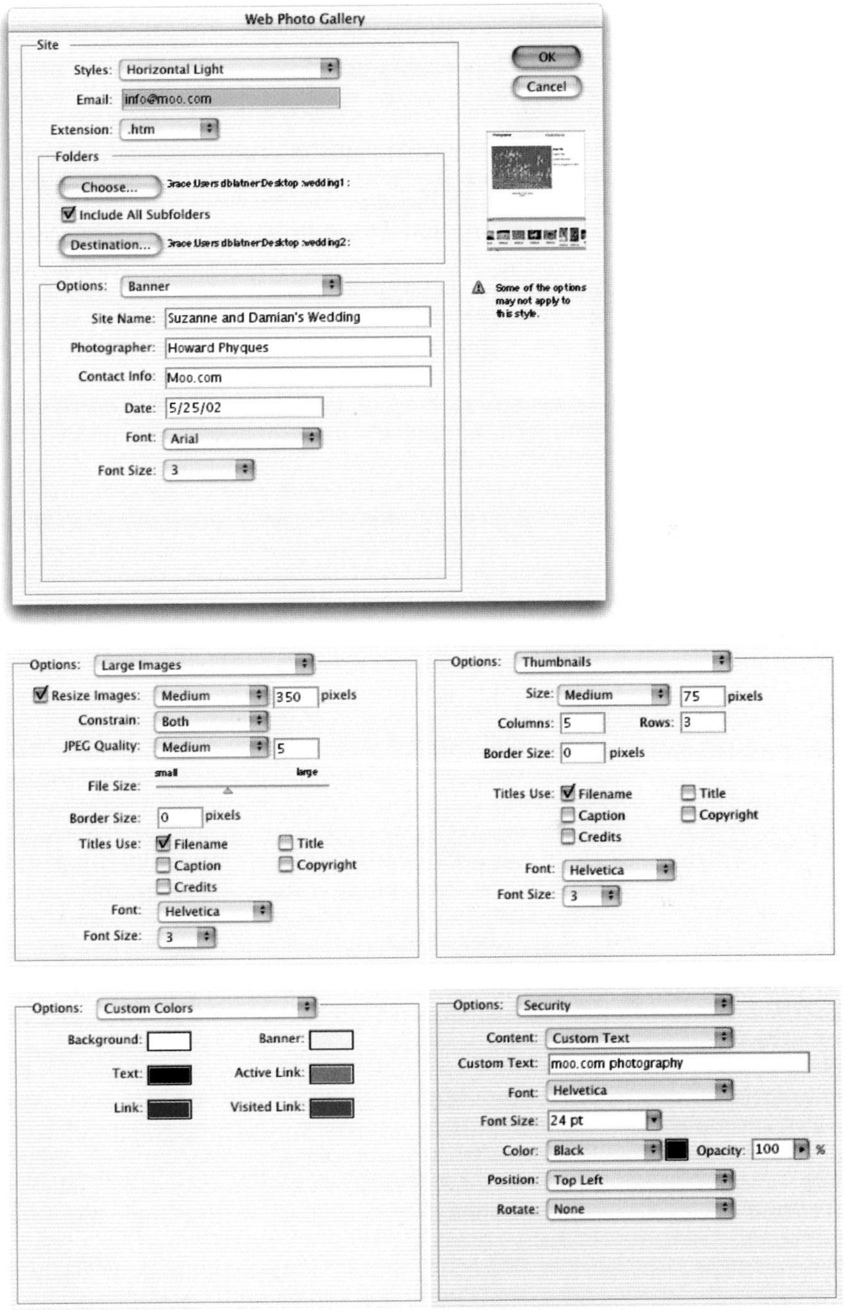

out the fields in the File Info dialog box (under the File menu), Photo-shop can use this data—just turn on the Title, Copyright, Caption, and Credits checkboxes.

The Security features let you tell Photoshop to add text to each image. For example, if you want your company name to be added in the lower-left corner of each image, you can select Custom Text from the Content popup menu. (You can also specify where you want Photoshop to place the text and in what font, size, and so on.) Of course, Adobe is using the word "Security" pretty loosely—there's no reason someone can't copy the image and just crop out your name. But something is certainly better than nothing in this game.

3. Click the Source and Destination buttons to specify a folder that contains all the pictures as well as a folder in which to put all the final files. If you want Photoshop to look inside subfolders, turn on the Include All Subdirectories checkbox. (Note that if you include an alias or a shortcut to another folder, Photoshop is smart enough to look inside those folders, too.)

After you click OK, Photoshop processes each of the images in your folder(s) and saves them as JPEGs (this is a good time to go grab a cup of coffee). The final result is three folders—one for the thumbnail images, one for the larger-size images, and one for the HTML pages that display the larger-sized images—plus two other text files. You can throw away the file called "UserSelections.txt." This is just a record of the settings you used in the Web Photo Gallery dialog box (we're not sure why it saves this, but there's probably a *really* good reason).

Tip: Count Your Pictures First. If you're going to use the Table or Simple gallery style, you should be sure to count the images inside the Source folder first. The reason: Photoshop needs you to type in the number of columns and rows for the thumbnail gallery. If you have 13 images in the folder, and you type 3 columns and 4 rows, then the program has to make a second thumbnail page (with a single thumbnail on it). If you know you've got 13 images, you might choose a different layout, like 4-by-4. We wish that Photoshop could count the images for us and suggest reasonable row and column values, but it ain't that smart yet. You can ignore the Row and Column fields for the frame-based styles; Photoshop does.

Tip: Customize Your Galleries. You don't like the galleries that Photoshop creates? Not jazzy enough for you? No problem, you can always edit the HTML files in GoLive, Dreamweaver, or some other editor later. However, if you're going to be making a lot of galleries, it would be more efficient to edit Photoshop's built-in templates instead.

1. Find the folder that contains the gallery templates (it's called Web Photo Gallery, and it's inside the Presets folder, in the main Photoshop folder).

2. Make a copy of one of the template folders here, and name the duplicate folder as whatever you want your template to be called in Photoshop's Web Photo Gallery dialog box.

3. Edit the files inside this folder using a text editor. You can edit them to some degree with Adobe GoLive or Macromedia Dreamweaver, but because these files are templates (rather than real Web pages), it's safer to make your changes in the actual HTML code.

   Note that the template works by replacing certain codes with the settings you make in Photoshop. For instance, the %%BGCOLOR%% code in the template automatically gets stripped out and replaced with the background color you chose in the Web Photo Gallery dialog box. If you always want the same background color, though, you can remove this code from the template and type in your own color.

Now, when you open the Web Photo Gallery dialog box, your new template should appear in the Styles popup menu. Obviously, making templates requires some knowledge of HTML, but it's surprisingly easy once you get the hang of it.

The Future of Publishing

While much of the wild rush to the Web has been driven by vague fears of being left behind by the competition, people are beginning to invent Web business models that actually make sense and occasionally even make money as well. Whatever your reason for being on the Web, one of the keys to success is to produce images that are small and compress well, yet still have impact. Photoshop gives you the tools to accomplish this. As for making money at it: if we knew how, would we have written this book?

Production Notes

How We Made This Book

In many ways, producing this book was as interesting as writing it. So we thought that something a bit more complete than a normal colophon was in order. What follows is an overview of the systems and procedures that we used to produce this book.

Our Systems

We're often asked about our personal system setups. Here's a quick rundown of what equipment we used while making this book. This isn't everything we use, of course . . . there's always some new toy.

Bruce. System 1: Power Macintosh G4/800MHz x2, 1.5 GB RAM, 570 GB hard drive space, LaCie electron22blue III and LaCie PhotonII 18 monitors, GretagMacbeth EyeOne spectrophotometer, LaCie BlueEye colorimeter, LaCie BlueEye and GretagMacbeth ProfileMaker Pro monitor calibration. **System 2:** Power Macintosh G5 2GHz x2, 3.5 GB RAM, 1.5 TB hard drive space, Sony Artisan and EIZO ColorEdge 21 monitors, GretagMacbeth ICColor 210 Spectrophotometer, Imacon Flextight 848 scanner. **System 3:** Apple PowerBook G4/1GHz 12-inch, 768MB RAM, 120 GB hard drive space. **System 4:** Power Macintosh G4/450, 1.5 GB RAM. 320 GB total hard disk space, Epson Stylus Photo 2200 printer, Apple LaserWriter Pro 630 laser printer, GretagMacbeth SpectroScan spectrophotometer.

David. Macintosh 17-inch PowerBook G4 with 1 GB RAM and Mac OS X 10.2, Sony Vaio SuperSlim Pro with Windows XP, Hewlett Packard Design-Jet 20ps, Epson Stylus inkjet printer, UMAX Astra scanner, Brother 1270N black and white laser printer, Palm Pilot Vx (with beta version of Photoshop for Palm).

Writing, Editing, and Page Layout

Originally, we wrote this book in Microsoft Word on the Mac. Previous editions were laid out with Adobe PageMaker; but for this edition, we opened those PageMaker files in Adobe InDesign CS. Then, some chapters were exported to Microsoft Word for editing, some were edited using Adobe InCopy, and some were edited directly within InDesign (using the Story Editor).

Design and Type

The body text typeface is Adobe Utopia (various weights)—9.8 on 15 for the main text, 8.8 on 12.5 for sidebars. Heads are set in ITC Optima Black. Figure callouts use Utopia Italic 9 on 12.

Images

Many of the images were scanned from film on a LeafScan 35, and more recently, on an Imacon Flextight Precision III. Prints were scanned on a variety of flatbed scanners, including an Agfa Arcus Plus, a Linotype-Hell Saphir Ultra, a Heidelberg CPS Opal Ultra, a UMAX PowerLook 3000, and a low-end UMAX Astra1220. We also used direct digital captures from Canon 300D, Canon 1Ds, Kodak DCS 420, Kodak DCS 460, Olympus DC265, Polaroid PDC-2000, Nikon/Fuji E2S and Nikon CoolPix 5000 digital cameras. The remaining images came from various CD collections (see "Image Credits"). We captured all the screen shots using the indispensable SnapzPro X from Ambrosia Software. All the images in this book started out in RGB form; we used no drum scans.

We placed all the color images as preseparated CMYK TIFFs (with the exception of duotones and graphics from Illustrator and FreeHand, all of which required that we use EPS).

Separations

All the color images in this book were separated in Photoshop using a variety of RGB Working spaces and one of two CMYK output profiles.

RGB Working Space. Most of the images in this book were edited in Adobe RGB (1998), or Kodak ProPhoto RGB. A few legacy images were edited in ColorMatch RGB or Bruce RGB. For monitor calibration, Bruce used Sony's Artisan colorimeter and software, EIZO's Color Navigator software with a GretagMacbeth Eye-One Pro, LaCie BlueEye software with a Sequel BlueEye colorimeter, and GretagMacbeth ProfileMaker Pro 4.1.5 with an Eye-One Display colorimeter. David tried to stay out of the way, while relying primarily on Adobe Gamma and his weary eyeballs.

CMYK Setup. Since the book was printed direct-to-plate, we printed GretagMacbeth's TC 6.05 profiling target on press. We built a set of ICC profiles with GretagMacbeth ProfileMaker Pro profiling software, using the average of five readings each from ten different press sheets for a total of 50 sets of measurements. We used a GretagMacbeth Spectrolino mounted on a GretagMacbeth Spectroscan xy table to automate the data collection. We built two profiles from this data set, one with light GCR for images, the other with heavy GCR for screen shots.

Preproofing

When we compared the test images on the print test with the digital files viewed on our reference monitor, we found that our custom ICC profile, in combination with solid monitor characterization, gave us a very accurate on-screen view of the CMYK data in Photoshop.

We also used our ICC profiles to provide accurate viewing of the color within InDesign CS. This proved surprisingly useful: in several cases we went back and edited the images after we had seen them in context on the page.

For hard-copy preproofing, we used the press ICC profile as our source profile and a custom profile for the Epson Stylus Photo 2200 printer with Epson Enhanced Matte paper that we built using GretagMacbeth's ProfileMaker Pro 4.1.5 software as our output profile.

For non-color proofing, we built PDF files for each chapter and emailed them to our editors. Our editors exported their comments as small Acrobat FDF files and e-mailed them to us; we reimported these comment files into the original PDF files before making final edits in pages. We killed as few trees as possible during the production of this book.

Author! Author!

Where to Reach Us

David Blatner is a Seattle-based consultant specializing in electronic publishing. He has authored or coauthored 13 books, including the award-winning *Real World QuarkXPress* (formerly titled *The QuarkXPress Book)*, *Real World InDesign CS*, *Real World Scanning and Halftones*, *The Flying Book*, *Judaism For Dummies*, and *The Joy of Pi*. Over a half a million copies of his books are in print in 12 languages. David is a contributing editor for *Macworld* magazine, and has presented at conferences around North America, South Africa, and Japan, including Macworld, Seybold Seminars, and The Photoshop Conference. His email address is *david@moo.com*.

Bruce Fraser spent 25 years in Edinburgh, Scotland before moving to the equally gray fog belt of San Francisco, which may explain his fascination with color. Bruce is currently a contributing editor for both *Macworld* and *www.creativepro.com*, and is coauthor of *Real World Color Management*. He has lectured on color reproduction in North America, Europe, and Australia, and is a founder and principal of Pixel Genius LLC. Bruce has been a Photoshop user since the program made its first appearance as BarneyScan XP, and was an alpha tester for Photoshop CS. You can reach him via email at *bruce@pixelboyz.com*.

We'd love to hear from you. While the e-mail addresses above are easiest, you can also contact us by mail here: c/o Moo.com, 18315 NE 198th St., Woodinville, WA 98077, or fax: 309/423-5256.

Image Credits

And Permissions

Earth image used on chapter opening pages, courtesy National Aeronautics and Space Administration.

Page 15. Farmington Cemetary, Maine©2002 David Blatner. Nikon CoolPix 5000 camera.

Page 17. Taj Mahal ©1995 Bruce Fraser, Imacon Flextight Precision II, Kodak Ektar 25.

Page 23. Stone Forest ©1999 Bruce Fraser, Imacon Flextight Precision II, Kodak EPP 100.

Page 30. From "Animals and Wildlife," courtesy Digital Stock.

Page 44. Mosaic, Madaba, Jordan ©2000 David Blatner, Olympus DC265 camera

Page 49. From "Visual Symbols Sampler 2," courtesy PhotoDisc

Page 51. Mosaic, Madaba, Jordan ©2000 David Blatner, Olympus DC265 camera

Page 55. From "Sharks and Whales," courtesy Digital Stock.

Page 71. Butchart Gardens ©2001 David Blatner, Nikon CoolPix 5000 camera.

Page 94. From "Retro Americana," courtesy PhotoDisc.

Page 95. From "Faces and Hands," courtesy PhotoDisc.

Page 96. From "PhotoDisc Sampler" courtesy PhotoDisc.

Page 97. Deep bitmap image courtesy Simon Tuckett.

Page 100. From "Fine Art and Historical Photos," courtesy PhotoDisc.

Page 101. From "Faces and Hands," courtesy PhotoDisc.

Page 104. From "Fine Art and Historical Photos," courtesy PhotoDisc.

Page 105. Bike Parts ©1991 MacUser Magazine, by Peter Allen Gould. Leafscan45, Kodak Ektachrome 4x5.

Page 106. From "Classic Sampler," courtesy Classic PIO Partners.

Page 114. Brick Wall ©2003 Bruce Fraser. Canon EOS 1Ds Camera.

Page 134. Curraghs ©1995 Bruce Fraser. Leafscan 35, Kodak Royal Gold 200.

Page 150. Chichen-Itza ©1999 Bruce Fraser. Imacon Flextight Precision III, Kodak PJA-100.

Page 195. Boothbay Harbor, Maine ©1993 Bruce Fraser. Leafscan 35, Kodak Lumiere 100.

Page 226. Golden Gate Park windmill, ©2003 Bruce Fraser, Canon EOS 1Ds camera.

Page 231-232. Valparaiso Moa, ©1994 Bruce Fraser, Imacon Flextight 848, Kodak EPP 100.

Page 234. Special collections division, University Washington Libraries. Photo by Cobb, UW negative #10509.

Page 235. "Dia" ©1994 Susie Hammond. Hewlett-Packard Scanjet IIcx, 4x6 print.

Page 235. Special collections division, University Washington Libraries. UW negative #80.A.W&S.

Page 243. Waterfall by Eric Wunrow, from "ColorBytes Sampler One," courtesy ColorBytes, Inc.

Page 245. Train by Eric Wunrow, from "ColorBytes Sampler One," courtesy ColorBytes, Inc.

Page 249. Boat by Eric Wunrow, from "ColorBytes Sampler One," courtesy ColorBytes, Inc.

Page 255. Building from "ColorBytes Sampler One," courtesy ColorBytes, Inc.

Pages 269. Cape Elizabeth Lighthouse, Maine ©1993 Bruce Fraser. Leafscan 35, Kodak Lumiere 100.

Page 271. Your's Ella by Drummond Shiels Studios, Edinburgh, Scotland, c. 1926. Photographer unknown. Agfa Horizon, 8x10 print.

Page 290. Alcatraz ©1995 Bruce Fraser. Kodak DCS 420 camera.

Page 299. Masked Dancer ©1994 Bruce Fraser. Leafscan 35 Kodak PJA 100.

Page 301. Conservatory, Golden Gate Park ©1995 Bruce Fraser. Nikon E2S camera.

Page 307. Seal Rock and Cliff House, ©2003 Bruce Fraser, Canon EOS 1Ds camera.

Page 308, 310. Arthur's Seat, ©2000, Bruce Fraser, Imacon Flextight 848, Kodak PJA 100.

Page 314. Rhyolite Windows ©1988 Bruce Fraser. Leafscan 35, Kodak Ektar 25.

Page 321. Machu Picchu 1 ©1998 Bruce Fraser. Imacon Flextight Precision III, Kodak PJA 100.

Page 323. La Paz Drummers ©1994 Bruce Fraser. Leafscan 35, Kodak PJA 100.

Page 327. Woman in Red Hat ©1990 Eastman Kodak Co., photographer Bob Clemens, Kodak Photo CD Sampler.

Page 332. "Dia" ©1994 by Susie Hammond. Hewlett-Packard Scanjet IIcx, 4x6 print.

Page 333. Conservatory, Golden Gate Park ©1995 Bruce Fraser. Kodak DCS 420 camera.

Page 334. Glass image ©Fuji Photo Film, Agfa Arcus Plus, 4x5 print.

Page 335. La Paz Street Vendor ©1994 Bruce Fraser. Leafscan 35, Kodak PJA 100.

Page 338. Dune, Death Valley, ©1998 Bruce Fraser, Imacon Flextight 848, Kodak EPP 100.

Page 342. Na Pali Coast ©2000 Bruce Fraser. Imacon Flextight Precision III, Kodak Ektar 25.

Page 348. Wedding Dress, ©2002 David Blatner, Nikon CoolPix 5000 camera.

Page 349. From "Visual Symbols Sampler 2," courtesy PhotoDisc.

Page 356. Blue Bottle, ©2002 David Blatner, Nikon CoolPix 5000 camera.

Page 362. From "Signature Series 8: Study of Form and Color," courtesy PhotoDisc.

Page 364. Bahai Temple, Haifa. ©2002 David Blatner, David Blatner, Olympus DC265 camera

Page 366. From "Sports and Recreation," courtesy PhotoDisc

Page 370. From "Fine Art and Historical Photos," courtesy PhotoDisc.

Page 374. From "Object Series 1: Fruits and Vegetables," courtesy PhotoDisc.

Page 379. From "Children of the World," courtesy PhotoDisc.

Page 381. Apples image from "The Painted Table," courtesy PhotoDisc.

Page 382. Fishing lure from "Object Series 4: Retro Relics," courtesy PhotoDisc.

Page 384. From "Object Series 1: Fruits and Vegetables," courtesy PhotoDisc.

Page 393. From "Visual Symbols Sampler 2," courtesy PhotoDisc

Page 394. From "Signature Series 8: Study of Form and Color," courtesy PhotoDisc.

Page 399. From "Visual Symbols Sampler 2," courtesy PhotoDisc, and "Streets of London," courtesy ImageFarm

Page 411. Mount Rushmore from Volume 5: Mountainscapes, 1993 courtesy ImageClub.

Page 415. Jerash Ruins, Jordan ©2000 David Blatner, Olympus DC265 camera

Page 417. From "Object Series 4: Retro Relics," courtesy PhotoDisc.

Page 418. From "Signature Series 8: Study of Form and Color," courtesy PhotoDisc.

Page 419. From "Signature Series 8: Study of Form and Color," courtesy PhotoDisc.

Page 421. Trees image from "Signature Series 8: Study of Form and Color," courtesy PhotoDisc.

Page 421. Sunset image from "Kai's Power Photos," courtesy HSC Software.

Page 423. Waterfall image from "Signature Series 8: Study of Form and Color," courtesy PhotoDisc.

Page 435. Blue Curragh ©1995 Bruce Fraser. Leafscan 35, Kodak Royal Gold 200.

Page 436. Connemara Fishing Boats ©1995 Bruce Fraser. Leafscan 35, Kodak Lumiere.

Page 446. Dawn at Varanasi ©1995 Bruce Fraser. Leafscan 35, Kodak PJA 100.

Page 448. From my deck, ©2003 Bruce Fraser, Canon EOS 1Ds camera.

Page 449. Men in Kilts ©1995 Pamela Pfiffner. Leafscan 35, Kodak PJA 100.

Page 454. Machu Picchu 3 ©1998 Bruce Fraser. Imacon Flextight Precision II, Kodak PJA 100.

Page 456. Golden Gate Fog, ©2003 Bruce Fraser, Canon EOS 1Ds camera.

Page 459. Lexxi ©2000 Alan Womack, used by permission.

Page 466. Chichen Itza Pyramid 1 © 2000 Bruce Fraser. Imacon Flextight Precision III, Kodak PJA 100.

Page 467. Kremlin Domes © 1997 Bruce Fraser. Imacon Flextight Precision, Kodak PJA 100.

Page 472. Sagebrush at Mono Lake, ©2003 Bruce Fraser, Flextight Precision 848, Kodak Portra 160 NC.

Page 389. Photo by Goetzman Photo.

Page 478. Frosted trees from "Color Digital Photos: Paramount," courtesy Seattle Support Group.

Page 479. Ship masts from "Color Digital Photos: Paramount," courtesy Seattle Support Group.

Page 480. Bird from "Color Digital Photos: Paramount," courtesy Seattle Support Group.

Page 482. Eye image ©1990 Eastman Kodak Co., photographer Bob Clemens, Kodak Photo CD Sampler.

Page 485. Trees image from "Signature Series 8: Study of Form and Color," courtesy PhotoDisc.

Page 485. Pumpkin image from "Object Series 1: Fruits and Vegetables," courtesy PhotoDisc.

Page 495. Golden Gate Park Windmill (detail), © 2003 Bruce Fraser, Canon EOS 1Ds camera.

Page 498. Alice-Anne, ©2000 Bruce Fraser, Nikon LS 4000, Kodak Portra 160 NC.

Page 501. Chichen Itza Pyramid 2 © 2000 Bruce Fraser. Imacon Flextight Precision, Kodak PJA-100.

Page 502. Niña con Conejo ©2000 Bruce Fraser. Imacon Flextight Precision, Kodak Lumiere.

Page 505. Golden Gate Bridge ©2000 Bruce Fraser. Kodak DCS 460 camera.

Page 520. Barn image from "Signature Series 8: Study of Form and Color," courtesy PhotoDisc.

Page 521. Leaf image from "Signature Series 8: Study of Form and Color," courtesy PhotoDisc.

Page 527. From "Signature Series 8: Study of Form and Color," courtesy PhotoDisc.

Page 531. Zabriskie Point, ©2001 Bruce Fraser, Flextight Precision 848, Kodak Portra NC.

Page 532. From "Signature Series 8: Study of Form and Color," courtesy PhotoDisc.

Page 535. From "Signature Series 8: Study of Form and Color," courtesy PhotoDisc.

Page 537. Hearst pool image from "Color Digital Photos: Paramount," courtesy Seattle Support Group.

Page 539. From "Animals," Dover Publications.

Page 549. From "William Morris: Ornamentation & Illustrations from The Kelmscott Chaucer," Dover Publications.

Page 552. From "Animals," Dover Publications.

Page 553. From "Animals," Dover Publications.

Page 554. Special collections division, University Washington Libraries. UW negative #10542.

Page 584. Koala, ©2003 Bruce Fraser, Canon EOS 300D camera.

Page 587. Clown Parrots, ©2003 Bruce Fraser, Canon EOS 300D camera.

Page 601. Painted Ladies (detail), ©2003 Bruce Fraser, Canon EOS 300D camera.

Page 632. "Seattle Lamppost" ©1995 David Blatner.

Page 634. "Debbie" by Donald Carlson, part of a collection by David Blatner.

Page 636. Seattle Sunrise ©2001 Debra Carlson, Olympus DC265 camera.

Page 639. Gabriel, ©2002 David Blatner, Nikon CoolPix 5000 camera.

Page 640. "Author at Work" by Howard Blatner, from Blatner family collection.

Page 644. Giant Snow Morels ©2001 David Blatner, Olympus DC265 camera

Page 646. From "Fine Art and Historical Photos," courtesy PhotoDisc.

Page 648. From "Fruits and Vegetables," courtesy PhotoDisc

Page 658. "Billboard" ©1995 David Blatner.

Page 676. From "Object Series 4: Retro Relics," courtesy PhotoDisc.

Page 685. From "Object Series 4: Retro Relics," courtesy PhotoDisc.

Page 685. Birthday Tulips ©2000 Debra Carlson

Page 746. "Edna Hassinger" courtesy Allee Blatner. Photographer unknown.

Page 769. Taj Mahal image ©1993 by Carol Thuman.

Page 793. Earth image courtesy National Aeronautics and Space Administration.

Page 811. From "PhotoDisc Fine Art Sampler," courtesy PhotoDisc.

Page 815. Volunteer Park Conservatory ©2002 David Blatner, Nikon CoolPix 5000 camera.

Page 845. Space Shuttle Atlantis image courtesy National Aeronautics and Space Administration.

Page 849. Day at the Ballpark ©2002 David Blatner, Nikon CoolPix 5000 camera.

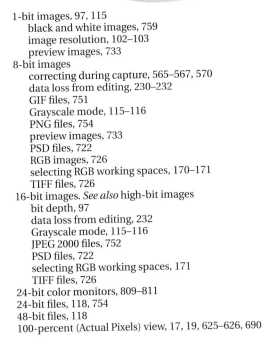

Index

O

object-oriented graphics. *See* vector graphics
object-oriented PICTs, 758
Off (policy), 202, 203–204
OK button, Camera Raw dialog box, 589
on-screen densitometers. *See* densitometers
on-screen output. *See also* monitor profiles
  file formats for, 721
  image resolution, 109
  spot colors, displaying, 523–525
one-shot cameras, 557, 558–559
OneClick, 699
online printing services, 799
opacity
  blending modes, 439–444
  brush opacity, 47
  controlling adjustment layer effects, 430, 431, 434, 437–438, 452
  converting to Grayscale, 629–631
  displaying in Info palette, 68
  drop shadows, 677, 678
  positioning composite images, 645
  solidity of spot colors, 510–511
opening files
  Color Management Policies. *See* Color Management Policies
  commands for, 718–719
  in current folder, 16
  EPS files, 655
  File Browser, 75, 621
  mismatched profiles, 83, 208–209
  missing profiles, 83, 210–211
  in multiple windows, 16
  PDF files, 655
  Photo CD images, 578–580
  PICT or TIFF previews, 656
operating system requirements, 2
OptiCal calibration package, 10, 156, 157
Optimize To File Size, 827
optimized GIF files, 827, 838
optimized JPEG format, 818, 838
optimized printing, 725
optimizing images
  automatic optimization, 294
  color images, 293–296, 463–469
  during image capture, 563
  manual optimization, 294
  optimizing tonal range, 256–267
  out-of-gamut colors. *See* out-of-gamut colors
  output sharpening, 485, 486, 487–488, 488, 489, 498, 500
  reference images, 464, 467–469
  for RGB output, 296
  soft proof images, 464–469
  using adjustment layers, 463–469
Options bar
  keystroke modifiers, 39, 41
  palette well, 58–59
  tool presets, 41
Optix calibration package, 10, 157
OS X. *See* Macintosh systems
out-of-gamut colors. *See also* gamuts
  gamut alarm, Info palette, 299, 303

gamut clipping, 294–295
gamut compression, 294–295
Gamut Warning, 80, 299, 304
rendering intents, 142–143
selecting and replacing, 324–325
output issues. *See also* output methods
  color correction considerations, 783
  contone images, 767–768, 776–777, 782, 783, 784
  halftones. *See* halftone images
  image mode considerations, 784
  image resolution. *See* image resolution recommendations
  multitone images, 534, 541–545
  on-screen output, 109, 523–525, 721
  optimizing images. *See* optimizing images
  saving CMYK multitone images, 541–542
  saving Duotone images, 541
  sharpening considerations, 783–784
  tonal correction considerations, 783
output levels, 246, 247, 251, 252–253, 254
output methods. *See also* output issues
  compensating for. *See* optimizing images
  hybrid screening methods, 777–781
  printing. *See* printing from page-layout programs; printing from Photoshop
  proofing output. *See* proofing output
Output options, Print with Preview, 787–795
output profiles
  previewing output. *See* soft proofs
  soft-proofing and, 466
  as working space, 179–180
Output Settings, 838, 839–840
output sharpening, 485, 486, 487–488, 488, 489, 498, 500, 503–504, 505
Output Space popup, 798
oval selections, 353
overlapping slices, 834–835
Overlay blending mode, 442, 450
Overprint dialog box, 525
overprints, 513–514
  drop shadows, 680
  estimating for CMYK working spaces, 187–188
  specifying overprint colors, 524–525
Override Printer's Default Curves, 791

P

padlocks, locked colors, 826
page-layout programs
  clipping path handling, 746–749
  converting pages to Web images, 812–813
  EPS file handling, 724–725
  EPS preview images, 732
  file formats for, 721
  halftone screen settings, 772
  JPEG 2000 file handling, 752
  JPEG file handling, 751
  PDF file handling, 740
  printing from. *See* printing from page-layout programs
  spot color names, 738
  text handling, 659–660
  TIFF file handling, 724–725
  ZIP compression and, 729